BEST PLACES®

VANCOUVER

BEST PLACES®
VANCOUVER

Edited by
KASEY WILSON

EDITION 3

SASQUATCH BOOKS
SEATTLE

Printed in the United States of America
Distributed in Canada by Raincoast Books Ltd.

Third edition.
04 03 02 01 00   5 4 3 2 1

ISSN: 1095-9087
ISBN: 1-57061-224-2

Series editor: Kate Rogers
Cover and interior design: Nancy Gellos
Cover photograph: Rick Dahms
Fold-out and interior maps: GreenEye Design

SPECIAL SALES

BEST PLACES® guidebooks are available at special discounts on bulk purchases for corporate, club, or organization sales promotions, premiums, and gifts. Special editions, including personalized covers, excerpts of existing guides, and corporate imprints, can be created in large quantities for specific needs. For more information, contact your local bookseller or Special Sales, BEST PLACES® Guidebooks, 615 Second Avenue, Suite 260, Seattle, Washington 98104, 800/775-0817.

SASQUATCH BOOKS
615 Second Avenue
Seattle, WA 98104
206/467-4300
books@SasquatchBooks.com
www.SasquatchBooks.com

CONTENTS

Contributors

Editor **KASEY WILSON** is an award-winning freelance food and travel writer, broadcaster, and author of several guidebooks and cookbooks. The Restaurant Association of BC and the Yukon awarded her the Media-Person of the Year for Outstanding Reporting in the field of Hospitality in 1996. She co-hosts a popular weekly radio show called "The Best of Food and Wine" on CFUN and has been featured on CNN, PBS, and NBC.

ANTHONY GISMONDI is Canada's most influential wine critic. A top-rated, award-winning freelance writer, broadcaster, and speaker, his understanding of wine is widely acknowledged throughout the international wine community.

NICK ROCKEL is an editor at *Vancouver* magazine. As a contributor to the Nightlife chapter, he holds a local record for most clubs visited in a single evening. He also spent his summer vacation writing Itineraries.

STEVEN THRENDYLE, author of the Recreation chapter, is a freelance writer/photographer whose work has appeared in *Men's Journal, Outside, Powder, Bike,* and *Snow Country* magazines. He is the 1999 winner of the Harold S. Hirsch award for excellence in snowsports journalism (magazine).

SARAH REEDER, who wrote the Shopping chapter, is associate editor and fashion editor of *Vancouver* magazine, while covering style, furniture, and design for *The Globe and Mail*.

Though he claims to be overfed and undernourished, **MURRAY MCMILLAN** attempts to keep abreast of Vancouver's booming dining scene both for his day job as food editor of the *Vancouver Sun,* and as a contributor to national magazines and international travel guides.

Greasy spoon writer **MARK LABA** is skinny enough to fit through a mail slot and is wondering where all the grease is settling. His food writing has appeared in various magazines and travel guides and his broadcasting work has surfaced on CFUN radio and CBC television.

Travel and cocktail book authors **ANISTATIA MILLER** and **JARED BROWN** contributed to the Whistler and Victoria chapters. They came to Vancouver on a three-week business trip and stayed for three years, dining in and travelling throughout BC.

À jogger constantly in search of a new path, **NOEL HULSMAN** stumbled upon most of the sites in the Exploring chapter while running off writer's block.

PETER MORGAN contributed to Planning a Trip and Lay of the City. He's the president of Morgan: Newsletters and a former editor of *BC Business Magazine*. He has been a journalist, writer, and news broadcaster for more than 30 years.

Food writer **ERIC AKIS** says please don't wake him, he's having a dream that someone's willing to pay him to consume, and then write about, the wonderful food and drink on picturesque Vancouver Island.

Acknowledgments

Many people contributed to *Vancouver Best Places* in many different ways. My thanks to Carellin Brooks, Dallas Harrison, QuBic Lam, Jena MacPherson, Jack Moore, Tod Maffin, Jodi Rock, Stephen Wong, and Ann Claggett. In addition, a special thank you to researcher/fact checker Peter Mitham for his diligence and commitment.

Another round of applause is due to all the great folks at Sasquatch Books, especially those who work in the trenches: assistant editor Justine Matthies and series editor Kate Rogers, who has always coaxed the critical path of *Vancouver Best Places* into a straight line—that's three down!

And last, but really first—Jason, Jeff, and Karen Meagan.

About Best Places® Guidebooks

People trust us. BEST PLACES® guidebooks, which have been published continuously since 1975, represent one of the most respected regional travel series in the country. Each guide is written completely independently: no advertisers, no sponsors, no favors. Our reviewers know their territory, work incognito, and seek out the very best a city or region has to offer. Because we accept no free meals, accommodations, or other complimentary services, we are able to provide tough, candid reports about places that have rested too long on their laurels, and to delight in new places that deserve recognition. We describe the true strengths, foibles, and unique characteristics of each establishment listed.

Vancouver Best Places is written by and for locals, and is therefore coveted by travelers. It's written for people who live here and who enjoy exploring the city's bounty and its out-of-the-way places of high character and individualism. These are the very characteristics that make *Vancouver Best Places* ideal for tourists, too. The best places in and around the city are the ones that denizens favor: independently owned establishments of good value, touched with local history, run by lively individuals, and graced with natural beauty. With this third edition of *Vancouver Best Places*, travelers will find the information they need: where to go and when, what to order, which rooms to request (and which to avoid), where the best music, art, nightlife, shopping, and other attractions are, and how to find the city's hidden secrets.

We're so sure you'll be satisfied with our guide, we guarantee it.

NOTE: *The reviews in this edition are based on information available at press time and are subject to change. Readers are advised that places listed may have closed or changed management, and, thus, may no longer be recommended by this series. The editors welcome information conveyed by users of this book. A report form is provided at the end of the book, and feedback is also welcome via email: books@SasquatchBooks.com.*

How to Use This Book

This book is divided into twelve chapters covering a wide range of establishments, destinations, and activities in and around Vancouver. All evaluations are based on numerous reports from local and traveling inspectors. BEST PLACES® reporters do not identify themselves when they review an establishment, and they accept no free meals, accommodations, or any other services. Final judgments are made by the editors. **EVERY PLACE FEATURED IN THIS BOOK IS RECOMMENDED.**

STAR RATINGS *(for Top 190 Restaurants and Lodgings only)* Restaurants and lodgings are rated on a scale of one to four stars (with half stars in between), based on uniqueness, loyalty of local clientele, performance measured against the establishment's goals, excellence of cooking, cleanliness, value, and professionalism of service. Reviews are listed alphabetically, and every place is recommended.

★★★★ The very best in the city

★★★ Distinguished; many outstanding features

★★ Excellent; some wonderful qualities

★ A good place

[unrated] New or undergoing major changes

(For more on how we rate places, see the BEST PLACES® Star Ratings box, below.)

PRICE RANGE *(for Top 190 Restaurants and Lodgings only)* Prices for lodgings are based on peak season rates for one night's lodging for two people (i.e., double occupancy). Off-season rates vary but can sometimes be significantly less. Prices for restaurants are based primarily on dinner for two, including dessert, tax, and tip. Call ahead to verify, as all prices are subject to change. **ALL PRICES ARE GIVEN IN CANADIAN DOLLARS.**

$$$ Expensive (more than $80 for dinner for two; more than $125 for one night's lodgings for two)

$$ Moderate (between expensive and inexpensive)

$ Inexpensive (less than $40 for dinner for two; $85 or less for one night's lodgings for two)

RESERVATIONS We used one of the following terms for our reservations policy: reservations required, reservations recommended. No information given means that reservations are either not accepted or not necessary.

ADDRESSES AND PHONE NUMBERS Every attempt has been made to provide accurate information on an establishment's location and phone number. But it's always a good idea to call ahead and confirm. For establishments with two or more locations, we try to provide information on the original or most recommended branches.

CHEQUES, CREDIT CARDS, AND DEBIT CARDS Many establishments that accept cheques also require a major credit card for identification. Note that some places accept only local cheques. Credit cards are abbreviated in this book as follows: American Express (AE); Carte Blanche (CB); Diners Club (DC); Discover (DIS); Japanese credit card (JCB); MasterCard

BEST PLACES® STAR RATINGS

Any travel guide that rates establishments is inherently subjective—and BEST PLACES® is no exception. We rely on our professional experience, yes, but also on a gut feeling. And, occasionally, we even give in to a soft spot for a favourite neighbourhood hangout. Our star-rating system is not simply a AAA-checklist; it's judgmental, critical, sometimes fickle, and highly personal. And unlike most other travel guides, we pay our own way and accept no freebies: no free meals or accommodations, no advertisers, no sponsors, no favors.

For each new edition, we send local food and travel experts out to review restaurants and lodgings anonymously, and then to rate them on a scale of one to four, based on uniqueness, loyalty of local clientele, performance measured against the establishment's goals, excellence of cooking, cleanliness, value, and professionalism of service. That doesn't mean a one-star establishment isn't worth dining or sleeping at—far from it. When we say that *all* the places listed in our books are recommended, we mean it. That one-star pizza joint may be just the ticket for the end of a whirlwind day of shopping with the kids. But if you're planning something more special, the star ratings can help you choose an eatery or hotel that will wow your new clients or be a stunning, romantic place to celebrate an anniversary or impress a first date.

We award four-star ratings sparingly, reserving them for what we consider truly the best. And once an establishment has earned our highest rating, everyone's expectations seem to rise. Readers often write us letters specifically to point out the faults in four-star establishments. With changes in chefs, management, styles, and trends, it's always easier to get knocked off the pedestal than to ascend it. Three-star establishments, on the other hand, seem to generate healthy praise. They exhibit outstanding qualities, and we get lots of love letters about them. The difference between two and three stars can sometimes be a very fine line. Two-star establishments are doing a good, solid job and gaining attention, while one-star places are often dependable spots that have been around forever.

The restaurants and lodgings described in *Vancouver Best Places* have earned their stars from hard work and good service (and good food). They're proud to be included in this book—look for our BEST PLACES® sticker in their windows. And we're proud to honor them in this, the third edition of *Vancouver Best Places*.

(MC); Visa (V). Debit cards are widely used in Vancouver; if an establishment accepts them, it is indicated. No debit card information means that the establishment was not accepting debit cards at press time.

EMAIL AND WEB SITE ADDRESSES Email and Web site addresses have been included for establishments where available. Please note that the World Wide Web is a fluid and evolving medium, and that Web pages are often "under construction" or, as with all time-sensitive information, may no longer be valid.

MAP INDICATORS The letter-and-number codes appearing at the end of most listings refer to coordinates on the fold-out map included in the front of the book. If an establishment does not have a map code listed, its location falls beyond the boundaries of these maps.

HELPFUL ICONS Watch for these quick-reference symbols throughout the book:

 FAMILY FUN Family-oriented places that are great for kids—fun, easy, not too expensive, and accustomed to dealing with young ones.

 GOOD VALUE While not necessarily cheap, these places offer you the best value for your dollars—a good deal within the context of the city.

 ROMANTIC These spots offer candlelight, atmosphere, intimacy, or other romantic qualities—kisses and proposals are encouraged!

 UNIQUELY VANCOUVER These are places that are unique and special to the city, such as a restaurant owned by a beloved local chef or a tourist attraction recognized around the globe. (Hint: If you want to hit several of these special spots at once, turn to the Top 20 Attractions in the Exploring chapter. They're all uniquely Vancouver!) The same icon is also used in the Whistler and Victoria chapters to signify places that are unique to those towns.

&. Appears after listings for establishments that have wheelchair-accessible facilities.

INDEXES In addition to a general index at the back of the book, there is an index of restaurants by location at the beginning of the Restaurants chapter.

MONEY-BACK GUARANTEE Please see "We Stand by Our Reviews" at the end of this book.

READER REPORTS At the end of the book is a report form. We receive hundreds of reports from readers suggesting new places or agreeing or disagreeing with our assessments. They greatly help in our evaluations, and we encourage you to respond.

PLANNING A TRIP

PLANNING A TRIP

How to Get Here

BY PLANE

VANCOUVER INTERNATIONAL AIRPORT (604/276-6101; www.yvr.ca; map:B5) is a major international airport with flights daily to every continent. (A travel tip: if your luggage is destined for Vancouver, make sure the tag on it has YVR as the initials.) The airport, located 15 kilometres (9 miles) south of downtown on Sea Island, completed an extensive renovation program in 1996 that included construction of a terminal dedicated to international flights. Both the older domestic terminal and its newer counterpart are modern and spacious. The major airlines of Canada, the United States, Asia, and Europe fly into Vancouver, providing regular service to 40 cities around the world. Annually, the airport handles approximately 15.5 million passengers. In recent years, international business passengers have ranked Vancouver International first among major North American airports, according to statistics compiled by the International Air Transport Association of Geneva, which represents 260 international air carriers.

After passing through the **CANADA CUSTOMS** checkpoint, travellers arriving from the United States and overseas enter the international terminal's reception lobby. The lobby has a tourist information counter, foreign-exchange kiosks, banking services, and access to ground transportation into the city and beyond. Porters and free baggage carts are available in both terminals. For advice and basic directions, newcomers can turn to an army of about 150 **GREEN COATS**, volunteer goodwill ambassadors for the airport authority who are on hand to greet every flight.

Several **CAR RENTAL AGENCIES** are located on the ground floor of a new, three-level parkade; these include Avis (604/606-2847), Budget (604/668-7000), Enterprise (604/231-9222), Hertz (604/606-3700), and National-Tilden (604/273-3121).

PARKING is available here by the half hour ($2 for self-serve or $2.50 with cashier service). The maximum daily charge on the second and third levels (P2 and P3) is $14; for the week, it's $91. There is no limit to parking charges on the first level, a measure designed to free up space for those who need it for only a few hours.

An "economy" parking lot farther away from the terminals, to which there is shuttle service, offers cheaper rates: $2 per half hour, $10 per day, $65 per week, and $170 per month. Valet parking is also available; the rates, not including taxes, are $25 for the first day (includes valet fee), $15 for the second and subsequent days. If you pick up your car within three hours of the start of the second or subsequent days, you are not charged for the day; otherwise, a half-hourly rate of $2.50 is charged, to a daily maximum of $15. Cash, Visa, MasterCard, and American Express are accepted methods of payment for parking services. Park 'n Fly (6380 Miller Rd, Richmond; 604/270-9395) is an off-site service that offers valet parking and shuttle service to the airport for $10.95 per day, $69.95 per week, and $279.80 per month.

The two major Canadian **AIRLINES**, Canadian International (604/279-6611) and Air Canada (604/688-5515), are planning to merge. These two carriers provide the bulk of travel along chief intercity routes within the country; in turn, each airline contracts or owns regional airlines that move people and freight within a region, a kind of hub-and-spoke situation. Air BC (604/688-5515 or 888/422-7533) is the main regional air carrier, connecting Vancouver via Vancouver International Airport with a number of larger BC cities and towns.

The major airlines of the United States, Asia, and Europe also have facilities at the airport. For a listing of current **ARRIVALS AND DEPARTURES** at Vancouver International Airport, log on to www.yvr.ca/FIDS/fidsarrivalsbytime.asp.

For travellers leaving Vancouver by air, an airport departure fee is charged. It's in addition to departure taxes, which are usually noted and paid for in your airplane ticket. The fee schedule: $5 for passengers travelling to a destination within British Columbia or the Yukon; $10 for passengers travelling to other North American destinations, including Hawaii and Mexico; and $15 for passengers travelling to destinations outside North America. You can't get on a flight out of the airport without paying the fee, and you do it at marked booths near the terminal gateways. Machines at the booth take major credit cards. There is no fee for arrivals.

Airport Transportation

Taxis, shuttles, limousines, and public transit are all available curbside in front of the terminals to take you downtown or anywhere else in the city. **TAXIS** from the airport to downtown cost $20 to $25. A 25-minute ride will take you through the Marpole neighbourhood (a favourite with university students), tony Shaughnessy, and the exclusive shopping strip of South Granville on your way downtown. For about half the price ($10 one way, $17 round trip), you can catch the **YVR AIRPORTER** (604/946-8866 or 800/668-3141). The distinctive green buses pull up outside the arrivals level of the terminals about once every 15 minutes. The service operates 6:30am to 12:10am daily, stopping at most of the main downtown hotels.

Instead of forking over $10 to the Airporter, hop on **BC TRANSIT**'s #100 bus (schedule info at 604/521-0400), which offers connections to the downtown core; the fare is $2.25 ($1.50 after 6:30pm). Make sure you have exact coin fare, since BC Transit drivers do not carry change.

VANCOUVER THROUGH TIME

16,000 to 11,000 BC The ancestors of the Squamish, Burrard, Tsleil-Waututh, Musqueam (Xw'muthk'i'um), Tsawwassen, Coquitlam (Kwayhquitlam), Katzie, and Semiahmoo Native bands—all segments of the Coast Salish people—arrive and establish settlements in and around the beaches and forests at the mouth of a big river emptying into a vast ocean.

AD 1792 British explorer Captain George Vancouver arrives on the West Coast, where he surveys Puget Sound, Burrard Inlet, and the island that will later bear his name.

1808 Simon Fraser, an explorer and fur trader, arrives at the village of Musqueam following an overland route by a river he thinks is the Columbia. Despite the error, the river he navigates is named for him.

1827 The Hudson's Bay Company builds a trading post on the Fraser River. It is the first permanent, non-Native settlement in the Vancouver area. Since 1893, the company has occupied a prime location at the corner of Georgia and Granville in Vancouver's downtown core, and they're still trading.

1858 The news that there is gold on the banks of the Fraser River raises a bit of interest. About 25,000 prospectors drop in to have a look.

1859 A talkative chap nicknamed "Gassy Jack" Deighton opens a saloon for forestry workers on the shore of Burrard Inlet. It becomes so popular, a community is built up around the place and calls itself Gastown.

1869 A two-and-a-half-hectare (six-acre) townsite, including Gastown, is incorporated as the town of Granville, named after the colonial secretary of the time.

1886 Granville is incorporated as the City of Vancouver. The first mayor is realtor M. A. McLean. Lucky him. On June 13, a brush fire gets away and burns the city to the ground in less than 30 minutes. McLean, knowing the value of real estate, starts rebuilding in a matter of days.

1887 The Canadian Pacific Railway's first train arrives; Vancouver is the terminus of the first transcontinental trip.

1889 The first Granville Street Bridge opens. The present one is the third.

1891 French actress Sarah Bernhardt stars in Fedora at the Opera House.

1898 The Nine O'Clock Gun is placed at Brockton Point. People still set their watches by it.

1904 The first automobile arrives using an overland route.

1908 The University of British Columbia opens its doors. A few students show up. There are 17,000 there now.

1909 The Dominion Trust Building, the city's first skyscraper, opens at Hastings and Cambie Streets.

1911 Canada's first artificial ice rink, the Arena, opens. People immediately begin skating around the edge counterclockwise.

1936 The new City Hall at 12th Avenue and Cambie Street is dedicated. It still looks like it belongs in Gotham City.

1939 The Lions Gate Bridge is officially opened by King George VI and Queen Elizabeth. It was built so a real estate company could sell the property it had bought on the North Shore. It was engineered to last about 50 years. The third (and present) Hotel Vancouver is completed. Almost immediately, it becomes a barracks for World War II soldiers.

1954 Roger Bannister and John Landry run the "Miracle Mile" in less than four minutes at Empire Stadium.

1958 The Second Narrows Bridge collapses, killing 18 workmen and 1 rescue worker.

1964 The Beatles visit.

1967 Anti–Vietnam War protest takes place. More follow.

1970 The Vancouver Canucks play their first National Hockey League game.

1979 The Vancouver Whitecaps win the North American Soccer League championship.

1980 One-legged runner Terry Fox begins his cross-Canada "Marathon of Hope."

1983 BC Place Stadium inflates, looking like a cake in the oven. Once up, it becomes the world's largest air-supported dome. It has 60,000 seats. Let's put that in perspective: if you put in it all the residents of Vancouver when the city was incorporated in 1886, you'd have 59,000 empty seats.

1985 Rick Hansen begins his around-the-world Man in Motion tour by wheelchair.

1986 Vancouver's centennial is marked by the transportation fair Expo 86, the largest special-category world exposition ever staged in North America.

1994 The Vancouver Canucks reach the Stanley Cup finals but lose in the final moments of the game. Disappointed fans riot in downtown Vancouver. The BC Lions football team wins the Grey Cup for the second time in its history.

1995 The new Vancouver Public Library building opens. General Motors Place, a venue for hockey, basketball, and musical performances, opens. The NBA franchise the Vancouver Grizzlies begins its inaugural season and nearly gets the award for the most losses by a rookie team. (It missed the record by one game.) The Ford Centre for the Performing Arts opens for what turns out to be three years, before its owners went bankrupt.

Board outside the terminals, ask for a transfer (good for 90 minutes), and get off at Granville Street and 70th Avenue. Transfer to a #8 Fraser bus to get downtown. If you stay on the #100 until it reaches the New Westminster SkyTrain station, you get a scenic tour of the city and can use your transfer to ride the SkyTrain rail transit system downtown (see Getting Around in the Lay of the City chapter).

Perimeter Transportation's **WHISTLER EXPRESS** (604/266-5386) shuttles travellers to the Whistler ski resort by bus five times a day for $43. **QUICK SHUTTLE** (604/940-4428) operates a service between the major downtown hotels, Vancouver International Airport, and various points in Bellingham and services Seattle eight times daily; a one-way ticket is about $45 (US $29). Reservations must be made in advance. If you need a quick link to Victoria, the province's capital, you can take advantage of any one of five daily flights from Vancouver International Airport to Victoria Harbour offered by **HELIJET AIRWAYS** (604/273-1414 or 800/665-4354; www.helijet.com). Regular one-way cost of the half-hour flight is $129. Victoria and several coastal communities are also served by several charter services.

By Charter or Private Airplane
North Vancouver Air (604/278-1608), Harbour Air Seaplanes (604/688-1277), and Vancouver Helicopter Tours (604/270-1484) all serve Victoria and other coastal communities. Private aircraft are welcome at Vancouver International's south terminal, but those coming from the United States or overseas should call Canada Customs (604/666-1805) prior to arrival in order to clear their entry into Canada. Otherwise, simply arrange arrival and parking privileges at the South Airport through the Flight Service Station (604/666-9403).

By Seaplane
Vancouver is one of the few major international airports to also operate a floatplane facility. For many communities along the province's rugged Pacific Coast, year-round floatplane access is more economical than building facilities for conventional wheeled aircraft. For further information, call the Flight Service Station (604/666-9403). Other seaplane connections to Vancouver are detailed under Air Tours in the Exploring chapter.

BY BUS

Located just east of the downtown core near the intersection of Main and Terminal Streets, the weathered but still graceful facade of **PACIFIC CENTRAL STATION** (1150 Station St; map:V6) welcomes travellers to the local terminus of several bus and rail services. The station is well served by taxis and public transit. City buses and SkyTrain, Vancouver's high-speed rail transit service, are only a block away.

Bus lines operating from Pacific Central Station include Greyhound (604/662-3222 or 800/661-8747; www.greyhound.ca) and Pacific Coach Lines (604/662-8074). **GREYHOUND** operates five trips daily between Vancouver and Seattle, with connections in Seattle to other U.S. points. The Greyhound depot in Bellingham, Washington, offers a convenient link with ferries travelling north to Alaska. **PACIFIC COACH LINES** (PCL) operates a modern, Greyhound-like bus service between Vancouver and Victoria via BC Ferries. Connections are available in downtown Victoria for points across Vancouver Island. Although most people board at Pacific Central Station, you can arrange to be picked up or dropped off at the airport or at specific city bus stops along the route in Vancouver, Richmond, or Victoria and its suburbs.

PCL buses depart Vancouver and Victoria for the Tsawwassen and Swartz Bay ferry terminals about an hour before each ferry departure. Since the ferries adjust their schedules seasonally, it is wise to verify departure times prior to travelling. The round-trip fare is $50 per person and includes the ferry. While aboard the ferry, you are free to go anywhere passengers are allowed on the ship. The ferry crew makes an announcement shortly before docking asking bus passengers to return to their coach; your driver will explain the procedure in detail before you board the ferry. The total travel time, one way, is about three hours (see Getting Around in the Lay of the City chapter).

BY TRAIN

VIA RAIL (1150 Station St; 800/561-8630; www.viarail.ca/en.trai.oues.html; map:V6) is Canada's national passenger rail service. The *Canadian*, the name of the transcontinental train, travels between Toronto, Ontario, and Vancouver, with stops in Sudbury Junction, Ontario; Winnipeg, Manitoba; Saskatoon, Saskatchewan; Edmonton and Jasper, Alberta; and Kamloops, BC. The *Canadian* leaves Vancouver on Fridays, Sundays, and Tuesdays and leaves Toronto on Tuesdays, Thursdays, and Saturdays. The entire journey takes three days: if you leave Toronto on, say, Tuesday at midday, you'll arrive in Vancouver on Friday morning. Two classes are offered aboard the *Canadian*: economy and first class, which is called Silver & Blue.

AMTRAK (1150 Station St; 800/872-7245; www.amtrak.com/trip/cascadacordor.html; map:V6) is the American passenger train service and part of Amtrak's Pacific Northwest route system that services Oregon and Washington State. Trains travel daily between Seattle and Vancouver. The fare ranges from $24 to $32 one way.

BC RAIL (1311 W 1st St, North Vancouver; 800/339-8752 within BC, 800/663-8238 outside BC; www.bcrail.com/bcrpass; map:E1) is the provincial railway operation. It provides comfortable passenger transportation between North Vancouver, just north of the city's downtown core, and the central interior city of Prince George. You ride aboard the *Cariboo Prospector* train on a fleet of self-propelled, air-conditioned passenger cars known as Budd cars. An additional summer train, the *Whistler Explorer*, which runs between Whistler and Kelly Lake, is used extensively by tour groups from overseas and the United States (see Exploring in the Whistler chapter). BC Rail also operates a popular turn-of-the-19th-century-style steam train called the *Royal Hudson* on excursions from North Vancouver to Squamish along scenic Howe Sound between June and September.

BY CAR

Two major highways connect Greater Vancouver to British Columbia, the rest of Canada, and the United States, offering drivers a panorama of farmland, towns, cities, and mountains. **HIGHWAY 99**, the main highway connecting Vancouver to Seattle and the rest of Washington State, leads south from the city across the fertile delta at the mouth of the Fraser River and connects with Interstate 5. It's about a three-hour drive between Vancouver and Seattle, crossing the international boundary at Blaine, Washington.

Highway 99 also connects Vancouver to the ski resort town of Whistler, about a two-hour drive north of the city. Offering some stunning views of the Coast Mountains, it's been dubbed the **SEA TO SKY HIGHWAY**. From Whistler, 99 arcs northeastward into the province's interior, joining Highway 97, the main north-south highway in BC, just north of Cache Creek.

HIGHWAY 1, the **TRANS-CANADA HIGHWAY**, winds through the Lower Mainland, up the Fraser River Valley, and east across the rest of Canada. The stretch from Vancouver to Chilliwack, an agricultural community about two hours east of Vancouver, is a divided freeway. The rest is a good two-lane highway with connections to Highway 97 at Cache Creek, Highway 5 (the Yellowhead) at Kamloops, and other roadways from Idaho and Montana. The Trans-Canada crosses the Rocky Mountains through the historic Rogers and Kicking Horse Passes, passing through Revelstoke, Golden, and Banff, Alberta.

RUSH HOUR in Vancouver starts about 7am and tangles up traffic until about 9am Monday through Friday. In the afternoon, it starts about 3:30pm and ends about 6:30pm. For regular updates on highway conditions in the Vancouver area and across the province, call 604/299-9000; the information is also available on-line, through the BC Ministry of Transportation (www.th.gov.bc.ca/bchighways/camroad/roadrpts.htm) and a private operator (www.bchighway.com/report/).

When to Visit

Keep in mind that airfares, hotel rates, and admission fees are often lower from November through February.

WEATHER

While the rest of Canada suffers from long winters, British Columbia, blessed by a temperate maritime climate, has become known as Lotus Land. Vancouver's weather is the mildest in Canada, thanks to ocean currents and major weather patterns that bring warm, moist air in waves from the Pacific all year-round. The city is the largest one in Canada with palm trees. (Don't believe it? There's one at First Beach in the downtown core's West End.) Spring comes early, with flowers generally in full bloom by early March. July and August are the warmest months. Late-summer and autumn days—through October—tend to be warm and sunny, with the odd day of showers. Winter is the rainy season, which starts about November and tapers off about March, but the rain usually falls as showers or drizzle. Heavy continuous downpours are rare, as are thunderstorms and strong winds. Of course, the amount of rain is what makes the Douglas fir trees grow so large on the mountainsides readily visible from Vancouver and what causes the area to look so lush to many visitors. If it's going to snow—and most of the time it doesn't—it will usually snow in late December or early January. Higher elevations experience the precipitation as snow, translating into excellent skiing on the area's three major ski hills during the winter. June, July, and August are the driest months.

Average temperature and precipitation by month

Month	Daily Average Temp. (Centigrade)	Daily Average Temp. (Fahrenheit)	Monthly Precipitation (in millimetres)	Monthly Precipitation (in inches)
JANUARY	3.0	37.4	149.8	5.9
FEBRUARY	4.7	40.5	123.6	4.9
MARCH	6.3	43.3	108.8	4.3
APRIL	8.8	47.8	75.4	3.0
MAY	12.1	53.8	61.7	2.4
JUNE	15.2	59.4	45.7	1.8
JULY	17.2	63.0	36.1	1.4
AUGUST	17.4	63.3	38.1	1.5
SEPTEMBER	14.3	57.7	64.4	2.5
OCTOBER	10.0	50.0	115.3	4.5
NOVEMBER	6.0	42.8	169.9	6.7
DECEMBER	3.5	38.3	178.5	7.0
ANNUAL	9.9	49.8	1,167.4	46.0

Source: Environment Canada

TIME

Vancouver is on Pacific Standard Time (PST), the same as Washington State, Oregon, and California. Residents enjoy long daylight hours in summer, with sunrises before 6am and sunsets as late as 10pm.

WHAT TO BRING

The best clothing for summer is lightweight shirts, shorts, blouses, and pants, plus a jacket for rain. For fall and winter, bring the type of clothing you can put on in layers, including long-sleeved shirts or blouses, as well as some additional clothing, such as sweaters and jackets. Pack an umbrella, a pair of waterproof shoes, and a rain jacket. Clothing is casual in virtually all parts of the city; even the most expensive restaurants allow patrons to wear jeans, and none require men to wear a tie.

General Costs

For the past couple of years, British Columbia, usually Canada's economic powerhouse, has been in the economic doldrums. There are a number of reasons for this, among them provincial-government policies, Asian economic troubles, and a relaxation in the demand for key commodities such as lumber and minerals. BC's economy has long been based on resource industries, primarily forestry, mining, and fishing. In the past decade, all of these have declined in strength as tourism became more important; it's now in the number-two position. During 1998, $8.8 billion was spent by 22 million overnight visitors travelling in the province. Forestry remains the province's number-one economic engine. It accounts for about $15.8 billion worth of activity annually, just under half of the province's manufacturing output. The production of mineral and petroleum products in BC is valued at about $4.6 billion per year.

British Columbia's population of four million continues to grow more diverse, with a steady influx of newcomers from other parts of Canada and around the world. The largest age group, 35 to 44, accounts for about 17 percent of that total. During the past 10 years, people coming from elsewhere have accounted for 77 percent of the province's population growth, with residents' own natural increase contributing the remaining 23 percent. The origin of non-Canadian immigrants to BC has changed during the decade. Historically, the bulk came from Europe; recently, more immigrants have come from Asia.

The Canadian dollar is worth only about half of the American dollar, which makes for great bargains for outside visitors. In addition to a low dollar, Vancouver has a wide and modern selection of goods and services. For example, the city's prices for legal music CDs are among the lowest in the industrialized world—you can buy four top sellers for the price of two in other countries. Most Greater Vancouver firms accept

U.S. dollars and the Japanese yen, and they usually offer reasonable **EXCHANGE RATES** (see the Foreign Visitors section under Tips for Special Travellers in this chapter). American coins work in most vending machines, as Canadian coins resemble American coins of similar value. For instance, an American and a Canadian quarter look similar and can usually be used interchangeably in vending machines. Same with dimes, nickels, and pennies. But don't expect to get an exchange rate when paying with coins. The Canadian dollar itself is no longer paper; it's a relatively large gold-coloured coin nicknamed the "loonie" because it features the aquatic bird on its face. There is also a distinctive two-tone $2 coin, a bit bigger and heavier than the $1 coin. It has various nicknames, the most prevalent being "toonie" (or "twoonie"), because it rhymes with loonie. Retailers say visitors often have trouble remembering which coin is what value, but here's a simple method: the $1 is one colour, the $2 is two colours.

Vancouver is ahead of the world when it comes to using **ELECTRONIC CASH** at retailers and restaurants. Debit cards can be used in virtually all retail shops and restaurants—even fast-food eateries—in Greater Vancouver. Cash machines (aka ATMs) are located throughout high-volume areas of the city and usually at each bank branch. As a result, few Vancouverites bother carrying a chequebook anymore. Major **CREDIT CARDS,** particularly Visa and MasterCard, are accepted virtually everywhere. American Express and Discover charge cards are accepted only at major retail locations and restaurants.

Three levels of **TAXATION** affect visitors to Vancouver. On the sale of most goods and the provision of most services, a 7 percent provincial sales tax (PST) as well as a separate 7 percent federal goods and services tax (GST) are levied. Even though governments claim they are trying to keep things simple, there are lots of untaxed exemptions, particularly when dealing with food. Typically, no tax is charged on food unless it's prepared food or small portions. Children's clothing is usually PST-exempt. PST on liquor is 10 percent instead of 7 percent. PST is not charged on accommodation; instead, there is a 10 percent accommodation tax that appears on hotel and motel bills. By law, retailers must show whether they are including the GST when they show prices, and the tax must be shown separately on bills or receipts. By convention, most prices are shown before tax; taxi fares (which include GST) are the notable exception, because it's more practical to pay the amount shown on the meter. With receipts, U.S. and international visitors to Vancouver can apply at Canadian Customs to have the GST returned to them (for items costing more than $50) when they leave the country. Forms are also available from a number of retailers in Vancouver. For details of how the **GST REBATE** works, contact Canada Customs and Revenue Agency's Visitor

Rebate Enquiries Line (800/668-4748 within Canada, 902/432-5608 outside Canada) or e-mail questions to visitors@rc.gc.ca.

Average costs for lodging and food

Double room:	
INEXPENSIVE	**$50–$70**
MODERATE	**$70–$100**
EXPENSIVE	**$100 AND UP**
Lunch for one:	
INEXPENSIVE	**$5–$10**
MODERATE	**$10–$15**
EXPENSIVE	**$15 AND UP**
Beverages in a restaurant:	
GLASS OF WINE	**$4–$7**
PINT OF BEER	**$5**
COCA-COLA	**$1.25**
DOUBLE TALL LATTE	**$3.53**
Other common items:	
MOVIE TICKET	**$9**
ROLL OF FILM	**$5**
TAXI PER KILOMETRE	**$1.25**
16 OZ. SMOKED SOCKEYE SALMON	**$20.95**
VANCOUVER SOUVENIR T-SHIRT	**$10–$20**

GRATUITIES are not mandatory for most services rendered, but tips of 10 to 20 percent on the pretax amount are encouraged when above-average service is encountered. An easy formula is to double the GST (federal tax) to equal 14 percent. Add a little and you have a decent tip on the pretax bill. It is courteous to tip hotel staff $1 to $5 depending on the service provided, such as baggage delivery ($1.50 per bag at top hotels) or room service.

Tips for Special Travellers

FAMILIES WITH CHILDREN

In an emergency, call 911, 24 hours a day. For answers to questions about your child's health, growth, or development, call the BC Children's Hospital (4880 Oak St; 604/875-2345). If you think your child has swallowed a toxic substance, call the Poison Control Centre (604/682-5050 or 604/682-2344). *West Coast Families* is an award-winning monthly publication full of event listings and information for parents. Published by Ideas Ink (604/689-1331), it is available free at most bookstores, children's retailers, community centres, and other locations throughout the

Vancouver area, as well as on-line (www. westcoastfamilies.com). Another useful magazine, published monthly, is *BC Parent* (604/221-0366; www.bcparent.com).

Most major hotels can arrange for child care if notified in advance. Travelling to special sights or events with kids is not a problem; children 4 years and younger ride free on BC Transit.

Watch for the icon at left throughout the book; it indicates places and activities that are great for families.

SENIORS

Seniors One-Stop Information Line (604/983-3303) and Seniors Information and Referral Services (604/875-6381) provide information about programs and services available to seniors in the Vancouver area. Seniors 65 and over with valid proof of age are eligible for concession fares on BC Transit vehicles; they vary according to time of day and distance travelled. On weekdays before 6:30pm, fares are as follows: one zone, $1; two zones, $1.50; three zones, $2. After 6:30pm and on weekends and holidays, the fare is a standard $1. A FareSaver booklet of 10 tickets is $10, and a daypass offering unlimited travel is $4. These can be purchased at "FareDealers," identified by a decal in windows of retail stores such as Safeway, 7-Eleven, and some gas stations.

PEOPLE WITH DISABILITIES

BC is home to more disabled people per capita than any other province in Canada, thanks to its mild climate and its efforts to accommodate the needs of residents and visitors. Most buses and businesses are wheelchair accessible, and a wide range of community and recreational services are available. Resource groups include the BC Paraplegic Association (604/324-3611), the BC Mobility Opportunity Society (604/222-1312), the Canadian National Institute for the Blind (604/431-2121, TTY 604/431-2131), and the Western Institute for the Deaf and Hard of Hearing (604/736-7391, TTY 604/736-2527).

Door-to-door transportation in lift-equipped vans is available for passengers in wheelchairs and others with restricted mobility, through HandyDART (604/540-3400), a service of BC Transit. Trips must be booked at least 48 hours in advance. The basic fare is $1.50, and a book of 10 tickets is available for $15. Vancouver Taxi (604/871-1111 or 800/969-8294) also carries wheelchair passengers, at no additional charge to the regular fare.

WOMEN

Vancouver is a safe city for female travellers, but extra precautions are always wise at night, especially in the city's many parks. Women should also be wary in the old industrial and warehouse district downtown east of Granville Street, north from the Granville Street bridge. Though relatively safe during the day, it takes on a more lurid cast in the evening. The

Rape Relief and Women's Shelter (604/872-8212) and Rape Crisis Centre (604/255-6344) are available to assist victims of rape and abuse. For health and reproductive services, call Planned Parenthood (604/731-4252). On a lighter note, a rich trove of reading material and resources of interest to women can be found at the Women in Print bookshop, located in Kitsilano (3566 W 4th Ave; 604/732-4128; map:B2).

PET OWNERS

Vancouver, with its glorious views, constantly green grass, and miles of beaches is dog heaven, as long as you use a leash. Your year-round best bets for **OFF-LEASH EXERCISE** are Pacific Spirit Regional Park (the UBC endowment lands), particularly nice in the summer as the big trees keep it cool, and Ambleside Park and beach in West Vancouver. The privileges are earned: scoop your pooch's doo. Off-leash times are posted at certain parks in Vancouver, too. Ross Powell's *Where to Walk Your Dog in Greater Vancouver* (Arcadian Productions, 1998) is a treat for all dog owners.

Visitors to Vancouver will delight in the fact that the **FOUR SEASONS HOTEL** (791 W Georgia St; 604/689-9333; map:S4) not only welcomes dogs but has a "Dog Recognition Program," including a handmade dog bowl by a local ceramic artist, biscuits made in the hotel's bakery (with recipe card), and bottled Evian water. Dog beds are available on request, as are dog walks. For more on accommodation, see Marg Meikle's *Dog City: Vancouver* (Polestar, 1997), which also covers resources from doo to don'ts, from photographers to psychics, and from taxis to training.

Dirty dog? Try **IT'S A DOG'S LIFE**, a self- or full-serve dog wash and consignment store (3428 W Broadway; 604/739-DOGS; map:C3).

Need pet day-care? Dogs need all standard shots and kennel cough vaccination. In the downtown area, **LAUNDERDOG DAY CARE AND DOG WASH** (1064 Davie St; 604/685-2306; map:R5) has small- and large-dog play areas. The dog needs a half-hour intro before the first-day stay. **DOG HOUSE DAY CARE** has two locations (2425 Manitoba, at W 8th; 604/708-6100; map:U8; and 105–1833 Anderson St, entrance to Granville Island; 604/737-7500; map:Q7).

Does your dog deserve a serious treat? Birthday cakes, personalized dog bones, and assorted homemade goodies are available from **THREE DOG BAKERY** (2186 W 4th Ave; 604/737-3647; map:N7).

GAYS AND LESBIANS

Vancouver is home to two distinctly different queer neighbourhoods. The West End is an exciting urban residential area long established as friendly to its substantial gay population and mainly centred around Davie and Denman Streets. Delany's on Denman (1105 Denman St; 604/662-3344; map:P2) is a cool coffee spot and meeting place for the gay and lesbian crowd. Gay men may prefer the catwalk atmosphere of Davie Street, a short strip scattered with gay-friendly cafes, brunch spots, and clothing stores and anchored by the city's gay bookstore, Little Sister's Book & Art Emporium (1238 Davie St; 604/669-1753; map:Q4). As clubs close, the Edge (1148 Davie St; 604/688-3395; map:R5) fills with club-weary revellers looking for a jolt of caffeine or a last chance at romance. Lesbians will feel most at home on Commercial Drive, an East Side artery offering a vibrant mix of authentic Italian and Portuguese cafes, stylish new restaurants, and small boutiques. Harry's (1716 Charles St; 604/253-1789; map:Z6) is a friendly coffee shop and community meeting spot. For club options, see the Nightlife chapter.

Xtra West (604/684-9696), a free gay publication, lists events, clubs, and community groups; it's available in stores and cafes in the West End. Visitors may also wish to drop by the Centre (1170 Bute St; 604/684-5307; map:Q4), which offers a library, or call Prideline from 7 to 10 pm (604/684-6869). Gay businesses and services are listed in the *GLBA Directory,* published by the Gay and Lesbian Business Association (604/878-4898), available free in many stores. Gay culture also thrives outdoors. Mostly men head to clothing-optional Wreck Beach, off Marine Drive below the University of British Columbia, or to Lees Trail near Second Beach in Stanley Park. In the summer months, lesbians congregate at Trout Lake at Victoria and 15th (near Commercial) or head up Highway 99 to the beach at Lions Bay. Gay bashing is uncommon but not extinct. If you are in danger, call 911; report incidents by leaving a message on the Bashline at (604/899-6203).

FOREIGN VISITORS

Vancouver is a cosmopolitan port city and offers a wide range of services to international visitors. Several **EXCHANGE FIRMS** have locations downtown, including the Thomas Cook Group (Pacific Centre Shopping Mall, 701 Granville St; 604/687-6111; map:T4; and Pan Pacific Hotel; 130–999 Canada Pl; 604/641-1229; map:U2), the International Securities Exchange (1036 Robson St; 604/683-4686; map:S4; 1169 Robson St; 604/683-9666; map:R3; and 1325 Robson St; 604/683-3817; map:R3), and Inter Currency Exchange Corp. (300–609 W Hastings St; 604/688-8668; map:U4). Banks are also able to exchange many currencies, and most businesses accept U.S. dollars (though at varying exchange rates, sometimes significantly different from the rate posted at banks and exchange offices). For a current quote on your money's worth, check the following Web site: www2.mybc.com/aroundtown/moneyweb/calc/currency.html.

Many **TRANSLATION SERVICES** operate in Vancouver. For names of accredited translators who will best serve your needs, call the Society of Translators and Interpreters of BC (604/684-2940). The College of Physicians and Surgeons (604/733-7758) provides a list of multilingual doctors, and some transit drivers are familiar with Asian languages.

For **CUSTOMS INFORMATION AND SERVICES,** call Canada Customs (604/666-0545). There are no embassies in Vancouver, but the city hosts more than 30 consulates.

WEB INFORMATION

It's hard to walk through some of Vancouver's trendier districts, such as Yaletown, and not spot a technology or graphic design company. The city is home to some of North America's most active animation, Internet, and software development firms. (It's also home to more Starbucks coffee outlets per capita than anywhere in Canada, which probably helps drive the fast-paced technology business.) A number of good Web sites disseminate the latest dirt on Vancouver. They include www.mybc.com, the main portal site, with movie reviews, sports events, and local news, and the content-rich information site www.vancouver.about.com. The hub of technology news for Vancouver is www.bctechnology.com.

For arts and entertainment news, log on to www.straight.com, the arts and entertainment weekly on-line, now part of mybc.com. Other Web sites useful for getting a good overview of Vancouver—both figuratively and literally—include www.localdir.com (the Vancouver Internet Directory); www.vancouvertourist.com/sat1.htm (for a satellite-eye view of Vancouver); www.telemark.net/cgi-shl/wc.pl (for a current look at Vancouver's Burrard Inlet); and www.vancouvertourist.com/photopages/photo index.htm (for some great-looking photos of interesting sights). For your own map of Vancouver (in PDF format, suitable for printing on your own printer), visit www.vancouvertourist.com/maps/vancouver.pdf or www.discovervancouver.com/maps/maps_index.html. For maps of the downtown core (including a map of the Robson Street retail area), Granville Island, Stanley Park, and the transit system of Vancouver, complete with bus routes, among others, check out www.tourism-vancouver.org/ (Tourism Vancouver's site). For an eclectic view of Vancouver, log on to www.rediguana.com/wbcity/map/map.html.

LAY OF THE CITY

LAY OF THE CITY

Orientation

Hold your right hand out, palm up and thumb out, so your thumb points straight ahead away from your body. That's what the city of Vancouver looks like from above. Your thumb is a peninsula jutting into the middle of the large **BURRARD INLET**, nearly splitting the inlet in half, and Vancouver's downtown core is the lower half of your thumb. To the north, in the direction your thumb is pointing, are Vancouver's trademark mountains—Cypress, Grouse, and Hollyburn—with their forested slopes, caps of clouds, and, in the fall, winter, and spring, snowy peaks. At their base, just beyond your thumbnail, are the suburbs of **NORTH** and **WEST VANCOUVER**, gathered like petticoats skirting the bottom of these megaliths. The rest of Vancouver, which is primarily residential (except for the business and retail sections along the main thoroughfares), is on your palm.

That may sound like quite a handful, but so is Vancouver. It's actually an extensive group of cities built on an ancient river delta that was formed, squished, pushed, and squashed by the Ice Age glaciers. The entire Lower Mainland, which encompasses Greater Vancouver and the once-rural but now bustling Fraser Valley to the east, has been built up on the outflow remnants of a vast, roaring river that burst out of central British Columbia during the Ice Age tens of thousands of years ago. The delta's geological origins made for rich, forested land, which became a magnet for settlers after the interior gold rush ended in the middle of the 19th century. Since then the population, economics, and politics of the region have moulded the delta's communities until they now form one giant metropolitan area.

The suburban communities of **BURNABY** and **NEW WESTMINSTER**, once separate cities in their own right and still maintaining their own urban governments, lie to the east of Vancouver, but only a map and the occasional road sign will let you know where their city limits begin. Along the south edge of Vancouver is the North Arm of the **FRASER RIVER**. It borders the north edge of the delta of the mighty Fraser, one of the world's largest rivers. Big as it is, it's only a remnant of the river that once flowed into a pristine fjord when the glaciers held sway. The delta's islands are now the huge suburbs of **RICHMOND, DELTA,** and **SURREY**. The City of Richmond is on Lulu Island, defined by the North and South Arms of the Fraser River, and Vancouver International Airport is on Sea Island, to its north.

Hold out your palm again. Remember that the lower part of your thumb represents Vancouver's downtown core. On the left side of it is Vancouver's heavily populated **WEST END**, a forest of apartment buildings

HOW TO ACT LIKE A LOCAL

Become ecologically friendly. They say you should never discuss politics or religion at a party. In Vancouver, add ecology to that list. This is composting country, the birthplace of Greenpeace, the home of David Suzuki, the land of lush temperate rain forests. Don't get us started.

Adopt laid-back living. Begin your weekend just after noon on Friday. Play hard all weekend. Then begin your work week just after noon on Monday.

Become a wine connoisseur. British Columbians drink the most wine per capita in North America, and they often order wine not by colour but by place and type. Here's a line to get you started: "Do you have any Oregon pinot noir or New Zealand sauvignon blanc?"

Wear Gore-Tex. On the street, you need to look as if you're ready to ascend Mount Everest—or at least one of the local mountains. Most popular are locally made TAIGA jackets, which sport all the requisite pockets, zippers, drawstrings, and Velcro fasteners. They come in emergency colours, so you'll never get shot in the woods wearing one.

Put on Birkenstocks. Like many of the locals, Birkenstocks are left over from the hippie days. Since the winters are mild, you can wear Birkenstocks year-round—with socks for half the year, without socks for the other half. Clutching a latte-to-go, sporting a TAIGA jacket, and wearing Birkenstocks, you'll pass for a local for sure.

Ski in the morning, swim in the afternoon. Shuttling between snow and sand is a local pursuit in spring. Head to the mountains in the morning for some skiing, doff the snowsuit and don the swimsuit, and head to Kitsilano Beach in the afternoon for some swimming.

Skate the seawall. On a nice summer day, the picturesque seawall around Stanley Park becomes a speedway for in-line skaters, and many locals have been handed "speeding tickets." If you don't own in-line skates, rent a pair and try to get your own ticket. Like the locals, you can then use it to prop up the leg of a wobbly table.

Jaywalk across Broadway. Locals are trusting. They expect drivers to slow down so they can cross Broadway or any other busy street. The most trusting simply saunter across. Your first attempt should be a dash.

Turn left on a red. Locals are intentionally colour-blind. They don't wait long to turn right at a red light or left on a one-way street. If no one is coming, why not turn? Come to a dead stop, gather your nerve, look both ways, and drive like a local.

—*Mark Laba*

on a grid of streets that have been retrofitted to keep traffic from roaring through the neighbourhood. In the middle of the lower part of your thumb is the business centre of the city, with skyscrapers up to 48 floors in height. On the right side of your thumb is what's called the **DOWN-TOWN EAST SIDE**, a blue-collar docks-and-warehouse area with a skid row and flophouse core. All along the right edge of the lower half of your thumb are waterfront docks.

At your thumb's pad and tip is **STANLEY PARK**, a 405-hectare (1,000-acre) forest of lush green pines, firs, and cedars interspersed with wonderful paths and meadows. On the left edge of your thumb, where Stanley Park meets the West End, is a rambling shoreline fronted by apartments, readily accessible public beaches, parks, and walking paths that, as they get to the base of your thumb, skirt the north shore of False Creek, an inlet packed with yachts, restaurants, and new high-rise condo complexes. Right at the eastern end of False Creek is the big, can't-miss-it, sparkly bubble of a building that houses **SCIENCE WORLD** (1455 Quebec St; 604/268-6363; map:V5), a great place for all members of the family to learn about science. Vancouver has an extensive network of parks that allow public access to the waterfront via large, well-lit, paving-stone paths. Many of these parks and paths, which wrap around much of the downtown waterfront, were built only in the past two or three decades. They make for a pleasant outing by foot or bike.

On the west side of the city (we're on your palm now) is an area called **KITSILANO**. Chock-a-block with friendly folk, it retains a whiff of the hippie culture that infiltrated it in the '60s in its funky retail stores. The sprawling campus of the **UNIVERSITY OF BRITISH COLUMBIA**, a city-within-a-city of 17,000 students during most of the year, is at the far western tip of Vancouver (and the fingertips of your palm). Officially, legally, it's not actually part of Vancouver, but everybody except City Hall bureaucrats pretends it is. To the east of the university is **KERRISDALE**, the affluent West Side of Vancouver. (Don't confuse Vancouver's West Side with the West End or West Vancouver; they are three entirely different areas.) And if you're going to tony Kerrisdale, take your credit cards. The working-class area of **EAST VANCOUVER** (there's only one East Van) is east of an invisible line that runs the length of Main Street as it cuts south through the city (across your palm from the very base of your thumb). **CHINATOWN** is (mostly) east of Main. A blue-collar area of East Van called **LITTLE ITALY** is just to the east of Chinatown, north and south of the fascinating intersection of First Avenue and Commercial Drive. **SOUTH VANCOUVER** is a combination of ethnic areas, including Punjabi Market, along 49th Avenue between Fraser and Main. It's about the middle of your palm, if you've still got it handy.

And that's the lay of your hand, er, Vancouver.

Visitor Information

Whether you're looking to climb Grouse Mountain, planning an evening out, or just going to the mall, go ahead and ask a passerby for advice. Vancouverites pride themselves on knowing their city well, and most will at least be able to steer you in the right direction. Otherwise, the **VANCOUVER TOURIST INFOCENTRE** (200 Burrard St; 604/683-2000; map:T2) offers a wealth of information about the city.

Getting Around

BY BUS

Although many Vancouver-area residents prefer to drive, the public transit system is one of the most effective ways to get around the city. **COAST MOUNTAIN TRANSLINK** (604/521-0400; www.bctransit.com or www. translink.bc.ca), the main subsidiary of the Greater Vancouver Transportation Authority (GVTA), covers more than 1,800 square kilometres (695 square miles) with three forms of transit: bus, SeaBus, and SkyTrain. At press time, TransLink had recently taken over transit services in the Lower Mainland from the government-owned company BC Transit (though locals still refer to it as BC Transit). Detailed information and transit maps are available at all visitor information centres, public libraries, city halls, a lot of magazine stores, and most ticket sellers. Call for route information or use the intuitive Web sites.

The current fare schedule, applicable to all three forms of transportation, is based on the number of zones travelled, as follows: one zone, $1.50; two zones, $2.25; three zones, $3. The off-peak fare, in effect through all zones after 6:30pm weekdays, on weekends, and on holidays, is $1.50. The concession fare, available to students and senior citizens with valid ID, is half the regular fare. A transfer, available from bus drivers at the time you pay your fare, is good for 90 minutes in any direction. Businesses identified by a special FareDealer decal sell tickets and passes: the most common retailers are Safeway supermarkets and 7-Eleven convenience stores. Validation machines at SkyTrain and SeaBus stations sell tickets and can make change for bills up to $20. Ticket booklets called FareSavers ($13.75 for one zone) and $6 day passes, which are great for visitors, are also available. Bus drivers are helpful, but they only accept exact change, tickets for the correct amount, or valid transfers.

BY SKYTRAIN

SkyTrain is Vancouver's fast, modern, and efficient rapid-transit system. Twenty-nine kilometres (18 miles) of route, most of it elevated on its own special tracks, run from the downtown core through Vancouver, across

21

Burnaby through New Westminster, and across the Fraser River to the Whalley area of Surrey. More routes are under construction. At the moment, there are 20 stops in all, each linked to the bus system; the trains halt at each stop for no more than three minutes, then glide away. All the SkyTrain stations have elevators (except the Granville station, map:S4, one of the four stations in the downtown core) and most have escalators. The other downtown stations are Waterfront (map:U2), Burrard (map:S3), and Stadium (map:T5). In the downtown core, the SkyTrain becomes a subway. The system is entirely computerized, with no drivers; proponents liken it to a horizontal elevator. The train cars, which can run individually or, typically, in batches of four, use a special electromagnetic system of propulsion, which gives the SkyTrain its distinctive sound. The last SkyTrain service out of downtown is 1:15am; from New Westminster into downtown, 1:29am; and from Surrey into downtown, 12:39am. Service from downtown resumes at 5:35am.

BY SEABUS

SeaBus is the only integrated marine bus system in the world. The SeaBuses are smallish foot-passenger ferries (up to 400 passengers) that cross Burrard Inlet between Vancouver's Waterfront station in the downtown core (north foot of Granville St; map:U2) and North Vancouver's Lonsdale Quay (south foot of Lonsdale Ave; map:E1). At either end, the terminals link directly to the regular bus system; on the Vancouver side, the terminal is also adjacent to stations for the SkyTrain and the *West Coast Express* (a regional commuter train). The SeaBus is wheelchair accessible, and bikes can be strapped into special racks onboard. The spectacular ride—you cruise around huge freighters and busy tugboats across one of the world's most impressive harbours, against a backdrop of tree-clad mountains and shining skyscrapers—takes 12 minutes.

The SeaBus runs every 15 minutes weekdays from about 6am to 6:30pm, then every half hour until 12:16am. Service on Saturdays is every half hour until 10:16am, then every 15 minutes until 6:16pm, at which time it reverts to half-hourly sailings. On Sundays and holidays, service is only at quarter-after and quarter-to the hour, from 8:16am to 11:16pm. If exact timing is crucial, double-check with the transit information line (604/521-0400) or the Web site (www.bctransit.com or www.translink.bc.ca), which can also outline possible connections to your destination with other forms of transit.

BY CAR

Unique among major North American centres, Vancouver has no freeways within city limits (that's what the suburbs are for, in the opinion of many Vancouverites), so traffic tends to move less than briskly during busy times. City engineers and even a few brave politicians have talked about building freeways, but plans get shot down by residents of the proposed location whenever the topic comes up. **RUSH HOURS**, which are particularly heavy and getting heavier, are from about 7 to 9am and 3:30 to 6:30pm Monday through Friday. Weekend mornings can be quiet; however, shoppers downtown on sunny Saturday or Sunday afternoons can often make it seem like rush hour. Fortunately you don't really need a car to get around, unless you're planning a trip outside the main areas of the city.

The **BC AUTOMOBILE ASSOCIATION** is the local affiliate of the Canadian Automobile Association; two branches are located on the West Side (999 W Broadway; 604/268-5600; map:R8; and 2347 W 41st Ave; 604/268-5800; map:C4). There are no downtown locations. For 24-hour roadside assistance, call 604/293-2222.

Several **RENTAL CAR AGENCIES** are located downtown, and some offer pickup and drop-off service. Call:

AVIS (Pan Pacific Hotel, 999 Canada Pl; 604/844-2847; map:T2; and 757 Hornby St; 604/606-2872; map:S3)

BUDGET (99 W Pender St; 604/683-5666; map:V4; and 501 W Georgia St; 604/668-7000; map:T4)

ENTERPRISE (585 Smithe St; 604/688-5500; map:S4)

HERTZ (1128 Seymour St; 604/606-4711; map:S5; and Westin Bayshore Hotel, 1601 W Georgia St; 604/606-3784; map:R2)

NATIONAL TILDEN (1130 W Georgia St; 604/685-6111; map:R3)

Downtown **PARKING** is available on the street (except during rush hour in places), in lots, or at parkades. The lots and parkades are relatively expensive—they range from $1.50 per half hour to $2.50 per 20 minutes—and metered curbside parking is often quite short-term, sometimes as little as 7 minutes at a time. (Beware: the streets are regularly patrolled by meter readers.) Good news for those who want to reduce the relatively low risk of car thefts and break-ins: many lots and parkades are now patrolled by parking guards.

Your car has disappeared from where you left it? First, find out if it was towed. Vancouver City Hall has a contract with a big towing company called Unitow (1717 Vernon Dr; 604/606-1255; map:Y6), so call there if you parked on a city street or lane. If it was on a private parking lot, call Busters (104 E 1st Ave; 604/685-8181; map:V6) or Drake's Towing (1553 Powell St; 604/251-3344; map:Z6). All three companies provide 24-hour towing within Vancouver. If none of them have your wheels, call 911, report the missing car to the police, and get on with your life. According to 1996 statistics, an average of 28 cars per day were reported stolen, with Vancouver Police recovering 93 percent of them.

You can buy **ROAD MAPS** at most newsstands, convenience stores, drugstores, and bookstores. If you're heading into more remote areas of the province, World Wide Books and Maps (736A Granville St; 604/687-3320; map:S4) and the Geographical Survey of Canada (101–605 Robson St; 604/666-0529; map:S4) sell detailed topographic maps.

BY TAXI AND LIMOUSINE

If anything, Vancouver may be a city of too many cabs. The phone book lists 19 taxi companies of various pedigrees, whose drivers must meet a set of standards formulated, in part, by the city's tourism groups. Besides cash, all drivers accept either Visa or MasterCard, and many take American Express. The four main companies serving downtown—and they'll take you to the surrounding communities, too—are Black Top and Checker Cabs (604/731-1111), MacLure's Cabs (604/683-6666), Vancouver Taxi (604/871-1111), and Yellow Cab Company (604/681-1111 or 800/898-8294). Vancouver Taxi specializes in wheelchair-accessible cabs, but all of the firms accommodate passengers with wheelchairs if you mention the requirement to the dispatcher when you call in. The fare is $1.25 per kilometre, plus a $2.30 flag or service charge. A cab from the airport to downtown costs about $25.

Rather pay by the hour and go first class? Star Limousine Service (604/685-5600) has been around for more than 15 years and has a fleet of more than two dozen limousines. Other companies offering prompt, reliable service include Classic Limousine (604/267-1441) and Air Limo (604/273-1331).

BY BICYCLE

Cycling is a popular method of getting to work in Vancouver, but you won't find a stream of cyclists negotiating rush hour traffic. Most people still opt to drive a car, take the bus, or find some other means of getting to the office. Part of the reason is that there are few bike lanes into the downtown core. On the other hand, 104 kilometres (65 miles) of bike paths wind through the city centre and surrounding areas, including 55 kilometres (34 miles) in Pacific Spirit Regional Park (map:B3), on the edge of the University of British Columbia campus. The City of Vancouver has done quite a bit to encourage bike travel on and off roads, and there's a comprehensive bike route network in Vancouver, featuring routes designed so bikes can share the road with cars. The city has also instituted some bicycle-activated signals, made some changes to the pavement, and given bicycles priority at some stop signs, traffic circles, traffic diversions, and medians. Fortunately—or unfortunately, depending on your point of view—these measures also reduce motor vehicle speed and volume.

Six of these **BIKE ROUTES** are now finished: the Adanac Bikeway, the Ontario Bikeway, the Off-Broadway Bikeway, the Cypress Bikeway, the Lakewood Bikeway, and the Heather Bikeway. Bike lanes along SW Marine Drive and along 37th Avenue should be finished soon. The east sidewalk of the Cambie Street Bridge (map:T6) is also an official bike route. Call the **BICYCLE HOTLINE** for details (604/871-6070) or drop by City Hall (453 W 12th Ave; map:D3) for a free map of bike routes.

The Seaside Bike Route, around the edge of Stanley Park from the Lost Lagoon area (map:P1) and along the north side of False Creek to Science World (map:V5), is one of the most popular and scenic bike routes in the city. It's a route that in part is also shared with pedestrians and in-line skaters, which makes it one of the most crowded in Vancouver. In a few years, a final piece of the route will be built, and once that's done, you'll be able to ride from Lost Lagoon to Vanier Park (map:P5), all of the route alongside a waterway.

The car vs. bike debate hasn't yet conceded all to bike riders, even on designated bike routes. Bicyclists still have to yield to pedestrians and watch for schoolchildren crossing the routes, and they are supposed to obey all other rules of the road—although quite a number of cyclists seem to disdain such regulations. In addition, cyclists are not allowed to wear headphones that cover both ears, and safety helmets, headlights, and taillights are required by law. Safety jackets, the kind that cover arms and have reflective tape on them, are recommended but optional. If you're thinking you'll just skip that helmet, forget it. There are about 60 police officers and a half-dozen parking meter staff that are on bikes instead of in squad cars, and they all enforce bike regulations.

There are many **BIKE RENTAL** facilities (which also rent bike safety equipment) around Stanley Park; the most popular are Spokes Bicycle Rental & Espresso Bar (1798 W Georgia St; 604/688-5141; map:Q2) and Bikes 'N' Blades (718 Denman St; 604/602-9899; map:Q2). Public **BIKE RACKS** are conveniently located throughout the downtown area, but bring a shackle-style U-lock if you plan to stop and shop or walk around. For additional information on biking in the city, see the Biking section of the Recreation chapter.

BY TRAIN

During the first half of the 20th century, passenger trains were a common way to get to and from Vancouver. But the advent of cars, buses, and aircraft travel sounded the death knell for many of those passenger trains. Now most of the trains arriving in Vancouver carry freight only. For information on trains in and out of Vancouver, see How to Get Here in the Planning a Trip chapter.

ROCKY MOUNTAINEER RAILTOURS (1150 Station St; 604/606-7200 or 800/665-7245; map:V6) operates a sight-seeing train from Pacific Central Station to Calgary via the breathtaking Rocky Mountains.

Within the city, the *West Coast Express* (199 Water St; 604/683-7245; map:T2) operates a weekday commuter rail service between Mission in the Fraser Valley and Waterfront Station in downtown Vancouver that offers various amenities, including cappuccino bars. Five morning trains head west from Mission beginning at 5:28am. Eastbound service begins in the afternoon and ends with the last departure from Waterfront Station at 6:15pm. Fare to Mission is $7 one way, $13.65 round trip. Interurban rates, as well as weekly and monthly passes, are also available.

BY FERRY

Vancouver is surrounded by water on three sides, but no large passenger ferries dock within the city. The government-run BC FERRIES (1112 Fort St, Victoria; 250/386-3431 or 888/223-3779; www.bcferries.com) operates a busy service that includes a minimum of eight daily sailings (more than a dozen in summer) between Tsawwassen (pronounced Swah-sehn), a town named after a local Native tribe that's located about a half-hour drive south of the city, and Swartz Bay, on Vancouver Island near Sidney, a town that's a similar distance from downtown Victoria. Travel time, city centre to city centre, is about three hours; about 90 minutes of that is on the ferry trip. The rate schedule covers three seasons. All fares are one way. WINTER: passengers are $7.50, cars $22.75 (weekdays) and $24.25 (weekends), SPRING AND FALL: passengers are $8.50, cars $27 (weekdays) and $28.75 (weekends), SUMMER: passengers are $9, cars $30 (weekdays) and $32 (weekends).

Other sailings go from Tsawwassen or Horseshoe Bay, north of Vancouver, to the "mid-Island" city of Nanaimo, the Gulf Islands, and the Sunshine Coast. The ferries provide a pleasant cruise through often awe-inspiring scenery, with amenities that include a cafeteria and (on some) buffet dining room, snack bar, newsstand, and promenade decks. Foot passengers can take either a West Vancouver Blue Bus (604/985-7777) to the Horseshoe Bay terminal, or a TransLink bus (604/521-0400) to Tsawwassen, or travel via Pacific Coach Lines (604/662-7575), which goes to Victoria, Nanaimo, the Sunshine Coast, and the Gulf Islands.

Essentials

PUBLIC REST ROOMS

Vancouver has no shortage of places to go. All of the major malls in Greater Vancouver have public facilities, and some large stores, such as Eaton's, the Bay, and Chapters, have rest rooms that are open to the public. Downtown, the most accessible public rest rooms are located on the Howe Street level of the Pacific Centre shopping mall (700 W Georgia St to 777 Dunsmuir St; map:S4) and the ground level of the Bentall Shopping Centre (595 Burrard St; map:S4).

MAJOR BANKS

Don't worry if you arrived with unfinished business: all the major Canadian banks and many foreign financial institutions provide a full range of financial services, including foreign exchange. There are also dozens of ATMs, or bank machines, scattered throughout the downtown core. Standard banking hours are from 9:30am to 4pm, though some downtown locations open as early as 8am.

POLICE AND SAFETY

In emergency situations, dial 911. For fire and ambulance, typical response times are within three to five minutes; for police, it depends on the situation, but three minutes is typical for an emergency. For non-emergency situations, call 604/717-3535. There are two police stations: the old one is in the rough section of town at 312 Main Street (map:V3), and the new, main one is at Cambie Street and Sixth Avenue (map:T7).

Greater Vancouver is among the safest cities in the world for residents as well as visitors. Men can safely walk in any area of the city at any time of the day or night, but should be wary in the skid row areas of Hastings Street (the three blocks either side of Main Street; map:V4) and on Granville Street between Nelson Street and the Granville Street Bridge (map:S5). Women should not walk alone in and, even in pairs, should avoid these areas after dark, particularly on Friday and Saturday nights. It is extremely unlikely that women, even if alone, would be attacked in these areas, which are well patrolled, well lit, and usually quite busy, but they are much more likely than men to be approached, panhandled, or hassled. Women should also avoid the several blocks of the red-light district that establishes itself in the late afternoon and evening on Richards and Seymour Streets between Drake and Nelson (map:S5) in the downtown core, in the three blocks of Hastings Street either side of Main (map:V4), in the half-dozen blocks around Broadway and Fraser (map:X8), or in a three-block radius around the industrial area of Sixth Avenue and Ontario Street (map:V7). During the daytime, it's quite safe in these areas.

Most panhandlers are courteous and focus on the downtown cores and malls. Pickpockets are not a great concern either, but there are a lot of drug-driven "smash-and-grabs" in cars and homes. Hotels, especially in the downtown core, are fairly protective, but you should not leave personal property of any value in a vehicle, and definitely not if it can be seen by passersby. Cars in park-and-ride lots near public transit are particularly vulnerable to thieves.

HOSPITALS AND MEDICAL/DENTAL SERVICES

We hope you don't need the information in this section, but just in case: the two largest hospitals are Vancouver General Hospital (855 W 12th Ave; 604/875-4111; map:D2), atop what's locally called Fairview Slopes overlooking the downtown core, and St. Paul's Hospital, in the city's heavily populated West End (1081 Burrard St; 604/682-2344 or 604/806-8011 for patient information; map:R4). The UBC campus on Point Grey is home to the University Hospital (2211 Westbrook Mall; 604/822-7121; map:A2).

Walk-in clinics, with no appointment necessary, include Carepoint Medical Centres (1175 Denman St; 604/681-5338; map:P3; 3419 Kingsway; 604/436-0800; map:F4; and 1623 Commercial Dr; 604/254-5554; map:Z6), Maple Medical Clinic (103–2025 W Broadway; 604/730-9769; map:C3), Medicentre (Bentall Centre, 1055 Dunsmuir St; 604/683-8138; map:S3), and Royal Centre Medical (238–1055 W Georgia St; 604/682-6886; map:S3). The College of Physicians and Surgeons of BC (1807 W 10th Ave; 604/733-7758; map:C3) has a list of doctors accepting patients.

POST OFFICE

The federal government owns the independent national company Canada Post, which has a monopoly on moving mail in the country. Canada Post's headquarters is a big, block-size, square building in downtown Vancouver (349 W Georgia St; 604/662-5722; map:T4). It's located across the street from Library Square and is one of two outlets the national postal service operates in the downtown core. The other is in the Bentall Centre (595 Burrard St; 604/482-4296; map:S3). Both have philatelic counters. Standard first-class postal rates, not including the 7 percent federal sales tax, are 46 cents within Canada, 55 cents to the United States, and 95 cents overseas. Mail bound outside Canada and requiring more than $5 postage is tax-exempt. Please note the obvious—but sometimes overlooked—point that all postage on mail that goes through the Canadian postal system must be Canadian.

GROCERY STORES

In addition to numerous produce shops, bakeries, and butcher shops, Greater Vancouver is fed by three major chain grocers: Canada Safeway, Overwaitea/Save-On-Foods, and IGA. Downtown, your best bet is Safeway, which has locations at 1641 Davie St (map:Q3) and 1766 Robson St (map:Q2). For cutting-edge foodstuffs—including farmers market–style produce displays, breads flown in from France, prepared luxe meals, and a wine bar and restaurant—Urban Fare in Yaletown (177 Davie St at Pacific; 604/975-7550; map:S6) is the stylish stop for grocery shopping. It's open 7am to midnight, seven days a week. The only 24-hour grocery store in the city is SuperValu (1255 Davie St; 604/688-0911; map:Q4). There are also a number of organic-food stores; perhaps the best known is Capers (1675 Robson St; 604/687-5288; map:Q2; 2285 W 4th; 604/739-6676; map:N7; and 2496 Marine Dr, West Vancouver; 604/925-3316).

BUDDHA IN A HOTEL AND OTHER PLACES OF WORSHIP

In the 1950s it was joked that you could stroll backward down the centre of Burrard Street on a Sunday morning and not get run over. You wouldn't get far now: Vancouver consistently finds itself among Canada's leading cities for religious absenteeism. Which is sad, because we have some of the nicest places to pray.

Christ Church Anglican Cathedral (690 Burrard St; 604/682-3848), built in 1889, is the oldest and undisputed granddaddy of Vancouver churches. When banks and office towers moved in, inflating property values and challenging the value of stained glass, even the diocese wanted to bring on the wrecking ball. Divine forces, or heritage planners, intervened at the last moment and the building was saved. It is also a heavenly setting for string quartet recitals and Shakespearean plays.

Oak Street is the heart of the local Jewish community, with the orthodox **Schara Tzedeck** (3476 Oak St; 604/736-7607) and the conservative **Beth Israel** (4350 Oak St; 604/731-4161) drawing the biggest crowds on Friday nights.

Tucked on a quiet street just north of Broadway is **Jamia Masjid** (655 W 8th Ave; 604/803-7344), where Muslims of Pakistani origin gather for weekly prayers. The tiny square edifice honours the rectilinear forms and uncluttered purity so treasured in Islamic architecture. Older, larger, and considerably more ornate is the local centre for adherents of the Sunni tradition, **Masjid at-Taqwa** (12407 72nd Ave, Surrey; 604/591-7601).

Bright watercolour paintings line the assembly hall of the **Unitarian Church of Vancouver** (949 W 49th Ave; 604/261-7204), whose congregation prides itself on intellectual enrichment and religious pluralism.

The Khalsa Diwan Society's **Gurdwara Sahib** (8000 Ross St; 604/324-2010) was designed by renowned local architect Arthur Erickson. Keeping with tradition, the *gurdwara*, meaning "prophet's door," has entrances on each side to signify that people from all points of the world are welcome.

Founded by his grace A. C. Bhaktivedanta Swami Prabhupada, the multidomed **Hare Krishna Temple** (5462 SE Marine Dr, Burnaby; 604/433-9728) claims one of the largest congregations in North America, drawing up to 10,000 on high holy days.

The Radisson President is the only hotel in the western hemisphere that is home to a genuine **Buddhist Temple** (8181 Cambie Rd, Richmond; 604/273-0369). Buddhist and non-Buddhist visitors alike enjoy a free vegetarian lunch after services. Bonsai plants grace the courtyard and dragons leap from the porcelain roof at the **International Buddhist Society Temple** (9160 Steveston Hwy, Richmond; 604/274-2822), perhaps the most impressive example of Ming architecture in Canada.

—Noel Hulsman

PHARMACIES

Shopper's Drug Mart and London Drugs both have several locations throughout Greater Vancouver and are mini-department stores as well as full-fledged and extensive pharmacies. Three Shopper's Drug Mart locations are open until midnight (1020 Denman St; 604/681-3411; map:P2; 4326 Dunbar St; 604/732-8855; map:B3; and 2947 Granville St; 604/738-3107; map:D3). There are at least two that are open 24 hours a day, 7 days a week (2302 W 4th Ave; 604/738-3138; map:C2; and 1125 Davie St; 604/669-2424; map:D4).

DRY CLEANERS AND LAUNDROMATS

The Valetor has helped Vancouverites keep their clothes clean for the past 50 years and has seven locations throughout the city, including one downtown at the Bay (W Georgia and Granville Sts; 604/681-6211; map:S4). Scotty's One Hour Cleaners (834 Thurlow St; 604/685-7732; map:R3) offers good service and a professional job. Wheely Clean (604/816-8721) will pick up and deliver dry cleaning to your home or downtown office at reasonable rates. Woodman's Cleaners (Bentall Centre 1, 505 Burrard St; 604/684-6622; map:S3; and Royal Centre, 1055 W Georgia St; 604/684-3623; map:S3) offer same-day dry cleaning or shirt laundry, as well as alterations and repairs.

Self-serve laundromats are few and far between downtown, but you can find a full range of cleaning services seven days a week at the Davie Laundromat (1061 Davie St; 604/682-2717; map:Q5). There are several laundromats across English Bay in the Kitsilano neighbourhood (all of which have drop-off services), including the Gold Coin Laundry (3496 W Broadway; 604/739-0598; map:C2), which claims to be the largest coin laundromat in western Canada and also has fresh cappuccino on hand.

LEGAL SERVICES

If you have a legal problem, the local branch of the Canadian Bar Association operates the free Dial-a-Law service, a library of recorded messages on various topics (604/687-4680 or 800/565-5297). The Law Students' Legal Advice Program (604/822-5791) offers a free consultation service, and the Lawyer Referral Service (604/687-3221) advises people seeking legal representation.

BUSINESS, COPY, AND MESSENGER SERVICES

It's two in the morning, you're just finishing up that report, and you need 20 copies for the meeting in the morning? Or you've brought your laptop but didn't think you'd need the printer? No problem. Most hotels have a business centre on the premises, but if you're not at a hotel or can't wait till dawn, head on over to any of Kinko's three locations (1900 W Broadway; 604/734-2679; map:O7; 789 W Pender; 604/685-3338; map:T3; and 811–5300 No. 3 Rd, Richmond; 604/303-0144; map:D7).

Need to get your documents on their way pronto? For fast, reliable service within the Greater Vancouver area, call Dwarf Courier (604/278-1935), PDX Courier (604/684-3336), Rush Courier (604/520-9444), or VIP Courier (604/899-8601).

Offices and meeting space in a professional atmosphere and with the necessary administrative and communications services are available at a number of downtown locations. Total Office (1300–666 Burrard St; 604/688-9276; map:R5), HQ (700–555 W Hastings St; 604/443-5000; map:T3), and Suite 400 Executive Offices and Secretarial Services (400–850 W Hastings St; 604/687-5516; map:T3) all offer short- and long-term rentals. Professional simultaneous translation services are available from ISTS (1475 E Georgia St; 604/255-1151; www.ists.com; map:Z4).

PHOTOGRAPHY EQUIPMENT AND SERVICES

Local camera buffs—or those needing quick, reliable film processing—head to Lens & Shutter (www.lensandshutter.com), which has two downtown locations (Pacific Centre Mall, 700 Granville St to 777 Dunsmuir St; 604/684-4422; map:S4; and 1112 Robson St; 604/681-4164; map:R3) and another shop at 2912 W Broadway (604/736-3461 or 888/736-3461; map:C2). Dunne and Rundle is an alternative, with locations in the Bentall Centre (595 Burrard St; 604/689-8508; map:S3) and at 891 Granville St (604/681-9254; map:S4). They also do repairs. London Drugs' three downtown locations have an exceptional selection of moderately priced cameras at competitive prices and also offer good prices on video transfers from film, slides, and photos.

COMPUTER REPAIRS AND RENTALS

CompuKits (4310 Fraser St; 604/879-9288; map:E3) and the Computer Service Centre (104–340 Brooksbank Ave, North Vancouver; 604/760-8949 or 604/980-6373; map:F1) service the major lines of hardware, including Apple, IBM, Okidata, Toshiba, and, in case the modem's acting a little "phoney," US Robotics. Need to rent a system? Pacific West Office World (211 Nelson St; 604/681-9666; map:S5) rents IBM-compatible systems, as well as printers, copiers, and office furniture, by the day, week, or month. A complete system with software and printer is about $100 a week. Staff members are accommodating and friendly—and they deliver, too! Central Computer (5U–555 W Hastings St; 604/684-4545; map:T3) also rents IBM and peripheral systems for about $150 a month, with delivery and setup service to boot. Mac users turn to Advantage Computers (1690 W Broadway; 604/714-5700; www.advantage.com; map:O8), WestWorld Computers (2151 Burrard St; 604/732-4499; www.westworld.ca; map:P7), and MacStation (207A–3430 Brighton Ave, Burnaby; 604/420-5224; www.macstation.com; map:G2). Kinko's rents Mac and PC stations for in-store use (see the Business, Copy, and Messenger Services section in this chapter).

PETS AND STRAY ANIMALS

Want to make sure your pets have as much fun as you do, but not necessarily with you? Hugs & Kisses Pet Sitters (604/731-1948) has a network of animal lovers who will take pets as temporary guests in their homes. They pick up and drop off your animal companions, too. If puss, pooch, or parrot gets sick while in Vancouver, call the West End Veterinary Clinic (1788 Alberni St; 604/685-4535; map:Q1) or the Animal Clinic (1236 Kingsway; 604/871-1110; map:E3; and 1855 Burrard St; 604/738-7600; map:B7). The Granville Island Veterinary Hospital (1635 W 4th Ave; 604/734-7744; map:P7) and Vancouver Animal Emergency Clinic (1590 W 4th Ave; 604/734-5104; map:P7) offer 24-hour care. And should your pet die here (though we hope not!), the Animal Grief Support line (604/985-7553) offers free counselling to bereaved owners.

Lost pets could end up at the city animal pound (1280 Raymur Ave; 604/251-1325; map:E2) or the Society for the Prevention of Cruelty to Animals, aka the SPCA (1205 E 7th Ave; 604/879-7721 or 604/879-7343 after business hours; map:Y7). In addition to a shelter, the society also operates an animal health clinic (604/879-3571). An excellent resource for dog owners visiting the city is *Dog City: Vancouver* by Marg Meikle (Polestar, 1997). Also see the Tips for Special Travellers section in the Planning a Trip chapter.

SPAS AND SALONS

Given the healthy Vancouver lifestyle, it's no wonder that day spas flourish here. Spa at the Century (1015 Burrard St; 604/684-2772; map:R4) is the best known in the city; it offers a full range of services to primp and pamper, with complimentary gourmet spa cuisine. There's a downtown spa, the Robert Andrew Salon & Spa in the Hotel Vancouver (900 W Georgia St; 604/687-7133; map:S3). Numerous other hair salons and aestheticians are located in downtown Vancouver. Some of the finest in the city are Tech 1 Hair Design (1057 Cambie St; 604/689-1202; map:T5) and Suki's, in the Pan Pacific Hotel (999 Canada Pl; 604/641-1342; map:T2). South Granville, the Kitsilano area, and W 10th Avenue are home to many top salons, including another branch of Suki's (3157 Granville St; 604/738-7713; map:D3), Raymond Salons (2825 Granville St; 604/482-3265; map:D3), and Eliane Hair Design (4353 W 10th Ave; 604/222-1511; map:B2). For more listings, see Skin and Hair Care in the Shopping chapter.

Local Resources

NEWSPAPERS AND MAGAZINES

Want to make sense of that long row of newspaper boxes outside your hotel? The *Vancouver Sun* (604/732-2111; www.vancouversun.com) is the city's main English-language daily, and is published every morning except Sunday. The *Province* (604/732-2222; www.vancouverprovince.com) is a tabloid newspaper, and its mandate is flashy, headline-grabbing journalism with an emphasis on sports and entertainment. Both are part of the Southam newspaper chain, which owns papers in most major cities across Canada, as well as one of the country's national newspapers, the newcomer the *National Post* (416/383-2300; www.nationalpost.com). The other national paper is the well-respected *Globe and Mail* (604/687-4435; www.globeandmail.com). Both publish Monday through Saturday.

The *Georgia Straight* (604/730-7000; www.straight.com) is a free entertainment weekly published on Thursdays. *Terminal City* (604/669-6910) is a similar free weekly that caters to an alternative audience. *Vancouver,* the city magazine, published 10 times a year, offers restaurant reviews, fashion and style reviews, and insights on the latest happenings around town. *Business in Vancouver* (604/688-2398; www.biv.com) is Vancouver's weekly business tabloid—and an excellent paper—and *City-Food* (604/737-7845) is a free insider's guide to cooking and dining.

There aren't many cities that have more daily ethnic newspapers than mainstream publications, as Vancouver does. The city has three thriving daily Chinese-language newspapers: *Sing Tao* (604/321-1111), *Ming Pao* (604/231-8998), and the *World Journal* (604/876-1338) offer news to Vancouver's large Chinese Canadian population. In *Sing Tao*, QuBic Lam writes the only regular wine column in the Chinese language in North America.

PUBLIC LIBRARIES

The Vancouver Public Library's main branch is in the dramatic Library Square (350 W Georgia St; 604/331-3600; map:T4), one of the city's architectural landmarks, and the strength and breadth of its multifloor collection reflects the importance the city puts on the value of reading. The bright, spacious building, designed by world-renowned architect Moshe Safdie, is open Monday to Thursday 10am to 8pm, Thursday to Saturday 10am to 5pm, and Sunday 1 to 5pm. (The library is closed Sundays from May through September.) There are 20 other branches of the library located throughout the city, all offering a wide selection of books, magazines, and audio and video recordings.

RADIO AND TV

Vancouver's radio airwaves are crowded with AM and FM stations that range from opera each Saturday afternoon on CBC-FM (which the CBC calls CBC Radio 2) to the in-your-face rap and hip-hop of Co-op Radio. There's mainstream music, talk, arts, and current affairs. CKNW is western Canada's most popular radio station, and it has been thus for decades, thanks in part to excellent and thorough news and sports coverage and, for the past two decades, open-line shows. A trio of multicultural and Chinese-language stations—CHKG, CJVB, and CHMB—thrive in their particular niche. CBC-AM (which the CBC calls CBC Radio 1) is commercial-free public radio with a patented series of 10-minute interviews for much of its programming. For up-to-the-minute food and wine news, tune into award-winning journalists Anthony Gismondi and Kasey Wilson (this book's author) on *The Best of Food & Wine,* on CFUN from noon to 1pm every Saturday.

Radio stations

ADULT FAVOURITES	600	CKBD AM
NEWS/TALK	690	CBC AM (Radio 1)
NEWS/SPORTS	980	CKNW AM
ALL TALK	1410	CFUN AM
COUNTRY	93.7	CJJR FM
TOP 40	95.3	CKZZ FM
ROCK	99.3	CFOX FM
CLASSIC ROCK	101.1	CFMI FM
ALTERNATIVE	102.7	CO-OP Radio FM
CONTEMPORARY	103.5	CHQM FM
CLASSICAL/ARTS	105.7	CBC FM (Radio 2)

TV stations

CBC ENGLISH	3	CBUT-2
CBUFT (CBC French)	7	CBUFT-26
VTV	9	Batch-32
ABC	10	KOMO-4
BCTV	11	CTV-8
CKVU GLOBAL	13	CKVU-10
UPN	14	UPN-10
CBS	15	KIRO-7
NBC	16	KING-5
CBC NEWSWORLD	26	NW
PBS	27	KCTS-9
CNN	33	CNN

INTERNET ACCESS

Most major hotels offer the option of Internet access with double phone lines in guest rooms, and several have business centres with computers (see the Lodgings chapter). Public library branches have a limited number of terminals that allow patrons to access the Internet, but there are also a handful of cafes that allow you to surf, including BC Internet Coffee (1104 Davie St; 604/682-6668; map:Q4), Digital U Cybercafe (1595 W Broadway; 604/731-1011; map:P8), and Kitsilano Cyber-Cafe (3514 W 4th Ave; 604/737-0595; map:B2). The rates at the cybercafes vary, but expect to pay about $5 per hour.

UNIVERSITIES

You won't have to study hard to find the University of British Columbia (604/822-2211; www.ubc.ca; map:A2). Founded in 1908, it's the oldest university in the province. The campus, perched on Point Grey overlooking Burrard Inlet, is one of the most attractive in Canada and offers amazing vistas of sea, mountains, and sky. It's also a bustling centre of research and learning in the humanities and sciences, and boasts an excellent library collection. It's not the only post-secondary institution in town, though: Burnaby-based Simon Fraser University (604/291-3111; www.sfu.ca; map:I2) has a campus downtown at Harbour Centre (515 W Hastings St; 604/291-5000; map:T3) in Gastown, and Regent College (5800 University Blvd; 604/224-3245; map:A2) on the UBC campus is well known in Christian circles for its theological teaching. The BC Institute of Technology (3700 Willingdon Ave, Burnaby; 604/434-5734; map:G3), which produces skilled high-technology grads, also has a campus downtown (555 Seymour St; 604/412-7777; map:T4). The Vancouver area also has its share of colleges, including Capilano College (2055 Purcell Wy, North Vancouver; 604/986-1911; map:F1), Douglas College (700 Royal Ave, New Westminster; 604/527-5400; map:I5), and Langara College (100 W 49th Ave; 604/323-5511; map:D4).

Important Telephone Numbers

EMERGENCIES—POLICE, FIRE, AMBULANCE	911
AIDS VANCOUVER HELP LINE	604/687-2437
ALCOHOLICS ANONYMOUS	604/434-3933
ANIMAL CARE (SPCA)	604/879-7721
ANIMAL EMERGENCY CLINIC	604/734-5104
ANIMAL POUND	604/251-1325
BC FERRIES	888/223-3779
BC RAIL	604/631-3500
BCAA	604/268-5600
BCAA EMERGENCY ROAD SERVICE (24 hours)	604/293-2222

BETTER BUSINESS BUREAU	604/682-2711
BUS, SEABUS, SKYTRAIN SCHEDULE INFO	604/521-0400
CHAMBER OF COMMERCE	604/681-2111
CITIZENSHIP AND IMMIGRATION	604/666-2171
COAST GUARD EMERGENCY	800/567-5111
CONSUMER AND CORPORATE AFFAIRS	604/666-5000
CRIMESTOPPERS (Police crime tip line for anonymous callers)	604/669-TIPS
CRISIS CENTRE	604/872-3311
CUSTOMS (Canada)	604/666-0545
CUSTOMS (U.S.)	604/278-1825
DIRECTORY ASSISTANCE (95 cents per call)	411
DOMESTIC VIOLENCE HOTLINE/Battered Women's Support Services	604/687-1867
GREYHOUND CANADA SCHEDULE INFO	604/482-8747
KIDS HELP LINE	800/668-6868
INFORMATION SERVICES VANCOUVER	604/875-6381
LEGAL SERVICES	604/687-4680
MISSING PERSONS	604/717-3535
PASSPORTS	604/586-2500
PLANNED PARENTHOOD	604/731-4252
POISON CONTROL CENTRE	604/631-5050
POST OFFICE INFORMATION	800/267-1177
POSTAL CODE INFO (75 cents per call, up to three codes)	900/565-2633
RAPE CRISIS CENTRE	604/255-6344
RAPE RELIEF	604/872-8212
RED CROSS	604/879-6001
ROAD CONDITIONS	604/299-9000
ROYAL CANADIAN MOUNTED POLICE ADMINISTRATION	604/264-3111
SENIORS INFO (Vancouver)	604/684-8171
SKI REPORT	604/986-6262
SUICIDE PREVENTION	604/872-3311
TAX (GST) **REFUNDS**	800/668-4748
TICKETMASTER	604/280-4444
TOURISM VANCOUVER	604/683-2000
VANCOUVER CITY HALL	604/873-7011
VANCOUVER CITY POLICE ADMINISTRATION	604/665-3535
VANCOUVER HEALTH DEPARTMENT	604/775-1866
VANCOUVER PARKS AND RECREATION BOARD	604/257-8400
VIA RAIL	800/561-8630
VITAL STATISTICS (birth, marriage, death certificates)	800/663-8328
WEATHER	604/664-9010
WOMEN'S SHELTER	604/872-8212

TOP 190 RESTAURANTS

Restaurants by Neighbourhood

BURNABY
The Bread Garden
Earls
Hart House on Deer Lake
Horizons on Burnaby Mountain
Kamei Royale Japanese
 Restaurant
The Pear Tree
Rainforest Cafe
Szechuan Chongqing Seafood
 Restaurant
Vassilis Souvlaki Greek Taverna
White Spot

CHINATOWN
Boss Bakery and Restaurant
Floata Seafood Restaurant
Hon's Wun Tun House
Kam Gok Yuen
Park Lock Seafood Restaurant
Phnom Penh Restaurant
Pho Hoang

DOWNTOWN
Aki
Allegro Cafe
Aqua Riva
Bacchus Ristorante
Bandi's
Bianco Nero
Bin 941 Tapas Parlour
The Boathouse
C
Cafe de Paris
Caffe de Medici
Cardero's Restaurant
Chartwell
Chili Club Thai Restaurant
CinCin Restaurant & Bar
Crime Lab
Da Pasta Bar
Delilah's
Diva at the Met
Dynasty
Earls
El Caravan
Ezogiku Noodle Cafe
The Fish House at Stanley Park
Five Sails
Fleuri
Flying Wedge
Fritz European House of Fries

Gotham
Great Wall Mongolian BBQ
 Restaurant
Griffins
Gyoza King
Hamburger Mary's
The Hermitage
Herons
Hy's Encore
Il Giardino di Umberto
J J's Dining Room
Joe Fortes
Just One Thai Bistro
Kamei Sushi
Kirin Mandarin Restaurant
Kitto Japanese House
Koji Japanese Restaurant
L'Arena
La Crepe Bretonne
La Terrazza
Le Crocodile
Le Gavroche
Liliget Feast House
Manhattan
Milestone's
Moutai Mandarin Restaurant
Musashi Japanese Restaurant
Nat's New York Pizza
Nikko Japanese Restaurant
900 West Restaurant &
 Wine Bar
Olympia Seafood Market & Grill
O–Tooz The Energie Bar
Piccolo Mondo
Picholine
Raincity Grill
Richard & Co.
Rodney's Oyster House
Romano's Macaroni Grill
Settebello
Shanghai Chinese Bistro
Stepho's Souvlakia
Subeez
Tanpopo
Tapastree Restaurant
The Teahouse at Ferguson Point
Victoria Chinese Restaurant
Villa del Lupo
White Spot
The William Tell
Won More Szechuan Cuisine
Wonton King

Yaletown Brewing Company

EAST VANCOUVER
Accord
Al Ritrovo
Alibi Room
Arirang House
Ashiana Tandoori
The Cannery Seafood House
Cipriano's Ristorante & Pizzeria
Dario's La Piazza Ristorante
La Villetta
Lok's Chinese Restaurant
Nazarre BBQ Chicken
Noor Mahal
The Only Seafood Cafe
Pho Hoang
The Pink Pearl
Rubina Tandoori
Sawasdee Thai Restaurant
Shanghai Garden Restaurant
Shil-La Korean Restaurant
Spumante's Cafe Ristorante
Sun Sui Wah Seafood
 Restaurant
Sun Wong Kee
Szechuan Chongqing Seafood
 Restaurant
Tak Sangka Indonesian
 Restaurant
Tio Pepe's
Tony's Neighbourhood
 Deli-Cafe
Vong's Kitchen
Wonton Noodle Restaurant
White Spot

GASTOWN
Borgo Antico
Raintree at the Landing
Water Street Cafe

GRANVILLE ISLAND
Bridges

LADNER
La Belle Auberge
Uncle Herbert's Fish & Chip
 Shop

NORTH SHORE
The Beach House at
 Dundarave Pier

Beach Side Cafe
Capers
Earls
La Cucina Italiana
La Toque Blanche
Moustache Cafe
The Salmon House on the Hill
Salute
The Tomahawk
White Spot

PORT MOODY
Caramba!

RICHMOND
Floata Seafood Restaurant
IKEA
Kamei Sushi
President Chinese Seafood
    Restaurant
Steveston Seafood House
Sun Sui Wah Seafood
    Restaurant
Top Gun Chinese Seafood
    Restaurant

SURREY
Earls
White Spot

WEST SIDE
Akbar's Own Dining Lounge
Annapurna Vegetarian Cuisine
    of India
The Avenue Grill

Bin 942
Bishop's
Bistro Ecco il Pane
The Bread Garden
Coco
Earls
Fatzo's Barbeque Smokehouse
Fiasco
Flying Wedge
Gianni Restaurant & Norcineria
Grand King Seafood Restaurant
Habibi's
Kalamata Greek Taverna
Kamei Sushi
King's Fare Fish & Chips
Landmark Hot Pot House
Las Margaritas
The Lazy Gourmet Bistro
Lorenzo
Lumière
Major the Gourmet
Meinhardt Fine Foods
Montri's Thai Restaurant
Moustache Cafe
Naam
Nat's New York Pizzeria
New Grand View Restaurant
Nyala Restaurant
Omnitsky Kosher Foods
The Original Tandoori K. King
Ouzeri
Pastis
Pâtisserie Lebeau

Perfetto Pizza
Phnom Penh Restaurant
Planet Veg
Provence Mediterranean Grill
Quattro on Fourth
The Red Onion
Sami's
Seasons in the Park
Shao Lin Noodle Restaurant
Shijo Japanese Restaurant
Sienna Tapas Bar & Grill
Singapore Restaurant
Smoking Dog Bar & Grill
Sophie's Cosmic Cafe
Surat Sweet
Szechuan Chongqing Seafood
    Restaurant
Tang's Noodle House
Tojo's
Tomato Fresh Food Cafe
Top Gun Chinese Seafood
    Restaurant
Vij's
White Spot
Won More Szechuan Cuisine
Wonton Noodle Restaurant

WHITE ROCK
Earls
Giraffe
White Spot

RESTAURANTS

Accord / ★

4298 MAIN ST; 604/876-6110

Behind white venetian blinds, this restaurant serves excellent Cantonese seafood. Try the live spot prawns steamed in the shell and brought to the table with a serrano-soy dipping sauce, or the beef tenderloin with pickled vegetables. The menu also includes a handful of Chiu Chow specialties from the southern coastal region of China. Accord is open till the wee hours—perfect for those late evenings when only Chinese food will do. Ask for the midnight snack menu, now available in English, which includes 68 half-size dishes between $5 and $8, including deep-fried spicy baby octopus, Chinese smoked pork with *gailan,* clams with black bean sauce, and a wonderful beef satay. *$$; MC, V; no cheques; dinner, midnight snacks every day; beer and wine; map:E3.*

Akbar's Own Dining Lounge / ★★☆

1905 W BROADWAY; 604/736-8180

Akbar's back on the scene and everything's remained the same— authentic Kashmiri and Mughlai cooking from northern India with its delicately balanced spices and flavours. Shrimp pakoras, zingy with ginger and green chiles, are crunchily wrapped in sesame seed batter. Lamb tikka has an equally surprising overcoat: a batter that hints at tandoori. Particularly good are the fiery prawn vindaloo or the more subtle prawn Kashmiri, cooked with butter, tomatoes, apples, and cream. Try the felicitous combination of lamb—either ground or in meltingly tender chunks—and spinach, perfumed with fresh fenugreek. The biryanis, heady with saffron and shot through with your choice of chicken, lamb, prawns, or vegetables, are exceptional. Vegetarian dishes include the irresistible *alu gobi*—chopped cauliflower and potato. *$$; AE, DC, E, MC, V; no cheques; lunch Mon–Fri, dinner Mon–Sat; full bar; map:O7.*

Aki / ★

745 THURLOW ST; 604/682-4032

After more than 36 years in Vancouver's Japantown, Aki has gone upscale and moved into the space formerly occupied by Naniwa-Ya Seafood. This intimate Japanese restaurant was the place where more than a few locals were introduced to the then-dubious joys of sushi and sashimi. Sophisticates that we are now, we still go back—for the same reasons we went in our student days: the food is good and the bill won't make a major dent in your pocketbook. The menu embraces all the favourites: teriyaki, sunomono, and those uniquely Japanese udon noodle dishes that manage to be both light and robust. A crisp and fragile batter lifts the tempura here far above the usual. Sushi choices let you stay with the tried-and-true or experiment with sea urchin or flying-fish roe. Service is concerned and consistently charming. *$$; AE, MC, V; no cheques; lunch Mon–Fri, dinner every day; full bar; map:R3.*

Al Ritrovo / ★
2010 FRANKLIN ST; 604/255-0916
Tucked away a half block off unfashionable E Hastings Street, this ivy-covered eatery is warm and inviting, the kind of place where you can relax over a glass of Chianti, eat heartily, and watch the colourfully mixed crowd. A sign on the roof identifies it as a really rare establishment these days: a place where you can dine and dance to live music—at least on Fridays, Saturdays, and Sundays. With its backlit paintings of moonlit piazzas; the odd string of fairy lights; Italian classics played on the accordion, guitar, and bass; and couples of all ages taking to the floor, the ambience seems to come straight from the cover of a romance novel. The mainstream Italian menu occasionally plays second fiddle to the dancing, with service scheduled around the sambas and tangos. Expect solid Italian cuisine like Mamma used to make. Servings of lasagne or tagliatelle *alla boscaiola*—pasta laden with bacon, mushrooms, and cream—are robust. A flavourful veal saltimbocca is aromatic with fresh sage. For lovers of old-time dancing, Al Ritrovo is heaven; go with a group. Pizzas are served after 10pm, and there is a minimum charge of $15 per person after 9pm. *$$; AE, MC, V; local cheques only; lunch Tues–Fri, dinner Fri–Sun (closed in Aug); full bar; map:Y4.*

Alibi Room / ★★★
157 ALEXANDER ST; 604/623-3383
The name has a deliciously furtive ring to it, but you won't need an alibi to cover your visit to the Alibi Room. As many a food-savvy Vancouverite will tell you, this recent arrival is serving gutsy, original fare in a transitional part of town. Wander east from the fringe of Gastown and you land among seedy commercial blocks mixed with ultraurban condos. Here the Alibi occupies an old brick building. Outside its thick, thick walls, railcars shunt back and forth; beyond them is the working harbour. Inside, the room is spare with an upbeat, youthful feel. It's popular with the film industry crowd (check the bookshelves for typescripts of your favourite movies), but chef Tim Hunt's cooking has wide appeal. Try starting with an assortment of "small bowls": the sautéed mussels are smashing; steamed, salted fresh soybeans (*edamame* on Japanese menus) could be addictive; same goes for the sinful onion rings, thick and sweet, hot, and spicy. (An alibi might be an idea if you overindulge!) Main courses have been consistent winners: the delicious "macaroni and cheese" with crab, shrimp, and shiitakes is unlike anything Mom ever made. Both the grilled beef tenderloin and grilled ahi tuna hit the mark on repeat visits. Don't overdo the early courses, because you need room for dessert—in particular the toffee bread pudding, which is too decadent

to be legal. Saffron-tinged white chocolate cheesecake with a rhubarb compote stands out as well. And the bill is just as satisfying: excellent value for dining of this quality. *$$; MC, V; debit cards; no cheques; lunch, dinner every day, brunch Sat–Sun; full bar; reservations recommended on weekends; www.alibiroom.com; map:V3.* &

Allegro Cafe / ★★
1G–888 NELSON ST; 604/683-8485
If a restaurant can be called a flirt, this is it. Tucked away in the courtyard of an office tower opposite the Law Courts, Allegro sometimes beckons with a warm, intimate appeal. Other times the flirting can seem forced. All decked out in curvy, dark green velvet banquettes; warm lighting; and red, green, and gold draperies, this restaurant is a hot spot for lawyers and the young urban set. Here restaurateur Michael Mitton (his newest venture is the Crime Lab) teams up with chef Barbara Reese (of the Reese Peanut Butter Cup family) to offer Mediterranean dishes with West Coast panache: flavourful soups (try the roasted garlic), creative pastas (capelli with grilled scallops, leeks, roma tomatoes, and tarragon in a mascarpone cream sauce with salmon caviar), and seafood and meat cooked to perfection. Reese has finesse with flavours. For instance, a charbroiled veal chop with Gorgonzola and whole-grain mustard cream sauce could have been a disastrous cacophony of flavours but instead was a symphony of subtlety. Pull up a stool at the bar, order a martini, and settle in for some serious people-watching. Yes, there's a peanut butter pie for dessert, and a wonderful bread pudding as well. *$$–$$$; AE, DC, E, MC, V; debit cards; no cheques; lunch Mon–Fri, dinner every day; full bar; reservations recommended; map:S4.* &

Annapurna Vegetarian Cuisine of India / ★
1812 W 4TH AVE; 604/736-5959
The Annapurna was the first restaurant in the Lower Mainland to tap into the most highly developed vegetarian cuisine in the world. Every vegetarian who has opened a menu at an Indian restaurant only to see the same standard meatless dishes just one too many times is going to like Annapurna a lot. There are unfamiliar dishes to try, and some of them—like the lentil dumplings soaked in yogurt with chickpeas and chutney—are especially good. Service is hit-and-miss. And the small dining room, its ceiling covered with lanterns, has a ringside view of a busy intersection. *$; MC, V; no cheques; lunch, dinner every day; full bar; map:O7.*

Aqua Riva / ★★
30–200 GRANVILLE ST; 604/683-5599
Like its siblings Salmon House on the Hill and Horizons on Burnaby Mountain, Aqua Riva boasts an outstanding view of the harbour and North Shore mountains. Executive chef Deb Connors rattles the pots and

pans and tends the wood-fired oven and rotisserie in this sparkling restaurant near Canada Place. Prices are reasonable for alderwood-grilled salmon, oven-baked pizzas, and slow-smoked barbecued ribs. Service is unfailingly friendly, and the stunning decor is especially soothing when you're settled into a booth with Dana Irving's art deco wraparound mural above you. Aqua Riva is very popular with the lunch crowd who inhabit the office tower atop the restaurant and tourists from hotels in the area. *$$; AE, DC, E, MC, V; no cheques; lunch, dinner every day, brunch Sat–Sun May–Oct; full bar; www.aquariva.com; map:T3.*

Arirang House / ★★

2211 CAMBIE ST; 604/879-0990

An unmistakable whiff of savagely good kimchi (pickled cabbage, red pepper, black beans, and garlic) greets you as soon as you walk in the door of this traditionally designed Korean restaurant at the south end of the Cambie Street Bridge. Despite a Japanese-style sushi bar, the Arirang House strives for Korean authenticity. In the evenings, the restaurant serves a dish revealingly called Jumuluck Garlic Lovers. Combining marinated beef, lettuce leaves, and vast quantities of raw garlic, it's a cook-it-yourself variation of traditional Korean barbecue. Less daunting are *bulgogi* (marinated filet of beef), *bulgabi* (ribs), or any of the other table-top-grill options. Sizzling and deeply flavoured hot pots and assorted seafood dishes round out the menu. Seating is in booths or private tatami rooms, and there's a karaoke room in case you feel like singing. The lunchtime barbecue buffet is an exceptional value. *$$; AE, MC, V; no cheques; lunch, dinner every day; full bar; map:T7.*

Ashiana Tandoori / ★★

1440 KINGSWAY; 604/874-5060
2006 W 4TH AVE; 604/730-5069

In a city blessed with Indian fare, Ashiana stands out. The tandoori dishes come sizzling from the oven to the table on cast-iron platters. The chicken tikka is tasty and moist, the lamb tikka superb—tender, fragrant, and rich from its marinade of yogurt, ginger, garlic, and spices. *Murg makhani*, one of 11 chicken curries, is luscious and sweet, delectable when eaten with *paneer* naan deftly flavoured with fresh coriander. Speaking of breads, the whole-wheat *paratha* with cheese is a must with the *channa masala*—chickpeas stewed with garam masala, onions, and tomatoes. This is food that makes you happy. *$$; AE, MC, V; no cheques; lunch, dinner every day; full bar; map:R3, O7.*

The Avenue Grill / ★★

2114 W 41ST AVE; 604/266-8183

For generations this was a neighbourhood burger joint. Later it went upscale. Three years ago, Herve Fabre took it over, looked around Kerrisdale, and saw a sufficiency of both burger joints and formal dining. So

GREASY SPOONS

Greasy-spoon restaurants are fast becoming an endangered species. But like an aging boxer, they refuse to go down, standing up to take one more punch from the cilantro-infested culinary contenders for the dining crown. With home-fried hospitality, they welcome you in from the technological wasteland of modern living, where you can sit back with a good cup of coffee minus the foam, the infusions, and the sprinkles to remember or just imagine days gone by. Here are some of Vancouver's finest.

Aristocratic Restaurant / 1465 W Broadway; 604/733-1515 Risty, the restaurant's mascot, may have moved from the famous Broadway-and-Granville location, but his heart's still in the right place. The famous neon featuring Risty the Rooster can still be seen upstairs in the Chapters bookstore that took their corner spot. Their famous $3.95 full breakfast with coffee is served daily from 9 to 11am. *Every day; map:Q7.*

Bert's Restaurant / 2904 Main St; 604/876-1236 This homey diner on Main Street proudly displays the Gold Cup Coffee Award it won in 1969. You can't go wrong. And the waitresses will capture your heart when they call you Mister. *Every day; map:E3.*

Bon's Off Broadway / 2451 Nanaimo St; 604/253-7242 A Californian Tuscan stucco interior with signed *X-Files* cast members' pictures on the walls and one of the cheapest breakfasts in town. All-night ravers mix with truckers and families, and the bottomless cups of coffee will keep you going for days. *Every day; map:F3.*

The Cottage Coffee Shop / 1441 Commercial Dr; 604/254-0306 Homemade ketchup! Homemade ketchup! Homemade ketchup! What more can you say? At this coffee shop run by the same family for more than 30 years, they still hand-cut their french fries for each order. The location on hip Commercial Drive makes for an interesting crowd, and the price of a burger and fries makes you wonder how they've stayed in business so long. *Every day; map:Z5.*

E & B Restaurant / 2066 Kingsway; 604/879-5625 The E & B has two important factors a greasy spoon must fulfill: a good sign and good food. Be sure to try the veal cutlets. *Every day; map:E3.*

Molly's Cafe / 1832 Columbia St; 604/874-5122 Decorated in cowboy paraphernalia that has attracted more than a few movie shoots, Molly's boasts one of the best chicken club sandwiches in town. Both Chinese food and standard greasy-spoon fare make Molly's the ultimate in deep-fryer fusion. The bacon, lettuce, and tomato fajita is truly a strange combo, especially with the addition of hoisin sauce. Plus you can hear all the day's news from the Global TV crowd that chows down here. *Every day; map:U7.*

Normandy Restaurant / 2675 Granville St; 604/738-3115 Nestled in an upper-crusty neighbourhood, the Normandy caters to the blue-haired-rinse set. Its pseudo Playboy mansion atmosphere and whitebread daily specials have made the

Normandy a small pocket of time in the world of retro fashion. *Every day; map:D3.*

Reno's Restaurant / 151 E Broadway; 604/876-1119 The huge picture windows give you the passing parade at the corner of Main and Broadway as you sip your coffee and play with your Jell-O. Cafeteria-style and just a block away from the bingo hall. *Every day; map:V7.*

Slickety Jim's Chat'n'Chew / 2513 Main St; 604/873-6760 Eclectic and eccentric, and a creative cook in the kitchen to boot, Slickety Jim's doesn't fall under the true definition of a greasy spoon. But with a foot in two worlds, it's still a place that would make Tom Waits proud. *Every day; map:V7.*

Varsity Grill / 4381 W 10th Ave; 604/224-1822 One of the true forerunners of Chinese Canadian cuisine, the Varsity is a landmark to timeless perseverance. Where else can you get old-fashioned milk shakes, wavy fries, and a fortune cookie on the way out? *Every day; map:B3.* —*Mark Laba*

he said to himself, "What this neighbourhood needs is a good bistro." And so it is: a place of relaxed atmosphere, good cooking, and a fine selection of wine by the glass. There are 45 different mix-and-match pasta combinations. The chalkboard specials are superb, with nothing over $14.95. "The Ave" is very casual, and it retains the 1950s-style neon sign it had when it was a burger joint. It's popular with the Kerrisdale crowd and one of the best places for weekend brunch (till 5pm), mainly because of the fluffy pancakes cooked with seasonal fresh berries, the eggs Benny, and the homemade marmalade. *$$; AE, MC, V; cheques OK; breakfast Mon–Fri, lunch Mon–Sat, dinner every day, brunch Sat–Sun; full bar; map:C4.*

Bacchus Ristorante / ★★★☆

845 HORNBY ST (THE WEDGEWOOD HOTEL); 604/608-5319
Wonderfully romantic, this richly decorated room is a triumph for Eleni Skalbania and chef Robert Sulatacky, whose contemporary French cooking is spectacular. Dark wood panelling and deep burgundy velvet couches are accented by huge bouquets of flowers, creating private niches. Booths along the wall are separated by upholstered floor-to-ceiling dividers, for even more intimate seating. At lunchtime, Bacchus attracts the legal beagles from the neighbouring courthouse for an ever-changing roast of the day, pizza Bacchus, or the superb tortelloni of sweet white corn. Afternoon tea (2 to 4pm) in front of the fireplace hits the spot, with finger sandwiches followed by freshly baked scones with dollops of Devon clotted cream, and tea pastries swished down by your favourite blend. The changing dinner menu might include terrine of Quebec foie gras, caramelized sea scallops, truffle and pistachio roasted breast of squab, or *daube*

de boeuf bourguignonne. Hope that the apple tarte Tatin happens to be on the menu, or surrender to the dark-chocolate hazelnut torte served with a milk-chocolate mousse and brandied cherries. Best of all, Bacchus offers fine French cheese, fine wines, and servers who cater to your every whim. Nightly except Sunday, a pianist tickles the ivories. Stogie aficionados have free rein in the cigar room. *$$$; AE, DC, MC, V; no cheques; breakfast, lunch, dinner every day, brunch Sat–Sun; full bar; www.wedgewoodhotel.com; map:S4.* &

Bandi's / ★★

1427 HOWE ST; 604/685-3391
You'll exit in a fog of garlic. At Bandi's, chef-owner Bandi Rinkhy produces the robust country food of Hungary, with maître d' and co-owner Kader Karaa's sense of humour providing the dash of paprika. Start with an excellent sour-cherry soup and the dangerously addictive *langos,* a deep-fried peasant bread served with raw garlic. (Order one for your friends, one for yourself, and one to take home.) Duck connoisseurs who haven't experienced Bandi's signature dish—crisp duck served with red cabbage braised in Tokay wine—should by all means do so. Goulash is presented in a little kettle set over a portable flame. Hungary's best whites are on the wine list. *$$; AE, MC, V; no cheques; lunch Tues–Fri, dinner Tues–Sun; full bar; map:R5.*

The Beach House at Dundarave Pier / ★

150 25TH ST, WEST VANCOUVER; 604/922-1414
On sunny days, this waterside favourite offers unequalled water views from its year-round heated patio. Misty nights, when dining is accompanied by the basso profundo of distant foghorns, it's just as appealing. Lovingly restored, the green, shake-clad heritage building that first opened as a teahouse in 1912 sits only metres from the waters of Dundarave Beach. At press time, chef Sonny Mendoza is departing after five years at the helm, and we predict some big changes in this West Coast kitchen. Managing partner Ken Brooks has put together an impressive wine list. It features many good wines by the glass, the best of BC estate wineries, an excellent mix of U.S. West Coast varietals, and a sizable number of bottles from around the world. *$$; AE, DC, MC, V; no cheques; lunch, dinner every day, brunch Sat–Sun; full bar.* &

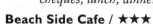

Beach Side Cafe / ★★★

1362 MARINE DR, WEST VANCOUVER; 604/925-1945
Chef Carol Chow and manager-sommelier Mark Davidson have turned this intimate Ambleside haunt into the area's most serious restaurant. The summertime deck rates among the best, with views of Stanley Park and Kitsilano across the water. Choices are plentiful, with emphasis on everyday specials, and there is a cutting-edge list of Canadian and

international wines. Start with the warmed potato cake with smoked salmon and sevruga caviar, or grilled Fanny Bay oysters with smoked-paprika mayonnaise. Definitely order sautéed BC prawn tails and seared scallops with a lemongrass ginger broth, or rack of lamb with porcini mushroom crust. Dessert lovers swear by the lemon meringue pie. Take advantage of the view, during a leisurely Sunday brunch, with a Brie-and-spinach omelet and freshly baked banana bread. A great place to do lunch, too. In any case, service is top drawer. *$$$; AE, MC, V; no cheques; lunch Mon–Fri, dinner every day, brunch Sat–Sun; full bar; map:D1.* &

Bianco Nero / ★★☆

475 W GEORGIA ST; 604/682-6376

Bianco Nero is food critic Jurgen Gothe's secret hangout. This boldly black and white canteen is the eatery of choice before the theatre for those seeking every Italian dish imaginable. Order the Pasta 95, a half-dozen pastas in a rosé sauce topped with spicy Italian sausage and grilled prawns, or the Trio—tiger prawns, scallops, and chicken in a mustard cream layered on egg-and-spinach fettuccine. This is *the* place for lovers of Italian wine; it boasts one of the most comprehensive selections in Canada, including a full range of vintage Barolo. An amiable serving crew get you to the Queen E with time to spare. *$$$; AE, MC, V; no cheques; lunch Mon–Fri, dinner Mon–Sat; full bar; map:T4.*

Bin 941 Tapas Parlour / ★★★
Bin 942 / ★

941 DAVIE ST; 604/683-1246
1521 W BROADWAY; 604/734-9421

The fact that this place is constantly packed attests to its popularity. It lures an attractive crowd, all in deep conversation that at first seems unlikely beneath the muscular yet unoppressive music. The setting is funky: a madcap mix of chrome-and-Naugahyde furniture, mismatched stools, and wild art, all crammed into a shoebox of a restaurant. The food of chef-owner Gordon Martin is both dazzling and an outrageously good value. Order a pound of Prince Edward Island mussels done (superbly) any of four ways for just 10 bucks. Two fat crab cakes served with a burnt-orange-and-chipotle sauce and charred baby bok choy cost a mere eight. Beef and fowl appear as well, in imaginative presentations; nothing is over $10. Shoestring french fries—a $3 haystack of Yukon Golds hand-cut, then hand-seasoned after frying—are the best-tasting potato bargain in town. Martin headlines his menu "tapatizers" because everything can be shared or enjoyed solo (sharing's best!) while you rub shoulders, unavoidably, with those at the next table. Seven whites and seven reds are all offered by both the bottle and the glass. A seat at the longer of the two bars gets you barlike conversation, but any of the three perches facing the open kitchen adds a free lesson in exquisite plate presentation as you watch the talented crew. The action continues late, making this one of the city's hottest hot spots. One price of popularity: Bin 941 doesn't take reservations. Martin's second location, Bin 942, opened in August 1999 with a similar menu and is open for lunch as well as dinner. *$$; MC, V; debit cards; no cheques; dinner every day (Bin 941); lunch, dinner every day (Bin 942); beer, wine, and liqueurs; www.bin941.com; map:R5, P7.* &

Bishop's / ★★★★

2183 W 4TH AVE; 604/738-2025
Where better to eat than in this simple two-level restaurant, long a fixture on busy W Fourth Avenue? "Nowhere" is the answer; John Bishop is the reason. Bishop has cooked for Presidents Clinton and Yeltsin, and Hollywood knows about Bishop's as well—Glenn Close, Robin Williams, Richard Gere, Robert De Niro, and others have been spotted here. Bishop warmly greets his guests (celebrity and otherwise) and, assisted by the most professionally polished young staff in the city, proceeds to demonstrate that he understands personal service, hovering over each table serving, pouring, discussing. Chef Dennis Green's entrees are uncomplicated. Dungeness crab is bathed in a saffron tomato broth, and wild salmon is grilled and brushed with a sesame ginger glaze. The rack of lamb with truffle and goat cheese mashed potatoes, and the pan-roasted halibut (in season) on a warm new-potato salad are standouts. So are the pan-seared scallops in a sweet red pepper and chive bisque, topped with a crisp potato pancake. Wonderful cooking! Everything bears the Bishop trademark of light, subtly complex flavours and bright, graphic colour. Desserts such as the toasted almond cake with poached apricots and homemade apricot ice cream, the moist ginger cake pooled in toffee sauce, and the Death by Chocolate are legendary. Manager Abel Jacinto oversees an eclectic list of fine wines including a breathtaking selection of 50 half-bottles. *$$$; AE, DC, MC, V; no cheques; dinner every day (closed for two weeks in Jan); full bar; inquire@bishops.net; www.bishops.net; map:O7.*

Bistro Ecco il Pane / ★★★

2563 W BROADWAY; 604/739-1314
Are we eating in a bakery or dining in a luxe bread and pastry shop? Does it matter? Vancouverites addicted to Ecco il Pane's superb rustic breads, biscotti, cakes, and tortas cheered when Christopher Brown and Pamela Gaudreault included a bistro at their second location, on W Broadway, a panino-toss away from posh Lumière. (The cafe at the original Ecco—238 W 5th Ave; 604/873-6888; map:V7—does panini, coffee, and other light meals, but its prime draw is baked goods.) Sumptuous Italianate appointments give the Broadway dining room the feel of some contessa's terrazza (all the more so on the patio in fine weather). Chef Rebecca

Olfert has a sure hand with meats and fish. The pan-roasted lamb sirloin with salsa verde–Dijon crust was memorable, and cioppino, a special one night, came loaded with clams, mussels, prawns, and halibut in an exquisite broth. Of course, there was lots of fine bread to soak up the latter. Definitely leave room for one of the desserts, served on hand-painted tiles. (The sour-cherry flan is a knockout.) And pick up a long green-olive *ficelle* on the way out—spicy, crusty perfection. *$$–$$$; MC, V; no cheques; breakfast, lunch every day, dinner Thurs–Sat, brunch Sat–Sun; full bar; reservations recommended on weekends; map:C3.* &

The Boathouse / ★★

1795 BEACH AVE (AND BRANCHES); 604/669-2225

When a spectacular sunset is taking shape over English Bay, nothing beats a window table in the upper-storey dining room at the Boathouse. (Downstairs holds a casual bistro and, outside, a deck—more on those in a moment.) Upstairs, all is shipshape: smooth, cordial servers, and an attractive-if-mainstream menu with a strong emphasis on seafood, as you'd expect. Seasonal special events feature wild salmon in summer, lobster in January, crab in the fall, and so on. But the menu constants in this large, warm room are reasonably consistent, especially the mildly spiced crab cakes and grilled king crab. Those who hanker for red meat will find (among several choices) rotisserie-roasted prime rib, a specialty. Desserts are enticing, or if you prefer a wee dram, select from 15 single-malt scotches. An upstairs/downstairs dichotomy makes the lower-level bistro and deck less inviting. Service can be curt, and the food seems an afterthought to the 14 martini variants offered. The views are still lovely, as are the fireplace and massive display bar. But there's better casual food at a corporate sibling, Milestone's, next door. The Boathouse dining room is a good beachside spot for families or for locals aiming to impress out-of-towners. There are also four suburban locations. *$$; AE, DC, DIS, E, JCB, MC, V; no cheques; lunch Mon–Sat, dinner every day, brunch Sun; full bar; reservations recommended, particularly for window tables; map:P3.*

Borgo Antico / ★★☆

321 WATER ST; 604/683-8376

It's like stepping back in time walking on cobbled sidewalks to the iron-gated entrance of Borgo Antico (which means "old quarter"), Umberto Menghi's Gastown *ristorante*. Inside, the dining room is separated by a series of arches and has a lively, colour-splashed decor. You'll find many of the same well-prepared dishes that Umberto has on the menu at Il Giardino, but the prices are lower here. We recommend the antipasto plate or the razor-thin carpaccio with arugula as a starter. Go with the chef's suggestions—a swordfish simply grilled or oven roasted, the risotto of the day, or the tagliolini with half a fresh lobster. Serious grape nuts are

49

drawn to the basement of this former Gastown warehouse not only to choose from an estimable wine list but to attend private wine functions. *$$; AE, DC, MC, V; debit cards; no cheques; lunch Mon–Fri, dinner Mon–Sat; full bar; www.umberto.com; map:U3.*

Boss Bakery and Restaurant / ★
532 MAIN ST; 604/683-3860

The Boss is a slice of Hong Kong life transplanted intact from Asia's distant shores. Once beyond the sandblasted glass door, with its tongue-in-cheek silhouette of a man in a bowler smoking a pipe, you can easily imagine yourself transported across the Pacific. In one booth is a group of young teenagers reading to each other from their Chinese comics. In another, a businessman is taking lunch with an associate, and next to them three older men are debating the prowess of their favourite race-horse of the day. The menu is uniquely and eclectically Hong Kong–style cafe—a strange hybrid of East and West. Spaghetti is topped with baked seafood; macaroni is served up in soup with crunchy Chinese meatballs or strips of ham. Chinese noodle dishes and *congees* are also offered. If you are visiting Chinatown, the Boss is a must. Besides, where else are you going to get Ovaltine served hot, iced, or with a raw egg? *$; cash only; lunch, dinner every day; no alcohol; map:V4.*

The Bread Garden / ★★☆
1880 W 1ST AVE (AND BRANCHES); 604/738-6684

The bakery-cafe concept started in Vancouver in the early '80s; the Bread Garden was the first in town, and now it's a robust restaurant chain with fully 10 locations, each as popular as the one that opened before. The Bread Garden caters to people looking for a late-night snack after an evening of dancing, a homey midweek dinner, a quick sit-down lunch, or just a muffin to go. The deli cases keep expanding, stuffed with salads, sandwiches, and ready-to-nuke fare such as quiches, frittatas, roast-vegetable lasagne, and burritos. You can have a wholesome muffin or scone, or throw caution to the winds and be tempted by the best carrot cake in the city (perfect for birthday celebrations) or a slice of warm apple pie with whipped cream. *$; AE, E, MC, V; no cheques; breakfast, lunch, dinner, midnight snacks every day (Granville and 14th branch only open 24 hours a day); beer and wine (1st Ave location only); map:O6.*

Bridges / ★★
1696 DURANLEAU ST; 604/687-4400

One of the city's most popular hangouts has a superb setting on Granville Island. Seats on the outdoor deck, with sweeping views of downtown and the mountains, are at a premium on warm days. Bridges is actually three separate entities: a casual bistro, a pub, and a more formal second-storey dining room. The bistro's casual offerings are the best bet; upstairs, the

kitchen takes its seafood seriously, but expect to pay top dollar for it. *$$;
AE, DC, MC, V; no cheques; lunch, dinner every day, brunch Sun; full
bar; www.bridgesrestaurant.com; map:Q6.* &

C / ★★★☆

2–1600 HOWE ST; 604/681-1164

Be prepared to spend an entire afternoon or evening on the patio at C,
because lunch or dinner is always an event at Harry Kambolis's restau-
rant. C offers contemporary and exotic seafood in Zen-like surroundings
with an unbeatable view of the busy entrance to False Creek and
Granville Island. Executive chef Robert Clark creates dishes that are as
dramatic on the palate as they are on the plate. Start with a taster box
filled with grilled Monterey Bay squid, halibut sashimi, ahi tuna tartare,
and crisp soft-shelled crab. And don't miss C's signature starters of caviar
in a gold-leaf pouch, lobster tail sashimi bathed in Cognac, or octopus-
wrapped scallops. A dim sum–style menu is served at lunch, featuring
tasty portions of spicy crab dumplings, subtle steamed lobster, and
macadamia nut miso buns, as well as crisp scallop and ahi tuna spring
rolls. Whatever the special is, order it. You can also expect the unex-
pected from C's eclectic wine list, composed by manager-sommelier Peter
Bodnar-Rod. His wine service is correct and informative without being
pretentious or intrusive. *$$$; AE, DC, E, MC, V; no cheques; lunch,
dinner every day; full bar; reservations recommended; www.crestaurant.
com; map:Q5.*

Cafe de Paris / ★★

751 DENMAN ST; 604/687-1418

Lace curtains at the window, paper covers on the table, a mirrored bar,
and Piaf or Aznavour on the sound system: this is the bistro that takes
you back to the Left Bank. Cafe de Paris's heart-of-the-West-End location draws locals and Francophiles alike. The *frites*—genuine french
fries—have become a Vancouver legend; crisp and light, they accompany
all entrees and have regulars begging for more. As in France, you can opt
for the three-course table d'hôte menu, or pick and choose from à la carte
offerings. Among the latter: a savoury bouillabaisse dense with prawns,
scallops, mussels, and monkfish, its broth infused with saffron and
Pernod, and a deeply comforting cassoulet. Chef André Bernier also creates his own contemporary French cuisine: orange-glazed salmon slices
perfumed with saffron and flashed under a salamander; smoked rack of
lamb. Table d'hôte offerings might include the leek-and-duck confit tarte,
a satiny hot-chicken parfait, or beef tenderloin with Cafe de Paris butter.
Try this bistro for lunch or dinner, *naturellement,* and be sure to glance
at the commendable wine list, which has several surprises in store. Check
out the couscous festival held in September. *$$$; AE, MC, V; no cheques;
lunch Mon–Fri, dinner every day, brunch Sun; full bar; map:Q2.*

Caffe de Medici / ★★★

1025 ROBSON ST; 604/669-9322

As you enter Caffe de Medici, you are immediately made to feel like a favoured guest. The high moulded ceilings, serene portraits of members of the 15th-century Medici family, chairs and drapery in Renaissance green contrasting with the crisp white table linens, and walls the colour of zabaglione create a slightly palatial feeling that is businesslike by day, romantic by night. Skip the soups and order the beautiful antipasto: a bright collage of marinated eggplant, artichoke hearts, peppers, olives, squid, and Italian meats. Pasta dishes with shellfish are flat-out *magnifico:* linguine with seafood in a white wine and Pernod sauce or the signature shellfish risotto with saffron. Both the osso buco Milanese-style and the Roman-style rack of lamb are must-orders. There's a solid, mostly Italian wine list. *$$$; AE, DC, DIS, JCB, MC, V; debit cards; no cheques; lunch Mon–Fri, dinner every day; full bar; www.medici.cc; map:S3.* &

The Cannery Seafood House / ★★★

2205 COMMISSIONER ST; 604/254-9606

Frederic Couton has been winning awards for his cooking since his arrival at the Cannery in 1996. (You can taste his signatures on Canadian International Airlines flights, too.) His culinary artistry makes the trek out to this relatively remote east-end dockside location unquestionably worthwhile. Serving "salmon by the sea" for more than 25 years, the Cannery resides in a building that has been cleverly refurbished to look and feel even older than that. On any given day, you'll find a baker's dozen of honestly prepared, high-quality seafood on the fresh sheet, including a delicate arctic char, a juicy grilled swordfish, and a meaty tuna. (You can order a trio of shellfish for $23.95.) Salmon Wellington has been a house specialty here since 1971; recently rematched with a pinot noir sauce, it's still a winner, yet our favourite is the buttery steamed Alaskan black cod. Those who don't go for fish are catered to with herb-crusted rack of lamb, a crispy seared duck breast, or a simple grilled beef tenderloin. Wine enthusiast Michael Mameli presides over the solid cellar, and his award-winning list is one of the city's best. Service is enthusiastic and friendly. *$$$; AE, DC, MC, V; debit cards; no cheques; lunch Mon–Fri, dinner every day; full bar; www.canneryseafood.com; map:F2.*

Capers / ★★

2496 MARINE DR, WEST VANCOUVER; 604/925-3374

Healthy, holistic, fresh, inventive—pick practically any current cuisine buzzword and Capers fits the bill. What sets Capers apart from virtually any other establishment in the city is that you can also shop here in a country-store setting for glorious produce, unusual condiments, and a broad assortment of take-out dishes (Mediterranean wraps, vegetarian chili, wild pecan rice). Less than a half hour from downtown, the Dundarave location wows with water and city views from the outdoor terrace. Generous helpings and low prices draw local residents, who come for the organic beef burgers or pita pockets stuffed with roasted free-range chicken salad. Vegetarian emphasis translates into big-flavoured dishes. For breakfast, there are organic blueberry pancakes, free-range eggs, and turkey bratwurst sausage. There's a Capers in Kitsilano and the West End, but Dundarave has the only full-service restaurant. *$; AE, MC, V; debit cards; no cheques; breakfast, lunch, dinner every day, brunch Sat–Sun; beer and wine.*

Caramba! / ★★
215 NEWPORT RD, PORT MOODY; 604/461-7676
Mario Enero has brought his successful Mediterranean-style restaurant concept from Whistler to Port Moody. Handsomely installed in Newport Village (across from City Hall), Caramba! has an open kitchen with a wood-burning pizza oven. Every night of the week, this high-energy spot with enthusiastic service draws a neighbourhood crowd for very good, reasonably priced food—free-range chicken that's crisp and juicy, homemade Italian sausages with baked beans, crusty roasts (lamb or pork), or mouth-watering grilled trout with bacon-and-onion mashed potatoes. The Fuego pizza is heaped with hot *cappicollo*, red onion, spicy eggplant, and chile peppers. Eat in or take out. *$$; AE, MC, V; debit cards; no cheques; lunch Mon–Sat, dinner every day; full bar; map:J2.* &

Cardero's Restaurant / ★☆
1583 COAL HARBOUR QUAY; 604/669-7666
Nothing looks more quintessentially Vancouver than this big-room newcomer built on pilings in Coal Harbour, with its wavelike roof, low-key maritime decor, menu showcasing seafood, and huge windows framing swaying yacht masts and floating gin palaces. Stanley Park forms a green backdrop to the racing sculls; beyond can be seen (weather permitting) the North Shore mountains. Sometimes the food lives up to the setting, sometimes not. It's brought by youthful servers, both the men and women dressed in crisp white shirts and ties, jeans, and long white aprons; the approach is courteous if sometimes aloof. At lunch, a salmon-and-shrimp sandwich is all tasteful simplicity, the seafood tossed with diced red onion, dill, and mayo, served on a large soft roll along with mixed greens. At dinner we've fared less well: ho-hum mushrooms from the wok menu were almost counterbalanced by tasty honeyed back ribs. But overcooked halibut was unforgivable, and lamb shanks were well beyond the advertised falling-off-the-bone. If the blueberry-lemon tart is on the dessert menu, indulge. The place is young and, given the great setting, the hope is that the kitchen finds a more even keel. *$$–$$$; AE, MC, V; no cheques; lunch, dinner every day, brunch Sun; full bar; reservations recommended; map:R2.* &

Chartwell / ★★★★

791 W GEORGIA ST (THE FOUR SEASONS); 604/689-9333

Chartwell remains in the bold forefront of excellent hotel dining, evoking an upper-class English men's club atmosphere with wood-panelled walls and classic furnishings. Executive chef Douglas Anderson (ex–Four Seasons Chicago) offers a fresh take on local ingredients, cooking food with direct flavours and a keen edge. His lemon-scented cauliflower custard with a lobster salad is very fine, as are his giant Vancouver Island scallops with roe, complemented by chopped apple and smoked bacon. Even something as rudimentary as beef comes alive in his kitchen. A sirloin, juicy and tender, served one evening with a vegetable pie, its accent avocado, was marvellous. Another night, the side was a beef bone filled with marrow custard stuffing—but it wasn't a bone after all; it was a cooked, hollowed-out potato. Finish with a goat cheese from David Wood on Salt Spring Island. Master host Angelo Cecconi and his talented staff give Chartwell its distinctive stamp of personal service—warm, discreet, and attentive. A pretheatre dinner menu with valet parking is an outstanding value. The wine list is an award winner, and the winemaker dinners are the most popular in the city. *$$$; AE, DC, DIS, JCB, MC, V; no cheques; breakfast, dinner every day, lunch Sun–Fri; full bar; www.fshr.com; map:S3.* &

Chili Club Thai Restaurant / ★★

1000 BEACH AVE; 604/681-6000

Despite the name, with a few noteworthy exceptions, Chili Club's fare is not particularly hot. The staff members, however, are well informed and helpful, and if you want it spicy, they'll gladly oblige. We've enjoyed pork satay and *tom yum goong* soup (prawns and mushrooms married in a good broth with hot spice and deep-scented lemongrass), and when giant smoked New Zealand mussels stuffed with a mild, thick curry paste are available, order them; the same goes for solidly spiced chicken curry, made with coconut milk and bite-size Thai eggplant. There's plenty to choose from. Popular wines and beers are available at realistic prices. For the best view of False Creek, try the holding bar upstairs, which has floor-to-ceiling windows on all sides. Even when the food is fiery, the decor is rather cold. Chili Club is located close to the water, under the Burrard Street Bridge. *$$; AE, DC, MC, V; cheques OK; lunch, dinner every day; full bar; map:Q5.* &

CinCin Restaurant & Bar / ★★★

1154 ROBSON ST; 604/688-7338

CinCin is a hearty Italian toast, a wish of health and good cheer, all of which is implied in this sunny Mediterranean space. The Italian- and French-inspired dishes are boldly flavoured by talented chef Romy Prasad. Launch your meal with his appetizer platter ($16 per person) which might include house-smoked trout, Prince Edward Island mussels, or a tomato and *bocconcini* crostini draped with Parma prosciutto. For entrees, savvy diners order Prasad's veal osso buco with fresh sage gnocchi. Wine takes centre stage at CinCin with sommelier Michael Dinn orchestrating the 10,000-bottle cellar, and it's good value because of a reduced markup. Linger at the bar over a Mandorla Martini or sip wine in the lounge (food's served until 11:30 pm). Dine outdoors on the heated terrace overlooking Robson Street. *$$$; AE, DC, MC, V; no cheques; lunch Mon–Fri, dinner every day; full bar; cincin@direct.ca; www.cincin. net. map:R3.*

Cipriano's Ristorante & Pizzeria / ★★

3995 MAIN ST; 604/879-0020

Don't expect to be impressed with this little trattoria's location—in an old nondescript building with a sagging neon sign on a featureless street corner. Inside, the overall impression is a little better, but not much. But you'd be hard-pressed not to enjoy the comfortable and casual ambience of the place. The giant Caesar salad (made to share), an exercise in excess, is garlic-laden and crammed with croutons. Deep-dish pizza, pasta puttanesca, and chicken cacciatore are all worthwhile, though some sauces can be remarkably familiar. Short routines from owner and onetime stand-up comedian Frank Cipriano punctuate the meal that his wife, Christina, prepares. Cipriano's has a devoted clientele, so reservations are necessary any night of the week. *$$; V; no cheques; dinner Tues–Sat; full bar; reservations required; map:E3.*

Coco / ★★★

1688 W 4TH AVE; 604/731-1185

Imagine for the moment that the spirit of a grand European apartment—say, Coco Chanel's—has been captured, then writ large on the walls of a nondescript box of a room in an equally unremarkable spot that's not quite Kitsilano, not quite Fairview. Add a long, sinuous bar (perfect for dispensing 18 varieties of martinis, including a "Chanel," and seating a dozen sippers or diners), some old-world decor, and cheerful service, and you have Coco—a bold new player in the tapas league. It's been booming since it opened in the spring of '99. Although called tapas, and priced at $6, $8, or $10, its dishes approach main-course size and burst with flavour. They include a salad of warm goat cheese crusted with almonds, served atop mesclun; blackened buffalo seared to perfect tenderness beneath a soy glaze, accompanied by a Thai green curry; and grilled musk ox with cherry-rhubarb chutney. Few regional alliances are apparent in this tiny, open kitchen—just lots of invention, mostly successful. The menu changes regularly, which suits loyal fans fine. The berry desserts are a big hit. *$$; MC, V; debit cards; no cheques; lunch Tues–Fri, dinner Tues–Sun; full bar; reservations recommended; map:P7.* ⅅ

Crime Lab / ★★★

1280 W PENDER ST; 604/732-7463

"Mr. Foreman, has the jury reached its decision?" "It has, milady. Based on all the forensic evidence before us, we find the Crime Lab acquits itself superbly, deserving its reputation as one of the hottest new spots in town." Case closed. But let's review the evidence: overindulging in any of the two dozen clever martinis offered ("Care for a Formaldehyde, sir? Perhaps a Rigor Mortis or an Autopsy?") might lead to unwanted crime lab interest, but chef Tyler Gordon's wild kitchen creativity sends taste buds flying in purely legal ways. Spicy tuna tartare on a sesame cracker with shiitake-soy vinaigrette is one charmer among a dozen fine starters. His affinity for seafood continues with such entrees as seared, chile-rubbed halibut in coconut lemongrass sauce. The angel hair pasta with smoked chicken in a light cream sauce was seductive. Ditto a creamy apple risotto that arrived ringed with six grilled garlic prawns. One caution: the kitchen likes to turn on the spice-driven heat, and the menu may not convey its full intensity. If you're not keen on heat, make that known, and the cordial staff will undoubtedly oblige. Desserts are consistently fine, and the only thing better at the end of the meal is the bill. With appetizers topping out at $7, dinners (except specials) pegged at $15, and desserts each $6, paying the bill can seem like getting off scot-free. Oh, yes: the wedgelike two-storey building was indeed once a crime lab. It remains a charming architectural oddity in a rather odd corner of town, and a return visit is definitely warranted to the scene of this Crime Lab. *$$; AE, DC, E, MC, V; debit cards; no cheques; dinner every day, brunch Sun; full bar; reservations recommended; map:R2.* &

Da Pasta Bar / ★★

1232 ROBSON ST; 604/688-1288
2201 W 1ST AVE; 604/738-6515

The concept of mixing and matching pasta with sauce isn't a new one, but it works better here than at most places. The can't-miss location on Robson Street, although cramped for space, draws everyone from the Docs-and-jeans set to kids with their elderly aunts; the ebullient, pasta-literate servers make all feel welcome. The pastabilities are endless, with six different pastas and 14 assorted sauces adding up, theoretically, to more than 80 different dishes, but servers are good at steering you to what best complements what. Perhaps they'll even suggest some intriguing fusions of West Coast produce and seafood with Asian ingredients. Da Pasta Bar offers good lunchtime deals on pasta combos ($6), and you can add a designer salad or soup for $1.50. *$; AE, DC, JCB, MC, V; debit cards; no cheques; lunch, dinner every day; full bar; www. dapastabar.com; map:R3, N7.*

Dario's La Piazza Ristorante / ★★
3075 SLOCAN ST (ITALIAN CULTURAL CENTRE); 604/430-2195
If you locate your restaurant inside Vancouver's Italian Cultural Centre, you had better be very good at producing and serving Italian food. That this restaurant has prospered for more than 20 years attests to its ability to meet all Italian standards. And it does so without pretension. Large tropical plants and floral displays complete the comfortable illusion of dining in a courtyard. There's an elaborate bar, glazed red brick underfoot, and whole walls of wine racks (housing the place's considerable vintage inventory). The menu is full of familiar favourites now considered out of vogue, among them fettuccine alfredo, risotto al funghi, and veal scaloppine with lemon and white wine. *$$; AE, DC, MC, V; no cheques; lunch Mon–Fri, dinner Mon–Sat; full bar; map:F3.* &

Delilah's / ★☆
1789 COMOX ST; 604/687-3424
This restaurant started life on the subsidewalk floor of a funky old West End hotel, and very quickly became the hippest hip venue in town for in-the-know party people. At its new location it's not quite so esoteric, but it is a carefully planned setting for a voluptuous evening for those of all persuasions. Despite the fact we're into the third millennium, there's an air of 19th-century elegance about the place. Check out the cheeky cherubs on the ceiling, the plush red-velvet banquettes, and Delilah's trademark superintimate curtained booths, for what could only be an extraspecial evening. Also a trademark is Delilah's martini list, the city's first. It contains more than 30 variations on the original gin-and-vermouth theme, and Delilah's martinis are often mentioned as the best in town. Food comes in small portions but is good and reasonably priced. Your menu is your bill; simply check off your selections and hand it to your waiter. The pumpkin tangerine soup is a good choice, and so is the grilled beef tenderloin with chanterelles in a Cinzano sauce. Since they only take reservations for larger parties, be prepared for a wait at the bar. *$$; AE, DC, E, MC, V; no cheques; dinner every day; full bar; reservations accepted for parties of 6 or more; map:P2.*

Diva at the Met / ★★★☆
645 HOWE ST (METROPOLITAN HOTEL); 604/602-7788
Diva is an airy, multitiered space with an exhibition kitchen that fires off daring West Coast fare. Whatever chef Michael Noble serves can be ranked with the best in town. The Alaskan black cod with a mussel, leek, and saffron soup is a standout, and Noble's version of rack of lamb is very creative. To it he adds a braised shank and complements the pair with an organic-barley and mushroom salad. For a zingy, refreshing dessert, try the citrus parfait set into a cool tangerine soup. Marvellous. Brunchers will swoon over the smoked Alaskan black cod hash topped

with poached eggs. All the desserts are winners, but the Stilton cheese-cake is a must-order. Hotel manager Jeremy Roncoroni stocks a deep cellar and delights in rarities (Venturi-Schultz from Vancouver Island among them). *$$; AE, DC, JCB, MC, V; no cheques; breakfast, lunch, dinner every day; full bar; reservations@divamet.com; www.metropolitan.com; map:S3.* &

Dynasty / ★★

888 BURRARD ST; 604/681-8283

Albert Cheung was first among a group of Chinese entrepreneurs to bring the Hong Kong style of fine dining to Vancouver. The decor is postmodern, the waiters are courteous and helpful, and the overall look is so glamorous that it makes the food appear to be more expensive than it actually is. We recommend the individual servings of shark's fin and shredded-chicken soup served in mini-clay pots (at a bargain price), tea-smoked squab, and the Buddha's eight vegetable treasures. The rock cod, lobster, prawns, and geoduck come to your table live in a plastic case for your premeal inspection (though you're welcome to skip the preview). Dim sum is first-rate, too. *$$; AE, E, V; no cheques; lunch, dinner every day; full bar; map:S4.* &

Earls / ★★

1185 ROBSON ST (AND BRANCHES); 604/669-0020

Among the region's upscale chains, Earls has refined a winning formula without being formulaic. "GREAT FOOD. GREAT PEOPLE," reads the slogan and, cockiness aside, it's apt. It's fast food, and it isn't. Each pearl in the Earls chain has the same sassy style and emphasis on high-quality, fresh-only, seasonal ingredients, whether on pizzas (from the open-to-view wood oven), in pastas, or with burgers. Earls follows food trends closely and trains its staff accordingly, once a year shipping the whole management team off to Tuscany (or wherever) to experience the cuisine first-hand. The team-training approach filters down and pays off. Servers are young, bright, attractive, and obviously enthused about what they're doing. A diner can't help but smile when an eager busperson asks: "Everything cool?" Atmosphere varies with location. Above happenin' Robson Street, a Mexican mode prevails, with big pottery pieces and a huge sombrero-topped pig in the centre of the room. In other locations the style is more refined. The menu caters to all tastes and ages, but Earls attracts mostly a younger crowd. Exclusive microbrews and a one-price list of wines at just over $20 (there's also a pricier reserve list) add to the appeal; most wines are available by the glass. There are now 22 Earls restaurants in BC, 15 of them in the Lower Mainland. The one on Robson Street is open until midnight; some locations stay open even later. *$$; AE, MC, V; no cheques; lunch, dinner every day; full bar; reservations accepted Sun–Thur only for groups of 8 or more; map:R3.* &

El Caravan / ★
809 SEYMOUR ST; 604/682-7000
Touted accurately as the best Middle Eastern restaurant in town, this
place also has the advantage of a fabulous location, right next door to
the Orpheum Theatre and handy to Robson Street shopping and other
city-centre amenities. It's a big space opulently decorated with items such
as feathery pampas plumes and pharaonic Egyptian prints. Chef Mona
Helfaoui is Lebanese and cooks the dishes she learned at her grandmother's
elbow. Partnering the usual Middle Eastern appetizers—hummus, baba
ghanouj, and grape leaves—are Mona's exceptionally spicy carrots.
Entrees include a choice of souvlakia, prawns, moussaka, and spinach
pie. *$$; AE, DC, MC, V; no cheques; lunch, dinner every day; full bar;
map:S4.*

Ezogiku Noodle Cafe / ★
1329 ROBSON ST; 604/685-8608
A small gem of a place operated for the benefit of Oriental food lovers
who don't want to spend a lot of money. This tiny place (only 70 seats, and
they're close together) displays only a modest awning saying NOODLE
CAFE, but regulars would say that doesn't start to describe its value. Sev-
eral varieties of ramen noodle dishes make up most of the menu, many
representing a clever combination of Japanese and Chinese culinary
tastes, and all come in huge, filling quantities. But there's also fried rice,
fried noodles, and wonderfully tasty gyoza. Be prepared to wait for a
seat. Other branches are in Honolulu and Tokyo. *$; cash only; lunch,
dinner every day; no alcohol; map:R3.*

Fatzo's Barbeque Smokehouse / ★★
2884 W BROADWAY; 604/733-3002
"BEST BUTT ON BROADWAY" brags the back of the server's T-shirt (cus-
tomers can buy one, too, of course), and regulars believe it. That's BBQ'd
Pork Butt—served chopped on a dinner platter or piled high and smoth-
ered in barbecue sauce on a sandwich combo plate. It's one of many
Southern specialties that create weekend lineups outside Fatzo's. Viewed
from north of the 49th parallel, Americans' debate-without-end over
what constitutes true barbecue seems one of those issues—like politics,
religion, and philandering—that can spark wars. When someone imports
great barbecue into the North, Canadians just give thanks and chow
down—on brisket, on ribs, on smoked-and-peppered turkey breast. All
the meals here let you choose two of nine side dishes. (One, a kid's beach
bucket filled with fries, easily feeds two or three.) Lurking among the
appetizers you'll find "quik fried dill pickles" (worth experiencing at least
once). Fatzo's decor is a paean to jazz and blues artists. A huge mural
salutes Mississippi John Hurt, Muddy Waters, Willie Dixon, and others;
soothing sounds fill the room and flow onto the sidewalk in fine weather.

$$; MC, V; debit cards; no cheques; lunch, dinner every day, brunch Sat–Sun; full bar; reservations accepted weekdays only; map:C3. ♿

Fiasco / ★★

2486 BAYSWATER ST; 604/734-1325

Officially named Mark's Fiasco, this place attached to a high-end men's clothing store in Kitsilano attracts an upscale and devoted clientele. It's a great big, wide-open room designed to be a casual meeting place for a not-quite-young but very hip clientele. Very urbane, very cool, very Kitsilano-verging-on–Upper West Side. The focus of the decor is a whopping old-fashioned bar flanked with television sets, where you'll find a goodly number of regulars at any hour of the day. The tables are comfortable, too, and spread right out onto the sidewalk when the weather is accommodating. A huge open kitchen provides almost as much entertainment as the bar, serving up Cal-Ital entrees that include esoteric and experimental pastas and calzone. Bargain seekers should look for weeknight specials. There's live entertainment Thursday through Sunday. *$$; AE, MC, V; no cheques; lunch, dinner every day, brunch Sat–Sun; full bar; map:C3.*

The Fish House at Stanley Park / ★★★

2099 BEACH AVE (ENTRANCE TO STANLEY PARK); 604/681-7275

Take your pick—the Garden Room surrounded by large trees, the intimate Club Room overlooking the tennis courts, or the formal Fireplace Room. Count on chef Karen Barnaby to cook seafood the way you like it, and an ardent staff to serve it. There's everything you'd expect (salmon cakes) and some things you wouldn't (halibut and "chips"). As an appy, share the prawns flambéed with ouzo or wood oven–roasted calamari with smoked-tomato vinaigrette. As an entree, ahi tuna comes as two-fisted loins (a pair), barely grilled through and fork-tender in a green-pepper sauce. It's the whole plate that impresses. Barnaby's vegetables aren't an afterthought; each is a discovery in itself. Examples include red cabbage with fennel-and-buttermilk mashed potatoes. Save room for comforting desserts—coconut cream pie or lethal chocolate lava cake. If you want recipes (and you will), pick up a copy of Barnaby's cookbook, *Screamingly Good Food. $$; AE, DC, E, JCB, MC, V; debit cards; no cheques; lunch Mon–Sat, dinner every day, brunch Sun; full bar; www.fishhousestanleypark.com; map:D1.* ♿

Five Sails / ★★★☆

999 CANADA PLACE (PAN PACIFIC HOTEL); 604/891-2892

The drop-dead-gorgeous harbour view may lure diners here for the first time, but it's the food that brings them back. Don't even think of not ordering the Alaskan black cod chowder. Or the napoleon of chilled Dungeness crab, or the seared Alaskan scallops atop a Grand Marnier–

marinated fresh foie gras, dressed with a sun-dried cherry sauce. Mussels presented with smoked bacon in a fumé blanc–based sauce are recommended, as is the filet mignon, pan-seared and bathed in a red-wine reduction. After your dinner, or even before, have maître d'hôtel and wine steward Stewart Warmbath do his dissertation on single-malt Scottish whiskies. He's worth the company. Become a member here of la Confrère du sabre d'or by ordering champagne and sabering the bottle. Free parking. *$$$; AE, DC, JCB, MC, V; no cheques; dinner every day; full bar; preserve@panpacific-hotel.com; www.panpac.com; map:T2.* &

Fleuri / ★★★⯪

845 BURRARD ST (SUTTON PLACE HOTEL); 604/682-5511

At press time, executive chef Kei Lermen has moved to the Ritz-Carlton in Philadelphia. The toque has been passed to Michael Deutsch, who has worked under Lermen and plans to continue in his footsteps. We hope he keeps the wild BC salmon roasted and served with sautéed bacon and garlic, and sauerkraut flavoured with Jerez vinegar on the menu. In the afternoon, hotel guests—corporate types and movie stars (celeb-spotting is a popular sport)—converse over traditional English tea in an atmosphere that is light and European. For $18, you can nibble on finger sandwiches, pastries, scones, and cream. On Friday and Saturday, tables are laden with seafood and fish for the "Taste of Atlantis." The Chocoholic Bar has become a legend on Thursdays, Fridays, and Saturdays, and the Sunday brunch has been rated as the number-one special-occasion place in town. *$$; AE, DC, DIS, JCB, MC, V; no cheques; breakfast, lunch, dinner every day, brunch Sun; full bar; info@suttonplace.com; www. travelweb.com/sutton.html; map:S4.* &

Floata Seafood Restaurant / ★★

400–180 KEEFER ST; 604/602-0368
1425–4380 NO. 3 RD, RICHMOND; 604/270-8889

Vancouver's historical Chinatown is home to the largest restaurant in western Canada. This cavernous, sparsely postmodern room seats 1,000 (yes, 1,000). The room is equipped with wall-to-ceiling partitions that can carve up the impressive space, to order, into restaurant-size private dining rooms, each equipped with its very own karaoke sound system. A brisk dim sum trade ensures fresh and very good nibbles for those who are here to enjoy this popular Chinese roving lunch-hour feast. Unfortunately, dinner experiences here have fallen short of the high quality one comes to expect at the group's other location in Richmond, where the succulent crispy-skin chicken, the tender lobster in cream sauce, the velvety braised Chinese mushrooms with mustard greens, and other Cantonese favourites are local standard-bearers of the cuisine. *$$; AE, DC, MC, V; no cheques; dim sum lunch, dinner every day; full bar; map:X4, D5.* &

Flying Wedge / ★

3499 CAMBIE ST (AND BRANCHES); 604/874-8284

Pizza is all they sell here. Both full-sized pies and generous slices (for $3.25) are available at no fewer than five locations (including downtown, Kitsilano, and even the airport). An evidently lighthearted atmosphere prevails, with a brightly coloured cartoon decor and, at the original location, what appears to be one of Buck Rogers's old spaceships in flight over the pizza counter. Standard pizzas are available, but you're urged to try something from the ever-changing parade of exotic concoctions—Deep Purple, heady with marinated eggplant, or spicy Sichuan chicken. Eat all you can Sundays for $7.29; eat *and* drink all you can for $7.99. The Royal Centre locale (1055 W Georgia St; 604/681-1233; map:S3) is closed Sundays, and Library Square (207–345 Robson St; 604/689-7078; map:T5) serves only lunch. *$; AE, MC, V; debit cards; no cheques; lunch, dinner every day (with exceptions); no alcohol; map:D3.*

Fritz European House of Fries / ★★☆

718 DAVIE ST; 604/684-0811

Near the corner of Davie and Granville Streets, potato history is being made. Within the humble confines of the Fritz European Fry House, a Belgian and Dutch tradition is reborn with these crispy take-out french fries, served in paper cones and accompanied by your choice of one of 13 dips. The crowd favourites seem to be the garlic lover's mayo and the mango chutney curry mayo, which are outstanding. Try a bit of Cajun ketchup to throw a little zing into the mix, and wash down your fries with a Barq's Rootbeer on tap. The king cone of fries here is the Montreal-style *poutine,* dripping with cheese curds from St. Albert, Ontario, and hot gravy. Variations include Italian-style and chili *poutine.* Portions of fries range in size from mini to large. Try the large fries with dip and drink for five bucks. Extra dips are 50 cents each. *Poutine* is $3.75 for a regular and $4.50 for a large. There's a wooden bench along one wall in case you want to dine in, complete with holes cut in the armrests for holding your cone of fries. *$; cash only; lunch, dinner every day; no alcohol; map:R5.* ♿

Gianni Restaurant & Norcineria / ★★★

2881 GRANVILLE ST; 604/738-7922

Spaghetti *al tartufo Norcina* or, to you and me, spaghetti with truffles. If for no other reason, visit Gianni's for this dish: you'll swear it was transported to earth by some heavenly messenger. Of course, the roasted meats, simple but packed with flavour, may also entice you, or the light-as-air tiramisu, or the good selection of Italian wines. The food is almost as appealing as the shy charm of chef-owner Gianni Picchi and his attentive servers. Gianni used to cook at Umberto Menghi's Il Giardino, and has brought all the lessons from that highly respected kitchen to a neighbourhood that sorely needed them. The classic dishes he serves are straightforward, husky, and simple, with strong, earthy flavours that will assure you this is just how food *should* taste. If you're shopping on South Granville, stop by the take-out window at noon for a vegetarian panini or a Roman-style pizza square. *$$$; AE, DC, MC, V; no cheques; lunch Mon–Fri, dinner Mon–Sat; full bar; map:D3.*

Giraffe / ★★

15053 MARINE DR (ACROSS FROM PIER), WHITE ROCK; 604/538-6878
Chef Corinne Poole sold this delightful, elegant neighbourhood restaurant in White Rock with a view of Semiahmoo Bay and moved to Seattle. Two energetic staff members took it over, and it is busier than ever. Poole's luxurious appetizers of crispy wonton skins filled with fresh crab and served with honey mustard, or a layered *torta basilica* of cream cheese, pesto, pine nuts, and sun-dried tomatoes with garlic crostini are still on the menu. New entrees include a provençal crusted lamb loin with apricot mint chutney, and a boneless chicken breast wrapped with prosciutto and stuffed with an artichoke-and-Brie mousse. Both are outstanding. Save room for "The Graze"—a dessert sampler with an array of sweets that might include cheesecake, fruit and berry sorbets, or a rich chocolate cake. *$$; MC, V; no cheques; lunch, dinner every day, brunch Sun; full bar; www.thegiraffe.com.*

Gotham / ★

615 SEYMOUR ST; 604/605-8282
The newest buzz in Vancouver, besides coffee, is Gotham. With a flashy interior built to the tune of $3 million, it's no wonder most of the people who dine here look as if they share an equally high tax bracket. The king of steakhouses, David Aisenstat, has turned his attention to creating a hipper-style Hy's. The result is a downtown dining experience that is every bit as alluring as its 22-foot ceilings. To capture an intimate atmosphere in such a large space, he's used dark woods, muted lighting, and a postmodern medieval touch that broadcasts subdued bacchanalia. Meat is the main course here, or USDA prime, to be precise. The standalone steaks (vegetables are à la carte) are even more beautiful than the people. From the New York strip ($34.95) to the splendid 24-ounce porterhouse ($37.95), it's a cattle drive for the taste buds. At $5.50 per order, you can share mashed potatoes, creamed spinach, or crispy french fries. It remains to be seen how the cholesterol-denying populace of Vancouver take to this red-meat renaissance. For sheer entertainment value, take a seat at the bar and engage in some of the best people-watching that Vancouver has to offer. Beware: this place prices under the assumption that everyone has a Swiss bank account. *$$$; AE, DC, MC, V; no cheques; lunch, dinner every day; full bar; map:S3.* &

Grand King Seafood Restaurant / ★

705 W BROADWAY (HOLIDAY INN); 604/876-7855

The bad news is that chef Lam Kam Shing, who wowed lovers of Chinese food in this well-established restaurant, is gone. The good news is that most of his creations will remain on the menu. One of our recent favourites is the Dungeness crab. The body meat is steamed in its shell, which is laced with the crab's rich roe, minced pork, and cellophane noodles and surrounded by its legs, crisp-fried with spicy rock salt. Another is the superb double-boiled winter melon soup, cooked inside the melon and laden with seafood. A dim sum standout are the steamed vegetarian dumplings, almost worth the trip in themselves. Have them as a first course. One more thing: you'll be happy to know that those addictive complimentary candied walnuts and the dynamite X.O. chile sauce are now bottled-to-go and available at the cashier's desk on your way out. *$$$; AE, DC, MC, V; no cheques; lunch, dinner every day; full bar; map:R7.*

Great Wall Mongolian BBQ Restaurant / ★★☆

717 DENMAN ST; 604/688-2121
2897 W BROADWAY; 604/739-4888

A casual place where locals come to fill up on all-you-can-eat Mongolian. This is interactive dining at its best. Pay no attention to the luncheonette-style decor. Pick up a bowl at the buffet. Add as much beef, pork, lamb, or chicken as you wish. Toppings include a selection of 20 very fresh vegetables, noodles, tofu, and 16 flavourful sauces. (Follow their excellent suggestions if you're not feeling creative.) When you're ready, the chef spills your creation onto a huge, sizzling-hot circular grill. He works it all the way around the grill with a pair of chopsticks. In under a minute your meal is fully cooked. Then, with a deft stroke of the sticks, he lands everything in a fresh bowl and hands it to you. Feel free to put together a small test bowl on your first round. Lunch includes soup and rice; dinner includes Mongolian bread (sort of sesame croissants), fried wontons, soup, and rice. *$; MC, V; debit cards; no cheques; lunch, dinner every day; beer and wine; map:Q2, C3.* ⅃

Griffins / ★★

900 W GEORGIA ST (HOTEL VANCOUVER); 604/662-1900

The eminently respectable Hotel Vancouver (one of the historic Canadian Pacific châteaus that dot Canada) houses a bright and lively bistro. With taxicab-yellow walls, griffin-motif carpet, and a feeling of urban action, the place has energy to burn. Three meals a day are served à la carte, but the buffet meals are the way to go. The breakfast buffet lets you veer toward the healthy (muesli, fresh fruit compote, and such) or the hedonistic (carved Pepsi Cola–glazed ham). An Asian corner supplies early birds with a fix of grilled salmon and toasted nori. Make a dinner of smoked salmon or roasted peppers with basil at the appetizer bar, or work your way through entrees of silver-dollar scallops in garlic sauce, an exemplary steak, or a pasta dish, then take a run or three at the pastry bar. *$$; AE, DC, E, JCB, MC, V; no cheques; breakfast, lunch, dinner every day; full bar; www.cphotels.com; map:S3.* &

Gyoza King / ★★
1508 ROBSON ST; 604/669-8278
Gyoza King serves outstanding Japanese "comfort food" such as two dozen varieties of gyoza: fried dumplings filled with prawns, pork, or vegetables along with ginger, scallions, and garlic, served with a soy dipping sauce. This casual hangout, which is perennially packed with Japanese students on vacation, also makes sushi, udon noodle soups, *katsu-don* (breaded pork cutlet over rice), and a hearty soup called *o-den*. Sit at the bar or at the low front table for a good view of the chef in action. There are Western-style tables as well. The other pluses here are late hours, reasonable prices, a very courteous staff, and a good selection of beers. *$; AE, MC, V; debit cards; no cheques; lunch, dinner every day; beer and wine; map:S4.*

Habibi's / ★★★
7–1128 W BROADWAY; 604/732-7487
Richard Zeinoun cooks from the heart at this casual Middle Eastern spot on W Broadway. There are all sorts of surprises, starting with the complimentary meze of olives, nuts, cucumbers, and onions. These refreshing tapas whet the appetite for *shinkleesh,* an aged goat cheese from the mountains of Lebanon; *balila,* warmed chickpeas in garlic-infused oil; or *warak anab,* grape leaves stuffed with mildly spiced rice and marinated in lemon juice. As well, there are falafels and both Lebanese- and Israeli-style hummus. Fresh pita bread and wines chosen to go with the food make Habibi's an unbeatable dining experience. Food is downright cheap; all dishes are $5.50 and the baklava is a buck. Friendly and enthusiastic service. There's live entertainment on weekends. *$; no credit cards; debit cards; cheques OK; lunch, dinner Mon–Sat; wine and beer; map:R7.*

Hamburger Mary's / ★
1202 DAVIE ST; 604/687-1293
Mary's is the diner we all grew up with gone upscale, with groovy chrome 'n' glass-block decor and heartachey songs on the jukebox. A West End fixture since 1979, Hamburger Mary's has stayed open by racing apace of fickle appetites. Thus, starters are whatever's hip, be it potato skins, chicken strips with plum sauce, or pot stickers. Big burgers are the major draw here, served with bacon, cheese, and just about any other combo that strikes your fancy, with The Works for the undecided and chicken burgers for the quasi-vegetarians. During the winter on Tuesdays and Wednesdays, the attraction is a selection of 12 kinds of pasta for just

$5.95. Not forgetting its diner roots, Hamburger Mary's also serves up chips with a side of mayo or gravy, and humongous milk shakes in chrome containers. Open till 4am on Friday and Saturday. *$; AE, DC, MC, V; no cheques; breakfast, lunch, dinner, midnight snacks every day; full bar; map:Q4.*

Hart House on Deer Lake / ★★☆

6664 DEER LAKE AVE, BURNABY; 604/298-4278

Twenty minutes from downtown is an urban getaway in a heritage Tudor country manor overlooking scenic gardens and Deer Lake. The menu features West Coast cooking with a focus on game and local seafood. Start with the carpaccio of musk ox and move into the sesame soy–glazed scallops and prawns or the Hart House signature—standing rack of lamb with fresh mint jus. There's great depth (many older vintages) in the California and Pacific Northwest cellar selections and one of the best BC lists in the province. If you request it in advance, they'll set up a croquet course under the willows on their lakeside lawn. Free parking. *$$$; AE, DC, MC, V; no cheques; lunch Mon–Fri, dinner every day, brunch Sun; full bar; www.harthouserestaurant.com; map:H3.* &

The Hermitage / ★★☆

115-1025 ROBSON ST; 604/689-3237

Hidden away at the back of a minimall just off Robson Street, the Hermitage, believe it or not, opened a decade ago as a coffee shop. Now it offers an intimate dining experience and a polished professional staff. Chef-owner Herve Martin (who was once chef to the late King Leopold of Belgium) sticks strongly by his French roots. This is the place to come for duck flambéed with Armagnac and sprinkled with crackling, pheasant served in two courses, or a seafood cassoulet in a delicate lobster sauce—that sort of thing. More than 350 wines (some from his family's vineyard in Burgundy) reflect Martin's eye for high-quality, good-value producers. Only a fool would pass up the crepe with fresh berries and a scoop of vanilla ice cream, warmed and served with a strawberry coulis. Although the Hermitage (as its name implies) may be hidden, it's well worth looking for. *$$; AE, DC, JCB, MC, V; debit cards; no cheques; lunch Mon–Fri, dinner every day; full bar; map:S3.*

Herons / ★★☆

900 CANADA PL (WATERFRONT HOTEL); 604/691-1818

In the Waterfront Hotel, Herons' high-ceilinged dining room is a multipurpose bistro and restaurant with an open kitchen. Everyone will appreciate chef Daryle Ryd Nagata's rooftop herb garden, which determines the everyday fresh sheet of contemporary Canadian cooking. Start with an appetizer of musk ox carpaccio. It gets a lift from a shaving of Parmesan cheese and a roasted bell pepper aioli. Or share the salmon sampler—

generous portions of salmon and Dungeness crab cakes, salmon tartare, Indian candy, warm pan-seared gravlax, alderwood-smoked salmon, and salmon-belly tempura. Or order a traditional clubhouse. On Sundays, a pianist plays during brunch. Warm, accommodating service despite the room's lack of intimacy, but stay tuned—a renovation is planned. Innovative food and wine promotions. *$$; AE, DC, E, MC, V; no cheques; breakfast, lunch, dinner every day, brunch Sun; full bar; www.cphotels. com; map:T3.*

Hon's Wun Tun House / ★★☆

108–268 KEEFER ST (AND BRANCHES); 604/688-0871

By serving the just-plain-good, basic Chinese specialties you'd find in hundreds of street-corner restaurants in Hong Kong, and by keeping prices to a comfortable minimum, what was once a small and steamy Chinatown noodle house has now become something of a restaurant empire, with seven branches located all over the Lower Mainland. One of the keys to Hon's success is that all the locations are unpretentious and comfortable. Dishes are prepared before your eyes in open kitchens. Wonton is just one of the more than 90 varieties of soup available, and there's a seemingly endless list of noodle dishes. The trademark pot sticker dumplings, fried or steamed, are justly famous. Hon's also offers takeout and a full line of frozen dim sum. Only the Robson Street location (1339 Robson St; 604/685-0871; map:S4) accepts credit or debit cards. *$; cash only (except Robson St location); lunch, dinner every day; no alcohol; map:V4.*

Horizons on Burnaby Mountain / ★★★☆

100 CENTENNIAL WY, BURNABY; 604/299-1155

You may need a map to find this place near the top of Burnaby Mountain, and when you do, the weather had better be clear or you'll miss the main attraction—a view of Burrard Inlet, the North Shore mountains, Stanley Park, the Strait of Georgia halfway to Nanaimo, and, of course, the city itself. If it's raining, you'll still find yourself in a well-designed, spacious setting surrounded by a lovely park. The menu features traditional Native alder-smoked and alder-grilled BC salmon, a perennial favourite, but other temptations include unique maple-roasted salmon, a scallop-and-prawn risotto, and a hearty West Coast bouillabaisse. Impressive wine list. *$$; AE, E, MC, V; no cheques; lunch, dinner every day, brunch Sun; full bar; map:I2.*

Hy's Encore / ★★★

637 HORNBY ST; 604/683-7671

Hy's has weathered the skinless chicken breast, vegetarian, and white wine fads of the past and is now revelling in the return of steaks, chops, and martinis. It's a classically masculine establishment: dark oak panelling, white linens, leather chairs, lamplight, and oil paintings. The aged steaks literally come in all shapes and sizes, from not-so-dainty charbroiled filet mignons to spicy steak au poivre to juicy châteaubriands. The chicken and seafood dishes on the menu are definitely made for light appetites but are not the reason local stockbrokers and visiting Japanese executives pack the place at both lunch and dinner. *$$–$$$; AE, DC, E, MC, V; no cheques; lunch Mon–Fri, dinner every day; full bar; reservations recommended; map:S3.*

IKEA / ★

3200 SWEDEN WY, RICHMOND; 604/273-2051
Why would we suggest a meal in a furniture store? Two reasons: first, if you've never wandered through this successful high-concept, low-priced, serve-yourself Swedish store, you're in for a treat. Second, and more to the point, it's the only place in and around Vancouver (it's 20 minutes from downtown via the Knight Street Bridge) that serves Swedish food. It's also the only cafeteria—let alone furniture store—we know of that lets you sip a glass of wine with your meal. You'll find a variety of spiced or marinated pickled herring, liver pâtés, cucumber salad, and red cabbage and *köttbullar* (Swedish meatballs). Open-faced sandwiches and children's box lunches are also available. Nearby you can gather an armload of such specialties as lingonberry preserves, Swedish flatbread, or a bottle of 38-proof Gammel Dansk bitters to take home. *$; MC, V; debit cards; cheques OK; lunch every day, dinner Mon–Fri; beer and wine; map:C6.* ఉ

Il Giardino di Umberto / ★★★

1382 HORNBY ST; 604/669-2422
Stars, stargazers, and the movers and shakers come to Umberto Menghi's Il Giardino to mingle amid the Tuscan-villa decor: high ceilings, tiled floors, winking candlelight, and a vine-draped terrace for dining alfresco (no better place in summer). The emphasis is on pasta and game, with an Italian *nuova* elegance: tagliolini in a lobster sauce, tender veal with a mélange of lightly grilled wild mushrooms, and osso buco with saffron risotto. Be warned: the prices on the specials are in their own category. For dessert, go for the prizewinning tiramisu—the best version of this pick-me-up in town. Expect swift, polished service and a solid wine list. One of Canada's best-known restaurateurs, Menghi has a syndicated TV show, has written three cookbooks, and owns Villa Delia, one of Italy's best cooking schools. *$$$; AE, DC, E, MC, V; debit cards; no cheques; lunch Mon–Fri, dinner Mon–Sat; full bar; map:R5.*

J J's Dining Room / ★

250 W PENDER ST; 604/443-8479

An ever-changing menu of Escoffier-level gourmet dishes at rock-bottom prices? There has to be a catch, right? Well, sort of. This restaurant is part of the downtown campus of Vancouver City College, and the dishes served at J J's are prepared by the students in that school's well-respected culinary courses. Because of this, the menu changes constantly, but at any time you'll be offered an entirely adequate bill of fare featuring upscale restaurant food at ridiculously low prices. The decor is simple to the point of being almost spartan, but it's a comfortable space nonetheless. One problem is a lack of signage, making it extremely difficult to find in the midst of a bustling postsecondary educational establishment. You may have to ask your way, but it's definitely a place worth finding. The Friday-night buffet is excellent. *$; MC, V; no cheques; lunch, dinner Mon–Fri; full bar; map:U4.*

Joe Fortes / ★

777 THURLOW ST; 604/669-1940

Don't be surprised to see Alice Cooper or the rock group AC/DC sitting at the bar out on the fabulous upstairs roof garden. Joe Fortes—named for the city's best-loved lifeguard—has a kind of high-energy, uptown-chophouse feel to it and is one of the city's hippest watering holes. The draw is more than the big U-shaped bar, where martinis and single-malt scotch are in equal demand. It's the oyster bar, too, dispensing dozens of faultlessly fresh varieties, all sold individually. Sipping, schmoozing, and sampling (starters include Dungeness crab cakes, beef carpaccio, and Joe's seafood tower) often segue seamlessly into the dinner hour. The fresh fish is a constant lure; order the chef's trio of grilled seafood, and $21.95 gets you your choice of shark, red snapper, salmon, halibut, mahimahi, sea bass, or swordfish. Attentive service and a solid wine list. At press time, a new chef has taken the helm. Stay tuned. *$$–$$$; AE, DC, JCB, MC, V; no cheques; lunch Mon–Fri, dinner every day, brunch Sat–Sun; full bar; map:R3.*

Just One Thai Bistro / ★

1103 DENMAN ST; 604/685-8989

A collection of porcelain and brass Buddhas set into illuminated wall recesses, fresh floral arrangements, slate floors, and palm trees create a peaceful setting at this informal Denman Street establishment. The house specialty is Thai barbecue. Meats, chicken, or seafood are marinated in mild curry, lime juice, and soy, then skewered, grilled, and served with a spicy peanut sauce. Thai-style curries ranging from medium-hot red to superhot green, subtly spiced stir-fries, crispy spring rolls, and steaming bowls of *tom yum goong* (a hot and sour prawn and mushroom soup) are favourites. Service is superb at both lunch and dinner. Early-bird and lunch specials are exceptionally good values. *$–$$; AE, MC, V; no cheques; lunch, dinner every day; full bar; map:P3.* ♿

Kalamata Greek Taverna / ★★

478 W BROADWAY; 604/872-7050

In a city with many Greek restaurants, Kalamata has been selected as the best restaurant of its kind in Vancouver for five straight years by an authoritative annual critics' poll. Owner and chef Stathi Rallis serves up excellent Greek classics with a modern touch, including dishes that were Greek favourites before souvlaki, moussaka, and dolmades were introduced. "I have 2,000 years of culinary history to work with," says Rallis. House specialties include bird's milk (egg white) avgolemono soup and skewers of delicious grilled artichoke hearts. The location is a bit unfortunate, right at a busy, loud intersection, and the service can be slow. But the truly good food and excellent prices make a visit worthwhile. *$$; AE, MC, V; no cheques; lunch Tues–Fri, dinner Tues–Sun; full bar; map:T7.* ♿

Kam Gok Yuen / ★

142 E PENDER ST; 604/683-3822

If you're ravenous from souvenir shopping in Chinatown and can no longer resist the beckoning of barbecued ducks hanging in food store windows, head to the no-decor Kam Gok Yuen for an affordable repast. Its famous barbecued meats are sold out every day, so a near-empty window is not suspect, but a sign that you should hurry in and order before the store runs out. Some of the best *congee* (rice porridge with meat or seafood) in town is cooked to order over hissing burners in the open kitchen up front. Watch as wontons and noodles are tossed, caught, and dropped into bowls with a magical ease that borders on showmanship. Be sure to ask about specials posted on the walls in Chinese, since they can be some of the tastiest items. Brisk service. *$; cash only; lunch, dinner every day; no alcohol; map:V4.*

Kamei Royale Japanese Restaurant / ★★

1030 W GEORGIA ST (AND BRANCHES); 604/687-8588

With three locations, Kamei may no longer be the best single Japanese restaurant in town, but its simple, westernized dishes certainly make it one of the most popular. The luxury-class Kamei Royale on W Georgia Street seats more than 300, with open and private tatami rooms. Combination platters contain all the standards, or try the red snapper *usuzukui*, thinly sliced and fanned on the plate, accompanied by a citrus sauce. Robata dishes are the special focus at the Broadway Plaza location (601 W Broadway; 604/876-3388; map:U7) and can be very good. *$$; AE, DC, JCB, MC, V; no cheques; lunch Mon–Sat, dinner every day; full bar; map:S3.* ♿

King's Fare Fish & Chips / ★

1320 W 73RD AVE; 604/266-3474

Enter this busy small restaurant and you'll immediately sense that this place means business. The staff hustle but still find the time to be polite, stopping to chat with the regulars, of whom there are plenty. Portions of cod and halibut are generous and the batter is perfect: light but not greasy, crisp but not overly so. The potatoes come from Ladner and are chipped in the kitchen. The coleslaw is made from scratch and served in portions you don't mistake for the coffee cream. Decent ale on tap adds that extra touch of authenticity. So do the "take-away" fish-and-chips wrapped in the funnies. *$; E, MC, V; no cheques; lunch, dinner every day; beer and wine; map:D5.*

Kirin Mandarin Restaurant / ★★★

1166 ALBERNI ST (AND BRANCHES); 604/682-8833

Kirin's postmodern decor—high ceilings, slate-green walls, black lacquer trim—is centred around the two-storey-high mystical dragonlike creature for which the restaurant is named. The menu reads like a trilingual (Chinese, English, and Japanese) opus spanning the culinary capitals of China: Canton, Sichuan, Shanghai, and Beijing. Live lobsters and crabs can be ordered in 11 different preparations. Remarkably, most of the vastly different regional cuisines are authentic and well executed, but the northern Chinese specialties are the best. Peking duck is as good as it gets this side of China, and braised dishes such as sea cucumber with prawn roe sauce are "royal" treats. Unlike in most Chinese restaurants, desserts can be excellent. Try the red-bean pie, a thin crepe folded around a sweet bean filling and fried to a fluffy crispness. The Western-style service is attentive though sometimes a tad aggressive. Unless you are in the mood to splurge, stay away from the Cognac cart. Here fresh seasonal seafood choices, such as drunken live spot prawns and whole Alaskan king crab, are often presented with dramatic tableside special effects. Kirin also has great dim sum (including a definitive *har gow* or shrimp dumpling). The other Kirin Seafood restaurants are at City Square (201–555 W 12th Ave; 604/879-8838; map:D3) and, the newest one, in Richmond (200–7900 Westminster Hwy; 604/303-8833; map:D6). *$$$; AE, DC, JCB, V; cheques OK; lunch, dinner every day; full bar; map:R3.* &

Kitto Japanese House / ★

833 GRANVILLE ST; 604/687-6622

Kitto thrives on theatre row downtown, and it's a great place before or after a movie. The reason for its success? Authentically flavoured, accessible Japanese food at rock-bottom prices There's sushi and sashimi, udons, ramens, sobas, and donburis—rice and noodle dishes that are fast and satisfying. Or try some robatas, which include smoky yakitori chicken with green onions; fleshy, velvety-fresh shiitake mushrooms; zucchini with dry bonito flakes; and an incredible dish of *hamachi* gill. Two or three with a bowl of rice make a wonderful meal, with dinner for two comfortably priced about $10 a person. *$; cash only; lunch, dinner every day; beer only; map:S4.*

Koji Japanese Restaurant / ★★
630 HORNBY ST; 604/685-7355

In our opinion, Koji has the most beautiful garden in a downtown Vancouver restaurant—an island of pine trees and river rocks on a patio above Hornby Street. The best seats are the ones by the windows looking out on the garden or at the sushi and robata bars. The rest of the restaurant is crowded and often full of Japanese tourists. The sushi is not the best in town, but selections from the robata grill are dependable; the grilled shiitake, topped with bonito flakes and tiny filaments of dry seaweed, are sublime. The Japanese boxed lunch might contain chicken *karaage,* superb smoked black cod, prawn and vegetable tempura, two or three small salads, rice with black sesame seeds, pickled vegetables, miso soup, and fresh fruit—all for about $10. Finish with green-tea ice cream. *$$; AE, DC, JCB, MC, V; no cheques; breakfast, dinner every day, lunch Mon–Fri; full bar; map:S3.* &

L'Arena / ★
300 W GEORGIA ST; 604/687-5434

Tucked into Library Square, L'Arena is a favourite among ticket holders heading to GM Place, BC Place, or the Queen E. Its mostly Italian menu features antipasto, pizzas, pastas, and seafood, but the real ticket here is the Gnocchi Bar ($16.95 at dinner, $12 at lunch). With house-made gnocchi, you get a choice of meat or seafood (prosciutto, grilled chicken, baby shrimp, or Italian sausage) and two vegetables (artichoke hearts, sun-dried tomatoes, black olives, or roasted bell peppers) added to your preference of a pesto, cream, or tomato sauce. Service is friendly (they anticipate and expect the theatre crowd) and the ambience is relaxed, so you don't have to worry about missing the curtain call. *$$; AE, DC, MC, V; debit cards; no cheques; lunch Mon–Fri, dinner every day; full bar; resos@larena.com; www.larena.com; map:T4.*

La Belle Auberge / ★★★
4856 48TH AVE, LADNER; 604/946-7717

Thirty minutes from Vancouver, famed chef-owner Bruno Marti serves traditional French-style cuisine with Asian tics at this 95-year-old Victorian manse in Ladner. Marti is well known to Vancouverites as a member and coach of the gold medal–winning teams at the Culinary Olympics. The duckling in blueberry sauce is, deservedly, his most popular dish on a superb menu offering rack of lamb, milk-fed veal, and some game dishes. Well-rounded wine list of Pacific Northwest and international wines.

*$$$; AE, DC, MC, V; no cheques; dinner Mon–Sun; full bar; bruno@
auberge.bc.ca; www.auberge.bc.ca.*

La Crepe Bretonne / ★☆

795 JERVIS ST; 604/608-1266

A husky-voiced chanteuse pouring forth *en français,* and walls washed
in sunshine yellow, combine to dissolve cares as you enter this cozy spot
steps away from bustling Robson Street. Maurice and Colette Sompayrac
(as Gallic as their names suggest) run this outpost of Brittany, serving ten-
der crepes from morning to night. There are just three dozen seats
indoors and a handful more outside, under cover, for diehards who can't
endure a meal without a Gauloise. (You might find the cook lighting up
beside you.) For a small meal, try a bagatelle—a length of baguette stuffed
with warm chicken or Black Forest ham and oozing melting Swiss or
Brie, accompanied by a green salad. Savoury crepes come with many fill-
ing options. Pretend it's Paris and follow the crepe with a mimosa salad
of butter lettuce and chopped egg—Dijon-drenched and oh-so-French.
To accompany the main event, there's special cider imported from France.
Finish with a huge, sweet, folded crepe. Fresh seasonal fruit and vanilla
ice cream is one flavourful filling option (add chocolate sauce at will). At
$5.75, the Continental breakfast beats any nearby hotel dining room, but
start the day late: opening time is 9am. For a dollar more, choose a break-
fast crepe, tea or coffee included. *$; AE, DC, E, JCB, MC, V; debit cards;
no cheques; breakfast, lunch, dinner Tues–Sun; wine, beer, and liqueurs;
map:R3.* ⅙

La Cucina Italiana / ★★

1509 MARINE DR, NORTH VANCOUVER; 604/986-1334

Stuck rather incongruously in the middle of North Vancouver's strip of
car dealerships and video shops, La Cucina Italiana has a rustic charac-
ter that manages to overcome its surroundings. The attractive dining
room has Italian opera playing at just the right volume. When it's available,
try *bresaola*—air-dried beef imported from Switzerland—as an appetizer,
or the antipasto. Pastas range from traditional spaghetti with tomato-
and-meat sauce to linguine with clams or fettuccine with pancetta. Fish
specials are usually good. Don't leave without sampling the homemade
marsala ice cream. *$$; AE, DC, MC, V; no cheques; lunch Mon–Fri,
dinner Mon–Sat; full bar; map:D1.* ⅙

La Terrazza / ★★

1088 CAMBIE ST; 604/899-4449

This new Yaletown dining room, with its romantic lighting, dark-painted
interior, heavy drapes, and many secluded nooks, could serve as the set
for a postmodern performance of *Romeo and Juliet.* Shakespeare's couple might well be nestled at the next table. La Terrazza lives up to its

name: in warm weather a row of French doors open onto a large terrace, which even adds an alfresco atmosphere to the inside tables. The cuisine is inventive, modern northern Italian. Start with the grilled eggplant stuffed with goat cheese, arugula, and sun-dried tomatoes; the tender beef carpaccio anointed with white truffle oil; or the steamed mussels served in a herb-scented tomato broth. The pasta dishes are inspired: fettucine with crayfish and avocado in a light cream sauce; linguine with prawns and scallops, finished in a crab bisque. However, for better or worse, the kitchen's creativity really comes through in the main courses: roasted pork tenderloin crusted with pink peppercorns served with a rich, intense espresso and port demi-glace (don't bother with an appetizer if you try this one); sea bass with a luxuriant Grand Marnier, champagne, and persimmon sauce; roast duck breast with a barbera and blueberry reduction. The service is discreet yet attentive, and the wine list is complete yet not overbearing. *$$–$$$; AE, DC, E, MC, V; no cheques; lunch, dinner every day; full bar; map:T5.* &

La Toque Blanche / ★★★

4368 MARINE DR, WEST VANCOUVER; 604/926-1006
One of Greater Vancouver's best-kept culinary secrets is hidden away amid evergreens, tucked behind a service station along West Vancouver's serpentine Marine Drive. But it's easy to find, not far from the city centre, and deserves much more acclaim. If the good burghers of West Van wanted to keep La Toque Blanche to themselves, who could blame them? Chef-owner John-Carlo Felicella, a veteran of topflight international culinary competitions, has a passion for detail, manifest in such appetizers as an eye-dazzling salad of smoked salmon, fennel, and orange, and a wickedly rich lobster bisque. His entrees exceed all expectations raised by the starters: lamb sirloin is roasted to perfection, then served with fresh morels and polenta; the Dungeness crab–potato gnocchi almost outshine the swordfish they accompany, both are so fine. The menu changes according to what's in the market and Felicella's imagination. Count on having dessert, particularly in fresh berry season. At every step of the meal, the staff are gracious and attentive. The best surprise may come at the end: prices for this kind of quality, detail, and presentation are a bargain by today's standards. *$$–$$$; AE, MC, V; local cheques only; dinner Tues–Sun; full bar; reservations recommended.*

La Villetta / ★★☆

3901 E HASTINGS ST; 604/299-3979
If there was ever any place in Vancouver specifically designed for romance, this is it. White walls, tiles on the roof and floor: it's a stylized copy of a small Italian village trattoria. When it's warm there's seating outside on a vine-covered patio, discreetly separated from Hastings Street by a high wall. When the weather isn't warm enough, you can cozy up by a sizable fireplace, and there are lots of quiet corners for those special one-on-one

evenings. The food is operatically Italian, ranging from pizzas and pastas to house-specialty dishes such as the prawns and scallops in a sambuca, saffron, and cream sauce. And, of course, there are lots of tables for two. Don't miss the tiramisu. *$$; AE, MC, V; local cheques only; lunch Mon–Fri, dinner Tues–Sun; full bar; map:G2.* &

Landmark Hot Pot House / ★★★

4023 CAMBIE ST; 604/872-2868

Hot potting—traditionally for the warming of body and soul on long wintry nights—seems to have transcended its seasonal limits to emerge as a Chinese culinary trend, and Landmark, Vancouver's first hot pot house, remains the best. If you are a Trekkie you might find yourself reaching for your com-badge upon first sight of the state-of-the-art-extraction units needed to regulate the air quality and temperature in the room. But it will not take you long to discover that the picture-perfect presentation and uncompromised freshness of the food are earthly delights that no replicator can hope to provide. The gas stove inset into your table provides the basis for healthy, fun, do-it-yourself, fondue-style cooking. The menus are simply lists of available ingredients and prices. Order the Duo Soup Base of satay and chicken broth, then, if it's your first time, start with the seafood combination. The initiated and unsqueamish should attempt to cook the still-writhing live prawns when in season or the superb whole geoduck presented sashimi-style—cooking strictly discretional. Finish with noodles and dumplings and a soulful bowl of the rich broth. The cooling sour-plum drink that follows is on the house. *$$; MC, V; no cheques; dinner every day; full bar; map:D4.* &

Las Margaritas / ★★☆

1999 W 4TH AVE; 604/734-7117

¡Olé! Mexican beer signs, Coca-Cola signs, sombreros hanging from the ceiling, red-tiled floors, and white stuccoed archways all add up to quintessential Mexican-restaurant decor in this lively Kitsilano cantina. The crowd changes with the hour. Early evenings, expect families (there's a good, inexpensive children's menu). Later, people come in for the margaritas: three sizes, eight flavours. This is a popular hangout for couples or the gang from the office. A little nacho-noshing or a few dips into a Mexican cheese fondue with optional chorizo takes the edge off the appetite while you mull the relative advantages of tacos and enchiladas. Chiles rellenos, chimichangas, and flautas—you'll find all the standards here, including combination plates for ditherers who can't decide. Servings are ¡muy amable! and the churros ¡muy bien! *$$; AE, E, MC, V; no cheques; lunch, dinner every day, brunch Sat–Sun; full bar; www.las margaritas.com; map:O7.*

The Lazy Gourmet Bistro / ★

1605 W 5TH AVE; 604/734-1396

There's nothing lazy about Susan Mendelson, owner of the Lazy Gourmet, Vancouver's best-known caterer. Her centrally located establishment has a catering kitchen, a bakery, and an open bistro kitchen with a wood-burning oven serving generous meals, mouth-watering takeaways, and homemade breads and desserts. Adults go here for the ultra-thin pizzettes, ziti with smoked chicken, and the white cheddar burger, and kids inhale the mac 'n' cheese. Everybody loves Susan's Nanaimo bars, that legendary trio of semisweet chocolate, creamy custard, and chocolate-nut layers that has become a trademark food of hers. *$–$$; AE, MC, V; debit cards; no cheques; lunch Mon–Fri, dinner Tues–Sun, brunch Sat–Sun; full bar; catering@lazygourmet.ca; www.lazygourmet. ca; map:P7.*

Le Crocodile / ★★★★

100–909 BURRARD ST; 604/669-4298

France without a passport—that's Le Crocodile. It was named after chef-owner Michel Jacob's favourite restaurant in his hometown of Strasbourg. His Franco-German culinary heritage is obvious. Everyone wants to order Jacob's savoury onion tart served with chilled Alsace Edelzwicker in green-stemmed glasses. Entrees of marvellously sauced classics such as duck (crisp outside, moist inside) in a reduction with olives, calf's liver with garlic spinach butter, and rabbit in a pinot noir sauce all pay their respects to tradition. He grills salmon "skin on" and pan-fries Dover sole to remember. Jacob's treasury of French cheeses makes a fine end to a meal or an even better prelude to a tangy lemon tart paired with house-made raspberry sorbet. The wine list is solid. Alsace Riesling, pinot blanc, and Gewürztraminer are proudly poured, but so are many others. France's Loire Valley, Bordeaux, and Burgundy are well represented, but so is California. The ever-professional service and chic European atmosphere make dinner at Le Crocodile an event—cause or setting for celebration. *$$$; AE, DC, MC, V; no cheques; lunch Mon–Fri, dinner Mon–Sat; full bar; map:R4.* &

Le Gavroche / ★★★

1616 ALBERNI ST; 604/685-3924

Arguably the most romantic restaurant in the city, Le Gavroche is one of the city's leading French kitchens (with a Pacific Northwest influence), enhanced by a discreet upstairs room and complete with blazing fire and glimpses of the harbour and mountains. For starters, try chef David Lane's fresh foie gras with endive, apples, and raisin marmalade. Entrees include rack of lamb with minted gnocchi, poached smoked Alaskan cod in a burnt-orange and anise coulis, or Thai curry lobster. For dessert, try the trademark lili cake—a soft almond-and-hazelnut meringue with an almond crème anglaise. Even *Gourmet* magazine requested the recipe. Le Gavroche has one of the city's better wine cellars (more than 12,000 bottles), with one of the largest selections of Bordeaux in the city. Service is formal but friendly and subtly attentive. *$$$; AE, DC, JCB, MC, V; no cheques; lunch Mon–Fri, dinner every day; full bar; map:Q2.*

Liliget Feast House / ★
1724 DAVIE ST; 604/681-7044
One culinary category that Vancouver has never been long on is the authentic food of the local aboriginal population. However, for more than 20 years there has been at least one downtown location that serves nothing else, and it most definitely qualifies as the site for a gourmet adventure. Under three different names (Muckamuck and Quilicum, and now Liliget), this restaurant provides as close as most people will ever get to dining in a real Native longhouse, even though it was designed by famed local architect Arthur Erickson. The menu includes salmon, of course, but also dishes most people have never tried: oolican, toasted seaweed, wild blackberry pie, and truly impressive bannock bread. The Liliget Feast platter for two ($42) is heaped with alder-grilled salmon, buffalo smokies, rabbit, halibut, and smoked oolican. *$$; AE, DIS, MC, V; debit cards; no cheques; dinner every day; full bar; map:P3.*

Lok's Chinese Restaurant / ★
4890 VICTORIA DR; 604/439-1888
There are plenty of small Chinese restaurants located in strip malls all over East Vancouver, but this one has had an especially devoted following for many years. The reason for this is simple—good solid Cantonese food at delightfully moderate prices and a staff that's only too happy to help you decide what to have for dinner. Among the popular entrees are clay-pot dishes, curry and satay specialties, the requisite range of noodle dishes, and an especially fine selection of seafood dishes, prepared as only Cantonese seafood lovers can cook them. And yes, they deliver. *$; MC, V; no cheques; breakfast, lunch, dinner every day; beer and wine; map:F4.*

Lorenzo / ★★
3605 W 4TH AVE; 604/731-2712
Make a meal of antipasto (an impeccable carpaccio, melon with prosciutto, mussels marinara) at the new lounge in Pasquale Di Salvo's neighbourhood eatery, where classic Italian has been the order of the day for the past 20 years. The scampi Lorenzo is indecently good. (Try it for an appetizer if you don't believe us.) The veal is always dependable (especially when stuffed with oyster mushrooms in a baritone sauce of marsala and wine), as are the rack of lamb and chicken stuffed with an aromatic pairing of spinach and prosciutto. A solid, mostly Italian wine list. *$$$; AE, DC, MC, V; debit cards; no cheques; lunch Mon–Fri, dinner every day; full bar; map:C2.* &

Lumière / ★★★★

2551 W BROADWAY; 604/739-8185

Rob Feenie serves up some of the very best food the city has to offer. The minimalistic elegance of this room showcases both the chef's exquisite creations and the Armani-clad clientele. The decor was a tad austere when Feenie first opened, but the room has been warmed up by the addition of tilted mirrors and wooden blinds. Food luxuriates in the skill of Feenie's contemporary French kitchen. Whether Feenie is preparing his chef's tasting menu of potato blini, grilled yellowfin tuna, five-spice duck consomme, braised short ribs, and desserts or something lighter, he always seems to achieve a perfect balance of flavours and textures. The vegetarian tasting menu will fill you up and you'll leave feeling virtuous. Spunked up by the success of his tasting menus, Feenie plans to eliminate the à la carte menu altogether. Rhonda Viani's brûlées (coconut and kaffir lime leaf), mousses (hazelnut mocha with double-milk ice cream), and panna cottas (light sour cream and cinnamon) will make you moan. There's an adequate wine list that's improving. The service is informed, attentive, and helpful. *$$$; AE, DC, MC, V; no cheques; dinner Tues–Sun; full bar; map:C2.* &

Major the Gourmet / ★

102–8828 HEATHER ST; 604/322-9211

Strictly speaking, this is not a restaurant, but the perennially busy headquarters of caterer-about-town Nicky Major. No matter. Savvy Vancouverites know that this is the place—in fact, in this mostly light-industrial area, the *only* place within blocks—for a lunch that's as interesting as it is fast. Major spins the ingredients so that the menu is rarely the same, and there is an ever-changing panoply of specials (though you can count on fish-and-chips on Fridays, and you're advised to get there before they're sold out). Grilled chicken might go on an everyday pizza, be featured in a salad, or go *mano a mano* with Thai noodles. Curried lamb might show up, or a chicken-and-broccoli pasta. Vegetarian and meat lasagnes, hearty pot pies, and shepherd's pie are staples. Desserts and soups change every day. Tables outside in warmer months, with limited seating inside. *$; MC, V; no cheques; breakfast, lunch Mon–Fri; no alcohol; map:D5.*

Manhattan / ★★☆

550 W HASTINGS (DELTA VANCOUVER SUITES); 604/899-3049

At press time, executive chef David Griffiths recently made the move from the Westin Grand Hotel to Manhattan, a sophisticated room tucked away on the second floor of the Delta Vancouver Suites. Manhattan has been known for imaginative and flavourful food, and we expect that Griffiths will continue in that tradition. The three-course prix fixe menu (including coffee or tea) is a bargain—it's $35 if you're solo, $33 per person for a couple, $32 each for a trio, and $30 each for four. The menu is under-going changes, but risotto is Griffiths' signature dish. You can also expect to find light fare with an ethnic flavour. Order the Manhattan wine flight ($30) that finishes with an Okanagan ice wine. *$$$; AE, DC, MC, V; no cheques; lunch Mon–Fri, dinner every day, brunch Sat–Sun; full bar; map:T5.* &

Meinhardt Fine Foods / ★★

3002 GRANVILLE ST; 604/732-4405

Linda Meinhardt, the force behind the Bread Garden chain, took a health food store on S Granville and created a food shopper's paradise. In this lofty, white-painted room, stainless-steel shelves carry the best in snack foods, sauces, spreads, oils, vinegars, dressings, and other condiments. Along with the small but well-stocked butcher shop, an extensive deli sec-tion offers excellent cheeses, olives, cold cuts, and sandwich fixings as well as prepared foods. There's a counter with 30 stools, so you can eat in or take out. Try the potato salad with blue cheese dressing, the chicken potpie with mashed yams, the Moroccan lamb ragout, or the gravlax. The best bakers in town supply Meinhardt's with fresh loaves every day, but get there early or all the baguettes will be sold out. The store also offers decadent desserts, including an otherworldly carrot cake that con-sists of several layers of rich cake separated by inches of tangy frosting. *$; AE, MC, V; debit cards; no cheques; breakfast, lunch every day; no alcohol; map:D3.*

Milestone's / ★★☆

1210 DENMAN ST (AND BRANCHES); 604/662-3431

Megaservings of food (and booze), priced inexpensively, are the draw at Milestone's, which, despite being a chain, consistently manages to impress with its witty takes on West Coast food trends. The breakfasts are out-standing (and cheap!) and the dinners unfailingly good. Witness the appetizers—most big enough for a light lunch—and the southwestern chicken strips with ancho chile barbecue sauce. Salads are generous: the Caesar apparently uses an entire head of lettuce, and the seafood fettuc-cine is lavish with shrimp, mussels, and salmon. The fashionable menu includes Triple A prime rib, quesadillas, and pizzas from the wood-burn-ing oven. Try the trademarked Rollups, especially the Thai chicken in a whole-wheat tortilla encasing chicken, cilantro rice, and carrots, served with a peanut and sesame-cucumber mayo. Fresh-fruit martinis, frozen "Bellinis" (peach schnapps, white rum, and sparkling wine topped with sangría), and sinfully good desserts. *$; AE, DC, MC, V; debit cards; no cheques; lunch, dinner every day, brunch Sun; full bar; map:P3.*

Montri's Thai Restaurant / ★★★

3629 W BROADWAY; 604/738-9888

Why go anywhere else for Thai food when Montri's is simply the best in town? When Montri Rattanaraj took a mid-'90s sabbatical, fans wept at losing their prime source of chile-induced tears. But when he reopened (in contemporary wicker-accented digs on Broadway near Alma), they flocked to his door: the food was better than ever. He presents an authentic cuisine not watered down for Vancouver tastes and with little touches all his own, like the salmon steak in red curry sauce. Thai cuisine is a careful balancing act based on six interconnecting concepts: bitter, salty, sweet, hot, herbaceous, and fragrant. The heat content is rated on a scale of one to five chile symbols, five being the level for masochists and Thai nationals. What to order? Everything is good. *Tom yum goong* is Thailand's national soup, a lemony prawn broth, and it lives up to its name— yum. The *tod mun* fish cakes blended with prawns and chile curry are excellent, as is the salmon simmered in red-curry-and-coconut sauce. Rattanaraj's Thai *gai-yang,* chicken marinated in coconut milk and broiled, is a close cousin to the chicken sold on the beach at Phuket. Have it with *som tum,* a green papaya salad served with sticky rice and wedges of raw cabbage; the cabbage and the rice are coolants, and you will need them (Thailand's Singha beer also helps). For a group of six or more, splurge for the *pla lard prig,* a whole rockfish or red snapper slashed to allow flavourings to penetrate, then very quickly deep-fried—ambrosial! *$$; MC, V; no cheques; dinner every day; full bar; reservations recommended; map:C3.* ♿

Moustache Cafe / ★★★

2118 BURRARD ST; 604/739-1990
1265 MARINE DR, NORTH VANCOUVER; 604/987-8461

Before or after a film at the Fifth Avenue cinema, you'll find more theatre next door in this Mediterranean restaurant with talented chef Don Letendre performing in the open kitchen. Serious mouths go for the everyday specials—brilliant and full of flavour—that Letendre invents, such as pan-seared scallops with vanilla basmati rice or smoked black cod layered with a mushroom duxelles wrapped in pâte with a caviar beurre blanc. For dessert, request the baked-to-order tarte Tatin and a glass of dessert wine from the more than 20 available by the glass. The wine list also features a good selection of champagne, half bottles, and older vintages of Barolo and Amarone. The hospitable staff appear to be hired for their sense of humour. *$$$; AE, MC, V; debit cards; no cheques; lunch Mon–Fri, dinner every day; full bar; map:O7, E1.* ♿

Moutai Mandarin Restaurant / ★

1710 DAVIE ST; 604/681-2288
The menu at this tiny restaurant was modelled after the one at the well-patronized Szechuan Chongqing. Now West Enders don't have to leave their territory to get good versions of old favourites such as green beans with plenty of chile pepper. We particularly like the specials: ginger beef and the blistering stir-fry with prawns known as *dai ching*. Moutai's acid-green tabletops and Arborite trim in a pebble-pattern grey are miles removed from the red-dragon-tacky or Hong Kong–slick styles that seem to dominate the city's Chinese eateries. Being a stone's throw from the very-downtown strutting beach at English Bay, it all somehow fits. *$; AE, MC, V; no cheques; dinner every day; full bar; map:P3.* &

Musashi Japanese Restaurant / ★★

780 DENMAN ST; 604/687-0634
Do you seek a sushi feast in intimate surroundings, with ethereal koto music caressing your ears and demure servers endlessly bowing? Then head elsewhere—and pay several times the price you would at Musashi. You'll find no frills here, but smiling, attentive staff make you feel welcome. The decor is universal neighbourhood eatery, Japanese-style, and high culinary art is offered nightly at amazing prices—usually to a packed house. Nigiri-sushi—shrimp, tuna, geoduck, sea urchin, and more—starts at $1 a piece and tops out at $1.60 for the deluxe *tsukimi ikura*. *Makis* (rolled sushi), yielding four bite-size pieces, range from $2.10 to $5.50 (for a megabite roll stuffed with tempura prawns, avocado, and mayo). A full range of soups, salads, appetizers, tempuras, rice and noodle dishes, and combination dinners are also available. Check for specials on the wall behind the 10-seat sushi bar (they're also on a list at each table). If you see barbecued fresh mackerel, go for it. Fresh, dense, and flavourful, it's a steal at $4.50. Musashi sits in a strip of four shoulder-to-shoulder Japanese restaurants on a street packed with eateries. It's been here forever, feeding ordinary folks who have fallen in love with sushi but know that at most places, a steady diet of it can prove costly. Here your hunger fades long before your wallet feels vaguely threatened. *$; AE, MC, V; no cheques; dinner every day; full bar; map:Q2.*

Naam / ★

2724 W 4TH AVE; 604/738-7151
A full 30 years ago, the stretch of Fourth Avenue between Macdonald and Burrard was Vancouver's hippie district, and the Naam, Vancouver's oldest vegetarian restaurant, is the last outpost of that era. With its funky decor and friendly staff, it's still a crowd-pleaser. Lineups are common (maybe because the service is so slack). Summertime, we try to nab a seat in the tiny private garden patio. Winters, the candlelit Naam is as cozy as a Gulf Islands cabin. You can still sip dandelion coffee and nibble at a

bee pollen cookie, but the menu has broadened considerably over the years. Habitués breakfast on a mishmash of eggs, cheese, tofu, mushrooms, and tomatoes on toast. The house salad—a toppling heap of red cabbage, shredded lettuce, thickly sliced tomato, and sunflower seeds— is humongous. The veggie burrito is the size of a neck pillow. The menu wanders lazily around the world, offering stops for nachos, hummus and pita, Thai and Caesar salads, sesame fries with miso gravy, and enormous pita pizzas. The Naam is open 24 hours. *$; AE, DC, MC, V; debit cards; no cheques; breakfast, lunch, dinner, midnight snacks every day, brunch Sun; beer and wine; map:C2.* &

Nat's New York Pizzeria / ★★

2684 W BROADWAY; 604/737-0707
1080 DENMAN ST; 604/642-0777
Cousins Nat and Franco Bastone headed to their uncle's pizza parlour in Yonkers, where he taught them how to create Naples-style pizza. Then they opened up Nat's and now serve up some of the best thin-crust pizza around. Take out, or pull up a chair under the Big Apple memorabilia and watch the world go by while you sink your teeth into some pie loaded with chorizo and mushrooms, or artichokes and pesto, or cappicolo and hot peppers. Or try the 5th Avenue (sweet onion, spinach, tomato, and feta cheese) or the Hot Veg (sun-dried tomatoes, hot peppers, and mushrooms). Top it off with the oven-baked garlic shavings or the selection of other condiments you can sprinkle on top. Avoid Nat's Broadway location on weekdays between 11:30am and 12:15pm when the local Kits high school breaks for lunch and the students take over. If you're there before they leave, you'll notice students squeezing honey on their leftover crust for dessert. *$; cash only; lunch, dinner Mon–Sat; no alcohol; map:C3.*

Nazarre BBQ Chicken / ★

1859 COMMERCIAL DR; 604/251-1844
There are rubber chickens on the turntables decorating the storefront, but only tender barbecued chicken finds its way onto your plate. French-born and Mexican-raised owner Gerry Moutal bastes the birds in a mixture of rum and spices in the rotisserie. The chickens drip their juices onto potatoes roasting and crackling below and are delivered with mild, hot, extra-hot, or hot-garlic sauce. There are a few other goodies (vegetarian empanadas, tacos), but it's the chicken you really should not miss. Eat in at one of the four tables—or take it to go. *$; cash only; lunch, dinner every day; no alcohol; map:Z7.*

New Grand View Restaurant / ★

60 W BROADWAY; 604/879-8885
This is almost like a granddaddy on the Chinese restaurant scene. They've added New to the name, but nothing else has changed—same

owner, same crew—for over 15 years. The New Grand View was among the first to introduce weekend northern-style dim sum brunches, serving steamed pork dumplings, robust beef noodle soups, and foot-long fried dough with soy milk—salted or sweetened for dunking. A separate "vegetarian delights" section on the menu includes meatless versions of the garlicky Sichuan eggplant, hot and sour soup, and the Mah Po bean curd. Departing from convention, the chefs quick-fry geoduck in a spicy garlic sauce and substitute squid for chicken in Kung Pao–style sauté. Lamb dishes and the Shanghai-style, doubled-cooked pork in garlic and chiles deserve kudos. *$; V; no cheques; lunch Mon–Fri, dinner every day; full bar; map:V7.*

Nikko Japanese Restaurant / ★★

1008 ROBSON ST; 604/683-6111

Climb one storey (by stairs or elevator) from pedestrian-packed Robson Street and there awaits a vast, modern, halogen-bright room where the ubiquitous dishes of Japan are turned out consistently well—and a few unusual offerings keep locals coming back. Among the latter: marinated black cod, also known as sablefish or butterfish (for very good reason—it melts on the tongue); shiitake and enoki mushrooms grilled in a little foil pouch, swimming in piquant sauce; and particularly good bowls of clams, steamed in garlic butter. At the next table a young Japanese student might be loudly slurping a large bowl of noodles. (Careful cooking and reasonable prices combine to attract a booming ex-pat clientele.) In a city where sushi bars proliferate like bamboo, Nikko does an exemplary job on some standards. The outsize Dynamite Roll (avocado, cucumber strips, and radish sprouts enveloping tempura prawns, all encased in sushi rice) is a bargain at $4.25; the spicy tuna roll is another favourite. Choose from a dozen nigiri-sushi (slices of seafood atop balls of rice) at 99 cents each for a custom, low-cost feast. Servers are cheery and obliging, though at times bridging the language gap can be a challenge. The light hit on your wallet more than compensates. *$$; AE, DC, E, JCB, MC, V; no cheques; lunch, dinner every day; full bar; map:S3.* &

900 West Restaurant & Wine Bar / ★★★☆

900 W GEORGIA ST (HOTEL VANCOUVER); 604/669-9378

The restaurant is reminiscent of a cruise-ship dining room, recalling the era of the great luxury liners. It would appear this lovely, refurbished dining room has quietly set on the back burner its well-publicized experiment with celebrity San Francisco chef Jeremiah Tower. It has brought in chef Dino Renaerts, from CP's Waterfront Centre Hotel, to cook. Good choice. Renaerts is creating several signatures, none of which should be missed: smoked black cod with braised greens and a crisp-fried noodle cake; prosciutto seared, then placed atop a tiny ball of mozzarella and served with a zucchini and tomato bundle dressed with basil oil and balsamic vinegar. Nor should you miss his mussel and clam hot pot in a ginger miso broth. Alongside the dining room is the chic Wine Bar, offering a well-chosen 350-plus international wine list. Within the impressive old- and new-world list, 900 West has assembled the most comprehensive cellar of Canada's best VQA (Vintners Quality Alliance) wines in the country. There are rarely fewer than 75 wines available by the glass, and there are ever-changing flights that include BC's renowned ice wine. Order a flight of caviar or the rare ahi tuna tower while you're there. Afternoon tea reigns supreme in the lounge with three to choose from— traditional, Asian, and West Coast. *$$$; AE, DC, E, JCB, MC, V; no cheques; lunch Mon–Sat, dinner every day; full bar; lcockburn@hvc. mhs.compuserve.com; map:S3.* ♿

Noor Mahal / ★

4354 FRASER ST; 604/873-9263

The owners are new at the Noor Mahal, but the same hospitable, helpful service is still there. The menu includes Sri Lankan, Malaysian, and Indian fare, and prices are a bargain at $7 to $14 per dish. These are all full-meal deals, complete with rice, roti, chutney, pappadam, and salad. The food is hot and spicy but adjustable to order. The portions are substantial. *Dosas*—South Indian flatbreads made from rice, wheat, and lentil flour—are the specialty here. They come rolled, like crepes, filled with your choice of 31 fillings, including chicken, shrimp, and vegetarian, and accompanied by *sambar* (a lentil stew) and its traditional condiment, *nariyal chatni* (coconut chutney). *$; MC, V; no cheques; lunch Sat–Sun, dinner every day; full bar; map:E4.*

Nyala Restaurant / ★

2930 W 4TH AVE; 604/731-7899

Many people are unaware that Ethiopia, like other African nations, has a cuisine all its own. The food here is served in traditional Ethiopian style—no knives, forks, or spoons. The *injera* (plate-size flatbread with a spongy, honeycomb texture) is the only utensil you need. Just tear off a little bit of bread, fold it around a bite-size portion of food, and pop the whole thing into your mouth. The food, mostly stewed or curried preparations of savoury goat, beef, ostrich, venison, lamb, chicken, fish, or vegetables, is served communally at each table on a large metal platter accompanied by an assortment of condiments (spicy sautéed cabbage, golden herbed bulgur wheat, gingered lentil purée). The decor here is simple; however, gracious host Assefa Kebede makes this a warm experience. There's a vegetarian buffet on Wednesdays and Sundays for $10.95. In the summer, the garden patio is the spot to be. *$; AE, DC, MC, V; debit cards; no cheques; dinner every day; full bar; www.nyala.com; map:C3.*

Olympia Seafood Market & Grill / ★★☆

820 THURLOW ST; 604/685-0716

A half block off crowded Robson Street, the compact Olympia (15 seats inside; three sidewalk tables) plays two roles: it's first a seafood shop, selling fresh fish, smoked salmon (packed for travel), pickled herring, salmon caviar, and the like. But for the price of a seafood appetizer in one of the city's posh rooms, you can park at a table or the window-view counter and enjoy crisp fish-and-chips—halibut, sole, cod, prawns, scallops, calamari, or whatever is the day's special. That might be marlin, tuna, shark, or catfish. A platter with lots of fish, a small tub of coleslaw, and fries that look like they were once actually part of a spud, plus a beverage, barely puts you over the $10 mark, so don't expect fancy surroundings—just good value. Soft drinks include Chinotto (Italian herbal- or fruit-flavoured sparkling water) and root beer. Eat in or take out, but do plan on an early dinner. Latest closing of the week is 9pm on Friday; Olympia closes an hour earlier other nights and 7pm on Saturday and Sunday. *$; AE, DC, E, MC, V; debit cards; no cheques; lunch, dinner every day; no alcohol; map:R3.*

Omnitsky Kosher Foods / ★★★☆

5566 CAMBIE ST; 604/321-1818

Haimish is the Yiddish word for comfort, and it's the word that best describes the experience at this eat-in or take-out deli. Omnitsky's is the next best thing to a home-cooked Jewish meal. Corned beef and other smoked meats are layered on incredible rye bread like Leaning Towers of Pastrami. Once you're into the dill pickles, chicken soup with knaidlach (matzoh balls) the size of tennis balls, and very good chopped liver, it'll seem like old times. Whatever you can't eat there, you can take home— knishes, kreplach (a Jewish version of ravioli), kasha and noodle shells, potato kugel (baked potato pudding), sweet lokshen (noodle pudding), and gefilte fish. Because Omnitsky's doubles as a kosher butcher shop, there are roasts, beef briskets, steaks, veal, and lamb, all custom-cut to order. Step into this heavenly noshery and hear the battle cry, "Eat . . . eat . . . eat some more." *$; MC, V; debit cards; no cheques; lunch Sun–Fri, dinner Sun–Thurs; no alcohol; map:D4.* &

The Only Seafood Cafe / ★

20 E HASTINGS ST; 604/681-6546

Since it is located in the very worst block of the very worst neighbourhood in the city, an evening at the Only Seafood Cafe scarcely qualifies as upscale gourmet dining. But the cafe itself is historic, being Vancouver's oldest existing restaurant, built in 1912. Easily recognizable by its old-fashioned seahorse neon sign, this is very much a no-frills establishment, the only hint of elegance being the original patterned-metal ceiling. Two tiny booths and a row of counter stools comprise the seating arrangements, and a locally famous hand-painted sign on the wall says SORRY—NO REST-ROOMS. But the food is both terrific and cheap—strictly seafood, strictly fresh (the fish are on ice in the window), and cooked on a huge old stove before your eyes. *$; cash only; lunch, dinner every day; no alcohol; map:U4.*

The Original Tandoori K. King / ★★☆

689 E 65TH AVE; 604/327-8900
The very pink Tandoori King gets low marks for decor, but if any place deserves to wear the tandoori crown, this is the spot. Don't be confused by the other Tandoori King around the corner. Just look for the restaurant whose sign is emblazoned with "The Original." A feud between two brothers led to this royal battle that borders on a saga, but it's the "Original" that plays a raga on the taste buds. Tender lamb *seekh kabab*, chicken tikka, and rich, layered breads from the Tandoori's oven are addictive, as is the smoky eggplant, roasted whole over the wood fire in the tandoor before being mashed and seasoned. Order a side of mango chutney for dipping. Cool off with a Kingfisher beer. Takeout is also available. *$$; AE, MC, V; no cheques; lunch, dinner every day; beer and wine; map:E4.*

O-Tooz the Energie Bar / ★

777 DUNSMUIR ST, PACIFIC CENTRE (AND BRANCHES); 604/684-0202
What started purely as a juice bar has become the darling of the health set, with its all-around-good-for-you-fast-food format. The mood and the decor are upbeat, with contemporary black bar stools for those with enough time to sit while they down their energy boosters. A simplified menu includes the tasteful and healthful rice pot—basmati served with a choice of spicy peanut, spinach basil pesto, or hummus sauce, accompanied by raw vegetables. The same ingredients are served in the wrap, a whole-wheat tortilla shell. Roasted chicken breast (the only meat you'll find here) is offered as an extra. Juices of choice are the BC trio of carrot, celery, and beet, and the Hi-C, with pineapple, orange, and carrot. The healthiest bar in town—with only a hint of salt. *$; MC, V; no cheques; breakfast, lunch, dinner every day; no alcohol; map:T4.*

Ouzeri / ★★

3189 W BROADWAY; 604/739-9378
Traditionally, the Greek *ouzeri* is a place to go to drink and eat tapas before going to dinner. In Vancouver, the Ouzeri is where you can go any time of the day and compose a meal of appetizers. The food here includes all the expected Greek specialties and then some. Moussaka Kitsilano-style is vegetarian; chicken livers are wonderful—crisp on the outside and tender on the inside. Prawns dressed with ouzo and mushrooms are simply amazing. Friendly, casual, happy (with surely the most reasonably

priced menu this side of Athens), Ouzeri proves that being Greek doesn't mean you can't be trendy. The tile floor can make it a bit loud. In summer, the restaurant opens onto the sidewalk and small patio. Open until 2am on weekends. *$$; AE, DC, MC, V; debit cards; no cheques; lunch, dinner every day; full bar; map:C3.* &

Park Lock Seafood Restaurant / ★★
544 MAIN ST; 604/688-1581
When we first climbed its steep, narrow stairs in the early '80s, Park Lock seemed frozen in time. Not any more. A face-lift and a new Hong Kong–style menu make Park Lock the most authentic Cantonese restaurant in Chinatown. No more egg foo yung on the menu (unless you ask for it), but the black-peppered flank steak or scallops and prawns with black-bean sauce still come sizzling to the table on scorching cast-iron platters. Top-quality Peking duck in two or three courses and shark's fin soup for 2 or 10 are less expensive than in the upscale restaurants outside Chinatown. The tasty, dainty dishes of steamed spareribs with yellow-plum sauce that are fast becoming an anachronism elsewhere are still proffered during the chaotic dim sum service every day. *$; AE, MC, V; no cheques; lunch every day, dinner Tues–Sun; full bar; map:V4.*

Pastis / [unrated]
2153 W 4TH AVE; 604/731-5020
An energetic duo—chef Frank Pabst (ex-Lumière) and attentive front man John Blakeley (ex-Diva)—in summer 1999 opened Pastis, a modern high-energy French bistro in Kitsilano. It's buzzing as West Siders and the men of the hot-stove league check out this Gallic guy on the block where Bishop's lives. You'll feel like you're in Paris sipping pastis, sharing an escargot-and-oyster-mushroom casserole and a tomato-and-tapenade tart. Our quartet was pleased with the fig and Belgian endive salad, the steak tartare, the duck breast with Quebec foie gras, and the thyme- and lemon-roasted free-range chicken. The Alice and Alison cheese plate is a fine finale. *$$$; AE, MC, V; no cheques; dinner every day, full bar; map:O7.*

Pâtisserie Lebeau / ★★★
1660 CYPRESS ST; 604/731-3528
Tucked into Kitsilano's small-but-booming northeast corner, this high-end bakery-cafe draws food mavens and off-duty chefs from across the city, especially for a casual weekend brunch. Seats number fewer than 20 but increase by a third in fair weather, when outdoor tables become an option. The decor is sleek but low-key—surely so it doesn't distract from the cooler cases holding shelf upon shelf of delicate European pastries, cakes, and other eye-popping desserts (fine conclusions for a dinner party). Good breads and excellent croissants await as well. A limited

menu offers six or eight whole or half sandwiches (at very attractive prices), plus classic quiche lorraine and croque monsieur hot from the grill, the *vrai* Gruyère snappingly crisp. Belgian waffles with sliced fresh fruit and whipped cream make wonderful Sunday brunch fare. Service can be brusque in a Continental way (and 50 cents for extra mustard or 20 cents for a paper cup seems petty), but there's no quibbling about the quality of the baker's art or the robust coffee. *$$; V; debit cards; no cheques; breakfast, lunch Wed–Sun; no alcohol; map:O6.* &

The Pear Tree / ★★★

4120 E HASTINGS ST, BURNABY; 604/299-2772

Sometimes you fall in love with a restaurant on your first visit. The atmosphere says, "Come in, sit down, relax, let us feed you," and the warm, professional staff meet (or exceed) all your expectations. True excitement comes when subsequent meals confirm your first crush. Since Scott Jaeger and Stephanie Millar (now Jaeger!) opened the Pear Tree in 1998, patrons have kept returning—for the elegant dishes he sends forth from a small open kitchen and for the finesse and charm with which she runs the dining room. It's small (two dozen seats); the walls are dappled the yellow of a ripe Bartlett and hung with dramatic art (with a pear theme, naturally). The fact that this tree has blossomed on a prosaic commercial strip in north Burnaby is cause for celebration. The chef's menu is taut but sparked with adventure. Where else might you find roast caribou with mashed potatoes and asparagus spears in a carrot *nage*? (Scott apprenticed with one of Canada's top European-trained chefs, and learned well.) Seafood receives equally skilful handling: for another main dish, he sears plump, sweet scallops until golden-edged but absolutely tender, then dots them atop orzo with a froth of truffle oil. It's difficult to imagine an ingredient he wouldn't handle well. Desserts are highly satisfying, especially the lemon tart that arrives beneath a lattice of caramelized sugar, with a garnish of sliced grapes and diced papaya. If you'd rather end on a savoury note, the cheese platter offers an excellent selection, accompanied by meticulously cut fruit and toasts. Most of the menu is available à la carte, but at $36, the three-course prix fixe is unbeatable (there's a modest supplement for the cheeses). You can't help but leave the Pear Tree smiling—the dining is first class, the quality unquestionable, and the skill and enthusiasm of the youthful proprietors assure you that patrons' palates should be in good hands for many decades. *$$–$$$; AE, DC, E, MC, V; debit cards; no cheques; dinner Mon–Sat; full bar; reservations recommended; map:G2.* &

Perfetto Pizza / ★★☆

4460 W 10TH AVE; 604/222-8080

Pizza joints proliferate much as sushi bars do—two or four or more per block in densely packed corners of town. So it's refreshing to find those that rise above the mediocre average. Perfetto performs, its business undoubtedly fed by pizza-craving students from nearby UBC. The classics are here, many updated, plus some intriguing vegetarian choices. The crust is crisp, the first layer of sauce intensely tomatoey, and a creamy layer atop forms the underpinning for many combos, such as Perfetto's special of grilled eggplant, roasted onions, fresh garlic, and sun-dried tomatoes. A pasta menu offers more basics (notable among them linguine with smoked salmon and pesto). The Caesar salad is huge (a half-order can feed two modest appetites), if not otherwise exceptional. Burnt-orange walls, farmhouse kitchen tables, and quarry tiles on the floor make for a rustic atmosphere. The place can be noisy if there's a rollicking bunch of kids nearby. Focus on the pizza, and all is *perfetto*. *$–$$; MC, V; debit cards; local cheques only; lunch, dinner every day; full bar; map:B3.* &

Phnom Penh Restaurant / ★★★

244 E GEORGIA ST; 604/682-5777
955 W BROADWAY; 604/734-8898

Phnom Penh was once a treasure Vancouverites kept to themselves, but this restaurant now continues to win a steady stream of accolades from sources as diverse as local magazine polls to the *New York Times*. The decor is still basic, but the menu has expanded from its original rice-and-noodle focus to include the cuisines of China, Vietnam, and Cambodia. Pineapple-spiked hot and sour soup, with your choice of chicken, fish, or prawns, is richly flavoured and redolent with lemongrass and purple basil. An excellent appetizer of marinated beef sliced carpaccio-thin is seared rare and dressed with nuoc mam (a spicy, fishy sauce—the Vietnamese staple). Sautéed baby shrimp in prawn roe and tender slivers of salted pork cover hot, velvety steamed rice cakes—a real masterpiece. Grandma's recipe of garlic chile squid, prawns, or crab with lemon pepper dip has been uniformly declared "unbeatable." The chicken salad with cabbage is a refreshing twist on a pedestrian vegetable, and the oyster omelette is a dream. If it's good enough for Julia Child, it should be good enough for you. Service is knowledgeable and friendly, and there's a second location on W Broadway. *$; AE, MC; no cheques; lunch, dinner Wed–Mon; full bar; map:V4, R8.*

Pho Hoang / ★

3388 MAIN ST; 604/874-0810
238 E GEORGIA ST; 604/682-5666

 As common in Vietnam as the hamburger is here, pho is a quick balanced meal or a heartwarming snack—and an incredible bargain besides. A large bowl of rich broth with rice-stick noodles and your choice of flank, rump, brisket, tripe, or meatballs, or a dozen other permutations of the aforementioned, will cost you just over $5. You're served a side dish of bean sprouts, fresh basil, sliced green chiles, and lime to garnish with as you see fit. A glass of superstrong Vietnamese coffee, filter-brewed at the table, sweetened with condensed milk, then chilled with ice is all you will need to complete a very satisfying meal. *$; cash only; breakfast, lunch, dinner every day; no alcohol; map:E3, V4.*

Piccolo Mondo / ★★★

850 THURLOW ST; 604/688-1633

Seldom do you meet people with as intense a dedication to fine food as that of the husband-and-wife team of George Baugh and Michele Geris, proprietors of this exquisite Italian restaurant. Their little world is one of Vancouver's best-kept secrets, a place where the setting is calm and elegant, the food absolutely authentic, the wine list phenomenal, and the service immaculate. This stately European room can seem stiff and formal at first. But just wait. Within minutes, Geris will have you feeling happy and comfortable, and by the time you've taken your first sip of wine, you'll be right at home. The wine list is a marvel that is yearly honoured by *Wine Spectator* magazine. It is Baugh's mission to assemble a collection that ranges from reasonable table vino through excellent Chiantis, brunellos, and pinot grigios to the $1,200 special vintages. As for the food, chef Stephane Meyer oversees a menu that is small but nearly perfect. Each dish is packed with the intense flavours of northern Italy, and the kitchen is dedicated to using only the best, freshest ingredients. To start, try the saffron-scented fish soup or one of the composed salads. Follow that up, perhaps, with the powerful risotto with duck, red pepper, and Gorgonzola; the veal osso buco with lemon and capers; or the house specialty, a creamy salted cod with pine nuts and raisins. By the time dessert comes around, you'll be convinced: this is the best of all possible worlds. *$$$; AE, DC, MC, V; no cheques; lunch Mon–Fri, dinner Mon–Sat; full bar; map:R3.*

The Pink Pearl / ★★★

1132 E HASTINGS ST; 604/253-4316

The Pink Pearl is better than ever under the ownership of Rick Hui and a gifted chef who wokked at the Kingsland. Tanks of fresh fish are your first clue that the Cantonese menu is especially strong on seafood. If you order the crab sautéed with rock salt and chiles, you'll be further con-vinced. It's a spectacular dish—crisp, chile-hot, salty on the outside, and moist on the inside. A good dim sum is served every day (be sure to arrive early on weekends to avoid the lineups), and the cart jockeys always seem to have time to smile as you choose among sticky rice wrapped in lotus leaf, stuffed dumplings, and fried white-turnip cakes. A great place for kids. Free patrolled parking lot. *$$; AE, DC, MC, V; debit cards; no cheques; dim sum lunch, dinner every day; full bar; map:Y4.* &

Planet Veg / ★★
1941 CORNWALL AVE; 604/734-1001

There's hope for the slender wallet at Planet Veg. This new, mostly Indian fast-food spot is located in the heart of health-conscious Kitsilano, and serves the juiciest veggie burger in BC. You can also get roti rolls (a meal in themselves), samosas, and potato salad. It's as inexpensive here as it is tasty. Inside seating is limited, so you may want to perch outdoors during the warmer months or avail yourself of its popular takeout. *$; cash only; lunch, dinner every day; no alcohol; map:O6.*

President Chinese Seafood Restaurant / ★★★
8181 CAMBIE ST (RADISSON PRESIDENT HOTEL), RICHMOND; 604/276-8181

It comes as no surprise that the Radisson President Hotel, located in the middle of "Little Asia" in Richmond, would harbour a great Chinese fine dining restaurant—in the view of many, perhaps one of the best in Greater Vancouver. Its dim sum menu, hands-on created and supervised by executive chef Ho Wing Li, is incredibly, classically good. And the remainder of its food, the province of co-executive chef Yuen Man Wai, is equally fine. Try suckling pig, roasted to parchment; Fried Crab Hong Kong Style (which really means it was devised in Hong Kong's Typhoon Shelter), dusted with flour and fried with garlic, salt, and chiles; or the shark's fin soup, a clear consommé filled with fin and bits of ham, pork, and conch. Adventurous eaters should try the deep-fried chicken knees with spicy salt. Perfectly done cooking. Be sure to finish with the popular Love Bird Fried Rice, topped half with creamy shrimp sauce and half with chicken-in-tomato sauce. The usual variety of dim sum is made to order. *$$; AE, DC, MC; no cheques; lunch, dinner every day; full bar; map:D5.* &

Provence Mediterranean Grill / ★★★
4473 W 10TH AVE; 604/222-1980

It's sunny here with chef Jean-Francis Quaglia and his wife, Alessandra, *en garde* at this university-district location. Provence rules in the antipasto: choose from a variety of baked, grilled, stewed, or marinated items; one item for $2.95, up to nine choices for $22.95. There's pissaladière, curried eggplant, squid, artichokes, and roasted tomato with bocconcini. Appetizers include an intense fish soup and warm goat cheese crusted with herbes de Provence on organic greens. Prices are fair—Jean-Francis's bouillabaisse, served with a garlicky rouille and shards of Gruyère, is only $21.95. Hope that you're here in August when Mme. Quaglia (Jean-Francis's mother) arrives and cooks up a storm with her son using ingredients and recipes from her restaurant in Marseilles. *$$$; AE, MC, V; debit cards; no cheques; lunch Mon–Fri, dinner every day, brunch Sat–Sun; full bar; map:B3.* &

Quattro on Fourth / ★★★

2611 W 4TH AVE; 604/734-4444

Antonio Corsi and son Patrick Corsi run one of the most comfortable Italian restaurants in the city, and you're pampered the minute you walk through the door. There's a high sense of *abbondanza* here. An impressive selection of antipasto includes no less than eight different carpaccio offerings. The razor-thin-sliced raw swordfish is superb; so, too, the grilled radicchio bocconcini and portobello mushrooms. Kudos for the grilled beef tenderloin cloaked in aged balsamic syrup, the pistachio-crusted sea bass, and the spicy deboned Cornish game hen. Spaghetti Quattro ("for Italians only") rewards with a well-spiced sauce of chicken, chiles, black beans, and plenty of garlic. Of course, the mostly Italian wine list is stellar, from a rustic Montepulciano D'Abruzzo (Illuminati Riparosso) to a 1990 Masseto Tenuta dell'Ornellaia (Marchesi Lodovico A.). The Corsis also have the largest selection of grappa in Vancouver. The heated patio seats 35. (See also Quattro in the Whistler chapter.) *$$$; AE, DC, MC, V; no cheques; dinner every day; full bar; map:C4.* ㅎ

Raincity Grill / ★★★

1193 DENMAN ST; 604/685-7337

Grape nuts love the extensive list of Pacific Northwest wines (more than 100 by the glass), but that's only one reason to visit this bright, contemporary restaurant. Fantastically situated at the happening intersection of Davie and Denman, Raincity provides diners with excellent views of English Bay all year-round: in winter, from its tall windows; in summer, from the outdoor patio. Now that Scott Kidd is in the kitchen, dazzled fans insist the food is better than ever. And they're right. At lunch, skip the turkey burger and order the grilled Caesar, the duck confit with macaroni and cheese, or the soothing shrimp risotto. At dinner, order the grilled Caesar, the seared veal liver, or the crispy Dungeness crab roll. A glass of dessert wine and the caramel nut torte or blueberry pie make a perfect finish. Expect ever-professional service. *$$; AE, DC, MC, V; no cheques; lunch, dinner every day, brunch Sat–Sun; full bar; map:P3.* ㅎ

Rainforest Cafe / ★

4700 KINGSWAY (METROTOWN SHOPPING CENTRE), BURNABY; 604/433-3383

With kids, half the fun is getting there, so hop on the SkyTrain and head to the jungle in Metrotown. A talking tree, Nile the Crocodile, and thunderstorms every half hour will vie for your youngsters' attention at the Rainforest Cafe. Chef Andrew Skorzewski was spirited away from Bridges to cook for kids and their parents. The kids' menu is gently priced at $5.99 and pleases with Gorilla Grilled Cheese, Three Amigos (three minidogs served on minibuns), and Jurassic chicken tidbits in dinosaur shapes. Adults go for the Primal Steak (12-ounce New York topped with red pepper–basil butter) and Mayapastalaya (linguine, chicken, and vegetables in a spicy Cajun sauce). Eat your veggies and you can have dessert—Gorillas in the Mist (a chocolate-topped banana cheesecake) or a Banshee Sundae. You're not finished yet. There's a wild place to shop for oversize mugs, kids' boxer shorts, even a leather jacket with the Rainforest logo for Mom or Dad. *$; AE, DC, JCB, MC, V; no cheques; lunch, dinner every day; full bar; www.rainforestcafe.com; map:G4.* &

Raintree at the Landing / ★

375 WATER ST; 604/688-5570
Bill Clinton ate vegetarian (and gorged himself on platters of dessert) at this beautiful Gastown restaurant. The heritage building, with exposed brick walls and two wood-burning fireplaces, overlooks the harbour and the North Shore mountains. At press time, Cale Gault is the promising new chef at the Raintree, and he's developing a menu with a strong West Coast focus. The wine list is exclusively Pacific Northwest, with an emphasis on BC wines. There's a smoker-friendly bar and bistro positioned in a separate room for hard-core puffers. *$$$; AE, DC, MC, V; debit cards; no cheques; lunch Mon–Sat, dinner every day, brunch Sun; full bar; map:U3.* &

The Red Onion / ★★

2028 W 41ST AVE; 604/263-0833
Forget drive-ins and head to Kerrisdale for the best double dogs in town. Two European-style wieners barely fit into the bun, with onions, grated cheddar cheese, and the Red Onion's special relish sauce to top it off. Keep this monster wrapped or it will end up in your lap. In fact, just about everything at the Red Onion tries to scoot off the bun at the first bite. Grilled-chicken burgers and hamburgers are delivered in foil pouches, piled high with all sorts of fixings. The french fries in a basket will easily feed two and are served with the best sour-cream-and-dill dip in town. Posters, hanging plants, and a Pabst Blue Ribbon neon beer sign complete the unpretentious atmosphere, enhanced by the aroma of grilling meats. Wieners and buns are made to the Red Onion's specifications, and the morning muffins and cinnamon buns are all baked on the premises. This is a hot dog eater's hedonistic paradise, and many have fallen to its charbroiled charms. *$; MC, V; no cheques; breakfast, lunch, dinner every day; beer and wine; map:C4.*

Richard & Co. / ★★☆
Picholine / ★★☆

451 HOWE ST; 604/681-9885
2385 BURRARD ST; 604/736-3760

Office workers are the long-haul truckers of the urban core. They roam the same territory week after week, learning the best places to stop for good food at reasonable prices. On the highway, a busy truck stop signals good eats are to be had; downtown, look for a well-dressed lineup in modest surroundings, and chances are you'll dine well for a song. That's definitely the case at Richard & Co., which bills itself as "an extraordinary soup and muffin shop." The muffins are there for a light start to the day. At lunch, you get in line to order and pay, then take a seat. Very soon a staffer calls your name and delivers your meal. Soups are indeed extraordinary—usually 10 or more listed on the day's chalkboard, all made from scratch each morning, at least half of them vegetarian. But there's much more: chiles, hearty stew, lasagne, numerous sandwiches (available on house-made focaccia), and simple salads (Caesar, house green, pasta). You can mix and match to fit your appetite and/or budget, but a substantial lunch seldom costs more than $8. The always-upbeat, friendly staff remember regulars' names, often writing them on each order as the customer struggles with the array of choices. No posh decor here, just honest lunch fare. Picholine, under the same ownership, has long provided equally good lunch food and service for the area around Broadway and Burrard, and now does dinner. *$; cash only; breakfast, lunch Mon–Fri, dinner Wed–Sun (Picholine); no alcohol; map:T3, P7.* &

Rodney's Oyster House / ★★

1228 HAMILTON ST; 604/609-0080

It's hard to find a spot at the bar as gamins of all persuasions eye the forearms of the young shuckers at this nautical Toronto transplant in Yaletown. A team of experts make careful cheques of temperature, freshness, and quality of more than a dozen briny bivalves (many from the East Coast). While the slogan here is "The lemon, the oyster, and your lips are all that's required," you'll be catered to, nonetheless, if you don't take them straight. Rodney's makes four sauces—you'll want the seawich if you grew up with cocktail sauce on your shrimp. There's also a choice of creamy chowders, steamed mussels and clams, local Dungeness crab, and East Coast lobsters. If you've got the dough, Rodney's will come to your home and set up a boat laden with oysters for 20 or more of your closest buddies. *$$–$$$; AE, E, MC, V; no cheques; lunch, dinner Mon–Sat; beer, wine, and scotch; map:S5.*

Romano's Macaroni Grill / ★

1523 DAVIE ST; 604/689-4334

At press time, Romano's is being renovated after a fire in this West End heritage mansion. The menu won't change, so look for pizzas, toothsome pasta dishes (ask for extra sauce), and a hearty breaded veal with tomato sauce or Asiago cream. Wine is measured by the inch, and just about everything is worth the fair price. A great family place. Reservations for parties of eight plus can choose a bargain family-style menu at dinner or at lunch. Don't miss the frozen Bellinis. On Sundays, there's a midday all-you-can-eat pasta bar. *$$; AE, DC, MC, V; no cheques; lunch, dinner every day; full bar; map:P3.* &

Rubina Tandoori / ★★

1962 KINGSWAY; 604/874-3621

Son Shaffeen Jamal is the congenial host; mother Krishna cooks the authentic East Indian fare. Rubina's menu is built around tandoori dishes, South Indian seafood, and Punjabi and Moghul dishes. Not surprisingly, tandoori breads are outstanding, and you can watch them being made in the tandoori oven at the entrance of the restaurant. Fish masala is worth trying, as is a dry curry with potatoes—or any of the dishes that include Rubina's homemade *paneer* cheese. If you're a beginner at Indian food, try a duet (for two or more)—for example, Moglai Magic, a great, not-too-hot introduction to the cuisine. Don't pass up dessert, since the *gulab jamun,* deep-fried milk dough smothered in syrup and scented with rose water, is a soothing finale. While you're there, pick up a copy of Krishna's *Heartsmart Flavours of India* cookbook. *$$$; AE, MC, E, V; debit cards; no cheques; dinner Mon–Sat; full bar; www.rubina.com; map:E3.*

The Salmon House on the Hill / ★★★

2229 FOLKESTONE WY, WEST VANCOUVER; 604/926-3212

Book a table at the Salmon House on the Hill. Any table. It's a great way to show off Vancouver to out-of-town pals. Northwest Coast Native arti-facts reflect the origins of chef Dan Atkinson's West Coast menu. It's worth the drive halfway to Horseshoe Bay (but only 10 minutes from downtown) to taste his wild BC salmon—marinated in rum, cane sugar, and dill, then perfectly grilled. There's a fresh sheet every day. Start with the crab, corn, and potato cakes with tamarind chutney and mango coulis. The wine list favours good BC, Oregon, and Washington wines. There's a striking entrance area, but the lounge gets smoky after eight o'clock and somewhat uninviting, despite the incredible view. Service is friendly and correct, and parking is free. Check out the annual salmon festival in October. *$$$; AE, DC, MC, V; no cheques; lunch, dinner every day, brunch Sun; full bar; www.salmonhouse.com.*

Salute / ★★

1747 MARINE DR, WEST VANCOUVER; 604/922-6282

This cozy, relaxed spot joins the growing number of excellent eateries sprouting alongside West Vancouver's Marine Drive. The elaborate bar puts out some great martinis. Owner and chef Gamal Hanna spent several years at one of Vancouver's respected trattorias honing his skills, as reflected in his version of carpaccio: lean and moist, attractively arranged, drizzled with piquant whole-grain mustard, and garnished with capers and fresh parsley, it's among the best around. A good list of pastas is punctuated by some more rustic dishes, such as *ciocicara,* a gutsy, earthy combination of fusilli pasta with potatoes and spicy sausage, or the Spaghetti Salute, a mix of chicken, pink and green peppercorns, garlic, chiles, black beans, and al dente pasta. A predominantly Italian wine list leans toward the high end, though there are some less expensive options. *$$; AE, MC, V; no cheques; dinner Mon–Sat; full bar; map:O7.*

Sami's / ★

986 W BROADWAY; 604/736-8330
1795 PENDRELL ST; 604/915-7264

Bicycles hanging from the ceiling and engaging art on the walls are all part of the casual intimacy of Sami's dining room. This Indo-American bistro sets the trend as a forerunner of some of the best fusion food in the city. East and West happily meet in a harmony of spices and fresh local ingredients that will dazzle you with their creative pairings. BBQ Crab and Shrimp Masala Cakes baked in naan, tandoori chicken and caramelized shallot-stuffed dumpling with cilantro-cashew pesto, and the melt-in-your-mouth beef short ribs braised in cumin and ginger fill the room with an aroma that's exotic enough to be erotic. Specials change daily, and a recent offering included an incredible appetizer of smoked salmon, capers, and red onion with a curry salsa, baked on a flatbed of naan. Spiced corn mulligatawny soup is a refreshing starter to the meal, and a selection of BC and California wines as well as local and imported beers are on hand for dousing the palate. Although it's ironically sandwiched between a 7-Eleven and a Pizza Hut, on the other side of Sami's door lies a laid-back elegance, hidden like a jewel in a sea of convenience food. Takeout is also available. *$$; DC, MC, V; no cheques; lunch, dinner every day; beer and wine; map:R7.*

Sawasdee Thai Restaurant / ★

4250 MAIN ST; 604/876-4030

The oldest Thai restaurant in Vancouver, Sawasdee doesn't offer the most sophisticated Thai food around, but it offers a friendly, upbeat environment in which to eat it. The *mee krob* appetizer—crisp noodles with shrimp, bean sprouts, dried tofu, and shredded red cabbage—will be either too sweet or addictive, depending on your taste. Order the chicken wings, deboned, stuffed with minced chicken and vegetables, and paired with a spicy dipping sauce. The chef's suggestion, *choo-chee talay,* combines a spicy curry with prawns, squid, clams, and fish. Relaxed but friendly service. Save room for the deep-fried banana fritters, which can be had with homemade coconut ice cream (have both). *$$; MC, V; no cheques; dinner every day; full bar; map:E3.*

Seasons in the Park / ★★★

CAMBIE ST AT W 33RD AVE (QUEEN ELIZABETH PARK); 604/874-8008
Considerable attention in the kitchen has contributed to Seasons in the Park's rapidly rising reputation. Although the Queen Elizabeth Park setting and the stunning view of downtown and the North Shore mountains still guarantee a line of tour buses outside, today's visitors to Seasons (including presidents Clinton and Yeltsin) come as much for the food as the view. Diners are treated to chef Pierre Delacorte's menu of just-picked produce, succulent seafood, and local wines. Popular dishes include a sun-dried tomato tart baked with Stilton, seared prawns and scallops sauced with Pernod and green peppercorns, and constantly changing wild or farmed Pacific or Atlantic salmon entrees. For dessert, the sunburned lemon pie with fresh fruit coulis will end the meal on a high note. Seasons is also a good place to get hitched—either on the patio or in the 60-seat gazebo. *$$$; AE, MC, V; debit cards; no cheques; lunch Mon–Fri, dinner every day, brunch Sat–Sun; full bar; seasons@settingsun.com; www.settingsun.com/seasons; map:E3.* &

Settebello / ★

1131 ROBSON ST; 604/681-7377
The bad news is that Umberto Menghi sold his most casual restaurant. The good news is that the new owners haven't changed things, and you'll still find on the menu the same pizzas and pastas you've always enjoyed. *Settebello* means "seven diamonds" or winning hand (from an Italian card game). Settebello is best on sunny days, as a respite from shopping, perhaps, when you can sit out on the rooftop patio nibbling at pasta or a collection of Italian tapas-style dishes. Begin with the fresh buffalo mozzarella with tomatoes, basil, and a touch of *balsamico* and extra-virgin olive oil. Then order the first-rate trio of pastas featuring creamy tortellini, fettuccine sauced with spicy tomatoes, and the linguine with pesto. Try the *salsiccia* pizza, with hot Italian sausage, spinach, sun-dried tomatoes, and chile peppers. Good prices on the wine list. *$$; AE, DC, MC, V; debit cards; no cheques; lunch, dinner every day; full bar; map:R3.*

Shanghai Chinese Bistro / ★★

1128 ALBERNI ST; 604/683-8222

Consistently good food and cheerful servers with a formidable collective memory have made this tasteful, airy, L-shaped "bistro moderne" a popular haunt for the downtown Chinese-food cognoscenti. The unique and magical nightly noodle show provides another excuse to bring visitors along for a good nosh before heading next door for a bellow of karaoke. Hand-pulled noodles Shanghai-style are a must, of course, and so are the chile wontons. Both the pan-fried live spot prawns with chile paste and soy, and the salt-and-chile crab, are finger-licking good. For a balanced meal, try a plate of pea shoots lightly touched with garlic. You can have a late-night snack of dim sum (from 10:30pm)—a welcome alternative to the otherwise desolate downtown choices of pizzas, salads, and almost-day-old pastries. *$$; AE, JCB, MC, V; no cheques; lunch, dinner every day; full bar; map:R3.*

Shanghai Garden Restaurant / ★★

3932 FRASER ST; 604/873-6123

For as long as we can remember, three restaurants have been located side by side on the east side of Fraser Street at 23rd Avenue. Like the three doors on the famous television game show, they don't always open to winners. In fact, doors one and three have changed hands so many times we've lost count. But door number two, the one in the middle, has always been a sure bet. Consistency and occasional brilliance are what one gets from Shanghai Garden's years of experience. Enter and you'll be rewarded with crispy fried duck so tender you'll be tempted to eat the bones. Tofu steamed over sautéed spinach, wonderful five-spice beef, fat juicy Shanghai noodles, and silky drunken chicken are some of the other prizes. If you want to hit pay dirt, try a live crab out of the tank, deep-fried in peppered salt and tossed in garlic and chiles. In a word: outstanding. *$; MC, V; debit cards; no cheques; lunch, dinner Thur–Tues; full bar; map:E3.*

Shao Lin Noodle Restaurant / ★

548 W BROADWAY; 604/873-1816

The noodle makers toss, stretch, spin, and cut your meal right before your eyes at this central Vancouver Chinese noodle shop. These tender strands of handmade pasta are combined with meats, vegetables, and seafoods into curries, soups, and other pasta dishes with names like drag- ging noodles, cutting noodles, pushing noodles, hela noodles, stewed noodles, cold noodles, and rolling noodles. Dim sum–style treats such as steamed vegetable buns and pork dumplings as well as rice dishes are also served in tasty, healthy portions. The atmosphere resembles a casual, neighbourhood coffee shop. The dark-panelled walls are filled with framed newspaper articles and photos. Ordering tea is half the fun of eating here: tea is poured from a metre-long pot like the one used to serve an 18th-century Chinese empress who felt that, even when serving, her staff should maintain a polite distance. *$; cash only; lunch, dinner every day; no alcohol; map:U7.*

Shijo Japanese Restaurant / ★★

1926 W 4TH AVE; 604/732-4676

Shijo is a pleasant, uncluttered sushi bar serving excellent sushi, sashimi, and robata. Oysters, grilled on the half shell and painted with a light miso sauce, are a good bet, as are butterflied tiger prawns or shiitake foilyaki—mushrooms sprinkled with lemony ponzu sauce and cooked in foil. Meals end in a refreshing manner at this second-floor perch, with orange sherbet served in a hollowed-out orange. *$$$; AE, JCB, MC, V; debit cards; no cheques; lunch, dinner every day; full bar; map:O7.* &

Shil-La Korean Restaurant / ★

208–333 E BROADWAY; 604/875-6649

Shil-La can easily be mistaken for a private club. This second-storey restaurant on E Broadway has minimal signage, and the entrance hall at street level looks as if it belongs to a local branch of H & R Block. Upstairs, private rooms surround a central area with booth seating dominated by a giant mirror ball and *bulgogi* grills on every table. The special combination for two (a hearty undertaking) is a bargain at $27: rib-eye steak slices, short ribs, chicken, prawns, and pork come neatly arranged on a large platter ready to be seared to taste, complemented by interesting side dishes of kimchi, pickled garlic, grilled dry minnows, sesamed spinach, and other vegetables. Sushi, tempura, and noodle dishes are also available, with sometimes inconsistent execution. But when they're good, they're very good. *$$; MC, V; cheques OK; lunch, dinner every day; full bar; map:X7.*

Sienna Tapas Bar & Grill / ★★

1809 W 1ST AVE; 604/738-2727

A new pocket of good eating has emerged west of Burrard on First Avenue, and Sienna holds down one corner. Fine bread and pastries can be had around the corner, good olives in the adjacent minimall. This large room, awash in mustard yellow and oversize French posters, carries a pan-Mediterranean theme through various main dishes, seven or eight pizzas, as many pastas, mussels prepared six ways (both half and full servings are generous), and tapas, hot and cold. (Tuesday is bargain night: all tapas $6 or less.) A wee bowl of olives and decent focaccia with olive oil and balsamic vinegar welcome you. Chef Geoff Laithwaite crafts a creamy stew of plump oysters accented with strips of tomato. Artichoke-and-roasted-fennel dip, served with greens and shards of grilled flatbread, makes a pleasant starter. Mussels steamed in bitter ale with miso, carrots, and onion develop a fine flavour interplay. Grilled lamb chops have been less successful, the promised Persian seasonings barely noticeable, although their bed of mashed spuds was fine. Sports fanatics can park at the massive bar and watch the playoff du jour on TV (it doesn't intrude elsewhere). Don't let the outside parade of lithe bodies going to and from the fitness centre upstairs guilt you into avoiding the enticing desserts. *$$; AE, DC, E, MC, V; debit cards; no cheques; lunch, dinner every day; full bar; reservations recommended on weekends; map:O6.* &

Singapore Restaurant / ★

546 W BROADWAY; 604/874-6161

The city at the crossroads of the world has bred a multicultural cuisine that's part Chinese and part Malaysian, yet has its own clear identity— as you'll discover at the Singapore. This small West Side eatery provides a cozy ambience, but it's the bargain-priced dishes, not the atmosphere, that keep customers coming in droves. Dishes are spice-rated with one to five stars; you decide how high to turn up the thermostat. At the top of the scale, *sambal bunchies,* a mix of green beans and pink prawns, can scorch your palate. Peanuty fried *hokkien mee*—noodles studded with squid and morsels of pork and omelet—offers a milder choice. Try the pungent Singapore eggplant, the satays, or the gado gado (spicy) salad. Other options? Smooth-as-a-kiss coconut milk–based curries; a complex yellow ginger rice; a pageful of clam, shrimp, and fish dishes; interesting noodles; and more. *$; MC, V; no cheques; lunch, dinner every day; full bar; map:T7.*

Smoking Dog Bar & Grill / ★★★

1889 W 1ST AVE; 604/732-8811

If it weren't for the lack of Gauloise fumes (the city being a nonsmoking zone), you might think you'd landed in a smart new bistro off the Boulevard St.-Germain; instead it's the *rez-de-chaussée* of a Kitsilano condo block (with patio, if you must eat and puff). But the waiters are oh-so-French and charming in their long white aprons and black vests, the music is oh-so-stereotypically French and soothing, the food so consistently Gallic, that the major clue that this isn't the Left Bank is the bargain prices. The real deal is the prix fixe special: choose an 8-ounce steak, breast of chicken, salmon steak, or the roast du jour (veal one day, maybe pork the next), which comes with a small haystack of very good *frites.* Then, in a separate bowl, to be properly enjoyed after the main course, a mimosa salad. It's long been a Jean-Claude Ramond signature: tender butter lettuce, a wedge each of tomato and hard-cooked egg, some grated egg among the greens, and creamy vinaigrette laden with Dijon. Total price: $16.99. The whole menu (much of it on chalkboards around the bright corner room) is more extensive, and worth exploring, both starters and main dishes. Order pâté maison and you receive a generous serving of two types—one fine, livery, and mousselike; the other more dense and country-style, with a peppercorn crust. The pâté is served alongside a small pile of greens in a pleasant vinaigrette, with tart ripe olives and puckeringly good cornichons. At lunch, the light, fluffy leek-and-onion tart is memorable, as is the tarte *au citron* among the seductive desserts. *$$; AE, DC, E, MC, V; debit cards; no cheques; lunch Mon–Fri, dinner Mon–Sat; full bar; reservations recommended; www.thesmokingdog. com; map:O6.* &

Sophie's Cosmic Cafe / ★★
2095 W 4TH AVE; 604/732-6810
The walls of this funky Kitsilano diner are the flea market of a kitsch collector's dreams. Old felt pennants, prehistoric 7-Up bottles, toys of all shapes: you name it and it's likely there. So don't worry about the wait—there's plenty to look at, including Sophie's collection of colourful lunch boxes and hats that were once stashed in her attic. Evenings, people are drawn by burger platters, pastas, and boffo spicy mussels (worth arriving early for—they sell out). Chocolate shakes are a balm for the tummy and hell on the diet (give in). On weekends, fans queue in the rain for stick-to-the-ribs breakfasts, especially the Mexican eggs (with sausage, peppers, and onions, spiced with hot-pepper sauce poured from a wine bottle—handle with caution: it's potent). There are plenty of vegetarian choices all day. Sophie's is a Kits institution, with the permanent mood of a mellow fiesta. A covered deck now accommodates all-weather puffers. *$–$$; MC, V; debit cards; no cheques; breakfast, lunch, dinner every day, brunch Sat–Sun; full bar; map:N7.* &

Spumante's Cafe Ristorante / ★★
1736 COMMERCIAL DR; 604/253-8899
A standout in a street of good solid Italian neighbourhood restaurants, Spumante's is a haven for the indecisive. Dark-trimmed green walls and gilt-framed paintings make for attractive surroundings, and the service is contagiously enthusiastic. (They love their food, and they want you to love it, too.) Meals kick off with a little plate of *stuzzichini*—starters—on the house, and there's a handful of appetizers. With the entrees (chicken, veal, lamb, pork chop, steak, shellfish), you have a choice of fettuccine alfredo, linguine al pesto, or *pennette al pomodoro*. Daytime regulars go for the inexpensive quick-lunch menu. *$$; AE, DC, MC, V; no cheques; lunch Tues–Fri, dinner Tues–Sun; full bar; map:Z6.*

Stepho's Souvlakia / ★★
1124 DAVIE ST; 604/683-2555
Known as much for its lineups as for its cheap and delicious Greek food, Stepho's remains a fixture in Vancouver's West End. Pungent tzatziki and the mandatory travel-agency images of Greece set the mood in this newly

renovated and expanded space. White stucco walls and arched doorways give the room a light, airy feel. Even with the added tables, the lineups persist. And for good reason. Huge portions of chicken, lamb, or beef brochettes fight for space on a plate loaded with rice pilaf, buttery roast potatoes, and a Greek salad, all served with tzatziki and hot pita bread. The hummus as an appetizer is outstanding. Check the everyday specials for the tender and toothsome baby back ribs. Prompt and polite service, generous portions at a cheap price, and a well-priced wine list have made Stepho's the budget eater's mecca for Mediterranean meals. *$; AE, MC, V; no cheques; lunch, dinner every day; full bar; map:Q4.* &

Steveston Seafood House / ★★☆

3951 MONCTON ST, RICHMOND; 604/271-5252

Appropriately located near the Fraser River and the fishing docks, the Steveston Seafood House continues to earn its reputation as "that great little seafood place in Richmond." The decor is funky, with a nautical motif featuring overhead nets, glass floats, and corny seashell knick-knacks. The seafood, simply prepared and generously served on large fish-shaped plates, delivers all it promises. We recommend any of the house specialties—even ones with names such as Jonathan Livingston Seafood (a mixed-seafood platter)—but you don't overlook simple dishes such as the juicy pan-fried halibut with lemon butter. *$$; AE, E, MC, V; no cheques; dinner every day; full bar; map:C7.*

Subeez / ★★☆

891 HOMER ST; 604/687-6107

With a clientele so hip their fashion is dated before they leave the restaurant, Subeez is the spot for the alternative urban dweller. Neogothic, postapocalyptic interiors complete with massive candelabras that would please Dracula set the scene for this millennial mausoleum. Almost everything in this 225-seater is constructed from recycled goods, including the bathroom sinks from Oakalla prison. A mishmash of styles is reflected in the food as well as the decor. Chicken and Brie sandwiches, curried-lamb burgers with mango chutney, and fries with a tantalizing garlic mayo dip will pop the piercings on any jaded slacker. Past, present, and future all come together in this theatre of art, music, and food. A well-priced wine list and local, microbrewed beers are available to ease millennial angst. Be prepared for the 30-speaker sound system that fills this massive space with an eclectic assortment of music that keeps urbanites on the edge. Subeez was one of the choices of the Spice Girls when they were in town. Need we say more? *$; MC, V; no cheques; lunch, dinner, midnight snacks every day, brunch Sat–Sun; full bar; www.subeez.com; map:S4.*

Sun Sui Wah Seafood Restaurant / ★★★

4940 NO. 3 RD (ALDERBRIDGE PLAZA), RICHMOND; 604/273-8208
3888 MAIN ST; 604/872-8822

The splashy Sun Sui Wah in Richmond, with its sail-like sculpture stretching across the glass-domed roof designed by Bing Thom, is fast becoming the talk of the town. Simon Chan brought the proven track record and signature dishes of this successful Hong Kong group to Vancouver a decade ago, and his team has been playing to packed houses ever since, both in Vancouver and Richmond. The reasons are legion: crispy, tender roasted squabs and sculpted Cantonese masterpieces such as the luscious broccoli-skirted steamed chicken interwoven with black mushrooms and Chinese ham; deftly steamed scallops on silky bean curd topped with creamy-crunchy *tobikko* (flying-fish roe) sauce; live Alaskan king crab dressed in wine and garlic; lobster hot pot with egg noodles; giant beach oysters steamed to perfection in black-bean sauce; and lightly sautéed geoduck paired with deep-fried "milk"—fragrant with sweet coconut in a fluffy crust. Reserve early, as these are now the hot spots in town for weddings. *$$; AE, MC, V; no cheques; lunch, dinner every day; full bar; map:D6, E3.* &

Sun Wong Kee / ★★☆

4136 MAIN ST; 604/879-7231

The Sun Wong Kee changed hands recently and the food is better than before, but not as inexpensive as it was. That said, a five-course seafood dinner for four can be had for less than $40. You'll still find minimal decor (although not as rustic) and maximum attention to what's cooking, especially the live crabs, rock cod, and lobsters priced just a tad above what they sell for at the market. The seafood is prepared several ways. You can have it steamed plain, served with butter and cream; baked with green-pepper and black-bean sauce; or baked with green onion and ginger—but the spicy, deep-fried version gets our vote. The 224-item menu runs the gamut of noodles, hot pots, *congee,* and pork, beef, and rice dishes; veers toward seafood (abalone to oysters); and includes such esoterica as fried milk with house special sauce. Open until 2am. *$; MC, V; no cheques; dinner every day; beer only; map:E3.*

Surat Sweet / ★

1938 W 4TH AVE; 604/733-7363

Formerly located in Vancouver's East Indian neighbourhood, Surat Sweet became so popular with West Siders, the owners decided to relocate to Kitsilano. Serving freshly made Gujarati food (and therefore, by definition, vegetarian), this updated 50-seat restaurant draws a steady stream of regulars looking for a curry fix. Samosas are fresh and commendably nongreasy. *Bhajia*—chickpea-floured potato slices—are deep-fried and served with tamarind sauce and freshly grated coconut. *Thalis* (trays, one

103

for each diner, consisting of small containers of food), depending on their size (the special feeds two), include one or two curries spiced with the subtlety of a maestro. The mind-blowingly sweet desserts are all good, but don't miss the *shrikhand*—thickened yogurt tinted with saffron and speckled with cardamom seeds and finely chopped pistachios. *$; DC, MC, V; no cheques; lunch Tues–Sat, dinner Tues–Sun; beer and wine; map:O7.*

Szechuan Chongqing Seafood Restaurant / ★★

2808 COMMERCIAL DR (AND BRANCHES); 604/254-7434 OR 604/879-8454

Dining at the Szechuan Chongqing has always been a Vancouver tradition for those who favour the searing heat of fresh and dry chiles. Today, there's a posh West Side branch (1668 W Broadway; 604/734-1668; map:P7) and the 280-seater in Burnaby (4519 Kingsway; 604/434-1668 or 604/434-2668; map:F3), making it that much easier to sate our cravings for those chile-spiked, garlicky green beans that had us lining up at its doors a generation ago. Added to the memorable repertoire of General Tso's Chicken, magnificent fried prawns with chile sauce, lingering orange beef, melt-in-your-mouth sliced pork with garlic, and rich, silky-crunchy Tan Tan noodles are popular seafood treasures, including steamed Alaskan king crab in garlic and braised sea cucumbers with black mushrooms. *$$; AE, MC, V; no cheques; breakfast, lunch, dinner every day; full bar; map:E3.*

Tak Sangka Indonesian Restaurant / ★★

3918 FRASER ST; 604/876-0121

After 30 years on Main Street, Vancouver's oldest Indonesian restaurant has moved to larger premises on Fraser at 23rd. But that's the only change you'll notice. It still has that simple elegance, is immaculate and comfortable, and is decorated with carefully collected Indonesian treasures. The service can be leisurely, but it is very friendly and warm—like the food. A great way to graze through the 50-item menu is to order the *rijsttafel*—the deluxe offers 12 dishes and a choice of four desserts, a symphony of tastes for $18 per person. Dishes include a superb spicy coconut curried chicken, an intense braised beef spiced with chiles, savoury prawns with garlic and tomatoes, and a vegetable chowder of corn, broad beans, red peppers, and cabbage subtly sweetened with coconut milk. Lively sweet pickles of cucumber and carrots cleanse the palate for the nutty, deep-fried, hard-boiled eggs marinated in sambal and the rich, crunchy gado gado (spicy) salad. And that's just half of it. So bring a friend or two, relax, feast, and plan your next trip to Bali. The food is prepared in accordance with Muslim halal dietary restrictions. *$$; AE, MC, V; no cheques; lunch Tues–Fri, dinner Tues–Sun; full bar; map:E3.*

Tang's Noodle House / ★
2807 W BROADWAY; 604/737-1278
As Vancouver's Asian population swells, noodle houses pop up overnight like mushrooms. Tang's is still one of the best, thanks largely to owner Eddie Tang's rigorous quality control (MSG is verboten) and insistence on giving good value. Here, in bubblegum-pink and grey surroundings, you'll find locals rubbing elbows with those who have trekked in from the distant 'burbs for a serving of fried spicy black cod or shredded pork in garlic and sour sauce. The 100-plus dishes on the menu include rice with barbecued duck, chicken, pork, or brisket; warming hot pots; and vegetarian dishes. Aficionados of incendiary dishes (thoughtfully marked with an H) shouldn't miss the wonton in spicy garlic and chile. Gentler flavours are found in the Singapore noodles—a golden, curry-flavoured dish crunchy with bean sprouts, green pepper, and onion and generously sprinkled with shrimp and slivers of barbecued pork. Terrific hot and sour soup and bargain-priced lunch specials. $; MC, V; no cheques; lunch, dinner Mon–Sat; beer and wine; map:C3.

Tanpopo / ★★
1122 DENMAN ST; 604/681-7777
Whether it's a weekend or a weekday, regulars are willing to wait 30 minutes or more to be seated for all-you-can-eat sushi at Tanpopo. Located on the second floor, this large, lively establishment overlooks Denman Street and even offers patio seating on warm days. Tuna and salmon sashimi, California and BC rolls, and fried gyoza are some of the more popular items you'll see being served by the dozen. Vegetable tempura, sticks of tonkatsu (breaded pork), chicken *karaage*, agedashi tofu, and broiled oysters on the half shell are also in abundance. The restaurant has a regular menu as well, featuring prawn tempuras, donburis, and other traditional dishes. $–$$; AE, DC, DIS, MC, V; debit cards; no cheques; lunch, dinner every day; full bar; reservations recommended; map:P3.

Tapastree Restaurant / ★★
1829 ROBSON ST; 604/606-4680
Ultrastarred chefs around North America may crow about their new "tasting menus," but the concept is not new. Spain long ago enriched the world with tapas, and on a quiet western stretch of Robson Street, steps from Harley-harassed Denman, Nicole Welsh and Mike Jeffs have created a showplace for the tapas art that's relaxed, gracious, informal—and full of flavourful surprises. Seafood figures in much of the room's bright contemporary art, and the arm-shaped candle sconces always draw a chuckle. Seafood also figures prominently on both the regular menu and specials sheet: nippy deep-fried calamari rings dijonnaise, seared ahi tuna with ponzu sauce and Chinese mustard (tapas may be Spanish, but Jeffs cooks globally), scallops with pickled ginger and mirin cream sauce. The

Mediterranean-tinged lamb chops are exceptional; ditto pork ribs with Chinese barbecue sauce. (Other meat and fowl dishes call for more visits.) The kitchen's sure style extends to tender treatment of vegetables, elevating such items as roasted potatoes to addictive status. If the choice is too much for you after a long day (a late closing numbers among Tapastree's many charms), the chef will make up a platter for you. In good weather, the patio allows full appreciation of the West End's passing parade. Service is hit-and-miss on busy nights. *$$; AE, DC, MC, V; debit cards; no cheques; dinner every day; full bar; reservations recommended on weekends; map:Q2.* &

The Teahouse at Ferguson Point / ★★
7501 STANLEY PARK DR; 604/669-3281
This stunning location in Stanley Park is a magnet for tourists, with its series of airy and light dining rooms, park setting, and spectacular view of English Bay, but a faithful following of locals attests to the consistency of fare and professional but warm service. Appetizers run the gamut from Teahouse stuffed mushrooms (crab, shrimp, and Emmentaler) to steamed mussels in a saffron-anchovy broth. Salmon is always a good bet, served with seasonal sauces, and the rack of lamb in a fresh-herb crust is a perennial favourite—even without the view attached. Desserts include a dark-and milk-chocolate *torta milano* with mascarpone mousse or the lemon *chiboust*. If you're planning a summer wedding, check out the sunset patio overlooking English Bay. *$$$; AE, MC, V; debit cards; no cheques; lunch Mon–Fri, dinner every day, brunch Sat– Sun; full bar; teahouse@ settingsun.com; www.settingsun.com/teahouse; map:C7.* &

Tio Pepe's / ★
1134 COMMERCIAL DR; 604/254-8999
A shoebox of a restaurant—one long, narrow room crammed full of tables, with the kitchen at the back—Tio Pepe's has reasonable prices and food unlike any other Mexican food in town. Start with margaritas and a double order of chicken flautas—some of the best around. Charbroiled lamb is marinated in wine and spices with a haunting, bittersweet taste of Seville oranges. *Pascaya con huevo*—date-palm shoots fried in an egg batter and served with tomato sauce—is an unusual appetizer, with a pleasantly astringent taste. The food is flavourful without being too spicy; it has a mildness typical of Yucatan cooking. If fire is your style, however, on your table you'll find a bottle of habanero hot sauce, distilled from the hottest peppers known to anyone. *$; MC, V; debit cards; no cheques; dinner every day; beer and wine; map:Z6.* &

Tojo's / ★★★★

202–777 W BROADWAY; 604/872-8050

Tojo Hidekazu is Tojo's. One of the best-known sushi maestros in Vancouver, this beaming mustachioed Japanese chef has a loyal clientele that regularly fills his spacious upstairs restaurant, though most people want to sit at the 10-seat sushi bar—not big enough for all his devoted patrons. He's endlessly innovative, surgically precise, and committed to fresh ingredients. Show an interest in the food, and he might offer you a bit of this and that from the kitchen: Tojo tuna or "special beef" (very thin beef wrapped around asparagus and shrimp) or shrimp dumplings with hot mustard sauce. Tojo-san created the BC roll (barbecued salmon skin, green onions, cucumber, and daikon) now found in almost every Japanese restaurant in Vancouver. Getting to be a regular is not difficult, and it's highly recommended. The dining room has a stunning view of the North Shore mountains and plenty of table seating. Japanese-menu standards like tempura and teriyaki are always reliable, and everyday specials are usually superb: pine mushroom soup in the fall, steamed monkfish liver from October to May, and cherry blossoms with scallops and sautéed halibut cheeks with shiitake in the spring. Cold Masukagami sake is hot at Tojo's. *$$$; AE, DC, JCB, MC, V; no cheques; dinner Mon–Sat; full bar; map:R7.* ♿

The Tomahawk / ★

1550 PHILIP AVE, NORTH VANCOUVER; 604/988-2612

Step inside the Tomahawk and be greeted by garden gnomes standing in a fountain of running water. This is only a prelude to the deeper level of kitsch that lies in wait. Fake Native carvings and paintings of the souvenir variety, spanning the spectrum from the stereotypical to the downright bizarre, fill every conceivable space in the restaurant. It's the Louvre of tacky art. The menu names are a match for the decor, with hamburgers named after Native chiefs. Legendary is the Yukon Breakfast, which is piled with five rashers of bacon, two eggs, hash browns, and toast, and is served all day. For lunch try the Big Chief Skookum Burger, if you can say it with a straight face, and chow down on a double beef-patty burger topped with a hot dog plus all the fixings, completed with a mountainous side order of fries, pickle, and slaw. For those who wish to eat something just a wee bit smaller, the Tomahawk offers a slew of sandwiches and other delicious, comforting fare. Cap your feast with one of the baked-on-the-premises pies (lemon meringue, Dutch apple, or banana cream). At this Vancouver institution for more than 70 years, there's no better experience than having breakfast as the morning mist slides across the North Shore mountains, a telltale totem pole casting a long shadow in the golden light. *$; AE, DC, MC, V; debit cards; no cheques; breakfast, lunch, dinner every day; no alcohol; map:D1.* ♿

Tomato Fresh Food Cafe / ★★

3305 CAMBIE ST; 604/874-6020
Chef-on-the-run Diane Clement, daughter Jennifer, and general manager Christian Gaudreault have doubled the seating and won an interior-design award for it. When you slip into a booth at this neighbourhood spot, you're in for some serious eating. For years, this was a greasy spoon; now it has an overlay of young, retro energy, most lucidly expressed in the big, chunky, wildly coloured bowls used for serving specialties such as "teapuccino"—cappuccino made with tea. Young waiters serve a variety of mom food: vegetarian chili with really good corn bread, a whacking slab of turkey in the turkey sandwich, and real milk shakes. There's also great takeout from Tomato to Go (open Mon–Sat), which has the best scones and muffins in the city. *$; AE, MC, V; no cheques; breakfast, lunch, dinner every day; full bar; map:D3.*

Tony's Neighbourhood Deli-Cafe / ★★

1046 COMMERCIAL DR; 604/253-7422
If you're looking for a real ham behind the deli counter, take a walk into Tony's Deli and look for co-owners David Kariatakis and Erle Dardick. These guys can entertain you as well as they feed you. Located in the heart of Little Italy on Commercial Drive, Tony's is housed in a beautiful turn-of-the-century building. Famous for panini, especially the Ivana—grilled chicken breast with a corn cilantro salsa, its name inspired, according to Kariatakis, by a beautiful woman who walked in the door one day and captured his heart. Now that's Italian! Insalatas and antipasto complete the trattoria offerings, and Tony's catering services to film crews and visiting celebrities keep the place hopping. If your name is Tony, they'll put your picture up on their "Tony Wall." *$; cash only; lunch every day; no alcohol; map:Z5.*

Top Gun Chinese Seafood Restaurant / ★★

2110–4151 HAZELBRIDGE WY (ABERDEEN SHOPPING CENTRE), RICHMOND; 604/273-2883
1316 W BROADWAY; 604/731-8382
A visit to Top Gun is never just a culinary experience, it's also a crash course in Pacific Rim culture. The Hong Kong–style Aberdeen Shopping Centre in which it's located, together with the adjacent Yaohan Centre and nearby Parker Place, is part of an area nicknamed "Little Asia." In these few square blocks are an education centre, a Buddhist temple, bookstores, barbecue shops, bakeries, video arcades, herbalist clinics, and even a bonsai studio. All this makes weekend dim sum here seem more like an excursion than a meal. Expect a lineup and sometimes indifferent service. The dinner menu is generic Cantonese, but specials can be quite interesting. Try sautéed spiced frogs' legs with *fagara*, baby abalone on mustard greens, or sea scallops with jackfruit and fresh pears in a potato

nest. For dessert, amble across the mall to Rhino's Cafe (next to the bowling alley) and try some of the unusual Eurasian cakes and pastries featured there. The W Broadway location offers an all-you-can-eat dim sum lunch for $9.95 ($10.95 on weekends), and in the evening there are half-price specials. *$$; V; no cheques; lunch, dinner every day; full bar; map:D5, Q7.* &

Uncle Herbert's Fish & Chip Shop / ★★
4866 DELTA ST, LADNER; 604/946-8222
At Uncle Herbert's, owner Ken Mertens has crafted an old-English-village atmosphere, with individually styled rooms lining either side of a main "street." The walls in one room are covered with tea towels from every English town big enough to print one, and the Windsor Room is stocked with royal memorabilia dating back to George V. Stop by from two to four for afternoon tea. For $3.25, you get a pot of tea, finger sandwiches, and scones with clotted cream. But it's the top-quality fish-and-chips (with lingcod or halibut) that draw the crowds. The roster of pub food includes Cornish pasties, English pork pies, Scotch eggs, sausage rolls, New England clam chowder, and Yorkshire fish cakes (two large slices of potato with fish between them, like a sandwich, battered and deep-fried). Mertens imports as many English beers as he can get. *$; MC, V; no cheques; lunch Tues–Sat, dinner Tues–Sun; beer and wine.*

Vassilis Souvlaki Greek Taverna / ★★
6558 KINGSWAY, BURNABY; 604/434-0626
You'll feel transported to the Mediterranean despite the tropical landscaping at this suburban outpost. Vassilis is one of Vancouver's original Greek restaurants. The menu is quite traditional, but the quality is consistent. Worthy starters include lightly battered calamari, pan-fried chicken livers and onions, and rich, salty, scalding-hot *saganaki* (Greek *kefalotiri* cheese fried in oil and sprinkled with lemon juice). Generous portions of souvlaki and the house special of Athenian chicken avgolemono are winning entrees. *$$; AE, MC, V; no cheques; lunch, dinner every day (opens at 1pm Sun); full bar; map:E3.* &

Victoria Chinese Restaurant / ★★
1088 MELVILLE ST (ROYAL CENTRE); 604/669-8383
This upmarket, well-maintained, professional restaurant in the Royal Centre adjacent to the Hyatt Regency Hotel is now a downtown favourite. Superb dim sum is made to order from a sizable menu featuring tasty bites such as shrimp salad roll, egg rolls with shrimp-and-mayonnaise filling, satay calamari, and, on a good day, ostrich pot stickers. The dinner menu samples all Chinese culinary regions. Standouts include finger-licking lettuce wrap with minced squab; succulent, perfectly cooked salt-and-chile black cod; creamy braised napa cabbage; and a superior pan-fried

prawns in soy. The older sister restaurant, East Ocean Seafood Restaurant (108–777 W Broadway; 604/876-8388; map:S7), was among the very first of the new-style Chinese dining rooms to cross the Pacific from Hong Kong, and remains one of the most popular. *$$; AE, MC; no cheques; lunch, dinner every day; full bar; map:S3.*

Vij's / ★★★☆

1480 W 11TH AVE; 604/736-6664

Where food writers impress informed eaters from out of town. Bombay native Vikram Vij dishes up imaginative home-cooked Indian fare that evolves at whim. His seasonal menu changes every three months but almost always includes a mean curry (lamb chops in a fenugreek-and-cream curry with turmeric potatoes) or a killer *saag* (pan-seared squab breast with rapini-and-cumin rice). The decor is minimalist, casual, and modern. Black walls and East Indian ornaments allow the food to take center spotlight. Start with a glass of Vij's refreshing fresh-ginger-and-lemon libation, and don't pass on the standout appetizer—small samosas filled with ricotta and served with a Bengali sauce containing a mixture of five spices called *panchpooran*. Courtesy and simplicity rule as Vik waits carefully on all who arrive early enough to get in—first greeting them with a glass of chai before discussing the menu. A small but excellent wine list. The prices are civilized, too. *$$; AE, DC, MC, V; no cheques; dinner every day; beer and wine; map:D3.* &

Villa del Lupo / ★★★☆

869 HAMILTON ST; 604/688-7436

Chef Julio Gonzalez Perini's dazzling experiments with flavour bring off-duty local chefs to this elegant Victorian townhouse. Order the veal steak, and marvel at the delicate blending of tastes and textures found in a sautéed morel stuffed with rich foie gras. Prices tend to be high, but so is the quality, and the portions are very generous. Almost everything else on the northern Italian menu is wonderful. The roasted sea bass wrapped with Parma ham, prosciutto, and sage is remarkable. The osso buco is a hearty house specialty and a consistent favourite. The wine list goes far beyond the Italian border. Grappa and eaux-de-vie are available as well. Service is always amiable and correct. *$$$; AE, DC, MC, V; no cheques; dinner every day; full bar; map:S5.*

Vong's Kitchen / ★★

4298 FRASER ST; 604/879-4298

Like the phoenix rising from the ashes, Vong's was born from modest beginnings. It was originally known as the Hold One Donut Cafe. The Vong family took it over in 1968 and through three historic decades have provided Vancouverites with homespun, imaginative Chinese cooking. Tony Vong, a kid when Vong's first opened, now handles the giant woks. Using knowledge gleaned from a stint in Hong Kong as well as a few secrets from Mom, he's the hippest Chinese chef in town. Tony's opening appetizer of deep-fried curried-beef wontons served with a sweet plum sauce is mandatory. Follow that with Jade Chicken, named for its deep-fried, crisp bed of spinach, which cradles tender morsels of Sichuan peppercorn-spiced chicken, and an order of spicy red snapper. Don't forget the honey-orange beef and the garlic-chile prawns. MSG is banned from the premises; Tony wields his cleaver over only the freshest of ingredients. You'll stuff yourself silly, but leave room for the banana fritters that arrive at the end of every meal. The low-key decor of Vong's Fraser Street locale is cheery and unobtrusive, the focus being on food and the families and friends who return year after year. *$; cash only; dinner Tues–Sat; no alcohol; map:E4.*

Water Street Cafe / ★☆

300 WATER ST; 604/689-2832

Across the street from Gastown's steam-powered clock, this small corner cafe is the restaurant of choice for homemade focaccia, buttery carpaccio, and southern Italian pastas. It's a delightful find, especially when you can sit outside at the sidewalk tables. (Best to call ahead and reserve one at lunch.) The menu is not long, but whether for lunch or dinner, there's always something that's exactly right: calamari, deep-fried and served with a cucumber-and-dill yogurt; salmon marinated in soy and balsamic vinegar, sautéed and served on a bed of greens; spaghetti tossed with chicken, sun-dried tomatoes, and fresh basil; and, for dessert, a rich, smooth tiramisu. The staff is warm and welcoming, providing a great place to dine *alla famiglia*. Two rooms upstairs (one seats 12 and has a fireplace; the other seats 45) are used for private parties. *$$; AE, MC, V; no cheques; lunch, dinner every day; full bar; map:U3.*

White Spot / ★☆

1616 W GEORGIA ST (AND BRANCHES); 604/681-8034

It's as much a part of the city as Stanley Park, and Vancouverites driving into town after months or years away have been known to stop first for a chocolate milk shake and a Legendary Burger Platter, which includes a Triple O Burger lavishly garnished with a "secret sauce." The first Spot opened as a hamburger joint in 1928, went on to become the first drive-in restaurant in Canada, and now has more than 53 family/casual-style restaurants and 10 Triple Os (express locations serving the best burger). It continues to be a fave among even the most fussy foodies. The freshly baked muffins, the clam chowder, the clubhouse sandwich, and the Pirate Pak for kids are the stuff of legend. You'll also find the ultimate in comfort foods: liver and onions, a hot turkey sandwich, meat loaf, and chicken potpie. Signature desserts include the cheesecake and the boysenberry pie. *$; MC, V; debit cards; no cheques; breakfast, lunch, dinner every day; full bar; www.whitespot.com; map:T4.*

The William Tell / ★

765 BEATTY ST (THE GEORGIAN COURT HOTEL); 604/688-3504

The Willian Tell is in a transitional period, with chef changes, but it's still special-occasion dining at its very best, thanks to owner Erwin Doebeli. The consummate restaurateur, Doebeli is possibly the most charming man in Vancouver and will personally ensure that you have a wonderful meal. His restaurant reflects his old-world dedication to excellent food and service. Its proximity to the Queen Elizabeth and Playhouse Theatres makes this a perfect place for a big night out—have an early dinner, then come back after the show for dessert and a spectacular flaming caffé diablo. Outstanding appetizers include rabbit rillettes in phyllo pastry and, as a special, the BC salmon tartare with fennel and wild mushrooms on toasted homemade brioche. The menu ranges from the traditional (chateaubriand for two) to Swiss-inspired dishes (veal scaloppine with morel mushrooms in cream sauce) to the light and flavourful, such as the potato-crusted salmon. The desserts are pure decadence: meringue glace au chocolat, hot fruit soufflés, and opulently rich crepes suzette prepared at your table. Erwin's son Philippe reigns over one of the best wine cellars in the city. (Aficionados should ask to see the reserved-wine menu.) Sunday night is family dining with a Swiss farmer's buffet (no à la carte menu). *$$$; AE, DC, MC, V; no cheques; breakfast, dinner every day, lunch Mon–Fri; full bar; map:T5.* &

Won More Szechuan Cuisine / ★

201–1184 DENMAN ST; 604/688-8856
1944 W 4TH AVE; 604/737-2889

Whether you eat in or take out, Sichuan is the fieriest of Chinese cuisines. Go for the diced chicken with hot garlic sauce, three-alarm spicy pork with peanuts and hot chile, or the spicy eggplant in black-bean sauce. For those looking to take a walk on the mild side, mu-shu shrimp or Singapore noodles, lightly curried and entwined with shrimp, barbecued pork, shredded omelet, and crispy bean sprouts, will turn your palate into a palace of wild flavour. Inexpensive, with a low-key decor and high-key cooking, there are two locations to choose from. The Denman Street spot is just a few steps from English Bay, where you can walk the beach and work off the pork; the Fourth Avenue location is a pleasant stroll away from the water, where a beautiful sunset sits well with the spice. *$; MC, V; debit cards; no cheques; dinner every day; beer and wine; map:P3, O7.*

Wonton King / ★★

620 SE MARINE DR; 604/321-4433

The sign of a good restaurant is a sea of Chinese faces, and you'll see them here until 2am. Skip the wonton and the regular menu, and ask for a translation of the preset special menu (changes daily) printed in Chinese. Don't miss the crispy, meaty, succulent spareribs in salt and chiles or the

THE GOURMET TRAIL

Vancouver Island is both beautiful and bountiful. The waters along its shores are rich with salmon and shellfish, the lush Cowichan Valley grasslands home to sheep and fallow deer, the fields of Salt Spring Island dotted with orchards. Food artisans attracted to these rural, off-the-beaten-path areas produce a variety of specialty items, including wines, ales, cheeses, salad greens, and more. Five world-class lodgings with fine restaurants and talented chefs, who imaginatively employ this bounty, have collaborated to provide a tour of this largesse. The route—ranging 206 miles and five hours, from the grande dame Empress Hotel in Victoria to the rustic-elegant Wickaninnish Inn on the island's wild western coast at Tofino—has been dubbed The Gourmet Trail. It's a journey catering to those who not only want to explore the island, but plan to give their taste buds a trip as well.

Included along the way are Hastings House, a Sussex-style manor house on Salt Spring Island; the Aerie, a fantasy-like retreat atop Malahat Mountain; and Sooke Harbour House, a Cape Cod–style inn perched on a promontory overlooking the Strait of Juan de Fuca. Group tours include visits with producers such as Salt Spring Island cheesemaker David Wood, a Royal Provisioner. Pricey for the complete guided tour ($2,675 per person, all inclusive, U.S. funds), off-season prices or independent visits to just a few properties make these luxury destinations affordable. For details, call 800/970-7722 or email hatchman@islandnet.com.　　　　　　　　　　　　　—Jena MacPherson

cool, velvety, hand-shredded chicken. For around $58, you get a full meal consisting of your choice of four dishes from about 40 selections, a double-boiled soup, and an appetizer of Peking duck in pancakes. It's enough to feed four to six. For the quality, it's a bargain. *$$; V; debit cards; no cheques; lunch, dinner Wed–Mon; full bar; map:E5.*

Wonton Noodle Restaurant / ★☆
4008 CAMBIE ST; 604/877-1253
1991 E HASTINGS ST; 604/253-8418

The decor at the Wonton is basic and the service, though pleasant, is brisk, but the food makes up for any shortcomings. The menu lists 186 items, and chances are good you'll find any Cantonese dish you've ever heard of—wonton soup, Peking duck, sweet and sour, hot and sour—and then some. Servings are generous. The medium-size bowl of Seaweed Bean Cake Seafood Soup, a bewitching complexity of textures and flavours, feeds three. The menu for chicken's feet, ducks' tongues, and various tripe dishes is written in Chinese only, but the staff are happy to make a stab at translation. Worth ordering (after 9pm) are the rock-bottom-priced, snack-size specials: a single crisp-skinned, butterflied quail or *pai dan*—

the preserved duck egg whose yolk is the colour of green marble. Worth trying, too, are the half-moon-shaped dumplings, the eggplant and deep-fried bean curd in hot garlic sauce, and the superlative pan-fried squid with salt and hot pepper. The second location on a charmless strip of E Hastings Street is out of the way but offers the same good food. *$; AE (Cambie location only), MC; debit cards (Cambie location only); no cheques; lunch, dinner every day, brunch Sat–Sun (Cambie location only); full bar; map:D3, E2.*

Yaletown Brewing Company / ★☆

1110 HAMILTON ST; 604/681-2739

Yaletown Brewing Company attracts the local architects and designers who work in the neighbourhood as well as sports fans attending games at the nearby BC Place Stadium and General Motors Place. The decor is casual and masculine: exposed-brick walls, wood floors, and heavy oak furniture. The microbrews made in Yaletown's own brewery range from lagers and light ales to bitters and stouts. (Ask the bartender for a setup of short samples to help you decide.) Pizzas and pastas predominate on the menu, but there are specialties like the grilled cumin-scented salmon filet and succulent baby back ribs. *$–$$; AE, MC, V; no cheques; lunch, dinner every day; full bar; reservations recommended; map:T5.*

LODGINGS

LODGINGS

Coast Plaza at Stanley Park / ★★

1733 COMOX ST; 604/688-7711 OR 800/663-1144

Situated just off Denman Street, the main artery through the vibrant West End, this monolithic grey former apartment tower offers 267 large rooms, including 170 suites—a dozen of them with two bedrooms. All guest rooms have balconies, and more than two-thirds of the rooms have complete kitchens, making this a great place for families vacationing and Hollywood film crews working in Vancouver. (The stars stay elsewhere.) Amenities include 24-hour room service and, in each room, a minibar and a small fridge. But the hotel's strongest point is its proximity to Stanley Park. Request a room with a park view. Guests are welcome at the adjoining health club, which is popular with local singles. *$$$; AE, DC, E, MC, V; cheques OK; www.coasthotels.com; map:P2.* &

Crowne Plaza Hotel Georgia / ★★

801 W GEORGIA ST; 604/682-5566 OR 800/663-1111

This attractive 12-storey stone hotel, built in 1927, had a complete face-lift recently, restoring it to its original wood-panelled grandeur. Each of the 313 guest rooms is outfitted with custom-built furnishings designed to reflect the 1920s look and feel. Upgraded features—such as multiline phones, voice mail, dataports, in-room coffee service, hair dryers, and irons—are now included in each room as well. The rooms with the best views face south to the Vancouver Art Gallery, but they are on a busy, noisy street. (Ask for an upper floor.) Executive-level rooms provide complimentary local calls, terry robes, and speaker phones and offer evening turndown service. The hotel is located right in the centre of everything. Its restaurant, As Time Goes By, serves European cuisine with Asian touches and afternoon tea; the Casablanca lounge off the lobby is an intimate spot for a nightcap and a light snack. *$$$; AE, DC, JCB, MC, V; no cheques; www.crowneplaza.com; map:S3.* &

Delta Vancouver Suites / ★★

550 W HASTINGS ST; 604/689-8188 OR 888/268-1133

Newly constructed in the heart of Vancouver's financial district, the Delta Suites offers luxury at surprisingly reasonable prices. The grand marble and atrium lobby includes Spenser's (a comfortably secluded cocktail lounge) and Manhattan (an elegant open dining room situated a few levels above the check-in area). The 226 business-style suites are of average size but large compared to those in other new suite hotels. They are well appointed, with blond-wood furnishings, tan upholstery, marble bathrooms, flexible workstations, two voice/data lines, a speaker phone, and

LOCATION, LOCATION, LOCATION

Although Vancouver is easily negotiable and not too spread out, sometimes it's nice to know you're staying as close to the attractions as you can get. Here are a few examples of local attractions and the lodgings nearest to them.

Stanley Park The Rosellen Suites were closest until the Westin Bayshore extended the Stanley Park seawall, planting itself within the boundaries of the 405-hectare (1,000-acre) park.

Vancouver Art Gallery We had to count the number of steps to determine that the Hotel Vancouver is closer than the Hotel Georgia to the gallery's front door. The Wedgewood comes in a close third.

Canada Place The Pan Pacific Hotel is right on the pier, rising up behind the five sails. The next closest hotel is the Waterfront Hotel, directly across the street.

Grouse Mountain/Capilano Suspension Bridge Thistledown House is right between these two major North Vancouver attractions. The Lonsdale Quay Hotel is just a few minutes away.

Financial District The Delta Vancouver Suites and the Sheraton Suites le Soleil have taken the front seat on Vancouver's financial exchange away from the aging Days Inn downtown.

BC Place Stadium The Georgian Court Hotel, directly across the street from the stadium, is a favourite of sports enthusiasts. However, the Westin Grand, a few blocks up Robson Street, might be close enough for anyone who still wants to be close to the Robson Street nightlife.   —Jared M. Brown

high-speed Internet access. The corner suites with king-size beds feature windows wrapping around the bed on two sides. The fitness centre is well equipped, with an indoor pool, weights, and stationary bikes. There is a full-service business centre with secretarial service and meeting rooms for up to 120 people. The hotel is connected to Simon Fraser University's new Centre for Dialogue, which includes a 154-person amphitheatre able to accommodate simultaneous four-language interpretation. $$; AE, DC, E, MC, V; cheques OK; www.deltahotels.com; map:T3.

English Bay Inn/ ★★★★
1968 COMOX ST; 604/683-8002

Owner Bob Chapin devotes meticulous attention to his romantic five-room English Bay Inn, and he has proven himself to be a top-rated innkeeper, year after year. Down comforters rest atop Louis Philippe sleigh beds beneath alabaster lighting fixtures. The pièce de résistance is a two-level suite on the top floor with a fireplace in the bedroom. Extras include terry robes, evening port or sherry, and phones in each guest room. All rooms have private baths, and two back rooms open onto a small garden. A fabulous breakfast is served in a formal dining room complete with gothic dining suite, crackling (albeit gas) fire, and ticking grandfather clock. Stanley Park and English Bay are just minutes away by foot. *$$$; AE, MC, V; cheques OK; www.englishbayinnvancouver. com; map: P2.*

The Four Seasons / ★★★★

791 W GEORGIA ST; 604/689-9333 OR 800/332-3442 (U.S. ONLY)

Guests wallow in luxury at this upscale Four Seasons hotel, which offers meticulous attention to detail. It's a modern tower that's connected to 165 shops in the Pacific Centre mall below it. Although the hotel is located smack-dab in the middle of the high-rise downtown core, many of the guest rooms and suites offer surprising views of the city as well as peeks at the harbour. Amenities include bathrobes, hair dryers, VCRs, shoe shines, 24-hour valet and room service, and complimentary morning coffee and tea in the lobby. Housekeeping takes place twice daily. Facilities include a year-round indoor/outdoor pool, a complimentary health club (with iced towels), and a rooftop garden. Kids are welcomed not only with milk and cookies on arrival, but also with a teddy bear in their crib, a step stool in the bathroom, and their own plush bathrobes. There's also a Dog Recognition Program (see Pets in the Planning a Trip chapter). Business travellers appreciate phones with voice mail in English, French, or Japanese; modular phone jacks for computer hookup; and full business services. Chartwell (see Top 190 Restaurants) is the best hotel dining room in the city. The Garden Terrace, just off the lobby, is a place to see and be seen. *$$$; AE, DC, JCB, MC, V; no cheques; www. fshr.com; map:T4.* &

Georgian Court Hotel / ★★★

773 BEATTY ST; 604/682-5555 OR 800/663-1155

Compared with the other pricey hotels in the city, there's good value to be enjoyed at this 180-room hotel, only a short walk from Gastown, Chinatown, Yaletown, and Robson Street, and across from BC Place Stadium and the Queen Elizabeth Theatre. All guest rooms have a masculine decor, featuring dark-wood furnishings, good writing desks, minibars, three telephones, nightly turndown service on request, and good reading lamps. Among Vancouverites, the Georgian Court Hotel is best known as the home of the William Tell Restaurant (see Top 190 Restaurants), where for years flamboyant owner Erwin Doebeli has set the standard for fine dining in Vancouver. A guest—or any visitor who might enjoy its classic Swiss fare—would be remiss if they failed to dine at the William Tell. Casual fare and sports talk are readily available in the Beatty Street Bar and Grill, also part of the hotel, though it has a separate entrance.

$$; AE, DC, DIS, E, JCB, MC, V; Canadian cheques OK; www.georgian court.com; map:T5. &

Hotel Dakota / ★

654 NELSON ST; 604/605-4333

The Granville Entertainment Group spent more than $2 million to completely renovate the interior and exterior of the original 1904 Barron Hotel. With a tastefully executed 1950s tropical decor that includes bamboo, equatorial prints, light-coloured furnishings, and brushed chrome, the 100 guest rooms appeal to a young-and-on-a-budget crowd. The hotel is a breakthrough in accommodations for the funky (or, if you prefer, mildly seedy) Granville Street entertainment area. Reasonably priced, it's located near hot nightclubs such as Babalu and the Roxy, and within blocks of the always interesting Yaletown district. Complimentary breakfast is served in the hotel's breakfast room and is included in the price. *$$; AE, DC, MC, V; no cheques; info@hoteldakota.com; www.hotel dakota.com/; map:S4.*

Hotel Vancouver / ★★★

900 W GEORGIA ST; 604/684-3131 OR 800/441-1414

One of the grand French château–style hotels owned by the Canadian Pacific Railway, the Hotel Vancouver dates back to 1887. The steeply pitched, green-patina copper roof of its current incarnation has dominated the city's skyline since 1939. A recent overhaul was more restoration than renovation, and the hotel is once again appropriately opulent. Stone arches, friezes, and other design elements hidden by earlier remodelling have been restored or re-created in the past few years. A new Lobby Bar with oversize club chairs and the elegantly casual 900 West restaurant (see Top 190 Restaurants) replaced the original main-floor lobby and Timber Club. The 11-store shopping arcade includes Louis Vuitton, Bally Shoes, Aquascutum, a jewellery store, a watchmaker, stores selling men's and women's apparel, and a Canadian Pacific Store, featuring private-label goods reminiscent of the early days of Canadian travel. The 508 spacious guest rooms retain their elegance. Dark-wood furnishings and comfortable seating are complemented by welcome touches, such as real cream for the in-room coffee service, thick terry robes, duvets, and a morning newspaper. There is a health club with a lap pool beneath skylights. Try to get a room high above the street noise. *$$$; AE, DC, DIS, E, JCB, MC, V; cheques OK; www.hotelvancouver.com; map:S3.* &

Hyatt Regency / ★★

655 BURRARD ST; 604/683-1234 OR 800/233-1234

No surprises here. This is a good Hyatt Regency, like all the others around the world. A modern white downtown tower, it's popular with conventions and tour groups yet continues to offer personalized service.

Adjacent to the Royal Centre mall and two blocks from the Pacific Centre mall, it is surrounded by great shopping. Good views of the harbour and mountains are available from north-facing upper floors. Try for a corner room with a balcony. The Regency Club floor, with special keyed access, has its own concierge, complimentary breakfast, midday cookies, and late-afternoon hors d'oeuvres. There's complimentary use of the health club and pool for all guests. Even the standard rooms are among the largest in the city. *$$$; AE, DC, DIS, E, JCB, MC, V; cheques OK; www.hyatt.com; map:S3.* &

Kingston Hotel / ★★

757 RICHARDS ST; 604/684-9024

Guests often comment that this centrally located inn reminds them of a European bed-and-breakfast, especially its façade of cut granite and heavy wood and its Tudor-style windows. Rooms with private baths have colour TVs; other rooms have hand basins and share bath and TV facilities. All rooms have phones. A Continental breakfast is served in the small lounge downstairs. Facilities include a sauna and a coin-op laundry. A neighbourhood pub, the Rose and Thorn, popular with a young crowd, is on the main floor. This three-storey bed-and-breakfast inn—warning: no elevator—continues to be a great downtown value, and it even offers seniors' discounts. *$; AE, MC, V; no cheques; www.vancouver-bc.com/kingstonhotel; map:T4.*

La Grande Résidence / ★★★★

845 BURRARD ST; 604/682-5511 OR 800/543-4300

Owned by the Sutton Place Hotel, La Grande Résidence provides all the amenities of a luxury hotel in 162 spiffy one- and two-bedroom apartments with kitchens and balconies. (It is, in fact, attached to Sutton Place.) Valet parking, a concierge, and secretarial, maid, laundry, and room services are all available. A state-of-the-art security system ensures privacy. Telephone calls and visiting guests are received by the hotel's front desk. The minimum stay is seven nights (starting at $169 per night). *$$$; AE, DC, DIS, E, JCB, MC, V; no cheques; www.travelweb.com/sutton.html; map:R4.*

Metropolitan Hotel / ★★★

645 HOWE ST; 604/687-1122 OR 800/667-2300

The Met has been a hit since owner Henry Wu began to woo Vancouverites and cosmopolitan travellers in 1995. Mandarin International built this richly appointed, 197-room hotel in time for Expo 86. Now, Metropolitan Hotels has brought back the sparkle, attention to detail, and personal around-the-clock service the hotel offered during the six-month celebration of transportation. Located in the heart of the downtown business and financial district, this red-brick tower offers outstanding concierge service, private Jaguar limousine service, nightly turndown service on request, 24-hour room service, a full-scale business centre, and one of the finest hotel health clubs in the city. You can even watch CNN in the sauna. There are 18 palatial suites; all other rooms are deluxe, with balconies and close-up views of the city, elegant contemporary appointments, European duvets, and Frette bathrobes. Technologically enhanced business guest rooms include laser printers and in-room faxes that deliver the latest-breaking news from the *Wall Street Journal* and Japan's *Yomiuri Report*. Diva at the Met (see Top 190 Restaurants) is the hotel's storefront bar and 116-seat restaurant; it has some of Vancouver's top chefs rockin' on the pans, a logo inspired by Picasso, and dessert plates inspired by Kandinsky. *$$$; AE, DC, MC, V; no cheques; reservations@ metropolitan.com; www.metropolitan.com/; map:T3.* &

"O Canada" House / ★★☆

1114 BARCLAY ST; 604/688-0555

Situated on a quiet street where the West End and downtown meet, this beautifully restored 1897 Victorian home is where the national anthem, "O Canada," was written in 1909. Filled with the comfort and grace one would expect in such a setting, the front parlour and dining room hearken back to gentler times. Potted palms nestled in Oriental urns; a welcoming fireplace; large, comfy chairs; and soft lights greet you at every turn, along with a glass of sherry in the evenings. A wraparound porch looks out onto the English-style garden surrounding the house. The late-Victorian decor continues into the six guest bed-cum-sitting rooms, which have private baths and modern conveniences such as a TV, VCR, fridge, and telephone. The South Suite has an additional adjoining sitting room. The Penthouse Suite offers two gabled sitting areas, skylights, and a view of the downtown area. The separate, diminutive guest cottage, a new addition, also has a gas fireplace and private patio. *$$$; MC, V; no cheques; www.vancouver-bc.com/OCanadaHouse/; map:R3.*

Pacific Palisades / ★★★

1277 ROBSON ST; 604/688-0461 OR 800/663-1815

Under new management by the San Francisco–based Kimpton Group, this hotel has long been popular with visiting movie and television production crews. Part of the appeal comes from the hotel's personal attention to guests' needs, though the major draw is its spacious rooms and balconies with panoramic views of the city and harbour. Decorated in pastels with light-wood furniture, all rooms are equipped with minikitchens that include a fridge, microwave, and coffee maker. There's a health club and one of the city's largest hotel swimming pools. The location on Robson Street is tough to beat if you want to be where the action is. Though the restaurant is undergoing renovations, the hotel offers room service from 6:30am to 11pm daily and is surrounded by a wide selection

---

ECOLOGICALLY INSISTENT

Are the hotels really greener north of the border? Environmental consciousness is one of the hottest new trends in the hospitality industry. As it should be. Hoteliers have discovered that many "green" solutions—such as recycling, designing rooms that automatically shut the lights off when the guest is out, encouraging guests to reuse clean towels, and the like—are saving vast quantities of natural resources. A few Vancouver hotels are pushing the standard, shaping the future for hotels in general. The **Fairmont Vancouver Airport Place,**, the **Hotel Vancouver,** and the **Waterfront Hotel** have added everything from discreet recycling baskets to superefficient laundry systems. The most surprising result? Better room rates, as hoteliers are discovering the beneficial effect their efforts can have on their bottom line.   —Jared M. Brown

---

of restaurants. *$$$; AE, DC, E, JCB, MC, V; no cheques; www.pacific palisadeshotel.com; map:R3.* &

Palisades Extended-Stay Suites / ★★★
Residences on Georgia / ★★★

1288 ALBERNI ST; 604/891-6111

Comprised of four modern hotel towers that surround a long row of equally modern townhouses as well as an 1897 landmark mansion, the Palisades Extended-Stay Suites and the Residences on Georgia occupy and entire city block and offer an impressive range of accomodations. The tower suites proffer commanding city and harbour views. The penthouses have sprawling rooftop terraces. The three-storey townhouses provide the added convenience of private street entrances.

The attractive decor eclectically blends classic and modern touches: Grecian vases and gilt-framed pictures are paired with sleek wood furnishings. The suites are loaded with hotel amenities (from toiletries to bottled water) and long-stay essentials like hair dryers, terry bathrobes, an iron, small storage room, in-room safe, washer and dryer, even a laundry basket. The full kitchens are equipped with Jenn-Air appliances, including dishwasher and microwave. The only thing missing is groceries, which can be ordered from one of the selection of delivery menus thoughtfully placed on the counter. There are conference rooms, videoconferencing facilities, and a high-tech screening room. Each of the towers has a cardio fitness room, plus there's a complete fitness center with a pool and spa in a separate building. Security is tight: and the garage has a double gate system. The elevators operate by key access, towers guests can also check the outside entry buzzer via closed-circuit TV. It's no wonder many of the guests are Hollywood stars, producers, and directors working on location in Vancouver.

This establishment is also pet friendly. The concierge can arrange for dog walking, as well as feeding and attention for pets, if guests are going away for the weekend. Rates include twice-weekly maid service. Parking in the underground garage is an additional $100 per month, and voice mail is $60 per month. *$$$; AE, DC, JCB, MC, V; Canadian cheques only; www.palisadesvancouver.com; map:R3.*

Pan Pacific Hotel / ★★★☆

300–999 CANADA PLACE WY; 604/662-8111 OR 800/663-1515, 800/937-1515 (U.S. ONLY)

No hotel in Vancouver has a more stunning location, a better health club, or a more remarkable architectural presence. As part of Canada Place, the Pan Pacific juts out into Vancouver's inner harbour with its five giant white sails—which are actually the roof for a huge convention centre. The pier, which is also the embarkation point for the thriving summer-time Alaska cruise ship market, hasn't achieved the fame of Sydney's architecturally similar Opera House, but Canada Place's five sails are gradually becoming the city's signature landmark. It's a little confusing when you first enter the hotel, though. Check-in is up the escalator to the third floor; guest rooms start on the eighth floor. Standard guest rooms are small, but the suites are spacious. The decor is flawlessly understated and intentionally muted, in tones of cream and beige. Nothing deters from the spectacular views. The best views face west, but you can't beat a corner room (with views from your tub). Watching the floatplanes come and go against the backdrop of Stanley Park, the Lions Gate Bridge, and the North Shore mountains is positively hypnotizing. A complete range of guest services is offered. The fine-dining restaurant, the Five Sails (see Top 190 Restaurants), has received much well-deserved recognition for its exquisite Pacific Rim cuisine. The Cascades Lounge, just off the lobby, is a must for watching ships sail into the sunset. *$$$; AE, DC, E, JCB, MC, V; no cheques; preserve@panpacific-hotel.com; www.panpac. com; map:T2.* ♿

Rosellen Suites / ★★★

2030 BARCLAY ST; 604/689-4807

Located on a quiet residential street a few hundred yards from Stanley Park, the Rosellen has been an apartment hotel since the 1960s. Although its rather plain façade makes it look like just another West End residential building, autographed celebrity photos in the manager's office attest to its popularity among Hollywood stars and production crews. Katharine Hepburn always stays in the penthouse when she's in town. (It's even named after her.) Privacy is the Rosellen's main appeal, and it's the perfect place for families. There is no lobby, and the manager's office is only open 9am to 5pm. Each guest gets a front-door key, a direct private phone number with free local calls, voice mail, and access to the laundry facilities. Maid service comes in twice a week, and dry-cleaning service is also available. Each of the 30 one- and two-bedroom suites has a spacious living room—some with fireplace—a television, a separate dining area, and a full-size, fully equipped kitchen. (Some have dishwashers, some feature a casual dining area.) There is a three-night minimum stay. Free parking in the rear of the building. *$$$; AE, DC, E, MC, V; no cheques; www.rosellensuites.com/; map:R3.* &

Sheraton Suites le Soleil / ★★★

567 HORNBY ST; 604/632-3000
Outside, it's easy to walk right by the bland façade of Sheraton Suites le Soleil ("the sun"). But inside, the decor demands attention. The high-ceilinged lobby is a study in gilded opulence. It features original oil paintings, a grand fireplace, and a cozy sitting area. Like the lobby, the 112 guest suites are a little on the small side. But with their efficient layouts, the loss of space is not as noticeable as the value for dollar is evident. Besides, the suites are beautifully decorated and furnished in tones of regal red and gold, focusing on le Soleil's solar theme. (France's "Sun King," Louis XIV, would've loved this place.) Some suites also have floor-to-ceiling windows and large balconies. Amenities include bathrobes, Aveda toiletries, and in-room coffee makers. Le Soleil guests have access to the state-of-the-art YWCA fitness centre next door. *$$$; AE, DC, MC, V; no cheques; www.lesoleilhotel.com; map:T3.*

Sheraton Wall Centre Hotel / ★★

1088 BURRARD ST; 604/331-1000 OR 800/663-9255
Just a few blocks from Robson Street, this stunning, 35-storey glass tower houses a wonderful addition to Vancouver's wide-ranging luxury-lodging scene. What distinguishes the Wall Centre from the competition is its stylish, avant-garde decor. The lobby area features furnishings in playful primary colours and dramatic marble, as well as blown-glass chandeliers and a gold-leaf staircase. Standard double rooms are small, although expansive views from the higher floors make them feel larger. Check in to a one-bedroom corner suite with a two-vista view; floor-to-ceiling windows face north up Burrard Street, with Grouse Mountain in the distance, and west to English Bay and the Coast Mountains beyond. Most suites feature a wet bar, a microwave, and a deep soaker tub in the marble bathroom. The complex also features a full health club with a 15-metre (50-foot) lap pool and a beauty salon. Complimentary morning newspapers are provided and turndown service is offered. All in all, this is a wonderful place to stay. *$$$; AE, DC, JCB, MC, V; no cheques; map:R4.* &

The Sutton Place Hotel / ★★★★

845 BURRARD ST; 604/682-5511 OR 800/543-4300

With its elegant interior and understated beige façade, Sutton Place would rank as a top hotel in any European capital. Each of the 397 soundproofed rooms and suites in this sumptuous residential-style hotel has all the amenities one could wish for, including newspapers (on request), umbrellas, and complimentary shoe shines. Housekeeping tidies up the rooms twice daily. The beds are king-size; the furnishings are museum-quality reproductions of European antiques. (There are plenty of spectacular original pieces throughout the hotel's public spaces as well.) There are 11 nonsmoking floors, the fastest elevators in town, a concierge, and bellhops who snap to attention when you arrive, whether you are wearing blue jeans and driving a beat-up truck or emerge in black tie from a limo. Sutton Place's Fleuri restaurant and its lounges have been popular with locals since the day they opened. Elegant meals, a civilized tea, and a chocolate buffet await those who venture into Fleuri (see Top 190 Restaurants). The richly panelled Gerard Lounge is ranked as one of the best watering holes in the Pacific Northwest. Le Spa is replete with a swimming pool, a fitness room, and beauty salons. Sutton Place also provides the best wheelchair-accessible rooms in the city. The city's best rental condominiums are located in a separate building connected to the hotel (see La Grande Résidence). *$$$; AE, DC, DIS, E, JCB, MC, V; no cheques; info@vcr.suttonplace.com; www.travelweb.com/sutton.html; map:S3.* &

Sylvia Hotel / ★

1154 GILFORD ST; 604/681-9321

This is a favourite for price and location more than for attentive service. The English ivy–covered, eight-storey historic brick hotel is a landmark adjacent to English Bay Beach, Vancouver's most popular sand-and-strutting grounds. Try for a south-facing room. A low-rise addition was built to accommodate guests in the busy summer season, when you might just need to settle for any room. Doubles begin at $65, and reservations are required well in advance. All 119 rooms, some of which are quite small, have private baths. Families or small groups should request the one-bedroom suites, which can sleep four and include a kitchen and living room. Covered parking—with no security (and that can be a problem)—is available for an extra charge. The hotel also offers room service, a restaurant, and a lounge. Legend has it that the first cocktail bar in Vancouver opened here in 1954. (On some winter afternoons, it looks as though the original clientele is still in situ.) The outstanding variety of cuisines available on Denman Street are more alluring. But the view of the bay at sunset makes a pre-dinner cocktail in the lounge a rewarding experience. *$; AE, DC, MC, V; cheques OK; www.sylviahotel.com; map:O2.*

Times Square Suites / ★★

200–1821 ROBSON ST; 604/684-2223

Located at the bustling corner of Denman and Robson Streets, Times Square offers apartment-style accommodations that are ideal for extended stays in the city's West End. The 42 one-bedroom suites are comfortably furnished, employing light woods and soft earth tones to lighten the atmosphere. A fireplace in each living room provides a cozy ambience on cold winter nights. A washer and dryer are also installed in each suite. The full-size, fully equipped kitchens have a dishwasher and a microwave. Each guest receives a private phone number, voice mail, and unlimited local calls. Some upper-floor rooms have a partial park and mountain view. For warm summer nights, the rooftop barbecue is open for guests' use. The building managers live on the premises for added 24-hour convenience. There's also maid service twice a week. Secure underground parking is included. *$$; AE, MC, V; no cheques; tsquare@ bc.sympatico.ca; map:Q2.*

Waterfront Hotel / ★★★

900 CANADA PLACE WY; 604/691-1991 OR 800/441-1414

The large and tastefully appointed rooms in the 23-storey Waterfront Hotel are among the best in the city. Underground walkways connect the Waterfront to Canada Place as well as to the Vancouver Convention and Exhibition Centre. Expect wonderful surprises, such as third-floor guest rooms with private terraces and herb gardens that supply Herons (see Top 190 Restaurants). Two Entree Gold Club floors cater to every whim, offering a private concierge, Continental breakfast, nightly hors d'oeuvres, and a private conference room. Of the 489 guest rooms, 29 are suites and one is fit for royalty. The works of Canadian artists are prominently displayed throughout the hotel's public spaces and guest rooms. Amenities include an excellent health club, an outdoor pool with its own spectacular view, nightly turndown service, nonsmoking floors, and rooms designed for people with disabilities. All harbourside rooms have upgraded amenities and dataports for business travellers. (This hotel gets packed during high season because of its across-the-street proximity to the Alaska cruise ship terminal.) *$$$; AE, DC, DIS, E, JCB, MC, V; no cheques; www.cphotels. com; map:T2.* ♿

The Wedgewood Hotel / ★★★

845 HORNBY ST; 604/689-7777 OR 800/663-0666

 Owner and manager Eleni Skalbania takes great pride in the Wedgewood Hotel, as well she should. This is a hotel you will want to return to time and again. It is ideally nestled in the heart of Vancouver's finest shopping district and across the street from the art gallery, the gardens of Robson Square, and the courthouse built of glass. The Wedgewood offers old-world charm and scrupulous attention to every detail. From its ideal downtown location to the renowned Bacchus Ristorante (see Top 190 Restaurants), this 93-room hotel is all that a small urban luxury hotel should be. This is the only upscale hotel in the city where you'll almost never find tour buses unloading swarms of visitors. The finely appointed rooms, which are surprisingly large and are decorated with vibrant colours and genuine English antiques, have the feel of a grand home. Nightly turndown service, a bare-essentials fitness room, and 24-hour room service are offered. Though the views are lost to taller buildings in the neighbourhood, this is the place to spend your honeymoon—and many do. For that matter, any weekend at the Wedgewood is a weekend to savour. *$$$; AE, DC, DIS, E, JCB, MC, V; no cheques; www. travel.bc.ca/w/wedgewood/; map:S4.* &

West End Guest House / ★★
1362 HARO ST; 604/681-2889
Don't be put off by the blazing-pink exterior of this early-1900s Victorian home, which is located on a residential street close to Stanley Park and just a block off Robson Street in the city's busy West End. Owner Evan Penner runs a fine eight-room inn (each room with private bath), and during summer a vacancy is rare. Rooms are generally small but nicely furnished, and there are antiques throughout the house. The staff members have all worked in major hotels and know what hospitality is. Sherry or iced tea is served in the afternoons on the covered back deck overlooking the verdant English-style garden. Nightly turndown service, feather beds and lambskin mattress covers, robes, telephones—even teddy bears!—are provided in every room. Breakfast is a bountiful cooked meal served family-style or delivered to your room. There is guest parking, which is a rarity in the West End. Families with children are accepted, but just be careful with the antiques. If you stay, be sure to take a stroll along the garden paths in Barclay Square, one block to the west, for a quick impression of how the neighbourhood looked in the early 1900s. *$$$; AE, DIS, MC, V; cheques OK; wegh@idmail.ca; www. bcbandb.com; map:Q3.*

Westin Bayshore Hotel / ★★
1601 W GEORGIA ST; 604/682-3377 OR 800/228-3000
The Bayshore (which at press time was undergoing major renovations inside and out, with completion slated for June 2000) sits on the southern shore of Coal Harbour next to the main entrance to Stanley Park. Set back from busy Georgia Street, this is the only downtown hotel that resembles a resort—children love it here. Rooms look out over a large outdoor pool, with Coal Harbour's colourful marina, Stanley Park, and the North Shore mountains beyond as a backdrop. At a kiosk near the indoor pool, you can rent bicycles, and if you're up for a one-hour ride, you can't beat the scenery along the nearby Stanley Park seawall. The

marina has moorage for visiting boaters and charter vessels for guests who want to get out on the water. Amenities include all that you'd expect from a Westin. Guest rooms in the tower all have balconies. There's also a full, newly upgraded health club. A currency exchange is on-site, and the major business and shopping areas of downtown are a pleasant 15-minute walk away. *$$$; AE, DC, DIS, E, JCB, MC, V; cheques OK; www.westin.com; map:R2.* &

The Westin Grand Vancouver / ★★★

433 ROBSON ST; 604/684-9393 OR 888/680-9393

The Westin's exquisite new boutique hotel is a welcome addition to Vancouver's hotel scene. This 31-storey, piano-shaped tower—hence the name—on the east end of Robson Street opened for business in spring 1999. A semicircular marble staircase rises from the dark-wood-panelled street-level entrance to the second-floor lobby, bar, and restaurant. (There's an elevator behind the stairs, if you prefer.) This theme of modern elegance is carried over into the 207 guest suites featuring blond-wood furnishings, grey fabrics, and spacious marble bathrooms. Picture windows highlight the city views from each room. There's a general abundance of comforts and amenities. Each suite comes equipped with two TVs, a kitchenette, a large soaker tub, bathrobes, cordless phones, two phone lines, a dataport, a large desk, and high-speed Internet access. Two suites per floor are outfitted for business travellers, with a fax machine, comfortable office chair, halogen desk lamp, and even basics like a stapler. The outdoor pool and Jacuzzi on the second-floor sundeck seem a world away from the street below. There's also a fitness centre, as well as a business centre with secretarial services. VODA, a popular upscale nightclub, is located at street level. Be sure to stroll next door to one of Vancouver's most striking landmarks, Library Square (see Exploring chapter). *$$$; AE, CD, E, MC, V; cheques OK; www.westin.com; map:S4.*

YWCA Hotel/Residence / ★★

733 BEATTY ST; 604/895-5830 OR 800/663-1424

Weary business travellers arriving late at the YWCA Hotel/Residence on Beatty Street may be somewhat flummoxed by the institutional-style security. (There are separate keys for the parkade, for the elevator, for your room, and for the hall baths; there is no direct elevator access to the parkade; and front-door entry is only available via intercom after 11pm.) It might help to know that the hotel was built in 1995 with safety and security in mind. The rooms are functional, immaculately clean, and reasonably priced for a downtown location. All rooms have sinks; baths are private, shared with another room, or "down the hall." Rooms with private baths have a TV. The residence is also remarkably quiet, and although it might not be quite the thing for those accustomed to amenities (no tissues, clocks, or coffee makers here), it does provide meeting rooms, kitchen and laundry facilities, and communal lounges. There isn't a gym, but you can work out for free at the YWCA Fitness Centre at 535 Hornby Street. Wheelchair-accessible rooms are available upon request. The residence is close to theatres, sporting venues, and the library. Underground parking is $5.35 per day. *$; MC, V; cheques OK for deposit only; hotel@ywcavan.org; www.ywcahotel.com; map:T5.*⎮

West Side

The French Quarter / ★★★

2051 W 19TH AVE; 604/737-0973

C'est magnifique! Ginette Bertrand's French country–style home—nestled in the historic, exclusive Shaughnessy district—has a delightful, cozy, well-appointed room in the main house, as well as a private poolside cottage with all the amenities: a queen-size bed, large closet and bathroom, fireplace, TV, VCR, refrigerator, and a complimentary sherry. The open kitchen, dining room, pool deck, and living room are spacious and offer privacy. A gourmet sweet-or-savoury breakfast menu, topped off with fresh fruit, is served from 8:30 to 10:30am. Access to a well-equipped fitness room is included. Ideal for a romantic getaway, though families with children eight and older are welcome. Some small pets are allowed. There's a minimum two-day stay during summer peak season. *$$$; MC, V; cheques OK; map:C3.*

Johnson Heritage House / ★★★

2278 W 34TH AVE; 604/266-4175

To say that owners Ron and Sandy Johnson are quite fond of antiques would be an understatement. They have restored a 1920s Craftsman-style home on a quiet street in the city's Kerrisdale neighbourhood and turned it into one of Vancouver's most intriguing bed-and-breakfasts. Everywhere you turn in the three-storey house, there are relics of the past: coffee grinders, gramophones—even carousel horses in the largest guest room. Above the front door, installed as the porch light, is a genuine old Vancouver street lamp. The rooms on the top floor and in the basement are cozy; the Carousel Suite, with its adjoining mermaid-theme en suite bath, is the grandest, with an antique slate fireplace. A separate guest telephone line, guidebook, and map to Vancouver in every room all contribute to the friendly atmosphere. Breakfast is served in a bright, airy, cottage-style room on the main floor. Suitable for families with children 12 and over. No pets. *$$; no credit cards; cheques OK; www.johnsons-inn-vancouver.com; map:D3.*

Penny Farthing Inn / ★★

2855 W 6TH AVE; 604/739-9002

This 1912 Edwardian home is an historic treasure in Vancouver's trendy Kitsilano district. Of the four guest rooms, try for Abigail's Suite, which has a sitting room, a fireplace, lovely views of the North Shore mountains, skylights, and a soft-pastel decor. A butler's pantry—stocked with coffee, tea, and cookies—is open day and evening for guests to help themselves. Owner Lyn Hainstock is a professional innkeeper with a wealth of information about Vancouver. Breakfast, served indoors or on the brick patio in season, is a gourmet's feast. All the rooms now have fridges and phones, and frolicking house cats entertain. *$$; no credit cards; cheques OK; farthing@uniserve.com; map:B2.*

Two Cedars Bed & Breakfast Suite / ★★

1423 WALNUT ST; 604/731-0785

Tourism- and hospitality-industry veterans Tracy Lott and Peter Burrow have a bright, airy suite for bed-and-breakfast guests in their renovated 1911 Kits Point–district home. Two Cedars' prime location—only a couple of blocks from Kitsilano Beach and Vanier Park, as well as Vancouver and Maritime Museums—is also within walking distance of Granville Island and buses going downtown. The guest suite has its own terraced garden entrance at the rear and a reserved parking spot to boot. The suite accommodates up to four adults. Kids are welcome. Special treats include Continental breakfast served in bed and wine tastings (on request). *$$; no credit cards; cheques OK; map:O6.*

University of BC Residences / ★

5961 STUDENT UNION BLVD; 604/822-1010

You could probably spend a whole vacation just exploring UBC's beautiful campus: the Museum of Anthropology, the Botanical Gardens, sports facilities, walking trails, and more. From May through August the university opens its student residences to travellers at bargain rates. Dormitory rooms, with two beds and bath down the hall, are as low as $24. Single travellers who want to meet people like the six-bedroom units that share a bathroom, fridge, and living room. There are also studios with bath and kitchenette or, all year-round, one-bedroom apartments that sleep four. Lots of dining facilities are available on campus and in the University Village nearby. For a small fee you can use the university's athletic facilities and swimming pool. Bus service from the campus to either downtown or Jericho Beach is very good, providing easy access throughout the day. Parking is free in the summer months at the Walter Gage Residence; otherwise, there's a charge of $4 per day. *$; MC, V; no cheques; www. conferences.ubc.ca; map:B2.*

North Shore

Capilano RV Park / ★

295 TOMAHAWK AVE, NORTH VANCOUVER; 604/987-4722

If you've brought your recreational vehicle or tent to Vancouver, this is the place to park it. Nicely situated on the Capilano River, just across the Lions Gate Bridge from downtown, this convenient camping facility operated by the Squamish Nation features a pool, playground, and Jacuzzi. The Park Royal Mall is a few blocks away. The noise from bridge traffic may not be obtrusive to RV guests, but tenters should consider camping elsewhere. Tenting sites are $22, partial hookup sites are $27, and full hookup sites are $32. Reservations are a must in summer for the RV sites, but there are no reservations for the tenting sites. Prices quoted are for two people; extra charges are $2–$3.50 for pets. *$; MC, V; no cheques; www.capilanorvpark.com; map:D1.*

Laburnum Cottage Bed & Breakfast / ★★

1388 TERRACE AVE, NORTH VANCOUVER; 604/988-4877 OR 888/686-4877

This elegant country home is set off by an award-winning English garden that has been tended with care for more than four decades by innkeeper Delphine Masterton, who raised five children here before opening the home to lodgers. The main house, furnished with antiques and collectibles, features four light and airy guest rooms with private baths and garden views. Two of these have a queen bed plus a single. The Summerhouse Cottage—situated in the midst of the garden and accessed by a footbridge that crosses a small creek—is a Rosamund Pilcher novel come to life, perfect for honeymooning couples. A larger cottage, the Carriage House, sleeps five and has a private entrance, kitchen, fireplace, and children's loft. Breakfast, prepared by a professional chef, might include mushroom crepes, Belgian waffles, or pancakes, served in the big country kitchen. Masterton's gift for being welcoming and her ability to turn strangers into friends over the cheerful breakfast table make a stay here like a congenial family reunion. *$$; E, MC, V; cheques OK; laburnum@ home.com; www.vancouver-bc.com/laburnumcottagebb; map:D1.*

Lonsdale Quay Hotel / ★

123 CARRIE CATES CT, NORTH VANCOUVER; 604/986-6111 OR 800/836-6111

Few visitors take the time to explore the North Shore, which has perhaps the best wilderness areas of any major North American city. The pleasant Lonsdale Quay Hotel is located atop the enjoyable Lonsdale Quay market, with its open stalls filled with everything from toys and crafts to produce and smoked salmon. The hotel is directly across Burrard Inlet from downtown Vancouver, yet only 15 minutes away via the SeaBus, which regularly scoots between the quay and the SeaBus terminal just east of the Canada Place pier. This hotel gives you a comfortable place to stay as long as you don't need to be pampered. French doors on south-facing rooms open to the Vancouver skyline, an especially dazzling sight at night when the lights reflect off the water. *$$$; AE, DC, DIS, E, JCB, MC, V; no cheques; lqh@fleethouse.com; map:E1.* &

Park Royal Hotel / ★★

540 CLYDE AVE, WEST VANCOUVER; 604/926-5511

The ivy-covered Park Royal Hotel is a study in contradictions. It's nestled into its own little forest of mature greenery just metres away from one of Vancouver's busiest freeways, but traffic noise never seems to intrude into your surroundings. Some of the 30 guest rooms are beautifully appointed with custom woodwork, exposed beams, classic 1920s wood furnishings, and bathrooms full of marble and brass. A few are still stuck in the '70s. Ask for one of the 12 riverside rooms that overlook the hotel's gardens and the Capilano River, which flows alongside. The coziness and romantic setting make it a popular place for weddings. The Tudor Room is open for breakfast, lunch, and dinner; the pub offers a chance to mingle with refined locals. We liked the genuinely friendly housekeeping staff. The legendary hospitality of owner Mario Corsi is, well, legendary. When he's around, things and people get looked after in a special way. *$$; AE, DC, E, MC, V; no cheques; map:D0.* &

Thistledown House / ★★★☆

3910 CAPILANO RD, NORTH VANCOUVER; 604/986-7173

There are five reasons to be in North Vancouver: Grouse Mountain, the Capilano Suspension Bridge, Capilano Regional Park, the Capilano salmon hatchery, and Thistledown House. Fortunately, this bed-and-breakfast is about as close to the other four as you can get. It's a gorgeous Craftsman-style home built in 1920 from timber cut on the nearby mountain. The home has been completely restored and luxuriously furnished. Antiques and period pieces intermingle with eclectic works of art gathered from around the world. The six guest rooms have private baths, soundproofed walls, thick terry robes, and either down or silk duvets. Two rooms have gas fireplaces and separate sitting areas. Our favourite, Under the Apple Tree, also has a two-person Jacuzzi and a private patio. One room even has a private porch. Owners Rex Davidson and Ruth Crameri are ideally suited to innkeeping: Ruth is a professional interior designer and comes from five generations of Swiss hoteliers; Rex is a genial former restaurateur and an expert on Scottish history. Afternoon tea, with complimentary sherry and fresh pastries, is served on the porch overlooking the flower garden or in the living room by the fireplace. Breakfast is a sumptuous four-course affair, over which guests like to linger to exchange travel stories. The morning menu might include homemade granola with mulled milk or stirred yogurt, a selection of breads and jams, sherried grapefruit, alder-smoked Pacific salmon, and fresh fruits. The service is so flawless, it's hard to believe this B&B opened just a few years ago. It's not so hard to believe that returning guests from the United States, England, Scotland, Norway, eastern Canada, and various other points of the compass are quickly becoming the majority of their business. *$$$; AE, DC, ER, MC, V; no cheques; davidson@helix.net; www.thistle-down.com/index2.htm.* &

Burnaby

Simon Fraser University Residences / ★

ROOM 212, MCTAGGART-COWAN HALL, BURNABY; 604/291-4503
Simon Fraser is located on top of Burnaby Mountain about half an hour from downtown. The campus is an architectural showpiece designed by Arthur Erickson, and in summer the residences offer budget accommodations. Single rooms are $27 if you want bedding and towels or $19 if you supply your own. Twin rooms with linen service are less than $50, and families can stay in townhouse units with four bedrooms, two baths, kitchen, and living room for $100. Bus service to downtown takes about an hour. The campus is self-contained, with cafeterias, a pub, and even fine dining. Parking is $3 per day. *$; MC, V; cheques OK; www.sfu.ca/ campus-community-services/conference-accommodation; map:I2.*

Airport Area

Delta Pacific Resort / ★★

10251 ST EDWARDS DR, RICHMOND; 604/278-9611 OR 800/268-1133
Formerly called the Delta Airport Inn, this is one of two Delta hotels in the vicinity of Vancouver International Airport. Both are well run and offer a wealth of recreational facilities. Unlike its business-oriented sibling, this four-hectare (10-acre) resort includes three swimming pools (one indoor), an indoor water slide, year-round tennis courts under a bubble, a play centre with spring-break and summer camp for kids ages 5 to 12, exercise classes, volleyball nets, and a golf practice net. As a massive sign on the side of the hotel implies to passing motorists, kids are most welcome here. There are meeting rooms and a restaurant, a cafe and a bar. As at its counterpart, Business Zone rooms with private faxes and other amenities are available for an additional $15. A $2 shuttle service goes between the hotel and the airport, as well as to nearby Richmond Centre mall. If you're driving, ask the clerk for directions from Highway 99; it's a bit tricky to get to the hotel, even when you can see it. Kids under 6 eat free in the Reflections restaurant. *$$$; AE, DC, DIS, E, JCB, MC, V; no cheques; www.deltahotels.com; map:D5.* &

Delta Vancouver Airport Hotel & Marina / ★★

3500 CESSNA DR, RICHMOND; 604/278-1241 OR 800/268-1133
This is the closest hotel to Vancouver International Airport, built on the banks of the Fraser River. Planes pass overhead but the rooms are sound-proofed. It has an outdoor pool, a bar, as well as bicycle and running trails. Not a bad place for a layover. Rooms on the east side face the hotel's marina, its popular seafood restaurant, and the river. Downtown is a little less than 30 minutes' drive away. The 415 guest rooms and the dozen or so meeting rooms are popular for conventions and with corporate travellers. Business Zone rooms, which include a fax machine, halogen desk lamp, cordless phone, and basic office supplies, are available for an extra $15. There's a small fitness centre on the top floor, or guests are welcome to take the shuttle to the more extensive facilities at the Delta Pacific Resort nearby. Kids under six eat free in the hotel's dining facilities. *$$$; AE, DC, DIS, E, JCB, MC, V; no cheques; www.deltahotels. com; map:D5.* &

Fairmont Vancouver Airport Place / ★★★

VANCOUVER INTERNATIONAL AIRPORT; 604/207-5200 OR 800/676-8922
While most airport hotels simply cater to harried business travellers, here is an oasis of tranquility. Rising above Vancouver's international terminal, it is the closest hotel to the airport. (You can check in at satellite counters situated in the domestic and international baggage claim areas. Plus, you can check your bags onto certain flights right from your room.) A waterfall in the lobby and floor-to-ceiling Vision Wall soundproof glass on all floors eliminate outside noise, whether you're in the restaurant or a guest room. The Globe, with its subtle aeronautical motif, is a reasonably priced restaurant with a full menu, plus gourmet pasta and pizza bars during lunchtime hours. Even if you're not a hotel guest, it's the perfect spot to while away spare boarding time, in front of the large fireplaces or at the bar. Also, nonguests can use the workout facilities, which include weights, treadmills, stationary bikes, rowing machines, a lap pool, saunas, hot tub, plus workout clothes and terry robes for lounging around the pool, all for $15. From poolside picture windows, you can languidly muse on the bustle in the terminal below. This is Canada's possibly most technologically advanced and environmentally sound hotel. The room heat turns on when you check in; the lights turn on when you insert your key into the door—and turn off when you leave; the DO NOT DISTURB sign illuminates from a central control panel on the nightstand (which also shuts off the doorbell and routes calls to voice mail). The Entree Gold rooms feature automated curtains, plus the phones have keyboards and LCD screens for sending faxes and checking email. *$$; AE, DC, E, MC, V; cheques OK; www.cphotels.com; map:D5.*

Radisson President Hotel & Suites / ★★

8181 CAMBIE RD, RICHMOND; 604/276-8181 OR 800/333-3333

We knew we were in for a treat at Richmond's Radisson President Hotel and Suites when we received impeccable directions to the hotel over the phone and gracious assistance with some rather unusual park-and-fly arrangements. The Radisson offers everything from excellent Cantonese cuisine in the President Chinese Restaurant (see Top 190 Restaurants) to meeting and conference rooms to shopping at the adjoining President Plaza. Staff handled even the most obscure requests with ease: customer service here is prompt and friendly. Rooms are spacious and well appointed (you can actually open the windows), and business-class accommodations cover small needs and large—from a free morning newspaper to dataport hookups for your laptop. Complimentary shuttle service to the airport is available every half hour. The atmosphere in Gustos' Bistro is bright and funky (we liked the colour scheme and the cheery round coffeepots), but breakfast prices are expense-account high. The appealing West Coast lunch and dinner menu created for the bistro offers a much better value. *$$$; AE, DC, DIS, E, JCB, MC, V; no cheques; map:E6.* &

South of the Airport

The Duck Inn / ★

4349 RIVER RD, WEST LADNER; 604/946-7521

The Fraser River delta teems with wildlife. From great blue herons to friendly flocks of ducks and swans, nature provides serenity in this setting, with the North Shore mountains serving as a backdrop. The Duck Inn's single riverside accommodation is perched one flight up over the water: a reasonably spacious, modern one-bedroom wood cottage that overlooks the delta. French doors off the living room open onto the balcony, which can also be accessed via a private outside staircase. Furnishings are simple yet comfortable: a wood-burning fireplace and an entertainment centre in the living room add a homey feel. There's a soaker tub in the bathroom and a king-size bed to make this retreat even more appealing. Outside, a gas barbecue and a hammock are set up under the weeping willow tree. Guests can use the inn's canoe to reach secluded beaches on nearby islands, or bike (they also have bikes) to Reifel Bird Sanctuary just a short distance away. Breakfast is left for you in the refrigerator, including homemade smoked salmon, farm-fresh eggs, home-baked breads and jams, plus coffee, tea, and a selection of local fruits. Complementary sherry and snacks are set out as well. The inn is located in Ladner, 20 minutes south of Vancouver International Airport, off Highway 99. *$$$; MC, V; no cheques.*

Ocean View Lodging / ★

246 CENTENNIAL PARK WY, TSAWWASSEN; 604/948-1750

Just north of the U.S. border, this immaculate B&B is on the edge of Boundary Bay, a major flyway for migratory birds. The wonderfully tranquil beach is right out the front door. The house is filled with antiques and has two fireplaces, a hot tub on the beach, a library, and a comfortable living room stocked with travel brochures and books. The dining room and most of the guest rooms have panoramic views of the water and the mountains beyond. (That's Mount Baker towering above the western horizon.) Rooms have king- or queen-size beds and are elegant and well appointed. The Master Suite is exceptional, featuring 5-metre (16-foot) bay windows, a round 8-metre (27-foot) rock fireplace, three decks, and two lofts. Owner Mary Lou Stewart is an inveterate amateur bird-watcher and an engaging host, making stays here particularly pleasant. Smoking is not permitted. *$$; AE, MC, V; no cheques.* &

River Run Cottages / ★★

4551 RIVER RD W, LADNER; 604/946-7778

The River Run Cottages on the Fraser River are nestled among a community of residential houseboats in historic Ladner. Thirty minutes' drive south of downtown Vancouver and close to the Tsawwassen ferry terminal, the four guest cottages offer nearness to nature. Ducks, swans, leaping salmon, and bald eagles may all put on a spontaneous show while you look from your deck toward the North Shore mountains and Vancouver Island. The complex features the floating Water Lily Cottage, which is ideal for two. On land, the Northwest Room has a wood-burning fireplace and French doors that open onto the water. The Keeper's Quarters has a hand-built driftwood bed and a Jacuzzi. The Netloft has a spiral staircase that leads up to a queen-size captain's bed as well as a Japanese-style soaker tub on the deck. A hot breakfast is delivered to your room with the morning paper. Bikes and a two-person kayak are available for exploring. No pets. *$$; MC, V; cheques OK; riverrun@direct.ca.*

EXPLORING

EXPLORING

Top 20 Attractions

1) GRANVILLE ISLAND AND FALSE CREEK

Beneath Granville Street Bridge to Science World; 604/666-5784
Whether you're looking for a few organic avocados or 5,000 tonnes of foundation-ready cement, Granville Island is the place to go. Originally called Industrial Island, this weekend shopping mecca was once an assortment of dusty factories and derelict warehouses. As Vancouver grew, most of the industries there left for cheaper and more spacious pastures, and the island became a grimy eyesore. That changed in the mid-1970s when two local visionaries decided the mudflat had development potential (to wit, location, location, location). The federal government got on board, a little imagination was employed, and those warehouses haven't been the same since. Out went the bolts, anvils, and boilers and in came the art supplies, organic fruit, and flame-juggling buskers.

Taking over the tin sheds of a rope depot on the north corner of the island is the **PUBLIC MARKET** (1689 Johnston St; 604/666-5784), the first new business venture to arrive. Here you will find more than 50 shops and stalls hawking fresh radishes, dolmades, freshly baked bread, fudge, salmon, pottery, art, and everything in between. The market is open daily. On Thursdays, from late May to October, there's the **TRUCK FARMERS MARKET** (1585 Johnston St) in the Arts Club Theatre parking lot, where BC farmers sell local veggies and flowers from the backs of their trucks. Nearby, the **NET LOFT** (1666 Johnston St) contains small shops and craft displays, with everything from beads to Northwest Coast carvings under one roof. All around are aromatic bakeries, bookshops, glass galleries, and pottery studios.

More of the same, for the little ones, can be found at the **KIDS MARKET** (1496 Cartwright St; 604/689-8447). The market is chock-a-block with games, gifts, hobbies, art and craft supplies, toys, and video games. Musicians and tightrope-walking buskers contribute to the lively atmosphere. In the summer months, a visit to the **WATER PARK** (604/666-5784) and adventure playground off Cartwright is a must for parents with young children. *Public Market open every day 9am–6pm; Kids Market and Net Loft open every day 10am–6pm; www.netminder.com/granville-island; map:Q6.*

As much as locals are loath to ever utter a bad word about Granville Island, we have to admit that parking here is a challenge. The problem is particularly tough on weekend mornings when the entire city seems to drop by. There's covered pay parking to supplement the free outside spaces, but if you're not having any luck finding a spot, try parking near

SERIOUS ARCHITECTURE

Marine Building / 355 Burrard St Dressed in stunning terra-cotta finery, this 25-storey terminal vista soars above the darkened stoops of Hastings Street. Soon after it was built in 1929—the tallest building in the British Empire at the time—Guinness boss A. J. Taylor set up a lavish penthouse pied-à-terre (which his terrified-of-heights wife made him abandon) in the building. It's still there, peeking out above the classical lines and elegant swirls that have placed this building in the pantheon of art deco architecture. Awash in aqua-green and blue, the lobby is meant to resemble a huge, treasure-filled Mayan temple.

Canada Place / 999 Canada Pl Not merely the most famous building in Vancouver, also the most versatile. What other local landmark could play host to 18 heads of state, 2,800 freighters and cruise ships, and Tchaikovsky's *The Nutcracker,* all within the same year, and still be admired for its graceful looks? The five stylized masts are a visual riff that has been copied around the world, although few recognise the design's home city. Built as the Canadian Pavilion for Expo 86, this $144.8 million leviathan encloses an all-star team of local tourism, tucking in a cruise terminal, convention centre, IMAX cinema, and the Pan Pacific Hotel beneath its gleaming white sails.

Vancouver Law Courts / 800 Smithe St Vancouver's Law Courts are unquestionably the coolest place in Canada in which to be handed a life sentence. This glass palace was designed to demystify the black-robed judiciary. Believing that justice should not only be done, but seen to be done, architects Arthur Erickson and Bing Thom wrapped the building behind a transparent facade. Finished in 1979, the final product is a radical departure from the original idea. Initially, the provincial government had visions of a 55-storey tower, but in 1973, Dave Barrett's New Democratic party won a surprise victory, fired the original architects, and knocked the plan on its side.

Library Square / 350 W Georgia St Designed by Moshe Safdie, Library Square is one of those rare buildings that can turn heads and change traffic patterns. Long considered the poorer cousins of Robson Street, the eastern flanks of the downtown strip have been revived by this Roman Colosseum copycat. Although Safdie's square has given people a reason to wander east, not everybody appreciates the library's styling, least of all Safdie, who insists there's no connection between his $100 million design and the Italian version. While the design community fights it out, the public has embraced the building's soaring atrium and comfortable piazza, not to mention the library's 1.2 million books. —*Noel Hulsman* the intersection of Fourth Avenue and Fir Street and take the #51 Granville Island bus. The **AQUABUS** (south foot of Hornby St; 604/689-5858) is a regular shuttle service across False Creek from downtown to the island.

Once you've gotten to the island, relax and soak in the views. Most restaurants on Granville Island have capitalized on the waterfront setting, and there's no shortage of sights to take in as you relax over coffee or a meal. There's also a pleasant **SEAWALL** (Kitsilano Beach to Canada Place), a wide waterfront walkway paved in a mixture of surfaces—flagstones, wood, or concrete—where you will find sheltered courtyards, inviting plazas, and grassy landscaped areas, as well as benches where you can sit and watch all the activity. Canada geese congregate on rocks rising from the large duck pond. Cormorants wait and watch for their dinners to swim by.

At the west end of the island is the waterside wharf, edging Broker's Bay. Millions of dollars' worth of yachts are berthed here, and it's a good place to rent or charter a boat. If you already own a boat (or are in the market for one), check out the aquatic bonanza on Duranleau Street, where boat shops and repair stores cluster. Three marinas line the shores of False Creek, and sailboats, canoes, and kayaks abound.

Despite the presence of all the seafaring vessels, it should be noted that False Creek is not actually a creek. The name comes from the logbooks of a long-since-forgotten naval officer who, thinking the passage was a creek, guided his ship into it. Alas, it is simply an inlet. And now it is only half its original size, having been filled in during the Great Depression to create an industrial area.

False Creek may have shrunk, but it is still a popular paddling site. Each June the **CANADIAN INTERNATIONAL DRAGON BOAT FESTIVAL** (122 W 4th Ave; 604/688-2382) takes place here. Slender, brilliantly coloured, exotically decorated boats come from around the world to take part in the races. Each one is paddled by 20 people, with rhythmic assistance from a drummer and a steersman. The best viewing is from the north shore of False Creek, near the **PLAZA OF NATIONS,** or near **LEG-IN-BOOT SQUARE** on the south side. The festival also includes an international food fair and entertainment stage. *Mid-June, annually; www. canadadragonboat.com; map:U5.* &

2) STANLEY PARK

West end of Beach and W Georgia Sts to Lions Gate Bridge; 604/257-8400 Stanley Park's 404 hectares (1,000 acres), just west of the downtown core, may be the most cherished acreage in British Columbia, if not the whole country. Described by one local writer as a thousand-acre therapeutic couch, this is the park where Vancouverites come to unwind, from the Howe Street financial barons jogging off their adrenaline at lunch to the young kids who play in the sand on the weekends. Thanks to the farsightedness of the city's founders, this sacred turf has remained parkland since it was permanently designated as such in 1886. That much is agreed upon. Everything else about the use of the park is a matter of debate. The park is so beloved by locals that any change to the natural landscape, beyond trimming the hedges, is an issue of study and contention. In recent years, a free-concert-in-the-park offer by hometown hero Bryan Adams was turned down (no Central Park hucksterism here, thank you), as was an entreaty by Jaguar Motorcars to use the seawall as a backdrop for the unveiling of its new line of snazzy coupes.

So what's all the fuss about? Well, it's about natural woodlands—this is one of the last places in the Lower Mainland where you can stroll amid old-growth forests. It's also about manicured gardens, quiet lagoons, ocean beaches, winding trails, summer theatre, totem poles, an aquarium, and wildlife. Like squirrels—lots of them. In 1909, the City of New York presented Vancouver with a gift of eight pairs of gray squirrels for the park. Now the place is riddled with the critters. They almost outnumber the Canada geese. No worries; both the squirrels and geese are grateful for the place and are more than happy to pose for photos. Park officials ask that you please don't feed them or they will become dependent on human food.

Like the squirrels, attractions are scattered throughout the park. The best place to start is the **SEAWALL**, along which you can walk, run, cycle, or in-line skate. (Bike rental outlets are at Georgia and Denman Streets near the park entrance.) The seawall, the longest in Canada, is 10.5 kilometres (6.5 miles) long and features separate lanes for pedestrians and those on wheels (cyclists and rollerbladers). Finally completed in 1980, it took 60 years to build. To allow undiminished views, there are no handrails around the wall. The paved path is nice and wide, so falling off is not a concern. Just don't go too fast if you're cycling.

The entire seawall can be walked in 2½ hours at a brisk pace. Or you can take a day to stroll around it, veering off to check out the surrounding attractions, stopping for coffee or lunch, or sitting in the sun marvelling at the views, which are always incredible. Horse-drawn tours around the park are available May to October through **STANLEY PARK HORSE DRAWN TOURS** (lower zoo parking lot; 604/681-5115; www.stanleypark tours.com).

Near a statue of Lord Stanley are the formal **ROSE GARDENS**, surrounded by a mass of perennial plantings, just a few minutes' walk from the seawall. A popular place to start a walk around the seawall is **LOST LAGOON**, home to most of the park's geese, as well as turtles, a few fish, and some trumpeter swans. The fountain in the centre, built in 1936 to mark the park's Golden Jubilee, is illuminated at night. (A separate path

runs around the lagoon.) Single sculls and eight-person sculls from the
VANCOUVER ROWING CLUB (604/687-3400; www.rowing.vancouver.
bc.ca) can often be seen skimming over the harbour waters. A statue of
Scottish poet Robbie Burns is opposite the rowing club. A couple of minutes' walk inland from the seawall, in a country-garden-like setting, is the
STANLEY PARK PAVILION CAFETERIA, built in 1932 and now a heritage
building. It looks out onto **MALKIN BOWL,** an outdoor theatre where
revivals of classic Broadway plays are staged during July and August.
Artists display their wares along a walkway in an informal, outdoor
gallery atmosphere.

Spectacular totem poles carved by the Squamish people, the earliest
inhabitants of this coast, stand near **BROCKTON POINT.** Featured on
many a postcard, these totems have become symbols of Vancouver. Bring
your camera, and in the evenings, maybe your ear plugs; nearby is the
NINE O'CLOCK GUN, an old English sea cannon placed in the park over
100 years ago. Once used to call fishermen home at night, the sound of
the gun is now an evening ritual in the West End. Residents can check
their watches by the boom at 9pm. Be warned: it is loud!

On summer weekends watch an unhurried cricket match at **BROCK-
TON OVAL.** Just offshore, you can see Vancouver's nod to Copenhagen.
Girl in a Wet Suit, a bronze statute created by Elek Imredy, is one of the
few pieces of public art in this city that is recognizable on sight and appreciated by all. Enjoyed equally well is the slightly more mysterious "fire-
breathing" dragon mounted on the seawall nearby. This wooden
figurehead is a replica of the one that once fronted the SS *Empress of Japan,*
an early passenger ship that used to visit Vancouver.

Another well-known feature is **LUMBERMAN'S ARCH,** made of
Douglas fir, erected in 1952 to pay tribute to those in the logging industry. It sits in a meadow that is perfect for picnics or playing, with a
delightful children's water park by the ocean and a busy concession stand
nearby. Watch for the brave bunnies that hop in and out of the bushes.
This lively area was once a Native village, and literally tonnes of shells
from the village midden were used to surface the first road into the park
in 1888.

The most developed area of the park is the **VANCOUVER AQUARIUM**
(604/659-3474; www.vanaqua.org; see Vancouver Aquarium later in this
section). Nearby is the delightful **MINIATURE TRAIN.** Kids of all ages love
the short but satisfying trip of 1.2 kilometres (0.75 mile), through forest
and lake (weather permitting). While waiting to board the train, visit the
petting zoo with its resident peacock and other creatures.

BEAVER LAKE, speckled with water lilies, is a quiet place for contemplation or a gentle walk. Numerous forest trails weave through hemlock, cedar, Douglas fir, maple, and spruce. The lake is situated inland,

and although the trails are extremely popular with walkers and joggers, they're a bit isolated and should not be tackled solo.

As well as offering a panoramic view of the North Shore, **PROSPECT POINT** (north of Beaver Lake on the seawall) displays a cairn in memory of the Pacific Coast's pioneer steamship, the SS *Beaver*, which met its watery ruin in 1888. Nearby is the Prospect Point Cafe, with an outdoor deck overlooking **LIONS GATE BRIDGE** and the large, grassy Prospect Point picnic area, suitable for groups. Stanley Park Drive leads past the remains of the once-mighty Hollow Tree, whose split trunk is wide enough for cars to cruise through. Nearby stands a huge red cedar, which has become known as the **NATIONAL GEOGRAPHIC TREE**. The National Geographic Society believes this red cedar, almost 30 metres (99 feet) around, is the largest tree of its kind in the world.

Along the northwest strip of the seawall is **SIWASH ROCK**, a rocky, offshore pinnacle that has withstood the harsh elements for centuries. Various Native legends have been spun around this bluff, which has one tiny tree clinging to its top. **THIRD BEACH**, a wide, sandy swimming area, is nearby. At **FERGUSON POINT**, locals take visitors to gaze at the views from the comfort of the **TEAHOUSE RESTAURANT** (7501 Stanley Park Dr; 604/689-3281 or 800/280-9893; www.cyberpathway.com/teahouse/).

SECOND BEACH is one of the best places in town to watch the sunset, and children love the playground and picnic area. Several nights a week in summer, the paved area is awash with dancers—Scottish dancers, ballroom dancers, and square dancers all kick up their heels here. This is also a sports area, with a shuffleboard, a lawn bowling green, and busy tennis courts. In addition, there's a pitch-and-putt golf course, bordered by a spring-blooming rhododendron garden. The excellent **FISH HOUSE AT STANLEY PARK** (8901 Stanley Park Dr; 604/681-7275 or 877/681-7275; www.fishhousestanleypark.com) is a good place for either a casual lunch or a more formal dinner.

Numerous annual events are held in Stanley Park; call the **PARKS AND RECREATION BOARD** office (604/257-8400) for information and maps. *Map:D1.*

3) VANCOUVER'S BOTANICAL GARDENS

Various locations When the Shaughnessey Golf Club moved a few kilometres south in 1960, the aim was to turn its 22.25-hectare (55.63-acre) course into a posh subdivision of sprawling mansions. The local gentry, unconvinced that their neighbourhood needed more homes, lobbied the city, the provincial government, and the Vancouver Foundation (led by Mr. W. J. VanDusen) to buy the grounds and turn them into a botanical garden. The result: a world-class bed of flowers and a ranking among North America's top 10 gardens. Set against the distant backdrop of the North Shore mountains, the **VANDUSEN BOTANICAL GARDEN** (5251 Oak

St; 604/878-9274) offers a collection of small, specialized gardens within the framework of the main garden. Among its famous flora are hundreds of variations of rhododendrons. In the springtime, the Rhododendron Walk blazes with colour.

Nearby, the hexagonal Korean Pavilion is a focal point for the garden's Asian plant collection. Sculptures abound on the lawns, under trees, between shrubs, and in the Children's Garden, where a chubby cherub presides over a wishing fountain. A latticework of paths wanders through 40 theme gardens, skirting lakes and ponds, crossing bridges, and winding through stands of bamboo and giant redwoods. There is also a maze, walled by 1,000 pyramidal cedars. Planted in 1981, the maze is a children's delight and a favoured location for local TV and movie producers who need a spooky setting. Once you've seen all the flowers, kick back at **SHAUGHNESSY RESTAURANT** (5251 Oak St; 604/261-0011), a nice spot in a serene garden atmosphere. *Every day; Oct–Mar 10am–4pm, Apr 10am–6pm, May 10am–8pm, June to mid-Aug 10am–9pm, mid-Aug to end of Sept 10am–6pm; www.vandusen garden.org; map:D4.*

Second only to VanDusen as an object of local devotion is the **UBC BOTANICAL GARDEN** (6804 SW Marine Dr; 604/822-9666). Spread over 28 rambling hectares (70 acres) overlooking the Strait of Georgia, the garden is festooned with over 10,000 different trees, shrubs, and flowers, including the largest collection of rhododendrons in the country. The grounds are divided into five distinct gardens, each with a different theme and character. The David C. Lam Asian Garden houses one of North America's leading collection of Asian plants. Surrounded by a second-growth coastal forest of firs, cedars, and hemlocks, the Asian Garden hosts maples, clematis, viburnums, and over 400 varieties of rhododendrons. Climbing roses and flowering vines twine around the trees, and the rare blue Himalayan poppy and giant Himalayan lily bloom here.

The BC Native Garden displays more than 3,500 of the plants found throughout the province. A sinuous stone path through 3 hectares (8 acres) of biodiversity offers great views of the bog laurel, Labrador tea, cranberry, and sundew. The E. H. Lohbrunner Alpine Garden lives up to the challenge of growing high-elevation plants at sea level. This garden has one of the largest alpine collections in North America; its west-facing slopes, specially imported soil, and boulders and rocks protect low-growing mountain plants from Australia, South America, Europe, Asia, and Africa. Based on a Dutch engraving, the Physick Garden re-creates a 16th-century monastic herb garden. The traditional plants, which grow in raised brick beds, can all be used for medicinal purposes. England's Chelsea Physic Garden is the source for many of the plants here.

The Food Garden is an amazing example of efficient gardening. Tucked into 0.10 hectare (0.75 acre), it's a patchwork of a dozen raised beds and more than 180 fruit trees, and successfully grows a cornucopia of crops, including warm-season ones such as cantaloupes. Fruit and vegetables are harvested regularly and donated to the Salvation Army. Regular lectures, on everything from pruning to growing trees in containers, are available for gardeners. *Every day; 10am–6pm; www.hedgerows. com/ubcbotgdn/index.htm; map:A3.*

4) GASTOWN

Hastings St and Water St between Homer St and Columbia St This is the edge of Vancouver, from which the city originally grew. Founded in 1867, the neighbourhood takes its name from its first notable inhabitant, Gassy Jack Deighton, a former river pilot famed for his verbal relentlessness (hence the nickname). After giving up the riverboat game, Gassy Jack started his own pub, the Globe Saloon. It was around this drinking hole that the community of Granville grew. In 1886, however, a Canadian Pacific Railway fire ripped out of control, destroying all but two of the original houses in less an hour. After the blaze, the city shifted westward and was rechristened Vancouver. Eventually, the old neighbourhood disintegrated into a beer-soused skid-row area.

In the late 1960s, renovation and restoration of the district began. The streets were paved with cobblestones and red brick, decorative street lamps were installed, and trees were planted in front of the boutiques and restaurants that had just moved in. In 1971, Gastown was designated a heritage site. Urban historians and heritage planners from across North America have since flocked here to study the stunning revival of the neighbourhood.

In Gastown, all streets—Carrall, Powell, Water, and Alexander—lead to Maple Tree Square. Nightclubs, art galleries, antique stores, coffee bars, and jazz and rock music clubs all add to the attraction of this vibrant place. Gassy Jack himself has not been forgotten—his statue stands proudly near the centre of Maple Tree Square.

The 2-tonne **GASTOWN STEAM CLOCK,** on the corner of Cambie and Water Streets, operates on steam tapped from the underground pipes of nearby buildings. The 5-metre (16.4-foot)-tall clock whistles every 15 minutes, sending forth clouds of steam every hour. With its big, four-sided glass face, 20-kilogram (44-pound) gold-plated pendulum, and Gothic roof, the clock is a popular stop for photographers. Around the corner and beside the train tracks, Ray Saunders, who designed the clock, has a store filled with antique timepieces.

Also nearby is **GAOLERS MEWS.** One of the few surviving legacies of the pre-1886 neighbourhood, this cobblestone, brick-strewn courtyard hosted the city's first ne'er-do-wells. The only remaining evidence of the mews' original purpose are the name and the cast-iron bars along the back of the Irish Heather. Swept up in Gastown's revamping, the mews now resembles some of the finer nooks of Old Montreal (complete with Victorian street lamps and potted plants). The cobblestone lanes continue out back to Blood Alley, without doubt the quaintest parking lot in the city. *Map:U3–V4.*

5) CHINATOWN

Between Abbott St and Heatley St, Prior St and Powell St No rickshaw drivers or chickens being chopped on the sidewalks, but as close as you'll get to Shanghai without a visa. Crowded between Carrall Street and Gore Avenue, Chinatown is the heart of a bustling bazaar of produce hawkers loudly promoting their wares. The market overflows with exotic vegetables, fruit, and seafood of various descriptions. It's easy to lose a few hours here, wandering through the tiny, incense-perfumed stores, examining the jade, ivory, rattan, brass, silk, and brocade. Navigate the busy sidewalks (dodging women laden with bulging shopping bags) and admire streetlights decorated with golden dragons, phone booths topped with pagoda-style roofs, and ornamental street signs, in both Chinese and English.

Enticing aromas waft from the bakeries and restaurants, with their steamed-up windows. Inside, Cantonese chefs are likely to be chopping at a furious pace, whipping up anything from stewed beef brisket to fried bean curd. The service tends to race at a Hong Kong clip, lightning fast, with little chatter. Orders occasionally get lost in the translation. You might get bruised gluten instead of braised eggplant, but the prices are generally cheap and the portions are generous. Culinarily speaking, the restaurants here are an ideal warm-up for anyone considering a trip to Asia.

This neighbourhood dates backs to the 1850s, when Chinese immigrants began arriving here to build the railways. By 1890, Vancouver's Chinese population exceeded 1,000, many of whom ran their own businesses. Now it is the second-largest Chinatown in North America, bustling with so many shops, restaurants, and cultural attractions that multilevel malls and parkades have been built to ease the congestion. Don't miss the open-air market, which runs from 6pm to midnight at Main and Keefer Streets during summer months.

Rumour has it that below these streets are hidden a slew of underground tunnels. Urban myth or local fact? It's a controversial mystery. One such passage did exist; it was inadvertently discovered below Alexandra Street by city work crews, who had cut through the pavement to find only air. The tunnel was quickly filled in.

On the corner of Pender and Carrall Streets is a building famous for being the world's narrowest. The **SAM KEE BUILDING**, built in 1913, is only 1.8 metres (6 feet) wide and two storeys tall. Once a store that sold beautiful silks, it is now an insurance office. *Map:U4–V4.*

6) GROUSE MOUNTAIN AND THE GROUSE GRIND

6400 Nancy Greene Wy, top of Capilano Rd, North Vancouver; 604/984-0661 Sailing 1,128 metres (3,700 feet) through the sky in an aerial tramway has to be one of the most breathtaking—and pleasurable—ways to ascend a mountain. Once at the summit of Grouse Mountain, you'll find the scenery amazing. Feathery firs stand just beneath you, the city spreads out at your feet, and Washington State's San Juan Islands—more than 160 kilometres (100 miles) to the south—are visible. Well-known as a snowboarding and skiing haven, Grouse Mountain offers a different scene in summer. For hiking diehards as well as those who prefer relaxing strolls, Grouse has the answer.

The **SKYRIDE**, an enclosed gondola, glides up the mountain and drops you into the centre of the alpine activities. A chairlift will take you right to the peak for additional breathtaking views and enchanting sunsets.

At the base of the mountain, a notice board outside the Skyride station has general information and a map of the trails. Once the lonely pursuit of the bushwhacking set, the **GROUSE GRIND** has recently become the city's sweatiest see-and-be-seen hiking strip. Last year, 140,000 enthusiasts scrambled up the rocky 2.9-kilometre (1.8-mile) incline, from the foot of Grouse to the beer and nachos nirvana of **BAR '98**. The Grouse Grind is a particularly popular evening hike. In the summer, the Skyride parking lot fills by 5:30pm, and within an hour, 400-plus are normally on the trail. But don't join the flock if you're not ready for a workout. It's not called the Grind for nothing. Staff recommend sensible shoes and at least one water bottle. One and a half hours is the average hiking time. Those in a rush should know the record: 27 minutes, 10 seconds. It's free to hike, but if you don't want to schlep back down, spend $5 to ride the gondola.

For the younger ones, there's an adventure playground at the top of Grouse. In summer, pony rides and horse-drawn wagons are there to entertain. There are also helicopter tours available if you want to go higher. Round out the perfect day with a visit to the multimedia **THEATRE IN THE SKY** or attend one of a series of summer concerts.

7) THE BRIDGES OF VANCOUVER

Various locations Blessed with an elegant wire-and-iron design—and a fabulous location—**LIONS GATE BRIDGE** is unquestionably one of the most beautiful bridges in Canada. It takes its name from the two mountain peak "Lions" on the North Shore. Connecting North Vancouver and downtown, this bridge is the stuff of countless postcards and endless intrigue, but now, nobody knows what to do with it. Recently, one lost soul flung himself off the 472-metre (1,548-foot) main span into the frosty, 13-km/h (24-mph) current of Burrard Inlet. Taunting death, he swam to shore. Like him, Lions Gate is a resilient enigma. Built in 1938 for $6 million, the big daddy of local bridges remains a conundrum: too narrow

147

for the amount of traffic it supports, too old to fix, too breathtaking to dismantle. With more than 60,000 to 70,000 cars crossing it daily, its future is a mystery waiting to be solved. *Map:D1.*

Neither as sleek nor as stylish as its colleague to the west, the **SECOND NARROWS BRIDGE** is wider and, unlike Lions Gate Bridge, able to handle heavy truck traffic; it receives most of the volume and is much safer during earthquakes. It wasn't always so secure. Midway through construction in June 1958, the north anchor arm buckled, killing 18 workers. It took $19 million, the lives of five more people, and two more years before the 3.2-kilometre (2-mile) span was finally finished. In 1994, the Second Narrows was renamed the Ironworkers Memorial Bridge. Once the heartbreak hill of the Vancouver Marathon, the bridge's steep, north-ward pitch recently forced the race to relocate. *Map:F1.*

If not the most visually dramatic toll bridge ever invented, the **CAPILANO SUSPENSION BRIDGE** (3735 Capilano Rd, North Vancouver; 604/985-7474) is certainly the most popular. Swaying 70 metres (230 feet) above the Capilano River Canyon, this skyway is built mainly of cedar and hemp. The bridge was inspired by an 1888 display at the Glasgow International Exhibition. A year later, Scottish engineer George Mackay moved to BC and began paving the Capilano Gorge. Stringing up the 137-metre (449-foot) span was his first step. It remains the longest and highest suspended footbridge in the world. Although always an enormous tourist attraction (830,000 visitors last year), this bridge gained further attention in 1999 when a 17-month-old infant fell from her mother's arms and miraculously survived a 47-metre (154-foot) plunge into the trees below. *Every day; winter 9am–5pm, summer 8:30am–dusk; www.capbridge.com; map:D0.*

Although shorter than its Capilano cousin a few kilometres away, the **LYNN CANYON SUSPENSION BRIDGE** is every bit as breathtaking. And even better, it's free of charge. Connecting Lynn Canyon Park with the fabulous hiking trails of Seymour Demonstration Forest, this narrow wooden walkway is very near the parking lot at the entrance of the park. Swinging 82 metres (269 feet) above Lynn Creek, the bridge offers spectacular views of the steep cliffs and tree-lined edges of the canyon. The bridge, park, and creek are extremely popular sites, attracting both tourists and locals year-round. *Map:G0.*

Originally designed with two decks—an upper level for cars and a lower level for trains—the **BURRARD BRIDGE** was built in 1932 to better serve the West Side "suburbs" of Kitsilano, Shaughnessy, and neighbouring areas. This bridge is distinguished by the huge concrete portals, complete with illuminated windows, at each end. In deference to the art deco style so popular at the time, the Vancouver Public Art Commission demanded that engineers build the portals to camouflage the bridge's steel structure and also insisted on a single deck. The bridge is now a major thoroughfare for downtown traffic. *Map:Q5.*

8) MUSEUM OF ANTHROPOLOGY

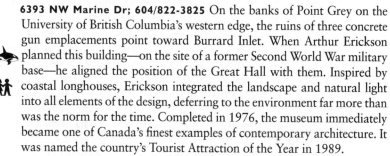

6393 NW Marine Dr; 604/822-3825 On the banks of Point Grey on the University of British Columbia's western edge, the ruins of three concrete gun emplacements point toward Burrard Inlet. When Arthur Erickson planned this building—on the site of a former Second World War military base—he aligned the position of the Great Hall with them. Inspired by coastal longhouses, Erickson integrated the landscape and natural light into all elements of the design, deferring to the environment far more than was the norm for the time. Completed in 1976, the museum immediately became one of Canada's finest examples of contemporary architecture. It was named the country's Tourist Attraction of the Year in 1989.

From the moment you walk through the museum's carved wooden doors, it is hard to tell which is more awe-inspiring—the building or its contents. In the **GREAT HALL**, monumental totem poles, studded with carvings of ravens, bears, eagles, frogs, and beavers, gaze into the distance, seemingly imbued with the spirit of Northwest Coast Native artisans. Spotlit on a podium is **THE RAVEN AND THE FIRST MEN** by Haida artist Bill Reid, depicting how the mythic Raven tricked the first people into emerging from their clamshell. Reid's smaller works, in gold, silver, wood, and argillite, are also on display. The museum uses a visible storage system. Visitors are encouraged to open any of the dozens of drawers that contain one of the most comprehensive collections of Northwest Coast Native artifacts in the world, as well as objects from other cultures for the purpose of comparison. The **KOERNER CERAMICS GALLERY** displays a collection of 600 European ceramics unique to North America, as well as specially commissioned ceramics and textiles by contemporary Vancouver artists. The **MASTERPIECE GALLERY** has carved works in silver, gold, stone, and wood. As well as this amazing permanent collection, there are ever-changing temporary exhibits and many special events. Even better, Tuesdays are free from 5 to 9pm. The gift shop is excellent.

Outside, between the museum and the Point Grey cliffs, is the outdoor sculpture garden, which includes 10 **TOTEM POLES** towering over grassy knolls and two beautifully carved Haida houses that blend perfectly into the cliffside setting. The work is by some of the finest contemporary First Nations artists of the coast, including Bill Reid, Douglas Cranmer, Norman Tait, Walter Harris, Joe David, Jim Hart, and the late Mungo Martin. Signs give information about the spirit beings represented on the poles, as well as the history of the buildings. You can enjoy the totem poles and the breathtaking views from this little park whether the museum is open or not. *Mid-May to Labour Day Wed–Mon 10am–5pm, Tues 10am–9pm; Labour Day to mid-May Wed–Sun 11am–5pm, Tues 11am–9pm; www.moa.ubc.ca; map:A2.*

9) LIGHTHOUSE PARK

Marine Dr to Beacon Ln, West Vancouver Driving along West Vancouver's Marine Drive, where houses are perched atop cliffs, you might expect to find a beach park, but instead you'll find a dense forest edged with rock. No logging has been allowed here since the area was set aside as a reserve in 1881. Numerous trails, long and short, meander through the park and to the tidal pools. Allow at least a half day for exploring. There are maps and information boards in the large parking lot, which can fill up early on summer Sundays. The main trail to the ocean and the **POINT ATKINSON LIGHTHOUSE** (built in 1914) is well marked, a mere 10-minute downhill walk through gigantic Douglas firs, some 61 metres (200 feet) tall and 2 metres (6.5 feet) in diameter. Tours of the lighthouse are given daily in summer—just show up. Take a sweater, since it can be cool in the woods. Unspoiled wilderness only 30 minutes from downtown Vancouver, spectacular sunsets. *www.vancouver-lodging.com/attractions.html.*

10) PACIFIC STARLIGHT DINNER TRAIN

1311 W 1st St, North Vancouver; 604/984-5246 or 800/363-3733 The Pacific Starlight Dinner Train follows the beautiful Sea-to-Sky coastline between North Vancouver and Porteau Cove, just south of Squamish. Operating Wednesday to Sunday evenings from June to October, the dinner train offers guests a three-course haute-cuisine meal and sumptuous views of the Pacific **COAST MOUNTAINS**, set against the waters of **HOWE SOUND**.

Purchased from the Spirit of Washington Dinner Train in 1997, the nine vintage stock cars, each named after a big-band tune or famous jazz locale—Manhattan, Moonglow, Indigo—are refurbished in the art deco style of the 1920s and '30s. Harking back to the days of rail romance, the coaches hug the cliff edges of the coast while chugging along to the boogie-woogie of the big-band era.

The evening starts just before 6pm at the **BC RAIL STATION** in North Vancouver. Limousines begin lining up in front of the station as anniversary couples, seniors' tour groups, and young tourists stream out of the backseats of stretch Caddies and make their way into the lobby. Officially, the limos have no connection with the dinner train, but they seem to be the most popular way of arriving, thus adding a certain elegance to the proceedings. The dress code verges on the semiformal: sport coats, summer frocks, and the occasional tux, but more casual than coattail. Inside the lobby, the jazz quartet Night Train swings through the standards as intrepid couples dance and everyone else mills around the station, waiting for the train to board.

Slightly after 6pm, guests are invited to find their seats. The train is divided into six salon coaches and three dome cars. Under a glassy sunroof, the dome cars offer better views and are slightly more expensive. At 6:15pm sharp, the trains pulls away from the station, dips under **LIONS GATE BRIDGE**, and heads toward the leafy boulevards and waterfront mansions of West Vancouver, passing so close you can see what people are having for dinner.

From there it's on to **HORSESHOE BAY** and **PORTEAU COVE**. ("Porteau" comes from the French phrase *porte d'eau,* meaning "water gate.") The swinging starts in earnest at Porteau Cove, as the band runs through popular dance classics near the front of the station. Alternatively, you can wander down to the pier for closer views of Howe Sound. Around 8:30pm, the train heads back down the coast toward **NORTH VANCOUVER**, finally pulling in 9:45pm.

The prices vary, according to the time of year, the dining car, and the nature of your excursion. The rates dip slightly in October for Sunday brunch on board, and are a bit more expensive for the Murder Mystery evenings. The standard price for a seat in the salon car is $82.95; for the dome car it is $99.95. This price includes meal taxes and tips. Beverages are extra.

Although the dinner train has only been running for a few years, it has become a popular excursion for Vancouverites. Far from being an attraction only for out-of-towners, the overwhelming majority of riders continue to be local. *www.bcrail.com/starlight/index.htm; map:D1.*

11) SEABUS AND LONSDALE QUAY

Burrard Inlet and North Vancouver Definitely the most affordable cruise in Vancouver, the **SEABUS** (Cordova St at Granville; 604/521-0400), also one of the most scenic, sails back and forth between the beautifully renovated **WATERFRONT STATION** in downtown Vancouver and Lonsdale Quay in North Vancouver. The station, a former Canadian Pacific Railway terminus, is now a destination in itself. Here, above small shops and coffee bars, a series of wonderful paintings depict the Rocky Mountains. The station is also the Vancouver terminus for the **SKYTRAIN** automated light rapid-transit service and the *West Coast Express* commuter train to the Fraser Valley. It's a gorgeous heritage building. If you want to buy blueberries and other fresh produce, hop the SeaBus and cruise over to Lonsdale Quay.

The SS *Burrard Beaver* and the SS *Burrard Otter*—little foot-passenger-only ferries—zip across the sheltered waters of Burrard Inlet in less than 15 minutes, much faster than their predecessors did at the turn of the last century. In 1900, years before any major bridges were built, a ferry chugged the same route. But the inlet wasn't as busy back then. Now the SeaBus must navigate through a thicket of freighters, cruise ships, sailboats, and even the occasional windsurfer. No need to worry—leave those distractions for the captain. Instead, simply enjoy the views.

To the north tower the Coast Mountains, to the west lies Stanley Park, framed by Lions Gate Bridge. Southward, office towers and high-rises cluster behind the shining sails of Canada Place. Dramatic during the day, the SeaBus is equally enchanting in the evening, when the city lights are reflected on the water. *Every day; hours vary; www.translink.bc.ca; map:U3.*

When the ride ends, you're at **LONSDALE QUAY MARKET** (123 Carrie Cates Court, North Vancouver; 604/985-6261), a multilevel mall of shops, boutiques, and restaurants. At ground level, the public market offers an array of fruits and vegetables, fish, breads, flowers, and meats. Have coffee outside in the sunshine and admire the stunning view. On the second floor are gift shops and boutiques, and on the third level is the entrance to the **LONSDALE QUAY HOTEL** (604/986-6111). *Lonsdale Quay Market open Sat–Thurs 9:30am–6:30pm, Fri 9:30am–9pm; www.lonsdalequay.com; map:E3.*

Make a left turn at the SeaBus terminal to get to **WATERFRONT PARK**. There's plenty to see along the paved walkway that surrounds this small park. Along the seawall, plaques identify several outstanding downtown buildings, and a huge modern sculpture, *Cathedral*, by Douglas Senft, sits on the lawn. At **SAILOR'S POINT PLAZA**, dedicated to those who have lost their lives at sea, sits an elegant sundial by Tim Osborne, titled *Timelines*. A plaque also commemorates **CAPTAIN GEORGE VANCOUVER**, the first English explorer to Burrard Inlet. At the far end of the park, the **PACIFIC MARINE TRAINING INSTITUTE** (265 W Esplanade, North Vancouver; 604/985-0622) is full of boats, ropes, and outboard engines for students working toward a marine career. During the summer this park is busy. Concerts are held on many Sunday afternoons, and numerous clubs hold festivals, exhibits, dances, and competitions here. *Map:E1.*

12) KITSILANO BEACH

Cornwall Ave and Arbutus St, bordering English Bay Named after Chief Khahtsahlano of the Squamish First Nation, Kits Beach has become an institution, a year-round haven for joggers, dog-walkers, and evening strollers. In the summer, they're joined by swimmers and sun worshippers in search of warm rays and safe swimming. The beach has become a top volleyball venue as well. Equally popular are the nearby tennis courts, basketball courts, and children's play area.

Open during the summer season, **KITSILANO POOL** (north foot of Yew St; 604/731-0011) is one of the largest outdoor pools in the city, with lanes for serious swimmers and a separate section for young splashers. Replacing the high-tide "draw and fill" basin carved into the banks of English Bay, this 1979 Kits addition has tried to stay true to its original roots. The pool fills up in the spring with saltwater, but now freshwater is pumped in to save the filters and foundation. Kits remains one of the last pools in North America to use the briny stuff. Its loyalty to swimmer-healthy seawater is appreciated; the pool averages over 150,000 visitors during its three-month season. At 133 metres (436 feet) in length, it almost triples the Olympic standard.

On the south side of the pool is the **KITSILANO SHOWBOAT** (2300 Cornwall Ave; 604/734-7332), a favoured venue for beachside entertainment since 1935. Three times a week, amateur troupes can be seen singing and dancing here, weather permitting. Nearby is the shoreline path beloved of dogs and joggers. The route curves along the main beach area, past the **MARITIME MUSEUM** (1905 Ogden Ave; 604/257-8300; www.vmm.bc.ca), the **VANCOUVER MUSEUM** (1100 Chestnut St; 604/736-4431; www.vanmuseum.bc.ca), and the **PLANETARIUM** (1100 Chestnut St; 604/733-6113; pacific-space-centre.bc.ca), all the way to Granville Island. The whole route is a pleasant 30-minute walk. *Map:N5–N6.*

13) SCIENCE WORLD/ALCAN OMNIMAX THEATRE

1455 Quebec St; 604/443-7443 Rivaling Canada Place as the architectural symbol of the city is **SCIENCE WORLD**'s geodesic white bubble, shimmering on the eastern edges of False Creek. To children, the futuristic dome means Science World, an interactive—and educational—playland of lights, sounds, and physics experiments. To longtime residents though, the "golf ball" is a pleasant reminder of the headiness of Expo 86. During the world's fair, the dome served as Expo Centre.

The dome is as busy and popular today as it was back then. Science World features permanent and travelling exhibits that dazzle the senses, offering hands-on experiences involve everything from real tornadoes to exploding frozen zucchinis. Three main galleries explore the realms of biology, physics, and music; the fourth gallery is reserved for travelling exhibits. There is also a great gift shop with, suitably enough, a science-oriented theme.

Equipped with an enormous wrap-around screen and a thunderous sound system, the **ALCAN OMNIMAX THEATRE** presents IMAX films. Admission to Omnimax and Science World is $14.75 for adults and $10.50 for students, children, and seniors; admission only to the theatre is $10 daily. Admission to double features on Wednesday and Sunday nights is $11.25 adults and $9 students, children, and seniors. Weekdays, 10am–5pm; Wednesday and Sunday double features start at 7:30pm. *Map:V6.*

14) VANCOUVER AQUARIUM

Stanley Park; 604/659-3474 The aquarium is in Stanley Park (covered earlier in this section), but it's such a favourite with locals and visitors that it deserves a ranking of its own. Many in the city have mixed feelings about the role of aquariums—do they preserve or imprison animals?

Regardless of the debate, this aquarium consistently ranks among the best in North America. Setting the tone, and guarding the entrance, is Haida artist Bill Reid's magnificent 5.5-metre (18-foot) bronze killer whale sculpture, in its own reflecting pool. Inside, the Arctic, the Amazon, and places in between await you. With more than 8,000 species of aquatic life from the world's seas and oceans, the aquarium has received kudos as an important educational and research facility. It provides tours, talks, films, and field trips.

A highlight of the aquarium is the beluga and killer whale shows, held in the $14-million marine mammal area. The whales eat up to 60 kilograms (132 pounds) of food each day. While cavorting as they would in the wild, breaching and performing other maneuvers, they also soak the unwary—the "splash area" by the pool is well named.

The **PACIFIC NORTHWEST HABITAT** area offers a close look at inhabitants from the local waters, including playful sea otters and gliding octopuses. Scuba divers feed the fish and harvest kelp fronds. The **AMAZON GALLERY,** 10 years in planning, is the only exhibition of its kind in Canada and re-creates part of the Amazon basin environment. Fish, reptiles, birds, insects, and plants thrive in the tropical humidity, created partly by computer-generated tropical rainstorms. The creatures in the gallery are amazing—four-eyed fish, scarlet ibises, anacondas, and fluorescent fish. The **ARCTIC CANADA** exhibition allows visitors to hear the language of the whales, walruses, and seals of the cold blue world beneath the northern ice. Fascinating displays illustrate just how fragile this hostile northern environment is. You can go nose-to-nose with a smiling, curious beluga whale. *Every day; June 25–Sept 7 9:30am–7pm, Sept 8–June 24 10am–5:30pm, Christmas and New Year's noon–5pm; www.vanaqua.org; map:D1.*

15) ROBSON STREET

Beatty St to Stanley Park If Vancouver is Hollywood North, Robson Street is our Rodeo Drive, a relentlessly trendy boulevard of pret-a-porter boutiques and swank eateries. Longtime residents mourn the loss of the schnitzel houses and Bavarian bakeries that once graced "Robsonstrasse," but the street now thrives with the fresh styles of a fashion catalogue. Saddled with some of the steepest commercial rents in the country, Robson retailers are comforted with a simple challenge: stay hip or find a cheaper strip. Success is rewarded—50,000 people stroll Robson's sidewalks on weekdays, 85,000 on weekends.

The street spans the city's central core, linking the entertainment district on downtown's eastern edges to Stanley Park in the West End. In between are shops, restaurants, and hotels. The street used to have a distinctly local, if slightly upscale, look. Over the past several years, though, the old wooden facades and two-storey stores and houses were bulldozed to make room for the glass and chrome cathedrals of international fashion. With the shift, window shopping has become a whole new experience. Robson is so popular with pedestrians that the stores of companies such as **SWATCH, NIKE,** and **GUESS** function more as 3-D advertisements than traditional shops. To stroll down Robson is to sample a series of walk-in billboards, sensory-enhanced environments designed to showcase merchandise (be it sneakers or swimsuits) and dazzle shoppers. Swatch features a marble floor from Italy. Nike displays the not-for-sale sneakers of NBA superstars. The street has morphed into a funky retail playland, where moving the goods is second to making a eye-popping, surround-sound statement.

In response, Vancouverites and tourists have voted with their feet. On weekend evenings in the summer, the crowds are so dense that the city posts cops at every corner just to keep the traffic moving. Some stores are flooded with up to 1,500 visitors a day. The two **STARBUCKS** outlets on the corner of Robson and Thurlow, combined, make more than 2,800 cups of java each day. *Map:Q2–V5.*

16) VANCOUVER ART GALLERY

750 Hornby St; 604/662-4719 Designed in 1907 by Victoria architect Francis Rattenbury—who also designed the Empress Hotel and the Parliament Buildings in Victoria—the former provincial courthouse, with its impressive stone lions and Greek columns, now houses the Vancouver Art Gallery. As part of the revamping of Robson Street, architect Arthur Erickson transformed the courthouse's cramped interior into four spacious floors, flooding them with light from the new glass-topped dome above the elegant rotunda.

The **EMILY CARR GALLERY** is filled with the work of British Columbia's most revered artist. A native of Vancouver Island, Emily Carr depicted the majesty of the coastal rain forests, towering totem poles, and the Natives who created them. Many of these works are from the turn of the last century. The other floors feature temporary exhibits. There is usually "one big show" each summer. Otherwise, there are travelling exhibits of photography, video, or sculpture, or selections from the gallery's permanent collection, which focuses on contemporary local, Canadian, and North American art. Other works in the collection are by the Group of Seven and European masters.

The **CHILDREN'S GALLERY** (604/682-5621) also has changing exhibits. Short talks are held several times a week. There are children's and adult workshops, as well as concerts, and one of the upper floors has a hands-on artists' studio in which children can create their own artworks.

The **GIFT SHOP,** off the main lobby, is an excellent place for unusual souvenirs, as well as postcards, posters, jewellery, books, and prints. Visit the **GALLERY CAFE** for coffee or lunch. Sit outside if weather permits and watch the crowds on Robson Street. On the Georgia Street side of the art gallery are attractive, well-kept gardens and the **CENTENNIAL FOUN-TAIN**. Surrounded by a blue, green, and white mosaic, the carvings on the rough-hewn rock in the centre depict Celtic legends. Designed in 1966 by R. H. Savery, the fountain commemorates the union of the Crown colonies of BC and Vancouver Island in 1866. *Fri–Wed 10am– 5:30pm, Thurs 10am–9pm, statutory holidays noon–5pm; www.vanart gallery.bc.ca; map:S4.* &

17) A TASTE OF THE ORIENT IN RICHMOND
Between Granville St and No. 3 Rd, Cook Rd and Cooney St Can't afford Hong Kong? Start your Asian tour in Richmond, at the **RADISSON PRESIDENT HOTEL** (8181 Cambie Rd, Richmond; 604/276-8181). This is Vancouver's new, postmodern Chinatown, where Asian pop culture meets the western strip mall. No dragons, Ming designs, or decorative shops here—this swath of parking lots and big boxes is, on one level, sub-urban planning at its bleakest. However, inside the several large shopping malls that form the core of so-called "Asia West," you can find convinc-ing iterations of suburban life in Tokyo (**YAOHAN CENTRE**, 3700 No. 3 Rd, Richmond; 604/231-0601), Taipei (**PRESIDENT PLAZA**, 3320-8181 Cambie Rd, Richmond; 604/270-8677), or Hong Kong (**ABERDEEN CEN-TRE**, 4151 Hazelbridge Wy, Richmond; 604/270-1234; **PARKER PLACE**, 2035-4311 Hazelbridge Wy, Richmond; 604/273-0276; and **FAIRCHILD SQUARE**, 4400 Hazelbridge Wy, Richmond; 604/273-1234). From the rambutans of Johor to the calligraphies of Shanghai, the wares of Asia are on sale. The humble food courts provide the widest range of Asian street food to be found outside that continent.

Don't miss the **BUDDHIST TEMPLE** in the President Plaza (the only mall in the Western hemisphere with one). The temple offers more than food for the soul. Buddhists and non-Buddhist visitors alike are offered free vegetarian lunch (with a view of the North Shore mountains) after the Sunday worship ceremonies that are conducted from 10am to 12:30pm. Select a fish from the tanks in the **T & T SUPERMARKET,** and they will deep-fry it for you while you shop. Or try the street food in the food courts: Sin-gaporean curries, Vietnamese pho, Northern Chinese dim sum, Chiu Chow stir-fries, Hong Kong coffee shop–style food, or Japanese yakitori. Order a Taiwanese pearl milk tea at the **LITTLE TEA HOUSE** or head to **TEN REN TEA & GINSENG.** They have complimentary ginger or ginseng tea on tap, but if you show even the slightest interest, you'll be invited to share a private tea ceremony. Before you leave, purchase stamps in Chi-nese for your postcards from the **CHINESE POST OFFICE.** *Map:D6.*

18) STEVESTON

Chatham Rd south to Fraser River Once the biggest fishing port on the West Coast, with over 50 canneries and 10,000 people crowding the boardwalks, Steveston is now bereft of active canneries. It remains a popular weekend destination for both tourists and locals, however, who buy prawns, crab, halibut, cod, and salmon fresh from the boats. Sitting at the mouth of the Fraser River, which still has the largest salmon run in North America, this community on the south side of Richmond is home to the largest fleet of commercial fishing vessels on Canada's west coast.

Parks Canada recently reopened the former **GULF OF GEORGIA CANNERY** (Fourth Ave, Steveston; 604/664-9009; www.harbour.com/parks can/ggc/) as a national historic site. Along with the historical fishing village, the cannery is a must-see on the Steveston itinerary. You may catch old-timers repairing an old wooden seiner in the massive **BRITANNIA HERITAGE SHIPYARD**.

Japanese Canadians helped build Steveston, and their heritage is still very much present in the community. They play an active role in the fishing industry, and nearby is the first **DOJO** (martial arts centre) to be built outside of Japan.

The **DIKES** that surround the southwestern edges of Steveston are ideal for a long stroll. Give yourself two to three hours to complete the walk. Great views of the waterfront can be found here, as well as glimpses of sea lions and blue herons. After your walk, pick up takeout at **DAVE'S FISH AND CHIPS** (3460 Moncton Rd, Steveston; 604/271-7555) or spoon chowder (in summer only) at **PAJO'S**, a boat restaurant anchored at the dock. *Map:C7.*

19) LOCARNO AND JERICHO BEACHES

NW Marine Dr between Trimble St and Blanca St The oldest settlement in Point Grey is **LOCARNO**. The beach, one of the most spectacular in the city, has bones and shells, once part of a Native midden, dating back 3,000 years. At low tide it appears possible to walk to West Vancouver, across miles of tide-rippled sand speckled with shallow tidal pools. Warmed by the sun, these pools are perfect for children. Seagulls stalk the water's edge, herons hunch in the shallows, and eagles sometimes circle overhead. A wide dirt path, well used by walkers and cyclists, runs along the top of the beach. Between the path and the road is a broad, grassy area with picnic tables and benches. A few trees bestow shade. All along this shoreline you can see the green of Stanley Park, the wilderness of Lighthouse Park, and the gleaming fingers of the high-rises in the West End.

Locarno and **JERICHO** beaches blend into each other. Jericho—the name is a corruption of Jerry's Cove, named for Jerry Rogers, who cut timber on the slopes above the cove in the mid-19th century—offers the same beautiful views as Locarno. A Japanese-style bridge arches over a pond shaded by willows that stand in the middle of the park just back from the beach. Together with **SPANISH BANKS BEACH,** the seemingly limitless shoreline offers a beach lovers', windsurfers', and sailors' paradise. *Map:B2.*

20) WRECK BEACH

Point Grey, Musqueam Reserve to Spanish Banks West Somewhere along the steep, muddy path that leads down the University of British Columbia's western bluff, the social fabric loosens and the tight stitches of inhibition tear open. By the time you're at the portable toilets near the edge of Wreck Beach, it's off with the modesty and into the full frontal— clothing is optional here. Aside from a few bundled-up rubberneckers scoping the shoreline, most Wreckies take full advantage of Canada's only Speedo-free beach. The 6-kilometre (3.6-mile)-long stretch of sand and rock, washed by the currents of the **FRASER RIVER, STRAIT OF GEORGIA,** and **ENGLISH BAY,** has become a mecca for an estimated 100,000 sun worshippers determined to avoid tan lines each summer.

Officially, the beach stretches from the Musqueam Reserve to Spanish Banks West, but each section is subtly divided up among the habitués. On the northern flank you tend to find a greater concentration of men, enjoying the wilderness and each other's company. (Although naturalism is encouraged, overt sexual activity runs counter to the Wreck way.) The central stretch, removed from the water, is Vendor's Row, an ad hoc food court of falafels, "buffalo burgers," Peruvian empanadas, and cool drinks. BC's stringent liquor laws aren't usually enforced down here, so there's usually a good supply of cold beer and wine in any of the iceboxes that are toted up and down the shore. On Wreck's southern edge, a carnival-style atmosphere prevails. Volleyball nets, boogie boards, Frisbees, and old hippies humming Neil Young tunes mix together happily. Body painting, boccie ball, and beach casino are also favoured pursuits. There's gambling, too, but this isn't Reno. The games are strictly "low stakes and no clothes."

Not only a local attraction, Wreck was named one of the world's great beaches by **LIFESTYLES OF THE RICH AND FAMOUS.** This is surely one of the few spots in Canada where you can lie on the beach and be served loose joints by a naked woman while eagles float by lazily overhead. A fun and laid-back place to hang out on a summer weekend, but don't expect complete anarchy. A strict code of conduct is upheld by the regulars who want to keep their stretch of sand peaceful and hassle-free. *Map:A2–A3.*

Neighbourhoods

No city is homogenous, particularly Vancouver. It's actually an amalgamation of neighbourhoods, each with its own defined residential and shopping areas. And each has an interesting story to tell. Here is the background for a handful of the 23 neighbourhoods of Vancouver City.

YALETOWN

By the time you've finished reading this paragraph, Yaletown probably will have changed again. Another upscale Italian furniture store will have opened, a skyscraping condo will have been added, or one more interior design firm will have decided that, yes, Yaletown is the only place for them. Unless you pine for the bruised and beaten warehouses of old, this heritage neighbourhood betwixt False Creek and downtown is a sterling case of gentrification gone right. Its narrow streets are living proof that the forgotten and the dilapidated can grow young again.

First settled in the 1890s by workers from the nearby Canadian Pacific Railway line, Yaletown evolved into the city's warehouse district before morphing into a yuppie hot spot with cafes, bars, billiard halls, boutiques, art galleries, studios, and offices. Led by the massive Concord Pacific development project, Yaletown emerged in the late 1980s as an urbane model of hip, high-density living (and a welcome alternative to the West End's stodgy apartment blocks). Locals jumped at the prospect of living in cozy lofts and glass-walled homes high above the city. Down below, designers and restaurateurs flocked to the cathedral ceilings and brick facades of the old warehouses.

The restaurant menus in this neighbourhood borrow from Bangkok (**THAI HOUSE**; 604/737-0088), Tokyo (**IZMI SUSHI**; 604/899-0366; **YOPO TEAHOUSE AND NOODLES**; 604/609-9676), Tuscany (**RUSTICA GOURMET PIZZA**; 604/688-5444), Northern California (**HAMILTON STREET GRILL**; 604/331-1511), and even the hardscrabble streets of New York (**DENIRO'S**; 604/684-2777). Recently though, the namesake of DeNiro's asked: "Are you talking about me? Are you talking about me?" His lawyers are on the case, and DeNiro's is now known as Section 3. The name may have changed, but the restaurant remains the same.

Mixed in among the restaurants are a number of fine spots for genuine microbrewed draft (**YALETOWN BREWING COMPANY**; 604/681-2739) or mocha latte (**CASALINGO**; 604/899-8090, **STARBUCKS**; 604/662-4030). For dessert consider the French pastries of **BOULANGERIE LA PARISIENNE** (604/684-2499). If you're young, stylish, and good-looking (or even if you're not), you can dance the rest of the evening away at **BAR NONE** (604/689-7000).

There's more to Yaletown than just munching and boozing. Behind the old brick facades is a high-tech cast of Vancouver start-ups that have resisted the Microsoft-style "glass campus in the suburb" approach to office space. Instead, they've gone for high-beam ceilings and character architecture, and more of them are coming. Their presence will ensure that Yaletown remains a bijou, a lively neighbourhood for years to come.

FALSE CREEK SOUTH

No neighbourhood has changed as dramatically as False Creek South, one of the largest urban redevelopment projects ever attempted in North America. Industrial land on both sides of False Creek disappeared in the 1970s and '80s, as Vancouverites reclaimed waterfront living. The first major phase of revamping the south shore was in the early 1970s, when the City Council began a concerted effort to clean up the smelly industrial wasteland, and the creek water turned from brown to green. Now, False Creek South is a parklike setting with strata-council apartments, co-operatives, and live-aboard marinas. On Fairview Slope, which forms the southern edge of the False Creek bowl, condos and townhouses have replaced old, crumbling houses. The new dwellings display an astonishing range of architectural styles and colours—some reminiscent of Mediterranean waterfronts. The population also keeps the core of the city alive and well, and has contributed to the success of Granville Island.

PUNJABI MARKET

Home to Vancouver's 60,000-strong Indo-Canadian community, the Punjabi Market is the place to go for great tandoori, a custom-fit *salwar kameez,* or the latest blockbuster from Bollywood on videotape. In south Vancouver at 49th Avenue and Main Street, the market is a *masala* mix of all-you-can-eat *thali* houses and sweet shops. This is the closest Vancouver gets to the authentic curries and cheap prices of northern India. South Indian chutneys and East African *halal* are also on hand. And there's more here than just food; sari boutiques, Rajastani jewellery stores, and travel agents offering cut-rate flights to Delhi pack the streets. Like the tightly packed bazaars of Bombay and Amritsar, the Punjabi Market is squeezed into a couple of blocks. A few hours of browsing here and you'll be ready for the subcontinent.

WEST END

This lively, vibrant neighbourhood in Vancouver's downtown core stretches from Coal Harbour to English Bay, with Stanley Park on one side and Burrard Street on the other. It's Canada's most densely populated area, an eclectic mix of graceful tree-lined streets, restaurants and shops, skyscrapers and low-slung apartments, and a few remaining Edwardian-style houses that were once residences of the city's wealthy class.

The residents here are predominantly young adults and seniors, with few children. The West End also has western Canada's largest gay and lesbian population. This odd combination has made it one of Vancouver's most livable, tolerant, and safe neighbourhoods. Simply going for a walk can be fascinating, but tennis, in-line skating, sailboarding, summer band concerts, and pitch-and-putt golf also keep residents on their toes.

There are three major streets, each seven blocks long: Denman Street, a strip with a smorgasbord of restaurants; Davie Street, with its busy shopping areas and nightlife; and Robson Street, with lots of coffeehouses, pizza parlors, and traffic. The English Bay popcorn vendor, usually found near the intersection of Davie and Denman, pops and butters year-round. BARCLAY HERITAGE SQUARE, a unique, parklike site that includes nine historic working-class houses and period landscaping, has preserved some Victorian charmers.

The West End is also one of the two areas of Vancouver (the other is Yaletown) envied by city planners in other parts of North America, particularly those whose cities become dark, scary holes after the evening rush hour. Here, the core is alive and busy, relatively safe, and lighted 24 hours a day.

For the past two decades, Vancouver's Pride Society has held an annual gay pride parade in the West End. Colourful floats and dancers in costumes pour down Denman, then Beach Avenue, before gathering for a mass celebration at Sunset Beach on English Bay. Historically, Vancouver's gay community has congregated in the West End. Many gay and gay-friendly businesses are still here, including LITTLE SISTER'S BOOK AND ART EMPORIUM (1238 Davie St; 604/669-1753; map:Q4) and a funky array of shops, cafes, restaurants, steam baths, and night nooks. Slightly smaller than San Francisco's Castro District, this neighbourhood remains "rainbow central," but an array of gay-centred hotels and dance bars have also begun to thrive in Gastown and Yaletown.

KITSILANO

Transient students and singles come and go, but a strong core of long-time residents still anchors in "Kits," one of the city's liveliest neighbourhoods, which overlooks the classic Vancouver view of sea, Stanley Park, and the North Shore mountains from Cornwall Street. Kitsilano Beach, Vanier Park (where the Vancouver Children's Festival is held each spring), and Vancouver's largest outdoor pool are big summer draws.

Kitsilano's main shopping thoroughfare, Fourth Avenue, put Kits on North America's counterculture map back in 1967 as Canada's Haight-Ashbury, but it has since become yuppified as baby boomers, who now comprise 56 percent of Kits's population, moved in and the hippies moved on. Broadway, with its own unique shops and a decidedly Greek flavour, runs parallel near the area's southern edge.

COMMERCIAL DRIVE

In multicultural Vancouver, few areas are as ethnically and politically jumbled as this busy street in East Vancouver. The Drive has long been the home of local lesbians and is beginning to sport some of the Good Vibrations look, with pink-triangle law firms and appliance shops, such as the popular Womyn's Ware. This street is also the epicentre of Sandinista-supporting eateries, pool halls that pay homage to Portuguese emperors, and cafes that tune into Italian and Brazilian *fútbol* matches. Greying curmudgeons sip espressos, pierced hipsters groove to techno, and grocers hawk cheap produce here—all within the same couple of blocks. Multiply that scene tenfold, toss in a repertory cinema, an alternative magazine joint, and some Nepali clothing boutiques, and you have a mix that would make Haight-Ashbury jealous. Whatever your ideology, there's a bumper sticker and a cafe here for you.

AMBLESIDE

What Commercial Drive is to bohemian subculture, this West Vancouver neighbourhood is to baby strollers and the British high street. If Marks and Spencer were urban planners, Ambleside would be the result, a sensible-shoe shopping district where ladies' garments and pork pie shops sit side by side. In the spirit of genteel living, the neighbourhood also sports a well-stocked greenhouse and a string of private art galleries.

Nearby, Ambleside Park is an ideal place to mosey along the seawall while watching bulk freighters from China and Liberia float by, past Stanley Park, under Lions Gate Bridge, and toward the city's skyline. For the athletically inclined, the park offers playing fields, pitch-and-putt golf, and jogging trails. Picnic areas and a playground wait nearby. The sandy dunes are popular year-round. In the summer, impromptu volleyball games can be found most evenings.

Museums

From large, world-renowned museums to tiny, specialized collections tucked into remote corners, Vancouver has a museum for just about everyone—aviation buffs, ancient-culture nuts, even those who are considering cloning a dinosaur.

BC MUSEUM OF MINING / Hwy 99 to Britannia Beach on Howe Sound; 604/688-8735 or 604/896-2233 Take an hour-long drive along the scenic Sea to Sky Highway toward Squamish to this mine and museum, now a national historic site. The old Britannia Copper Mine, which in the 1920s was one of the largest copper mines in the world, once processed more than 6.4 million kilograms (14.1 million pounds) of ore daily. Guided underground tours on electric trains give a glimpse of what working life was like for the miners, and there are demonstrations of diamond drilling and copper mining. The museum exhibits include hundreds of old photographs, artifacts, and a slideshow. You can also pan for gold ($3.50); "recovery guaranteed" means visitors are sure to find traces of gold dust in their pans. It's cool in the underground mines, so bring a light jacket or sweater. Admission is $9.50 adults; $7.50 children, seniors, and students; children under 3 free, family rate $34. Days and hours vary; call for information. *Every day from Mother's Day to Canadian Thanksgiving; www.mountain-inter.net/bcmm.*

BC SPORTS HALL OF FAME AND MUSEUM / Gate A, BC Place Stadium (east foot of Robson St), 777 Pacific Blvd S; 604/687-5520 This is the home of BC's most extensive collection of artifacts and archival materials on the province's professional and amateur sports and recreation history. Multimedia exhibits showcase BC's Olympic, Commonwealth, Stanley Cup, and Grey Cup champions. The heroic journeys of BC disabled athletes Terry Fox and Rick Hansen are commemorated in special galleries. Hands-on exhibits allow visitors the chance to test their skill at climbing, throwing, or racing like the pros. Admission is $6 adults; $4 children, seniors, and students; children under 5 free, family rate $15. *Every day; map:T5.*

BURNABY VILLAGE MUSEUM / 6501 Deer Lake Ave (Canada Wy at Sperling Ave), Burnaby; 604/293-6501 If the kids ever bug you about what life was like way, way back before the dawn of time, this open-air museum provides painless answers to their questions. This delightful re-creation of a turn-of-the-19th-century town was built to honour BC's centennial in 1958. Step back through time and visit a blacksmith's shop, an 1890s dentist's office, a sawmill, and a printer. In all, there are more than 30 buildings and outdoor displays, depicting daily life from 1890 to 1925. Authentically costumed "residents" welcome you into their homes—which might be a pioneer log cabin—and workplaces. A church, which can be booked for weddings, and a schoolhouse have also been re-created, and the ice-cream parlour (available for birthday parties) is operational. A lovingly restored 1912 carousel, called Carry-us-All, was once an attraction at the Pacific National Exhibition. Kids and adults alike will delight in a ride on this beautiful antique. Admission is $6.45 adults, $3.85 children, $4.35 seniors, $4.45 students, children under 6 free, family rate $3.85 per person. *Days and hours vary, call for information; www.museumsassn.bc.ca/~bcma/museums/bvm.html; map:I3.*

CANADIAN CRAFT MUSEUM / 639 Hornby St (in courtyard of Cathedral Place); 604/687-8266 Located off an elegant courtyard tucked behind the impressive facade of Cathedral Place, the Canadian Craft Museum is Canada's first national museum devoted to crafts. Local, national, and international pieces emphasize the beauty of handmade items and reflect the patience and care that go into these mostly one-of-a-kind pieces. A permanent collection and changing exhibits include everything from fragile glass perfume bottles to large pieces of furniture. Exhibits include tapestries, pottery, glass, jewellery, baskets, and sculptures. There is an excellent gallery gift shop. Admission is $5 adults, $3 seniors and students, children 12 and under free. Admission by donation Thursdays after 5pm. *Every day; map:S3.* &

THE CANADIAN MUSEUM OF FLIGHT / Hangar 2, Langley Airport, 5333 216th St, Langley; 604/532-0035 A fascination with vintage aircraft is evident at this mainly outdoor museum. The collection of over 50 examples of early aircraft includes a Tiger Moth, a Sopwith Camel, a Harvard, and an Avro Canuck. The transparent skin of a lumbering Second World War supply plane, the Lysander, reveals just how they do fly. Those interested in the technical side of things can browse in the library and the gift shop. The museum is an hour's drive from downtown Vancouver. Admission is $5 adults, $4 seniors and youth, children under 6 free, family rate $12. *Every day; www.canadianflight.org.*

FORT LANGLEY NATIONAL HISTORIC SITE / Mavis St, Langley; 604/513-4777 This former Hudson's Bay fur-trading post is the quickest route to the frontier days of 19th-century British Columbia. The 1839 storehouse is all that remains of the original compound, but Parks Canada has carefully reconstructed several nearby buildings. While interpreters in colonial garb will happily explain Fort Langley's historical significance as the place where Britain first laid territorial claim to BC, in 1858, your children will probably want to get their hands dirty by gold-panning, or make like voyageurs by hoisting a few bales of (fake) fur. Vivid re-enactments of life at the fort take place on holidays such as BC Day on the August long weekend. Admission is $4 adults, $3 seniors, $2 children 6–16, under 6 free, family rate $10. *Every day Apr 1–Oct 31, Mon–Fri Nov–Mar; www.users.uniserve.com/~gborden/gb-intrp.htm.*

GEOLOGICAL SCIENCES MUSEUM / Geological Science Centre, UBC, 6339 Stores Rd; 604/822-2449 Pieces of glowing amber and 80-million-year-old Lambeosaurus dinosaur bones are just some of the treasures to be found in this fascinating place. Displays of glittering crystals and minerals, as well as fossils that are so beautiful they outshine gemstones, encompass about 4.5 billion years of mineral and fossil history. More than 9,000 specimens are exhibited. Admission is free. *Mon–Fri; map:A2.*

HASTINGS MILL STORE MUSEUM / 1575 Alma St; 604/734-1212 The handmade glass is wavy and distorts the beach scene visible through the windows, but it only adds to the charm of this cluttered museum inside Vancouver's oldest building, one of only a handful to survive the fire of 1886. Set in a little park beside the Royal Vancouver Yacht Club, this building started life as a company store for a lumber operation and, before Vancouver became a city, was the first post office in the fledgling town, called Granville. Old muskets, Native baskets, satin clothing, chiming clocks, and a coach are only some of the items sheltered in the cool, dim interior. Admission by donation. *Tues–Sun June–mid-Sept, Sat–Sun rest of year; map:C2.*

MUSEUM OF ANTHROPOLOGY / 6393 NW Marine Dr, UBC; 604/822-3825 See Top 20 Attractions in this chapter.

PACIFIC SPACE CENTRE / 1100 Chestnut St; 604/738-7827 Sending your offspring into space (for the afternoon, at least) has never been so easy. Besides housing the **H. R. MACMILLAN PLANETARIUM** and the **GORDON SOUTHAM OBSERVATORY,** the Pacific Space Centre lets visitors experience the reality of life among the stars. In the **COSMIC COURTYARD,** exhibits include hands-on shuttle-docking simulations and a space suit from the Apollo launches, while **GROUNDSTATION CANADA** offers daily live demonstrations and multimedia shows about space travel. Unflappable family members can take a ride off-planet, on the Virtual Voyages Motion Simulator. For anyone too cool for school, the Planetarium hosts 40-minute evening laser concerts, featuring music by a range of artists, such as Pink Floyd and Britney Spears. Admission is $12.50 adults, $9.50 seniors and youth, $8.50 children 5–10, under 5 free, family rate $40. *Every day; www.pacific-space-centre.bc.ca; map:P5.*

SCIENCE WORLD/ALCAN OMNIMAX THEATRE / 1455 Quebec St; 604/268-6363 See Top 20 Attractions in this chapter.

VANCOUVER MARITIME MUSEUM AND ST. ROCH / 1905 Ogden St; 604/257-8300 Vancouver's seagoing tradition is spectacularly documented in this museum, suitably perched on the southern shore of English Bay. A Kwakiutl totem pole stands near the entrance, a replica of the 30.5-metre (100-foot) pole presented to Queen Elizabeth to mark BC's 1958 centennial. The museum is the home of a 1928 ketch, the *St. Roch,* now a national historic site. This Royal Canadian Mounted Police patrol boat was the first sailing vessel to navigate the Northwest Passage from west to east, a dangerous voyage of 28 months. The museum's permanent displays honour the city's growth as a port, the modern fishing industry, and 18th-century explorers. The museum also holds workshops, talks, and demonstrations—all with a nautical flavour.

At the **CHILDREN'S MARITIME DISCOVERY CENTRE,** your little Ahabs can step aboard a full-scale tugboat, peer out at Vancouver harbour through a powerful telescope, send a remote-controlled robot to the depths of the ocean—and those are just the beginning. Other permanent exhibits include the interactive Pirates Cove, where recreational choices run from digging up buried treasure to walking the plank. Stroll along the docks of the heritage harbour for an ever-changing view of vessels, both historic and modern. Admission is $6 adults, $3 seniors and youth, children 5 and under free, family rate $11. *Every day Victoria Day–Labour Day, Tues–Sun rest of year; map:O5.*

VANCOUVER POLICE CENTENNIAL MUSEUM / 240 E Cordova St; 604/665-3346 Even young people who weren't raised on a diet of *Cops* and *America's Most Wanted* will find this place fascinating, provided they have a strong stomach and a healthy sense of irony. "Mystery, History and Intrigue" is the motto here; cases full of seized weapons and counterfeit currency share this red-brick, former coroner's building with police artifacts, archival photographs, and a rather grim forensic exhibit (don't worry, it's a mannequin). Meanwhile, several displays of real crime-scene evidence invite visitors to put their sleuthing skills to work. At the end of it all, take home a souvenir from—where else?—the **COP SHOPPE.** *May–Labour Day Mon–Sat, Mon–Fri rest of year; map:V4.*

Galleries

Inside, outside, upstairs, and downstairs, Vancouver has a wealth of public and private galleries. Many of the city's commercial galleries are located on S Granville, between the Granville Street Bridge and 16th Avenue; others are scattered throughout downtown, in Gastown, or on Granville Island, site of the Emily Carr Institute of Art & Design and the Charles H. Scott Gallery.

Native galleries present art by members of the Northwest Coast First Nations, as well as the Inuit of Canada's far north. Craft galleries offer an eclectic mix of colourful, creative, and even functional pieces. Artist-run spaces include the refreshingly irreverent **WESTERN FRONT** (604/876-9343), now a quarter century old, **VIDEO IN/VIDEO OUT** (604/872-8337), and **ARTSPEAK** (604/688-0051). The **CONTEMPORARY ART GALLERY** (604/681-2700) is an independent, publicly funded art gallery, presenting a diverse program of regional, national, and international art.

ART BEATUS / 1M-888 Nelson St; 604/688-2633 Art Beatus seeks to present and promote contemporary international art. Its special focus is on artists of Asian origin, both local and offshore. The first Art Beatus opened in Hong Kong in 1992. *Tues–Sat; map:R4.*

BAU-XI GALLERY / 3045 Granville St; 604/733-7011 The Bau-Xi specializes in the works of Canadian artists such as Tom Burrows, Joe Plaskett, and the late Jack Shadbolt. Paintings are displayed in an uncrowded manner against a minimalist background, and open storage allows visitors access to a lot more than what's on display. This is one of Vancouver's oldest private galleries. *Mon–Sat; map:D3.*

BUSCHLEN-MOWATT GALLERY / 111-1445 W Georgia St; 604/682-1234 This modern gallery on the edge of Stanley Park, overlooking Coal Harbour, focuses on international contemporary art, from the truly challenging avant-garde to huge, splashy, romantic works. Artists include Boaz Vaadia, Bernard Cathelin, Yehouda Chaki, Otto Rogers, and Mark Gaskin, to name a few. *Every day; map:R3.*

CANADIAN CRAFT MUSEUM / 639 Hornby St (in courtyard of Cathedral Palace); 604/687-8266 See Museums in this chapter.

DIANE FARRIS GALLERY / 1565 W 7th Ave; 604/737-2629 The almost industrial feeling of this gallery is not an accident. Farris specializes in artists who work on enormous canvases, and the movable walls and high ceilings are essential. Farris has featured many young artists, including enfant terrible Attila Richard Lukacs, who had the international art world lining up at his Berlin studio door and is now in New York. Other artists include Dale Chihuly and Lawrence Paul Yuxweluptun. Farris's gallery is on the cutting edge of contemporary local and international art. *Tues–Sat; www.dianefarrisgallery.com; map:P7.*

DOUGLAS REYNOLDS GALLERY / 2335 Granville St; 604/731-9292 You'll find strictly Northwest Coast art here, including masks, totem poles, prints, and an exceptional selection of gold and silver jewellery. *Every day; www.douglasreynoldsgallery.com; map:P7.*

EQUINOX GALLERY / 2321 Granville St; 604/736-2405 Another long-established, serious Vancouver gallery, the Equinox Gallery handles only the very best North American painters and graphic artists. Works are beautifully displayed in serene surroundings. *Tues–Sat; map:P7.*

GALLERY OF BC CERAMICS / 1359 Cartwright St; 604/669-5645 The teapot as a functional work of art is quite the norm in this Granville Island gallery, which showcases the sometimes-amazing pottery of more than 60 BC artists. From funky to beautiful, useful to decorative, there isn't a clunky piece in sight. *Tues–Sun (extended summer hours); map:Q7.*

HEFFEL GALLERY / 2247 Granville St; 604/732-6505 Elegantly housed in an historic stone building, the Heffel Gallery specializes in international works by the august Group of Seven and many other respected Canadian landscape artists. Exhibits can be spread over its two floors, and there are lots of little spaces for quiet contemplation of a special work. *Mon–Sat; map:P7.*

INUIT GALLERY / 345 Water St; 604/688-7323 or 888/615-8399 This longtime Gastown gallery has a well-deserved reputation as North America's leading Inuit art gallery. Collectors from around the globe buy here, and some of the beautifully produced exhibition catalogues are collectors' items. The Northwest Coast work here includes masks, wood carvings, and jewellery. Gallery employees know their subject and are usually delighted to share their knowledge. *Every day; gallery@inuit.com; www.inuit.com; map:T3.*

JOHN RAMSAY GALLERY / 2423 Granville St; 604/737-8458 This gallery has an exciting roster of contemporary artists. Their work may be bold and beautiful or small and exquisite, but it is always respected across the continent. Shows range from cool still-lifes to starkly contemporary pieces. *Tues–Sat; map:P7.*

LEONA LATTIMER GALLERY / 1590 W 2nd Ave; 604/732-4556 See Native Arts & Crafts in the Shopping chapter.

MARION SCOTT GALLERY / 481 Howe St; 604/685-1934 One of the oldest galleries in the city, Marion Scott concentrates solely on Inuit art, and always has some absolutely stunning works. *Every day; map:S3.*

MONTE CLARK GALLERY / 2339 Granville St; 604/730-5000 One of the city's most influential gallery owners, Monte Clark has a great eye for emerging talent and has put Canada on the artistic map. He presents contemporary avant-garde artists, not only from Canada, but also from the United States and Europe. *Tues–Sat; map:P7.*

MORRIS AND HELEN BELKIN ART GALLERY / 1825 Main Mall, UBC; 604/822-2759 The former UBC Fine Arts Gallery features ever-changing exhibitions of contemporary art, and hosts lecture series and special events. *Tues–Sun; map:B2.*

OR GALLERY SOCIETY/KSW / 103 400 Smithe St; 604/683-7395 (Or), 604/688-6001 (KSW) Conceptual, quirky, and cutting-edge, the Or is a great showcase for local artists and it's a must-see for the best in contemporary art. Located at the back of the Or Gallery is the Kootenay School of Writing. Known as KSW, this is the place to go for the extreme in experimental poetry and fiction. Obscure, obtuse, and mind-bending in its approach to writing, KSW is one of the pulses of the literary fringe. Check its listing in the *Georgia Straight. Tues–Sat; www.ksw.net; map:T4.*

PRESENTATION HOUSE / 333 Chesterfield Ave, North Vancouver; 604/986-1351 This is a long-standing venue for photographic art. From elegant black-and-white to contemporary full-colour photographs,

Presentation House showcases exciting and beautiful exhibitions in this attractive older building. *Wed–Sun (summer hours vary); map:E1.*

ROBERT HELD ART GLASS / 2130 Pine St; 604/737-0020 Watch how glass is blown in this cavernous workshop/studio, where the red-hot furnaces lend an unreal background to the exquisite works of art created by local artisans. Elegant vases, goblets, glasses, candlesticks, and decorative pieces are swirled through with colour, emphasizing their unique, fragile shapes. *Mon–Sat; map:P7.*

SURREY ART GALLERY / 13750 88th Ave, Surrey; 604/501-5566 This cool, spacious gallery is part of the Surrey Arts Centre and benefits from strong community involvement. Exhibitions range from soothing to cutting-edge, and from local to international. The gallery and the arts centre hold imaginative art-appreciation programs for adults and children. *Every day; map:K6.*

THREE VETS / 2200 Yukon St; 604/872-5475 Vancouver's best-kept Northwest Coast art secret. Behind all the outdoor equipment, clothing, and great little gadgets is a gallery/storage room filled with art from more than 300 of BC's Native peoples. Paintings, prints, masks, carvings, jewellery, rattles, talking sticks, bowls, and plaques are all represented. The work has been collected over a 10-year period by curator Jerry Wolfman. *Mon–Sat; map:U7.*

VANCOUVER ART GALLERY / 750 Hornby St; 604/662-4719 See Top 20 Attractions in this chapter.

WITTMAN LAWRENCE GALLERY / 105-1529 W 6th Ave; 604/730-2875 Keep your eye on this young gallery, run by Jennifer Wittman and Tracey Lawrence. Their focus is on early to mid-career Canadian and American artists who are pushing the boundaries of art. *Tues–Sat; map:P7.*

Gardens

Vancouver's temperate climate and soft, plentiful rains encourage exuberant growth in limitless combinations of species. All over the city, gardens, parks, and green spaces are tucked into the corners of lots, squeezed between houses, stretched across a campus, or set in front of public buildings. High on a mountainside or beside the ocean are tiny private domains as well as sprawling hectares for public pleasure. The dogwood is British Columbia's provincial flower, and in spring, spreading trees are clothed in the fragile, creamy blossoms. Following are descriptions of some of Vancouver's wonderful gardens.

DR. SUN YAT-SEN CLASSICAL CHINESE GARDEN / 578 Carrall St; 604/662-3207 This authentic Ming dynasty garden is the first of its kind to be built either inside or outside China since 1492. Rocks, wood, plants, and water are used with deceptive simplicity but, gradually, contrasts are revealed—large and small, dark and light, hard and soft, straight and curved, artificial and natural. Windows frame courtyards, intricate carvings, or a rock whose heavily textured surface changes with the play of light. Pavilions connected by covered walkways edge the milky jade waters of the pond, whose surface is speckled with water lilies. Most of the materials were imported from Suzhou, China's foremost garden city. Adjoining this serene, starkly elegant garden is Dr. Sun Yat-Sen Park, a simplified version of the main garden. *www.discovervancouver. com/features/chinatown/chinatown.shtml; map:V4.*

NITOBE MEMORIAL GARDEN / UBC; 604/822-6038 This tranquil garden should be explored at leisure. As you stroll along the gently curving paths, note the care that went into the placement of every rock, tree, and shrub. Each element harmonizes with nature. Wander around, accompanied by the soothing sounds of the lake, waterfalls, and tiny streams; the gardens move from a beginning, through growth and change, to an ending. Native and imported plants and trees, azaleas, flowering cherry, irises, and maples provide colour year-round. *www.hedgerows.com; map:A3.*

PARK AND TILFORD GARDENS / 440 333 Brooksbank Ave, North Vancouver; 604/984-8200 Created in 1968, these glorious gardens are a popular place for summer weddings, and it's easy to understand why. A choice of eight theme gardens provides the perfect setting—from a stunning display of roses to the cool formality of the White Garden. The Display Garden features colourful spring bulbs and spreading annuals. The Oriental Garden showcases traditional bonsai trees and a tranquil pond, and in the Native Garden, a footpath winds through a small, aromatic Pacific Coast forest. There's also the Herb Garden and the shady Colonnade Garden, with its soothing rock pool and numerous other botanical delights. The gardens are located on the site of a former winery/distillery, which is now a shopping centre and movie studio complex. *www.north shore-online.com/park_tilford; map:F1.*

UNIVERSITY OF BRITISH COLUMBIA BOTANICAL GARDENS / SW Marine Dr, UBC 604/822-9666 See Top 20 Attractions in this chapter.

VANDUSEN BOTANICAL GARDENS / 5251 Oak St; 604/878-9274 See Top 20 Attractions in this chapter.

Parks and Beaches

Whether you're looking for a seaside stroll or a strenuous workout, dazzling views or deep aromatic forests, tennis courts or a shady picnic spot, one of Vancouver's more than 160 parks will deliver it. And, most likely, it'll have a beach nearby, for good measure.

AMBLESIDE PARK / Along Marine Dr, turning south at 13th St, West Vancouver This aptly named West Vancouver park is an ideal place to amble along the seawall, enjoying the superb scenery that forms a backdrop for the marine traffic. For the energetic, there are playing fields, pitch-and-putt golf, a fitness circuit, and jogging trails, as well as picnic areas and a playground. The beach is popular with families on summer days. Impromptu volleyball games take place most evenings. Bird-watchers appreciate the bird sanctuary on an artificial island in the tidal slough. *www.findfamilyfun.com/amblesidebeach.htm; map:D1.*

BARNET BEACH PARK / East along Inlet Dr to Barnet Rd, Burnaby Once the site of a busy mill town, this heritage park in north Burnaby is the perfect place to spend a day by the water. Traces of the old mill workings, which resemble a medieval castle, are a joy to youngsters. Safe, guarded swimming areas, a wharf for fishing and crabbing, picnic areas, barbecue pits, and a nonpowered boat launch area make this park a local favourite. On summer weekends the parking lot is often full, but there's plenty of parking on nearby side streets. *Map:I2.*

BELCARRA REGIONAL PARK / Along Hastings St to Barnet Hwy, turn north on Ioco Rd, and north to 1st Ave (follow signs); 604/432-6352 (group picnic reservations) It's well worth the hour's drive from downtown Vancouver to this park, which is really two parks in one—Belcarra and **WHITE PINE BEACH**. The huge, grassy sweep of the Belcarra picnic area slopes gently down to Indian Arm on Burrard Inlet and is ideal for individual and group picnics. **SASAMAT LAKE** has one of the warmest beaches on the Lower Mainland. There are also well-marked trails that edge the ocean at White Pine Beach, and the sheltered caves make perfect picnic and sunning spots. Tidal pools with their varied marine life are an endless source of entertainment. Crabbers and fishers bask in the sunshine on the dock, waiting for a bite (permits required). Kids love the imaginative adventure playground. Mudflats on the southern tip of Bedwell Bay provide interesting beachcombing. Busy on weekends. Signs along Ioco Road tell you if the park is full. *www.gvrd.bc.ca/board/members/belc.html; map:I1–J2.*

CAPILANO RIVER REGIONAL PARK / Along Capilano Rd N between Edgemont and Montroyal Blvds, North Vancouver This park spans North and West Vancouver and ranges from the urban to the wild. The immense Cleveland Dam, named after Vancouver's first water commissioner, Ernest Cleveland, harnesses the Capilano River and supplies Vancouver's water. There are great viewpoints of the spillway from clearings beside the dam. Pleasant picnic areas abound near the colourful flower gardens. Follow signs through the woods to the **FISH HATCHERY** (604/666-1790), where a glass-fronted observation area shows the fishways that assist salmon battling their way upriver to return to their birthplace. Displays chronicle the life cycle of the Pacific salmon, and breeding tanks hold minute salmon and trout fry. Below the hatchery is wilderness, with long and short hikes beside the rushing river as well as inland. The **CAPILANO SUSPENSION BRIDGE** (604/985-7474) is a swinging, 137-metre (450-foot) bridge that spans the Capilano River Canyon and is the area's oldest tourist attraction. Fishing in the Capilano River can be rewarding. *www.findfamilyfun.com/capsuspbridge.htm; map:D1.*

CENTRAL PARK / Between Boundary Rd and Patterson Ave, Kingsway and Imperial St, Burnaby One of the oldest parks in the city, straddling the boundary between Vancouver and Burnaby, this lovely park was named after its New York counterpart. Once a military reserve for the defence of New Westminster, the park has an award-winning playground specially designed to include children with disabilities. Longer trails for joggers and cyclists meander through the park. Horseshoe pitches, pitch-and-putt golf, tennis courts, a swimming pool, and lawn bowling greens ensure this park has something for everyone. Vancouver's professional soccer team, the 86ers, play their home games at **SWANGARD STADIUM** during spring and summer. *www.burnabyparksrec.org/central/central. html; map:G4.*

CYPRESS PROVINCIAL PARK / Take exit #8 off Hwy 1, then drive to top of Cypress Bowl Rd, West Vancouver; 604/926/5612 This West Vancouver park is perfect for those who like their wilderness manageable. Trails are steep and can be muddy and rough, but they are well marked. Trees are huge and old, with thick, textured bark. Swirling mist in the treetops adds to the feeling that you are a long way from civilization, when, in fact, the parking lot is a short walk away. Cypress Creek has carved a deep, narrow canyon, and the roar of the water foaming through the steep walls echoes around the park. From the canyon, the creek plunges in a spectacular cascade to the wide creek bed and its smooth, waterworn boulders. The main trail, which can be muddy and slippery, climbs steadily upward through heavy forest and underbrush, occasionally opening into natural viewpoints. Downhill and cross-country skiing, and tobogganing, are popular activities at the Cypress Bowl Ski Area in winter. *www.cypressmountain.com; map:C0.*

DAVID LAM PARK / Pacific Blvd, at south foot of Homer St and Drake St Named for a Chinese Canadian philanthropist and former lieutenant governor of BC, this park is one of the biggest green spaces in the mammoth Concord Pacific redevelopment of the south shore of False Creek. *www.concordpacific.bc.ca/inourcommunity/davidlam.html; map:S6.*

ENGLISH BAY BEACH / Along Beach Ave, between Denman St and Burrard St In the 1920s and '30s, throngs of Vancouverites would gather on this wide, sandy beach and along the pier. Plays were performed on the roof of the 1931 English Bay bathhouse, where a windsurfing school now operates. A Jamaican seaman, Joe Fortes, lived in a little cottage on the beach and for 25 years was a self-appointed lifeguard, teaching many youngsters to swim. A bronze drinking fountain in tiny Alexandra Park, across Beach Avenue, stands in tribute to Fortes. There is also a delightful gingerbread-embellished bandstand here, where a band plays on warm Sunday afternoons. The pier is gone, but crowds still come to swim and sunbathe. In July and August, English Bay is the setting for the **BENSON & HEDGES SYMPHONY OF FIRE** (604/738-4304), an international fireworks competition that takes place over four nights. On the last Sunday in July, the annual **NANAIMO-TO-VANCOUVER BATHTUB RACE** finishes near Kitsilano Beach on the south side of the bay. Dozens of hardy souls brave the Strait of Georgia in motorized bathtubs. Every New Year's Day, Vancouver's traditional **POLAR BEAR SWIM** takes place near the bathhouse off Beach Avenue. The number of onlookers is always larger than the number of brave swimmers who begin the year with a chilly dip. *www.englishbay.com/eb/walk1.htm; map:O2–P3.*

GARRY POINT PARK / 7th Ave at Chatham St, Richmond This park on the extreme southwestern tip of Lulu Island is rich with the history of boatbuilding and the lore of fish canneries. At the turn of the 19th century more than 2,000 fishing boats waited at the mouth of the Fraser River to set out into the Strait of Georgia. The nearby town of Steveston is preserved much as it was a century ago, when the first cannery went into operation. It is still an important fishing area. You can buy fish fresh off the boat from Steveston quay or enjoy a meal in one of the many excellent fish-and-chip restaurants nearby. This is also the perfect place to watch freighter traffic heading up the main arm of the Fraser. Equally popular is picnicking in one of the many sandy bays that edge this park (beach fires permitted). A small Japanese garden is evidence of the strong Japanese presence in Steveston. Kite fliers flock to the open, grassy field where steady breezes from the strait provide a challenge. North of the park are scenic riverside trails that run along Richmond's dykes, which are well used by walkers and cyclists. *www.findfamilyfun.com/garry point.html; map:B7.*

GEORGE C. REIFEL MIGRATORY BIRD SANCTUARY / Follow Westham Island Rd to Robertson Rd, Ladner; 604/946-6980 A bird-watcher's paradise. The 260 hectares (650 acres) of former tidal flats were reclaimed through dyking and were eventually transformed from a hunting ground to a rest stop for hundreds of species of migrating waterfowl and other winged creatures. (See also Nature Observation in the Recreation chapter.) *www.discovervancouver.com/places/tourist_attractions/bird_sanctuary.html.*

IONA BEACH PARK / Along Ferguson Rd near south terminal of Vancouver International Airport, to Iona Island Causeway, Richmond
Based on the premise that if you can't hide it, flaunt it, one of Vancouver's major sewage outfall pipes has been transformed into a unique walking and cycling path that extends 4 kilometres (2.5 miles) into the Strait of Georgia. The pathway, which is on top of the pipe, evokes the sensation of being at sea on an ocean liner. At the end of the walkway, a viewing tower gives a bird's-eye view of the strait and, on clear days, distant glimpses of Vancouver Island and the mountains of the Olympic Peninsula. Beaches are sandy and flat, ideal for kite flying, swimming, and sunning. The waters are sheltered, good for canoeing and kayaking. Driftwood rims the shore, and the river marsh on the island's south side is a haven for migrating birds that stop over on their way to and from Arctic breeding grounds. Ducks, songbirds, and sandpipers congregate here in vast numbers. *www.gvrd.bc.ca/parks/bro/pkion.html; map:B4.*

KITSILANO BEACH / Cornwall Ave and Arbutus St, bordering English Bay See Top 20 Attractions in this chapter.

LIGHTHOUSE PARK / Marine Dr to Beacon Ln, West Vancouver See Top 20 Attractions in this chapter.

LOCARNO AND JERICHO BEACHES / NW Marine Dr between Trimble St and Blanca St See Top 20 Attractions in this chapter.

LYNN HEADWATERS REGIONAL PARK / On Park Rd, past Lynn Valley Rd
The Lynn Canyon Suspension Bridge and Ecology Centre is near the entrance to the 250-hectare (617-acre) Lynn Headwaters Regional Park. The **ECOLOGY CENTRE** (604/981-3103), an educational resource and interpretive facility, is considered the ideal location to begin a hike. Guided walks are available. *www.bcadventure.com/adventure/explore/vancouver/parks/seymour.htm; map:G1–H1.*

MOUNT SEYMOUR PROVINCIAL PARK / Along Mt Seymour Pkwy, north on Mt Seymour Rd At Mount Seymour Provincial Park, downhill and cross-country skiing are popular in the winter (604/986-2261). When the snow melts, it's a prime location for hiking. On a clear day, BC's Gulf Islands and Washington State's San Juan Islands can be seen in the distance from several trails and lookouts. Farther down the mountain, in the 5,600-hectare (14,000-acre) **SEYMOUR DEMONSTRATION FOREST** (604/987-1273), you will find some of Vancouver's most popular routes for in-line skating and mountain biking. *www.bcadventure.com/adventure/explore/vancouver/parks/seymour.htm; map:G1–H1.*

PACIFIC SPIRIT REGIONAL PARK / Between NW Marine Dr and SW Marine Dr, Camosun St and UBC Pacific Spirit is one of the Greater Vancouver Regional District's newest parks, offering more than 800 hectares (2,000 acres) of wilderness. Adjacent to the University of British Columbia, some 55 kilometres (34 miles) of trails (designated for walkers, cyclists, and horseback riders) plunge through thick second-growth forest, edge deep ravines, and wind along cliff tops that overlook beaches with spectacular views of English Bay, Howe Sound, and the north arm of the Fraser River. There's plenty of small wildlife here, and early in the morning you may even catch a glimpse of a coyote. Just above the Locarno Beach cliffs on the Spanish Trail is an open area covered with wild roses, fireweed, and salmonberry bushes. It's called the Plains of Abraham, and a dairy farm operated here at the turn of the last century (traces of the brick foundation remain on the south edge). A serene forest on the edge of the city, Pacific Spirit Regional Park is well named. *Map:B3.*

STANLEY PARK / West end of Beach and W Georgia Sts to Lions Gate Bridge; 604/257-8400 See Top 20 Attractions in this chapter.

VANIER PARK / Just west of Burrard Street Bridge, north of Cornwall Ave at Chestnut St The ocean breezes that blow over this wide, grassy space on English Bay make it one of the best places in town to fly a kite. There's also the **H. R. MACMILLAN PLANETARIUM** (604/738-7827), considered one of the best planetariums in North America and a main attraction of the Pacific Space Centre. The planetarium and the **VANCOUVER MUSEUM** (604/736-4431), which has displays chronicling the history of Vancouver and the Lower Mainland, offer frequently changing shows. Both are in the building with the conical roof, which was designed to resemble the shape of a traditional, Native cedar-bark hat, a fitting tribute to the coastal people who oringinally lived on this tip of land. Outside the building is the wishing pool guarded by George Norris's stainless steel fountain, *Crab.* On the west side of the museum parking lot is the **MARITIME MUSEUM** (604/257-8300), which shelters the historic RCMP vessel the *St. Roch,* as well as offering fascinating information about Vancouver's seagoing heritage. Nearby is Heritage Harbour, where a unique collection of ordinary and unusual vessels are moored. At the end of May, families flock to the red-and-white-striped tents of the **VANCOUVER INTERNATIONAL CHILDREN'S FESTIVAL** (604/687-7697), where performers from around the world entertain multitudes of children with an amazing variety of theatre, music, dance, circus, storytelling, and multimedia productions. During the summer months, Shakespearean plays are presented by the **BARD ON THE BEACH** troupe (604/739-0559). *www.discovervancouver.com/places/tourist_attractions/vanier_park.html; map:P5.*

WRECK BEACH / Point Grey, Musqueam Reserve to Spanish Banks West See Top 20 Attractions in this chapter.

Organized Tours

The ideal way to explore Vancouver is on foot, but if the sky is crying and the winds are howling, then it's time to check out some of the more comfortable options. The choices range from a walking adventure through historic Gastown to a wild helicopter ride across the glaciers of the Coast Mountains. Some local companies offer tours of their operations, letting you discover something about the daily workings of the city. The Port of Vancouver (1300 Stewart St; 604/665-9179; www.portvancouver.com), for example, offers tours during regular business hours to groups of 10 or more, and self-guided tours to individuals. Both are free. Agricore, which operates the Cascadia grain terminal, also offers tours on Tuesdays and Thursdays at 10:30am and 1pm (on Commissioner St; 604/293-6222). The Greater Vancouver Regional District (604/432-6430; www.gvrd.bc.ca) offers guided bus tours of the two watersheds that supply the district, the Capilano and Coquitlam. Turning from water to wine, Domaine de Chaberton in Langley (1064 216th St; 604/530-1736 or 888/332-9463; www.domainedechaberton.com) offers tours of its winery at 2pm and 4pm on weekends and holidays. Still looking for things to do?

AIR TOURS

GLACIER AIR / 604/898-9016 or 800/265-0088 Providing both helicopter and airplane excursions, this company specializes in icy explorations. Packages include flights around the Tantalus mountain range followed by a quick landing and a walk on the Serratus Glacier. Their tours feature views of volcanic rock formations, hanging glaciers, and high-elevation waterfalls.

HARBOUR AIR SEAPLANES / Coal Harbour Rd (1 block west of Canada Place), Vancouver; 604/688-1277 You can cover a lot of ground in an airplane and avoid traffic problems to boot. Harbour Air offers two tours around the Vancouver area; the Vancouver Panorama tour costs $76 per person and runs 30 minutes; an aerial tour of glaciers north of the city is 75 minutes and costs $199 per person. *Map:T2.*

BOAT TOURS

AQUABUS / South foot of Hornby St; 604/689-5858 Vancouver's cutest way to get around. The fleet of 12-passenger ferries serves a network of five stations along the False Creek shoreline, leaving every 15 minutes between 10am and 5pm daily. Sight-seeing minicruises of False Creek on the 22-seat ferry are offered year-round from the landing point outside the public market on Granville Island. Cost of the 20-minute excursion is $3 for kids, $6 for adults. *Map:Q6.*

HARBOUR FERRIES / North foot of Denman St; 604/688-7246 or 800/663-1500 Take to the water in another way—Harbour Ferries offers a 75-minute tour of the city three times daily aboard the MPV *Constitution*, a delightful paddle wheeler that churns through Burrard Inlet. The cost is $18 for adults, and $15 for children and seniors. The company also offers dinner cruises between May and October. Boarding takes place at the north foot of Denman Street at 6:30pm, and the yacht leaves at 7pm, tracing a route around Stanley Park toward West Vancouver's Ambleside Park, then back to English Bay. It returns at about 10pm. Dinner is buffet style, and features a singer performing contemporary hits. *www.boatcruises.com; map:Q1.*

LOTUS LAND TOURS / 1251 Cardero St, Ste 2005; 604/684-4922 or 800/528-3531 Lotus Land's "paddle power" four-hour guided tours, on the waters of Indian Arm, are just the thing for those seeking something more relaxing than "pedal power." Lotus Land uses two-person, folding kayaks: small craft that are wide and stable like a canoe, yet sleek like a kayak. Prior experience is not necessary, but comfortable shoes, clothes, and a windbreaker are. *www.lotuslandtours.com; map:I0.*

MV QUEEN OF DIAMONDS / West end of Granville Island; 604/218-9777 Board this luxury dinner cruise at Granville Island and sail around scenic False Creek before rounding Stanley Park for a tour of Burrard Inlet. As the sun begins to set over the city, the boat returns to English Bay. Enjoy the buffet dinner. The three-hour cruise is $50 per person; be sure to check the cruise schedule for special events. The ship is also available for charter cruises. *www.mvqueenofdiamonds.com; map:Q6.*

CYCLING TOURS

VELO-CITY CYCLE TOURS / 6400 Nancy Greene Wy, North Vancouver; 604/924-0288 The **GROUSE MOUNTAIN WEST COASTER** is billed as Vancouver's first gravity-assisted mountain-bike adventure tour. The 25-kilometre (15.5-mile) downhill trek begins at the summit of the Grouse Mountain peak and takes riders at an unhurried pace to the bottom of the North Shore via its rain forests and river canyons. The 4½-hour guided tour includes use of a 21-speed mountain bike and transportation on the Grouse Mountain Skyride aerial tram. Tours run rain or shine, May through September, beginning at 10am and 3pm. Pickup service is available at local hotels throughout the downtown core. The tour price— $50 for kids, $75 for adults—includes a light snack. *www.velo-city.com; map:G1.*

HORSE-DRAWN TOURS

STANLEY PARK HORSE DRAWN TOURS / Lower zoo parking lot, Stanley Park; 604/681-5115 The easiest way to enjoy the serenity of Stanley Park, March through September. A one-hour tour by horse-drawn carriage leaves the lower zoo parking lot at regular intervals and meanders through this 1,000-acre park. A professional guide narrates the trip, which visits all the main points of interest. Adults pay $14.95, students under 18 pay $13.95, and the fare for kids between 3 and 12 is $9.95. The family rate for two adults and two kids or students is $46.69. *Map:Q1.*

MOTOR TOURS

PACIFIC COACH LINES / Pacific Central Station, 1150 Station St; 604/662-7575 or 800/661-1725 PCL offers two tours, from a short tour of major attractions to an all-day tour that includes taking the Aquabus to Granville Island and a trip on the Grouse Mountain Skyride. *www. pacificcoach.com; map:V6.*

WEST COAST CITY AND NATURE SIGHTSEEING / Stanley Park; 604/451-1600 Tour the city by minibus, stopping at museums and other attractions. There are several tour options, including one focussing on the culture of BC's First Nations people. This tour begins at the totem poles in Stanley Park, then heads to the University of British Columbia's Museum of Anthropology. After a walking tour of the museum's collection of Northwest Coast artifacts, you'll visit the nearby Native Education Centre. The four-hour tour costs $43 for each adult, $27 for each child. There are also student and senior rates. Dinner at the Hiwus Feasthouse atop Grouse Mountain is an optional component of the tour and adds five hours to its length, for a total cost of $109 (kids, $65). *www. vancouversightseeing.com; map:Q1.*

TRAIN TOURS

ROYAL HUDSON / W 1st St between Pemberton Ave and Philip Ave, North Vancouver; 604/984-5246, 800/339-8752, or 800/663-8238 It's a steamy experience—riding the rails on the *Royal Hudson* steam train. Engine 2860, the sole survivor of the 65 steam trains that crisscrossed Canada 50 years ago, takes you on a majestic trip along spectacular Howe Sound to Squamish, 65 kilometres (40 miles) north of Vancouver. There's a 90-minute stop in Squamish for sight-seeing and lunch. From June to September, reservations are essential. Passengers have the option of booking the return trip through Harbour Cruises (604/688-7246) aboard MV *Brittania*. It's almost the same scenic trip, but cruising on the water offers a different perspective. *www.bcrail.com/bcrpass/ bcrhudsn. htm, www.boatcruises.com/prod03.htm.*

TROLLEY TOURS

VANCOUVER TROLLEY COMPANY / 875 Terminal Ave; 604/451-5581
Take a jolly ride upon a trolley. It's an ideal way to familiarize yourself with the myriad charms of Vancouver. At any one of 15 stops, you can jump off and explore some of Vancouver's favourite attractions, catching the next trolley 30 minutes or even three hours later—and you pay only once. Reproductions of the trolleys that were common on Vancouver's streets around 1890, these bright red and gold vehicles trundle you unhurriedly through the city. A relaxing, fun way to explore. Standard fare is $10 for kids 4 to 12 years and $22 for adults. Sunset tours are also available, the Decadent Sunset Tour running $16 for kids and $28 for adults. *www.vancouvertrolley.com; map:V6.*

WALKING TOURS

HISTORIC VANCOUVER / 604/720-0006 Guides dressed in period attire will lead you on this adventure through downtown Vancouver. The itinerary features buildings and streets of historical and architectural interest. Hear tales and the folklore of the city's early pioneers while walking by their local haunts. Tours leave three times daily from Pacific Centre, meeting at the glass cupola at the corner of Howe and Robson Streets. The two-hour tour is $15 for adults, $6 for kids, with a maximum charge of two kids per family. Children under 5 are free. *Map:S3.*

WILDERNESS TOURS

ROCKWOOD ADVENTURES / 1330 Fulton St, West Vancouver; 604/926-7705 An opportunity for visitors to get out of the city without going very far at all. All year-round, Rockwood offers **RAINFOREST WALKS**, tours by knowledgeable guides through Stanley Park, Capilano River Canyon, Lighthouse Park, Lynn Canyon and Cypress Falls, and Bowen Island in nearby Howe Sound. Hiking experience is not necessary, as Rockwood allows participants to savour the stunning, temperate rain forest at a leisurely pace. Frequent stops are made along the trails for brief, informal nature lectures or to view wildlife. Any of the Rainforest Walks are the ideal way to cap a visit to the Lower Mainland, though the Lighthouse Park tour is a favourite. The last old-growth forest in the area is home to towering cedars, Douglas firs, and hemlocks, some of which are 600 years old and taller than many of the downtown buildings that can be seen in the distance from the rocky shoreline. Half-day or full-day tours available. Meals are included (owner Manfred Scholermann is a Culinary Olympics chef), as is the shuttle bus from downtown hotels. The Bowen Island trek includes a ferry ride, though seaplane transportation is optional. The price of most tours is $45. The Bowen Island tour is $95, but this doesn't include seaplane transportation.

VANCOUVER ALL-TERRAIN ADVENTURES LTD. / 4191 Dominion St, Burnaby; 604/434-2278 or 888/754-5601 This outdoor outfit specializes in wilderness explorations for city slickers. Included among their tours are a rain-forest adventure excursion to Bowen Island, via a private sea-plane or the ferry. The Bowen Island trip features a hike through a pristine forest followed by a gourmet picnic. This company also offers sea kayaking tours of Indian Arm, Canada's southernmost glacial fjord, and guided mountain-bike tours of Vancouver. Prices vary according to the package you choose, but tours generally last three to five hours. *www.all-terrain.com; map:G3.*

SHOPPING

SHOPPING

Shopping Areas and Malls

DOWNTOWN VANCOUVER

The **DOWNTOWN** area of Vancouver (map:N1–V5) has experienced a lot of growth and has seen many changes in the past few years. But, as it has in many urban centres, the shopping action (with the exception of Robson Street) has moved underground, into the malls: Pacific Centre, Vancouver Centre, Royal Centre, Bentall Centre, Sinclair Centre, and Harbour Centre.

ROBSON STREET is the meeting place of cultures and couture, as thousands of locals and tourists can be found strolling among its many shops every day. Weekends are very crowded, but there's lots to see, since the street runs from Granville Mall in the east, to Denman Street in the west (map:Q2–U4). You'll find art books, jewellery, and gifts by local artists at the Gallery Shop in the Vancouver Art Gallery and, on Robson Street, a string of flagship stores for international fashion companies (Inwear/Matinique, Zara, Banana Republic, Nike, French Connection, Gap, Club Monaco), local fashion chains (Aritzia, Zioni, Boys' Co.), and lots of family-friendly restaurants. For groceries, there is a Safeway at the foot of Robson near Denman, with an adjoining liquor store. In the other direction, at Robson and Homer Streets, you'll find the splendid Vancouver Public Library with its store, Bookmark, which has gifts for literary folk. On Robson and Burrard Streets you'll find a Chapters megabookstore.

Once just a cluster of dilapidated warehouses across the tracks from False Creek's mills and factories, **YALETOWN** (map:S5–T6) is now a highly desirable piece of history-crammed real estate. Traditionally the city's garment district, its brick warehouses have been converted into loft apartments, ad agencies, multimedia firms, and the occasional designer showroom. Though the area was slow to attract a retail market (like most garment districts, don't expect much action before noon), it now houses a number of ultrahip clothing stores (Global Atomic Designs, Atomic Model, Uncle Otis), a high concentration of high-end home furnishings (Chintz and Company, Liberty, Maison V), and a thriving restaurant and bar scene at night. Urban Fare, a new gourmet grocery store and restaurant, has finally moved into the neighbourhood to help yuppie loft-dwellers make better use of their stainless-steel kitchen appliances.

PACIFIC CENTRE / 700 W Georgia St to 777 Dunsmuir St; 604/688-7236 is downtown's biggest and busiest mall, which connects The Bay and the former location of the now bankrupt Eaton's department store. The mall includes designer department store Holt Renfrew and a food court, and connects to Vancouver Centre mall. With a 200-name list of outlets, it's not surprising that Pacific Centre is crowded all year-round. There is mall access on Granville, Howe, Dunsmuir, and Seymour Streets. *Every day; map:T4.*

SINCLAIR CENTRE / 757 W Hastings St; 604/659-1009 is not a large shopping centre, but it bears a look for two very good reasons. First, it is a striking example of the reclaimed-heritage school of architecture, where fine old buildings are put to alternative use without destroying their charm. Second, it contains the high-end designer department store Leone, as well as Plaza Escada and the Dorothy Grant boutique. Grant is a Haida fashion designer whose button-blanket garments and spruce-root hats are collected internationally. *Every day; map:T3.*

Historic Districts

Downtown Vancouver also encompasses historic **GASTOWN** (map:T3–V3), a quaint and cobbled tourist destination. The old warehouses and office buildings have been restored and refurbished, and summer and weekends find the streets bursting with visitors seeking food, fashion, and souvenirs of the smoked-salmon and maple-syrup variety. Drop by The Landing, just east of Waterfront station, to see a particularly handsome refit of an antique structure. While the building is beautiful, however, the shopping is mediocre. If you're up to the adventure, drop by one of the hemp cafes on the 100 block of Hastings Street, part of local marijuana crusader Mark Emery's legacy.

Although the Chinese-Canadian population of Vancouver is now concentrated in Richmond, the old **CHINATOWN** is still a vital and interesting area to visit and shop in. You'll find it a few blocks east and west of Main Street on Pender and Keefer Streets (map:U4–V4). The Chinese groceries and apothecaries have been there for generations, and many display remnants of Vancouver's recent-past status as a neon mecca. The Dr. Sun Yat-Sen Classical Chinese Garden at 578 Carrall Street, which took six years to plan and two to build, is a must-see. Many of the buildings in this area were built by Chinese artisans in a style not found outside China. Stores to check out include the original Ming Wo cookware shop at 23 E Pender Street, Cathay Importers at 104 E Pender, and Chinese Jade and Crafts at 38 E Pender. Be sure to stop for lunch at the original Hon's Wun-Tun House at 268 Keefer Street or 288 E Pender Street. Try the Man Sing Meat Centre at 224 E Pender Street for a little barbecued pork or duck, and the Ten Ren Tea & Ginseng Co. at 550 Main Street. Various Chinese apothecaries have herbalists who can be consulted without an appointment—try Tung Fong Hung Medicine Co. at 536 Main Street. During the summer, there's a night market around Main and Keefer on Friday, Saturday, and Sunday nights from 6:30pm to 11:30pm. The merchandise is mostly cheap Hong Kong imports and fake luxury goods, but the bustling atmosphere, neon lights, Asian languages and food, and steamy, wet streets are like a scene from the classic 1982 sci-fi film *Blade Runner.* Not uncoincidentally, Philip K. Dick, the author of the book on which the movie was based, spent several months living in the area in the 1970s.

Neighbourhoods

Under the Granville Street bridge on **GRANVILLE ISLAND** (map:Q6–Q7), warehouses and factories have been transformed into a public market and craft shops. Locals and tourists flock to this lively place for a tremendous selection of fresh food and gourmet items, musicians and street theatre. A walk off the beaten path through the corrugated-steel warehouses will furnish a glimpse of metalworkers, glassblowers, weavers, and other artisans at work; many of them have storefronts. Some of the best local designers are located in the Net Loft building, and there are more than 50 shops catering to the marine industry. Most of the stores are closed Mondays during winter. The Granville Island Information Centre number is 604/666-5784.

SOUTH GRANVILLE, from Granville Bridge toward 16th Avenue (map:D3), borders on the prestigious Shaughnessy neighbourhood and has traditionally catered to the carriage trade. It is sometimes referred to as Gallery Row, but while the art galleries represent internationally renowned painters and photographers, equally impressive is a new crop of Occidental antique stores—to supplement the existing British ones— that import treasures from Japan, Indonesia, and India. Top eateries (Vij's and Gianni), the newly refurbished Stanley Theatre, the elegant Meinhardt's Fine Foods, design supply store Paperhaus, and the boutique of local jewellery and housewares designer Martha Sturdy make this strip one of the best areas for a stroll early in the evening. Also, you can find top international designer clothing here (Boboli and Bacci's).

A visit to the malls that make up Richmond's **ASIA WEST** district (Aberdeen Centre, Yaohan Centre, President Plaza, and Parker Place; map:D5) is an experience unique in North America. The malls sprung up along a stretch of No. 3 Road between Capstan and Alderbridge Ways in the mid-1990s to service a newly settled community of mostly Hong Kong expatriates. The malls house Chinese herbalists, huge all-Asian supermarkets, inexpensive Japanese housewares, toys and candy, designer luggage, and lots of fashion-forward clothes and shoes for petite women. Do not be dissuaded by the marked prices—a simple inquiry will often bring them down substantially. Do be persuaded to stay for lunch—

the food courts offer a tempting variety of Asian street foods at bargain prices. Finish your visit with an intriguing bubble pearl tea, a fad that has been imported from Taiwan.

Apart from the massive Park Royal Shopping Centre, the shops along Marine Drive in **WEST VANCOUVER** (map:C1–D1) reflect the British heritage of the area's original European settlers. The stores are quaint but, in general, carry a good stock of quality merchandise. There are some nice little restaurants and galleries, too. West Vancouver is one of the more prestigious neighbourhoods in the Lower Mainland, so expect prices that reflect this fact.

LONSDALE QUAY MARKET / 123 Carrie Cates Ct, North Vancouver; 604/985-6261 This market is a delightful conclusion to a SeaBus ride, and its open-market concept contains a surprising number of intriguing shops. There are lots of food outlets, fashions for adults and kids, fresh and dried flowers and specialty shops (Girder & Beams Construction Toys and The Games People). Parking is abundant. *Every day; map:E1.*

PARK ROYAL SHOPPING CENTRE / 100 Park Royal S, West Vancouver; 604/922-3211 Park Royal has the distinction of being Canada's first shopping mall as well as the North Shore's largest and most prestigious shopping centre. It straddles Marine Drive in West Vancouver, just across Lions Gate Bridge. (Out-of-town visitors note: it's too far to walk, so take the bus or drive.) Parking is free and plentiful, there's an open-air food market in summer. Be thankful for the numerous spots to buy comfort shoes here (Rockport, Ingledew's, Clarks of England); you may be covering acres of shops. *Every day; map:D1.*

Shops from A to Z

ACCESSORIES AND LUGGAGE

BIG TOP HAT SHOP / 73 Water St; 604/684-7373 Two young local milliners joined forces to launch this Gastown hat shop, inspired by the images and colours of the Victorian circus. Styles range from 17th-century tricornes to 1950s saucers to berets, fedoras, and cowboy hats. *Every day; map:U3.*

EDIE HATS / 11 1666 Johnston St; 604/683-4280 Owner Edie Orenstein has been a mainstay of the local fashion scene for years. The store carries her own delicious creations as well as those of other local milliners. Imports, too. *Every day; map:Q6.*

SATCHEL SHOP / 1024 Robson St (and branches); 604/662-3424 A local favourite for purses, handbags, good-looking backpacks, and luggage. Lots of convenient locations. *Every day; map:R3.*

WESTON LUGGAGE REPAIR / 103-1111 Homer St; 604/685-9749 Weston has a well-established reputation for suitcase repairs. Most repairs completed while you wait. *Mon–Sat; map:S5.*

ANTIQUES

CANADA WEST ANTIQUES / 4430 W 10th Ave; 604/222-9190 Authentic pine antiques from eastern Canada mix with country furniture and decorator pieces. Be sure to see the selection of grandmotherly folk crafts—quilts, hooked rugs, and more. *Every day; map:B3.*

FOLKART INTERIORS / 3651 W 10th Ave; 604/731-7576 Besides antiques, this charming and fanciful place features unique pieces of folk art that are simply irresistible. There's a good selection of pine furniture as well. *Every day; map:B3.*

R. H. V. TEE & SON (ENGLAND) / 7963 Granville St; 604/263-2791 The provenance of this stately shop goes back almost as far as some of the antiques. The current Mr. Tee is the fourth generation of his family in the business, and he personally selects the pieces for the shop on his many trips to England. *Tues–Sat; map:D4.*

UNO LANGMANN LTD. / 2117 Granville St; 604/736-8825 This long-established, internationally recognized gallery specializes in European and North American paintings from the 18th, 19th, and early 20th centuries. Langmann also features furniture, porcelain, and silver. *Wed–Sat; map:P7.*

APPAREL

ARITZIA / 1110 Robson St (and branches); 604/684-3251 Six locations feature high-end, high-tech fashions for women. Hot, in, definite fashion statements for the very brave or the very young. Brands change seasonally, but look for the exclusive Talula Babaton and Kookai labels. *Every day; map:C4.*

BACCI'S / 2788 Granville St; 604/733-4933 Avant-garde designers who appeal to the city's fashion-conscious Asian population are a specialty—UK handbag designer Anya Hindmarch, Jean-Paul Gaultier, Moschino, Daryl K, and Helmut Lang are just a few. The adjoining Bacci's at Home boutique holds exquisite gift items, such as Japanese ceramics, locally designed Koo Koo bed-and-bath linens, and Kiehl's New York skin care line. *Mon–Sat; map:D3.*

BEBE / 1000 Robson St; 604/681-1819 Founded in San Francisco in 1976, this is the highly successful women's clothing company's first Canadian store. A hit with Japanese tourists, the look is body-conscious and logo-laden, with an emphasis on trendy separates. *Every day; map:R3.*

BETSEY JOHNSON / 1033 Alberni St; 604/488-0314 Known for irreverent New York–style, ruffly dresses and signature hot-pink shopping bags,

Johnson's gone from designing patterns for Butterick in the 1970s to choosing paint colours for Mercedes in the 1990s. *Every day; map:S4.*

BOBOLI / 2776 Granville St; 604/736-3458 The stone archway gracing the entrance to this high-end designer store is fabled to have come from a ruined Mexican cathedral. Inside, exclusive fashions and footwear await discriminating shoppers. The adventurous gentleman will find many imports, including Issey Miyake, Pal Zileri, and Fuji Wara. Ladies can rub fashionably clad elbows with such names as Blumarine, Missoni, and Alberta Ferretti; there are also shoes, jewellery, and a new La Perla lingerie boutique. *Mon–Sat; map:D3.*

BOYS' CO / 1044 Robson St (and branches); 604/684-5656 The venerable king of men's ready-to-wear in Vancouver, Murray Goldman, spawned this upmarket, youth-oriented store, run by son David. Denim, clubwear, and suits imported from Germany, England, and Italy, as well as a top-quality house sportswear label, too. *Every day; www.boysco. com; map:S4.*

CABBAGES & KINX / 315 W Hastings St; 604/669-4238 Gear for Goths, neopunks, and Mods, some new, some vintage. Leather, lace, combat boots . . . you get the picture. *Every day; map:U4.*

CAN AMERICA CUSTOM SHIRTMAKERS / 609 W Pender St; 604/669-1128 The staff has more than 60 years of experience, through high collars and button-downs, so you know you're in good hands. The selection of cotton and polyester/cotton is very good. Both men's and women's shirts are available here, but their clientele is largely made up of businessmen. *Mon–Sat; map:T3.*

CHANEL / 755 Burrard St; 604/682-0522 Vancouver's iteration of the far-flung empire carries Chanel fashions, accessories, cosmetics, and perfume, and its ebullient francophone staff is a pleasure to visit. *Mon–Sat; map:S3.*

CHEVALIER CREATIONS / 620 Seymour St; 604/687-8428 Definitely for the man on the way up. Custom suits from tailor Gabriel Kalfon in linen or mohair blends, or 100 percent wool. Custom-made shirts in silk, linen, or cotton. Make an appointment. *Mon–Sat; map:T4.*

DKNY / 2625 Granville St; 604/733-2000 The ever expanding Donna Karan empire now has a Vancouver address: men's and women's DKNY, plus Pure and Jeans collections, shoes, and accessories. Coming soon are DKNY lingerie and children's wear (infant to 7 years). *Every day; map:D3.*

EDWARD CHAPMAN LADIES SHOP / 2596 Granville St (and branches); 604/732-3394 For more than a century, this name has been synonymous with quality imported women's wear. Somewhat conservative in its selection, the store carries top names from England and Europe (notably

VINTAGE CHIC

The demand for mid-century props and wardrobe by the movie industry plus the general run on anything that resembles modernist design or Austin Powers equals dozens of vintage stores opening up every year. Below are the spots (some of which have been around since the '70s) that are owned by people who do their research, stock quality items, provide unique services, and genuinely love their work.

Burcu's Angels / 2535 Main St; 604/874-9773 The staff at this clothier describe it as an "organic entity" rather than a store, as evidenced by the 24-hour "free box," the fact that it carries large sizes as a service to bigger women and transvestites, and the owner's penchant for magic tricks. *Every day; map:D3.*

Collect-o-rama / 2507 W Broadway; 604/732-7701 A crowded hole-in-the-wall dedicated to vintage moderne furniture but dealing mostly to film industry rentals. The best selection of vintage lighting in the city from the '30s to the '50s and custom lighting is available as well. *Wed–Sun; map:N7.*

Corazon / 3683 Main St; 604/873-8874 This new shop specializes in vintage lingerie, bed linens, and housewares. The brilliant touch, however, is that owner Fiona Curtis repackages mismatched china plates and bowls into colour-themed sets of four and makes new sets out of different antique sheets and pillowcases. Next door, Curtis's brother operates Big Daddy, a vintage clothing store for men. *Tues–Sun; map:D3.*

Déjà Vogue / 1485 W 11th Ave; 604/736-8100 Find well-gleaned treasures, mostly glamourous-vintage lingerie, tuxedos, cigarette holders, cuff links, wedding dresses, and lots of glittery people who come to hang out with the gregarious proprietor, Monika Taylor. Prices are extremely reasonable and custom tailoring is available. *Every day; map:P7.*

Deluxe Junk / 310 W Cordova St; 604/685-4871 This vintage consignment store has suppliers in far-flung areas of the province who scour rural thrift shops and jumble sales for pristine vintage finds. The store stays au courant by forecasting fashion trends into the next season, then filling the store with a huge selection just in time for the trend to hit. *Every day; map:U3.*

The Good Jacket / 225 E Broadway; 604/872-5665 This self-described "vintage pop-culture clothier" located at Dysfunction Junction (the off-beat retail triangle at Broadway and Main) sells pre-'80s clothing and collectibles, toys and novelties. The owner has a talent for digging up dead stock—brand-new vintage items forgotten about in some warehouse for 30 years, and often still with their original price tags. *Tues–Sun; www.goodjacket.bc.ca; map:V7.*

The Hound Dog / 2306 W Broadway; 604/734-9393 Situated on a heritage block in Kitsilano, this is the oldest vintage store in the city. There's a good selection of dishes (such as Fiestaware), glasses, and decorative items from the '30s to the '60s. *Every day; map:N7.*

Metropolitan Home / 450 W Hastings St; 604/681-2313 This 15-year-old store specialized in midcentury modern furniture well before it was all the rage, lately moving away from '50s-kitchen style and toward slick modernism. *Every day; map:S3.*

Panther Décor / 2924 W 4th Ave; 604/733-5665 This large Kitsilano furniture spot is known for carrying large pieces and complete sets such as art deco sofas with matching chairs, or chrome and Formica dinettes and chairs. *Tues-Sun; map:C2.*

Populuxe / 302 W 2nd Ave; 604/879-2665 Find '50s kitsch, pop art, Lucite lamps, streamlined '30s stoves and fridges (restored to perfect working order by the store's owners), reupholstered '40s club chairs, dial telephones the colour of peach sorbet, and a superb collection of vintage microphones. *Every day; map:T6.*

True Value Vintage / 710 Robson St; 604/685-5403 An underground emporium of vintage stuff for guys and girls, from beaded shell tops to leather blazers, with an emphasis on the '60s, '70s and '80s. A locked collector's room with a Japanese-only sign holds real Cowichan sweaters, rare Levi's, and authentic '50s Hawaiian shirts. *Every day; map:R4.* —*Sarah Reeder*

Germany), in well-cut, well-made fashion. The new Circa Ici shop, connected though the back, is where you'll find local designer clothes. *Mon–Sat; map:D3.*

EDWARD CHAPMAN MEN'S WEAR / 833 W Pender St; 604/685-6207 Traditional in every sense of the word, Edward Chapman has been the place for classic British and American clothing for four generations. *Mon–Sat; map:S3.*

ENDA B / 4346 W 10th Ave; 604/228-1214 A warning to casual browsers: this store has a large selection of designer, natural fibre fashions and the savviest wardrobe consultants in town. Don't enter unless you're fully prepared to walk out with something you love. You'll also find accessories and jewellery, a good shoe section, a children's play area, and a cappuccino bar. *Every day; map:B3.*

ERMENEGILDO ZEGNA / Pacific Centre, top floor; 604/681-7988 The first Canadian store for this 88-year-old Italian textiles-and-clothing manufacturer houses upscale menswear collections and has retained its traditional cachet by resisting putting its name on colognes or underwear. Cashmere cloth is a specialty. *Every day; map:D4.*

FORMES / 2985 Granville St; 604/733-2213 This Parisian maternity store has a large roster of U.S. customers, not to mention the hundreds of local mothers-to-be who covet the discreet French styling of narrow leather pants, slinky dresses, and the store's best-selling maternity item— the business suit. *Every day; www.formes.com; map:D3.*

HILL'S OF KERRISDALE / 2125 West 41st Ave; 604/266-9177 A local institution since the 1930s, this mini-department store stocks men's, women's, and children's designer clothing plus private-school uniforms. Top-quality labels such as Wilke Rodriguez, Replay, A-Line by Anne Klein, and Teenflo; shoes from Nine West and others. Local jewellery designs bedeck counter displays, and the store also houses an Aritzia boutique (see listing in this section). *Every day; map:C4.*

JACQUELINE CONOIR BOUTIQUE / 3035 Granville St; 604/732-4209 High-quality, authoritative clothing by renowned local designer and owner RozeMerie Cuevas, whose suits are worn by local news anchors. *Every day; map:D3.*

LEONE / Sinclair Centre; 604/683-1133 Definitely worth a visit—and not just for the sheer architectural splendour of it all. Set like a jewel in the exquisite Sinclair Centre, this store showcases international men's and women's designers in separate galleries—Gianni Versace, Mui Mui, Prada Sport, Dolce & Gabbana, and many more. Shoes and accessories round out the main floor, while Versace housewares are on the top floor. The basement houses the original AWear boutique, the store's own, more affordable label. *Every day; www.awear.com; map:T3.*

MARGARETA / 1441 Bellevue Ave, West Vancouver (and branches); 604/926-2113 Design Classics, designed and manufactured for the store's own label. Styles range from the elegant to the casual. Custom-made and custom-fitted fashions are a specialty. *Every day; map:D1.*

MARIA JUNG / 2567 W Broadway; 604/737-8795 This celebrated Miami-based bridal designer has 30 years' experience custom tailoring dresses. Jung's daughter oversees the fitting of classic, couture wedding gowns at this stunningly minimalist Kitsilano boutique. *Mon–Sat; map:C2.*

MARK JAMES / 2941 W Broadway; 604/734-2381 (and branch) His name is synonymous with both men's fashion-forward dressing (suits from DKNY, Byblos, and Hugo Boss, sportswear from Diesel and Armani Sport) and brew pubs. The original Broadway store adjoins Fiasco's restaurant; the Yaletown location enters into James's highly successful Yaletown Brewing Company. *Every day; www.markjamesgroup.com; map:C3.*

MAXMARA / 2756 Granville St; 604/257-2350 Associated with its neighbour, Boboli, this women's clothing shop stocks the entire MaxMara clothing and accessory line. These chic but casual Italians include SportMax, Weekend, and Blues Club. *Mon–Sat; map:D3.*

MINICHIELLO DESIGNS / 1108 Homer St; 604/682-6800 Italian suits woven with clay or copper fibres to keep you cool and protect from UV rays are exclusive to this men's and women's high-end store. *Every day; map:S5.*

NANCY LORD / 1666 Johnston St; 604/689-3972 or 800/586-8555 There have been some monumental and technological changes in this one-of-a-kind store. Although it's known for its soft, supple leather fashions in classic and eclectic styling, it also creates women's fashions in Italian and Swiss fabrics personally selected in Europe. The colours are beautiful and the quality is high. *Every day; map:Q6.*

ROOTS / 1001 Robson St (and branches); 604/683-4305 The Vancouver area boasts 11 of this popular Canadian chain's shops, carrying casual, ruggedly styled clothes and shoes for men, women, children, and a certain Olympic snowboarder. The Robson location also carries Roots furniture and accessories for weekends in the great outdoors. *Every day; www.roots.com; map:R3.*

SALVATORE FERRAGAMO / 918 Robson St; 604/669-4495 Extraordinary fashions in an exclusive international boutique. This is the only Canadian operation of this company, which can be found in major cities around the world. *Every day; map:S3.*

VERSUS / 1008 W Georgia St; 604/688-8938 Kitty-corner from two of Vancouver's larger hotels, this men's and women's shop caters lavishly to the tourists and to well-clad locals. Versus, Versace Jeans Couture, and Gianni Versace perfumes and cosmetics. *Every day; map:S3.*

WEAR ELSE? / 2360 W 4th Ave (and branches); 604/732-3521 The dependable fashion consultants here can outfit you with an entire wardrobe—or the classic pieces that will be its foundation. Both international and Canadian designers are represented, and there is a large selection of shoes and accessories. Wear Else Weekend is available at the W Fourth Avenue location, and deals can be had at Wear Else Clearance at 78 E Second Avenue. *Every day; map:N7.*

 ZONDA NELLIS / 2203 Granville St; 604/736-5668 Unique loomed fabrics are used to create simple yet distinctive fashions. Nellis is a local designer with an international clientele. *Mon–Sat; map:Q7.*

AUCTIONS

LOVE'S / 1635 W Broadway; 604/733-1157 Since 1912, Love's has been helping bargain hunters get the best prices on all kinds of items. Auctions are held every other Wednesday at noon and at 7pm. Love's also does appraisals. *Mon–Fri; map:Q7.*

MAYNARD'S / 415 W 2nd Ave; 604/876-6787 Another longtime Vancouver fixture, Maynard's has been around since 1902. Auctions are held every other Wednesday at 7pm (absentee bids are accepted), and you're invited to view your potential treasures on Tuesdays between 10am and

6pm. The store also has a large retail area, where liquidated inventories (from tents to bikes to Paul Smith dress shirts) go for below cost. *Every day (retail only Sat–Sun); www.maynards.com; map:U7.*

TYLDESLEY'S / 1055 Vernon; 604/254-2111 The store may have been around since 1917, but it has kept up with communications technology. Auctions are held every Tuesday; viewing of items is Monday and Tuesday afternoons. *Mon–Fri; map:Y6.*

BAKERIES

ECCO IL PANE / 238 W 5th Ave (and branches); 604/873-6888 Christopher Brown and Pamela Gaudreault, the hardworking duo behind Ecco il Pane, create wholesome Italian country breads in their upscale west side bakery cafes. Our favourite, *dolce mio,* is a buttery and fragrant version of raisin bread with orange zest, anise, marsala, currants, and walnuts; the fantastic chocolate cherry loaf comes in a very close second. Wonderful Christmas gift packs and biscotti are available, and the Broadway location has an adjoining bistro. *Every day; map:U7.*

LA BAGUETTE ET L'ECHALOTTE / 1680 Johnston St; 604/684-1351 Owners Mario Armitano and Louise Turgeon create classic French-baked goods, such as their *pain de campagne,* a country-style baguette, decadent chocolate truffles, and seasonal fruit flans. For those on special diets, they bake loaves with no yeast, no sugar, and no salt. *Every day; map:Q6.*

SIEGEL'S BAGELS / 1883 Cornwall Ave (and branches); 604/737-8151 For bagel-bingers who love a chewy Montreal-style bagel with a handmade look. Siegel's bagels come in pumpernickel, cinnamon-raisin, caraway, multigrain, onion, sesame, orange poppyseed, and more varieties. Also find knishes stuffed with potato or spinach, and a vegetable roll. Try the Montreal smoked meat or lox and cream cheese. Eat in or take out 24 hours at this location. *Every day; map:O6.*

TERRA BREADS / 2380 W 4th Ave (and branches); 604/736-1838 Michael Lansky's Terra Breads has an avid clientele for its crusty hearth-baked breads, which are baked fresh every morning in a stone-deck oven and naturally leavened by a slow process using natural yeast starters. Terra's French baguettes are made in the authentic French tradition—the bakers use only unbleached flour without additives, fillers, or preservatives. Among the exceptional breads are white or levain rounds, fabulous black olive or rosemary and olive-oil loaves, Italian cheese bread, raisin rye, fig with anise, a very fine focaccia, and a grape-and-pine-nut loaf. *Every day; map:Q6.*

THREE DOG BAKERY / 2186 W 4th Ave; 604/737-3647 Most of these treats look tastier than human food, but pupcakes and bulldog bars are baked here for yuppie puppies. Let Rover cool his paws in the doggy lounge while you peruse the all-natural, low-fat goodies. *Every day; map:C2.*

UPRISING BAKERY / 1697 Venables St; 604/254-5635 A well-known Vancouver establishment, Uprising features the best in wholesome breads, buns, and goodies. An expanded retail area now includes a selection of cheeses, cakes, cheesecakes, and German chocolate, among other items. There's a full range of deli salads and spelt-flour bread for those with allergies. *Every day; map:Z5.*

BOOKS, MAPS, AND MAGAZINES

AEROTRAINING PRODUCTS / 4680 Cowley Cres, South Terminal, Vancouver International Airport; 604/278-8021 Appropriately located at the airport's south terminal, this store has really taken off. It has increased its sections on the technical aspects of aviation, which should thrill engineers, designers, and mechanics. Also, shelfloads of handbooks, regulation books, maintenance manuals—even video-format pilot training programs. *Mon–Sat; map:C6.*

ALBION BOOKS / 523 Richards St; 604/662-3113 A very personal place for people who love old books and jazz, and like to talk about them with kindred souls. The big difference between this used bookstore and others is its selection of sheet music, jazz on vinyl, and CDs, which Albion employees will cheerfully play for you. *Every day; map:T3.*

BARBRA-JO'S BOOKS TO COOKS / 1228 Mainland St; 604/688-6755 Find an excellent selection of culinary titles by local and celebrity chefs. Bonus: wine tastings and cooking demonstrations in the test kitchen often accompany book signings. *Every day; www.bookstocooks.com; map:S5.*

BANYEN BOOKS / 2671 W Broadway; 604/732-7912 Along with its extensive stock of New Age and self-help books, Banyen also has a great selection of vegetarian cookbooks, religious texts, and tarot cards. **BANYEN SOUND** (2669 W Broadway; 604/737-8858), next door, has New Age music recordings and spoken-text cassette tapes. *Every day; www.banyen.com; map:C2.*

BOOK WAREHOUSE / 632 W Broadway (and branches); 604/872-5711 Known for minimal merchandising (hence lower prices); expect to pay at least 10 percent less than at other stores for best-selling hardcovers and paperbacks. *Every day; map:D2.*

CHAPTERS / 788 Robson St (and branches); 604/682-4066 This ever expanding chain of superstores has spelled the demise of many small, neighbourhood magazine stores and bookshops, but if you like your best-sellers attractively merchandised, this is where to find them. Each store also contains a Starbucks coffee outlet. *Every day; www.chapters. ca; map:R3.*

THE COMICSHOP / 2089 W 4th Ave; 604/738-8122 For 25 years this unique little spot has served Vancouver's comic connoisseurs with new issues and collector's items. *Every day; comicshop.daconline.net; map:O7.*

DUTHIE BOOKS / 2239 W 4th Ave; 604/732-5344 The true bibliophile must make a pilgrimage to Duthie's last existing location, or its virtual bookstore that exists only in pixels (www.literascape.com). Since 1957, Duthie Books has been serving the literati and hoi polloi alike with its comprehensive selection of the popular and the obscure; in 1999 it was forced to close all but this location due increased competition in the marketplace. Helpful, knowledgeable staff. *Every day; infodesk@duthiebooks. com; map:S4.*

GRANVILLE BOOK COMPANY / 850 Granville St; 604/687-2213 This store is a browse-fest for book lovers, with a good selection of the latest best-sellers and a very good sci-fi/fantasy section. *Every day; www. granvillebooks.com; map:S4.*

HAGER BOOKS / 2176 W 41st Ave; 604/263-9412 This cozy Kerrisdale shop contains all the latest best-sellers and has an excellent children's selection. *Every day; map:C4.*

INTERNATIONAL TRAVEL MAPS AND BOOKS / 552 Seymour St; 604/687-3320 Wherever you're going, this store can help you find your way. It has one of the largest map and travel guide selections in Canada. *Every day; www.itmb.com; map:T4.*

KIDSBOOKS / 3083 W Broadway (and branches); 604/738-5335 To say this store is dedicated to children's literature is to make a terrible understatement. There are books and book talks, book readings and book launchings. And did we mention the books? The staff are especially helpful in choosing gifts for out-of-town children. *Every day; map:C3.*

LITTLE SISTER'S BOOK AND ART EMPORIUM / 1238 Davie St; 604/669-1753 You don't have to be gay to enjoy Little Sister's, but it helps. Little Sister's is the only gay and lesbian bookstore in Western Canada, and it is lavishly stocked with books on subjects ranging from coffee-table erotica to travel. Every cranny is filled with divertissements—calendars, T-shirts bearing slogans such as "Queerly Canadian," candles, Sex Grease, sex toys, and greeting cards. *Every day; www.lsisters.com; map:Q4.*

MACLEOD'S BOOKS / 455 W Pender St; 604/681-7654 Walking into MacLeod's is like walking into a Dickens novel: layers and mazes of books are piled to the ceiling. Each area of antiquarian books and collectibles is meticulously classified, and the store is heavily into history: British Columbian, Asian, military, marine, Native (Plains, Northeast, et cetera). Ninety percent of the stock is used and/or out of print. *Every day; www.abebooks.com; map:T4.*

MAGPIE MAGAZINE GALLERY / 1319 Commercial Dr; 604/253-6666 An intimate neighbourhood magazine store with a bookstore atmosphere, Magpie has halogen track lighting, a background of jazz music, and a curious and attentive staff, who will track down even the most obscure rag. Send a friend e-mail on the Magpie computer terminal for a buck per half hour. *Every day; map:Z6.*

MAYFAIR NEWS / 1535 W Broadway (and branches); 604/738-8951 Can't find your hometown newspaper? Need a copy of an obscure magazine? Try the Mayfair News collection of more than 3,000 periodicals. *Every day; map:S3.*

THE TRAVEL BUG / 2667 W Broadway; 604/737-1122 Off to the Serengeti? The Outback? The Bronx? Owner Dwight Elliot can find you just the right travel guide and foreign-language phrase book from his stock of more than 6,000 titles. Then he'll equip you with the essential travel accessories, from money belts (security holster, sock safe) to tele-plug-ins for computers to travellers' sleep sacks (an essential item for the hosteller). He can even provide the carry-on luggage in which to stow it all. *Every day; map:C2.*

UBC BOOKSTORE / 6200 University Blvd; 604/822-2665 For a bookstore, the one at UBC is huge—the biggest in western Canada, though most of the floor space is devoted to university logowear and student supplies rather than books. If you can muster the strength, peruse the more than 100,000 titles, from anatomy to zoology. Veer off into another section and you'll find BC pottery, varsity jackets, art supplies, cameras, fax machines, and a major computer department. Don't let the fact that it sounds like a mall put you off. The staff is dedicated to books, and there are comfy chairs where you can sit and read. *Mon–Sat; www.bookstore. ubc.ca; map:B2.*

WANDERLUST / 1929 W 4th Ave; 604/739-2182 When it's time for those boot heels to go wandering, Tony McCurdy and his helpful staff can make sure you're prepared. They carry thousands of books about foreign lands, with entire bookcases devoted to some countries. Travel accessories include water purifiers, mosquito nets, safety whistles, convertible packs, and language tapes. *Every day; map:O7.*

WOMEN IN PRINT / 3566 W 4th Ave; 604/732-4128 Books by women, for women, on women's issues. Also books by men on topics of interest to women, plus novelty T-shirts, cards, and puzzles. *Every day; map:B2.*

CANDIES AND CHOCOLATE

BERNARD CALLEBAUT CHOCOLATERIE / 2698 Granville St (and branches); 604/736-5890 Yes, there really is a Bernard Callebaut, and he supplies his stores with what may be the best chocolate in the world. (We know everyone says that, but we can't find anyone to argue with this claim.) *Mon–Sat; map:D3.*

CHOCOLATE ARTS / 2037 W 4th Ave; 604/739-0475 Greg Hook collaborated with native artist Robert Davidson to open this sweet shop, and has created fabulous-tasting chocolates that look like fine art. The perfect gift to impress out-of-towners is chocolate medallions with Haida designs, and the liquor-laced truffles are incredible. *Every day; map:N7.*

DANIEL LE CHOCOLAT BELGE / 1105 Robson St (and branches); 604/688-9624 In 1987, Daniel supplied his secret-formula chocolates to heads of state who were attending Vancouver's Commonwealth Conference, testimony to his highly developed sense of presentation, packaging, and decoration—not to mention his exquisite array of hazelnut paste, creamy caramel, delicious ganache creams, and liquor truffles, sleekly enrobed in pure, rich chocolate. *Every day; map:S3.*

THE LAZY GOURMET / 1605 W 5th Ave; 604/734-2507 Tops, locally, for a unique BC delicacy—a chocolaty, gooey, almost-too-sweet (but that never stopped us) confection—the Nanaimo bar. *Every day; map:P7.*

LEE'S CANDIES / 4361 W 10th Ave; 604/224-5450 A local legend, Lee's Candies is located next to the Varsity Theatre and is the mainstay of many a chocolate-starved UBC student. All candies are handmade on the premises. Seconds sell for $6.45 a pound and are bagged each Saturday, when they usually sell out fast. Lee's has the largest selection of chocolate moulds in the city. *Mon–Sat; map:B3.*

OLDE WORLD FUDGE / 1689 Johnston St (and branches); 604/687-7355 Here's the most reliable source we know for fabulous fudge. More than 10 varieties are available, with special novelty types for sale from time to time. *Every day; map:Q6.*

PURDY'S / Pacific Centre (and branches); 604/681-7814 A Vancouver institution and the place to fill up a stocking or Easter basket. The factory store (2777 Kingway St) always has prepackaged seconds, as well as a clerk who will parcel up what you want from loose seconds. *Every day; map:T4.*

SUTTON PLACE CHOCOHOLIC BAR / 845 Burrard St, in Fleuri restaurant; 604/682-5511 A legend in its own time, this decadent buffet of desserts simply overwhelms. Fresh fruit, French crêpes made to order, a variety of cheesecakes and squares, passion fruit, raspberry, or chocolate sauce, and a selection of liquor syrups await. *Thurs–Sat; map:S3.*

CHILDREN'S CLOTHING

BRATZ / 2828 Granville St; 604/734-4344 Stroll south down Granville (past 12th Avenue), until you come to a window full of colourful, adorable, definitely wearable children's clothing. Haircuts specifically for tots also available. *Every day; map:D3.*

ISOLA BELLA / 5692 Yew St; 604/266-8808 Exclusive designer togs for tots—much of the stock is imported from France and Italy—of European quality. You'll also find footwear for fashionable little feet and beautiful gift items for children. From newborn to size 16. *Mon–Sat; map:C4.*

KIDZ BIZ / 1210-6551 No. 3 Rd, Richmond (and branches); 604/276-8289 Brand-name duds for preemies to trendy preteens (Champion, Body Guard, Tommy), priced well below the competition. A modest markup policy and suburban locations keep the prices down. *Every day; map:C6.*

PLEASE MUM / 2951 W Broadway (and branches); 604/732-4574 Fun and functional clothing for the junior jet set. *Every day; map:B3.*

SPOILT / 734 Park Royal N, West Vancouver; 604/922-0750 Designed and made locally, these classic children's fashions are constructed to last through several hand-me-downs. The helpful staff is very tolerant of tired and temperamental tots. *Every day; map:D4.*

CONSIGNMENT

HAPPY THREE / 3629 W 4th Ave (and branches); 604/730-9638 Not only are there great designer bargains here (Chanel, Jean-Paul Gaultier, Gucci), there are racks of new samples of designer knockoffs from Hong Kong factories. Little sweater sets and trendy nylon sling bags are a bargain. Sizes are mostly on the small side. *Every day; map:C3.*

KISA'S OF KERRISDALE / 2352 W 41st Ave; 604/266-2885 Down the stairs through the ivy-bedecked entrance, you'll find a very nice selection of designer consignment fashion, jewellery, shoes, handbags, and accessories. Owner Barbara McDonald has an eye for the unique and offers new or gently worn clothing with well-known labels, many from Europe. *Mon–Sat; map:C4.*

MACGILLYCUDDY'S FOR LITTLE PEOPLE / 4881 Mackenzie St; 604/263-5313 A consignment store for children's wear, selling clothing, footwear, furniture, and some hand-knit pieces. *Mon–Sat; map:C4.*

SECOND SUIT / 2036 W 4th Ave; 604/732-0338 Although the quality of the consignment goods here is good and styles are no more than one season old, the real draw are the samples for men and women from the Yaletown showrooms for the upcoming season. As a bonus, the clothes are organized by colour rather than style so you can steer completely clear of canary yellow if you wish. Also find designer sunglasses and jewellery. *Every day; map:O7.*

TURNABOUT COLLECTIONS LTD. / 3060 W Broadway (and branches); 604/731-7762 High-quality consignment, carrying some designers. The W Broadway store is casual, fun, and funky for men and women (jeans, sportswear, bathing suits). At South Granville it has prestige labels, such as Donna Karan, Issey Miyake, and Armani, with an emphasis on eveningwear. *Every day; map:D3.*

COOKWARE

BASIC STOCK COOKWARE / 2294 W 4th Ave (and branches); 604/736-1412 Rack after rack of shining pots and pans of every size and description, and every gadget you could ever want to clutter your kitchen drawers. A selection of coffees and teas, and everything you need to make them in, is also offered. *Every day; map:N7.*

COOKWORKS / 1548 W Broadway; 604/731-1148 Find high-end kitchen tools such as retro-style chrome spa juicers and ice crushers from New York, professional cookware lines Henkel and Calphalon, stainless-steel salad spinners (and a cord-pull variety designed especially for arthritis sufferers) as well as Martha Stewart's favourite, the Donvier Shakemate. *Every day; map:C2.*

DRINKWATER AND CO. / 3036 W Broadway; 604/224-2665 The Drinkwater family embarked on this venture to fill a void in the market for high-quality, affordable home textiles. Find hand-printed and hand-woven tablecloths, curtains, and cushion covers in butter yellow or apple green arriving weekly in burlap bundles from India, as well as exotic accessories, such as Indonesian coconut-shell salad tongs. *Every day; map:C2.*

MING WO / 23 E Pender St (and branches); 604/683-7268 Since 1917, Ming Wo has maintained the highest standards of quality in the cookware and kitchenware it carries. A large stock of hard-to-find items and a reputation for value have kept Vancouverites (especially university students) loyal to the store. You'll find Ming Wo in suburban shopping centres and several Vancouver locations, but the shop in Chinatown is the original. *Every day; map:U4.*

TOOLS & TECHNIQUES / 250 16th St, West Vancouver; 604/925-1835 This West Van neighbourhood kitchen store concentrates on domestic and imported pots, pans, cooking aids, food processors, and cookbooks, but also offers specialty food items. Classes and book signings by respected Vancouver cooks take place in the well-equipped demonstration kitchen. *Every day; map:E3.*

DEPARTMENT STORES

ARMY AND NAVY / 27 W Hastings St (and branches); 604/682-6644 This generations-old Vancouver institution (owned by Jacqui Cohen-Herrendorf, one of Vancouver's leading socialites) got a boost during the "grunge look" era of the early 1990s, when rich kids flocked to this east-side store in search of work pants, plaid shirts, and steel-toed boots. All these things are still available—along with great bargains on fishing gear, shoes, and bed linens—albeit in a less proletarian environment, courtesy of a swish new marketing campaign. *Every day; map:U4.*

THE BAY / 674 Granville St (and branches); 604/681-6211 The Hudson's Bay Company has a long and romantic past, having served Canadians in one capacity or another for more than 300 years. Although the downtown store hasn't been around quite that long, it is a handsome heritage building. The times have caught up with the Bay gracefully; when the Granville SkyTrain station was planted practically in its basement, the owners transformed the lower level into a series of bright and attractive boutiques. The other floors in the store have also received renovations to keep them up-to-date. The Bay is the only store in town that carries authentic Hudson's Bay blankets, with their distinctive coloured stripes on a cream background, as well as jackets made from the same material. The store is connected to Pacific Centre. *Every day; map:T4.*

HOLT RENFREW / 633 Granville St; 604/681-3121 This prestigious national chain is Vancouver's largest designer department store for men and women, housing boutiques for Prada, Tiffany's, Louis Vuitton, Gucci, Hermès, and more. The Brown's shoe department is the best spot in town for designer shoes (Manolo Blahnik, Patrick Cox), the house label of women's sportswear is excellent and well priced, and the cosmetics department carries make-up artistry lines such as Bobbi Brown and Makeup Forever. *Every day; map:S4.*

FLORISTS AND GARDEN SHOPS

THE AVANT GARDENER / 1460 Marine Dr, West Vancouver (and branches); 604/926-8784 This is a great store for the serious gardener or the confirmed browser (and what gardener isn't both?). Gardening stock and patio furniture sit alongside decorator accents and designer T-shirts. *Every day; map:C1.*

DIG THIS / 1551 Johnston St; 604/688-2929 This is a faux-ivy-covered cottage on Granville Island offering supplies for indoor and outdoor gardening, as well as a variety of beautiful stone garden fountains. A large stock of garden and outdoor furniture can be found. *Every day; map:Q6.*

HILLARY MILES FLOWERS / 1 1854 W 1st Ave; 604/737-2782 Bouquet impresario Hillary Miles has been collaborating with fashion designers for more than 20 years, and creates floral chefs d'oeuvre for movie sets, weddings, special events, and, if you're lucky, maybe even your living room. *Mon–Sat; map:O6.*

SOUTHLANDS NURSERY / 6550 Balaclava St; 604/261-6411 Under the skilful guidance of renowned local gardener and florist Thomas Hobbs, the nursery offers indoor and outdoor plants—plus the perfect containers in which to display them. Hobbs is known for his expertise with (and fondness for) orchids, so expect a good selection. *Every day; map:C4.*

THOMAS HOBBS FLORIST BY MAUREEN SULLIVAN / 2127 W 41st Ave; 604/263-2601 or 800/663-2601 Though now under the ownership of Maureen and Jim Sullivan, this remains one of the finest florists—and certainly the best-known one—in the Vancouver area. Tasteful and creative arrangements are presented in handsome containers. *Every day; map:C4.*

GIFTS AND JEWELLERY

ATKINSON'S / 1501 W 6th Ave; 604/736-3378 Originally an executive gift service, the family-owned store holds two floors of European crystal, silver, china, and even a children's gift boutique. Splurge on Lalique, Baccarat, Christofle, and Limoges, or treat yourself to bed, table, and bath linen imported from Pratesi of Italy, and double-damask Irish table linens. *Tues–Sat; map:P7.*

BIRKS / 698 Hastings St (and branches); 604/669-3333 When Henry Birks opened his doors in the beginning of the last century, he could hardly have known that one day his empire would stretch from sea to sea. Birks stores are found in every major Canadian city. For generations, brides have received their engagement rings here (especially since Birks teamed up with renowned local jeweller Toni Cavelti), have registered here, and have received their subsequent anniversary presents from this store—all items coming in that distinctive blue box, which carries a cachet as exciting as the gift it holds. *Every day; map:T3.*

BLUE RUBY / Oakridge Centre (and branches); 604/269-BLUE An outcrop of the successful jewellery counter at Hill's of Kerrisdale, this boutique banked on the trend in the accessories market away from austerity and toward glamour: lush alcoves mimic a 1940s boudoir, while the focus is on high-quality fashion jewellery (most in sterling silver with semiprecious stones) aimed at the under-30 set. *Every day; map:D4.*

CHACHKAS / 1075 Robson St; 604/688-6417 Whether you're looking for the perfect little gift for a friend or a selfish little treat for yourself, you'll find plenty to choose from at this shop, which carries a large selection of jewellery, decorative items, prints, and imports. *Every day; map:R3.*

GEORG JENSEN / Pacific Centre; 604/688-3116 Jensen's classic turn-of-the-century designs—all executed in silver—vie for attention with modern styles. This store is part of the international chain founded by the

Danish designer and features high-quality jewellery, crystal, and decor items. *Every day; map:T4.*

HAMMERED AND PICKLED / 1494 Old Bridge St; 604/689-0615 Three young female jewellery designers have teamed up in this Granville Island studio where you can watch them make and polish pieces by hand before putting them into the display cases. Working mainly with silver and semi-precious stones, each designer has a distinctive style, and many of the pieces are one-of-a-kind. *Every day; map:Q6.*

KARL STITTGEN GOLDSMITHS / 2203 Granville St; 604/737-0029 A local favourite with a far-reaching reputation, designer Karl Stittgen creates fabulous handmade jewellery of gold and gems. Singularly handsome pieces are often one-of-a-kind. *Tues–Sat; map:P7.*

LIGHTHEART & CO. / 535 Howe St; 604/684-4711 or 800/474-4711 Divine ready-made gift baskets for every occasion. Owner Sherri Lightheart, born into Vancouver's Murchie's-coffee family, has earned a devoted clientele through high standards of customer service, which includes a bridal registry, a special discount for the bride, free gift wrapping and delivery, and a fabulous selection of crystal, china, decorative items, and linen. *Every day; map:T3.*

MARTHA STURDY ORIGINALS / 3039 Granville St; 604/737-0037 A local star with international appeal (Tokyo and New York are her biggest markets), Sturdy's bold metal and cast-resin jewellery was a staple gift 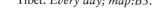 for retiring *Vogue* editors in the 1980s, and has appeared in Marc Jacob's runway shows. Now her sculptural housewares and furniture, also mostly made of metal and acrylic, are design items coveted the world over as well. *Every day; map:D3.*

MOULÉ / 1994 W 4th Ave (and branches); 604/732-4066 As well as attracting unique pieces from local artists and artisans, the owners of Moulé have scoured the globe and returned with exotic treasures, plus modern dinnerware from Calvin Klein and Nan Swid. *Every day; map:O7.*

PALLADIO / 855 W Hastings St; 604/685-3885 Vancouver's Bosa family of developers continue to build on their prospects with this latest jewellery venture, named for northern Italian architect Andrea Palladio. Semiprecious and precious stones, gold watches, and a good selection of pieces in the au courant metal, platinum. *Every day; map:R2.*

HOME FURNISHINGS

BALI BALI GALLERIA / 4462 W 10th Ave; 604/224-2347 A favourite importer of the exotic and the exciting; a delightful source of handicrafts and objets d'art from the fabled East, including Bali, Java, India, and Tibet. *Every day; map:B3.*

BERNSTEIN & GOLD / 1168 Hamilton St; 604/687-1535 Everything in this lifestyle store is keyed to the cream and gold decor—for a luxe appeal. Overstuffed and slipcovered furniture is made in BC, accessories are imported from Europe, and linens and bedding are of very high quality. *Every day; map:T5.*

COUNTRY FURNITURE / 3097 Granville St; 604/738-6411 If anything is going to convince you of the beauty and simplicity of pioneer life, it's a visit to this store. Faux-finished reproduction tables, decorative folk art, painted cabinets, and leather club chairs are the types of things you'll find in this laid-back, somewhat crowded store. *Every day; map:D3.*

FREEDOM / 1150 Hamilton St; 604/688-3163 An eclectic mix of home furnishings and accessories are selected by the owners during their extensive travels and combined with pieces from local artists; they're then arrayed in themed displays (the Garden of Eden, Morocco, et cetera) in this Yaletown store. *Every day; map:T5.*

INFORM / 97 Water St; 604/682-3868 Canada's most famous furniture designer, local Niels Bendtsen, founded this sleek store that stocks both his own line and dozens of carefully chosen others—all contemporary, some with a modernist influence. It's the kind of place where your purchase comes with a numbered authentication certificate, and is signed by the designer. Find Philippe Stark, Mies van der Rohe, Alias, Agape, and the like. Stock is mostly from Italy, with pieces from England, Scandinavia, and New York. Every single piece in the store is akin to art (several pieces are in fact in the permanent collection of New York's MOMA), and celebrities—such as Bryan Adams—ship purchases to homes as far away as London. *Every day; map:U3.*

KAYA KAYA / 2039 W 4th Ave; 604/732-1816 Beautiful Japanese imports, such as currently popular ceramic tea and sake services, are far less expensive here than in designer stores, and these ones are authentic. *Mon–Sat; map:N7.*

LIBERTY / 1295 Seymour St; 604/682-7499 This immense home store became an instant shopping landmark when it grew out of its former South Granville atelier and into its present 1,080 square-metre (12,000-square-foot) Yaletown building. The Gothic-themed main floor holds overstuffed velvet couches, a giant stone fountain, and stuffed crows in the rafters. The bright, naturally lit second floor displays iron beds, luscious linens, a children's furniture section, and shelves of decorative items sourced from around the world. *Every day; map:S4.*

MONTAUK / 1062 Homer St; 604/331-2363 The all-white Yaletown store is a West Coast first for the Montreal-based furniture manufacturer that was inspired by the American beach town of Montauk. Understated and contemporary, the hardwood, coil supports, and goose-down elements of the slipcovered sofas, chairs, and ottomans are guaranteed for 24 years. *Tues–Sun; map:S5.*

RESTORATION HARDWARE / 2555 Granville St; 604/731-3918 An IKEA for baby boomers that specializes in Mission-revival and Arts and Crafts–style furniture, plus hundreds of gifts and gadgets collected from all over the world. Although the company was started by a husband-and-wife team out of their garage, an average of 20 stores open per year in the United States (this is the first in Canada), making this hardly your average mom-and-pop operation. *Every day; map:P8.*

SENGARA PASSAGE THROUGH INDIA / 1525 W 6th Ave; 604/733-9992 Just in time for the Madonna-fueled run on South Asian furniture and textiles, Kim Sengara gave up Asian Studies at UBC to import artifacts from India, her parents' homeland. Find 1920s hand-embroidered wedding garments from Rajasthan sewn into wall hangings and cushions, architectural pieces, wall panels, and ornate dancers' boxes for storing jewellery. *Tues–Sun; map:P7.*

UPCOUNTRY / 2210 Cambie St; 604/875-9004 This elegant, multilevel store specializes in contemporary, Canadian-made furniture geared toward modular- and loft-living spaces. It's also a showcase for local talents, such as photographer Rob Melnychuk and home furniture designer Matthew Quetton. *Every day; map:T7.*

LINGERIE

DIANE'S LINGERIE AND LOUNGEWEAR / 2950 Granville St; 604/738-5121 You'll receive kid-glove treatment from the helpful staff when choosing a gift. The store offers a large selection of underpinnings in all sizes, from well-known manufacturers, as well as sleepwear ranging from prosaic jammies to sexy negligees. It also enjoys the distinction of having the largest selection of brassieres in western Canada. *Mon–Sat; map:D3.*

LA JOLIE MADAME / Pacific Centre; 604/669-1831 Ultra-feminine lingerie in a wide range of sizes. Much of the stock is imported. Friendly, knowledgeable staff. *Every day; map:T4.*

NATIVE ART AND CRAFTS

HILL'S INDIAN CRAFTS / 165 Water St; 604/685-4249 Located in Gastown, Hill's is famous for its wide selection of aboriginal art and handiwork, spread over three floors. It's somewhat infamous too, given that Bill Clinton picked up a carving here to give Monica Lewinsky when he was in town for APEC. Art ranges from original paintings and limited editions to gold and silver jewellery (the designs are carved into the metal, not cast). Each piece is signed. Hill's is also the best-known source for beautiful, durable Cowichan sweaters. *Every day; map:U3.*

LEONA LATTIMER / 1590 W 2nd Ave; 604/732-4556 This small gallery features aboriginal art of an extremely high calibre. Many items are purchased for collection. You'll find carvings, jewellery, prints, ceremonial masks, and drums and totems—all created by Native artists in the traditional motifs of the Northwest Coast peoples. *Every day; map:P7.*

THE MUSEUM OF ANTHROPOLOGY / 6393 NW Marine Dr, UBC; 604/822-5087 In addition to a fine selection of Northwest Coast art and books, the museum shop features Inuit prints, soapstone sculpture, and other handmade craftwork. It also happens to be situated in one of the most beautiful examples of modern architecture in the city. *Every day; map:A2.*

ONE-OF-A-KIND SHOPS

BUDDHA SUPPLIES CENTRE / 4158 Main St; 604/873-8169 At Chinese funerals, people burn joss—paper replicas of earthly belongings—to make the deceased more comfortable in the afterlife. At this tiny store, you'll find combustible cell phones, fax machines, and even a miniature cardboard penthouse apartment with a Mercedes in the driveway. *Every day; map:V7.*

THE FLAG SHOP / 1755 W 4th Ave; 604/736-8161 This is where you'll find flags for the country, the province, and the city—as well as a number of nonflag items such as pins, crests, decals, and wind socks. The shop will take orders by phone. *Mon–Sat; map:P7.*

FRANKLIN COVEY / 1018 W Georgia St; 604/669-6950 An organizer/planner store offering tools for becoming—you guessed it—a highly effective person. Features such seven-habit spinoffs as productivity-training kits and electronic organizers. *Mon–Sat; map:S4.*

FUTURE BEYOND INTELLIGENCE / 1463 Robson St; 604/642-0324 Microcameras, home-invasion security devices, high-tech spying gadgets, and books with titles such as *How to Get Anything on Anyone* show just how far we've come since the Whisper 2000. To put paranoid shoppers at ease, the store is laid out according to the principles of feng shui, complete with trickling fountain. *Every day; map:P2.*

GOLDEN AGE COLLECTABLES / 830 Granville St; 604/683-2819 It's hard to say which age these folks consider golden, but they do have a fine selection of movie posters, baseball and other sport cards (some bearing autographs), and other flotsam of youth. There are also lots of comic books and posters, and T-shirts with comic—and comical—designs. *Every day; map:S4.*

THE UMBRELLA SHOP / 534 W Pender St; 604/669-9444 Given Vancouver weather, it's easy to believe that this shop has been in business for over 50 years. You'll find a veritable deluge of bumbershoots in all sizes, shapes, and fabrics. Many of the umbrellas are constructed on the premises, will last for years, and can be repaired at the shop. *Mon–Sat; map:T3.*

RECORDINGS, CDS, TAPES, AND INSTRUMENTS

A & B SOUND / 556 Seymour St (and branches); 604/687-5837 You can't always get what you want, but chances are you'll leave satisfied. These stores boast a large stock of records, tapes, and CDs at great prices, as well as a good selection of electronics and even a small bookstore with good discounts. Their biannual sales draw lineups several blocks long. *Every day; map:T3.*

BASSIX / 217 W Hastings St; 604/689-7734 If you're a DJ, or simply aspire to be, this is the spot for danceable beats and rare grooves, much of it American hip-hop and European electronic music. A gathering spot for recuperating ravers, it's a good source for scoop about upcoming parties and club nights. Concert tickets and turntables also available. *Mon–Sat; map:T3.*

BLACK SWAN / 3209 W Broadway; 604/734-2828 If you're tired of browsing your local chain store hoping for some international jazz or world music, check out Black Swan, which specializes in these, plus folk and blues. The store carries some rare recordings and many hard-to-find numbers. Mail order is available. *Every day; map:C3.*

D & G COLLECTORS RECORDS LTD. / 3580 E Hastings St; 604/294-5737 You'll find original discs from the 1950s and 1960s, including many classics of that era, and CD reissues of discs from the 1920s and beyond. Mail-order service and special orders, too. *Every day; map:F2.*

HIGHLIFE RECORDS AND MUSIC / 1317 Commercial Dr; 604/251-6964 This shop carries music from around the world—specializing in Latin, African, and Caribbean—as well as a selection of vintage instruments. *Every day; map:Z6.*

THE MAGIC FLUTE / 2203 W 4th Ave; 604/736-2727 Predictably, this store carries an extensive selection of classical and jazz music. It's a great gathering place for true classics fanatics, and it contains a good selection of CDs and videos. *Every day; map:N7.*

NEPTOON RECORDS / 5750 Fraser St; 604/324-1229 An eclectic mix of just about everything, especially rare and out-of-print vinyl. You'll find lots of music-related memorabilia, including some hard-to-find concert posters from as far back as the 1960s. *Every day; map:E4.*

SAM THE RECORD MAN / 568 Seymour St (and branches); 604/684-3722 Sam is the godfather of retail music in Canada. Unlike megastores like Virgin, Sam's doesn't look like a nightclub, and it doesn't constantly play the Top 40. Instead, this family-run business has knowledgeable employees and a real feel for musicalia. The four-storey downtown location also

205

has a good stock of VHS and laser-disc movies for sale. *Every day; map:T3.*

TOM LEE MUSIC / 929 Granville St (and branches); 604/685-8471 Tom Lee Music has the largest selection of musical instruments in the Lower Mainland and several floors from which to choose. Find Yamaha, Petrof, Steinway, and others. *Every day; map:S4.*

VIRGIN MEGASTORE / 788 Burrard St; 604/669-2289 On the site of the former main branch of the Vancouver library, you'll find the first Virgin Megastore in Canada. Occupying three levels, Virgin carries the largest selection of music and entertainment in the country: more than 125,000 music titles on CDs and cassettes; 20,000 movie and music titles on video and laser disc; the largest selection of entertainment multimedia software for IBM and Mac. There's an in-store DJ booth, 140 listening stations at which customers may sample music, and 20 video/laser disc viewing stations. *Every day; map:S3.*

ZULU RECORDS / 1972 W 4th Ave; 604/738-3232 New wave, punk, electronic, techno, hip-hop, rap, and other modern sounds. There's an excellent secondhand section in the back, and the store doubles as a ticket venue for concerts. Zulu also carries its own label of independent recordings. *Every day; map:O7.*

SEAFOOD

THE LOBSTER MAN / 1807 Mast Tower Rd, Granville Island; 604/687-4531 Buy your lobsters while they're still kicking. In addition to live lobsters, The Lobster Man sells a wide variety of seafood-related gift items (utensils, accessories, and spices, among other things) for those hard-to-please friends. They'll even pack your crustaceans, at no extra charge, for travel or shipping. *Every day; map:Q6.*

LONGLINER SEA FOODS / 1689 Johnston St, Granville Island; 604/681-9016 The Longliner is one of the best fish markets on Granville Island. Expect to find Vancouver's professional cooks eyeing the goods alongside you. The staff is generous with cooking advice. *Every day (closed Mon in winter); map:Q6.*

THE SALMON SHOP / 1610 Robson St (and branches); 604/688-FISH Once upon a time, The Salmon Shop ran its own fishing boats, but alas, no more, and the prices reflect that change. Still, if you want premium quality, it's here for the taking. Stock includes mahimahi and swordfish, as well as the best of the local catch, such as octopus, lingcod, and salmon. The smoked salmon is wonderful. *Every day; map:Q2.*

SHOES

BENTALL CENTRE SHOE REPAIR / Bentall Centre, lower level; 604/688-0538 If your sole needs a little TLC, this little shop can help you out in its downtown location and make repairs while you wait. *Mon–Fri; map:T3.*

DAYTON SHOE CO. / 2250 E Hastings St; 604/253-6671 These boots were made for working, but they're now a staple for neopunk rockers, Goths, and fashion mavens all over the world, and they're made right here in a little shop on the East Side. Extremely durable, yet far more attractive than Doc Marten's, Dayton puts a lifetime guarantee on its products. *Mon–Sat; map:E2.*

JOHN FLUEVOG / 837 Granville St; 604/688-2828 The undisputed leader in footwear innovation in the country. Fluevog still lives and work here, even though his sculptural creations are just as famous in New York and London. Find the classic Angel boots and shoes, snowboarding boots, or go for a pair of indescribably funky "wok and roll" Japanese-style wooden shoes. *Every day; map:S4.*

SILVANO'S SHOE RENEW / 520 Robson St; 604/685-5413 Cobbler services while you wait. *Mon–Fri; map:S4.*

SIMARD / 1049 Robson St; 604/689-2536 Fashion- and quality-conscious men and women enjoy these stylish shoes. Well-made imports are a specialty. *Every day; map:D4.*

STEPHANE DE RAUCOURT / 1067 Robson St (and branches); 604/681-8814 Locals are fanatical about footwear from this retailer. The fashionable, high-quality women's shoes are made in Italy for the Raucourt label, and the majority of styles, quite smartly, are offered in black only. Lesser retailers have been spotted here recently buying samples to knock off for their own lines back in the United States. *Every day; map:R3.*

SKIN AND HAIR CARE

L'OCCITANE / 3051 Granville St; 604/734-4441 A longtime favourite of *Vogue* editors in New York, this new-to-Vancouver store has already got a strong following who have heard about its luxurious *eau de linge* (scented ironing water) and verbena-infused candles through international word-of-mouth. It's the French equivalent of The Body Shop, but the company practiced nonexploitative trade well before eco-marketing was all the rage. Known for its use of traditional Provençal soap-making techniques, and natural ingredients such as African shea butter and French lavender, the company also prints some of its labels in Braille. The men's line of skin care products is exceptional, too. *Every day; map:D3.*

LUSH / 3084 Granville St (and branches); 604/608-1810 Lush carries skin care and bath products that pamper and please, and all are made locally. Their bread-and-butter is the Bath Bomb, a richly scented concoction that makes the most mundane ablution a wickedly wonderful experience. *Every day; map:D3.*

OPTADERM / 355 2184 W Broadway; 604/737-2026 This skin care shop, and the skin care products and cosmetics of the same name, have garnered a fanatical following. Drop by for one of the shop's luxurious European facials and pick up some fabulous lotions and potions; they're happy to supply samples. All products are made locally. *Tues–Sat; map:N7.*

ROBERT ANDREW SALON AND SPA / 900 W Georgia St; 604/687-7133 Located in the Hotel Vancouver, this total body care salon will indulge you head to toe, seven days a week, with its own skin care line and treatments from Dermalogica and Hathor. Also on offer are full hair care services, plus hot-rock massage and hydrotherapy, in an environment that won a national award for its interior design. *Every day; map:S3.*

SPA AT THE CENTURY / 1015 Burrard St; 604/684-2772 The city's most-difficult-to-get-into spa has earned its clientele by offering a whole slew of complimentary services, such as light meals, eucalyptus steams, makeup application, and use of an ozonated swimming pool, with the purchase of spa treatments. Other draws are a Vichy shower, availability of the self-tanning process used for *Baywatch* cast members, and a roster of celebrity endorsements (Gwyneth Paltrow, Gillian Anderson) lining the lobby walls. *Every day; map:R4.*

SUKI'S / 3157 Granville St (and branches); 604/738-7713 Suki's has long been an established name in Vancouver for exceptional haircuts and care. Here you are assured the best cut and the best head massage (called a shampoo) at any one of its locations. The state-of-the-art South Granville shop was designed by noted local architect Arthur Erickson; that's where you'll find haircutter extraordinaire Suki, who is also a nail technician and aesthetician. The salons are open seven days a week (and some evenings) for busy clients. *Every day; map:D3.*

TECH 1 HAIR DESIGN / 1057 Cambie St; 604/689-1202 The comfort of the clientele is all-important at this salon. From the sophistication of the slate and granite floors to the genteel act of tea served in china cups, everywhere you'll find a relaxing ambience. As well as offering the best hair colouring from resident technicians, a full-service aesthetician offers manicures and makeup application. *Tues–Sat; map:T5.*

SPECIALTY FOODS

ALL INDIA FOODS / 6517 Main St; 604/324-1686 At this supermarket-size Indian food emporium in the heart of the bustling Punjabi Market (around Main Street and 49th Avenue), you'll find unlimited choices of specialty foods and seasonings. The narrow aisles are crowded with a vast array of chutneys, curry powders, cardamom seed, saffron, chiles, and other items—in more varieties, sizes, and forms than you'll find anywhere else in town. There are also bulk foods, fresh produce, and some of the cheapest milk prices around. Next door, All India Sweets offers confections and a warm, hospitable sit-down cafe. *Every day; map:E4.*

FAMOUS FOODS / 1595 Kingsway; 604/872-3019 The key to Famous Foods' bargain prices is its repackaging of bulk quantities into small packages, reducing the time spent measuring and weighing. The savings are passed along to the customer. Unlike bulk food outlets, there's no worry about bin contamination, and constant turnover ensures that grains, pasta, and spices are fresh. Added to its superior stock of spices are special deals on bulk peanut butter, honey, and grains, as well as an impressive assortment of cheeses. *Every day; map:E3.*

THE FIRST RAVIOLI STORE / 1900 Commercial Dr; 604/255-8844 Vancouver's oldest and most popular Italian supermarket presents an impressive array of fresh pasta and sauces. People crowd the aisles on weekends in pursuit of unusual canned items, olive oils, imported pasta, marinated vegetables, and deli meats. *Every day; map:Z7.*

FUJIYA / 912 Clark Dr (and branches); 604/251-3711 These stores are the best source for Japanese foods and pearl rice in town. They also have weekly specials and carry a wide variety of inexpensive kitchenware, including steamers, woks, and kitchen tools. You'll find some of the best buys in sushi supplies here, such as bamboo mats for rolling rice in nori. Take-out sashimi available. *Every day; map:Z4.*

GALLOWAY'S / 904 Davie St (and branches); 604/685-7927 The combination of herbs, spices, Indian chutneys, curry pastes, and dried fruit make this place an aromatic spot for leisurely shopping. This is also the place to find that elusive Mexican vanilla and crunchy Indian snacks, such as roasted green peas, pumpkin seeds, and nuts. *Mon–Sat; map:R4.*

GOURMET WAREHOUSE / 1856 Pandora St; 604/253-3022 This bulk gourmet store run by food maven Caren McSherry stocks hard-to-find items, imported mostly from France and Italy, in a no-frills environment that doesn't inflate the price stickers. *Mon–Sat; map:F3.*

LESLEY STOWE FINE FOODS / 1780 W 3rd Ave; 604/731-3663 When Buy and Lie is the best revenge, head to this top-notch take-out (or eat-in) and catering establishment. The shop is brimming with myriad starters, main courses, breads, specialty foods, fine cheeses, and not-to-be-missed decadent chocolate and luscious lemon desserts. *Every day; map:P7.*

MEINHARDT FINE FOODS / 3002 Granville St; 604/732-4405 There's a good selection of gourmet and imported goodies, and a very nice deli with take-out in this South Granville supermarket. (See Meinhardt Fine Foods in the Restaurants chapter.) *Every day; map:D3.*

THE MENU SETTERS / 1780 W 10th Ave; 604/732-4218 Say cheese at this catering hot spot owned by mother-daughter team Alice and Allison Spurrell. It's a favourite among Vancouver's top chefs because of the selection, quick turnover and the affordable prices of their 400-plus cheeses. The Spurrells will also guide you to a great wine to partner your cheese selection or anything from their catering menu. *Every day; map:B3.*

MINERVA'S MEDITERRANEAN DELI / 3207 W Broadway; 604/733-3956 If you don't feel like cooking up a Grecian feast from the imported foods available, just visit the deli section and pick up something tasty. For do-it-yourself types, olives, olive oils, cheeses, and other necessities are all here. You can also linger on the heated deck outside and sip a traditional Greek Nescafe or savour an ice cream. *Every day; map:C3.*

PARTHENON WHOLESALE & RETAIL FOOD / 3080 W Broadway; 604/733-4191 It's not a Greek island, but on a rainy day it's great to make-believe while nibbling such delicacies as taramasalata, baklava, dolmades, Greek olives, and shockingly good feta. Mediterranean expats travel from all over the city for their inexpensive soaps made from olive oil and basil. *Every day; map:C3.*

QUE PASA MEXICAN FOODS / 1647 W 5th Ave; 604/730-5449 Que Pasa is Vancouver's best source for the elusive spices and ingredients needed for Central American cooking. This small shop carries a variety of Mexican deli items and fresh vegetables for Mexican cooking: tomatillos, chilies, cactus, and jicama. There are many brands of salsa, including the store's own chunky style (in hot, medium, and mild) as well as its superior tortilla chips. In addition, we've discovered piñatas, Mexican candles, and margarita glasses. Que Pasa also sells a practical *molcajete*—a kind of mortar and pestle for grinding rice into flour—and has a good stock of Mexican cookbooks. *Every day; map:P7.*

URBAN FARE / 177 Davie St; 604/975-7550 Located in Yaletown, Urban Fare is the slickest supermarket in the city and the only one where you can sip a glass of wine with your crab cakes. In addition to supermarket items, there's organic produce (including Asian), a pasta bar, an olive bar, and lots of ethnic foods and spices. It's a hip, attractive source for prepared food selections for an inspired breakfast, lunch or dinner- to-go or to eat in the Urban Fare restaurant. While the store bakes its own breads, it also brings in sourdough rye, currant, and walnut from Poilâne—one of France's best bakers. There's live entertainment on Wednesdays and weekends. Yes, they deliver. *Every day; map:S6.*

THE STOCK MARKET / 1689 Johnston St; 604/687-2433 Owners Georges and Joanne LeFebvre used to delight guests with their culinary expertise at their restaurant, Le Chef et sa Femme. Now they help you delight your guests with the complete selection of stocks, sauces, dressings, and marinades available at their Granville Island shop. Everything is fresh and made with no preservatives, so selection depends on the season, but you can depend on finding and enjoying their soups made every day. *Every day; map:Q6.*

YAOHAN SUPERMARKET AND SHOPPING CENTRE / 3700 No. 3 Rd, Richmond; 604/276-8808 Where can you find more than 20 varieties of Japanese soy sauce, fresh wasabi root, matsutake mushrooms, or squid with smelt roe? Try the Yaohan Supermarket at the Yaohan Centre—the first Canadian branch of one of the largest department store chains in Asia. Here you can also find ready-for-the-pot precut sukiyaki beef; sashimi-grade salmon, tuna, geoduck, black cod, snapper, pomfret, mackerel, mushrooms, and napa cabbage. This may be the largest supermarket fish department in the Lower Mainland. Across the concourse, in the food court, 15 outlets provide a smorgasbord of Asian street foods. *Every day; map:D6.*

SPORTS EQUIPMENT AND SPORTSWEAR

CHEAPSKATES / 3644 W 16th Ave (and branches); 604/222-1125 This cluster of sporting goods consignment shops all within a stone's throw of each other (Cheapskates Too, 3, and 19) saves locals many bucks when shopping for bikes, skates, ski equipment, and so on. Used gear is priced to clear, with prices dropping the longer unsold merchandise stays in the store. *Every day; map:B3.*

COAST MOUNTAIN SPORTS / 2201 W 4th Ave (and branches); 604/731-6181 Affordable camping, hiking, climbing, and travel gear. Boots, sleeping bags, water purifiers, and high-tech items, such as freeze-dried food, and satellite tracking systems. Knowledgeable staff. *Every day; map:O7.*

CYCLONE TAYLOR SPORTING GOODS / 6575 Oak St (and branch); 604/266-3316 This shop is known as the place for skating gear. You can suit up a hockey team (ice or in-line), get your figure skates sharpened, or find safety equipment for a whole family of rollerbladers. The second location is in the Richmond Ice Centre. *Every day; map:F7.*

THE DIVING LOCKER / 2745 W 4th Ave; 604/736-2681 Equipment sales, rentals, and instructions. The Diving Locker has been in business more than 27 years. *Every day; map:C2.*

LULULEMON ATHLETICA / 2-2108 W 4th Ave; 604/732-6111 If you're a keener for the latest sports trends, this is where you'll find the gear: entire sections are devoted to Tae Bo, yoga, and rowing. Sport-specific brands include Gaia (for ultimate), Hind (for running), and Cannondale (for cycling). Look for the lululemon house label—store owner Chip Wilson was the mastermind behind Vancouver's world-famous skate- and snowboarding shop, West Beach. *Every day; map:O7.*

MOUNTAIN EQUIPMENT CO-OP / 130 W Broadway; 604/872-7858 Join for a few dollars, then shop to your heart's content amid racks of all the gear you'll need to enjoy the great outdoors. The store is huge, reflecting the enormous popularity of adventure sports and their trappings, whether your idea of an adventure is battling the current in a kayak or taking the bus to UBC. *Every day; map:U7.*

RUDDICK'S FLY SHOP / 1654 Duranleau St; 604/681-3749 The first—and many say the best—fly-fishing shop in western Canada. It's the exclusive licensed retail outlet for Orvis rods, clothing, and accessories. The shop also sells custom-tied flies and offers classes in fly tying and fly casting, as well as group expeditions to famous fishing locations. *Every day; map:Q6.*

TAIGA / 390 W 8th Ave; 604/875-6644 This local manufacturer with an international reputation sells high-quality tents, sleeping bags, and sportswear. It also has a great range of fashions in Gore-Tex, fleece, and Polartec. *Every day; map:T7.*

THREE VETS / 2200 Yukon St; 604/872-5475 One of the oldest and most respected outfitters in the area, Three Vets is famous for its low prices. You'll find good-quality basic equipment for entry-level campers and hikers. Check out the store's secret back room of Native art. *Every day; map:T7.*

WESTBEACH / 1766 W 4th Ave; 604/731-6449 Boarders chill out by the in-store half pipe and oil their wheels while young Japanese exchange students buy up a storm in the front. Phat pants, hoodies, bikinis, and Hawaiian shirts, as well as excellent technical snowboarding clothes and hardware. *Every day; map:P7.*

STATIONERY AND ART SUPPLIES

BEHNSEN GRAPHIC SUPPLIES LTD. / 1016 Richards St; 604/681-7351 This is a store for serious graphic artists and designers, but rank amateurs will find a wealth of inspiring colours and supplies. There are Saturday seminars on how to use art supplies, and graphic artists will appreciate the store's hardware and software offerings. *Mon–Sat; map:S5.*

OPUS FRAMING AND ART SUPPLIES / 1360 Johnston St; 604/736-7028 Opus is ideally situated on Granville Island across the street from the Emily Carr Institute of Art & Design. A discount art supply and do-it-yourself framing shop, Opus offers the lowest prices in the city and is an unparalleled source for art and framing supplies—more than 8,000 in-stock items. Most of the knowledgeable staff have art or design degrees. Don't overlook the Starving Artists' Table for samples and damaged goods at rock-bottom prices. Other locations are in Victoria and Langley, and there's a mail-order number (800/663-6953). *Every day; map:Q6.*

PAPERHAUS / 3057 Granville St; 604/737-2225 It's no surprise that the entire crew of London's *Wallpaper* magazine recently traipsed through the Seattle incarnation of this store—it's a design-junkie's fantasy. Row upon perfect row of aluminum portfolio cases, acid-free paper, preservation-quality storage boxes, and minimalist notebooks, all from internationally recognized lines such as Pina Zangaro. *Every day; www.paper haus.com; map:D3.*

PAPER-YA / 1666 Johnston St, Granville Island; 604/684-2531 You'll find a terrific selection of Japanese rice paper and paper-related gifts from around the world, as well as papermaking kits for fledgling artists. *Every day; map:Q6.*

RETURN TO SENDER / 1076 Davie St; 604/683-6363 A tasteful and not-so-tasteful selection of greeting cards, gift wrap, notepaper, magnets, stickers, and party supplies for every occasion, gay or straight. *Every day; map:Q4.*

THE VANCOUVER PEN SHOP / 512 W Hastings St; 604/681-1612 The giant pen in the window is your first clue to the giant selection offered here: Sheaffer, Montblanc, Cross, Waterman, and Dupont pens as well as inks and cartridges. The shop also stocks sketching tools and lower-priced pens. *Mon–Sat; map:T3.*

WINTON'S SOCIAL STATIONERY / 2529 W Broadway; 604/731-3949 These helpful people can supply your personal invitations in a matter of days, or you can choose from their extensive selection. They also sell blank greeting cards that are extremely laser printer–friendly. Guest books, picture frames, and other related gifts. *Every day; map:C3.*

THE WRITE PLACE / 2843 Granville St; 604/732-7777 Custom stationery, hilarious cards, writing implements, and gifts. *Every day; map:D3.*

TOYS

KABOODLES / 4449 W 10th Ave; 604/224-5311 This is the perfect store for stocking goody bags for kids' parties, but there's much, much more than a great selection of low-cost crowd-pleasers. Check out the umbrellas, the backpacks, and the colourful stuffed toys. Cards and gift wrap too. *Every day; map:B3.*

KIDS MARKET / 1496 Cartwright St; 604/689-8447 Not just toys, of course. The market features more than 20 specialty shops and services, including clothing, art supplies, and more. It's where you'll find the best kite shop in the city, and kids just love to visit. *Every day; map:Q6.*

THE TOYBOX / 3002 W Broadway; 604/738-4322 High-quality toys, and lots of them (except toy guns, which they don't stock on principle). Some of the merchandise is upmarket (read: expensive), but lots of lower-priced items will please. Games galore. *Every day; map:C3.*

SHOPPING

WINE, BEER, AND SPIRITS

BC SPECIALTY LIQUOR STORES / 5555 Cambie St (and branches); 604/266-1321 The Cambie Street liquor store, the flagship government-operated retail outlet, is a 15-minute drive from the downtown core. Located at the corner of 39th Avenue, it contains well over 2,500 products, including wine, beer, cider, coolers, and spirits. Wine enthusiasts will be impressed by the variety of wines for sale from all over the world. Often labels that have long since disappeared from London, New York, and San Francisco await the keen wine buff. Other specialty outlets are located at 1120 Alberni Street (604/660-4572) and 570 Park Royal Shopping Centre North, West Vancouver (604/981-0011). *Every day; map:D4.*

DUNDARAVE WINE CELLARS / 2448 Marine Dr, West Vancouver; 604/921-1814 Stephen Bonner runs this upscale wine shop in the West Vancouver village of Dundarave. You'll find a bit of everything here, although West Coast wines from British Columbia to Chile dominate. *Every day; map:C0.*

EDGEMONT VILLAGE WINES / 3050 Edgemont Blvd, North Vancouver; 604/985-9463 If you are looking for homegrown British Columbia Vintners Quality Alliance (VQA) wines, this is the place to head. You'll find just about everything that's produced in the province at the first all-VQA wine store in the Lower Mainland, including an extensive array of ice wine. *Every day.*

LIBERTY WINE MERCHANTS / 4583 W 10th Ave; 604/224-8050 Robert Simpson is the man behind the wines at Liberty. Hip, savvy, and blessed with a fine palate, he encourages his store managers to do their own thing—and they do. There's a fine core selection of champagne, Burgundy, and Bordeaux wines as well as a strong California/Northwest section; the rest varies to reflect the manager's taste. Also located in Park Royal Shopping Centre North, West Vancouver (604/925-3663) and Park and Tilford Centre, North Vancouver (604/988-2424). *Every day; map:B3.*

MARQUIS WINE CELLARS / 1034 Davie St; 604/684-0445 Look for an eclectic mix of hard-to-find international wines at this West End private wine shop, which has a strong representation of wines from the Pacific Northwest, Santa Barbara, and Australia. Top-of-the-line stemware and very knowledgeable staff. *Every day; map:R5.*

PERFORMING ARTS

PERFORMING ARTS

In spite of year-round competition from sporting events and outdoor activities, the Vancouver performing arts community is alive and thriving. Some enterprising theatre, dance, and musical groups have even turned the city's natural charms to their advantage: in any given week during the summer, you might catch Shakespeare on the beach, opera by the lake, or a symphony in the mountains. Indoor theatres and concert halls are busiest September through May, when Vancouverites cut back a little on the cycling and rollerblading—hey, it's raining—and show themselves to be enthusiastic patrons of the arts.

The daily and weekly newspapers do a good job of providing current listings for a broad spectrum of happenings, but the **ARTS HOTLINE,** 604/684-ARTS, is probably the best source of up-to-date information. Staffed by the Alliance for Arts and Culture, an umbrella service organization for hundreds of members, the hotline is accessible 24 hours a day. You may also visit the alliance's office at 938 Howe Street (map:S4) or check its very comprehensive Web site at www.culturenet.ca/vca. For tickets to many of the events described in this chapter, call Ticketmaster at 604/280-3311 or access its Web site, www.ticketmaster.ca.

Theatre

Vancouver's theatre scene offers a mosaic of live performances that range from glorious extravaganzas to impromptu events and include practically everything in between. Two large-scale companies and many small, innovative groups keep theatregoers entertained year-round. Until recently, the Ford Centre for the Performing Arts hosted big-budget musicals, but it has been sitting empty since its owners became embroiled in a financial scandal. The University of British Columbia, Simon Fraser University, Langara College, and Capilano College mount excellent theatre productions, dance recitals, and jazz concerts while classes are in session. Theatre at UBC's season runs September through April at the Frederic Wood Theatre and the Chan Centre's BC Tel Studio Theatre. During the same months, performances take place at the SFU Theatre, Langara's Studio 58, and the Capilano College Performing Arts Theatre. Other companies, performing in Vancouver and on tour, include Touchstone Theatre (604/709-9973); Ruby Slippers Productions (604/602-0585); Pink Ink Theatre (604/872-1861); Headlines Theatre Company (604/871-0508), which does "powerplay theatre," concentrating on plays about social issues; and Tamahnous Theatre (604/708-0799), which gave much of the city's senior talent its start. Listed below are some of Vancouver's main venues and festivals featuring live theatre. The Firehall

CELEBRITY HANGOUTS

Crashing a Vancouver movie location might work, but it's by no means the only way to catch a glimpse of your favourite Hollywood star. With a steadily increasing number of high-profile actors, musicians, and athletes either visiting the city or living and working here, celebrities are everywhere—eating in restaurants, misbehaving at nightclubs, and working out at the local gym. A big reason for this phenomenon is Vancouver's absence of paparazzi: unlike in New York or L.A., famous people can actually walk the streets here unmolested. That's where you come in. A few celeb hot spots:

Good Mediterranean food and a central location have made **CinCin** (1154 Robson St; 604/688-7338) a perennial destination for Hollywood actors and pro athletes. Other restaurants with celebrity-heavy reservation books include **Bishop's** (2183 W 4th Ave; 604/738-2025), which has served everyone from Alice Cooper to Robert De Niro, and **Tojo's** (202–777 W Broadway; 604/872-8050), where there's often someone outrageously famous sitting at the sushi bar. **Vij's** (1480 W 11th Ave; 604/736-6664) can count among its patrons the newsworthy duo of Gwyneth Paltrow and Sarah McLachlan. It's also a safe bet that the award-winning **Lumière** (2551 W Broadway; 604/739-8185) and **C** (2-1600 Howe St; 604/681-1164) host their share of A-list tables. Film types such as investor Jason Priestley (a local boy) congregate more visibly at the **Alibi Room** (157 Alexander St; 604/623-3383), though they're most likely to be of the common or Vancouver variety.

Like it or not, the two Vancouver nightspots that probably share the record for (mostly male) celebrity visits are the strip clubs the **Marble Arch** (518 Richards St; 604/681-5435) and the **No. 5 Orange** (203 Main St; 604/687-3483): Ted Danson, Richard Dreyfuss, Dennis Rodman, and members of Motley Crüe and Aerosmith are just a few of the big names who've been caught ogling the onstage talent. A little more discreet is cozy **Gerard Lounge** at the Sutton Place Hotel (845 Burrard St; 604/682-5511), where management simply refuses to acknowledge that Hollywood's finest often stop by for drinks after a day on the set. Unconfirmed celeb sightings abound at clubs such as **Richard's on Richards** (1036 Richards St; 604/687-6794) and Yaletown's **Bar None** (1222 Hamilton St; 604/689-7000). The Vancouver club with the most eclectic list of famous patrons may be the late-night **Sugar Refinery** (1115 Granville St; 604/683-2004): Billy Idol, the Chemical Brothers, and Maureen McCormick (aka Marcia Brady) are a representative sampling.

Another place to rub shoulders with celebs: **Spa at the Century** (1015 Burrard St; 604/684-2772), where Gillian Anderson, Ethan Hawke, Ashley Judd, and many others have checked in for a facial or a deep-tissue massage. *—Nick Rockel*

Arts Centre is listed under Dance later in this chapter. For information on the Vancouver International Children's Festival, see Vanier Park in the Exploring chapter.

ARTS CLUB THEATRE / 1585 Johnston St; 604/687-1644 Situated in the heart of lively Granville Island, the Arts Club Theatre and the neighbouring Arts Club New Revue Stage, both run by Bill Millerd, have become local institutions. The Arts Club is also the largest regional theatre in western Canada. In the fall of 1998, Millerd opened a third stage in the refurbished Stanley Theatre, on Granville Street near 13th Avenue (2750 Granville St; 604/687-1644; map:D2). At the Stanley, productions run from contemporary drama to Shakespeare to big-budget musicals. 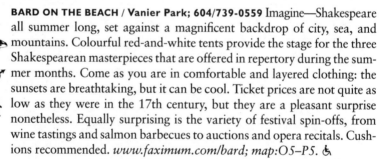 The yearlong offerings on the main Granville Island stage include a smorgasbord of drama, comedy, and musical classics, with a focus on 20th-century works. For those who enjoy a drink during the show, the cabaret-style Revue Stage is the perfect spot for light theatre and musical comedy; it's also the home of the Vancouver TheatreSports League. Intermission on the False Creek dock or at the bustling Backstage Lounge is an added attraction. The lounge, which supports the theatre, has its own entertainment and is a popular hangout spot for artists and musicians. *Map:Q6.* &

BARD ON THE BEACH / Vanier Park; 604/739-0559 Imagine—Shakespeare all summer long, set against a magnificent backdrop of city, sea, and mountains. Colourful red-and-white tents provide the stage for the three Shakespearean masterpieces that are offered in repertory during the summer months. Come as you are in comfortable and layered clothing: the sunsets are breathtaking, but it can be cool. Ticket prices are not quite as low as they were in the 17th century, but they are a pleasant surprise nonetheless. Equally surprising is the variety of festival spin-offs, from wine tastings and salmon barbecues to auctions and opera recitals. Cushions recommended. *www.faximum.com/bard; map:O5–P5.* &

QUEEN ELIZABETH THEATRE / Hamilton St at W Georgia St; 604/665-3050 On the Queen E.'s spacious stage, gorgeous glitz and glitter are commonplace. This elegant, comfortable, 2,900-plus-seat theatre is still one of Vancouver's main venues for lavish touring musicals each spring and summer, and dance, rock, and pop concerts and many multicultural shows the rest of the year. It's also home to Vancouver Opera and Ballet British Columbia (see Classical Music and Opera, and Dance, in this chapter). The Vancouver Playhouse (see separate listing) is next door. And just a few blocks away, the William Tell Restaurant (765 Beatty St; 604/688-3504; map:T4), offers a preshow table d'hôte starting at 5:30pm, with the option of returning later for dessert. If you're in the mood for a postshow drink, check out nearby VODA (783 Homer St;

604/684-3003; map:T4), an elegant lounge in the Westin Grand Hotel. A more casual option is Pit Barbecue and Brewery (871 Beatty St; 604/682-2739; map:T4). *www.city.vancouver.bc.ca/theatres; map:T4.* &

SHADBOLT CENTRE FOR THE ARTS / 6450 Deer Lake Ave, Burnaby; 604/291-6864 Housing two theatres, banquet facilities, and multi-use studios, this busy performance and teaching centre in Burnaby's Deer Lake Park is named in honour of the late BC painter Jack Shadbolt and his wife, writer and curator Doris Shadbolt. Although it hosts theatre performances, concerts, literary events, and an annual summer arts festival, the Shadbolt focuses on teaching. Classes include dance, acting, music, and the visual arts. Michael J. Fox and the Kimura Parker brothers have taken part in centre activities. *www.burnabyparksrec.org; map:H4.* &

STANLEY THEATRE / 2750 Granville St; 604/687-1644 See the Arts Club Theatre listing above.

THEATRE UNDER THE STARS / Malkin Bowl, Stanley Park; 604/687-0174 The sweetly familiar strains of "Some Enchanted Evening" take on new meaning at a performance of Theatre under the Stars (TUTS). Two Broadway musicals are offered in repertory from mid-July through mid-August each summer in Canada's only truly open-air theatre. Casts feature a combination of professional and amateur performers, lending the event a wonderful enthusiasm that makes for perfect family entertainment. Festival seating accommodates some 1,200 people, and the backdrop of forests, stars, and the moon is spectacular. Who could ask for anything more? Bring a cushion and warm clothing and be sure to wear socks to protect your ankles from the mosquitoes. *www.tuts.bc.ca; map:Q1.* &

VANCOUVER EAST CULTURAL CENTRE / 1895 Venables St; 604/254-9578 This beautifully restored 1914 church is one of Vancouver's most intriguing performance venues, where the tried-and-true shares the stage with the brand-new. Known to locals simply as the Cultch, the centre, which opened in 1973, makes diversity the key ingredient in its programming. Daring dance, alternative theatre and performance art, as well as music to keep your toes tapping or your heart swelling, all comes alive in this intimate 350-seat theatre space. The popular Kids' Series offers theatre, music, and madness for children, including a performance by the highly acclaimed resident company Green Thumb Theatre for Young People, which specializes in developing lighthearted and intelligent scripts based on complex social issues. The Cultch is also home to theatre companies Battery Opera and Touchstone Theatre, dance troupe the Holy Body Tattoo, the Little Chamber Music Series That Could, and Vancouver New Music (see Classical Music and Opera in this chapter). *www.vecc.bc.ca; map:E2.* &

VANCOUVER FRINGE FESTIVAL / Various locations; 604/257-0350 The good, the bad, and the adventurous are "Alive on the Drive" every September at the second-largest fringe theatre festival in North America. Billed as "an uncensored opportunity for performers to express ideas, challenge conventions, and stage innovative works with minimum finan-

cial risk," this extravaganza features all ages and levels of experience. At least 500 performances take place over 11 days in 10 indoor theatres and outdoor stages (some are wheelchair-accessible) on and around Commercial Drive. The 100-odd companies are accepted on a first-come, first-served basis—there is no jury process—and content includes everything from outrageous comedy to challenging drama to performance art. Admission is extremely reasonable. *www.vancouverfringe.com; map:Z3–Z7.*

VANCOUVER INTERNATIONAL COMEDY FESTIVAL / Granville Island; 604/683-0883 They call it the funniest festival of all. For 10 days in late July and early August, Granville Island is transformed into a veritable comedy lover's paradise. With dozens of free daily shows and some 30

ticketed events, mime artists, jugglers, and comedians seem to be everywhere. From noon to five each afternoon, roaming performers entertain onlookers, and each evening paying audiences savour the humour at the Arts Club New Revue Stage and Performance Works Theatre. Guests hail from around the globe but, as the saying goes, the language of a smile is universal. *www.comedyfest.com; map:Q6–R7.* &

VANCOUVER NEW PLAY FESTIVAL / 1405 Anderson St; 604/685-6228 For a week in May at Granville Island's Festival House, the Playwrights Theatre Centre breaks the seal on the very newest works by established and aspiring dramatists. The PTC is known for its active role in developing Canadian playwrights: festival participants, who must first submit their scripts for consideration, get help with the creative process through staged readings, workshops, seminars, and talks with the public. The more self-assured stage their work at the Playwrights' Cabaret, a showcase of the festival's most polished pieces. *Map:Q6.* &

VANCOUVER PLAYHOUSE / Hamilton St at Dunsmuir St; 604/873-3311 The Vancouver Playhouse Theatre Company produces six shows during its October-through-May season. One of western Canada's largest regional theatre companies, the playhouse blends the classic and the modern in its repertoire, including Canadian premieres and Broadway plays. The 670-seat theatre (every seat a good one) is home to many of Canada's finest actors, and productions are invariably top quality, with spectacular sets, luscious costumes, and terrific soundscapes. Friends of Chamber Music and the Vancouver Recital Society (see Classical Music and Opera in this chapter) as well as dance companies also use the space. *www.vancouverplayhouse.com; map:T4.* &

VANCOUVER THEATRESPORTS LEAGUE / 1585 Johnston St; 604/738-7013 Murder, talk shows, politics—nothing is sacred in the hands of Vancouver TheatreSports. A six-time world improvisational champion, TheatreSports offers hilarious, affordable entertainment at Granville Island's Arts Club New Revue Stage. The content of this Canadian creation varies. On any given night the 30-member ensemble might improvise on a specific theme, satirize the hottest TV shows, or stage competitions in which three-member teams vie for audience approval as they create vignettes based on audience suggestions. For mature audiences, there's also the Late Show, weekends at midnight. *www.vtsl.com; map:Q6.* ♿

Classical Music and Opera

During the past decade, Vancouver has seen its classical-music community grow in breadth and depth. Institutions such as the Vancouver Symphony and Vancouver Opera have spread their wings, and smaller chamber music series are flourishing. Choral music also enjoys a healthy local following. Both amateur and professional groups, including Chor Leoni Men's Choir, the Elektra Women's Choir, musica intima, the Vancouver Bach Choir, the Vancouver Cantata Singers, the Vancouver Chamber Choir, and the Vancouver Men's Chorus, perform at theatres, hotels, and churches throughout the city. Several of these groups regularly tour Europe and North America and have won prestigious international awards. The Little Chamber Music Series That Could is held at the Vancouver East Cultural Centre (see Theatre section of this chapter). For classical, opera, and choral events listings, call the **ARTS HOTLINE** at 604/684-ARTS. Listed here are some of the main venues, series, and organizations that enliven Vancouver's classical-music scene.

CHAN CENTRE FOR THE PERFORMING ARTS / 6265 Crescent Rd, UBC; 604/822-2697 An architecturally impressive building on the University of British Columbia campus, the Chan Centre hosts year-round performances by local, national, and international orchestras, chamber groups, and choirs. Its 1,400-seat Chan Shun Concert Hall is regarded as one of the continent's finest concert spaces. During a typical season, the program might include a visit from the Academy of St. Martin in the Fields, a series of summer concerts by the Vancouver Symphony Orchestra (see separate listing), and several distinguished soloists presented by the Vancouver Recital Society (see separate listing). The Chan Centre also hosts concerts by the UBC School of Music, and its 300-capacity BC Tel Studio Theatre hosts plays by Theatre at UBC. *www.chancentre.com; map:A2.* ♿

CHINESE CULTURAL CENTRE / 50 E Pender St; 604/687-0729 Chinese opera is just one of the many events presented at this centre by local organizations in the Chinese community and groups from around the world. The centre is also a venue for fascinating exhibitions of paintings and photography as well as book launchings and dance programs. It offers classes in language and arts and crafts as well. *www.cccvan.com; map:V4.* &

EARLY MUSIC VANCOUVER / Various locations and UBC School of Music Recital Hall; 604/732-1610 In times past, early music seemed to be the domain of a select following, but more and more converts are discovering these sublime sounds. Early Music Vancouver presents a series of performances, including various recitals, chamber orchestras, and choirs, in churches and concert halls throughout the city from fall through spring. Music from the Middle Ages to the 18th century is performed on original instruments by some of the finest early-music specialists. As an extension of the organization's main season, each summer the Early Music Summer Festival presents the sounds of harpsichords, lutes, and violas da gamba on the UBC campus. From mid-July through mid-August, local and international proponents of early music share the stage and classrooms, providing a feast of musical pleasures for everyone from the novice listener to the advanced music scholar. *www.earlymusic. bc.ca.; map:A3.* &

ENCHANTED EVENINGS / Dr. Sun Yat-Sen Classical Chinese Garden, 578 Carrall St; 604/662-3207 During summer, the Dr. Sun Yat-Sen Classical Chinese Garden (see Gardens in the Exploring chapter) presents a Friday-night concert series. It includes recitals of Asian classical music performed on traditional instruments by groups such as Silk Road and the Vancouver Chinese Music Ensemble. The grounds are illuminated with lanterns, providing a soft glow for music and a chance to wander through the garden. *www.discovervancouver.com/sun; map:V4.* &

FRIENDS OF CHAMBER MUSIC / Vancouver Playhouse, Hamilton St at Dunsmuir St; 604/437-5747 Devotees of chamber music may feel they have discovered manna with this 10-concert series. From September through May (all concerts are on Tuesdays), Friends of Chamber Music presents the crème de la crème of chamber music ensembles, such as the Emerson String Quartet. The group has received accolades for its special presentation of the complete Beethoven quartets, featuring the renowned Bartok String Quartet. *www.culturenet.ca/fcm; map:T4.* &

MUSIC IN THE MORNING / Vancouver Academy of Music, 1270 Chestnut St, Vanier Park; 604/873-4612 Experience the grace of the European salons of the 18th century with a visit to one of Music in the Morning's 10am concerts. Born in the living room of artistic director June Goldsmith more than a decade ago, the concert series has blossomed into a well-respected and innovative event. Its repertoire includes the old and the new, performed by local and imported artists. The society also presents the Musical Appreciation series for those who want to learn more about music in a relaxed setting. *www.musicinthemorning.org; map:P5.* ♿

VANCOUVER CHAMBER MUSIC FESTIVAL / Crofton House School, 3200 W 41st Ave; 604/602-0363 See the Vancouver Recital Society listing below.

VANCOUVER EARLY MUSIC SUMMER FESTIVAL / Various locations, UBC; 604/732-1610 See the Early Music Vancouver listing above.

VANCOUVER NEW MUSIC / Various locations; 604/606-6440 Eclectic, alternative, on the cutting edge—whichever expression you choose, Vancouver New Music has earned a reputation for presenting the hottest composers of contemporary music on an international scale. In attending its concerts, you might well be hearing music history in the making: recent commissions include the opera *Elsewhereless*, by local composer Rodney Sharman and filmmaker Atom Egoyan. The majority of concerts are staged at the Vancouver East Cultural Centre, where the intimacy of the hall makes for a wonderful ambience. Performances also take place at other venues scattered throughout the city. Every second summer, the society produces the Vancouver International New Music Festival. *www.newmusic.org.* ♿

VANCOUVER OPERA / Queen Elizabeth Theatre, Hamilton St at W Georgia St; 604/682-2871 Opera is once again firmly entrenched in the Vancouver arts scene. Once the domain of the "ladies who lunch," it is now one of the hippest tickets in town. Thanks to clever marketing, a re-evaluation of the organization's artistic vision in recent years, and the influence of megamusicals such as *Phantom of the Opera*, a new audience is flocking to Vancouver Opera in droves. The company presents four or five productions each season (a mix of contemporary and traditional works) as well as a fund-raising gala concert and recitals by distinguished soloists such as Richard Margison and Bryn Terfel. The sets are spectacular and the artists—including some of North America's brightest singing talents—are of international calibre. *www.vanopera.bc.ca; map:T4.* ♿

VANCOUVER RECITAL SOCIETY / Vancouver Playhouse, Hamilton St at Dunsmuir St; 604/602-0363 For a preview of who's going to be big in the classical-music world in the years to come, catch one of the dozen or so concerts in this recital series. Artistic director and general manager Leila Getz seems to have an uncanny sixth sense about young, up-and-coming artists, and that, matched with her impeccable taste, has enabled Vancouver audiences to hear some of today's foremost performers when they were aspiring musicians. In addition, the society presents a handful of superstars each season—for example, the enchanting singer Cecilia Bartoli, pianist Jon Kimura Parker, and violin master Itzhak Perlman. The Vancouver Playhouse is a principal venue, but concerts also take place at the Chan Centre for the Performing Arts (see separate listing) and the Orpheum Theatre (see next listing). In late July and early August, the Vancouver Recital Society invites a group of the brightest young talents in the chamber music world to perform at the Vancouver Chamber Music Festival, a six-concert series at Crofton House School (3200 W 41st Ave). *www.vanrecital.com; map:T4.* &

VANCOUVER SYMPHONY ORCHESTRA / Orpheum Theatre, Granville St at Smithe St; 604/876-3434 This granddaddy of the classical-music scene makes its home in the magnificent 1927 Orpheum Theatre, where thick red carpets, ornate rococo gilding, and sweeping staircases transport you to an earlier, more gracious era. Under the leadership of new music director Bramwell Tovey, the 74-member orchestra should continue to pursue the artistic heights aspired to by outgoing maestro Sergiu Comissiona. More than 10 subscription series offer music lovers a wide variety of aural delicacies, from traditional symphonic fare to a more adventurous repertoire to pops concerts featuring Dixieland, Celtic fiddling, and Latin jazz. An ever-increasing focus on Canadian artists and compositions has added a new dimension to the VSO's offerings, although a number of illustrious soloists, such as Yo-Yo Ma, Isaac Stern, and Pinchas Zukerman, continue to grace the Orpheum stage. The popular Kids' Koncerts provide an opportunity for children to experience the joys of symphonic music in a fun, relaxed atmosphere.

In addition to its main-stage concerts and special events, the VSO performs in the parks and on the beaches of the Lower Mainland during the summer. The high point of a symphonic summer is the annual Whistler mountaintop concert, where glorious music resounds amid the mountain peaks. The orchestra also plays series in New Westminster and Surrey, and tours the province every year. *www.culturenet.ca/vso; map:S4.* &

Dance

Vancouver is developing a reputation as a world centre of contemporary dance, attracting dancers and independent choreographers from all over Canada, the United States, and abroad who offer lively and original performances to appreciative audiences. The city is also a training ground for new artists, through organizations such as Main Dance and the Simon Fraser University School for the Contemporary Arts. Look for regular programs by Vancouver-based choreographers Karen Jamieson, Judith Marcuse, and Jennifer Mascall, as well as companies such as the Holy Body

Tattoo, Kinesis Dance, and Kokoro Dance. For information on upcoming dance events, call the umbrella organization, the **DANCE CENTRE**, at 604/606-6400 or check out its Web site, www.vkool.com/dancentre. The following are the main dance companies, festivals or series, and venues in Vancouver.

BALLET BRITISH COLUMBIA / Queen Elizabeth Theatre, Hamilton St at W Georgia St; 604/732-5003 Since its inception in 1986, BC's premier contemporary-ballet company has earned a glowing reputation for its bold, exciting performances. Under the artistic directorship of noted choreographer John Alleyne, Ballet BC offers dance enthusiasts a potpourri of modern and classical dance each September through June as part of its popular danceAlive! series. Guests range from the Royal Winnipeg Ballet to the Moscow Classical Ballet, along with master choreographers such as William Forsythe and James Kudelka. The company itself performs two programs each season, including Canadian or world premieres of innovative works. *www.discovervancouver.com/balletbc; map:T4.* &

DANCING ON THE EDGE FESTIVAL / Various locations; 604/689-0926 Dubbed North America's largest festival of independent choreographers, this two-week celebration of new dance, held each July, attracts first-rate talent from around the globe. Always fresh and daring, its 60 to 70 shows are offered throughout the day, from early afternoon to the wee hours of the morning. Venues can be as adventurous as the dance itself—from Vancouver's incomparable beaches to city street corners. Most performances, however, take place on the traditional stage of the Firehall Arts Centre (see listing below). *www.mcsquared.com/edge.* &

FIREHALL ARTS CENTRE / 280 E Cordova St; 604/689-0926 The Firehall Arts Centre Dance Series is best known as a vehicle for emerging dance artists. If a name will be on everyone's tongue tomorrow, that person is on the boards (or behind the scenes) at the Firehall today. From October to June you can catch the Firehall's contemporary-dance productions, including works by such well-established Vancouver companies as Karen Jamieson Dance, JumpStart Performance, and Kokoro Dance. The Firehall also presents several theatre productions each season, with an emphasis on Canadian theatre that reflects the cultural diversity of the nation. *www.mcsquared.com/firehall; map:V4.* &

THE KISS PROJECT / 1218 Cartwright St, Granville Island; 604/606-6425 From mid-January to the last week of February every year, the Kiss Project celebrates dance, theatre, and music at Granville Island's Performance Works theatre. The heart of the festival is the Kiss Commissions, in which 10 choreographers and 10 playwrights each produce a five-minute piece that includes a kiss. These works are performed during the festival's last two weeks. What makes the Kiss Project unique is the hands-on—or should we say feet-on—workshops that invite audiences to try flamenco or ballroom dancing, play improvisational theatre games, or simply bang some Japanese *taiko* drums. The program also includes plenty of performances and workshops for children. Kiss is produced by Judith Marcuse's Dance Arts Vancouver. *www.dancearts.bc.ca/kiss.htm; map:Q7.* &

VANCOUVER EAST CULTURAL CENTRE / 1895 Venables St; 604/254-9578 From September to June, the Vancouver East Cultural Centre presents the finest Canada has to offer in contemporary dance. If it's on the cutting edge, you'll find it at the Cultch. Past programs have included innovative dance and theatre artists from Montreal, including La La La Human Steps, Paul-André Fortier, and Peggy Baker, as well as the cream of Vancouver's rich dance scene and some international artists. See also Theatre in this chapter. *www.vecc.bc.ca; map:E2.* &

Film

When people describe Vancouver as Hollywood North, they're exaggerating. But the city's history as a movie location does date back to 1935, when MGM mogul Louis B. Mayer sent cast and crew northward to shoot Mountie scenes for his classic film *Rose Marie*. In 1969, director Robert Altman encountered Vancouver's adaptable charms while filming *That Cold Day in the Park;* he returned the following year to shoot *McCabe & Mrs. Miller.* Since then—with help from Canada's free-falling currency—the BC film industry is now a billion-dollar business, attracting countless productions from the United States and around the world. Vancouver is also beginning to develop its own film and television infrastructure, complete with influential directors, producers, writers, and actors working on their own projects.

For locals, all this means that celebrity-spotting isn't the novelty it was a decade ago (see sidebar, Celebrity Hangouts). In fact, the list of stars who have worked and played in the area during recent years grows steadily: Gwyneth Paltrow, Bridget Fonda, Ethan Hawke, Warren Beatty, Mel Gibson, Goldie Hawn, Alicia Silverstone, Robin Williams, Brad Pitt, John Travolta, Richard Gere, Sharon Stone, Steve Martin, Uma Thurman, Robert De Niro, Sean Penn, Jodie Foster, Sylvester Stallone. A few local film and TV actors—Michael J. Fox, Cameron Bancroft, Jason Priestley, and Cynthia Stevenson—have made it big in Hollywood after beginning their careers in Vancouver. There's also a new crop of indigenous acting talent with huge potential: Carrie-Anne Moss, Barry Pepper, Will Sasso, and Devon Sawa are among those with a shot at the A-list. Meanwhile, local directors such as Mina Shum, Lynne Stopkewich, and Bruce Sweeney have made a name for themselves.

Recent features filmed in and around Vancouver include *Reindeer Games, Mission to Mars, Lake Placid,*, and *Snow Falling on Cedars*. American producers also flock to the city to shoot an ever larger number of TV series and movies-of-the-week. (They say we have some of the most interesting alleys in North America for movie shoots.) Although *The X-Files* has departed to L.A., several TV series shoot their entire seasons here, among them *The Outer Limits, Poltergeist, Sliders, Stargate SG-1,* and *The Crow*. Some of the most-used locations in Vancouver are the Vancouver Art Gallery on Hornby Street, Blood Alley just off Carrall Street in Gastown, and the alley south of Hastings Street between Cambie and Abbott Streets. Finding a shoot is easy: just look for big white trailers lining the block and people in headsets keeping an eye on curious passersby. For updates of movies and TV series currently filming in the city, call the **BC FILM COMMISSION HOT LINE** at 604/660-3569 or access its Web site, www.bcfilmcommission.com. The local media has grown a little jaded about the film biz, but you can find industry news in the magazine *Reel West* (www.reelwest.com), which appears five times a year. *Reel West Digest*, published annually, lists production personnel, studios, performers, writers, and agents. Look for it at most major newsstands or order a copy by calling 604/451-7335.

If you'd like to see yourself on the big screen as an extra, there are lots of opportunities here. You'll like the work if you're already financially secure, your ego is intact, and you don't take the whole thing too seriously. The hours are long, the food's mediocre (you don't get to eat with the stars), the money isn't always great (extras earn anything from minimum wage to $22 an hour), the work is sporadic, and you'll be herded around like a heifer on a cattle drive. But hey, you might get to meet your favourite star. **EXTRAS CASTING** is done by several local agencies. Try Local Color at 604/685-0315 or Keystone Extras at 604/685-2218. You'll need a few head shots for their files, and you might be required to pay a one-time fee (usually about $25) to register. Other talent agencies include Characters (604/733-9800), Lucas Talent (604/685-0345), Twenty-First Century Artists Inc. (604/736-8786), and Hodgson Management Group (604/687-7676).

Film aficionados frequent the **DUNBAR THEATRE** (4555 Dunbar St; 604/228-9912; map:B3), **VANCOUVER CENTRE CINEMAS** (650 W Georgia St; 604/669-4442; map:S4), the **PARK THEATRE** (3440 Cambie St; 604/290-0500; map:D3), the **VARSITY THEATRE** (4375 W 10th Ave; 604/222-2235; map:B3), and **FIFTH AVENUE CINEMAS** (2110 Burrard St; 604/734-7469; map:P7), all of which screen an eclectic selection of new and recent independent movies. For $12, patrons can purchase an Alliance Cinemas membership that entitles them to reduced admission prices at the Fifth Avenue and Park Cinemas, plus concession-stand discounts. The **RIDGE THEATRE** (3131 Arbutus St; 604/738-6311; www.site geist.com/ridge; map:C3), the **HOLLYWOOD THEATRE** (3123 W Broadway; 604/738-3211; map:C3), and **DENMAN PLACE DISCOUNT CINEMA** (124–1030 Denman St; 604/683-2201; map:P2) are home to the popular, inexpensive, second-run double bill. The **PACIFIC CINÉMATHÈQUE** (1131 Howe St; 604/688-FILM; www.cinematheque.bc.ca; map:R4) is touted as a year-round film festival offering retrospectives of important directors, lecture series, classic foreign films, and a variety of independent and experimental Canadian films. Screenings are evenings only, six days a week, excluding Tuesdays, when the mainstream theatres drop their prices. Vancouver's newest independent movie house, the **BLINDING LIGHT!! CINEMA** (36 Powell St; 604/878-3366; www.blindinglight.com; map:V3), specializes in avant-garde features, shorts, and documentaries both old and new. On Thursday's BYO8 Night, audience members are encouraged to bring their own Super 8, 16mm, and VHS films.

Downtown, mostly in the two-block stretch of Granville Street between Georgia and Smithe, and in many suburban malls, you'll find multiplex theatres, run by corporate giants Cineplex Odeon and Famous Players, screening Hollywood's latest extravaganzas. Two of the biggest are the **GRANVILLE 7 CINEMAS** (855 Granville St; 604/684-4000; map:T4) and **STATION SQUARE 7 CINEMAS** (in Burnaby's Metrotown; 604/434-7711; map:G4). At press time, plans were well underway for a new 16-screen entertainment complex at the corner of Burrard and Robson Streets, complete with an IMAX theatre. The **ALCAN OMNIMAX THEATRE** at Vancouver's Science World (604/268-6363; www.scienceworld. bc.ca; map:V6) and **CN IMAX THEATRE** at Canada Place (604/682-IMAX; www.imax.com; map:T3) both offer new releases every few months. Both are legacies of Expo 86. The Vancouver suburbs of Richmond and Langley are also home to IMAX screens, at **SILVERCITY RIVERPORT** (No. 6 Rd and Steveston Hwy; 604/277-5993; map:E7) and the **COLOSSUS** (200th St and Hwy 1; 604/513-1610).

The **VANCOUVER INTERNATIONAL FILM FESTIVAL**, in late September and early October, is the third largest in North America and typically presents more than 400 screenings of some 275 films from more than 50 countries. At seven centrally located theatres (some with wheelchair access), viewers can catch dramatic features, documentaries (the VIFF has the biggest documentary section of all North American festivals), comedies, and animated shorts, theatrically grouped under categories such as Dragons and Tigers: The Cinemas of East Asia, Walk on the Wild Side (a sometimes risqué midnight series), and the Best of Britain. The Vancouver International Film Festival also features a three-day trade forum. For more information, call 604/685-0260 or log on to www.viff.org.

Other local film festivals include the **VANCOUVER JEWISH FILM FES-TIVAL** (604/257-5111), held in May at the Norman Rothstein Theatre (950 W 41st Ave; 604/257-5111; map:D4), and Pacific Cinémathèque, which gathers together work from countries such as Canada, France, Germany, Israel, and the U.K. Every June at Pacific Cinémathèque, the **CHINESE FILM FESTIVAL,** 604/688-FILM, shows 20-plus features from China, Hong Kong, and Taiwan—including several premieres—as well as animated shorts. Beginning in early August, the **VANCOUVER QUEER FILM + VIDEO FESTIVAL,** 604/688-WEST, ext. 2014 or 2299, offers some 150 screenings of 30 international films and videos at various venues. The **VANCOUVER UNDERGROUND FILM FESTIVAL** takes place in mid-November at the Blinding Light!! Cinema. A popular indie-film night—and a chance for film biz hipsters to socialize—is the **CELLULOID SOCIAL CLUB,** held once a month at the Purple Onion Cabaret (15 Water St; 604/734-8339; map:U3). In addition to being a venue for exhibitions, installations, and festival screenings, film co-op **VIDEO IN STUDIOS** (1965 Main St; 604/872-8337; www.video-in.com; map:V6) hosts Thursday producer nights.

Literature

Finally, the rest of the world has caught on that Vancouver is a hotbed of writing talent: authors such as Douglas Coupland, William Gibson, W. P. Kinsella, Evelyn Lau, Shani Mootoo, Bill Richardson, and Michael Turner now have international followings. Locally, the literary scene stays healthy largely thanks to the efforts of regional book and magazine publishers, a growing community of writers, and widespread enthusiasm for readings and other public events celebrating literacy. For the scoop on Vancouver writers, pick up a copy of Alan Twigg's quarterly *BC Bookworld* (604/736-4011), which contains profiles, interviews, gossip, literary polemics, and reviews of the latest BC books.

Besides its thriving poetry slam scene, Vancouver has enough reading series to satisfy even the most voracious literary appetite. Although they're a source of consternation for some local booksellers, **CHAPTERS** book superstores (various locations; www.chapters.ca) regularly host in-store readings and book signings. A smaller, homegrown alternative is **BLACK SHEEP BOOKS** (2742 W 4th Ave; 604/732-5087; www.black-sheepbooks.com; map:C2), which on Friday nights crams audiences into its small confines for appearances by seasoned and up-and-coming fiction writers, poets, and singer-songwriters. The **VANCOUVER PUBLIC LIBRARY** (350 W Georgia St; 604/331-4101; www.vpl. vancouver.bc.ca; map:T4) is a busy venue for local, national, and international authors.

CITY ARTS AND LECTURES

We know you didn't come to Vancouver to be lectured, but here are a few options for anyone craving an educational talk, a heated debate, or simply some old-fashioned intellectual stimulation. Several of these events will provide you with a deeper understanding of the city, and all of them help keep Vancouver connected to the greater world of ideas.

The **Vancouver Art Gallery** (604/662-4719) regularly hosts curator's lectures and artist's talks coinciding with major exhibitions. Also at the VAG during spring and summer: daily tours of selected current exhibitions (on Thursday evenings, these tours are offered in Chinese and Japanese). Several other galleries throughout the city host panel discussions and artist's lectures, among them the **Charles H. Scott Gallery, the Morris and Helen Belkin Gallery, Presentation House Gallery,** and **Western Front.** For updates of art gallery lectures, visit the Alliance for Arts and Culture Web site at www.culturenet.ca/vca or call their Arts Hotline at 604/684-ARTS.

The City Program During the academic year, Simon Fraser University's downtown Harbour Centre campus (515 W Hastings St; 604/291-5098; www.sfu.ca/city) sponsors several free public lectures as part of the City Program's attempts to foster a better understanding of Vancouver and its future. If discussions of city planning and economic development sound a little too dry, the program also offers brief and affordable courses in urban photography, urban landscape drawing, and Vancouver architecture.

MacMillan Bloedel Lectures on Architecture Organized by the Vancouver League for Studies in Architecture and the Environment (whew!), this well-attended series of a dozen or so free lectures between October and April brings in prestigious guest speakers from as far away as Helsinki and Tokyo. The idea is to encourage public debate about Vancouver's triumphs and follies in the realms of contemporary architecture and design. Another component is the **Builders of Vancouver** series, which includes panel discussions and symposia on everything from street design to public art. Lectures are held at the Robson Square Conference Centre (800 Robson St; 604/874-4499; www.vanmuseum.bc.ca/urbanar.htm).

The Opera Club If you're game for a night at the opera, why not an afternoon? Installments of the Western Canadian Opera Society's Sunday series—held monthly starting at 2pm from September to June—could include historical talks, audiovisual presentations, and an aria or two from a top-flight soprano. For its annual Western Canadian Opera Lecture, the society hosts a luminary from the international opera world. The Opera Club also organizes group opera tours. Meetings are held at SFU's Harbour Centre campus, and some events at the Robson Square Conference Centre.

Philosophers' Cafes This series of public discussions, held year-round in restaurants, coffee shops, and bookstores (and even at the beach during the summer), proves that philosophy needn't be boring or stuffy. The moderator introduces an invited guest, who briefly introduces the evening's burning issue—anything from censorship to (you guessed it) the existence of God—before opening the floor to debate. No philosophical training required, just the ability to eat, drink, and be talkative. For more info, phone 604/291-5237 or check out www.sfu.ca/cstudies/arts/philosopherscafe.

Unique Lives & Experiences High-calibre guests—from Mia Farrow to Maya Angelou to Margaret Thatcher—save the Vancouver chapter of this North American women's lecture series (www.uniquelives.com) from being simply an expensive pep rally. After speakers share their life stories, audience members are invited to ask prying questions during a Q&A period. The monthly evenings typically run September through June at the Orpheum Theatre (Granville St at Smithe St). Tickets are available from Ticketmaster, 604/280-4444. —*Nick Rockel*

Poetry at the Shadbolt, held the last Friday of the month at Burnaby's Shadbolt Centre for the Arts (see Theatre in this chapter), features readings by Vancouver poets and out-of-town guests, plus an open-mike session. Poetry collective the **KOOTENAY SCHOOL OF WRITING** (103–400 Smithe St; 604/688-6001; www.ksw.net; map:S5) welcomes heavy hitters from the North American poetry scene. **LAST FRIDAYS** at **GALLERY GACHET** (88 E Cordova St; 604/687-2468, www.gachet.org; map:U3) is an open-mike series for poets, prose writers, and performance artists. The **HELEN PITT GALLERY** (882 Homer St; 604/681-6740; map:S4) opens its doors for happenings such as pan-poetics, a fusion of words, images, and live music. Restaurants and cafes where you'll find readings and other spoken-word events include **DV8** (515 Davie St; 604/682-4388; map:R5) and, of course, **BUKOWSKI'S** (1447 Commercial Dr; 604/253-4770; map:Z6).

If screenwriting is your game, the stylish **ALIBI ROOM** restaurant (157 Alexander St; 604/623-3383; www.alibiroom.com; map:V3)—Gillian Anderson, Jason Priestley, and Tom Skerritt are investors—hosts a Sunday script read-through series. Every Thursday from late May through early September at the **ANZA CLUB** (3 W 8th Ave; map:V7), the Spincycle film and theatre society presents the cold reading series, a chance for screenwriters and playwrights to have their works-in-progress performed by local actors. Second Night, another Spincycle event held three times during the summer, mounts full-length scripts by established screenwriters. For more information about both events, call 604/450-6870. Readings at the **PRAXIS CENTRE FOR SCREENWRITERS** (300–12 Water St; 604/682-3100; www.sfu.ca/praxis; map:U3) are closed to the public, but the Praxis script library of 1,500 feature films, TV series, and documentaries is an excellent resource for writers and directors. Access to the library is free, and visitors can sign out scripts for a $30 membership fee. These three local festivals also celebrate the written word.

SUNSHINE COAST FESTIVAL OF THE WRITTEN ARTS / Rockwood Centre, Sechelt; 800/565-9361 Every year in August, 20 or so highly regarded Canadian authors and their fans gather at Sechelt's picturesque Rockwood Centre, on the Sunshine Coast (about 90 minutes north of Vancouver by car and ferry), for a long weekend of readings, book signings, and lively discussions over drinks. Nightly author receptions make this an excellent opportunity to mingle with the writers in an intimate setting, and the festival ends with a barbecue dinner. *www.sunshine.net/ rockwood.* &

VANCOUVER INTERNATIONAL WRITERS (& READERS) FESTIVAL / Granville Island; 604/681-6330 Canada's second-largest literary event, this annual Granville Island festival features poets, playwrights, and novelists from across Canada and around the world. Highlights include the Poetry Bash, the Literary Cabaret, and the Duthie Lecture, held in honour of late Vancouver bookseller Bill Duthie. The five-day festival usually takes place at the end of October. Guests could include anyone from the hottest new author on the circuit to CanLit heavyweights Margaret Atwood or Vikram Seth. *www.writersfest.bc.ca; map:Q7.* &

THE WORD ON THE STREET / Library Square, 350 W Georgia St; 604/684-8266 On the last Sunday in September, the downtown Vancouver Public Library and adjacent CBC Plaza host this one-day book and magazine fair, which coincides with similar events in other Canadian cities. Besides dozens of exhibitors from the local publishing community, participants include literacy organizations, booksellers, and roving performers. Among the other attractions: the Authors Tent, writers' workshops, a poetry stage, a cooking stage at CBC Plaza, and, of course, the chance to get a book autographed by your favourite writer. *wotsvan@ infinet.net; map:T4.* &

NIGHTLIFE

NIGHTLIFE

Music and Clubs

History shows that Vancouver nightclubs will try anything once, provided someone else tries it first. During the past several years, the city's after-dark scene has embraced the grunge aesthetic of its close U.S. neighbour, Seattle; launched a lounge revival hot on the heels of Los Angeles; and succumbed to the hypnotic beat of electronica, originally nurtured in New York, London, and Detroit. But still, the local nightlife has established an identity of sorts. On an evening out in Vancouver, you can enjoy just about every clubbing experience imaginable, from an old-time rock 'n' roll bender to a no-holds-barred striptease show, to a till-dawn rave in a factory warehouse. And you can rest assured that when the next big thing comes along, Vancouver club owners and promoters will be right there to make it their own.

Recently, the city has seen many of its live-music venues close or change format as a new generation of clubgoers faithfully queue up outside the downtown dance spots with the hottest DJs. One exciting development: the city is finally going ahead with its plans to create a downtown entertainment district on Granville Mall. Several new clubs are expected to open along the strip during the next couple of years.

Vancouver enjoys a growing international reputation among aficionados of electronica and rave culture, which (let's face it) are now about as mainstream as Coca-Cola. Meanwhile, tired of listening to music they don't understand, slightly older folks have taken to drowning their sorrows at the city's many bars and turning late-night restaurants into their personal playrooms. Night owls of a certain age tend to haunt cocktail lounges (most of them found in hotels) or bend an elbow at the local pub, the best examples of which are in suburbs like Coquitlam, Burnaby, and North Vancouver.

Given their notoriously fickle patrons, Vancouver nightclubs, pubs, bars, and lounges can assume a new identity—or simply disappear—almost overnight. Before visiting any of the establishments mentioned in this chapter, you might want to call ahead to make sure the circus hasn't picked up and left town. Otherwise, the best print sources for up-to-date listings are the *Georgia Straight* (www.straight.com), and the Thursday entertainment section of the *Vancouver Sun* (www.vancouversun.com). Online, the Telus Web site www.mybc.com and the relatively new vancouvertoday.com both carry nightlife information. For daily updates of concert announcements, visit the Ticketmaster Web site (www.ticket master.ca).

ALIBI ROOM / 157 Alexander St; 604/623-3383 Like its Seattle cousin (and unlike, say, Planet Hollywood), the sleek, modern Alibi Room is a restaurant where real film people can be seen enjoying a real meal. No wonder: the food's good, Jason Priestley and Tom Skerritt are among the investors, and there's a script library in the middle of the dining room. But beyond its Hollywood cachet, this is an excellent place to meet a group of friends for drinks and/or dinner—provided no one minds shouting over the outré electronica that's often blaring from the sound system. If you want to hear more, head downstairs to the ultra-hip lounge, which in a strange role reversal is often more subdued than the restaurant. Attention screenwriters: last Sunday of the month is the Alibi Unplugged Script Reading Series. *MC, V; debit cards; every day; full bar; map:U3.*

BABALU / 654 Nelson St; 604/605-4343 Word is that when folks graduate from the Roxy down the block, they put on their glad rags and join a dressier lineup outside Babalu. Fortunately, this club's Cuban-themed decor hasn't led to an influx of male patrons who look and act like Ricky Ricardo. Tuesday through Thursday, the house band, a snappy jazz combo appropriately named Smokin' Section, shoos couples onto the dance floor. A DJ—and a more rock 'n' roll vibe—take over for the weekend. Until Sunday, that is, when free swing lessons give even the ungainly the chance to learn a rudimentary Charleston. One of the few dance clubs in town where over-35s can be spotted in numbers. *AE, MC, V; debit cards; every day; full bar; info@babalu.com; map:S4.*

THE BLARNEY STONE / 216 Carrall St; 604/687-4322 Thursday through Saturday, the *Riverdance* phenomenon isn't lost on the hundreds of attractive 19- to 30-year-olds who pour into this rollicking Gastown club. The Olde Irish pub decor makes for a mead-hall atmosphere, complete with a sturdy house band eager to turn every weekend into a St. Paddy's Day celebration and every patron into an honorary native of the Emerald Isle. The crowd may be on the young side, but don't be surprised to see entire families partying together. *AE, MC, V; Tues–Sat; full bar; map:V3.*

BOONE COUNTY COUNTRY CABARET / 801 Brunette Ave, Coquitlam; 604/525-3144 Why do cowboy hats turn up at the sides? So four people can fit into a pickup and 300 into Boone County on weekends. This place is raucous, with a cramped layout that makes it seem busier than it really is. A large square bar fills much of the back half of the place, and raised tables and a decent-size dance floor take up the rest. Depending on your skill (or your liquid courage), you may want to join in on some country line dancing. Weekends are so busy you'll have to grease your chaps to slide into a standing-room spot, so mosey in early to grab a seat. *AE, MC, V; debit cards; Mon–Sat; full bar; map:K2.*

CELEBRITIES / 1022 Davie St; 604/689-3180 Since its auspicious beginning as the Retinal Circus, where the Grateful Dead came to play and the '60s hippies came to trip out, this club has been best known for its revolving marquee. A massive two-storey room, centred around a giant dance floor and a raised DJ booth, Celebrities is now Vancouver's hottest place to dance. Although it's "officially" a gay club, Celebrities welcomes patrons of all persuasions—especially on Fridays, the hugely popular Rehab night, which sees the place literally packed to the rafters with stylish young funksters hungry for the very newest electronic dance mixes. Other nights include '80s retro and the decidedly gay Planet Fag. *V; debit cards; Mon–Sat; full bar; map:R5.*

THE CELLAR JAZZ CAFE / 3611 W Broadway; 604/738-1959 Now that they finally have some nightlife, Kitsilano residents just can't get enough. Instead of heading downtown, they flock to neighbourhood spots like the Cellar, which shakes up a residential stretch of W Broadway with live jazz, funk, blues, and hip-hop seven nights a week. The raging red walls of this tiny basement are usually covered with someone's art exhibition, while carefully placed mirrors give the welcome illusion of a second room next door. A sometimes boisterous crowd—which may be dominated by older hipsters or younger funksters, depending on the night's entertainment—packs the zebra-skin booths and low-slung tables, sipping martinis that come in a colour for every week of the year. Jazz jam session Sundays. *AE, MC, V; debit cards; every day; full bar; jazzcel@aol.com; map:C3.*

CHAMELEON URBAN LOUNGE / 801 W Georgia St; 604/669-0806 Deep in the bowels of the Crowne Plaza Hotel awaits the Chameleon. The room itself is a narrow space dripping in cool basic black, with only red-velvet antique couches and splashes of halogen-lit original art to warm the visual landscape. Here the crowd is as cool as the black marble underfoot. Well-dressed, very urban 20- to 40-year-olds congregate to sip the latest trendy beverages and groove to music ranging from hip-hop to drum 'n' bass to live Latin jazz. You won't find much of a dance floor, but you're more than welcome to sway where you stand. A lounge lizard lineup is in place from 9:30pm till 1am on weekends, so slither in early. *AE, MC, V; debit cards; every day; full bar; map:S3.*

THE COMMODORE BALLROOM / 868 Granville St; 604/739-SHOW The Commodore reopened in late 1999 after sitting empty for three years, during which it narrowly escaped a makeover as an upscale cowboy bar. Fortunately, the Calgary entrepreneur who plotted that heinous crime withdrew his plans after noisy protests. The legendary live venue is now in the hands of local promoter and manager Bruce Allen, nightclub mogul Roger Gibson, and House of Blues Concerts Canada. With management

POOL HALLS

Automotive / 1095 Homer St; 604/682-0040 The pool hall used to be strictly a male domain—a place where monosyllabic greasers, smelling of hair oil and leather, would congregate to smoke, squint, and swear. Not so this hip Yaletown billiard room, ensconced in a former auto dealership. White walls, a high ceiling, and abundant windows keep it bright and cheery, and the original garage door swings open (weather permitting) to keep the air as fresh as the juices and bistro snacks that are offered up front. You'll wait about 15 minutes in the '60s-furnished holding lounge if you arrive between 8pm and 1am. *Every day; map:S5.*

Soho Cafe & Billiards / 1144 Homer St; 604/688-1180 This establishment was the first of the city's upscale pool haunts. Since day one, the seats and pool tables have been full of Kitsilano yupsters and Yaletown hipsters. The walls are clad in the original rustic brick, and the place looks and feels super. The food alone is worth a visit. *Every day; map:S5.*

like this, it's no wonder the 990-capacity Commodore has picked up where it left off, bringing in some of the world's best rock, pop, blues, and jazz artists. The club is also a coveted stage for up-and-coming and established local acts. While the room has been restored to an opulent version of its1930s art-deco glory (with an updated light and sound system, of course), the fabulously springy dance floor remains the same. *AE, MC, V; debit cards; open 5 to 7 nights a week (call for concert dates); full bar; www.commodoreballroom.com; map:S4.*

LAVA LOUNGE / 1176 Granville St; 604/605-1154 One of the city's best live venues, in a Howard Johnson hotel? Don't laugh: this big room greets visitors with sensational decor and sight lines. A wall of weathered brick and a long bar with recessed lighting line one side, and the large elevated stage is easily seen from every seat in the house. The Lava Lounge books original local acts and occasional touring biggies, while entertainment on other nights could be stand-up comedy, a swing extravaganza, or a bout of "New Waveaoke." The club, which is part of the Stages entertainment complex, has a habit of changing names: if you see the HoJo sign, you've come to the right place. *AE, MC, V; debit cards; every day; full bar; map:R5.*

LUV-A-FAIR / 1275 Seymour St; 604/685-3288 Luv-A-Fair plays host to a young crowd dressed in trendy threads, who bop nonstop to equally trendy tunes played at ear-splitting—but crystal-clear—volume. The differently themed nights run from industrial to Britpop to '80s alternative; all of them feature an opportunity for self-aware patrons to gyrate on platforms above the heavily strobed dance floor. If you'd rather keep a low profile, take things upstairs to the caged-in second level and shoot a game of pool. One of the busiest places in town; there's usually a line out the door. *MC, V; debit cards; every day; full bar; map:S5.*

MONTANA'S / 135 W 1st St, North Vancouver; 604/980-7722 Montana's—a sports bar? Perhaps, if they include the act of picking up someone as a form of weightlifting. Until then, Montana's remains simply the hottest "meating" place on the North Shore. This was one of the first nightspots to set an age requirement of 25 years or older on weekends, and according to management, the move has virtually eliminated fights and unruly behaviour. Though the younger set has taken to referring to Montana's as the "Prune Saloon," the place is a huge success. A large dance floor throbs to the beat of R&B and Top 40, while a pair of satellite dishes and a few pool tables offer diversion to the rhythmically challenged. Weekends are jammed, so get an early start to avoid the lineup. Large menu of pizza and pastas. *AE, V, MC; debit cards; Wed–Sat; full bar; map:E1.*

NUMBERS CABARET / 1042 Davie St; 604/685-4077 Regulars of all ages squeeze into denim and leather and cram into a room that's as intriguing as the gay clientele. Corridors connect four split-levels and a pair of bars. Grab a stool down below in the Kok-Pit or head up top and practise your stroke on one of the pool tables. The tunes are cranked up at 10pm nightly, and the midlevel dance floor fills until closing with swaying bodies. Cover charge on Friday and Saturday only. *No credit cards; debit cards; every day; full bar; map:R5.*

THE ODYSSEY / 1251 Howe St; 604/689-5256 At the Odyssey, a large contingent of bisexuals mingle with gays and a growing number of straight patrons, which sometimes motivates management to pluck gay people from the ever-present line (99 cents cover on Tuesdays). Work up a sweat on the dance floor and then cool off by stepping outside to the rear garden. Or, if you've put in your time at the gym, strip naked and lather yourself in an elevated shower, starting at midnight on Thursdays. The Odyssey also features a disco night and drag shows, as well as plays and film screenings. *V; debit cards; every day; full bar; map:R5.*

THE PALLADIUM CLUB / 1250 Richards St; 604/688-2648 Fridays, this humongous warehouse-size club hosts live local and touring acts, but on other nights the Palladium puts its powerful sound system to the test, as guest and resident DJs delve deep into their record collections. Expect evenings devoted to break-beat, progressive dance, and Gothic industrial, with attendant hordes of appropriately dressed followers. If you find all this genre-splitting confusing, there's also an '80s dance party. Between turns on the dance floor, relax in the carpeted lounge section or get a ventilator's-eye view of the action from upstairs. A line forms by 10pm on weekends. *MC, V; debit cards; every day; full bar; map:R6.*

THE PURPLE ONION CABARET / 15 Water St; 604/602-9442 In the heart of Gastown, two flights up from historic Water Street, the Purple Onion offers two great choices to suit your mood. For live music, check out the lounge, where local players come to show off their jazz, funk, and R&B chops. Watch white-bread, suburban kids enter and seemingly transform from geek to chic quicker than you can say Thelonious Monk. If folks with instruments aren't for you, the cabaret across the hall just might be. This place is crammed with tony and well-toned 19- to 25-year-olds. Indulge in a selection of pizzas, sandwiches, sushi, and daily specials between shaking a leg to house, hip-hop, Latin jazz, Top 40, or even a poetry slam. The Purple Onion is one of Vancouver's hot spots, so expect to cool your heels in a two-hour lineup on Friday and Saturday. *AE, MC, V; debit cards; every day; full bar; www.purpleonion.com; map:V4.*

THE RAGE / 750 Pacific Blvd S; 604/685-5585 The rumour is that house lights dim in a 12-block radius when the Rage turns on its sound system. Five separate bars and promotional tie-ins with a local dance station are two other reasons why its DJ nights are a hit with packs of trendy suburban kids, out to sample brand-new vinyl they can't hear back home. In a different life, this club at the Plaza of Nations uses its 1,000-plus capacity as a live venue for touring pop, rock, and blues acts. *AE, MC, V; debit cards; Fri–Sat and concert nights; full bar; map:U6.*

THE RAILWAY CLUB / 579 Dunsmuir St; 604/681-1625 This casual, second-storey spot is long and narrow, with a large, long bar cutting the room in two. The caboose shape makes it an intimate setting for innovative live entertainment, which over the years has included dozens of up-and-coming rock, pop, folk, and blues artists. Try to arrive early enough to grab a seat in the front section next to the stage; chances are you'll be glad you did. Otherwise you might find yourself in the quieter back forty, or around the corner in the retro cocktail lounge—hey, life could be much, much worse. Although the Railway is a club, nonmembers are welcome, at a slightly higher cover charge. *MC, V; every day; full bar; map:T4.*

RICHARD'S ON RICHARDS / 1036 Richards St; 604/687-6794 Better known as Dick's on Dicks, this is Vancouver's quintessential "meet market," a place where young folks who drive expensive cars come to boogie down to house DJs and add some zest to their social lives. Richard's is also a popular and intimate live venue, with the accent on local groups and some hot touring artists. The second level offers a shooter bar and a bird's-eye view of the dance floor, so if you're wearing something filmy and skin-tight, count on being ogled from above. Only open on weekends, so expect long lines. *AE, MC, V; debit cards; Fri–Sat; full bar; map:S5.*

THE ROXY CABARET / 932 Granville St; 604/684-7699 After the young suburbanites hit the mall and the college crowd hits the books, they all hit the Roxy for classic rock. This place has been drawing massive line-ups since forever, and its owners aren't about to mess with a simple but successful formula. Behind three bars the gin slingers do their Tom Cruise imitations, juggling joy juice, catching bottles behind their backs, and clanging a hanging bell whenever a generous donation makes its way into their tip jar. A pair of fiendishly competent cover bands split the week. Casual dress, with the latest Robson Street looks in abundance. *AE, DIS, MC, V; debit cards; every day; full bar; map:R5.*

SHARK CLUB BAR AND GRILL / 180 W Georgia St; 604/687-4275 Frantically busy when the Canucks or the Grizzlies play a home game at nearby GM Place, the Shark Club is an upscale, tiered sports bar offering a soothing decor of oak and brass, punctuated by an array of sports memorabilia. In addition to the usual assortment of interpersonal games being played among the crowd, you'll find 30 TV screens showing games of other kinds, along with the requisite pool tables. The long oak bar delivers 22 beers on tap, and the kitchen pumps out tasty food for lunch and dinner. Thursday is live-music night; other evenings, a DJ fires up Top 40 and classic rock and the dance floor fills fast. All 180 seats are occupied and a lineup in place Thursday through Saturday, when valet parking is available. *AE, DC, MC, V; debit cards; every day; full bar; map:T5.*

SONAR / 66 Water St; 604/683-6695 A huge uproar followed the announcement that one of Vancouver's premier live venues, the Town Pump, was going to be remodelled as a dance bar. In retrospect, it was a brilliant idea. Sleek, comfortable, and ultramodern, Sonar gives local DJs and their followings a place to call home, and keeps a respectable enough profile abroad to attract vinyl-spinning legends from the United States and Europe. The week's lineup is literally an education in house music and electronica, with a generous helping of jazz, hip-hop, and reggae to keep it real. Not only that, the owner works in the store: co-owner Luke McKeehan (also a partner in the Chameleon Urban Lounge and local record label Mo'Funk) mans the turntables some nights. Sonar has been named one of the world's top 20 dance clubs by Britain's *Ministry* magazine. *AE, MC, V; debit cards; Mon–Sat; full bar; www.sonar.bc.ca; map:U3.*

THE STARFISH ROOM / 1055 Homer St; 604/682-4171 Live pop, jazz, and electronica are the lures that attract schools of new-music aficionados to the Starfish. It's intimate, smoky, and high-volume, with good sight lines to the stage. Expect fine local talent and some stellar international acts, but be cautious on the dance floor—it can fill up with an eel-like tangle of moshing maniacs. Also be wary of the men's washroom, which often looks like somebody couldn't find the toilet. Cover charge varies. *MC, V; Wed–Sat; full bar; map:S5.*

VODA NIGHT CLUB AND LOUNGE / 783 Homer St (Westin Grand Hotel); 604/684-3003 Los Angeles chic touches down in Vancouver. This cavernous hotel lounge—just across the street from the downtown public library—is one of the city's best places to get caught being young and modern. Accordingly, the space-age rec-room decor is straight out of *Wallpaper* magazine: rosewood panelling, a backlit bar complete with cascading water, big angled beams, and loads of candles. Ditto for VODA's clientele, who Thursday through Saturday turn the lineup into a fashion show and the room into a somewhat frosty nightclub (with some help from the rotating house DJs). Other nights can be as dead as a Chevy Chase double bill—ideal if you're in the mood for a quiet drink while gawking at the expensive scenery. *AE, MC, V; Mon–Sat; full bar; map:T5.*

WETT BAR / 1320 Richards St; 604/662-7707 This swish dance club may no longer be called MaRS, but spending an evening here can still be an interplanetary experience. That's partly thanks to the whirling, space-craftlike lights and effects system suspended from the ceiling above the dance floor, and a 6.5-metre (22-foot) fibre-optic screen shot through with mind-altering images, courtesy of local "atmosphere designers" Urban Visuals. But perhaps the most attractive feature of all is the sound system (designed for a Michael Jackson tour), which pumps out distortion-free music that centres on the dancers and keeps the level tolerable elsewhere in the room. Wett Bar's DJs spin drum 'n' bass, house, funk classics, and even the occasional Top 40 smash. Anticipate a lineup, even when the place is half-empty. If you want to save yourself a hefty cover, call ahead to make sure no one's hosting a special event. *AE, MC, V; debit cards; Mon, Wed, Fri, Sat; full bar; map:R6.*

YUK YUK'S / 750 Pacific Blvd S; 604/687-LAFF This venue originated as the Flying Club during Expo 86 and is still going strong as a member of the world's largest comedy club chain. It's the perfect place for comedy, just the right size (218 seats), with a theatre-style setting that ensures a perfect vantage point from any seat in the house. Hilarious (or at least here's hoping) touring acts from across the continent appear Wednesday through Saturday. Reservations recommended on weekends. *AE, MC, V; debit cards; Wed–Sat; full bar; map:U6.*

Bars, Pubs, and Taverns

BAR NONE / 1222 Hamilton St; 604/689-7000 A brick-and-beam Yaletown gathering place from the mists of the early '90s, this lamplit living room still has members of the well-dressed, well-coiffed, and well-toned under-40 set queuing up to arrange themselves along its lengthy bar. The stage (really a part of the floor) is occupied by a house jazz-funk band Mondays and Tuesdays; other nights it stands conspicuously empty until patrons are emboldened by the DJ's thoughtful offerings of soul, house, Top 40, and other danceable grooves. Try to hang loose, but do keep your stomach sucked in. *AE, MC, V; debit cards; Mon–Sat; full bar; map:R6.*

THE BRICKHOUSE BAR / 730 Main St; 604/689-8645 Until the Brickhouse came along, there was nowhere on this gritty stretch of Main Street to enjoy a quiet drink—let alone a safe one. The thoughtful owners have created a welcoming atmosphere in the small, narrow room by following the simple principle of not overdoing things. All the same, there is a cigar humidor and a nice selection of scotch, as well as dartboards and pool tables for those who don't want to stick with the pleasures of good old conversation. Make sure you check out the wall of fish tanks. Upstairs is another find: the candlelit Brickhouse Bistro, serving great West Coast food until 2:30am most nights. If you're worried about your car (and in this neighbourhood you should be), there's a secured lot out back. And, wonder of wonders, the foyer has a bike rack. *MC, V; debit cards; every day; full bar; map:V5.*

THE CECIL EXOTIC SHOWLOUNGE / 1336 Granville St; 604/683-5029 As strip joints go, the Cecil is a palace: well-lit and friendly, with good pub grub and eye-poppingly attractive performers. And since Canadian laws allow exotic dancers to take it all off, the place is often packed with American tourists pinching themselves under the table to make sure they're not dreaming. If you're here for the entertainment (and who isn't?), there's a good view of the stage—outfitted with a shower *and* a hot tub—from just about anywhere in the room. Want to get a little closer to the action? The roving hostesses (and some mainstage performers) offer private dances in a VIP area. Another way to zoom in is by grabbing a seat in the "tipping section" around the edge of the stage. Just be prepared to lay down some bills. *MC, V; debit cards; every day; full bar; map:R5.*

THE CREEK RESTAURANT BREWERY & BAR / 1253 Johnston St; 604/685-7070 Part of the Creek Restaurant in the Granville Island Hotel, this woody meeting spot for up-and-coming (i.e., just-turned-30) stockbrokers, lawyers, and entrepreneurs has great views onto False Creek and a decent selection of brewed-on-the-premises lagers and ales. In summer, there's a smashing outdoor patio; in fall and winter, the combination of DJ and crackling fireplace make for a kind of Gen-X drawing room. And all year-round, you'll meet (or at least hear) people who bear absolutely no resemblance to the laid-back Vancouverites of legend. *AE, MC, V; debit cards; every day; full bar; map:Q6.*

DIX BARBECUE AND BREWERY / 871 Beatty St; 604/682-2739 The latest addition to clothier Mark James' roster of comfortable, nonthreatening restaurants and brew pubs, Dix manages not to offend just about everyone. That's why on a good night, you'll find the tables and bar stools of this handsome, brick-lined Yaletown gathering spot filled with everyone from fashionable twentysomethings to recalcitrant boomers. Many of them are here for the barbecue—slow-smoked ribs, pork shoulder, and brisket straight from the Southern Pride cooker, along with the obligatory sides of collard greens and creamed corn. Of course, the food cries out for one of the brewed-on-the-premises lagers, or perhaps a shot or two of Kentucky bourbon. Attentive staff can be over-friendly, but they mean well. *AE, MC, V; every day; full bar; www.markjames.com; map:T5.*

THE DRAKE SHOW ROOM / 606 Powell St; 604/254-2826 When they say their staff bends over backward to satisfy the customer, they're not kidding. The servers at this busy peeler bar are known as "the Drakettes," and when they're not whizzing to your table with refreshments, they're doffing their uniforms (invariably something clingy and low-cut) onstage. The main stage, ironically shaped like a cross, is flanked by a pair of 1-metre (3-foot) hexagonal ministages. Private shows are available from dancers working the room. Sports on TV screens, pool tables, and decent pub grub. *AE, V; debit cards; every day; full bar; map:X3.*

THE FAIRVIEW / 898 W Broadway; 604/872-1262 The Ramada Inn may seem like an unusual location for a blues club, but this is one bar that showcases some of the city's best players. Although not comfy enough to be considered intimate, the room is just the right size and there's hardly a bad seat in the house. A small dance floor sits in front of the tiny stage, and when the band gets cooking, so does the crowd. The atmosphere is casual, so come as you are. Blues jam Sundays. *AE, DIS, V; debit cards; every day; full bar; map:S7.*

FRED'S UPTOWN TAVERN / 1006 Granville St; 604/331-7979 After running the gauntlet of panhandlers on Granville Street, you'll want to catch your breath and a cool one downstairs in Fred's Tavern, cunningly designed to make first-time visitors believe they've wandered onto the set of *Cheers*. Belly up to the large rectangular bar that dominates the centre of the room or perch on the periphery at a table. At Fred's, the usual ceiling-mounted TV screens have been eschewed in favour of built-in mahogany bookshelves and high-quality TVs, which show an eclectic mélange of rock videos, cartoons, and other short cinematic surprises. The canned tunes are equally diverse: everything from modern rock to '60s numbers and TV themes are all delivered at a comfortable volume. Surprisingly good grub from the open kitchen helps keep the 19- to

LATE-NIGHT EATS

Late-night dining in Vancouver has improved dramatically during the past few years. Sure, there have always been Chinese restaurants that serve decent food after midnight, but the city now offers a wealth of other options for hungry clubgoers, insomniacs, and people who didn't eat enough at dinner. So if you're not willing to settle for Denny's, take a look at this list. All of the restaurants on it serve good food in comfortable surroundings, and at least one of them is sure to suit your tastes and your budget.

Benny's Bagels / 2503 W Broadway; 604/731-9730 A mellow, many-cornered place to work on your novel or fill up on dough after the clubs close. *Open until 3am Sun–Thurs, 4am Fri and Sat; map:C2.*

The Brass Monkey / 1072 Denman St; 604/685-7626 The solid bistro menu comes with a smart wine list. No, you are not dining on a film set. *Open until 2am Mon–Sat (kitchen closes at 1:30am), midnight Sun (kitchen closes at 11:30pm); map:P3.*

The Brickhouse Bistro / 730 Main St; 604/689-8645 Candlelit upstairs dining room offers entrées, appetizers, and desserts almost too good for a place open this late. Great specials and prices. *Open until 2:30am Tue–Sat; map:V5.*

Elwood's / 3145 W Broadway; 604/736-4301 A little like dining in someone's converted garage. Wings, burgers, nachos, and other hangover-fighters share the menu with surprisingly sophisticated tapas. *Open until 2am Mon–Sat, midnight Sun; map:B2.*

Gyoza King / 1508 Robson St; 604/669-8278 Gyoza of every description, sushi, noodle soups, and a big serving of stylish young Japanese folks. *Open until 2am Mon–Sat, midnight Sun; map:R3.*

The Living Room Bistro / 2958 W 4th Ave; 604/737-7529 One of the first local restaurants to reinvent Spanish tapas. The room, meanwhile, is pleasingly retro and laid-back. *Open until midnight Sun–Thurs, 1am Fri–Sat; map:C2.*

Martini's / 151 W Broadway; 604/873-0021 Good whole-wheat pizza, Greek dishes, and reasonably priced drinks. *Open until 2am Mon–Thurs, 3am Fri–Sat, 1am Sun; map:U7.*

Monsoon / 2526 Main St; 604/879-4001 Clean-lined, attractive room with an equally attractive South Asian menu and excellent fresh-fruit drinks. *Open until 1:30am Mon–Thurs, 2am Fri–Sat, midnight Sun; map:V7.*

The Sugar Refinery / 1115 Granville St; 604/683-2004 Second-floor lounge is one of the grooviest places downtown to grab a snack postclub or postmovie. *Open until 3am or 4am every night; map:R5.*

WaaZuBee Cafe / 1622 Commercial Dr; 604/253-5299 Always-lively neighbourhood gathering place, with a wide-ranging menu featuring lots of vegetarian options. *Open until 1am Mon–Sat, midnight Sun, map:Z6.*

Wonton Noodles / 4008 Cambie St; 604/877-1253 Just like the name says, but also hot pots, congee, and barbecued meats. *Open until 3am every day; map:D3.*

—Nick Rockel

50-year-old customers well fed and friendly. *AE, MC, V; debit cards; Mon– Sat; full bar; map:S5.*

THE JOHN B NEIGHBOURHOOD PUB / 1000 Austin Ave, Coquitlam; 604/931-5115 Live classic rock and a boisterous but well-mannered contingent of 25- to 40-year-old regulars keep the energy level high here. A freestanding gas fireplace dominates an upper no-smoking section; 16 stools await those who choose to stay close to the gorgeous oak bar with its ceiling-high backdrop of liquor bottles. The patio wins awards for its garden, and there's a dandy wine shop next door. The food's great, too, with Wing Night every Monday and a selection of stick-to-your-ribs barbecue dishes. Live music Thursday through Saturday. *AE, DC, MC, V; debit cards; every day; full bar; map:J3.*

THE MARBLE ARCH / 518 Richards St; 604/681-5435 Businessmen and visiting rock stars alike love this strip joint's downtown location. Lunchtime finds them seated suit to suit, shoulder to shoulder. All 280 seats are well served by not one, but three stages, which are often found in simultaneous operation—an event known as "triple stage mania." The nearsighted may arrange for a private dance in an adjoining curtained room. Between the action, keep busy with sports TV screens, video games, pool tables, and pub grub. *AE, MC, V; debit cards; every day; full bar; map:T4.*

THE MET HOTEL BAR & GRILL / 4011 Columbia St, New Westminster; 604/520-1967 New Westminster isn't exactly famous for its snazzy drinking establishments, but the Met has raised the stakes considerably. A 150-seat pub with a back patio and a wraparound oak bar, it shows off the recent award-winning renovations to a 106-year-old hotel once owned by the family of actor Raymond Burr. At lunch and dinner, you'll find judges and city councillors mixing with students and construction workers, all feasting from a menu that covers standard pub fare but also dishes up a mean braised lamb shank with garlic mashed potatoes. Or they're quaffing a pint while glued to one of eight TVs broadcasting satellite sports events. The Met offers drink specials every day, plus peel-and-eat prawns on Tuesdays and a Wing Night on Thursdays. And remember, if you've had one too many, there are 30 comfortable hotel rooms upstairs. *AE, MC, V; debit cards; every day; full bar; map:I5.*

THE MOUNTAIN SHADOW INN / 7174 Barnet Rd, Burnaby; 604/291-9322 Clad in weathered wood and stained glass, this Tudor-style inn is as good-looking as the 20- to 35-year-olds who fill it to the rafters. There's an upper level that overlooks an open centre section, allowing you to either hide away upstairs for a long view of the frivolities or mix it up in the action on the main floor, where there's a pool table and dartboards. Live music occasionally. Weekends are jam-packed. *AE, MC, V; debit cards; every day; full bar; map:I2.*

THE NO. 5 ORANGE / 203 Main St; 604/687-3483 Vancouver peeler bars: where women shower for men who don't. This hallowed hall of hedonism has been fuelling fantasies for more than 25 years—meaning that it's older than most of the ladies who dance here. The decor and food are okay, but the location is on the grotty side. *No credit cards; debit cards; every day; full bar; map:V3.*

SAILOR HAGAR'S / 86 Semisch Ave, North Vancouver; 604/984-3087 On-site microbreweries, like the gleaming stainless-steel example on display at Sailor Hagar's, have elevated the downing of beer to a high art. These days, discussions of sports and fast cars are liable to give way to fervent discourse on the colour, clarity, and head of one of the on-tap elixirs. Sailor Hagar's boasts of stocking the city's largest selection of West Coast cottage, microbrewed, and import beers, in addition to a fine array of wines, ciders, and coolers. The beer is pushed through temperature-controlled lines to a set of original British beer engines and taps. Just a two-block stroll from Lonsdale Quay and the SeaBus, this brew pub offers inviting decor, featuring a solid-oak carved fireplace and bar, an excellent menu of pub fare and Scandinavian delights, satellite-TV sports, and a heated patio with an outstanding view of Vancouver. Thursday night is the hot time to hoist a few. *AE, DC, MC, V; debit cards; every day; full bar; map:E4.*

STEAMWORKS BREWING COMPANY / 375 Water St; 604/689-2739 Standing guard at the entrance to Gastown is the Steamworks Brewing Company. The main floor holds a pub that has the ambience of an old English study; antique books line one wall, waiting to be read (don't hold your breath), while a bank of windows offers a semicircular vista of railway yards, Burrard Inlet, and the North Shore. If you venture down the set of spiral mahogany stairs, you'll find an even cozier 35-seat lounge.

Pull up a cushy leather chair, sink in, and divide your attention between the inlet view and the thermal charms of a rock fireplace. Or you can shoot some stick at a pair of pool tables and shoot the breeze with one of the 25- to 45-year-old suits who make this place hop. Friday is the big night, especially 4:30 till 9pm (with a queue in place 5:30 till 7pm). Try their home brew—it's justly famed—or take advantage of the fine on-site restaurant. *AE, JCB, MC, V; every day; full bar; www.steamworks. bc.ca; map:T3.*

THE YALE / 1300 Granville St; 604/681-YALE To fully appreciate the blues, they should be enjoyed in the same atmosphere in which they were created—a tattered old place in a tough part of town. Welcome to the Yale. The building has been around for more than 100 years, and so, it seems, have many of the imported blues musicians who play here. The room is long and narrow, with a teeny stage that's hard to see from the back, but you can always squeeze yourself onto the stage-front dance floor for a closer peek. Suburban blues lovers and seedy-looking characters share the surroundings. *AE, MC, V; debit cards; every day; full bar; www.theyale.com; map:R5.*

YALETOWN BREWING COMPANY / 1111 Mainland St; 604/681-2739 The other half of a busy Yaletown restaurant, the YBC's pub has stuck with the same exposed-brick and polished-wood decor it had when it opened in the early '90s—which is apparently just fine with its loyal patrons, many of whom have come to find even the red terrycloth table coverings endearing. But the real attractions are the friendly service, the beer-friendly grub (try the thin-crust pizzas), and the half-dozen or so tasty lagers and ales dispensed from copper kegs on display at the back. By early evening the place fills up with the suits, shoppers, and software workers who keep the Yaletown business district humming. *AE, MC, V; debit cards; every day; full bar; www.yaletownbrewingco.com; map:S5.*

Lounges

ARTS CLUB BACKSTAGE LOUNGE / 1585 Johnston St; 604/687-1354 Originally designed as a spot where theatre patrons could exit a play and then embark on a little play of their own, the Arts Club Backstage Lounge has succeeded almost too well. So many young and old West Siders pop by this Granville Island haunt on weekends to listen to live blues that the theatregoers can barely squeeze in. The room is simple, the crowd is well mannered and jubilant, and the grub's not bad, either. Tuesday finds students from the nearby Emily Carr art school hoisting cheap pints, grooving to a DJ, and spilling out onto one of the best waterfront patios in town. *AE, MC, V; debit cards; every day; full bar; map:Q6.*

BACCHUS LOUNGE / 845 Hornby St; 604/689-7777 Nestled in one of the city's best hotels, the Wedgewood, this elegant retreat is a 60-seat sensation. A piano player rules the roost weekdays during cocktail hours (5 to 8pm), and a combo often sets up on weekends to serenade imbibers with everything from soft rock to old standards. Attire is dressy, with wall-to-wall suits in attendance Friday and Saturday nights. Call ahead for a reservation. *AE, DC, DIS, E, V; debit cards; every day; full bar; www. wedgewoodhotel.com; map:S4.*

CLOUD 9 LOUNGE / 1400 Robson St; 604/687-0511 Every city should have one: a slowly revolving lounge, 40 storeys or so above street level, with an easygoing atmosphere and a view that goes on for miles. This perfectly describes Cloud 9, which by day treats tourists and locals to a spectacular 90-minute round trip that encompasses English Bay, the North Shore mountains, and downtown (go on a sunny afternoon). After dark, the ride continues, with the added bonus of live jazz later in the week. Seen the city lights go by one too many times? Order a refill, kick back in your armchair, and gaze into the twinkling constellations on the ceiling. *AE, DC, JCB, MC, V; every day; full bar; map:R2.*

THE GARDEN TERRACE / 791 W Georgia St; 604/689-9333 Sure to impress those out-of-town guests, the Garden Terrace, in the Four Seasons Hotel, is a stunning destination. A towering, atrium-style roof covers 120 seats set in what seems like a jungle but is actually an award-winning garden full of rare flora from Africa. The result is a soothing lounge, where the soft clinking of cocktail glasses mingles with the soft tinkling of a grand piano. A drink will cost you what a case used to, but the decor is impressive, and the full restaurant menu offers another excuse to drink it all in. *AE, DC, DIS, MC, V; Mon–Sat; full bar; map:S4.*

GEORGIA STREET BAR AND GRILL / 801 W Georgia St; 604/602-0994 A rich ribbon of oak, the bar snakes its way through this tastefully appointed watering hole. Choose your poison from hundreds of backlit bottles lining the wall, then choose your roost from a selection of fireside tables, cozy nooks, window seats, and bar stools. Suit-clad lawyers, brokers, and bankers peruse, schmooze, and nosh their way through burgers, appies, panini, and other bistro offerings. The hottest times are Thursday and Friday after work, and Thursday through Saturday after 10pm, when the jazz band starts cooking and the overflow from the Chameleon Lounge downstairs makes its way up here. *AE, DC, E, MC, V; debit cards; every day; full bar; map:S4.*

GERARD LOUNGE / 845 Burrard St; 604/682-5511 How does the other half live? Very well, thank you, if this lounge in the Sutton Place Hotel is any indication. The decor is posh, with an understated elegance— about what you'd expect from western Canada's best place for celebrity-

VANCOUVER AFTER HOURS

Most Vancouver bars and nightclubs close at 1 or 2am, but your evening by no means has to end at the hot-dog stand. Besides legitimate late-night hangouts such as **DV8** (515 Davie St; 604/682-4388) and the **Sugar Refinery** (1115 Granville St; 604/683-2004), on any given Friday or Saturday there may be as many as 30 illegal after-hours clubs open throughout the city. Of course, these places don't want their names and addresses mentioned in this book. And true to their secretive nature, they can disappear or change location literally from week to week. As a general rule, however, many of Vancouver's busiest after-hours haunts are found downtown, in two main areas: near the intersection of Hastings and Cambie Streets, and on Richards and Homer Streets at the edge of Yaletown. If you run into the right person or wander down the right back alley, chances are you'll find a place where you can keep partying till the break of dawn.

Cover charges can be substantial, especially if there's a DJ or a band performing. More often than not, these clubs are just someone's apartment or studio, so don't be shocked if your $10 or $15 buys you access to a mediocre loft party hosted by a stoned dude selling cans of warm beer. Also, keep in mind that the police have been known to drop by on occasion and arrest people for whooping it up beyond the long arm of the law. And, of course, exercise judgment: we accept no responsibility should your after-hours venue of choice turn into a crackfest or an extreme-fighting match.

On weekends the Vancouver area is also home to a healthy number of all-night dance parties, or raves, as they're often called. In fact, largely thanks to its beautiful natural surroundings, the city has a burgeoning international reputation as a great place to rave. Although some of them operate along the lines of the after-hours booze cans, Vancouver raves can range in size from an intimate get-together at a downtown warehouse to an elaborate outdoor festival attracting thousands of people and DJs from London, Chicago, and San Francisco. Lately, Richmond has been a hot spot, but would-be partyers can also expect to travel as far as Chilliwack, or even Squamish, where full-moon parties take place during the summer months. Organizers often wait until the night of the event to reveal its location. Expect to pay an admission of anywhere between $5 and $40, depending on the guest DJs and the scale of the party. A good way to get up to speed on the scene is to visit rave-friendly record stores such as **Bassix** (217 W Hastings St; 604/689-7734) and **Futuristic Flavour** (1020 Granville St; 604/681-1766), or restaurants such as **Subeez** (891 Homer St; 604/687-6107), where colourful handbills and knowledgeable scenesters are in abundance. Those same scenesters also regularly distribute flyers outside several downtown nightclubs. For schedules of upcoming Vancouver-area raves, visit the Web sites www.loungex.com and www.foraver.com.

—Nick Rockel

watching. After a hard day on the set, the movie crews and stars repair to Gerard to let their famous butts sink into the comfy couches around the fireplace. Cameron Diaz, Gwyneth Paltrow, John Travolta—if they're in town, eventually they'll pay a visit. There are only 50 seats, but a promenade with 25 more awaits, and you'll still hear the piano from there. *AE, DC, DIS, MC, V; every day; full bar; www.suttonplace.com; map:R4.*

GOTHAM STEAKHOUSE AND COCKTAIL BAR / 615 Seymour St; 604/605-8282 Next door to a proletarian SkyTrain entrance, the upmarket Gotham Steakhouse targets people who can actually afford to pay $50 for a sirloin with the trimmings, namely American tourists and high-rolling locals. Its dramatic, slender bar—affectionately known as the G Spot—is often jammed with the latter, in particular that fastidious variety of 30- to 50-year-old male who can look good even in a pair of sweatpants. Which isn't to say there aren't plenty of cocktail dresses and Italian blazers to go with the deep-red walls and obligatory cigars. Or that there aren't a few surgically enhanced female faces in the crowd, waiting to be noticed by a Rolex-sporting gentleman. If you get elbowed as you battle toward that elusive seat at the far end of the room, it'll be in the nicest possible way. *AE, MC, V; every day; full bar; map:T3.*

JOE FORTES / 777 Thurlow St; 604/669-1940 Lawyers, stockbrokers, and even decent people start their weekend festivities with a visit to the lounge area of this gorgeous restaurant, named after a turn-of-the-19th-century Vancouver lifeguard. Friday afternoon finds it packed with well-heeled movers and shakers clad in suits and well-cut business attire. The mood is jubilant, and the decor resembles that of a U.S. chophouse. *AE, DC, DIS, E, MC, V; every day; full bar; map:R3.*

900 WEST LOUNGE AND WINE BAR / 900 W Georgia St; 604/669-9378 In many ways, downtown Vancouver hotel lounges are ideal places for a quiet drink: the chairs are comfortable, the service is gracious, and you get those little plates of salty nibblies with your beverage. In ideal circumstances, they also feature a top-notch wine list and exceptional food. Such is the case with Hotel Vancouver's 900 West. Its wine bar has received a *Wine Spectator* Award of Excellence, and the food is prepared by the chefs of 900 West restaurant, whose delicious appetizer menu complements the many wines by the glass. On weekends, both the lounge and the wine bar are prime spots for people-watching: you'll not only see some of the city's movers and shakers raising a toast to themselves, but also young couples having a tête-à-tête and groups of chainsmoking Japanese businessmen making themselves right at home. And you get to enjoy all this in the lavish heritage surroundings of Hotel Vancouver, which helps make for the somewhat expensive drink prices. *AE, JCB, MC, V; debit cards; every day; full bar; map:S3.*

THE SUGAR REFINERY / 1115 Granville St; 604/683-2004 It may not have a back-alley entrance any more, but this second-floor lounge on the seediest part of Granville Street has somehow retained its after-hours cachet. The obvious reason: it still stays open until 3 and even 4am some nights, attracting bohemians, ravers, club-hoppers, and curious movie-goers from the cinemas that are a few blocks away. The Sugar Refinery also keeps its edge by boldly going where other clubs won't. A happy fusion of bar, restaurant, chill-out space, art gallery, and live venue, it can surprise you with a top-notch photography exhibit one visit and a way-out-there electronic performance the next. *V; debit cards; every day; full bar; map:S4.*

THE URBAN WELL / 1516 Yew St; 604/737-7770 It's a given that any place this close to Kits Beach will be jumping during the summer months—especially when the cramped patio has a perfect view of the sunset and all those toned, tanned bodies making their way home up Yew Street. But the Urban Well manages to keep up the energy all year-round with a decent dinner and tapas menu; a good selection of wines, scotch, martinis, and international beers; and a happy-go-lucky vibe aided by a dance floor in the middle of the velvety room. Most evenings a DJ spins funk, acid jazz, retro, and the like, transforming the restaurant/lounge into a nightclub. On Tuesdays, the dance floor becomes a stage for some of the city's best—and some of its worst—comedians, plus out-of-town guests. You may find your menu (not to mention some of the patrons) annoyingly cute, but generally speaking this is a lively, enjoyable spot offering good value and a vivid glimpse of Kitsilano nightlife. Expect line-ups on weekends and on Comedy Night. A second location recently opened downtown at 888 Nelson Street, 604/638-6070. *AE, MC, V; debit cards; every day; full bar; map:N6.*

THE WHIP GALLERY CAFE / 209 E 6th Ave; 604/874-4687 The artists, designers, and photographers who live and work in the Main-and-Broadway area have made the Whip their communal living room. Don't be intimidated, though: chances are nobody is going to shun you for not knowing who Le Corbusier is or treat you to a public display of his or her rattled artistic nerves. In fact, the congenial thirtysomething patrons are here to get away from all that: to sink into a comfy chair, down a pint or two of microbrew, and (a little later on, perhaps) order the right appe-tizer to help soak up the alcohol. In keeping with the communal-living-room theme, you'll find vintage furnishings here that look as if they've been borrowed from a dozen different apartments. If you come during warm weather, you'll also find the French doors open and tables out on the street. Live music occasionally. *MC, V; debit cards; every day; beer and wine; map:V7.*

UNCLE CHARLIE'S LOUNGE/LOTUS SOUND LOUNGE / 455 Abbott St; 604/685-7777 Perched where Chinatown, skid row, and downtown converge, the antiquated Heritage House Hotel is a bright spot in a blighted part of town. On the main floor is Charlie's Lounge, a toasty hideaway that caters to a gay crowd. A pair of opulent chandeliers, gorgeous antique furnishings, and warm colours complete the room. Snuggle into a cushy corner and swoon as the croon of Nat King Cole oozes from the speakers. Prices are reasonable. Down a flight of marble stairs is the Lotus Sound Lounge, a small, pillared room where the ceiling is low and the attitude high. A mixed crowd dances to drum 'n' bass, deep house, and funk on the smallish dance floor Tuesday through Saturdays. Friday night is women-only. *MC, V; debit cards; every day; full bar; map:U4.*

Coffee, Tea, and Dessert

BEAN AROUND THE WORLD / 4456 W 10th Ave (and branches); 604/222-1400 Together with its sister stores on Granville Street and in West Vancouver, this retail roasting shop helps supply Vancouver's addiction to fresh roasted beans. It's an inviting, cozy-sweater kind of place that serves a mix of sippers: early-bird exercisers, retired folk, students, and parents with kids in tow. This coffeehouse gives its beans a slightly lighter roast than many other beaneries. Not only does this preserve varietal distinctions, it provides more caffeine kick in the cup. Forty varieties of take-home beans are offered, along with the very popular fruit pies and rhubarb muffins. There's a 20-cent discount on take-out coffee (you provide the mug) and 65-cent refills. Curl up by the roaster and warm your cheeks over a latte served in a filling, consoling bowl. *Every day; map:B3.*

BON TON PASTRY & CONFECTIONERY / 874 Granville St; 604/681-3058 Mr. Notte came from Italy, Mrs. Notte came from France, and sometime in the early 1930s they opened a tea shop. Second-generation Nottes still labour away behind the scenes, creating the kind of picture-perfect pastries you remember from your childhood. Unless you're heavily into plastic geraniums, the backroom tearoom is unassuming at best. But here, motherly waitresses serve up some of the most wickedly delicious pastries in the city: mocha filbert meringues, chocolate éclairs, cream puffs, Napoleons, and diplomat cake. A selection, under a plastic dome, gets left on your table. Only the most ascetic person can stop at one. This place is a Vancouver tradition, and around teatime you can have your tea leaves or tarot cards read by itinerant fortune-tellers. *Tues–Sat; map:S4.*

FLEURI / 845 Burrard St, at the Sutton Place Hotel; 604/682-5511 See listing in Top 190 Restaurants chapter.

HOTEL VANCOUVER / 900 W Georgia St; 604/684-3131 See listing in Top 190 Restaurants chapter.

JOE'S / 1150 Commercial Dr; 604/255-1046 Intellectuals, bohemian philosophers, poets, feminists, and political agitators mix with cue-hustling locals at this vigorous pool hall and cafe. Joe's doesn't glamorize espresso or otherwise try to be popular; it just happens. All Joe needs to do is serve up his comely drinks with the famed foam. Despite the seedy decor and laundromat lighting, this place is a well-worn neighbourhood hangout. Knowing, deliberate hands prepare espresso standards, along with hybrids like Espresso Bica, Double Cappuccino, and Butterscotch Milk. The Carioca lait-coffee is a dwarf-size latte that can be ordered with a refreshing slice of lemon. (For coffee abstainers, juices, pop, flavoured malts, and average snacks are offered.) But be prepared—after the last mouthful . . . clank! Cup and saucer are jettisoned out from under you and whisked back to the bar. This encourages you to get up and take part in the activity (i.e., playing pool)—or to leave. *Every day; map:Z6.*

LA CASA GELATO / 1033 Venables St (and branches); 604/251-3211 If you are seeking a slightly different taste, be sure to visit this ice cream emporium. It has 168 flavours of ice cream, many of which (we guarantee) you have never tried. How about ginger-garlic? Or wasabi, wild asparagus with sun-dried cranberries, or lemon tarragon? Luckily, they'll let you taste as many as you want before you buy. *Every day; map:Y5.*

MURCHIE'S TEA & COFFEE / 970 Robson St (and branches); 604/669-0783 The current coffee scene reveals how the city is flavoured by Europe these days, yet Vancouver has strong British roots, some of which were brought over by John Murchie in the late 1800s. After working for the Melrose Tea Company in his native Scotland, John and family emigrated to British Columbia and opened the first Murchie's Tea Shop in New Westminster in 1894. In 1908, John began roasting fine coffee beans at his first Vancouver location—an oasis in an otherwise bleak coffee scene. Murchie's has chosen a lighter roast to bring out and preserve varietal nuance, and beans are always fresh (they get dumped after seven days). Choose from more than 40 blends and varietals, including the house blend (Murchie's Best). There are some 50 varieties and blends of tea, loose or bagged. John Murchie's No. 10 blend is literally world renowned—it's sold by mail in more than 40 countries. This longtime merchant has assembled an engaging collection of brewing paraphernalia and gifts, from clay teapots and English bone china to samplers, gift boxes, and traditional chocolate-coated ginger. *Every day; map:S3.*

SECRET GARDEN TEA CO. LTD. / 5559 West Blvd; 604/261-3070 This is the place to sip perfectly brewed tea and nibble pastries, and scones. Snugly settled in staid Kerrisdale, the Secret Garden offers a choice of more than 100 types of tea from around the world and traditional treats baked right on premises. *Every day; map:C4.*

SWEET OBSESSION / 2603 W 16th Ave; 604/739-0555 Lorne Williams and Stephen Greenham turn out some of the best-tasting, most addictive desserts in town from this bakery in the bistro Trafalgar's. Try their triple-chocolate mousse and creamy fruit cheesecakes and you'll understand why they supply the finest Vancouver restaurants with finales. Sweet Obsession is also known for homemade lemon curd, biscotti, and hazelnut sponge with Frangelico and chocolate hazelnut cream. Everything is made from scratch with the finest ingredients, including the tasty bistro menu at lunch and dinner, which makes a nice prelude. Or just skip right to dessert—we understand. *Every day; map:C3.*

TEAROOM T / 2460 Heather St (and branches); 604/874-8320 It's nice to find people who take an interest in their work, but these folks are obsessed—in a sedate, polite way, of course. This tea shop offers 250 different kinds of tea leaves and blends, including noncaffeinated, fruit tisanes, and herbals. Drop by for a tasting on the first Sunday of the month, or take a tea tour. And if you're just coming in for an afternoon cuppa, they'll do their best to do it the traditional way; either English, with locally made scones and Devonshire cream, or in a special Chinese tea service that gets the most from each infusion. They carry an extensive selection of teaware, cups, pots, and kettles from Alessi, Cardew, and Prandelli. Expert staff are happy to make up gift baskets or put together a mail order. *Every day; map:S7.*

TEN REN TEA & GINSENG CO. / 550 Main St; 604/684-1566 Bordered by the sensory pleasures of Chinatown and the squalor of Vancouver's skid row, a visit to Ten Ren is a unique, vigorous experience. You'll find no chrome tea balls or cozies here. One of 78 shops worldwide, Ten Ren offers many varieties and grades of Chinese tea: loose or in bags, green, baked, or fermented. Popular are Ti Kwan, jasmine, and King's Tea (the Ten Ren blend). As you browse, fortify yourself with a ginger or ginseng tea on tap. To the newcomer, the shop's staff can seem anxious for you to buy—it's really just enthusiastic to share its delicious teas. The north wall showcases many types and grades of ginseng, most of it not from the Far East, but from the ideal climate and soil of Wisconsin. Many tiny clay pots are presented—hand-crafted works of art. Those burdened with cash can drop $300 on a service for six. *Every day; map:V4.*

TRUE CONFECTIONS / 866 Denman St (and branches); 604/682-1292 These dessert outlets sell 20 kinds of grand cheesecakes, mile-high chocolate cakes, Belgian mousse tortes, pies, and more than 70 other desserts. *Every day; map:B3.*

WEDGEWOOD HOTEL / 845 Hornby St; 604/608-5319 See listing in Top 190 Restaurants chapter.

ITINERARIES

ITINERARIES

Vancouver is Canada's third-largest metropolitan area, but even on a short stopover, visitors can take in most of its essential sights, landmarks, and neighbourhoods. This chapter outlines a three-day tour of Vancouver plus an alternative "family day," with suggestions for lunch, dinner, and late-night entertainment. For Day Three, which involves a trip to the North Shore, you'll need a car; wheels are also useful for the afternoon in Steveston and Richmond described in Family Day. Otherwise, a willingness to ride the public transit system (one of the safest anywhere), a good pair of walking shoes, and a reliable map are all that's required. That, and some breathable rain gear if you're visiting between the months of October and April. Information about most of the places shown in boldface can be found in other chapters of the book (Top 190 Restaurants, Shopping, Exploring, and Nightlife). And, of course, feel free to create your own itinerary by mixing and matching these day trips and outings. Happy trails!

DAY ONE

On your first day in Vancouver, you'll spend a lot of time downtown and close to the water, getting a feel for the city's beautiful setting and some of its livelier shopping districts. This day also includes the option of an easy afternoon trip out of town.

MORNING: Locals can't fault you for starting the day—and your tour of Vancouver—at touristy **GRANVILLE ISLAND**. On weekends they head to this heart-of-the-city market in droves, which explains the shortage of free parking spaces. Even on a weekday it's hard to find a spot, so taking a bus is recommended: from downtown, take the #4 UBC and get off at the corner of Fourth Avenue and Fir Street, or take the #50 False Creek to the entrance of the island. There are also two easy ways to get to Granville Island by boat. False Creek Ferries (604/684-7781) depart every five minutes from the Aquatic Centre at the corner of Thurlow and Beach; the nearby Aquabus (604/689-5858) makes the trip every three minutes. Both are a cheap way to spend some time on the water, however brief, and get a look at the undersides of the Granville and Burrard Street Bridges.

The **GRANVILLE ISLAND PUBLIC MARKET** (1689 Duranleau St; 604/666-5784) opens at 9am. Filled with bustling stalls selling everything from ocean-caught salmon to artisan cheese to berries in season, it's a good place to turn breakfast into a progressive meal; a cappuccino at the **BLUE PARROT ESPRESSO BAR** (604/688-5127), grape focaccia from **TERRA BREADS** (604/685-6102), candied salmon from **SEAFOOD CITY** (604/688-1818). Once you've found what you like, have a seat outside on the wharf, being ever mindful of dive-bombing seagulls. Early morning is a good time to explore the market and Granville Island's dozens of shops, studios, and galleries. But you can also take a stroll along the False Creek seawall, where to the east you'll catch sight of the silver dome of Science World. If you'd rather just sit in a restaurant, **BRIDGES** (1696 Duranleau St; 604/687-4400) and **THE CREEK RESTAURANT BREWERY & BAR** (1253 Johnston St; 604/685-7070) serve weekend brunch. Both have large patios on the water with yachts passing by that are as close as the next table.

AFTERNOON: Here are two great ways to spend an afternoon. The first option takes you to Gastown, Chinatown, and/or Lonsdale Quay. The second takes you farther afield, across Burrard Inlet and up to Grouse Mountain.

Option 1: From the entrance to Granville Island, take a #50 Waterfront Station bus downtown and get off at the corner of Granville and Robson Streets. That way, you'll be close to the relatively new **LIBRARY SQUARE** complex, the centrepiece of which is the Colosseum-style public library. Nearby are a couple of *real* circuses: 19,000-seat **GENERAL MOTORS PLACE**—home to the NHL Vancouver Canucks and the NBA Vancouver Grizzlies—and larger **BC PLACE STADIUM**, where the BC Lions of the CFL host visiting teams. Walk downhill on Granville until you reach Hastings Street. If it's a clear day, drop $8 and ride the glass elevator 167 metres (548 feet) to the top of **HARBOUR CENTRE TOWER** (555 W Hastings St; 604/689-0421) for a 360-degree view of the city. Just north of Hastings (at Granville) is the Waterfront Station, the former Canadian Pacific Railway station, which is now a terminus for the Sky-Train, SeaBus, and a commuter train called the West Coast Express. To the west are the sails of Canada Place, docking point for the Alaska cruise ships; to the east, the entrance to Gastown.

First impressions to the contrary, **GASTOWN** is not just a place where dozens of tacky tourist shops flog T-shirts, mugs, and trinkets to unwary visitors. And there's more to do here than aim your camera at the **GAS-TOWN STEAM CLOCK** (well, OK, if you must) while waiting anxiously for it to whistle and belch steam on the quarter hour. Behind all the bric-a-brac are some of the city's oldest buildings, as well as finds such as the **INUIT GALLERY** (354 Water St; 604/688-7323), a showcase for exquisite northern Native sculpture, prints, and ceremonial masks. Gastown is also the home of Bryan Adams's state-of-the-art recording studio, **THE WARE-HOUSE** (100 Powell St), though you may have trouble gaining admission unless you do a good Rod Stewart impression. Warning: Gastown borders on the city's skid row district, so it's best to follow the main drag, Water Street, to its end at the intersection known as **MAPLE TREE SQUARE**.

If you're ready for lunch, right across from the Steam Clock is the **WATER STREET CAFE** (300 Water St; 604/689-2832), an airy West Coast–Italian restaurant with an excellent patio. Another busy Gastown

VANCOUVER HERITAGE WALK

Once visitors get over gawking at Vancouver's dramatic natural setting, they start noticing the richness and depth of its architectural landscape. For example, in the downtown core you'll find everything from brand-new (and often unsightly) office towers to elegant early 20th-century hotels to shining examples of high modernism. Because Vancouver is such a young and rapidly changing city, buildings constructed in the 1950s and '60s are as vital to its architectural heritage as those from the late 1800s. Getting a sense of all this history is as easy as taking a walk by (and a look inside) some of the downtown buildings on the city's heritage list.

A good place to start is Vancouver's oldest standing church, **Christ Church Cathedral** (690 Burrard St), completed in 1895 and now an island of antiquity amid a sea of traffic and glass high-rises. Christ Church is worth a visit for its beautiful stained-glass windows and the recent renovations to its exposed-beam, Gothic Revival structure. Just across the street, **Hotel Vancouver** (900 W Georgia St) opened for business in 1939: its richly detailed, château-style exterior (complete with verdigris roof) is matched by an equally lavish interior restoration. Also nearby is the old **Vancouver Public Library** building at the corner of Burrard and Robson. Although it hasn't vanished like so many of the city's other modernist landmarks, this clean-lined 1957 building has had a recent makeover as the location of a Virgin Megastore, the studios of local station VTV, and Planet Hollywood. For comparison's sake, it's worth a look at the new **Library Square** (350 W Georgia St), which—no matter what anyone says—bears a strong resemblance to the Roman Colosseum.

From the corner of Georgia and Burrard Streets, head south to the **Marine Building** at 355 Burrard. From a distance this 21-storey art deco treasure, built in 1929–30, looks like something out of Gotham City. But comic book analogies fail when you examine the exterior, inlaid with richly detailed terra-cotta friezes, and the opulent green- and blue-tiled foyer. Several blocks east on Hastings Street, the **General Post Office** building (757 W Hastings St), completed in 1910, is now part of the Sinclair Centre retail complex; its corner clock tower makes dramatic use of double columns and arcades, finishing in a dome and weather vane. Close by is the colonnaded former **Canadian Pacific Railway station** (601 W Cordova St), whose airy 1914 hall houses shops, offices, and the entrance to Waterfront Station (SkyTrain and SeaBus). From here it's a short walk east to Gastown. Along Water Street you'll find some of the city's oldest hotels and warehouses, many of them refurbished as lofts and offices. Another promising route lies south on Granville Mall, home to numerous heritage buildings, including the **Orpheum Theatre** (884 Granville St). Finished in 1927—and rescued from demolition during the 1970s—this one-time vaudeville theatre has a low-key facade but houses a spectacular mix of baroque styles.

If you want an expert guide, July through September the **Architectural Institute of BC** offers six rotating walking tours of Vancouver neighbourhoods, including downtown, Chinatown, the West End, and Strathcona. Tours depart between 1 and 1:30pm, several days a week, from the institute's offices at 101–440 Cambie Street. For more information, call 604/685-8588, or log on to www.aibc.bc.ca for a virtual walking tour of 10 significant buildings. Another option is to pick up a copy of *Exploring Vancouver: The Essential Architectural Guide* (UBC Press), by Harold Kalman, Ron Phillips, and Robin Ward, to enhance your own walkabout.   —*Nick Rockel*

lunch spot is **STEAMWORKS BREWING COMPANY** in the Landing Shopping Complex (375 Water St; 604/689-2739), which has tasty beers, good food, and spectacular views of Burrard Inlet.

Next stop: **CHINATOWN,** a short cab ride east or several blocks north of the Main Street SkyTrain station. (You can catch the SkyTrain at Waterfront Station.) Chinatown is also just 15 minutes from Gastown by foot, but be advised that you might encounter scenes of squalor on your trip through the intervening neighbourhood. Don't miss the guided tour through the **DR. SUN YAT-SEN CLASSICAL CHINESE GARDEN** (50 E Pender St; 604/687-0729) and a steamed bun from one of Chinatown's many bakeries. Haven't had lunch yet? Go for dim sum at the 1,000-seat **FLOATA SEAFOOD RESTAURANT** (400–180 Keefer St; 604/602-0368), or noodles and pot stickers (Chinese dumplings) at the inexpensive **HON'S WUN-TUN HOUSE** (108–268 Keefer St; 604/688-0871). After lunch, browse in packed-to-the-rafters shops along the frenzied streets, which rival Hong Kong in their smells and crowds. For jade treasures, don't miss **CHICOCHAI ANTIQUES,** at 539 Columbia Street (604/685-8116).

Option 2: Get out of the city for a while by taking a harbour cruise on the **SEABUS,** which departs every 15 to 30 minutes from Waterfront Station. The 12-minute crossing to North Vancouver's **LONSDALE QUAY** is a great way to get a view of the city, its natural surroundings, and the daily goings-on in one of the world's biggest harbours. The public market at Lonsdale Quay might remind you of the one on Granville Island, but with downtown much farther out of reach across the water. Also out of reach are both bridges servicing the North Shore, so stick with the SeaBus when it's time to go back downtown.

Downtown is certainly worth exploring, but for many visitors a trip to Vancouver isn't complete without a closer look at the natural setting that makes it such a beautiful city. Lonsdale Quay has a bus connection to **GROUSE MOUNTAIN.** But you can also get there by heading north from downtown through **STANLEY PARK** and crossing historic **LIONS**

GATE BRIDGE. As long as you avoid rush hour on the bridge, the drive to the north end of Capilano Road takes about 15 minutes. If you don't have a car, catch the #246 Lonsdale Quay/Highland bus from downtown and transfer to the #232 Grouse Mountain at Edgemont and Ridgewood.

The trip across Lions Gate Bridge makes for picture-postcard views of the North Shore, Stanley Park, and Burrard Inlet. On the way up Capilano Road is **CAPILANO REGIONAL PARK,** home to a fish hatchery, the huge Cleveland Dam, and the 137-metre (450-foot) **CAPILANO SUSPENSION BRIDGE** (3735 Capilano Rd; 604/985-7474), which dares tourists to walk its undulating span high above the river canyon. Stopping to take in these sights might help prepare you for an 1,100-metre (3,600-foot) ascent of Grouse Mountain in the Skyride gondola (604/984-0661). A less direct route to the top is the gruelling 880-vertical-metre (2,880-foot) Grouse Grind hiking trail, a weekly endurance test for hundreds of Vancouverites. Either way, on a clear day at the top of Grouse you'll enjoy a superb vista of Vancouver and the Lower Mainland. The casual Bar 98 restaurant (604/984-0661) is open for lunch.

EVENING: Vancouverites are dedicated shoppers, but it took millions of international tourists to make **ROBSON STREET** one of the world's premier retail strips. That said, the first landmark you'll encounter as you walk along Robson west of Granville is the steps of the **VANCOUVER ART GALLERY** (750 Hornby St; 604/662-4700). Shopping rules beyond that point: witness the former Vancouver Public Library building at the corner of Burrard Street, which now houses the **VIRGIN MEGASTORE** (788 Burrard St; 604/669-2289), a **PLANET HOLLYWOOD** restaurant (969 Robson St; 604/688-7827), and local television station **VTV.** Grab a latte at one of the two **STARBUCKS** locations kitty-corner at the intersection of Robson and Thurlow; during the late afternoon and early evening here, the people-watching can be a sociologist's dream (or nightmare). Beyond, it's chic boutiques, stylish crowds, and cruising automobiles all the way down to Bute Street, where a steep hill thins out the storefronts and foot traffic.

Make your way down the hill to Denman Street—where foot traffic picks up again—and head south to the beach at **ENGLISH BAY,** the focal point of the densely populated **WEST END.** Depending on your blood-sugar level and the hours of daylight left, you might want to take a run at the 10.5-kilometre (6.5-mile) **STANLEY PARK SEAWALL.** Otherwise, it's time to look for dinner. The West End isn't exactly a hotbed of great restaurants, but there are a few exceptions. The **RAINCITY GRILL** (1193 Denman St; 604/685-7337) offers contemporary West Coast cuisine, a formidable Pacific Northwest wine list, and a fabulous view of the bay. Across the street, the darker, funkier **BRASS MONKEY** (1072 Denman St; 604/685-7626) serves appetizing bistro food. If the weather is co-operating, watch out for the English Bay sunset. A good spot to enjoy it (and an after-dinner drink or two) is the lounge of the ivy-shrouded **SYLVIA HOTEL** (1154 Gilford St; 604/681-9321), a short walk along the edge of Stanley Park from the corner of Denman and Davie Streets. Back up the hill on Davie (flag a cab), you'll find a busy after-dark scene. **CELEBRITIES** (1022 Davie St; 604/689-3180), a straight-friendly gay nightclub, spins some of the city's best dance music; Friday nights are hugely popular with patrons of all persuasions. If you prefer a live show—pop, jazz, or an evening at the symphony—ask the cab driver to take you to Granville Street. There, the **COMMODORE BALLROOM** (868 Granville St; 604/739-SHOW), the **ORPHEUM THEATRE** (corner of Smithe and Seymour Streets; 604/665-3050), and the **VOGUE THEATRE** (918 Granville St; 604/331-7909) sometimes have last-minute tickets available before 8pm.

DAY TWO

On this day, you'll explore Vancouver's West Side, blessed with beaches, great shopping, and one of the world's greenest university campuses. Then it's on to the bohemian delights of Commercial Drive.

MORNING: If you had to pick the quintessential Vancouver neighbourhood, **KITSILANO** would be it. Close to the water, packed with shops and restaurants, and home to some very attractive and truly awful examples of West Coast architecture, Kits was a low-rent haven for hippies in the '60s and '70s. The yuppies have since taken over, along with a sizable contingent of college students and fun-loving twentysomethings who firmly believe the exorbitant rent (much of it collected by the yuppies) is well worth the proximity to the beach. Wander down to **SOPHIE'S COSMIC CAFE** (2095 W 4th Ave; 604/732-6810) for breakfast on a Friday or Saturday morning (take the #4 UBC bus from downtown), and you'll wait in line with a good cross section of Kitsilano's population. Sophie's serves big portions of eggs, pancakes, and waffles; its bustling, kitschy interior (no, those metal lunch boxes will *not* fall off the wall onto your head) will help keep any kids in your party entertained.

Sophie's is also a good starting point from which to explore Kitsilano. A block west on Fourth Avenue is Yew Street, a steep incline plunging down to busy Cornwall Avenue and **KITSILANO BEACH**. By late morning on a warm, sunny day, the restaurant patios lining the lower blocks of Yew fill with neighbourhood residents and visitors chowing down on breakfast before, after, or during their inevitable stroll, jog, or cycle along the beach. Or even on a not-so-warm day: just as Vancouverites are known to wear shorts in just about any weather, they'll sit on an unheated patio in February if it feels like the rain is going to let up. Provided you're visiting during the three warm-weather months it's open, saltwater **KITSILANO POOL** (2305 Cornwall Ave; 604/731-8628) rates high as a morning refresher. If it's summer, you'll see volleyball and basketball players warming up along the beach's eastern stretch. Watch out for the cyclists and in-line skaters who share the pathways with pedestrians.

Back up on W Fourth, it's still possible to find a flower-power—or make that hemp-power—boutique reminiscent of the neighbourhood's hippie heyday. But much of the street's retail space is now given over to restaurants, trendy clothing and home accessories stores, and food shops such as the pristine **CAPER'S** supermarket (2285 W 4th Ave; 604/739-6676), where you can assemble a picnic lunch of organic and other goodies. Or let the hip-era folks at **NAAM** (2724 W 4th Ave; 604/738-7151) whip up a veggie burrito for you to enjoy in this granola-head hot spot. Continuing west on Fourth, you'll encounter a steep downhill crowded with recent condo developments illustrating those regrettable West Coast architectural styles mentioned earlier. If you're not anxious to hop on a bus to the next part of the tour, at the bottom of the hill is **BLACK SHEEP BOOKS** (2742 W 4th Ave; 604/732-5087), a well-stocked independent bookstore that feels like a survivor from the counterculture days.

AFTERNOON: Catch the #4 UBC bus heading west through Point Grey to the bus loop at the **UNIVERSITY OF BRITISH COLUMBIA** campus. Bastion of middlebrow academic respectability that it is—not to mention home to the infamous 1997 police pepper-spraying of APEC protesters—UBC also boasts a couple of attractions that appeal to visitors without a scholarly bent. At both of these, it's possible to spend an hour or three just looking, provided you don't touch. The first, clothing-optional **WRECK BEACH,** is a brisk 15- to 20-minute walk southwest from the bus loop, then down a winding cliffside staircase. On summer afternoons, Wreck has the atmosphere of a medieval fairground and is a perfect place to eat lunch and watch the world go by—completely naked. For those who didn't bring a picnic, the roving vendors sell just about everything (and we do mean *everything*). Back up the cliff and a 10-minute walk north of Wreck Beach along SW Marine Drive (remember to put your clothes back on), the **UBC MUSEUM OF ANTHROPOLOGY** houses jaw-droppingly impressive First Nations artifacts in a setting so beautiful that even the most garrulous member of your party will be at a loss for words. (Note: If you've extended your Kitsilano walking tour west into the beaches of Point Grey, the #42 Chancellor bus runs along NW Marine Drive, stopping at both the Museum of Anthropology and Wreck Beach on its way to the UBC Botanical Garden.)

By now it's 3pm or so, which means that everyone on **COMMERCIAL DRIVE** will be out of bed. That may be a bit of an exaggeration, but Vancouver's designated slice of bohemia doesn't really start to simmer until early afternoon. The fastest bus route to Commercial from UBC is the frequent 99 B-Line express, an articulated double bus that makes only a few stops along Broadway. (Catch it back at the UBC bus loop.) On the way east, you might want to stop again in Kitsilano. Get off at Macdonald to explore the lively shopping and restaurant strip nearby. The 99 B-Line also stops in the city's "midtown" district at the intersection of Granville and Broadway, an area known for its tony clothing shops and its many commercial art galleries. Continuing east, stay on the bus until you reach the Broadway SkyTrain station at the corner of Commercial. Don't be put off by the sometimes seedy activities going down outside the busy SkyTrain station: get on a #20 Downtown bus (usually crowded) and head north to enter "the Drive."

Like Kitsilano, Commercial Drive once had another identity—it used to be the hub of Little Italy, home turf to hundreds of Italian families, most of whom have since moved east to the suburbs. Many Italian restaurants, bakeries, and cafes remain along the strip, coexisting peacefully with newer organic-food co-ops, import boutiques, and vegetarian eateries, as well as businesses representing Vancouver's many other cultures. In recent years, the neighbourhood has become slowly gentrified as upwardly mobile families move in, attracted by the relatively cheap housing prices. But if you're looking for the old Italian flavour of the Drive, no place is more authentic than the statue-filled **CALABRIA BAR** near the corner of First Avenue (1745 Commercial Dr; 604/253-7017). We suggest you stop there for a cappuccino and a noisy introduction to the area's inhabitants, who range from lesbian couples and earnest young intellectuals to single moms and dignified old European gentlemen.

North of First and Commercial expect crowded sidewalks, especially at the fruit-and-vegetable markets along the east side of the street. Shops and restaurants here are of varying quality, but browsing will give you a good idea of the Drive's ethnic mix—Italian, Portuguese, Greek, Latin American, Caribbean, Vietnamese, Filipino, plus a large population of Anglo-Saxon folks indulging their alternative lifestyles. Weekends, for a dose of old-world charm—plus a shouting match or two—wander east along Charles Street and watch the Italian men playing an involved game of boccie ball in a small neighbourhood park. Or continue north and venture into **GRANDVIEW PARK**, where hackysackers encroach on the children's playground and someone can usually be found espousing a political cause.

EVENING: Just opposite Grandview Park is **HAVANA** (1212 Commercial Dr; 604/253-9119), a Cuban-themed restaurant serving decent food at reasonable prices. (At dusk, the sidewalk patio has a pretty view of downtown.) Stop by **MAGPIE MAGAZINE GALLERY** (1319 Commercial Dr; 604/253-6666) for your favourite off-the-wall 'zine. Commercial also has several good Italian restaurants; one of the best is **SPUMANTE'S**

CAFE (1736 Commercial Dr; 604/253-8899), which offers dozens of combinations of pasta and meat, fish, or vegetables. The more adventurous can hop in a cab and spend the evening at **AL RITROVO** (2010 Franklin St; 604/255-0916). Several nights a week (call ahead), this ambitiously retro dine-and-dance spot serves up generous helpings of Italian and Latin music to go with its pleasantly conservative menu. Sadly, the Commercial Drive area boasts very little in the way of pubs. One exception is the **PORTUGUESE CLUB** (1144 Commercial Dr; 604/251-2042), inevitably stocked with working-class folks, young hipsters, and even people of Portuguese extraction. Other neighbourhood hangouts include the funky **WAAZUBEE CAFE** (1622 Commercial Dr; 604/253-5299), where there's usually something decent for dessert (warning: the music can be deafening). Otherwise, the **VANCOUVER EAST CULTURAL CENTRE** (1895 Venables St; 604/254-9578) is as good a reason as any to spend an evening on the Drive. Even if you don't have tickets, it's worth a call or a look in to see what's showing—the Cultch, as it's affectionately known, has a reputation for booking some of the best dance, theatre, and live music in North America (much of it local).

DAY THREE

Because you'll be venturing away from Vancouver proper on Day Three, it helps to have a car and a detailed map of the region. After getting to know the parks of the North Shore, stop for dinner in West Vancouver or spend the evening discovering Yaletown.

MORNING: First, use those wheels to go for breakfast at the Fifth Avenue location of the **ECCO IL PANE** bakery (238 W 5th Ave; 604/873-6888), near Main Street in the heart of artists'-loft country. Ecco sells some of the best baked goods you'll find anywhere, including a small, perfectly chewy cherry-chocolate loaf that makes a great snack for later in the day. Then it's off to **DEEP COVE** on the North Shore. Drive north on Main through Chinatown and turn right on E Hastings Street. About 5 kilometres (3 miles) east, a few blocks past Renfrew Street, turn left onto Highway 1 and the **IRONWORKERS MEMORIAL BRIDGE** (commonly known as the Second Narrows Bridge).

At the other side of the bridge, take the first right exit, marked #23, onto Dollarton Highway, which runs east and then north to Deep Cove along the shores of Burrard Inlet and Indian Arm. Dollarton Highway passes through waterfront **CATES PARK,** an interesting side trip. Oil storage facilities on the opposite shore and the remains of the Dollar Lumber Mill give it the atmosphere of an industrial suburb—albeit a very green one. Step down to the beach for a close look at rusty freighters lying at anchor in the inlet, and for a distant view of downtown Vancouver, hemmed in behind the Second Narrows Bridge (Ironworkers Memorial Bridge). There's also a 15-metre (50-foot) war canoe on display, and a manicured forest walk dedicated to alcoholic British author Malcolm Lowry, who wrote most of his famous novel *Under the Volcano* while living nearby in a squatter's shack during the 1940s.

While Lowry's ghost may haunt the woods of Cates Park, there isn't a hint of gloom in the town of Deep Cove. Tucked away from the city on a steep hillside facing the spectacular, forested slopes of Indian Arm, this pleasant little community attracts visitors and recreational boaters with its shopping and dining area, seaside park, and sheltered marina. Deep Cove is also a prime launching area for sea kayaking day trips. The catch: you'll have to arrive before 9am, have some previous kayaking experience, and call ahead to **DEEP COVE CANOE AND KAYAK CENTRE** (2156 Banbury Ave; 604/929-2268) to make a reservation. Chances are you won't need lunch reservations at any of the restaurants and cafes by the water. Another option is to backtrack a short distance for some grub at the **RAVEN NEIGHBOURHOOD PUB** (1060 Deep Cove Rd; 604/929-3834), an English-style alehouse overlooking Indian Arm.

AFTERNOON: For a look at a few of the other places where Vancouverites go for a walk in the park, follow Deep Cove Road south out of town and take a right on Mount Seymour Parkway. About 1 kilometre (0.6 mile) down the parkway lies Mount Seymour Road, the turnoff to **MOUNT SEYMOUR PROVINCIAL PARK**. Or keep heading west another 6 kilometres (3.7 miles) and you'll reach Lillooet Road, which leads to the 5,600-hectare (14,000-acre) **SEYMOUR DEMONSTRATION FOREST**. A mecca for the mountain bikers and in-line skaters who frequent its trails and paved pathway, the forest is also a favourite location for some of the many cheesy sci-fi TV shows filmed in Vancouver. Still farther west is **LYNN CANYON PARK**. To get there, turn right at the Mountain Highway exit, located off Highway 1 (also known as the Upper Levels Highway). Beside the entrance to the park, you'll find the **LYNN CANYON SUSPENSION BRIDGE AND ECOLOGY CENTRE**. A concession stand is open during the summer months. Unlike Capilano Suspension Bridge, the Lynn Canyon bridge is free. All three of these parks are excellent places to hike—try the lookouts on Mount Seymour—assuming you've had lunch or brought along some trail food.

From Lynn Valley Road, keep going west on Highway 1 for about 6 kilometres (3.7 miles), then turn left on Capilano Road to enter **WEST VANCOUVER**. Turn right on Marine Drive and you'll soon be in picturesque **AMBLESIDE**. Its modesty belies its location in the Vancouver area's wealthiest neighbourhood, which stretches several hundred metres up the mountainside in a veritable rabbit warren of poshly appointed streets, lanes, and subdivisions. **AMBLESIDE PARK** is worth a visit for its seawall and its magnificent sea-level view of Stanley Park, Lions Gate Bridge, and Kitsilano. During the summer months, you might also spot a cruise ship or two. Otherwise, the busy shopping and restaurant district along Marine Drive has the feel of an English seaside town with too many (and too many expensive) cars. By all means, take a look around, but just pray that no one confuses you with the help.

Farther west, Marine Drive becomes a crazily winding country road giving access to dozens of palatial waterfront estates. There are also several turnoffs leading up the mountain, but count on getting lost if you explore them: most residential areas of West Vancouver appear designed to discourage Sunday driving. About 10 kilometres (6.2 miles) west of Ambleside Park is Beacon Lane, the entrance to **LIGHTHOUSE PARK**. The 1914 lighthouse and the rocky outcrop of Point Atkinson are a short walk from the parking lot, down a gently rolling trail sheltered by tall trees. If you still haven't had your fill of stunning city views (and trust us, no one ever does), this one is a keeper. It's enough to make you understand why Vancouverites risk getting stuck on Lions Gate Bridge to drive out here for a Sunday picnic. And speaking of the bridge, don't bother trying to cross Lions Gate between 4 and 6pm on weekdays, when afternoon rush hour traffic is at its busiest.

EVENING: After spending a day behind the wheel roaming the far reaches of the North Shore, you might want to put off thinking about the bridge and instead have dinner in West Vancouver. If so, the **BEACH HOUSE AT DUNDARAVE PIER** (150–25th St; 604/922-1414) offers yet another beautiful view, excellent seafood dishes, and a killer wine list. Back in Ambleside, an equally good bet is the **BEACH SIDE CAFE** (1362 Marine Dr; 604/925-1945), where during summer you'd be wise to enjoy the inventive West Coast menu out on the deck. For a casual dinner or dessert and coffee, you can't beat the **SAVARY ISLAND PIE COMPANY** (1533 Marine Dr; 604/926-4021).

But for those who can't wait to get back to the city, **YALETOWN** is the next destination. After crossing Lions Gate Bridge and going through Stanley Park, drive southeast through downtown along Georgia Street. After turning right on Richards Street, look for parking in the area (there are several lots and garages). Head southwest until you reach Nelson Street, the northern boundary of Yaletown. From there it's easy to find Hamilton and Mainland Streets, the two short business and residential strips that anchor this ultrahip neighbourhood.

Yaletown used to be the city's warehouse district. Now its old red-brick buildings house upscale furniture stores, clothing boutiques, fashion showrooms, galleries, lofts, offices, bars, and restaurants. If you want to keep your dinner options open, try the candle-lit **BRIX RESTAURANT AND WINE BAR** (1138 Homer St; 604/915-9463). This place has it all: inventive tapas and entrees, a tasting menu, more than 50 wines by the glass, and one of the city's best patios during summer. A lively social scene is inevitable at the **YALETOWN BREWING COMPANY** (1111 Mainland St; 604/688-0039), a casual restaurant and brewpub with a huge patio. The people at the next table might be wearing suits, but they could just as easily be decked out in the most fetching of athletic attire. Across the street is **CIRCOLO** (1116 Mainland St; 604/687-1116), gastronomic guru Umberto Menghi's chic new restaurant. Stop by for dinner or a glass of his Tuscan Bambolo wine at this vibrant gathering spot.

Managed to hold off on dessert? Enjoy a pastry at the unbelievably chic **DON'T SHOW THE ELEPHANT** (1201 Hamilton St; 604/331-1018)—the washroom alone is worth a visit. Or take a walk down to Pacific Boulevard for a look at **CONCORD PACIFIC**, North America's largest—and, arguably, its most successful—downtown residential development. Among the elegant highrises you'll find **URBAN FARE** (177 Davie St; 604/975-7550); this cleverly designed supermarket has a small, licensed restaurant in front and live music on weekends. But this is no time to be picking up a quart of milk. Yaletown-area nightclubs include the fairly straight-laced **BAR NONE** (1222 Hamilton St; 604/689-7000), and new addition **VODA** (783 Homer St; 604/684-3003), where the clientele tends to be future. For something in between, checkout the bar at cavernous **SUBEEZ** (891 Homer St; 604/687-6107), a restaurant that wishes it could be an after-hours party.

FAMILY DAY

If you have young children, you can bring them along for most of Days One through Three without fear they'll be absolutely bored out of their little skulls (we hope). But it also helps to have a backup day, as it were, planned specifically with them in mind. By and large, Vancouver is a kid-friendly city. During spring and summer there are countless family events, including the **VANCOUVER INTERNATIONAL CHILDREN'S FESTIVAL** at Vanier Park (late May and early June; 604/687-7697) and the **ALCAN DRAGON BOAT FESTIVAL** (604/688-2382), which takes place in late June at the Plaza of Nations. If your kids don't go in for those kinds of things—meaning that they wouldn't be caught dead taking part in an official family outing—here are some other ways to keep them occupied.

MORNING: Here are two options, the first focusing on the arts and sciences (with a bit of consumer culture thrown in), the second leaning toward history and industry (but not excluding shopping, of course).

Option 1: We know it's not haute cuisine, but kids don't seem to have a problem with **WHITE SPOT**, the local restaurant chain that has attuned the taste buds of generations of Vancouverites to its hamburger slathered in Triple-O sauce. In the morning, the big location downtown at the corner of Georgia and Seymour Streets (580 W Georgia St; 604/662-3066) serves pancakes, eggs, and other breakfast foods guaranteed to appeal to young palates. It's also close to the **GRANVILLE SKYTRAIN**

STATION, the fastest and most exciting way to get to **SCIENCE WORLD**. Jaded as your children may be by life in the 600-channel universe, there's at least a glimmer of hope that a ride on the SkyTrain (seats near the front and back windows are great) will get them pumped for a look under the silver geodesic dome, which houses the **ALCAN OMNIMAX THEATRE** and an ever-changing series of exhibits.

What's more, you don't have to leave Science World the way you came. **FALSE CREEK FERRIES** (604/684-7781) and the **AQUABUS** (604/689-5858) shuttle passengers to downtown and **GRANVILLE ISLAND**, where the several storeys of **KIDS MARKET** (1496 Cartwright St; 604/689-8447) stretch even the briefest of attention spans with toy and hobby shops, a jungle gym running the height of the building, and a snack bar at the very top. (Another way to get to Granville Island is the Downtown Historic Railway (604/325-9990), which during summer weekends and holidays departs from Science World every 30 minutes between 1 and 5pm.) If it's turning out to be a hot day, the **FALSE CREEK COMMUNITY CENTRE** (1318 Cartwright St; 604/257-8195) offers playgrounds and the continent's biggest free **WATER PARK**. The **GRANVILLE ISLAND PUBLIC MARKET** (1689 Duranleau St; 604/666-5784) is probably your best bet for lunch, bearing in mind that even adults have a hard time keeping their bearings among the dozens of stalls. Kids love to wolf down minibagels with cream cheese from Bageland (604/685-1618), glazed donut holes from **LEE'S DONUTS** (604/685-4021), and seasonal berries from any produce stall.

Option 2: For families with a car, the picturesque fishing village of **STEVESTON** is a half-hour drive south of downtown on Highway 99, across the Oak Street Bridge and west on Steveston Highway. The promise of fish-and-chips for lunch will probably help make the journey a pleasant one: two good options are **DAVE'S FISH AND CHIPS** (3460 Moncton Rd; 604/271-7555) and **JAKE'S ON THE PIER** (3866 Bayview St; 604/275-7811). Historical attractions in Steveston include the **BRITANNIA HERITAGE SHIPYARD** (604/241-9453), a re-creation of a turn-of-the-century shipyard complete with workers refurbishing antique fishing boats. The 19th-century **GULF OF GEORGIA CANNERY** (12138 4th Ave; 604/664-9009) offers guided tours and demonstrations. And the **STEVESTON MUSEUM** (3811 Moncton St; 604/271-6868) contains the original manager's office of Steveston's first bank, plus restored living quarters upstairs.

But if your child's day just isn't complete without a trip to the mall, head back east along Steveston Highway, turn left onto No. 3 Road, and visit Richmond's **ASIA WEST** district between Capstan and Alderbridge Ways. Here, a cluster of shopping centres—**YAOHAN CENTRE, PRESIDENT PLAZA, PARKER PLACE,** and others—offer bargain-priced clothing; supermarkets selling live fish, crabs, and other animals; and huge food courts serving a bewildering variety of Asian fast food. A definitely cool beverage is a bubble pearl tea, imported from Taiwan, a fad among young Chinese. Who says going to the mall can't be educational?

AFTERNOON: Whether or not you initiate an earnest discussion about the pros and cons of keeping whales in captivity, the **VANCOUVER AQUARIUM MARINE SCIENCE CENTRE** (604/659-3474) in **STANLEY PARK** is sure to be a big hit with your kids. During summer, the aquarium organizes children's workshops, field trips, and even sleepovers beside the whale pools. An equally big hit is the **CLAM SHELL GIFT SHOP**, which you'll have to negotiate in order to leave the building. But Stanley Park has several other attractions to snag young people whose spirits might be flagging a little by this point in the day. Near the aquarium, a **MINIATURE TRAIN** (604/257-8531) departs—provided it's not raining— for a 1.2-kilometre (0.75-mile) trip through the woods. Right next to it is a petting zoo and close by, at Lumberman's Arch, you'll find a children's **WATER PARK**. Across the park, at **SECOND BEACH**, there's a swimming pool, a playground, and room to eat a picnic lunch. And, of course, active families will want to strap on the Rollerblades for a whiz around the seawall or rent bikes on nearby Denman Street.

EVENING: As everyone knows, our market-driven world has made children easily distracted by the messages of advertising and other mass media. At the end of a long day in Vancouver, that's a good thing: just head for **ROBSON STREET** and let your offspring do as much window-shopping as they can handle. If the family unit makes it as far as the corner of Burrard Street, the kids will probably drag you into the **VIRGIN MEGASTORE** (788 Burrard St; 604/669-2289)—or perhaps it will be the other way round. But the real reason you're on Robson is to get some dinner. Not only does **EARLS** (1185 Robson St; 604/669-0020) welcome small children, but its affordable menu will also appeal to discriminating adults. If your kids have more adventurous tastes, take them to **HON'S WUN-TUN HOUSE** (1339 Robson St; 604/685-0871). They'll enjoy the bustling atmosphere of the big, Hong Kong-style dining room, and pictures on the back of the menu let them choose from several types of soup noodles. Oh, and the service is fast. Real fast. A short detour off Robson is **ROMANO'S MACARONI GRILL** (1523 Davie St; 604/689-4334), a mansion full of singing wait staff, Caesar salads, and lots of pasta and garlic bread.

If you're not completely and utterly exhausted by now, nearby **GRANVILLE MALL** is home to several cinema multiplexes, as well a couple of budget repertory theatres. (At press time, plans were being made to construct a huge entertainment complex at Robson and Burrard, complete with 16 screens and an IMAX theatre.) Further afield, the 12-screen

TINSELTOWN megaplex opened in late 1999 at International Village, near the Stadium SkyTrain station. And if it's early enough in the evening—and they haven't packed up and moved stateside—the perennially under-500 **VANCOUVER GRIZZLIES** play to some pretty cheap seats at nearby GM Place. Granville Mall is also home to about 20 holes-in-the-wall serving 99-cent pizza slices, in case someone decided to play with their dinner instead of eating it. But don't say we didn't warn you: a combination of loitering street kids, panhandlers, and incipient pub-crawlers doesn't make Granville Mall the ideal family environment. Come to think of it, TV back in the hotel room may be a better option—with milk and cookies delivered to your room before bed.

VICTORIA
AND BEYOND

VICTORIA AND BEYOND

How to Get Here

BY FERRY

BC Ferries (www.bcferries.bc.ca) ships depart the mainland from Tsaw-wassen (38 kilometres/24 miles south of Vancouver) to Swartz Bay (32 kilometres/20 miles north of Victoria) eight or more times a day (sched-ules vary seasonally). For details, call 250/386-3431 (or 888/223-3779 in BC only). Regular fares are $32 one way for the car and driver and an additional $9 for each passenger; children under 11 are $4.50; children under 5 travel free. If your time is money, ante up $15 more to reserve a space (604/444-2890) and avoid a wait in line. BC seniors travel free Mondays through Thursdays. The scenic trip takes 95 minutes, but allow about three hours each way to include the drive between downtown and the ferry terminal at both ends as well some waiting time at the docks. Loading begins about 20 minutes before departure, so be sure to arrive ahead of time. Each of the ferries is equipped with many conveniences: indoor lounge seating, outdoor benches, a cafeteria, a gift shop, a chil-dren's play area, and a video arcade.

An alternative offered by BC Ferries is the Horseshoe Bay–Nanaimo ferry, which passes by Bowen and Gabriola Islands during its 95-minute voyage. The waterfront village of Horseshoe Bay in West Vancouver mer-its a visit while you're waiting for the ferry to begin boarding. However, you should allow about five hours each way for this trip if your destina-tion is Victoria or if you are starting from Victoria and want to end up in downtown Vancouver. The 111-kilometre (66-mile) drive between Nanaimo and downtown Victoria is along the picturesque Trans-Canada Highway (Highway 1). It winds through the pastoral Cowichan Valley, over a mountain range to the spectacular Malahat Summit, and through the lush rain forest of Goldstream Provincial Park. During the summer and on holiday weekends, arrive at the terminal at least an hour before sailing: Vancouver Island is a popular destination for throngs of main-land locals and neighbouring Washingtonians.

BY BUS

Another way to make the crossing is by bus. Pacific Coach Lines (604/662-8074) offers frequent, reliable service via the Tsawwassen–Swartz Bay BC Ferries route. You board the bus at the Vancouver bus terminal (Pacific Central Station, 1150 Station St; map:V6) and are deliv-ered to the Victoria bus depot (710 Douglas St) behind the Empress Hotel in about three and a half hours; the fare is $26.50 one way.

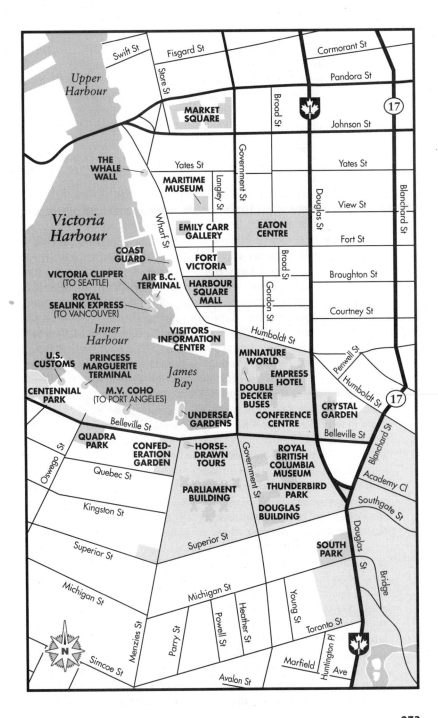

Swift St
Fisgard St
Store St
Cormorant St
Pandora St
Broad St
17
Johnson St
Upper Harbour
MARKET SQUARE
Yates St
Yates St
Government St
View St
Langley St
Douglas St
Blanchard St
THE WHALE WALL
MARITIME MUSEUM
Victoria Harbour
EMILY CARR GALLERY
EATON CENTRE
Fort St
Wharf St
FORT VICTORIA
COAST GUARD
Broad St
Broughton St
VICTORIA CLIPPER (TO SEATTLE)
AIR B.C. TERMINAL
HARBOUR SQUARE MALL
Gordon St
Courtney St
ROYAL SEALINK EXPRESS (TO VANCOUVER)
VISITORS INFORMATION CENTER
Humboldt St
Inner Harbour
MINIATURE WORLD
Penwell St
U.S. CUSTOMS
PRINCESS MARGUERITE TERMINAL
James Bay
EMPRESS HOTEL
Humboldt St
CENTENNIAL PARK
M.V. COHO (TO PORT ANGELES)
DOUBLE DECKER BUSES
17
Belleville St
UNDERSEA GARDENS
CONFERENCE CENTRE
CRYSTAL GARDEN
Belleville St
QUADRA PARK
Oswego St
CONFEDERATION GARDEN
HORSE-DRAWN TOURS
Government St
ROYAL BRITISH COLUMBIA MUSEUM
Blanchard St
Academy Cl
Quebec St
PARLIAMENT BUILDING
THUNDERBIRD PARK
Southgate St
Kingston St
DOUGLAS BUILDING
Douglas St
Superior St
Superior St
SOUTH PARK
Bridge
Michigan St
Michigan St
Menzies St
Parry St
Powell St
Heather St
Young St
Toronto St
Huntington Pl
N
Simcoe St
Avalon St
Marfield
Ave

BY AIR

The fastest link to Victoria (inner harbour) is a 35-minute harbour-to-harbour flight by **FLOATPLANE OR HELICOPTER.** Contact Harbour Air Seaplanes (800/665-0212) and West Coast Air (604/800/347-2222) for flight information; one-way fare is $84. Helijet Airways' helicopter service (800/665-4354) is about $129 one way. (Helijet also offers direct service between downtown Victoria and Vancouver International Airport.)

Orientation

Victoria, BC's capital city, was ranked by *Condé Nast Traveler* magazine readers as one of the top 10 cities in the world to visit, and number one in the world for ambience and environment. The city is a mecca for tourists seeking a slower, genteel pace. They come to stroll the endless sculptured gardens, to shop for Irish linens and Harris tweeds, to sip afternoon tea, to dine on fresh seafood, to meander along the inner harbour. And whether you make the trip by ferry, coach bus, floatplane, or helicopter, getting to Victoria is half the fun. At the turn of each corner you'll find a landscape from a romantic novel. The distant snowcapped Olympic Mountains of Washington State are right out of E. M. Forester's *A Passage to India.* The inner harbour seems to have leapt out of the pages of James Clavell's *Tai-pan.* There are mansions and houses that look as if they had been transported from the town of Weatherbury in Thomas Hardy's *Far from the Madding Crowd.* And one would expect Wolf Larsen from Jack London's *Sea Wolf* to be sailing the Strait of Juan de Fuca in the cutter *Ghost* with his love, Maude Brewster, by his side. But don't get us wrong. Victoria is definitely not a large-scale retirement village, as some people would lead you to believe.

Victoria's backyard encompasses a variety of landscapes, from the nearby Saxe Point naval base to the wild West Coast just around the southern tip of Vancouver Island (see Sooke in this chapter). Once you've strolled around the inner harbour on your first day, it's worth going a little farther afield to discover what lies beyond.

Everything in Victoria fans out from the inner harbour. Ground zero in this seeming maze of tiny streets and alleyways is intersected by only three main thoroughfares. Stand on the sidewalk in front of the Empress Hotel, facing the inner harbour. The street in front of you is **GOVERN-MENT STREET.** To the right, it leads north through the downtown's busy shopping area, Old Town's restored heritage buildings, and Chinatown's landmark sights. To the left, this same street leads south past the provincial Parliament Buildings on Belleville Street to the residential James Bay neighbourhood. Rimming the harbour and running parallel to Government Street to the west, Wharf Street merges with Government Street at its southern end and terminates to the north at the Johnson Street Bridge.

Another main business thoroughfare is **DOUGLAS STREET**, which parallels Government Street to the east. The southern terminus is where the Trans-Canada Highway begins, at the Mile 0 marker on Dallas Road, overlooking the vast Strait of Juan de Fuca. To the northward, outside the city limits, Douglas becomes the multilane Highway 1, leading to Nanaimo. Blanshard Street parallels Douglas Street. Southward, it merges with Douglas at the entrance to Beacon Hill Park on Southgate Street. To the north, it becomes Highway 17, leading to Butchart Gardens, near the Victoria International Airport, and the Swartz Bay ferry terminal.

Visitor Information

Your first stop in the city should be the **TOURISM VICTORIA VISITOR INFOCENTRE** (812 Wharf St; 250/953-2033). The well-versed staff here dispense useful information on the sights to see, can book last-minute accommodations (accommodation hotline 800/663-3883), and will update you on special events. For a listing of local happenings, the free *Monday Magazine* offers the city's best weekly calendar of events; pick it up at various locations throughout the city.

Getting Around

Walking is by far the best way to get around Victoria. Limited on-street parking is only half the reason: most attractions, restaurants, and services are within a 12-square-block radius. But if you plan to see beyond the main core, there are alternative forms of transportation that will save your soles.

The **VICTORIA REGIONAL TRANSIT SYSTEM** is operated by BC Transit (250/382-6161) and has 40 bus routes through greater Victoria, running 6am to midnight. Pick up a copy of *Explore Victoria by Bus* at the Tourism Victoria Visitor InfoCentre. It spells out exactly how to get to every attraction, neighbourhood, and park by bus. Fares are calculated on a per-zone basis. A one-way, single-zone fare is $1.75; two zones are $2.50. Transfers are good for travel in one direction only with no stopovers. A day pass ($5.50)—also available at the InfoCentre and at ticket outlets displaying the Fare Dealer symbol—covers unlimited travel throughout the day. There are discounts for children and seniors.

The miniature **FERRYBOATS** (each seats 12) operated by Victoria Harbour Ferry Company (250/708-0201) squire passengers to and from shore points all along the inner harbour for about $12 per person (half-fare for children). You can get on at any stop and take a round-trip, 45-minute cruise, or you can hop on and cross the inner harbour for $3. Sailing every 15 minutes, from 10am to 10pm (off-peak season 11am to

GHOSTLY VICTORIA

The Old Cemeteries Society (Fairfield Rd at Memorial Dr; 250/384-0045) offers **Lantern Tours of the Old Burying Ground** at 9:30pm each evening during July and August from the Cherry Bank Hotel (825 Burdett St). The society also conducts walking tours of Victoria's many cemeteries on Sundays (and on Tuesday and Thursday evenings during the summer), but the majority of tours—with good cause—go to Ross Bay Cemetery. It's a veritable who's who of Victoria (and BC for that matter), including coal magnate Robert Dunsmuir, Billy Barker (a canalboat sailor from Cambridge, England, who struck it rich when he discovered the Cariboo's largest gold claim, then spent it all and died a pauper), and Victoria-born artist Emily Carr. You can also buy a booklet on self-guided tours at Munro's bookstore and go around on your own. The annual Ghost Walk takes place on October 31. Call 250/ 384-0045 for meeting locations.

6pm), the little blue craft dock at the Empress, Coast Harbourside Hotel, and Ocean Pointe Resort Hotel.

Within the downtown area, you can generally get from place to place via **TAXI** for less than $6, plus tip. It's best to call for a cab; drivers don't always stop on city streets for flag-downs, especially when it's raining, as they're usually responding to calls. Call Empress Cabs (250/383-8888) or Blue Bird Cabs (250/382-8294).

For **BIKES AND SCOOTERS,** Victoria has bike lanes that run through the city, as well as paved paths along parks and beaches. There are a few basic cycling rules here: helmets are mandatory, and it's illegal to cycle on sidewalks, except those designated as bike paths. You can rent bikes for around $6 an hour ($20 a day) at Budget Rent-A-Car (250/953-5300). Budget also rents motorized scooters for $10 an hour ($45 a day). Some visitors rent scooters for the half-hour ride up to Butchart Gardens via Beach Drive, along the waterfront. It's also possible to rent baby strollers for $6 per day.

Traffic is often heavy and **PARKING** is scarce in downtown Victoria. It helps if there's parking at your lodgings. If not, be prepared to circle around awhile for metered, on-street parking. There are parking lots on View Street between Douglas and Blanshard, on Johnson near Blanshard, on Yates near Bastion Square, and at the Bay—the department store—on Fisgard at Blanshard. Most major **RENTAL CAR** agencies have downtown pick-up/drop-off locations, including Avis (800/879-2847), Budget Rent-A-Car (800/268-8900), Hertz Canada (800/263-0600), and Tilden International (800/387-4747). If you are a AAA or CAA member, ask the reservations agent for a member discount.

Essentials

PUBLIC REST ROOMS

Hotel lobbies are your best bet downtown. Shopping centers also have public facilities. Restaurants and service stations are required by law to provide public facilities for their patrons' use.

MAJOR BANKS

Royal Bank (1079 Douglas St; 250/356-4500) is located in the heart of downtown Victoria, along with the Bank of Montreal (1225 Douglas St; 250/389-2400) and the Toronto Dominion Bank (1080 Douglas St; 250/356-4000). All have branches scattered throughout the Greater Victoria area.

POLICE AND SAFETY

Crimes of opportunity, such as property theft from unlocked cars, occur in this heavily touristed city. Use common sense. There are also transient panhandlers working the street corners around the downtown and Old Town areas, but they are usually not aggressive. Dial 911 for fire, police, ambulance, or poison control. Lost property should be reported to the Victoria City Police (250/995-7654). The Royal Canadian Mounted Police (250/380-6261) should also be contacted regarding lost property or crime.

HOSPITALS AND MEDICAL/DENTAL SERVICES

Most major hotels have a doctor and dentist on call. The James Bay Treatment Center (100 230 Menzies St; 250/388-9934) is open daily, including holidays. Cresta Dental Centre (3170 Tillicum Rd in the Tillicum Mall; 250/384-7711) is open daily. Hospitals within the downtown vicinity include Royal Jubilee Hospital (1800 Fort St; 250/370-8212) and Victoria General Hospital (35 Helmcken Rd; 250/727-4181).

POST OFFICE

The main post office (714 Yates St; 250/595-2552) is not the only place to purchase stamps or mail packages. Shopper's Drug Mart (1222 Douglas St; 250/384-0544) and other stores displaying a Canada Post "postal outlet" sign can also provide these services.

GROCERY STORES

One of Canada's best-managed companies, Thrifty Foods, offers quality food products, friendly staff, and well-stocked stores in Victoria and on Vancouver Island.

PHARMACIES

Shopper's Drug Mart (1222 Douglas St; 250/384-0544) is open daily until 7pm. McGill and Orne (649 Fort St; 250/384-1195) is open daily until 6pm.

DRY CLEANERS AND LAUNDROMATS
There's a laundromat under the Tourism Victoria Visitor InfoCentre on Wharf Street, next door to Milestones.

LEGAL SERVICES
Dial-A-Law (800/565-5297) operates 24 hours a day offering general information on legal topics. The call to the service is free; lawyers charge $10 for a half hour of legal advice. Dial-A-Law is sponsored and operated by the Canadian Bar Association (BC branch).

BUSINESS, COPY, AND MESSENGER SERVICES
J&L Copy and Fax (777 Fort St; 250/386-3333) is open Monday to Saturday and also does repairs.

PHOTOGRAPHY EQUIPMENT AND SERVICES
Lens & Shutter (615 Fort St; 250/383-7443) sells and services camera and video equipment; it's open Monday to Saturday.

COMPUTER REPAIRS AND RENTALS
If you're in Victoria, a range of IBM and Macintosh systems are available for rent from Compu Lease Ltd. (2001E Douglas St; 250/388-7114 or 800/747-7114; www.vvv.com/~compulea/index.html). WestWorld Computers has a wide selection of Macintosh systems at its Victoria location (2001A Douglas St; 250/386-6665; www.westworld.ca).

PETS AND STRAY ANIMALS
Call the SPCA (250/385-6521) for any animal emergency.

SPAS AND SALONS
Ocean Pointe Resort Hotel and Spa (45 Songhees Rd; 250/360-2999) has a complete European spa, including aesthetics and massage.

Top 20 Restaurants

Cafe Brio / ★★★
944 FORT ST; 250/383-0009

Owners Greg Hays and Silvia Marcolini literally invite you into their home when you visit this lively Antique Row restaurant, serving *cucina domestica* (Italian cuisine focussing on seasonal foods from the region). Bathed in warm terra-cotta and mustard yellow tones, this comfortable room exudes life. Several pieces from Marcolini's personal art collection that decorate the walls are illuminated by turn-of-the-century shaded torchlights. Chef Sean Brennan mirrors the change of seasons in his West Coast (with Tuscan touches) menu. Appetizers include smoked ivory salmon, seared Alaskan scallops, and crispy quail. Local organic grower Tina Frazer supplies a range of specialty produce for Brennan's entrees, which range from rack of lamb served with a caramelized onion and goat cheese tart and olive vinaigrette, to delightful and affordable dinner selections like the spaghettini with fried bread crumbs, anchovy, chiles, and olives. The wine list is well chosen, with a good selection of West Coast wines and minimal markups. *$$–$$$; AE, MC, V; debit cards; no cheques; lunch Tues–Fri, dinner Mon–Sat; full bar; downtown.* &

Carden Street West / ★★★
1164 STELLYS CROSS RD, BRENTWOOD BAY; 250/544-1475
Make sure you've got the right address before heading north from Victoria along W Saanich Road to this rural restaurant, just past the town of Brentwood Bay on the Saanich Peninsula. The name doesn't relate to its current address, but instead to its original site, the still-popular Carden Street Cafe in Guelph, Ontario. When owners Paulette Jolley and Micheal Mino decided to move to Vancouver Island four years ago and open Carden Street West, they brought with them the philosophies that made their first effort so successful: personalized service and delicious food. Area residents are frequent visitors to this establishment, housed in a charming, almost farmhouse-looking structure (the building was once a fruit stand). The 40-seat dining room is gardenlike and full of rich, tropical colours. This lively look perfectly matches chef Connie O'Brien's main menu, which the owners describe as "spicy international"—inspired by their many travels—and includes outstanding West African and Southeast Asian–style curries. A daily specials sheet offers a range of less spicy, but full-flavoured tastes from around the world. The wine list is limited, but there is a good choice of beer and fruity drinks that go well with spicier flavours. Richly flavoured desserts, such as cheesecake, chocolate mousse and a light-as-air pavlova are made on the premises. *$$$; AE, MC, V; debit cards; no cheques; dinner Tues–Sat; beer and wine; reservations recommended; at W Saanich Rd.* &

Cassis Bistro / ★★☆
253 COOK ST; 250/384-1932
This popular neighbourhood bistro in Victoria's Cook Street Village offers good food and good fun in a warm and relaxing atmosphere. Chef-owner John Hall runs the kitchen and his wife, Lisa, takes charge out front (she also scans local antique and secondhand stores for the unique dinnerware used in the restaurant). Cassis serves up true bistro fare, such as free-range chicken from Cowichan, topped with caramelized onions, and BC salmon, simmered in vermouth and served with a shallot and sorrel sauce. The wine list is small, but offers a good selection in a variety of price ranges. *$$$; MC, V; debit cards; no cheques; dinner every day, brunch Sun; full bar; reservations recommended; at Fairfield Rd.* &

Christie's Carriage House Pub / ★

1739 FORT ST; 250/598-5333

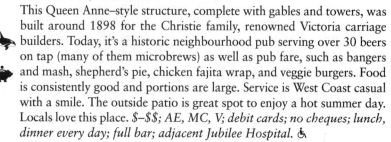

This Queen Anne–style structure, complete with gables and towers, was built around 1898 for the Christie family, renowned Victoria carriage builders. Today, it's a historic neighbourhood pub serving over 30 beers on tap (many of them microbrews) as well as pub fare, such as bangers and mash, shepherd's pie, chicken fajita wrap, and veggie burgers. Food is consistently good and portions are large. Service is West Coast casual with a smile. The outside patio is great spot to enjoy a hot summer day. Locals love this place. *$–$$; AE, MC, V; debit cards; no cheques; lunch, dinner every day; full bar; adjacent Jubilee Hospital.* ⅄

Deep Cove Chalet / ★★★

11190 CHALET RD, SIDNEY; 250/656-3541

Chef-owner Peter Koffel has brought a little European opulence to this stunning, rural seaside setting in nearby Sidney. (Don't be surprised if he jumps out of the kitchen to ceremoniously decant a bottle of wine.) The large windows of this chaletlike structure overlook meticulously kept lawns and a splendid view of the Saanich Inlet. Guests sometimes stroll the scrupulously manicured lawns between courses, wineglass in hand. Lobster bisque, cheese soufflé, scrambled eggs and caviar, sautéed oysters with béarnaise sauce, and beef Wellington are just a few of the classic dishes served here. Finish with crêpes suzette or cherries jubilee. The extensive wine list offers fine vintages from Burgundy, Bordeaux, and California. A private dining suite upstairs can be booked by groups for lunch or dinner. *$$$; AE, MC, V; debit cards; no cheques; lunch Wed–Sun, dinner Tues–Sun; full bar; reservations recommended; 40 km (25 miles) north of Victoria, call for directions.* ⅄

The Dining Room at the Aerie / ★★★

600 EBEDORA LN, MALAHAT; 250/743-7115

Perched high upon Malahat Mountain, the Dining Room at the Aerie (see Lodgings in this chapter) is as spectacular and inspiring as the view of the mountains and Spectacle Lake that it offers. Even with an expansion, the dining room still feels intimate. Wild mushrooms and other forest edibles are incorporated into the menu, which changes seasonally, creating an imaginative, regional cuisine. Poached Saanich Peninsula rock sole with Qualicum scallops in Dungeness crab broth, BC salmon with parsley and olive emulsion, roast Arbutus Ridge pheasant breast with barley risotto—these are just a few of the entrees you'll find. The multicourse, "tasting" menus (including a luscious vegetarian one) are a good way to sample all this kitchen has to offer. Think again before you pass up a dessert of warm Callebaut truffle and white chocolate pudding. Service is top-notch, and there's a superb wine list, with plenty of notable

Northwest wines. *$$$; AE, MC, V; debit cards; no cheques; lunch, dinner every day; full bar; reservations required; 30–40 minutes from downtown Victoria, take Spectacle Lake turnoff from Trans-Canada Hwy.* ᪲

Don Mee Seafood Restaurant / ★★

538 FISGARD ST; 250/383-1032
Located in Chinatown, Don Mee has the most extensive dim sum offered in Victoria. In business for over 60 years, it serves some of the only dim sum in the city that's made on the premises. There is no menu during lunch, just a never-ending variety served from carts that ceaselessly circle the room: fried pork dumplings with Chinese vinegar, steamed buns filled with chicken, curried pork puffs, rice wrappers stuffed with shrimp and dipped into hot sauce, and sticky rice wrapped in banana leaves. Arrive at the restaurant before 11:30am to ensure you get a table. Don Mee's dinner menu focuses on Cantonese and Sichuan dishes, such as steamed lobster in minced garlic sauce and sizzling scallops on a hot iron plate. Beware of ordering too much food; the portions are huge. Service is fast and efficient, no matter what time of day you arrive. *$–$$; AE, MC, V; debit cards; no cheques; lunch, dinner every day; full bar; Chinatown.*

Herald Street Caffe / ★★★

546 HERALD ST; 250/381-1441
This lively Old Town restaurant has served fine, innovative West Coast cuisine to locals and visitors alike for more than a decade. The interior is filled with grand floral arrangements and an eclectic collection of local art. Appetizers such as Dungeness crab cakes with cilantro-lime pesto and tomato salsa, and the alder-smoked salmon on apple potato latkes, are absolutely delicious. The Caesar salad is probably the best in town. Chef Mark Finnigan's menu is filled with longtime favourites, such as his signature bouillabaisse, cashew-crusted chicken, rack of lamb with mint and whole-grain mustard, and beef tenderloin stuffed with pâté. Shaker lemon pie is still one of the most popular desserts, but the homemade ice creams and sorbets are also definitely worth trying. An excellent wine list matches the eclectic menu. Knowledgeable, courteous service makes for an above-average dining experience. Tables may be a little close together, but on busy nights the atmosphere is quite electric. Later hours (Wed–Thurs till 1:30am, and Fri–Sat till 2am) make this an ideal venue for the post-theatre crowd. *$$–$$$; AE, DC, E, MC, V; debit cards; no cheques; lunch Wed–Sun, dinner every day; full bar; reservations recommended; at Government St.* ᪲

Il Terrazzo Ristorante / ★★☆

555 JOHNSON ST; 250/361-0028
A true taste of Italy is what you'll find in this beautiful restaurant tucked away on Waddington Alley, a short walk from Market Square. Surrounded

by five outdoor fireplaces and an abundance of plants and flowers, Il Terrazzo offers a haven of privacy in busy Old Town Victoria. (Alfresco dining on the covered, heated terrace is possible nearly year-round as well.) Lunch chef Max Leroy and dinner chefs Steven Usher and Daniele Mereu exude tremendous passion, creating a northern Italian cuisine that bursts with flavour. Classic minestrone soup, char-grilled baby squid, creamy risotto Milanese with seafood, wood-oven pizzas, marvelous pastas, and exquisite meat dishes such as veal marsala attest to the menu's diversity. The service is not always swift; patience is sometimes needed for the pasta dishes made to order. An extensive wine list showcases a range of fine Italian wines. *$$–$$$; AE, MC, V; debit cards; no cheques; lunch Mon–Sat, dinner every day; full bar; reservations recommended; near Market Square.* ⅍

J & J Wonton Noodle House / ★★

1012 FORT ST; 250/383-0680

You might easily walk past this popular Chinese restaurant with its unassuming facade. But when the door opens and the tantalizing aroma of ginger, garlic, and black beans embraces your senses, you'll be drawn in. This busy, modest, spotlessly clean restaurant treats you to the flavours of Hong Kong, Singapore, Sichuan cooking, and northern China. A large kitchen window lets you watch the chefs busily preparing wonton soup, imperial prawn with spicy garlic wine sauce, spicy ginger fried chicken, or Sichuan braised beef hot pot. Noodles are a specialty and are made fresh daily on the premises. Service is friendly, efficient, and knowledgeable. *$; MC, V; debit cards; no cheques; lunch, dinner Tues–Sat; beer and wine; between Vancouver and Cook Sts.* ⅍

Kaz Japanese / ★★

1619 STORE ST; 250/386-9121

The center of attention in this small, understated restaurant is its soft-spoken, humble owner, Kaz Motohashi. The Japanese community rank his sushi among the city's best. Although a traditionalist, Motohashi has adapted his menu to western tastes. Along with fine nigiri sushi such as *sake* (salmon), *tako* (octopus), and *ahi* (Hawaiian tuna), you'll find a range of North American–style rolls, such as prawn tempura roll and California Roll (made with real crab). The menu offers other delicacies, such as noodle soup, curry rice, and teriyaki. Start with the addictive chicken *karaage* (deep-fried marinated chicken wings) or the light and crispy tempura. Order the Bento Box at dinner and sample a superb array of Kaz's finest treats. *$–$$; AE, MC, V; debit cards; no cheques; lunch, dinner Mon–Sat; beer and wine; at Fisgard St.* ⅍

Med Grill / ★★
1010 YATES ST; 250/360-1660
Owner Paul Simpson transformed a defunct carpet store into a Mediterranean paradise. Skylights and massive windows illuminate the terracotta floor, rich wood trim, and lively yellow walls. Diners can have a cocktail at the black marble horseshoe-shaped bar before being seated in either the upstairs or downstairs dining areas. A statue of the wine god Bacchus greets diners ascending to the cozy upstairs room that overlooks the main dining area. The menu offers a wide array of moderately priced Mediterranean dishes, from pizza to pasta to spit-roasted meats. (A side order of Med bread is a must.) From martinis to wines by the glass, the drinks are attractively priced. Service sometimes slows when the place is packed and can be a bit too familiar for some. The large outdoor patio is open during summer months for alfresco dining. A second location (4512 Saanich Rd; 250/727-3444) offers the same tasty food in a more intimate, rural setting. *$–$$; AE, MC, V; debit cards; no cheques; lunch, dinner every day; full bar; reservations recommended; at Vancouver St.* ♿

Point-No-Point Resort / ★
1505 WEST COAST RD, SOOKE; 250/646-2020
The quaint dining room at the Point-No-Point Resort is a great place to experience a little civilization after a day in the wilds of Vancouver Island's southwest coast. The small menu is carefully prepared and elegantly presented, especially the creamy seafood chowder served with homemade soda bread, grilled salmon on a baguette, or local smoked salmon on a bagel with organic greens. The dinner menu (Wednesday through Sunday, in summer only) offers Continental fare, such as beef tenderloin stuffed with Stilton, and tequila-lime prawns served on linguine. Desserts of chocolate ganache cake, and crème caramel with Grand Marnier sauce don't disappoint. The wine list is small, but has a good range of choices. Service is kind and unobtrusive. Binoculars provided on each table allow guests to view the local killer whales as they pass. *$$–$$$; AE, MC, V; debit cards; no cheques; lunch, afternoon tea every day, dinner Wed–Sun; beer and wine; dinner reservations required; Hwy 14, 24 km (15 miles) west of Sooke.* ♿

Re-Bar Modern Foods / ★
50 BASTION SQUARE; 250/361-9223
This is the place to go when you're feeling low—on energy, that is. Victoria's original vegetarian, health-food, smoke-free restaurant, located in Bastion Square, is packed with lunchtime crowds (lineups are common). Sip one of the refreshing fresh fruit drinks, such as the Atomic Glow (apple, strawberry, and ginger juices) or the Soul Charge (carrot, apple, celery, ginger, and Siberian ginseng) while perusing the menu. Delicious pizzas topped with oyster mushrooms, Anaheim chiles, tomatillo salsa,

Asiago, and Monterey Jack are house specialties, along with pastas, oriental salads, and black bean chili. Breads are all homemade; the honey-cornmeal and rosemary-walnut ones are filled with an exotic assortment of tastes and textures. Lemon tahini dressing and basil vinaigrette are delicious salad-toppers. Friendly, helpful service exemplifies the Re-Bar's philosophy. *$; AE, MC, V; debit cards; no cheques; breakfast, lunch, dinner every day; beer and wine; reservations recommended for Sat-Sun brunch; at Langley St.* &

Sam's Deli / ★
805 GOVERNMENT ST; 250/382-8424

As so many downtown office workers can attest, this 20-year-old restaurant offers the most bang for your buck in the city. Located a stone's throw from the Empress Hotel and the inner harbour, this busy deli offers cafeteria-style service. The shrimp and avocado sandwich is an all-time favourite; so are the large tureens of the daily soup. The ploughman's lunch—a selection of meat or pâté, two different cheeses, kosher dill pickles, fresh fruit, and sourdough bread—is another popular choice that can be upgraded to include soup. Spinach salads, pastrami or roast beef on dark rye, desserts, and a range of local draft beer, natural fruit juice, and specialty coffee are also available. Large indoor windows and a sizable outdoor patio provide great spots for people-watching, or do take-out and head to the inner harbour for a picnic. *$; MC, V; debit cards; no cheques; lunch, dinner every day; beer and wine; at Humboldt St.* &

Sooke Harbour House / ★★★★
1528 WHIFFEN SPIT RD, SOOKE; 250/642-3421 OR 800/889-9688

Sinclair and Frederica Philip, along with their team of chefs, have garnered international attention for their rare dedication to the freshest local ingredients, blended with a good deal of energy and flashes of searing innovation. Be it the root, flower, leaf, or stem, organically grown edible plants from the inn's own gardens complement what dedicated Island farmers, fishermen, and the wilderness provide. Entrees range from cold-cured sockeye salmon tartare, served with zucchini blossoms stuffed with goat-cheese polenta, to pan-seared Qualicum Beach scallops, to roast sirloin of Cedar Glen Farm veal. Sooke's award-winning wine list features excellent French wines and an impressive array of Vancouver Island wines. You'll pay dearly for all this attention to detail, but the commitment to flavours may make you forget the high tariff. Reservations are recommended, especially in July, August, and September. *$$$; AE, JCB, MC, V; debit cards; no cheques; dinner daily; full bar; reservations recommended; off Highway 14.* &

Spice Jammer Restaurant / ★★
852 FORT ST; 250/480-1055
This pretty little Indian restaurant, with very atypical western decor, is overseen with effervescent charm and good humour by manager Amin Essa. His wife, Billie, is the chef. With her excellent curries and his good service you just can't go wrong. A window onto the kitchen provides a behind-the-scenes look at the cooks busily preparing east Indian and east African dishes, with an emphasis on tandoori-style cooking (naan, chicken tikka, spicy prawns). Appetizers range from vegetable, chicken, or beef samosas to fried *mogos* (an east African dish of fried cassava-root wedges served with tamarind chutney). The curries come as you like: mild, medium, hot, and, if you dare, extra hot. There are vindaloos and marsalas, as well as Bhunna beef, *palak* lamb, *aloo gobi,* and rice pilaf, cooked with cardamom, cumin, saffron, and cinnamon—all of which wake up the senses. There are token alternatives for those who don't like curries, but don't give them a second glance. You're here for the curries. *$–$$; AE, MC, V; no cheques; lunch Tues–Sat, dinner Tues–Sun; full bar; downtown.* &

Spinnakers / ★
308 CATHERINE ST; 250/386-2739
One of the first brew pubs on the Island, Spinnakers has been around since 1984. Situated right on the inner harbour, it has the best view of any pub in Victoria. In the Tap Room upstairs, traditional pub fare is the order of the day, with rather ho-hum fish-and-chips, burgers, pastas, and curries, but good salads. Noggins chowder is fresh and consistently tasty. (You'll also find pub games here.) Downstairs in the dining room (where you can bring minors) you'll find a very similar menu, with the addition of potpies, stir-fries, and the inevitable ploughman's lunch. Both levels serve beers brewed on site, including raspberry ale, oatmeal stout, and Scottish ale. A gift/bake shop at the entrance sells baked goods created in-house, Spinnaker's own bottled beer and malt vinegar, and all forms of pub memorabilia, from clothing to glassware. *$; AE, D, DC, MC, V; debit cards; no cheques; breakfast, lunch, dinner every day; full bar; near Chinatown.* &

Victorian Restaurant at Ocean Pointe Resort / ★★★
45 SONGHEES RD; 250/360-2999
Here's an elegant space with an unsurpassed view, located in one of Victoria's finest hotels (see Lodgings in this chapter). Unquestionably one of the best chefs in Victoria, Craig Stoneman has created a superb menu, from the maple-glazed caribou steak and game sausage to the baked macadamia-nut-crusted salmon and lobster in a Pernod lime cream. His fruit salad, of sautéed jumbo prawns in a citrus curry dressing, prepared tableside, is magical. Can't make a decision? Opt for the reasonably

priced—and creative—three-, four-, or five-course table d'hôte menu. Desserts (rhubarb and blackberry frozen parfait and sour-cherry consommé, white chocolate raspberry torte with a saffron crème anglaise) are well crafted and artistically presented. Stop the cheese wagon—it contains superior handmade local cheeses from Salt Spring Island. Menu prices are noted in Canadian and U.S. dollars. Jacques Forest, the charming maître d'hôtel, does a remarkable job of pairing food and wine, and his servers are among the most polished in town. *$$$; AE, DC, JCB, MC, V; debit cards; no cheques; dinner Mon–Sun in high season (winter hours may vary); full bar; across Johnson St Bridge from downtown.*

The Windsor House Tea Room / ★

2540 WINDSOR RD; 250/595-3135

Tucked away in Oak Bay is a joyful restaurant that's quintessentially English and oozes Victorian charm, in the form of lead-pane windows, lace tablecloths, and teapots with tea cozies. The soups are sensational. So are the wonderful homemade steak and kidney pie (by far the best in town), chicken potpie (laden with chicken and veggies simmered in a white wine sauce and topped with a flaky crust), ploughman's lunch, and Welsh rabbit. A small kitchen makes for a small menu (and the reason the dessert pies are not homemade), but the sandwiches couldn't be fresher. If an English tea is what you're looking for, homemade scones and buttered crumpets with jam and clotted cream are sure to appeal. This is a place where people come to talk, and with pictures of the royal family on almost every wall and a hot cup of tea in hand, there's always something to talk about. Afternoon tea is served throughout the day. *$; MC, V; no cheques; lunch, afternoon tea Mon–Sat; beer and wine; lunch reservations required; corner of Newport Ave.* &

Lodgings

Abigail's Hotel / ★★★

906 MCCLURE ST; 250/388-5363 OR 800/561-6565

Abigail's is all 1920s Tudoresque gables, gardens, and crystal chandeliers. There are 16 odd-shaped rooms in the original three-storey building; the adjacent new three-storey building contains an additional 6 spacious rooms and from the exterior replicates the look and feel of its older neighbour. The Celebration Rooms on the third floor of the old building are grand: crystal goblets, down duvets, wood-burning fireplaces, and fresh flowers grace each room. Our favourite rooms are the spacious Coach House Suites in the new building. Dark wood wainscotting is married with William Morris print wallpaper and fabrics, as well as Art and Crafts stained-glass lamps, a king-size canopied bed, writing table, wet bar, armoire, and leather loveseat. The combination creates a stately

British ambience. Much of the traffic noise from busy Quadra Street is muffled by the tapestry drapes and good soundproofing in the older building, but light sleepers may want to request a room as far from the street as possible. Fruit is served as the first breakfast course in the small, airy dining room that looks onto the patio garden. The choice of breakfast entrees prepared by the resident chef range from chocolate-and-vanilla waffles served with a mango salsa to a fresh herb-and-garden-vegetable quiche. Although children over 10 are accepted, this romantic-getaway establishment is more suited for adults. Abigail's also manages a two-bedroom beach house 10 minutes from downtown Victoria that's perfect for families, and a ski lodge in Whistler. *$$$; AE, MC, V; no cheques; innkeeper@abigailshotel.com; www.abigailshotel.com; at Vancouver St.*

The Aerie / ★★★

600 EBEDORA LN, MALAHAT; 250/743-7115

The Aerie is the successful expression of an unlikely dream: to build a European-style luxury resort on an arbutus- and fir-mountainside. Opened in the early 1990s (and expanded twice since), the resort looks as if it had been transplanted from Monte Carlo. The view over Finlayson Arm far below is magnificent on a fine day; in mist and cloud, you feel insulated from the cares of the world. The Aerie has 23 spacious rooms and suites in three buildings; some have Jacuzzis and fireplaces and most have balconies or sun decks. Look for Persian and Chinese carpets, furniture from Asia and Europe, four-poster king-size beds, and prices that soar soar up to $425 a night. There's an indoor pool, and outdoor tennis court, and a spa that offers services such as facials, massage, and manicures. The top-rated Dining Room at the Aerie serves seasonal regional cuisine (see Top 20 Restaurants in this chapter). *$$$; AE, MC, V; no cheques; aerie@relaischateaux.fr; www.integra.fr/relaischateaux/aerie; take Spectacle Lake turnoff from Trans-Canada Hwy.*

Andersen House / ★★

301 KINGSTON ST; 250/388-4565

Andersen House combines the best of both the 18th and 19th centuries. Modern creature comforts, like telephones, jacuzzis, and CD players, are placed alongside an eclectic mix of antiques and modern art in each of the five rooms, which all have private entries. Built in 1891 for a wealthy sea captain, this Queen Anne–style Victorian wooden structure has 3.6-metre (12-foot)-high ceilings, stained-glass windows, and hardwood floors. Our favourite suite is the teakwood cabin on the 15-metre (50-foot) 1927 motor yacht *Mamita*, which is fitted with Art Deco antiques from stem to stern, and docked two blocks away in the inner harbour. You'll have to stroll to the house to breakfast with the other guests in the morning, but the fresh-baked muffins are worth the walk. *$$$; MC, V; cheques OK; andersen@islandnet.com; www.islandnet.com/~andersen/; at Pendray St.*

The Beaconsfield / ★★★

998 HUMBOLDT ST; 250/384-4044

Tree-lined Humboldt Street is closer to downtown than its quiet demeanor would suggest, so the Beaconsfield's location, just two blocks from beautiful Beacon Hill Park, is prime. The decor is meant to convey a sense of romance and hideaway, and does, in all nine antique-filled bedrooms, which feature private baths and down comforters. The Attic Room, which has a jacuzzi, is exceedingly private. The Duchess Room, which has an unusual wood-enclosed period bathtub, provides a half-canopied, queen-size bed with inlaid mahogany pieces. There are modern comforts to be found here as well, such as steam-heated towel racks and the Ralph Lauren fabrics used in the decor. There are no telephones or televisions in the rooms, but there are fireplaces. The dark, gleaming mahogany in this stately 1905 Edwardian home was originally commissioned as a wedding gift, and the seemingly heavy interior is offset by the classic, sunny conservatory, where breakfast and afternoon tea—both included in the rate—are often served. The Beaconsfield also offers a cozy beach cottage for two near the University of Victoria with a Jacuzzi, outdoor hot tub, kitchen, and TV/VCR. *$$$; MC, V; cheques OK; beacons field@islandnet.com; www.islandnet.com/beaconsfield; at Vancouver St.* &

Craigmyle Guest House / ★

1037 CRAIGDARROCH RD; 250/595-5411 OR 888/595-5411

Built as a guest house early in the 20th century, the Craigmyle stands next to Craigdarroch Castle (see Top 10 Attractions in this chapter) and close to the Art Gallery of Greater Victoria, in the Rockland district, about 1.6 kilometres (1 mile) from downtown. The best rooms face the neighbouring castle. A large breakfast with homemade preserves and good coffee is served, and the main lounge features traditional wainscotting, lofty ceilings, an enormous fireplace, and annoying easy-listening music. Reasonably priced, the Craigmyle is one of the few guest houses in Victoria that allows children. *$; AE, MC, V; no cheques; craigmyle@vicsurf.com; www.bctravel.com/craigmyle.html; off Fort St.*

Dashwood Manor / ★★

1 COOK ST; 250/385-5517 OR 800/667-5517

Built in 1912, the Tudor-style Dashwood Manor overlooks the Strait of Juan de Fuca and the Olympic Mountains from its waterfront location. The dark oak panelling and burgundy carpeting of the lobby only hint at what you'll find in each of the hotel's 15 suites. Stay in one of the upstairs suites, where the view is more than worth its weight in gold on a sunny day. Each has a queen-size bed and a kitchen that is stocked with coffee and tea, and includes breakfast service in the price. Some suites have extra touches, such as a Jacuzzi, a private balcony, or a fireplace. Guests are greeted in the evenings with a complimentary glass of sherry, port, or wine in the lobby. *$$; AE, DC, JCB, MC, V; no cheques; www.dashwoodmanor.com; at Dallas Rd.*

The Empress / ★★★

721 GOVERNMENT ST; 250/384-8111 OR 800/441-1414

Canadian Pacific has owned this ivy-covered landmark hotel since the day it opened in 1908. This is where the Nixons honeymooned and Bob Hope once hit golf balls off the front lawn. With its commanding, front-seat view of the provincial government's Parliament Buildings and the inner harbour, the Empress stands like a grande dame before an admiring audience. It was one of the final flourishes of the Victorian era (even though it's technically Edwardian). The opulent marble lobby and grand staircase sweep visitors up to the Tea Lobby and Bengal Lounge (see Top 10 Attractions in this chapter), or to one of the 474 rooms or suites. Guest rooms are furnished with restored Victorian antiques, including ceiling fans—you don't usually need air-conditioning in Victoria's temperate climate. The deluxe rooms have harbour views. Accessed by a private stairway, the eight honeymoon suites have four-poster canopy beds. The Entree Gold rooms have the nicest furnishings and the best views; they also come with private check-in and concierge services, upgraded amenities, and a separate lounge, where a complimentary continental breakfast is served. From October to May be sure to ask for reservations at the "best room rate;" there are often unadvertised specials. Pack your marriage licence between November 1 and January 1 and, depending on occupancy through March, you can check into the hotel paying the equivalent of the year you married as room rate (maximum of three nights): if you married in 1958, you pay only $58 a night. *$$$; AE, DC, MC, V; cheques OK; cdick@emp.mhs.compuserve.com; www.vvv.com/empress; Inner Harbour.*

The Gatsby Mansion / ★

309 BELLEVILLE ST; 250/388-9191

Across the street from the Seattle ferry terminal, there's an 1897 heritage hotel that's been faithfully restored and preserved to resemble a cozy seaside resort out of the Roaring Twenties. A hand-painted, ceramic-tiled fireplace, rich wood panelling, crystal chandeliers, restored ceiling frescoes, and stained-glass windows are just a few of the fine touches found in the public areas. The 20 guest rooms feature down duvets and a few select antiques. Some rooms offer private parlours, and some have harbour views. The Gatsby's dining room serves breakfast (included in your room charge), as well as lunch and dinner daily. It features simple fare, such as pastas and steaks. There's also a licensed lounge with a good martini menu. *$$$; AE, DC, JCB, MC, V; no cheques; across from Seattle ferry terminal.*

The Haterleigh / ★★

243 KINGSTON ST; 250/384-9995

The Haterleigh House was built in 1901 by Thomas Hooper, an architect who designed many of the city's Victorian homes. The house and intimate garden have been well preserved and well restored. Fine, curved, stained-glass windows grace the parlour. Geared toward romance, all six rooms are spacious, and charmingly decorated with antiques. Ground-floor rooms have 3.6-metre (12-foot)-high ceilings. And four rooms have a Jacuzzi. We especially like the Secret Garden Room, which has a lovely view of the Olympic Mountains. Breakfast might include goldenrod eggs (a variation of eggs Benedict), a fruit plate, and homemade baked goods. Upon arrival, guests enjoy a glass of sherry and samples of rich Rogers' chocolates, made in Victoria. *$$$; MC, V; no cheques; paulk@tnet.net; www.vvv.com/~paulk; at Pendray St.*

Heritage House / ★

3808 HERITAGE LN; 250/479-0892

This 1910 beauty is 5 kilometres (3 miles) from downtown. The four rooms (which share three baths) have been redecorated to the house's original Craftsman style, and are enchanting. So is the Garden Room, a reading room with three walls of windows. Downstairs, the fireplace parlour is a cozy place; a wraparound porch provides ample seating for those who appreciate gardens—and the one here is splendid. Gourmet breakfasts consist of several courses and—if you're lucky—a much-praised salmon quiche. Two-day minimum stay. *$; MC, V; no cheques; www. victoriabc.com/accom/heritage.html; off McKenzie Ave.*

Joan Brown's B&B / ★★

729 PEMBERTON RD; 250/592-5929

Joan Brown may monopolize the conversation at the breakfast table, but most visitors enjoy listening to her tales. This lovely wisteria-draped house is in the renowned Rockland neighbourhood, a short drive from downtown. The spacious rooms—a few are ballroom-size—and Joan's quirky ways of running an inn (and her eccentric sense of humor) make this stately bed-and-breakfast a comfortable stay for those who prefer a traditional B&B with lots of personality. Our choice of room is the one with the Second Empire flavour, furnished with a king-size bed, fireplace, bath, and bay window. Nothing could be better for a rainy afternoon than a perusal of the well-stocked library. *$$; no credit cards; cheques OK; off Fort St.*

Laurel Point Inn / ★★★

680 MONTREAL ST; 250/386-8721 OR 800/663-7667

Laurel Point's modern, angular construction rests on a promontory, offering views of the inner harbour or the ship channel from each of its

ROUGHING IT IN LUXURY

At $1,200 (U.S.) per day, the **NIMMO BAY RESORT** (250/956-4000 or 800/837-HELI; heli@nimmobay.bc.ca) isn't cheap. But what a day! At this luxurious hideaway, which clings to the edge of the rugged forests of Mackenzie Sound, a day includes fly-fishing a river so high in the mountains it's accessible only by helicopter, lunch on a glacier at 2,100 metres (7,000 feet), beachcombing along the remote sand beaches of Vancouver Island's west coast, and a hot tub by a waterfall and dinner flawlessly prepared by a name chef at the end of it all. At Nimmo Bay, guests whirl off daily in six-passenger choppers, the pilots their personal guides. Is it worth it? There are poems of praise from corporate movers and shakers and a 75 percent return rate. Jimmy Pattison took George Bush to Nimmo Bay to heli-fish with owner Craig Murray, who says his 16-year operation offers "the inside of joy." Joyous nonfishing experiences include heli-ventures such as white-water rafting, whale watching, spelunking (otherwise known as caving), kayaking, and hiking. Naturally, at these rates, everything's included—fabulous meals, private-label wines, and all your heli-activities.   —*Kasey Wilson*

130 rooms and 72 suites. We like the junior suites in the newer, south wing, which are beautifully appointed with graceful, modern Japanese decor and huge, furnished, glass-enclosed balconies with floor-to-ceiling windows. Spacious marble bathrooms are fitted with soaker tubs and sexy, peekaboo stall showers. The channel-side rooms have the best view of the boats, seaplanes, the Olympic Mountains, a reflecting pool, and a sculptured Japanese garden at the water's edge. Rooms in the older, north wing are average, although some have a nice view of the inner harbour. Facilities include a heated indoor pool, sauna, and fitness center. The dining room, Cafe Laurel, is a wicker-and-fern affair, with good food. *$$$; AE, DC, JCB, MC, V; no cheques; laurelpoint@ampsc.com; www.island net.com/~cvcprod/laurel.html; at Belleville St.* &

Oak Bay Beach Hotel / ★★
1175 BEACH DR; 250/598-4556 OR 800/668-7758
This Tudor-style hotel, presiding over Haro Strait, is in the loveliest part of Victoria and is a nice place to stay if you want to be out of the downtown core. Even so, it's a busy spot—especially its bar. It evokes a British world; handsome Victorian and Edwardian antiques dot the comfortable rooms that are full of nooks and gables. The best rooms are those with private balconies and a water view. Some of the rooms seem a little down-at-heel. The hotel's private yacht can be booked for dinner cruises, sightseeing, and fishing charters. A new chef has put the dining room, Bentley's on the Bay, back on the culinary map. For a casual atmosphere,

opt for libations in the inviting English pub, Snug, where you can sit before the fire with your pint. Across the street is the private Victoria Golf Club, dramatically bordered by the sea (ask about their golf getaway package). And do enjoy the hotel's afternoon tea—a proper affair that deserves (but doesn't require) proper attire. *$$$; AE, DC, MC, V; cheques OK; near Oak Bay Ave.*

Ocean Pointe Resort / ★★

45 SONGHEES RD; 250/360-2999 OR 800/667-4677
You can't miss Ocean Pointe Resort as you enter the inner harbour from the sea. The massive 250-room, 34-suite waterfront resort stands as a modern counterpoint to the classic Empress and the provincial government's Parliament Buildings on the other side of the harbour. The lobby is elegant, with lots of marble and dramatic flower arrangements. The guest rooms themselves are understated, in pale earth tones and light furnishings, and the ones facing the harbour have a great view. Stay at Ocean Pointe to enjoy its facilities, especially the pool and the luxurious European spa. There's a choice of restaurants for fine or informal dining (see Top 20 Restaurants in this chapter). It's a short walk over the Johnson Street Bridge to the heart of downtown, or you can hop on a harbour ferry at the hotel's own dock. *$$$; AE, DC, JCB, MC, V; no cheques; ocean_pointe@pinc.com; www.oprhotel.com; at Esquimalt Rd.* &

The Prior House / ★★

620 ST CHARLES; 250/592-8847
No imitation here: this grand B&B occupies an English mansion built during the Edwardian period for the king's representative in British Columbia. It's in the quiet Rockland neighbourhood, about 1.6 kilometres (1 mile) from downtown. Many of the rooms have fireplaces and views of water; the Lieutenant Governor's Suite has an extravagant bath with a whirlpool tub, gold fixtures, and crystal chandeliers. Innkeeper Candis Cooperrider prepares a full breakfast that may be taken in the dining room or in the privacy of your room. Afternoon tea is served at 4pm. Families with children older than 9 years may stay in one of the lower-level Garden Suites, which have private entrances and full kitchens. *$$$; MC, V; Canadian cheques only; innkeeper@priorhouse.com; www. priorhouse.com; at Rockland Ave.*

Ramada Huntingdon Manor / ★

330 QUEBEC ST; 250/381-3456 OR 800/663-7557
Don't be misled by the Ramada name: this is not a typical chain motel. A comfortable antique-furnished parlour with a blazing log fireplace and an indoor whirlpool and sauna make for a pleasant stay. Rooms are nicely furnished, some with four-poster beds, and the spacious two-storey gallery suites have bedroom lofts. A good choice for families, and kids under 18

stay free. This is a full-service hotel with a reliable restaurant, and some rooms even have kitchen facilities. The location, a block from the Victoria Clipper terminal, is convenient yet fairly quiet. *$$; AE, DC, MC, V; no cheques; huntingdon@visual.net; www.visual.net/store front/huntingdon; at Oswego St.* &

Swans Hotel / ★

506 PANDORA AVE; 250/361-3310 OR 800/668-7926
Behind the traditional facade of this 1913 building hide 29 modern suites, complete with kitchen facilities and living areas. The two-bedroom suites are an especially good deal for families, as they don't cost much more than a studio and can sleep up to six—although there is an additional charge for more than two people in a room. The decor is bland, but you get plenty of room to spread out. Especially in summer, be sure to ask for a room away from the pub; it can be noisy. Remember, as well, like most hotels in Victoria, Swans does not have air-conditioning. The downstairs cafe and pub (which serves beer brewed on the premises) are lively gathering spots. In the pub, the menu matches in quality and preparation the ales, lagers, and stouts from the on-site brewery. A glassed-in terrace allows diners to watch the action without being blown away on a windy day. *$$; AE, DC, JCB, MC, V; no cheques; swans@islandnet. com; www.islandnet.com/~swans; at Store St.*

Top 10 Attractions

1) VICTORIA'S HISTORIC BUILDINGS

From Point Ellice to View Royal, but mostly downtown The 19th-century Scottish and British immigrants who settled Vancouver Island left their physical mark on this city, building everything from humble thatched cottages to magnificent mansions and opulent public buildings.

You can start a tour of these heritage buildings by boarding the little **VICTORIA HARBOUR FERRY** (250/708-0201) at the inner harbour for the 10-minute cruise up the Gorge (a long, narrow, saltwater inlet) to the **POINT ELLICE HOUSE** (2616 Pleasant St; 250/387-4697). There, you step up onto the landing dock and back into the 19th century. (Tip: Arrive by water, not by land. Neighbouring auto repair garages could spoil the mood.) Until 1977, Point Ellice was the home of the gardening-besotted O'Reilly family, whose slip into genteel poverty meant subsequent generations never replaced the original Victorian furnishings. Sir John A. Macdonald, Canada's first prime minister, once dined at this spot. June is when the thick scent of old-fashioned damask roses permeates the air from the garden. Sundays are best, and quietest, as Point Ellice is the last bastion of peace on the now quite noisy Pleasant Street. Afternoon tea is still served, during the summer only, on the croquet lawn from 1 to 4pm Thursday through Sunday (reservations are suggested). *Admission charged (children under 6 free); Thurs–Mon, 11am–5pm (summer).*

Take the ferry back to **THE EMPRESS HOTEL** (721 Government St; 250/384-8111). It was designed by architect Francis Mawson Rattenbury. Rattenbury, a story unto himself, obtained his first commission after his arrival from England at the age of 25. The commission? The provincial government's **PARLIAMENT BUILDINGS** (501 Belleville St; 250/387-3046 for tours) in 1897. The beautiful Empress Hotel, which was completed by the Canadian Pacific Railway in 1907, shows off its finest during December, when it's decorated for Christmas. Whether you arrive that month or during the bright, sunny days of summer, you should take a peek back into an earlier, gentler time at this heritage building. Check the hotel's archives on the lower level to learn about the days when a suite cost $15, when the king of Siam and Rudyard Kipling stayed in this opulent edifice, when the William F. Tickle Orchestra played, and when wartime menus urged, "All persons in ordering their food ought to consider the needs of Great Britain and her Allies and their Armies for wheat, beef, bacon, and fats."

AFTERNOON TEA is served in, of course, the **TEA LOBBY**. In high season (May through October), the six-course, traditional menu is more than a meal and carries a hefty $39 per-person price tag. First the hotel's private blend of tea is served. Then a fresh fruit compote arrives. Sparkling wine, sherry, and port are offered, but not included in the prix fixe. Next a three-tiered tray arrives, bearing a series of savoury and sweet delights. Crustless sandwiches range from traditional cucumber to salmon-and-cream-cheese rolled in whole-meal bread. The scones are served with the requisitely rich clotted cream and strawberry preserves. The layered cakes are frosted with the butteriest lemon- or chocolate-cream frosting. The plate of crisp tea biscuits bring you back down to earth as they accompany your departing sips. **BENGAL LOUNGE** also offers a lunch buffet, featuring a lovely assortment of curries for $15.95. A dress code at the Empress calls for "smart casual" attire and includes jeans, but not running shoes, short shorts, or tank tops. *Afternoon tea in the Tea Lobby every day at 12:30pm, 2pm, and 3:30pm; reservations required. Bengal Lounge open every day 11am–midnight.*

The 19th-century painter and notorious eccentric Emily Carr was born in **CARR HOUSE** (207 Government St; 250/387-4697). This is where her father's gardening habits inspired her to comment that her father "was more British than Britain." (She's often wrongly credited with making this observation about Victoria.) When she wasn't creating one of her magnificent paintings later in life, she ran a James Bay boarding house. Terrorizing the guests with her menagerie—which included a monkey, a white rat, stray cats, and bobtailed sheepdogs—Carr once turned a garden hose on a boarder who refused to bring in his washing. *Admission charged; every day (last weekend in May–second weekend in Oct).*

The residence of a pioneer doctor who settled here during the 1850s can also be viewed. **HELMCKEN HOUSE** (675 Belleville St, behind Thunderbird Park; 250/387-4697) still contains the original imported British furnishings and the good doctor's medicine chest. *Admission charged (children 6 and under free); Thurs–Mon 11am–5pm (summer).*

Head east to the four-storey-tall **CRAIGDARROCH CASTLE** (1050 Joan Cres; 250/592-5323), which was built during the 1880s to serve as Robert Dunsmuir's home. This Scottish coal-mining magnate had the 39-room, Highland-style castle decorated like the interior of a Gothic novel to induce his wife, Joan, to stay in the "wild west." It worked: she stayed until her death in 1908. Detailed woodwork, Persian carpets, stained-glass windows, paintings, and sculptures fill every regal corner of this monument to one man's devotion. *Admission charged (children 5 and under free); every day, 9am–7pm (Sept–mid-June 10am–4:30pm).*

It's a bit of a drive to see how rural Victorians lived, but it's worth it to see **CRAIGFLOWER FARMHOUSE** (110 Island Hwy, View Royal; 250/387-3067). Built in 1856, the house and grounds still contain many of the furnishings and tools imported by the original Scottish owner when he settled here. *Admission charged (children 5 and under free); Thurs–Monday 11am–5pm summer.*

2) ROYAL BRITISH COLUMBIA MUSEUM

675 Belleville St; 250/387-3701 or 800/661-5411 The Royal British Columbia Museum is one of the finest of its kind in the country. Outside the entrance to this contemporary concrete-and-glass museum is a glass-enclosed display of Native totem poles and large sculptural works. Displaying dramatic dioramas of BC's temperate rain forest, sea coast, and ocean floor, as well as a full-scale reconstruction of Victorian-era downtown and Chinatown inside, it's definitely a must-see. Of particular interest: the **NORTHWEST COAST FIRST NATIONS** exhibit, which is rich with spiritual and cultural artifacts. There's also an IMAX theatre and **THUNDERBIRD PARK**, where the Mungo Martin longhouse and a handful of totem poles remind visitors of the city's original heritage. Admission tickets are good for 24 hours so if you go after noon, you can go back the next morning. *Admission charged (children 4 and under free); every day (except Christmas and New Year's Day), 9am–5pm; www.rbcm1.bcm. gov.bc.ca.*

3) BUTCHART GARDENS

800 Benvenuto Ave, Brentwood Bay; 250/652-4422 Butchart Gardens is a mecca for gardening enthusiasts from every corner of the globe. At the turn of the century, cement manufacturer Robert Butchart exhausted the limestone quarry near his home. Rather than leaving the land to waste, his wife, Jenny, relandscaped the quarry into what was named the Sunken Garden, which opened to the public in 1904. Jenny's gardening prowess was widely acclaimed, inspiring her to add an English rose garden (populated with ducks, peacocks, and trained pigeons), as well as two sections designed in Italian and Japanese styles on the remaining 20 hectares (50 acres). Eventually the Butcharts realized they'd gotten carried away and opened their house and gardens as an attraction. Their grandson now owns and manages this year-round floral spectacle with a million-plus plants. Consider visiting in the evenings, when the gardens are illuminated with thousands of coloured lights, crowds are thinner, and entertainers give free performances. **FIREWORKS DISPLAYS**, set to music, add further sparkle on Saturday nights in July and August. Lunch, dinner, and **AFTERNOON TEA** are offered in the **DINING ROOM RESTAURANT** (reservations 250/652-8222) located in the historic residence. A more casual menu is served in the **BLUE POPPY RESTAURANT**; you can get a quick snack in the **QUARRY COFFEE HOUSE**. At the **SEED AND GIFT STORE**, you'll find a fine selection of plant seeds, gardening books, cards, calendars, and other collectibles. The gardens are 20 minutes from downtown Victoria. Take Blanchard Street (Highway 17) north toward the ferry terminal. Turn left on Keating Crossroads. Admission is charged for adults, and children 5 and older. Tickets are good for 24 hours, so if you go after noon, you can go back the next morning. *Admission charged (children 4 and under free); every day, from 9am (call for seasonal closing times).*

4) CHINATOWN

Store St to Douglas St, Johnson St to Fisgard St North America's oldest Chinatown was established in Victoria in 1858. The first settlers were mostly men, seeking their fortunes in gold by prospecting or railroad work. But once these work opportunities disappeared, they were employed as servants, dockworkers, and factory laborers. (Sunday was their official day off, starting after lunch and ending Monday morning. Consequently, polite society in Victoria didn't entertain callers on Sunday afternoons because their servants weren't available.) Although Chinatown covers only about six blocks, centering on Fisgard and Government Streets, this area still speaks of its rich heritage. Newly arrived mainland Chinese got their first break, in the form of spiritual and physical aid, in a balconied building on Government Street, the **CHINESE SETTLEMENT HOUSE** (1715 Government St). A Buddhist temple was on the ground floor; living quarters and social services were offered until a job was secured and living quarters were arranged. The original temple has since been moved to the second floor.

A half-block along, at 36 Fisgard Street, is another historic building. The pagoda-style **CHINESE IMPERIAL SCHOOL** (*Zhongua Xuetang*) was constructed by the Chinese Benevolent Society in 1908, the year after the Victoria School Board banned non-Canadian-born Chinese children from attending public school. Today it offers standard classes, as well as Chinese language instruction, for all ages on weekends.

Arching the entry to Fisgard Street at the corner of Government Street is the dragon-headed **GATE OF HARMONIOUS INTEREST**, completed in 1882 and restored in 1997 by the Chinese Benevolent Society to commemorate the visit of Princess Carolina Louise Alberta. The two stone lions that guard the foot of the gate were imported from Suzchou, China.

About halfway down the block is **FAN TAN ALLEY**, Canada's narrowest thoroughfare. It's nestled between Fisgard Street and Pandora Avenue, about a half-block west of Government Street. It measures just 1.2 metres (4 feet) across at both ends, although it widens to 1.8 metres (6 feet) in the center. Its doorways still bear their original Chinese signage and lead to a labyrinth of small courtyards that were once home to a factory that legally produced opium (until 1907), and ran gambling parlours and bachelor rooming houses. Those enterprises have been replaced by craft shops and clothing stores, such as **HEART'S CONTENT** (18 Fan Tan Alley; 250/380-1234), which purveys hip apparel like Doc Marten shoes and Ray Troll T-shirts. The alley's exotic allure has all but vanished, although **TURTLE EXPRESS** (3 Fan Tan Alley; 250/384-2227) offers southern Asian imports such as jewellery, fabric, and decorative items.

There are all sorts of imported Chinese items that can be purchased on Fisgard Street, ranging from food and medicinal herbs to dishware and furniture. **MAGPIE GIFT STUDIO** (556 Fisgard St; 250/383-1880) carries small, decorative Chinese and Japanese antiques and reproduction items such as rosewood boxes with jade and brass inlay. **EASTERN INTERIORS** (572 Fisgard St; 250/385-4643) is housed in a former Buddhist temple. It purveys large, museum-quality furniture and accessories.

MARKET SQUARE (560 Johnson St; 250/386-2441) is home to 45 craft, toy, and gift shops, as well as restaurants. Back in 1887, this is where 23 factories produced 90,000 pounds of opium for Canada's legal trade of the narcotic. Today, artist Bill Blair and partner Shelora Sheldan fill the tiny, colourful **HOI POLLOI** (Market Square; 250/480-7822) with weird and wonderful goodies, from his birch-bark lamp shades with Rosemarie-era Mounties painted on them to Mexican Day of the Dead skull-headed figures, as well as an artful selection of postcards.

If you'd like to take a guided stroll through the neighbourhood, call **LES CHAN** (250/383-7317) to see if he's running one of his popular tours of tea shops, temples, and herbalists, which include a scrumptious dim sum lunch at **KWONG TUNG SEAFOOD RESTAURANT** (548 Fisgard St; 250/381-1223).

5) MARITIME MUSEUM OF BRITISH COLUMBIA

28 Bastion Square; 250/385-4222 In under an hour, you can walk across downtown or stroll along most of the waterfront, past the sailboats and floatplanes to Bastion Square and the former provincial courthouse. That's where one of Victoria's lesser known but fascinating attractions is—the Maritime Museum. The museum houses more than 5,000 artifacts, including the *Trekka*—a 6-metre (20-foot) ketch that sailed solo around the world during the 1950s, and *Tilikum*—a converted 11.5-metre (38-foot) Native dugout canoe that made an equally impressive two-year passage to England at the turn of the century. *Admission charged (children 5 and under free); every day (except Christmas Day), 9am–4:30pm.*

6) BEACON HILL PARK

Southgate St to Dallas Rd, between Douglas and Cook Sts It's a fairly short walk from downtown and the Royal British Columbia Museum to the 75-hectare (187-acre) Beacon Hill Park. The park has splendid ocean views, as well as impressive stands of indigenous Garry oak trees. These distinctive-looking—and protected—trees are found in BC only on Vancouver Island and two of the Gulf Islands (Salt Spring and Hornby). Donated to the city by the Hudson's Bay Company in 1882, the park also features manicured lawns, ponds, colourful floral gardens, picnic tables, and a 100-year-old cricket field. It's a lovely spot to escape from the downtown shopping mania. The **BEACON HILL CHILDREN'S FARM** (Circle Dr; 250/381-2532) offers a wading pool, pony rides, and a petting zoo filled with friendly barnyard animals. *Admission by donation; every day (mid-March to Sept), 9am–5pm.*

A city of many beautiful outdoor gardens, Victoria even has a notable indoor one. Designed by architect Francis Rattenbury (he of Parliament Buildings and Empress Hotel fame), the **CRYSTAL GARDEN** (731 Douglas St; 250/381-1277) first opened as a huge saltwater pool in 1925. In fact, older locals remember when the 1930s *Tarzan* star, Johnny Weismuller, competed in it. It now houses a tropical rain forest and is filled with all sorts of exotic fauna and flora. Don't let the street-level souvenir shops deter you from visiting it. The array of coral flamingoes, macaws, butterflies, and jungle foliage can be a welcome ray of sunshine on even the dreariest rainy day. *Admission charged; every day, 10am–5:30pm.*

7) ART GALLERY OF GREATER VICTORIA

1040 Moss St; 250/384-4101 This gallery features one of the world's finest collections of Oriental art and the only Shinto shrine in North America. Housed in a contemporary structure that extends into the Edwardian-style Spencer mansion (which was donated to the city in the 1950s), it includes nearly 10,000 works of art, including paintings and drawings by premier BC artist Emily Carr, European painters, and contemporary Canadian artists. The museum store is a wonderful place to shop. *Admission charged (children 11 and under free); Mon–Wed and Sat 10am–5pm, Thurs 10am–9pm, Sun 1pm–5pm.*

8) THE ROYAL LONDON WAX MUSEUM

470 Belleville St; 250/388-4461 This wax museum is worth a visit—and a chuckle—even if you've seen the original Madame Tussaud's in London. The 300 hand-crafted wax figures were imported from the famed waxworks, including a few gory favourites from her infamous Chamber of Horrors. *Admission charged; every day, 9am–7:30pm; www.wax world.com.*

9) FISGARD LIGHTHOUSE NATIONAL HISTORIC SITE & FORT RODD HILL

603 Fort Rodd Hill Rd; 250/478-5849 The Fisgard Lighthouse, perched on a volcanic-rock point, has guided ships toward Victoria's sheltered harbour since 1873. This is Canada's oldest beacon on the Pacific. Displayed on two floors of the lightkeeper's house are the stories of the lighthouse, its caretakers, and the terrible shipwrecks (more than 2,000!) that gave the Vancouver Island coastline the ominous name "the graveyard of the Pacific."

Fort Rodd Hill is so close to the lighthouse that the concussion from the artillery guns once blew out the lighthouse windows. The exciting history of this 1890s coastal artillery garrison can be viewed from its original guns, camouflaged searchlights, and underground magazines. Multimedia presentations, room re-creations, and artifact displays inform and entertain. Bring a lunch so you can picnic on the grounds, where military concerts are held on summer Sunday afternoons. *Admission charged (children 5 and under free); every day, 10am–5:30pm.*

10) PACIFIC UNDERSEA GARDENS

490 Belleville St; 250/382-5717 If living creatures are to your liking, you will be pleased to know that about 5,000 different species feed, play, hunt, and, um, court in the protected waters of the inner harbour. Wolf eels, sea anemones, sea stars, sturgeon, stonefish, sharks, seals, and salmon are just a few of the denizens to be found when you descend into the Pacific Undersea Gardens via a sloping stairway that leads to a glass-enclosed, underwater viewing area. Injured and orphaned seal pups are rehabilitated in holding pens alongside the observatory as part of a provincial marine-mammal rescue program. *Admission charged (children 4 and under free); every day, 9am–5pm (10am–5pm Sept–April).*

Shopping

A few of the retail shops along Government Street take you back to Queen Victoria's era. You'll pass heritage buildings with gleaming brass, mahogany, and stained-glass interiors. One of these is the century-old **MORRIS TOBACCONIST** (1116 Government St; 250/382-4811). It ships custom-blended tobaccos throughout the world, offers both Cuban and non-Cuban cigars, and stocks nifty shaving gear, smoking accessories, seltzer bottles, and walking sticks. **MUNRO'S BOOK STORE** (1108 Government St; 250/382-2464), which *Maclean's* columnist Allan Fotheringham once called "Canada's best bookstore" is a real book-lovers' bookstore—a great selection of literature and children's books. There's also **ROGERS' CHOCOLATES** (913 Government St; 250/384-7021; www.rogerschocolates.com), whose chocolate-covered Victoria creams—in many flavors such as raspberry, mint, and coffee—are nearly the size of hockey pucks. They have even been shipped to Buckingham Palace.

Modern-day Scottish, Irish, and English jackets, sweaters, kilts, and blankets can be found at **PRESCOTT & ANDREW** (909 Government St; 250/384-2515). **THE EDINBURGH TARTAN SHOP** (921 Government St; 250/388-9312) purveys a fine selection of Highland items, including kilt pins, ties, and woollen scarves in every conceivable weave of clan tartan.

The **VICTORIA EATON CENTRE** (Government St between Fort St and View St) houses **BRITISH IMPORTERS** (250/386-1496), whose present store, complete with Italian leather floor tiles and handmade lighting fixtures, won a national design award. Its exclusive line of products goes beyond sturdy English brollies and Bally shoes to Armani and Valentino couture.

Serious antique hunters should head for **ANTIQUE ROW,** in the 800 to 1100 blocks of Fort Street. **LIBERTY VICTORIA ANTIQUES AND ART** (826 Fort St; 250/385-6733) has a beautiful collection of interior-decorator-quality, Edwardian-era furnishings and accessories. **HIBERNIA ANTIQUES** (1034 Fort St; 250/286-0911) is filled with Scottish and Irish antiques from the Victorian and Edwardian periods.

If your shopping tastes lean toward indigenous crafts, then head to the **COWICHAN TRADING COMPANY** (1328 Government St; 250/383-0321) and the **INDIAN CRAFT SHOPPE** (905 Government St; 250/382-3643), both of which stock some of the finest, warmest Cowichan sweaters available. Traditional animal and geometric motifs are knitted by local Native women into these thick, one-piece, wool, jacket-style garments. This shop also carries Native carvings, moccasins, and jewellery. Nova Scotia woollens, maple-sugar candy, salmon jerky, and other Canadian-made delights are offered at the **JAMES BAY TRADING COMPANY** (1102 Government St; 250/388-5477).

Victoria has more than a dozen places to appreciate and purchase Yuletide ornaments and decorations, including **THE SPIRIT OF CHRIST-MAS** (1022 Government St; 250/385-2501) and the gift shop at the **ART GALLERY OF GREATER VICTORIA** (see Top 10 Attractions in this chapter).

Aviation buffs will enjoy **CONTRAILS—THE AVIATION STORE** (19 Bastion Square; 250/361-4745), where pilots from the First World War to the Gulf War have signed the logbook. Posters, books, insignia, and loads of aviator history abound here. **DIG THIS** (45 Bastion Square; 250/385-3213) is a gardener's dream come true for tools, plants, seeds, containers, furniture, and lawn ornaments.

Performing Arts

Built at the turn of the century and renovated during the 1970s, the **ROYAL THEATRE** (805 Broughton St; box office 250/386-6121) presents concerts by the Victoria Symphony, as well as dance recitals and touring stage plays. The **VICTORIA SYMPHONY ORCHESTRA** (846 Broughton St; 250/385-9771) performs frequent evening concerts on weekdays and weekends from August through May. The orchestra kicks off its season with its internationally acclaimed Symphony Splash. It's a free concert on the waterfront, performed at the inner harbour. Tickets for most other concerts are about $12.

The box office for the Royal Theatre is located at another performing-arts venue, the **MCPHERSON PLAYHOUSE** (3 Centennial Square; 250/386-6121). This garishly ornate Edwardian edifice, built as North America's first Pantages Vaudeville Theatre in 1914, is the home of the Pacific Opera Victoria and the Victoria Operatic Society. The box office is open Monday through Saturday, 9:30am to 5:30pm (6 to 8:30pm on performance days). **PACIFIC OPERA VICTORIA** (1316B Government St; 250/385-0222) presents three different productions during the months of September, February, and April. Five performances of each production, which range from Mozart and Tchaikovsky to Gilbert and Sullivan, are performed at the McPherson Playhouse. Tickets range from $15 to $50. The **VICTORIA OPERATIC SOCIETY** (798 Fairview Rd; 250/381-1021) mounts Broadway musical performances such as *Evita* and *Into the Woods* year-round at the same theatre. Ticket prices range from $12 to $20.

When the lights go down low, head for **BELFRY THEATRE** (1219 Gladstone Ave; 250/385-6815) in the village of Fernwood. It's a wonderful converted heritage church, where nationally acclaimed productions of drama and music draw Vancouverites across the Strait of Georgia from October to April. Tickets average $16 per person; seniors and students get discounts. The box office is open every day from 9am to 5pm.

The annual **VICTORIA FRINGE FESTIVAL** takes place from late April through mid-September. Hosted by the Intrepid Theatre Company (Fringe Theatre, 602-620 View St; 250/383-2663), the festival has events scheduled from noon to midnight each day and includes the work of 50 international alternative-performance companies at seven different downtown venues. Tickets are $8 or less, with proceeds going to the performers. The Intrepid Theatre Company hosts a **SHAKESPEARE FESTIVAL** at the water's edge at the inner harbour during the month of August. Tickets are $10 for most performances.

Tiny, quirky, 50-seat **THEATRE INCONNU** (Market Square; 250/380-1284) likes to take risks with new playwrights, occasional nudity, and Shakespeare. It performs in the square itself and elsewhere in town on an irregular basis. The lead actor may be the person who takes your under-$10 ticket or serves coffee at intermission. The **VIC THEATRE** (808 Douglas St) shows higher-brow, alternative, and art films.

Nightlife

Contrary to the city's quiet nighttime reputation, there's a thriving jazz scene. The **TERRIFVIC DIXIELAND JAZZ FESTIVAL** (250/381-5277) takes place for five days during late April. An international entourage of musicians perform swing, Dixie, honky-tonk, fusion, and improv at venues all over Victoria. The **INTERNATIONAL JAZZ FEST** (250/388-4423) continues the beat during June. Swing, bebop, fusion, and improv are presented at noon-hour and evening performances at Market Square and other venues around the city. **SUNFEST** (250/953-2033) is an end-of-summer jazz festival that's held the third weekend of August at Market Square.

Sporting a laid-back ambience, **HERMANN'S DIXIELAND INN** (753 View St; 250/388-9166) is a low-lit Dixeland supper club. Dinners are reasonably priced (under $20 per entree) and so are drinks. The framed photos and posters plastered all over its walls are a "who's who" of the international talent that has performed here. It's open Monday 5pm to 12am, Tuesday to Friday 11:30am to 12:30am, and Saturday 4pm to 12:30am.

There are other forms of nighttime entertainment to be found in Victoria as well. **PAGLIACCI'S** (1011 Broad St; 250/386-1662) is a brash, loud Italian restaurant that's packed with people nearly every night. Imagine yourself in a Little Italy hot spot in Manhattan and you'll get the picture. Live musical entertainment changes the conversational pace Sunday through Thursday nights.

PLANET (15 Bastion Square; 250/385-5333) is a big-club, waterfront venue for high-profile performers like B. B. King and the Crash Test

Dummies. Hot local bands play anything from reggae to rock here as well. DJs take the stage Thursday, Friday, and Saturday nights. Admission ($3 to $15) depends on who's playing, and drink prices are reasonable.

SWANS BREW PUB (506 Pandora St; 250/361-3310) offers bluegrass and reggae in a laid-back, fern-and-brass atmosphere, combined with good pub food and great microbrews. **SWEETWATERS NITECLUB** (570 Johnson St in Market Square; 250/383-7844) is a basement-level singles hangout that spins Top 40 dance tunes from the last three decades from Tuesday to Saturday. Drinks start at $3 and admission is about the same.

Sooke

From Victoria, drive north on the Trans-Canada Highway (Highway 1) to the Colwood Sooke exit; drive west on Sooke Road (Highway 14) for about 45 minutes.

Sooke sits on Vancouver Island's wild and rugged west coast, but it's less than an hour away from downtown Victoria. Thanks to the protective (and scenic) curve of Washington's mountainous Olympic Peninsula, which looms only 15 miles across the water, much of Sooke is sheltered from the heavy surf, rain, and strong winds associated with the coast at Tofino, farther north. Excellent parks and trails can be accessed at Sooke and the neighbouring communities of Jordan River and Port Renfrew (the southern trailhead of the grueling, world-famous West Coast Trail). All Sooke Day, held the third Saturday in July, is the longest running logger sports event in Canada, attracting about 10,000 visitors annually

EAST SOOKE REGIONAL PARK (East Sooke Rd off Gillespie Rd), with 1,422 hectares (3,512 acres) of natural and protected coastal landscape, is another popular hiking spot. In fact, East Sooke's Coast Trail is one of Canada's premier day hikes. The 10-kilometre (6-mile) trip is challenging for even experienced hikers. Aylard Farm is the starting point here for easy, brief excursions out to a series of ancient Native petroglyphs.

Ask at the **SOOKE INFOCENTRE,** housed at the Sooke Region Museum (Phillips Rd, just off Hwy 14, near the lighthouse), for directions to **FRENCH BEACH PROVINCIAL PARK** and Sandcut Beach (it's easy to miss the sign), for **CHINA BEACH PROVINCIAL PARK** (which has a 15-minute trail that takes you to a secluded sandy beach, with a hidden waterfall at its west end), or for **MYSTIC BEACH** (a rugged 20-minute trail takes you there). Beware of the incoming tide at Mystic; it has trapped unwary people on rocks and sandbars.

The **SOOKE REGION MUSEUM** (250/642-6351) is open Tuesday through Sunday and well worth a stop. Phone first, to ensure you arrive in time for a 20-minute dramatized tour (10am and 4pm) of the restored, turn-of-the-century Moss Cottage. Step over the threshold and you're welcomed into the year 1902. The museum displays Native Indian arti-facts as well as logging equipment, and it sponsors BC's largest juried fine arts show, held every August in the Sooke Arena.

The **GALLOPING GOOSE TRAIL**, a scenic, 60-kilometre (35-mile) unpaved path, was formerly the rail line between Victoria and the appe-tizingly named Leechtown, just north of Sooke. You can, as they say, "walk the Goose, cycle the Goose, or ride the Goose on horseback." The easternmost access to the trail is located across from Six-Mile House on Sooke Road (Highway 14). The stretch that heads east of Sooke along Sooke Basin is the only section of the trail with a waterfront view. A good section heads north to Leechtown, passes through the Sooke Potholes (diving pools and grottoes), goes past the abandoned but still spectacu-lar Deer Trails Conference Centre, and crosses the Tod Creek Trestle. You can rent a bike from Sooke Cycle (5941a 6707 West Coast Rd; 250/642-3123; westwebb.com/sookecycle/). A Sooke Cycle employee will escort you to the trail.

Take a break at the **COUNTRY CUPBOARD CAFE** (402 Sheringham Point Rd, at West Coast Rd; 250/646-2323). The menu is simple: steamed Sooke clams and locally smoked salmon as well as creatively composed sandwiches (think pesto mayo, smoked chicken, herbed sour-dough) are served on their patio at lunchtime during the summer. The decor looks as if it came out of a country-style decorator book: Raggedy Ann dolls and toddler-size tea sets, potbelly stove and dried flowers, heart-shaped stencils and garage-sale knickknacks. But that doesn't keep the local logging contingent from showing up with muddy boots, lured here by the fabulous mile-high, liqueur-infused cheesecakes and crumble-topped pies.

Another spot for a tasty and reasonably priced meal is the **GOOD LIFE BOOKSTORE AND CAFE** (2113 Otter Point Rd, downtown; 250/642-6821). It's obvious by the name that you'll be surrounded by books while munching in this store that's been converted from an old house. At lunchtime, choose from lox quesadilla (with apple, tomato, red onion, and provolone wrapped in a flour tortilla) or a grilled vegetable Wellington (marinated vegetables folded in puff pastry and drizzled with a roasted-garlic cream sauce). The dinner selections, such as a rich bouil-labaisse (made with local seafood and fish in a rich broth) or a grilled rib-eye steak (with mushrooms, pearl onions, and horseradish sauce), are a pleasant surprise.

If it's all too beautiful to leave behind at the end of the day, there are places to stay and dine in Sooke that are destinations in themselves. You'll have to book way-y-y in advance to stay at **SOOKE HARBOUR HOUSE** (1528 Whiffen Spit Rd; 250/642-3421; www.sookeharbourhouse. com), but it has a cornucopia of rewards. Perched along the waterside at the end of a residential road, the original white clapboard farmhouse, which serves as the main building of this peaceful inn, dates back to 1929. There are 30 unusually designed and decorated guest rooms—they modestly call them rooms, but in reality they're all suites—that take their names from the selection of original Native and local art housed in each one. The Victor Newman Longhouse Room gives you an idea of what to expect from this hotel: the room has a serene ocean view, stunning Native ceremonial masks, a two-sided fireplace, a soaker tub, a private balcony, a wet bar, and plenty of comfortable seats for curling up and reading. Bouquets of fresh flowers, a decanter of fine port, fresh-baked butter cookies, books and magazines, a telephone, and soft terry bathrobes provide the frosting on this fabulous cake. Take a stroll along the adjacent Whiffen Spit, which extends out into the harbour from the inn's front yard; during the night listen to the melodic waves singing as they draw away from the pebbly shore. A lavish breakfast, such as hazelnut–maple syrup waffles with loganberry purée, or fresh garden vegetable quiche with scones and preserves, is delivered to your room in the morning. An outstanding box lunch, prepared upon request, is far superior to the food offered on the ferry to Vancouver. Both meals are included in the price of your stay. Dinner at Sooke Harbour House is exquisite—see Top 20 Restaurants in this chapter for a full review.

If you desire an English country-garden setting with a chocolate Labrador at your side, book into **MARKHAM HOUSE** (1853 Connie Rd; 250/642-7542; mail@markhamhouse.com; www.markhamhouse.com). The Lab is Virgil and he's as welcoming as his owners. Innkeepers Lyall and Sally Markham know when to leave you to yourself and when to sit and chat with you on the veranda of their Tudor-style B&B. People go to Markham House for its gentle pleasures: fireside port before turning in, feather beds, country hospitality. The immaculately groomed grounds encompass a small river, a trout pond, a putting green, and glorious iris gardens (home to more than 100 species). There are two bedrooms with private baths and the Garden Suite, which has a double Jacuzzi and overlooks the trout pond. There's also the self-contained Honeysuckle Cottage, spotlessly clean and filled with antiques.

If you prefer an adults-only retreat, the new, 210-metre (700-foot) garden hideaway at **RAY AND ANN HARTMANN'S B&B** (5262 Sooke Rd; 250/642-3761; www3.bc.sympatico.ca/hartmann/) is perfect. Nestled in the wooded hills with distant views of the water, this small bed-and-breakfast in a stone house offers lounging on the patio in pristine white wicker furniture above a trellised garden of flowers, herbs, and vegetables. Breakfast, prepared with fruits and herbs straight from the Hartmanns' garden, is a thoroughly gourmet affair: spiced rhubarb parfait, shrimp omelets with artichokes, and strawberry waffles.

Vancouver Island's Soderberg family owns 1.6 kilometres (1 mile) of beachfront and 16 hectares (40 acres) of wild, undeveloped, wooded coastline. Perched among the trees and near the cliff side is their **POINT-NO-POINT RESORT** (1505 West Coast Rd, 15 miles west of Sooke; 250/646-2020). The 20 reasonably priced rustic cabins with kitchens and fireplaces are in a corner of natural beauty. The only distractions you'll hear are the crashing of the waves and the crackle of the fireplace. (Firewood is supplied.) .

Tofino and Long Beach

From Vancouver, take the ferry from Horseshoe Bay to Nanaimo. Drive north on the Island Highway (Highway 19) to the Parksville bypass. Turn west, onto Highway 4, to cross the island (which takes approximately two and a half hours). Continue on Highway 4, past the Ucluelet junction, north to Tofino. North Vancouver Air (800/228-6608) flies to the Tofino/Long Beach airport from Vancouver International Airport in about 50 minutes.

Winter gusts often reach up to 100 kilometres (60 miles) per hour on Vancouver Island's wild west coast, where the next stop in the vast Pacific Ocean is Japan. As dense as Lyle Lovett's hair, scrubby shore pine permanently bend back, proof that they know which way the prevailing wind blows. Behind them, old-growth cedars and firs grow hundreds of feet high, giving the shoreline a steeply rising appearance, while creating a towering wonderland beneath the forest canopy. Curiously, the ocean waves come directly from the Antarctic or, after mid-October, from Alaska. It's the long Antarctic swells—15 seconds apart—that have made this coast famous for its thousands of shipwrecks and has turned Tofino into Canada's surfing capital. Local entrepreneurs have made this area the winter storm-watching capital of the Pacific Northwest, and the storms are definitely worth watching.

However, most of the 600,000 people who find their way to Vancouver Island's **PACIFIC RIM NATIONAL PARK** every year still arrive between April and October. The park is segmented into three parts: the Broken Group Islands in Barkley Sound, Long Beach, and the West Coast Trail. If your destination is Tofino or Ucluelet, you'll quickly discover why Long Beach epitomizes many people's concept of the wild and untrammeled northern Pacific. This destination might seem to define the word "remote," but the drive there is at times so spectacular that the trip lives up to the adage that life is the journey as much as the destination. Highway 4, which crosses Vancouver Island, winds along rivers and lakes, past soaring snow-covered peaks, through a stand of giant western red cedars that are on par with California's Avenue of the Giants, then on beneath more and more peaks. Locals claim the road is well maintained and passable year-round (although one of them admits you might get an opportunity to test the four-wheel drive on your rental sports-utility vehicle on some of the higher elevations in the winter). Try to avoid making this drive at night, as the scenery is not to be missed, nor are the highway's many winding curves.

The small towns of **UCLUELET** and **TOFINO** bracket Pacific Rim National Park's Long Beach division, and both towns celebrate the **PACIFIC RIM WHALE FESTIVAL** from mid-March to mid-April. That's when 20,000 Pacific grey whales—virtually the world's population of these mammals—pass by on their annual migration from Baja, Mexico, to the Arctic Ocean. Ucluelet, at the park's south end, is closer to Highway 4 and claims to be the world's whale-watching capital. (It is BC's third-largest port for landed fish catch.) But you can watch whales from Tofino too, and Tofino has infinitely more charm. Spring is best for whale watching, but some companies—and there are many—guarantee sightings into October. Check with the **TOFINO INFOCENTRE** (380 Campbell St; 250/725-3414). The tour guide nicknamed Pipot, at **REMOTE PASSAGES ZODIAC ADVENTURES** (71 Wharf St; 800/666-9833), is particularly good with kids. This same outfitter conducts guided sea kayaking trips to Meares Island and around Clayoquot Sound. Tip: 12-passenger rubber zodiacs offer a more thrilling encounter, but the bounce can be tough on people with back problems.

Tofino is also the gateway to Clayoquot Sound (pronounced "KLY-kwot"), which is home to Vancouver Island's largest remaining intact ancient temperate rain forest. (Its future is under hot dispute by environmentalists and forest companies.) Stop at the **PACIFIC RIM PARK INFOCENTRE** (just five minutes up the road after turning north to Tofino from the Highway 4 junction; 250/726-4212). Anyone parking within the park must buy a $5 day pass from dispensers (with a Visa card or cash), so you may want to set aside a full day to explore the park. (Except for the camping available at **GREEN POINT CAMPGROUND**, 800/689-9025 all accommodation lies outside park boundaries.)

Inside the park, don't miss the self-guided, three-quarter-kilometre (half-mile)-long boardwalk loop through the weirdly shaped woods on **SHOREPINE BOG TRAIL**, where the stubby, broccoli-like stands of hemlock, yellow cedar, and red cedar are centuries old. Outside the park, the **WILLOWBRAE TRAIL** traces part of the route that villagers trudged before 1942, when the road between Tofino and Ucluelet was built. The shorter **HALF MOON BAY TRAIL** winds through twisted stands of cedar and hemlock to reach a stairway. It descends past giant Sitka spruce before it opens out onto a sandy beach.

The best beaches are: **LONG BEACH**, all 19 sandy kilometres (11 miles) of it, for just about everything; **COX** and **CHESTERMAN BEACHES** for booming breakers; **MACKENZIE BEACH** for relative warmth; and **TEMPLAR BEACH**, a small, peacheful spot. **FLORENCIA BAY** (also known as Wreck Bay), former home to hippie squatters, is a local favourite—no crowds, and the tidal pools teem with marine life.

The stretch of surf-swept sand that is **LONG BEACH** is best explored by hiking the beach, its headlands, and their woodland trails, so pick up a free hiker's guide at the Tofino InfoCentre, or, better yet, buy the *Official Guide: Pacific Rim National Park Reserve* or veteran writer Bruce Obee's excellent *The Pacific Rim Explorer*, which is loaded with history, practical tips, and even the nitty-gritty on how whales do it. Ask for tips on whale watching and where to see the permanent colonies of basking sea lions. There are also daily interpretive lectures at **GREEN POINT THEATRE** (Green Point Campground; 800/689-9025) in the evening and occasional guided storm walks.

WICKANINNISH INN is a splendid, $9-million oceanfront inn, built on a point at **CHESTERMAN BEACH** just 5 kilometres (3 miles) south of Tofino. (Chesterman is the longest beach outside of the park.) The inn's name may be confusing to those who haven't visited the area in the past five years. The original inn on Long Beach was a haven to world travellers until 1977, when Pacific Rim National Park was created. Longtime resident Dr. Howard McDiarmid was behind the park's creation and now he, his sons, and investors are behind the new inn with the beloved old name.

The old inn was torn down and the massive timbers, rafters, and stone hearth were recycled into the building of the **WICKANINNISH INTERPRETIVE CENTRE** (at the end of Long Beach Rd; 250/726-7333), which is situated on the original, picturesque Long Beach point. It is well worth a stop. Operated by Parks Canada (closed in winter), the centre's revitalized exhibits explain the life of the area's Native whalers and their European successors. It also presents documentary films about the many indigenous marine animals that visitors might encounter on this remote island peninsula. Check out the telescopes on the observation decks as well. This centre also includes a restaurant. It's a decent place to get fish-and-chips or more formal entrees, along with a martini or a microbrewed ale (if you don't plan to picnic outdoors). Beach fires are allowed, but you'll need to gather firewood while it's still daylight if you plan to picnic here.

Once you arrive at the only traffic light in the town of Tofino (population 1,103), hang a right, drive down to the dock, and you've arrived at the end of the road. The best view in Tofino is right across from you, at the **HOUSE OF HIMWITSA** (300 Main St; 800/899-1947), which has a Native art gallery, a restaurant, and accommodations. If you're looking for an off-the-beaten-path experience, you can't do better than the Nuu-chah-nulth people's guided tours to Meares and Flores Islands. For schedules, ask at **TOFINO INFOCENTRE** (380 Campbell St; 250/725-3414) or the House of Himwitsa.

Tofino is a relaxed and walkable little town that is also a popular reprovisioning spot for sailors circumnavigating Vancouver Island. You'll find locals (read: hippies) at the **COMMON LOAF BAKE SHOP** (180 First St; 250/725-3915) behind the bank. This meeting spot is the place to find out what's happening on the environmental front. The bake shop has wonderful cheese buns, and come summer nights, bread dough becomes pizza dough. Locals also congregate at the organic-foods pink-and-turquoise **ALLEY WAY CAFE** (305 Campbell St; 250/725-3105), where everything, including the mayonnaise on the clam burgers, is made on the premises. The **COFFEE POD** (151 4th St; 250/725-4246) serves breakfast, lunch, and the celebrated "podwich"—their take on panini.

Be sure to visit **EAGLE AERIE GALLERY** (350 Campbell St; 250/725-3235), owned by renowned native artist Roy Henry Vickers. The gallery was constructed in traditional longhouse style and features adze-shaped cedar. Drop by the **COAST GUARD RESCUE STATION** (250/725-3231) during the informal daily open house (10am to 12pm) and imagine turning turtle (upside-down in the ocean) in the self-righting rescue vessel. Next door, you can rent a kayak and take lessons at **TOFINO SEA KAYAK-ING** (320 Main St; 250/725-4222) or sip a cappuccino at the tiny seaside espresso bar. Sunday nights, the Legion hosts entertainers called Java Jam; kids get in free.

Another must is sailing, cruising, or flying to **HOT SPRINGS COVE**, which has an unforgettable forest hike in to 43°C (109°F) waterfalls and pools. These are shared by tourists, shampooing boaters, and anglers. Bring a bathing suit. **SEASIDE ADVENTURES** (300 Main St; 250/725-2811) makes runs to the hot springs.

If you can't bear to leave, you can book into the acclaimed **WICK-ANINNISH INN** (Osprey Lane at Chesterman Beach; 250/725-3100) which offers a roaring fire in the tranquil lobby when it's howling out-side; a 100-seat, sea-view restaurant (The Pointe) and bar (On-the-Rocks), constructed by hand with red cedar and accented with butter-toned yel-low cedar, and stretching out over the rocks so that the surf pounds all around; a complete health spa (**ANCIENT CEDARS SPA**); and 46 comfy guest rooms. Each has an ocean view, a private balcony, a minibar, a gas fireplace, a soaker tub for two (with its own ocean view in many rooms) in the slate bathroom, soft terry robes, and a romantic, peaceful ambi-ence. Rain slickers and boots are provided for winter storm watching.

Make reservations to dine in **THE POINTE**, where Chef Jim Garraway offers his interpretation of Pacific Northwest cuisine, accompanied by an impressive wine list. Starters that are sure to awaken your palate: apple-wood-smoked rock scallops with frizzled onions and strawberry and red plum salsa, or fried smoked salmon and brie, served with sun-dried sour-cherry relish and salmon caviar crackers. Entrees—such as the Wickaninnish Potlatch (a bounty of local seafood in a tomato and vegetable stew) and rack of lamb in a dried-wild-mushroom crust served with caramelized onions, crisp potatoes, and a sun-dried blueberry and mint jus—make it easy to understand why it's the busiest restaurant in the area.

The inn with the best guest lounge is minutes away, at the delightful oceanfront Ralph Lauren–inspired **MIDDLE BEACH LODGE** (400 Mackenzie Beach Rd; 250/725-2900; www.middlebeach.com), where guests disappear into down-filled easy chairs and ottomans by the great rock fireplace, or snooze in broad-armed, wooden Adirondack chairs on the deck. Suite numbers are carved into canoe paddles mounted on dark green wood. The 25 guest rooms in the adults-only beach lodge are on the small side, except for the very romantic Honeymoon Suite, which has a kitchenette and a king-size bed. Nearby, the family-oriented Headlands lodge has 20 guest rooms, two suites with balconies, soaker tubs, gas fire-places, and new semidetached units with cliffside settings. If you want the pounding roar of open ocean, you won't find it here; instead, the gentle wash of waves on tiny Templar Beach lull you to sleep. Breakfast is included, and dinner (at very reasonable prices) is served at the Headlands up to five nights a week in the high season, as well as Saturday nights during the off-season. Otherwise, you can forage at local restaurants.

For fine dining in a casual atmosphere, it's hard to beat the **RAIN-COAST CAFE** (101 120 4th St; 250-725-2215). There's no red meat here, but you won't miss it when you taste their seafood and vegetarian dishes. For Dungeness crab, head to the **WEST COAST CRAB BAR** (601 Campbell St; 250/725-3733), and for oysters and local seafood, you'll want to check out the First Nations–run **SEA SHANTY RESTAURANT** in the **HIMWITSA LODGE** (300 Main St; 800/899-1947; www.himwitsa.com). Charleton Heston stayed here while filming *Alaska*. The four upstairs guest rooms are bright, spacious, and simply furnished. Each has a kitchenette, a private deck, a hot tub, and a queen-size bed.

WHISTLER

WHISTLER

How to Get Here

BY CAR

From Vancouver, it's a 90-minute drive up the scenic **SEA TO SKY HIGH-WAY** (Highway 99) from West Vancouver through Squamish to North America's top-ranked ski resort. The 125-kilometre (75-mile) route winds through the lush forests that rim Howe Sound and the perennially snowcapped Coast Mountains. Whether you travel by car, bus, or train, you'll find the route to Whistler is only a visually awe-inspiring overture to the majestic beauty you'll find at journey's end. If you're driving, don't get distracted by the breathtaking views—the curves of the road demand constant attention.

Along the way, you'll pass the quiet residential communities that surround Howe Sound, such as Horseshoe Bay, Lion's Bay, Porteau Cove, and Furry Creek. **BRITANNIA BEACH**, about a half hour north of Horseshoe Bay, was once the largest processor of copper in the British Empire. It has a mining museum as well as a few places to grab a snack: **MOUNTAIN WOMAN** for great burgers and fries, **SHERRY'S CAPPUCCINO AND SHEER CREATION** (604/896-1554) for bagels and stained-glass art, and **THE 99ER** (604/896-2497) for quick, cheap coffee to go. If you want serious food in a seriously casual setting, drive about 15 minutes farther and stop at the **ROADHOUSE DINER** (604/892-5312) overlooking Shannon Falls. It's open from 7am to 9pm, and kids of all ages will love the hundreds of rabbits that inhabit the surroundings. After lunch, visit **SHANNON FALLS** and take a stroll along the base of this beautiful waterfall. Six times the vertical drop of Niagara Falls, it's the fifth-largest waterfall in the world, plummeting 335 metres (1,100 feet).

Drive up Highway 99 a bit farther to watch rock climbers from around the world scale Smoke Bluffs (lobbying to be the first national park designated for climbers) or the imposing 650-metre (2,133-foot) granite mass that is **STAWAMUS CHIEF** (reputedly the second-largest granite monolith in the world after the Rock of Gibraltar). You can also view the climbers while having lunch at the **HOWE SOUND INN AND BREWING COMPANY** (604/892-2603), where wonderful hand-crafted ales are served in both a charming brew pub and **RACHEL'S RESTAURANT**, which has an inventive menu and features good prices, specializing in regional fare.

If you're a trainspotter from way back or want to introduce your kids to this tradition, turn west on Centennial Way, approximately 3 kilometres (2 miles) north of McDonald's on Highway 99 in Squamish, to the **WEST COAST RAILWAY HERITAGE PARK** (604/898-9336; www.wcra.org). This 5-hectare (12-acre) park houses Canada's second-largest collection of railway rolling stock. Its 58 vintage railway cars and locomotives, in various stages of restoration, are set in a beautiful natural landscape. Admission is $4.50 for adults or $12 for a family, with a $1 surcharge to ride the miniature railway.

The remaining 40-kilometre (24-mile) stretch to Whistler winds its way past the town of Brackendale, home of the annual bald eagle count, and Alice Lake and Brandywine Falls Provincial Parks, both of which border on Garibaldi Provincial Park before reaching Alta Lake and Whistler's town limits. (Garibaldi's looming Black Tusk mountain, according to Native legend, was the home of the Thunderbird, which made thunder with its wings and shot lightning bolts from its eyes.)

BY BUS

If you don't want to miss a single second of spectacular scenery but don't want to drive, take the bus to Whistler. A 3½-hour trip is offered by **PERIMETER TRANSPORTATION** (604/266-5386 in Vancouver, 604/905-0041 in Whistler), which ferries passengers daily between Vancouver International Airport and the Whistler bus loop. The bus is a popular form of travel for Whistler locals, so reservations are required year-round. One-way fares are $43 for adults, $25 for children.

MAVERICK COACH LINES (Pacific Central Station, 1150 Station St, Vancouver; 604/482-8747 in Vancouver, 604/932-6236 in Whistler) whisks you from the Vancouver bus depot to the Whistler bus loop. The trip takes about three hours. Buses leave six times daily from Vancouver between 8am and 7pm. Return trips leave the Whistler bus loop six times daily between 5am and 7:15pm. One-way fare is $18 for adults.

BY TRAIN

For a romantic alternative, take **BC RAIL**'s *Cariboo Prospector* (604/984-5246; www.bcrail.com), which departs the North Vancouver train terminal (1311 W 1st St) daily at 7am, wending its way up the Howe Sound coastline through the Cheakamus River Valley and Garibaldi Provincial Park. The 2½-hour trip includes a leisurely breakfast, reaching the Whistler train station on Lake Placid Road at 9:34am. The return trip leaves Whistler at 6:20pm and includes dinner, returning to North Vancouver at 9:05pm. A one-way ticket (including meal) is $31 for adults. Discounts are available for seniors and children.

BY PLANE

WHISTLER AIR (604/932-6615) offers a 30-minute floatplane service between Vancouver and Whistler ($125 one way) twice daily from June 1 to September 30.

Orientation

Way back in 1914, Alex and Marybeth Philip bought 4 hectares (10 acres) of land on Alta Lake for $700. They spent the summer building a ski resort and named it Rainbow Lodge. It attracted an enthusiastic audience of Europeans, Americans, and Canadians who had taken up skiing—a hot new sports craze at the time. There weren't many groomed trails on nearby London Mountain (now called Whistler Mountain) when the Philips first opened, but that changed pretty quickly when skiing became a popular winter pastime after the Second World War. In 1964, a group of investors began developing the valley, and in 1965 it was officially renamed Whistler after the indigenous hoary marmot, which is known for its shrill, whistling noise.

The area's reputation soared during the 1980s when nearby Blackcomb Mountain opened, doubling the overall skiing acreage and boasting a mile-high vertical drop: North America's highest. For several years, the twin glacial peaks of Whistler and Blackcomb Mountains have been rated North America's number-one ski resort by numerous ski and travel magazines, and it's also gained a reputation as a world-class year-round resort. In ski season, you'll hear plenty of foreign accents in the chairlift lineups, along with those of the many Aussie lifties. The **HORSTMAN GLACIER** on Blackcomb Mountain is open for skiing and snowboarding as late as mid-August. And if you're seeking mountain air, Whistler is an ideal summer getaway for visitors who want to hike, fish, mountain bike, paddle, raft, or simply experience the incredible beauty of the Coast Mountains during the spring, summer, and fall.

Surrounded by the 10,000-foot peaks of Garibaldi Provincial Park, Canada's first resort municipality is actually four cheek-by-jowl communities: **WHISTLER VILLAGE** (the main hub), **UPPER VILLAGE** (at the base of Blackcomb Mountain), **CREEKSIDE** (the southernmost community, at the original gondola base of Whistler Mountain), and **VILLAGE NORTH** (the northernmost development, which consists of the Marketplace and Town Plaza). Although the areas have grown exponentially with the completion of a number of multimillion-dollar condos, retail stores, and restaurants, walking in the pedestrian-only villages still evokes the intimate feel of a European resort. Sociable plazas are accessed via broad pedestrian-only boulevards, unexpected byways, and pathways that connect the various communities. Both mountains can be accessed from any of the four villages, thanks to a well-organized series of interconnecting high-speed lifts and gondolas. Free shuttle buses link each village, and local buses connect outlying residential areas to each village. The result of all this careful planning is a place where transportation is not needed to get to food, lifts, or nightlife: everything is a pleasant 2- to 10-minute stroll from your hotel or condo.

Visitor Information

The **WHISTLER VISITOR INFO CENTRE** (2097 Lake Placid Rd, Whistler Conference Centre; 604/932-5528) provides information about accommodations, restaurants, outfitters, and special events year-round. It's open daily from 10am to 6pm. From mid-May until early September, an information kiosk (at corner of Village Gate Blvd and Whistler Wy) is open daily from 10am to 6pm. The **WHISTLER RESORT ASSOCIATION** (4010 Whistler Wy; 604/932-3928) can help you book last-minute accommodations and special-event tickets as well as provide you with information about the resort's numerous activities.

Getting Around

The walk between Whistler Village and the Upper Village takes about five minutes. Similarly, Village North can be reached on foot from either Whistler Village or the Upper Village in about five to seven minutes. Free shuttle buses also link each village. If you're staying in any of the outlying neighbourhoods, such as Creekside, Nester's Village, Alpine Meadows, Emerald Estates, White Gold Estates, or Tamarisk, consider using the year-round public transit service. These **WHISTLER TRANSIT SYSTEM** buses (604/932-4020) operate daily with frequent stops right at the gondolas, providing an efficient and economical alternative to hunting down a parking space. One-way fares are $1.50 for adults, $1.25 for seniors and students, free for children under 5. Discounted TripCards for 5 rides, 20 rides, or 30 days are also available.

Whistler's **TAXIS** operate around the clock. Not only can Airport Limousine Service (604/273-1331), Whistler Star Express (604/685-5546), and Sea to Sky Taxi (604/932-3333) shuttle you between destinations, these companies also offer taxi tours, golf course transfers, and transport to Vancouver International Airport. Go first-class with Extreme Limousine (604/434-2278) if you want to stretch out in style.

Trips to outlying Pemberton, Mount Currie, or Lillooet require a car. Both Budget Rent-a-Car (Holiday Inn Sunspree, 4295 Blackcomb Wy, Upper Village; 604/932-1236) and Thrifty Car Rental (Listel Whistler Hotel, 4121 Village Green, Whistler Village; 604/938-0302) have reservation agents to book **RENTAL CARS** or SUVs for side trips.

Essentials

PUBLIC REST ROOMS

Most rest rooms in Whistler are provided for customers only. However, public rest rooms are available at the Whistler Conference Centre (2097 Lake Placid Rd) and at the base lodges for both the Whistler and Blackcomb lifts.

MAJOR BANKS

The Royal Bank has ATMs near Carleton Lodge in Whistler Village and near the Husky station in Creekside. Toronto-Dominion Bank has ATMs at the IGA store in the Marketplace, Village North; at Club Intrawest in the Upper Village; and at the Delta Whistler Resort in Whistler Village.

POLICE AND SAFETY

Dial 911 for police, fire, and ambulance. For nonemergency police services, call 604/932-3044. Whistler Search and Rescue can be reached at 604/932-2338. Whistler is a very safe community. However, you must still remain mindful that crimes of opportunity (property theft, mostly) can and do happen even in places like this.

HOSPITALS AND MEDICAL/DENTAL SERVICES

General medical services can be found through family physician Dr. E. F. Ledgerwood (203–2011 Innsbruck Dr, Creekside; 604/932-4404). You can also try the Town Plaza Medical Clinic (Town Plaza, Village North; 604/905-7089). Dental services are available through Creekside Dental (2011 Innsbruck Dr; 604/938-1550).

POST OFFICE

The main post office (the Marketplace, Village North; 604/932-5012) is not the only place to purchase stamps or mail packages. Other stores displaying the red CANADA POST POSTAL OUTLET sign can also provide these services (see also Pharmacies, below).

GROCERY STORES

The Grocery Store (Whistler Village Sq; 604/932-3628), the IGA Food Store (the Marketplace, Village North; 604/938-2850), and Nester's Market (Nester's Village; 604/932-3545) are super outlets for food and dry goods.

PHARMACIES

Pharmasave has outlets in both Whistler Village Square (Crystal Lodge; 604/932-2303) and at the Marketplace, Village North (604/932-4251).

DRY CLEANERS AND LAUNDROMATS

Many accommodations offer laundry facilities for their guests. Dual Mountain Dry Cleaners (the Marketplace, Village North; 604/932-7050) also offers laundry and dry-cleaning services.

BUSINESS, COPY, AND MESSENGER SERVICES

Whistler Office Services (the Marketplace, Village North; 604/932-5114) can help you with a variety of business, copy, and shipping services.

PHOTOGRAPHY EQUIPMENT AND SERVICES

Slalom 1-Hour Photo (the Marketplace, Village North; 604/938-9090) and Whistler's Foto Source (Crystal Lodge, Whistler Village Square; 604/932-6612) offer photofinishing as well as film.

PETS AND STRAY ANIMALS

Bow Wow (the Marketplace, Village North; 604/938-9663) has pet supplies and foods. Veterinarians can be found at Whistler Animal Health Clinic (1100 Millar Creek Rd; 604/905-5088) and Coast Mountain Veterinary Services (2011 Innsbruck Dr; 604/932-5391). Whistler Animals Galore (604/938-8642) is the local animal shelter.

SPAS AND SALONS

The Spa (Chateau Whistler Resort, Upper Village; 604/905-2086) offers massage, reflexology, hydrotherapy and herbal treatments, exfoliations, body wraps, as well as aesthetic services.

Top 20 Restaurants

Araxi Restaurant & Bar / ★★★

4222 WHISTLER VILLAGE SQ; 604/932-4540

A cousin to Vancouver's top-rated CinCin, the newly renovated and perennially trendy Araxi not only attracts a young, beautiful, and well-dressed crowd, it's also one of Whistler's long-standing culinary cornerstones. In a town with more restaurants per square foot than just about anywhere else, sticking around means something. It's located in the centre of "action central"—Whistler Village Square—with sought-after patio dining during the summer. (It can be jam-packed and hectic some nights, but be patient; or grab a seat at the bar.) The softly illuminated interior features rich earth tones as well as dark wood accents. Chef James Walt concocts surprising starters such as blue-shell mussels steamed in a curry-scented broth accented with clover honey and basil, or spring rolls stuffed with homemade sausage, prawns, and vegetables, served with a ginger-and-cilantro sauce. Entrees are equally entertaining. The juicy slow-roasted venison strip loin is served with woodland mushroom–and–provolone ravioli, spaghetti squash seasoned with a warming touch of nutmeg, and a bright cranberry–blood orange chutney. And Walt's version of paella combines local fish, shellfish, chorizo, and chicken in a saffron-laced risotto. Araxi's impressive wine list is big, changeable, and fairly priced, with lots of wine by the glass as well as tasting flights. Dessert? Share the rich chocolate espresso mousse served with mascarpone cream and delicate butter biscuits, or the ginger-scented crème brûlée. *$$$; AE, DC, MC, V; no cheques; lunch, dinner every day May–Oct, dinner only Dec–April (closed in Nov some years); full bar; reservations recommended; araxi@direct.ca; www.araxi.com; Whistler Village.* &

Auntie Em's Kitchen / ★

129–4340 LORIMER RD; 604/932-1163

This hip, cozy coffee shop wins the prize for wholesome comfort food (box lunch–style). Patrons order at the counter and seat themselves at the simple wood tables positioned so everyone can people-watch in comfort. Made-on-site baked goods, soups, sandwiches, salads, and vegetarian dishes are served up with coffees, fresh-pressed juices, smoothies, and shakes. (The Black Forest ham on home-baked rye topped with tomatoes and sprouts went perfectly with a piping hot cup of vegetable soup.) Breakfast is served all day for those who just can't resist eggs, bacon, and toast after noontime. Eat in or take out. *$; AE, DC, MC, V; debit cards; no cheques; breakfast, lunch, dinner every day; no alcohol; the Marketplace, Village North.* &

Bear Foot Bistro / ★★★

4121 VILLAGE GREEN (LISTEL WHISTLER HOTEL); 604/932-3433

André St. Jacques, the irrepressible manager at the Bear Foot Bistro, goes to great lengths to provide luxe wining and dining at luxe prices. The room is sophisticated and the pace is relaxed, though the service is attentive and professional. This bistro offers inventive Pacific Northwest cuisine with decidedly French influences. (No surprise, since head chef Eric Vernice was spirited away from the legendary French restaurant Troisgros.) Appetizers include Atlantic salmon and yellowfin tuna parfait with beluga caviar, and a marbled foie gras and red-deer terrine in red-beet-and-truffle jus. Main courses range from a sublime Muscovy duck with caramelized pears and toasted gingerbread in a honey lavender jus to exotic (and extremely popular) wild Northwest Territories caribou to a straightforward U.S. prime beef tenderloin cooked to perfection. The award-winning 1,100-bottle wine cellar is a small museum for oenophiles, with collections like Château Lafite Rothschild, back to 1911, and Dom Perignon to 1966. The dessert menu changes daily at the whim of the talented pastry chef. After dinner, head to the state-of-the-art smoking room, where you can sample a fine stogie (including prewar Cubans), or to their wine bar (see Nightlife in this chapter) for live jazz. *$$$; AE, DC,*

MC, V; debit cards; no cheques; lunch, dinner every day; full bar; reservations recommended; at Whistler Wy, Whistler Village. &

Caramba! / ★★

12–4314 MAIN ST; 604/938-1879

This fun, boisterous, Mediterranean-influenced restaurant reflects owner Mario Enero's ability to wow even those who are on a modest budget. He's combined high-energy service with big, soul-satisfying portions of down-home pasta, pizza, and roasts. Start with the savoury baked goat cheese served with a tomato coulis and garlic toast points. Then delve into the Fettuccine Natasha, accented with chunks of fresh salmon and a peppery vodka-and-tomato cream sauce. Munch on a Melanzana pizza heaped with roasted eggplant, roma tomatoes, and goat cheese. Or try the mouth-watering grilled bay trout with bacon-and-onion mashed potatoes. The open kitchen, earthen hues, and alderwood-burning pizza ovens lend a warm, casual tone to the room. Can't stay? They'll whip up a take-out meal in 15 minutes. Kids and adults both love the platter of three-cheese macaroni after a strenuous day on the slopes. *$; AE, MC, V; debit cards; no cheques; lunch, dinner every day; full bar; Village North.* &

Chef Bernard's / ★★

1-4573 CHATEAU BLVD; 604/932-7051

Chateau Whistler's former executive chef, Bernard Casavant, is now Whistler's foremost caterer. When you walk into Chef Bernard's, you enter Casavant's kitchen. Fortunately he included a few wooden tables and a take-out counter. The lights are a little bright and '80s rock wafts from a portable radio, but the food is truly outstanding. With an emphasis on farm-fresh local produce, Casavant creates a flawless fusion of classic French and Pacific Northwest cuisines. Start with the brie and carrot soup or the organic field lettuce salad with herb-crusted chicken breast. Try the pan-seared wild salmon fillet in a lemongrass and star anise marinade served with basmati rice and a spicy orange-ginger sauce. Chef Bernard keeps locals coming back for his fried free-range egg sandwich made with aged cheddar and bacon on a toasted granola bun. Fresh baked pies are a treat for the dessert lover. BC wines and beers dominate the beverage list. *$; AE, MC, V; no cheques; breakfast, lunch, and dinner every day; beer and wine; Upper Village.* &

Dubh Linn Gate / ★★

4320 SUNDIAL CRES (PAN PACIFIC LODGE); 604/905-4047

Homesick denizens of the Emerald Isle find a wealth of good cheer, fine "slow-pour" drafts, and heaping mounds of finely prepared pub fare in this transplanted bit of ole Ireland. Is it authentic? The pub's entire interior, including the unfinished-wood floors and lots of stained glass, was built back in the old country and imported to its prime base-of-the-mountain location. The patio, right at the bottom of the slopes, is crowded with ski instructors and their grown-up students. Live Celtic music serenades après-skiers indoors during the evening hours while they consume generous portions of steak-and-ale pie, "fat of the land" Irish stew, ale-battered halibut-and-chips, or a spilling-over-with-filling lobster-and-prawn croissant sandwich. The spinach salad with bacon and boiled eggs tossed with a red-wine vinaigrette is a meal in itself. (So are the starter portions of baby scallops and oysters in Irish whisky.) But be forewarned: the service is inconsistent and can be slow at times. (Granted, they have to find you in one of the numerous private nooks that constitute most of the pub's immense space.) *$$; AE, DC, MC, V; debit cards; no cheques; breakfast, lunch, dinner every day; full bar; Whistler Village.* &

Edgewater Lodge / ★★★
8841 HWY 99; 604/932-0688
Fabulous mountain and lake views: this is one of the few spots with a good view of both Whistler and Blackcomb. But the view is only one of the many reasons to drive out to Edgewater Lodge (see Lodgings in this chapter). Wallowing in the solitude of its own undeveloped 45-acre Green Lake estate, this intimate restaurant (with only 12 tables, plus seasonal lakeside garden seating) features memorable cuisine and outstanding service. This is the perfect spot for a private, relaxed, romantic sunset tête-à-tête. The menu is very traditional but remarkably appealing. Start with chef Thomas Piekarski's pan-seared Camembert. Progress to the schnitzel topped with a hunter's mushroom sauce and accompanied by rich mashed potatoes, or order the sweet and tender venison, raised on the lodge's own ranch in northern BC. Finish the evening with a slice of the luscious signature dessert: Black Tusk chocolate cake. *$$; MC, V; debit cards; Canadian cheques only; dinner every day; full bar; jays@whistler.net; www.whistler.net/resort/accommodations/edgewater/; 6 km (3.6 miles) north of Whistler Village, across from Meadow Park Sports Centre.* &

Hoz's Pub & Creekside Grillroom / ★
2129 LAKE PLACID RD; 604/932-4424
Good old basic fare in a down-to-earth atmosphere might seem hard to find in Whistler, but the locals have a hidden spot that pleases just about every palate. From deluxe burgers, barbecued chicken, and ribs (served with beans, hand-cut fries, and slaw) to cod or salmon fish-and-chips, Hoz's leaves you feeling satisfied. There are some surprises, like the Rahm Schnitzel (pork cutlet topped with a mushroom and port sauce) and the New York Neptune (a charboiled strip steak topped with white asparagus, baby shrimp, and hollandaise). Wear your best flannel shirt, and

check any pretensions at the door. If you're in the mood for a steak where the prices are tamer than Hy's, check out the Creekside Grillroom; Ron "Hoz" Hosner has spiffed up his eatery next to the pub and is serving up first-rate boneless prime rib and pepper steak. The wine list offers a good West Coast selection. Hoz also has a beer-and-wine store on-site, open from 11am to 11pm. *$; AE, DC, MC, V; debit cards; no cheques; breakfast, lunch, dinner every day; full bar; Creekside.*

Hy's Steakhouse / ★★★

4308 MAIN ST (DELTA WHISTLER VILLAGE SUITES); 604/905-5555
The perfect spot to indulge your guilty carnivorous pleasures is Hy's, delivering beef better than some of the finest traditional Manhattan and Midwestern establishments that specialize in the same tender subject. The steaks served at this white-linen, warm cherry wood–panelled establishment (with supple leather chairs) range in size from not-so-petite filet mignons and New York strips (executed au poivre with cracked black peppercorns and a smooth green-peppercorn sauce) to we-couldn't-finish-it chateaubriands. It's one of the few places left in North America where you can order a steak "blue" and not end up with medium rare. Nonsteak types find that the kitchen also knows its way around seafood. The Caesar salad is a crisp garlic lover's delight that doesn't skimp on shaved Parmesan and croutons. The prawn cocktail and starter portion of blackened ahi tuna are similarly generous and delectable. Hy's offers an excellent variety of Pacific Northwest wines, but why not elevate dinner with a pedigree Bordeaux? *$$$; AE, DC, MC, V; debit cards; no cheques; dinner every day; full bar; reservations recommended; Village North.* &

Il Caminetto di Umberto / ★★

4242 VILLAGE STROLL; 604/932-4442
This slice of the Tuscan countryside is the ubiquitous Umberto Menghi's answer to fine dining in Whistler. If you don't already know about him, he also owns the casual Trattoria di Umberto in Whistler Village (see review in this chapter) as well as some famous Vancouver spots (see the Restaurants chapter), and leads culinary tours of Italy. Not surprisingly, few things can top an après-ski meal here of fresh pasta and a bottle of Umberto's own Bambolo wine, even though the tables at this perennial favourite are too tightly packed together, and noise from the bar and cabaret interferes with table talk. Aside from pasta, aim for other Tuscan-style specials such as the roasted rack of lamb with rosemary-and-garlic crust. Or savour the rich flavours of Milanese-style osso buco served with sautéed vegetables and a saffron-tinted risotto. Leave room for the mascarpone cheesecake. Expect ever-professional service. *$$; AE, DC, MC, V; debit cards; no cheques; dinner every day; full bar; Whistler Village Square.* &

La Brasserie des Artistes / ★★

4232 VILLAGE STROLL; 604/932-3569

Locals breakfast here (8am to 3pm) before hitting the slopes, or while away the afternoon at small, crowded tables over coffee or a glass of wine. Thanks to efficient outdoor heating units and plenty of overhead coverage, the patio is open for eating and people-watching year-round. The young-and-casual lunch and dinner crowds (served by the equally young-and-casual staff until midnight) come for the Meat Lover Cannelloni, stuffed with beef, spinach, and cottage cheese and topped with rich tomato sauce, herbs, and cheese. The Gobble Gobble is another fave: roast turkey on grilled focaccia with lettuce, tomatoes, and onion, accompanied by a tangy cranberry chutney. (If you're superhungry, add an appetizer portion of *poutine*, a Quebecois specialty combining thick french fries with gravy and rich cheese curds.) *$; AE, DC, MC, V; debit cards; no cheques; breakfast, lunch, dinner every day; beer and wine; Whistler Village Square.* ໄ

La Rua / ★★★

4557 BLACKCOMB WY (LE CHAMOIS); 604/932-5011

Mario Enero runs a stylish but comfortable restaurant in Le Chamois hotel (see Lodgings in this chapter) that prides itself on snap-of-the-finger service and a great wine list. Chef Tim Muehlbauer has devised some superb dishes served in portions that will satisfy the most ravenous skier or mountain biker. Start with duck breast served on truffle potatoes topped with raspberry jus and hazelnut oil; or savour the port-marinated ostrich carpaccio that comes with capers and shallots. No one makes better lamb, serving a Washington State rack with mint pesto or a shank set atop a mound of root vegetables and lentils; their venison medallions aren't bad either. Toothsome pastas, such as butternut squash agnolotti with smoked duck in a curry cream sauce, are sure to win your heart. Save room for the homemade biscotti and chocolate truffles. When the weather warms up, cigar aficionados leave the deep-red dining room (filled with bold works of art) and hit the deck for a smoke and a glass of ice wine or port. *$$$; AE, DC, MC, V; debit cards; no cheques; lunch, dinner every day; full bar; reservations recommended; www.whistler. net/larua; Upper Village.* ໄ

Las Margaritas Restaurante y Cantina / ★★

2021 KAREN CRES (WHISTLER CREEK LODGE); 604/938-6274

Tucked away on the edge of the road at Creekside village, Las Margaritas, a big open room filled with sturdy oak tables and chairs, has a classic cantina atmosphere. It gets crowded, but who cares if you can't hear yourself think? Locals flock to Las Margaritas for its namesake cocktails, among them the Rosarita Margarita (Sauza Conmemorativo, Cointreau, fresh lemon and lime juice, and a splash of cranberry juice) or a Cactus

Pear Martini (El Jimador Blanco Tequila and cactus pear nectar). The cuisine is Northern Mexican, Baja, and Southern Californian. For starters, try the Fiesta Platter, with samplings of guacamole, chicken wings, cheese quesadillas, chicken taquitos, and mini chimichangas, along with sweet jalapeño salsa, sour cream, and salsa *de aguacate*. Besides some unique twists on tacos, enchiladas, chimichangas, and quesadillas, this cantina offers good sirloin steak or chicken breast fajitas. The grilled-salmon burrito, salmon marinated in cilantro pesto sauce, is served with black beans and house salad. Service at this cantina is as warm and friendly as the cuisine and the atmosphere. *$$; AE, DC, MC, V; debit cards; no cheques; dinner every day; full bar; Creekside.* &

Portobello / ★★

4599 CHATEAU BLVD (CHATEAU WHISTLER RESORT); 604/938-2040
Whether you're on holiday or at home, it's hard to find a restaurant that will appeal to both you and your kids. In Whistler, this becomes even more difficult if you've tired of hamburgers, spaghetti, and pizza before they have. Portobello offers an easy solution, with a marketplace theme. The kids' menu includes chicken fingers, hot dogs, and hamburgers. The economical family meals serve up a choice of roast chicken or meat loaf accompanied by a variety of hot and cold side dishes. The market-style layout doesn't stop there. Individual stations offer a wide variety: chowder and stew; fresh fish and seafood; dim sum; grilled chops, steaks, and chicken; shepherd's pie and lasagne; pastas; and a huge salad bar. Bakery desserts and a nice selection of wines and beers top off the afternoon or evening without breaking the bank. *$; AE, DC, MC, V; debit cards; no cheques; lunch, dinner every day; full bar; Upper Village.* &

Quattro at Whistler / ★★★

4319 MAIN ST (THE PINNACLE INTERNATIONAL HOTEL); 604/905-4844
Right from the start, carbo-loading skiers loved to slide into Antonio Corsi's restaurant at the Pinnacle (see Lodgings in this chapter). His Vancouver restaurant, Quattro on Fourth, is frequently rated among the city's best (see the Restaurants chapter). Quattro at Whistler is upbeat, it's vibrant, and it's innovative. La Cucina Leggera, or "the healthy kitchen," is the motto of Quattro, a concept that fits the West Coast sensibility like a good set of ski boots. Funghi fanciers love the carpaccio featuring sliced portobello mushrooms topped with flavourful white truffle oil and shaved Asiago. Kudos also for the prawns sautéed with thyme, garlic, and a sprinkle of fresh lemon, served with a painstakingly prepared creamy herb risotto. Corsi's pasta dishes are equally inspired. Try the gnocchi al Gorgonzola, an idyllic marriage of tender potato and semolina dumplings and sharp Gorgonzola topped with roasted pecans. Entrees of braised lamb shank simmered with root vegetables and porcini mushrooms served over a creamy polenta, or roasted lean duck breast

accompanied by sun-dried cherry and grappa syrup, are irresistible. The portions are generous, and the *l'abbuffata* sampler menu for four or more very hungry people will not disappoint. The mainly Italian wine list is stellar. The staff is knowledgeable, friendly, and attentive. Desserts (which change daily) are stunning. *$$$; MC, V; debit cards; no cheques; dinner every day; full bar; reservations recommended; Town Plaza, Village North.* &

Rim Rock Cafe and Oyster Bar / ★★★

2101 WHISTLER RD (HIGHLAND LODGE); 604/932-5565

Filled to the rafters with a hip local crowd, this cozy cafe with a stone fireplace has been dishing out great food for years. Split into two levels (smokers in the downstairs bistro), the Rim Rock is housed in the unprepossessing Highland Lodge near Creekside. Bob Dawson and Rolf Gunther's restaurant is remarkable proof that fresh seafood and wondrous cuisine are not anomalies in the mountains. The fresh sheet features starters such as raw Fanny Bay oysters topped with vodka, crème fraîche, and caviar. Main events range from herb-infused salmon to pan-fried mahimahi in an almond-ginger crust to a mouth-watering grilled filet mignon topped with either a fresh herb butter or a creamy tricoloured peppercorn sauce. The Death by Chocolate dessert can make grown men cry. During the summer, book a table on the cozy back patio and dine amid the fresh herbs in the chef's garden. Service is top-drawer—knowledgeable but not arrogant. *$$$; AE, MC, V; debit cards; no cheques; dinner every day; full bar; reservations recommended; Creekside.*

Splitz Grill / ★★

4369 MAIN ST (ALPENGLOW); 604/938-9300

It's been a long time since a hamburger (or any of its '90s-style chicken, salmon, or lentil cousins) has been this thick, juicy, and utterly tantalizing. Chef Trevor Jackson has struck the right chord in the hearts of locals and visitors by offering a not-so-humble grilled sandwich on a crusty bun with your choice of toppings, which range from chili, garlic mayo, ketchup, tahini, sauerkraut, and hummus to fresh tomato, sprouts, avocado, salsa, and kosher pickles. The thick, house-cut fries still have their skins. Even including a soft drink, you haven't spent $10 and you're more than satisfied (although dessert does beckon in the form of ice cream sundaes, floats, shakes, cones, and a caramelized banana split). Maybe that's why more than 44,000 burgers were sold from this tiny spot (with only eight counter seats) in its first year. *$; AE, MC, V; debit cards; no cheques; lunch, dinner every day; no alcohol; Town Plaza, Village North.*

Sushi Village / ★★

4272 MOUNTAIN SQ (WESTBROOK HOTEL); 604/932-3330

Where do the locals go to satisfy their appetite for healthy portions of "down-home" Japanese cuisine? Sushi Village. You can't miss it, even though it's perched on the second floor of the Westbrook Hotel. You'll see ravenous young skiers and snowboarders patiently waiting along with upscale sophisticates to get a table. It's worth the wait. The simple Japanese-style decor allows for privacy even with large parties. The staff is knowledgeable, gracious, and familiar year after year. Consistently delicious and extremely fresh sushi, sashimi, and *maki* platters, as well as abundant combinations served in wooden sushi boats, are prepared by animated experts at the counter. Tempura, gyoza, yakitori, teriyaki, and satisfying meal-sized noodle soups are just a few of the home-style hot dishes offered. The food is straightforward, dependable, and a truly good deal. Semiprivate tatami rooms and takeout are both available. *$$; AE, DC, MC, V; debit cards; no cheques; lunch Wed–Sun, dinner every day (weekends only in off-season); full bar; reservations accepted for parties of 4 or more; Whistler Village.* &

Trattoria di Umberto / ★★★

4417 SUNDIAL CRES (MOUNTAINSIDE LODGE); 604/932-5858

Two large, romantically lit dining rooms separated by a massive open kitchen welcome you as you enter this busy, lively, very northern Italian establishment. Animated conversation is as much a part of the atmosphere as the potted plants and sculptures, the poolside view, and the rustic Italian decor. The service is fast and friendly, adding to the congeniality. Classic Tuscan starters such as beef carpaccio topped with shaved Parmesan, accompanied by a mélange of aromatic vegetables, or their hearty Tuscan bean soup, warm both heart and soul. But it's entrees like the grilled quail with sage or the cioppino (a saffron- and fennel-laced stew combining crab, prawns, mussels, and a variety of fish in a rich tomato broth) that will leave you singing the kitchen's praises. No trattoria can exist without pasta and risotto dishes: smoked-duck-and-portobello risotto, and penne with pesto and smoked salmon, are just two examples of Umberto's Italian comfort food. A respectable wine list and desserts large enough to share, along with the requisite cappuccino and espresso, complete the experience. *$$$; AE, DC, MC, V; debit cards; no cheques; lunch, dinner every day; full bar; reservations recommended; Whistler Village.* &

Val d'Isère / ★★★☆

4314 MAIN ST (BEAR LODGE); 604/932-4666

Relocated from Whistler Village Square to Village North's Town Plaza, Val d'Isère offers a grand combination: fine dining and people-watching. Nearly every seat has a street-level view of the plaza. The interior is intimate: a provençal motif tastefully executed in muted tones of blue and gold, illuminated by table lamps. Superchef Roland Pfaff still presides over this French kitchen with overtones of Alsace, offering palate-pleasing delicacies. His starter of Queen Charlottes smoked herring and Granny Smith apple salad served in a buttery potato mille-feuille with a smoked-mussel vinaigrette is a heartwarming experience. For entrees, we couldn't resist the delicately seared Alaskan scallops, topped with a champagne sauce and accompanied by Israeli couscous, or the richly flavoured braised duck legs, enhanced by a duck stock and rosebud reduction, paired with bulgur risotto. Wines from France, the United States, and Canada grace the impressive cellar list, providing selections to complement each dish. Pfaff's signature dessert—a chocolate cream–centred chocolate cake presented on a custardy crème anglaise—will leave you breathless. *$$$; AE, DC, MC, V; debit cards; no cheques; dinner every day (closed after Canadian Thanksgiving and open again before American Thanksgiving); full bar; reservations recommended; Town Plaza, Village North.* &

Lodgings

Chateau Whistler Resort / ★★★

4599 CHATEAU BLVD; 604/938-8000 OR 800/606-8244

This is the place to see and be seen in Whistler—where a valet parks not only your car but also your ski gear or mountain bike. The hotel's 558 rooms are steps away from the base of Blackcomb Mountain. You enter into the Great Hall, which has a floor of giant slate slabs covered with oversize hooked rugs, two mammoth limestone fireplaces, and a 12-metre (40-foot)-high beamed ceiling. Folk art birdhouses and weathered antique furnishings warm up the lodge-style grandeur. The spa is especially swank, offering various facials, body wraps, herbal and aesthetic treatments, as well as massage and shiatsu. The health club has a heated pool flowing both indoors and out, allowing swimmers to splash away under the chairlifts or soak in the Jacuzzi under the stars. Other services include a multilingual staff, baby-sitting, room service, and a dozen or so exclusive shops. The guest rooms are light and reasonably sized. Suites are elegantly appointed, offering comfortable sitting rooms (some have fireplaces) and bedrooms as well as spacious European-style bathrooms. The duplex suites on the top floor are grand in size and comfort. The Entree Gold Floors offer a wood-panelled lounge with a fireplace where a fully stocked honour bar and hors d'oeuvres are available in the evening, and a Continental breakfast is offered in the morning. The resort even has its own 18-hole golf course (designed by Robert Trent Jones Jr.). The on-site restaurants—The Wildflower, the Mallard Bar (Robin Leach proclaimed this "the premier address at Whistler"), and Portobello (see Top 20 Restaurants in this chapter)—complete this impressive overall picture. *$$$; AE, DC, MC, V; no cheques; www.cphotels.ca; Upper Village.* &

Durlacher Hof / ★★★

7055 NESTERS RD; 604/932-1924

Shoes off. *Halflingers* on. Hospitality at Durlacher Hof begins in the traditional Austrian fashion with the donning of these hand-knit slippers, which gain guests (including bad boy Sean Penn) entrance into Erika and Peter Durlacher's immaculate inn. Their Austrian pension is a short ride from Whistler Village. Eight guest rooms (some are suites) invoke the original 1970s spirit of Whistler with hand-carved pine furniture and comfortable beds with goose down duvets. Part Mother Teresa who just can't do enough for her guests and part sergeant-major with a relentless drive for perfection, Erika never stops. Her lavish breakfasts are a new reason to smile when the sun comes up: a groaning sideboard holds a feast filled with special dishes she prepares for each guest, perhaps *Kaiserschmarren* (pancakes with stewed plums), freshly baked breads, and lean *Schinkenspeck* ham. An honour bar and a warm fire welcome guests home at night. A hot tub and sauna are available to warm weary bones in addition to the soaker tubs found in some guest rooms. From the moment the Durlachers get up before daybreak to bake the day's bread to the last cup of *Glühwein* late at night, sharing the Hof with them is a joy. *$$$; MC, V; cheques OK; durlacher_hof@bc.sympatico.ca; www.durlacherhof.com; Nester's Village.* &

Edgewater Lodge / ★★

8841 HWY 99; 604/932-0688

The 12-room Edgewater Lodge is nestled in the solitude of its own 19-hectare (45-acre) estate on the shores of Green Lake. It's a low-key resort, eschewing the highly competitive atmosphere of the village proper. There's no grand lobby or room service. Each guest room has its own outside, private entrance. The furnishings are nothing to write home about, and there aren't any fireplaces. Each room has a television, but the unobstructed view of the lake, the snowcapped mountain, and the wildlife that visits the grounds daily are far more entertaining. The outdoor Jacuzzi provides a serene place to commune with nature for an hour or two. The Edgewater's restaurant (see Top 20 Restaurants in this chapter) offers memorable cuisine, a limited wine list, and outstanding service. *$$$; MC, V; cheques OK; jays@whistler.net; www.whistler.net/resort/accommodations/edgewater/; 6 km (3.6 miles) north of Whistler, across from Meadow Park Sports Centre.* &

Le Chamois / ★★

4557 BLACKCOMB WY; 604/932-8700 OR 800/777-0185

This six-storey condo hotel, which is dwarfed by its gargantuan neighbour, the Chateau Whistler, is not as luxurious as its exterior implies. Rooms are reasonably sized. Light, airy, and clean, the 62 studio, one-bedroom, and two-bedroom suites feature simple Euro-style furnishings and pastel colour schemes. Single bedrooms are built to accommodate four; each includes a living area with either a fold-out sofa bed or a Murphy bed. Every room has a view, though views of the mountain cost more. During high season, the hotel requires a minimum stay of two nights. All guest rooms are privately owned condos. Some incorporate personal touches: one three-bedroom corner suite is furnished with a piano, and another displays photos of the owner posing on the slopes. The compact Pullman-style kitchens feature all the things you need for preparing quick meals, including a microwave, a refrigerator, and all utensils. Some two-bedroom suites offer full kitchens equipped with a dishwasher and an oven. But don't miss the two restaurants downstairs. The elegant La Rua (see Top 20 Restaurants in this chapter) specializes in Mediterranean-style cooking with a Continental flair, while Thai One On offers more casual dining. Other amenities include a small conference area, a very small fitness room with an outdoor pool, and a Jacuzzi. Children under 12 stay free. *$$$; AE, DIS, MC, V; no cheques; powder@ whistler.net; www.whistler.net/resort/accommodations/powder; Upper Village.* &

Pan Pacific Lodge / ★★★

4320 SUNDIAL CRES; 604/905-2999 OR 800/327-8585

The Pan Pacific's first resort lodge has nabbed one of the most desirable locations in Whistler: it's just a few paces from both the Blackcomb and Whistler gondolas in Whistler Village. Each of the 121 studio, one-bedroom, and two-bedroom suites has a fireplace, fully equipped kitchen, and dishwasher. The cream-coloured walls attract light into the guest rooms through massive double-paned windows. The maple-hued wood furnishings evoke the sturdy yet comfortable Mission design style. Some rooms have a balcony where you can relax after a day on the slopes. Guests have access to a small but adequate fitness centre, steam room, two outdoor Jacuzzis, swimming pool, laundry room, ski and bike lockers, and the Dubh Linn Gate (see Top 20 Restaurants in this chapter), which serves hearty, well-prepared Irish pub food. Ask about special romance and activity packages. *$$$; AE, MC, V; Canadian cheques only; whistler@ panpacific-hotel.com; www.panpac.com; Whistler Village.* &

The Pinnacle International Hotel / ★★★

4319 MAIN ST; 604/938-3218 OR 888/999-8986

The Pinnacle's name and logo have little to do with the size or shape of this centrally located, four-storey hotel. However, they properly represent the level of comfort you'll find in all 84 studios. Each guest room has a gas fireplace, a balcony, a fully equipped kitchenette, a TV and VCR, voice mail and dataports, deluxe amenities, in-room coffee and tea service, and a double Jacuzzi soaker tub. Light-wood furnishings, pale cream interiors, and soft floral textiles exude a spacious, airy atmosphere even on a rainy day. The heated outdoor pool, hot tub, and guest laundry facilities are welcome touches, as is the room service offered by the house restaurant, Quattro at Whistler (see Top 20 Restaurants in this chapter). Even though it's a 20-minute walk to the Whistler Village base, this is an outstanding getaway for skiers. *$$$; AE, MC, V; Canadian cheques only; www.pinnacle-hotels.com; Town Plaza, Village North.* &

The Summit / ★★

4359 MAIN ST; 604/932-2778 OR 888/913-8811

Situated right on Main Street, the Summit's understated facade and lobby conceal a welcome surprise. The 81 one-bedroom, executive studio, and studio suites in this full-service hotel are beautifully designed, featuring soft earth tones, rich wood furnishings, fireplaces, fully equipped kitchenettes, and comfy marble bathrooms. Unlike its immediate neighbours, the Summit delivers more than just good value for every dollar spent. All the comforts of home can be found in each suite: kimonos, hair dryers, an iron and board, TV and VCR, balcony, in-room coffee and tea service, voice mail, and phones with dataports. Amenities such as a concierge, bell service, ski or bike storage, laundry facilities, sauna, heated outdoor pool, hot tub, valet service, playpens, and a free ski shuttle add to the value of your stay. A complimentary Continental breakfast is included in the rate as well. *$$$$; AE, MC, V; no cheques; summitlodge@uniserve. com; www.summitlodge.com; Town Plaza, Village North.* &

Exploring

Cradled among mountains that rise majestically above the tree line to permanently snowcapped peaks, Whistler is a mecca for skiers, snowboarders, ice skaters, and other snow enthusiasts. In recent years, however, this winter resort has also attracted thousands of year-round visitors who aspire to less frosty pursuits such as sight-seeing, hiking, running, kayaking and canoeing, fly-fishing, rollerblading, horseback riding, tennis, cycling, shopping, and dining and dancing.

It's impossible not to be drawn outdoors into this merry blend of natural serenity and hedonistic bustle. Unlike most ski resorts, Whistler can easily be strolled from end to end. Pedestrian-only thoroughfares meander past endless shops and cafes. Here you can also find many outfitters offering guided excursions of all kinds, from helicopter skiing (and picnicking) to fly-fishing via snowmobile to paragliding above the slopes. You can arrange a white-water rafting or jet boat trip, dogsledding, or even a showshoeing tour. You can rent mountain bikes or in-line skates (the village is crisscrossed with terrific trails, which lead out to longer, more challenging rides), skis, snowboards, and just about any other piece of outdoor sports equipment. Or, if just reading this leaves you exhausted, you can find a table at a sun-drenched slopeside cafe, order a latte, and simply watch the world go by.

Even if you're a nonskier, Whistler and Blackcomb Mountains (604/932-3141; www.whistler-blackcomb.com) are excellent places to take in the view. Lift tickets for **MOUNTAINTOP SIGHT-SEEING** are less than those for skiing: $21 for adults during the day and $16 for adults during the evening. Discounts are available for seniors and children. The **WHISTLER INFORMATION AND ACTIVITY CENTRE** (604/932-2394) can supply you with information on guided hiking and cycling tours offered by outfitters on both mountains.

If you're dying to get a glimpse of the wilderness beyond Whistler, hop a ride on **BC RAIL'S** *Whistler Explorer* (604/984-5246; www.bcrail. com), which transports you from the Whistler depot through the Pemberton Valley and up more than 900 metres (3,000 feet) along the Gold Rush Trail to Kelly Lake. Depart at 8am and have a Continental breakfast on the train. You'll reach Kelly Lake at 12:15pm and have enough time to take a leisurely stroll before reboarding the train at 1pm for lunch and the return trip. The *Whistler Explorer* returns to the Whistler depot at 5:30pm. It's operated from late May until late September, and the round-trip fare (which includes both meals) is $114 for adults and $78 for children.

To find out what Whistler was like before the skiers arrived, visit the **WHISTLER MUSEUM & ARCHIVES SOCIETY** (4329 Main St, Village North; 604/932-2019). Established in 1986, the museum presents the culture of the Native people who have lived in both the Whistler and Pemberton Valleys for thousands of years. The village's turn-of-the-19th-century settlement by Scottish and British workers who were lured by the railway and logging companies is re-created in its exhibits. Learn how the Philips changed the face of Whistler when they built their Rainbow Lodge, through pictures, artifacts, and stories. The museum is open Sunday to Thursday 10am to 4pm, Friday and Saturday 10am to 6pm. Admission is by donation.

Feeling flush? **HELICOPTER TOURS** of the surrounding mountains are provided by Blackcomb Helicopters (604/938-1700) or Pemberton Helicopters (604/932-3512). Glacier tours (see sidebar), ice climbing, heli-picnics, and snowshoeing are all available.

During the third week in July, the villages host Whistler's **ROOTS WEEKEND** (604/932-2394), when you can listen to Celtic, zydeco, bluegrass, Latin, and world-beat music at free as well as ticketed events.

To sample the best of local fields and orchards, stroll through the **FARMERS MARKET** during the summer. It's open Sundays at the base of Blackcomb. The **ALPINE WINE FESTIVAL** (604/932-3434) takes place on Whistler Mountain during the first weekend in September. A late-summer classic, the festival features wine tastings and events that highlight North America's finest vintages, including many from BC's own vineyards. In November, it's **CORNUCOPIA** (604/664-5625 or 800/944-4783)—Whistler's food and wine celebration. This delicious fall escape offers Whistler visitors three days of BC's finest food and wine, plus a gala reception, seminars, workshops, and cooking demonstrations by local chefs and food personalities.

Recreation

SKIING/SNOWBOARDING

If you don't already know, there's more to snow sports than just downhill skiing. And Whistler offers every type of snow enthusiast a great place to play. Owned and operated by Intrawest, **WHISTLER MOUNTAIN** (604/932-3434, snow report 604/687-6761; www.whistler-blackcomb. com) has a 1,530-metre (5,020-foot) vertical and 100-plus marked runs for downhill and telemark as well as a huge half pipe, terrain park, and a mini park and pipe for snowboarders. At the lower elevations, outfitters can be booked and equipment rented for snowshoe excursions.

The mountain is serviced by high-speed gondolas, high-speed quads, chairs, and T-bars. Helicopter service provides access to another 100-plus runs on the nearby glaciers. Near the top, the **ROUNDHOUSE LODGE** (604/905-2367) has seven restaurants offering everything from lattes and cookies to barbecued chicken, Chinese stir-fries, sushi, deli sandwiches, burgers, and a licensed dining room, plus a gift shop and nearly 360 degrees of both indoor and outdoor seating with excellent views of the surrounding mountains. (Surprisingly, prices are on par with venues down at the base.) **HARMONY HUT** (at the Harmony Express chair), **RAVEN'S NEST** (at the top of the Creekside gondola), as well as **WORLD CUP CAFE** and **DUSTY'S** (at the base of Creekside) also serve food on the mountain; as does the **GARIBALDI LIFT COMPANY BAR & GRILL** (at the Whistler Village base).

Also owned by Intrawest, **BLACKCOMB MOUNTAIN** (604/932-3141, snow report 604/687-7504; www.whistler-blackcomb.com) has a 1,609-metre (5,280-foot) vertical and another 100-plus marked runs as well as two half pipes and a park that are serviced by a high-speed gondola, high-speed quads, chairs, and T-bars. There's a connector gondola situated at the base of Whistler Village that also transports you to Blackcomb, so you don't have to shoulder your skis and hike to the Upper Village. Blackcomb also has a small area open for night skiing and boarding on Wednesday and Saturday nights (which is good if you want to give either a try for the first time). Nine restaurants serve visitors, including the **WIZARD GRILL, MERLIN'S, ESSENTIALLY BLACKCOMB CAPPUCCINO BAR,** and **18° BELOW** (for teens only) at the base. Up toward the top, eating establishments include Glacier Creek Lodge's **RIM ROCK CAFE & OYSTER BAR** and **GLACIER BITE,** the Rendezvous Lodge's **CHRISTINE'S DINING ROOM** and the **MOUNTAIN GRILL, HORSTMAN HUT,** and **CRYSTAL HUT.**

Whistler has developed year-round recreation and is as busy in the summer as it is during the ski season. Blackcomb Mountain's **HORSTMAN GLACIER** is open from May to mid-August for snowboarders, skiers, and snowshoers. During the summer, lift tickets are $30 per day for adults. Discounts are available for seniors, students, and children ages 7 to 12. Summer-season passes and multiday passes are also offered. Saturday nights during the summer are a special treat, when Blackcomb Mountain conducts weekly guided stargazing and moonrise tours (604/938-7747).

For skiers and snowboarders, winter **LIFT TICKETS** are $57 per day for an adult dual-mountain pass. Discounts are available for seniors, students, and children 7 to 12. A three-day adult dual-mountain pass is $168, and four- and six-day dual-mountain passes are available for $220 to $312. Season passes and express card discounts for multitrip visitors are also offered. Sight-seeing tickets are also available for $29. Free **GUIDED SKI TOURS** are available to show intermediate and expert skiers and boarders how to maximize their ski time and get the most out of the mountains (truly worth doing!). These ambassadors and ski hosts can also direct you to the hottest ski day routes with names like the Grand Tour, the Weather Chaser, and Expedition Extreme. From late November until late January, **GONDOLAS** for both mountains are open weekdays 9am to 3pm, weekends 8:30am to 3pm. From late January to mid-June, Whistler Mountain operates weekdays 9am to 3:30pm, weekends 8:30am to 3:30pm; Blackcomb Mountain operates on this same schedule until late April. From mid-June to mid-August, Horstman Glacier on Blackcomb Mountain is accessible from noon to 3pm.

Cross-country skiers will appreciate the 32 kilometres (19 miles) of well-marked seasonal trails groomed for both **NORDIC AND SKATE SKIING** that run throughout the Whistler municipality, as well as the 35

GRAB A GLACIER!

Glaciers—those magnificent remnants of the last Ice Age—are as much a part of the Sea to Sky landscape as the waters of Howe Sound and the volcanoes at Black Tusk and Mount Garibaldi. One good place to get an idea of how extensive glaciation has been in this area is just off Highway 99 north of Squamish. The **Tantalus Range Viewpoint** provides a panoramic perch from which to see some of the province's wildest and most challenging mountains.

Glacier Air (800/265-0088) in Squamish offers a deluxe package that includes a glacier landing in the Tantalus Range, with a gourmet lunch and amusing "glacier games" such as golf, Frisbee, and badminton. Other flightseeing outfits in the region include Whistler Air (604/932-6615), Blackcomb Helicopters (604/938-1700), Whistler Heli-Hiking (604/932-4105), and Pemberton Helicopters (604/932-3512). Heli-flights can range from 15 minutes to a half day, depending on the activities you wish to partake of en route.

Three day-hikes stand out above the rest when it comes to seeing the glaciers at close range. The trail to **Cheakamus Lake** in Garibaldi Provincial Park is flat, easy, and one of only two trails in the park open to mountain bikes. (Rentals are available in Whistler.) At the head of the lake, the hiker/biker is greeted by glacier-clad peaks such as Castle Towers, the Musical Bumps on the backside of Whistler Mountain, and the McBride Range. Distance to the western end of the lake is 6 kilometres (3.7 miles), with negligible elevation gain. The view of Matier Glacier at **Joffre Lakes,** located 23 kilometres (14.3 miles) east of Pemberton (just off Duffey Lake Rd) is enough to make anyone lace on their hiking boots. If you're into relaxing, you can even enjoy the view from a roadside rest stop. This 6-kilometre (3.7-mile) (one-way) trail goes past three gorgeous alpine lakes, ending at a well-defined landmark known as the Rockpile, where you can almost reach out and touch the Matier Glacier. The twin peaks of Matier and Joffre are excellent mountaineering objectives but should not be attempted by inexperienced hikers.

Due to their relatively modest nature, the Cheakamus and Joffre Lakes hikes can be quite crowded. More glacial scenery can be found at **Wedgemount Lake,** where the Wedge Glacier used to cascade right down to water's edge. (It has since receded.) Crowds are nonexistent, especially on weekdays, because the stiff climb of 1,200-plus metres (4,000 vertical feet) in just over 6.4 kilometres (4 miles) demands better-than-average hiking fitness.

Finally, you can even glacier-ski in the summertime. The **Horstman Glacier** on Blackcomb Mountain is open to the public as well as to ski and snowboard training camps. Check for hours beforehand by calling Whistler-Blackcomb Mountains (604/932-3434).

—*Steven Threndyle*

kilometres (21 miles) of trails at the Mad River Nordic Centre. A super-popular route in town is the 15-kilometre (9-mile) Lost Lake circuit of easy to very difficult marked trails, which you can enter across the street from the Blackcomb Mountain parking lot. A 4-kilometre (2.5-mile) portion of this trail is illuminated for night skiing as well. Passes are $8 per day, and a one-hour Nordic or skate lesson costs about $35.

The village's Valley Trail system connects the municipality's various communities from Alta Lake to Green Lake; in winter it's transformed into a trail groomed for both Nordic and skate skiing that can be accessed for no charge. **GARIBALDI PROVINCIAL PARK** (604/898-3678) maintains 7 kilometres (4.2 miles) of marked, groomed trails at Singing Pass and another 10 kilometres (6 miles) at Cheakamus Lake Trail. On Highway 99 north of Mount Currie, **JOFFRE LAKES PROVINCIAL PARK** (604/924-2200) is a tranquil forested area with a few short trails that wind deep into the forest and circle the glacial lakes.

SNOWSHOERS who want to hike Whistler Mountain must book a hike with Outdoor Adventures@Whistler (Whistler Mountain; 604/932-0647; www.adventureswhistler.com). Otherwise, you're free to trek in designated areas at Mad River Nordic Centre and the Lost Lake circuit. Call the Whistler Activity and Information Centre (604/932-2394) for information on **PARAGLIDE LESSONS** (with or without skis), **DOGSLED TRIPS, SNOWSHOE HIKES, SNOWMOBILE TOURS,** and **SLEIGH RIDES.** Whistler Backcountry Adventures (4314 Main St, Town Plaza, Village North; 604/938-1410; www.fish-bc.com) is a reputable outfitter that books **HELI-SKI TRIPS** for skiers and snowboarders, as well as dogsled and snowshoe tours to the nearby glaciers. Located 5–6 kilometres (3.5 miles) from the village, the **MEADOW PARK SPORTS CENTRE,** 604/938-PARK, is Whistler's outstanding aquatic, ice, and fitness facility, offering **ICE SKATERS** a place to lace up their skates and stretch their legs. Call ahead to get times for public sessions.

MOUNTAIN BIKING

Diehards can ski Horstman Glacier until mid-August, but come summer, do what the locals do. Turn your back on Whistler Village Square and head for either mountain, the Valley Trail, or the road to Pemberton on your mountain bike. In the summer, mountain-bike rentals are available at Whistler ski shops, at the base of the Whistler gondola, and on Blackcomb at the Glacier Shop (604/938-7744).

For $24, the **WHISTLER MOUNTAIN BIKE PARK** (800/766-0449) is accessible via the Whistler Village gondola and features over 100 kilometres of single-track trail as well as an unusual skills-development course. Exhilarating descents back to the village are possible on both single- and double-track trails. Camps and instructional programs are available as well.

HIKING

Hike through the lush alpine meadows if you prefer to stop and smell the wildflowers. Besides hikes in the immediate vicinity, the two- to three-hour hike up into the glorious **ANCIENT CEDARS** grove on Cougar Mountain (off Hwy 99, up a gravel road off the north shore of Green Lake) is well worth it; you can smell the grove before you see it. For a much flatter stroll, take the pleasant half-hour walk to the dramatic waterfalls at **NAIRN FALLS PROVINCIAL PARK** 32 kilometres (20 miles) north of Whistler. Access is on the right-hand side of the highway as you drive from Whistler toward Pemberton.

RIVER RAFTING

The stunning Coast Mountains provide the scenic backdrop for rafting on several rivers in the Whistler area, north of Vancouver. Trips range from white-knuckle excitement on the Green, Birkenhead, or Elaho Rivers to placid float-trips down the Squamish and Lillooet Rivers. **WHISTLER RIVER ADVENTURES** (604/932-3532; www.whistler-river-adv.com), and **WEDGE RAFTING** (604/932-7171; www.whistler.net/wedge rafting), operate trips daily from late spring to the end of September. During the winter, guided river-rafting trips down the Squamish are operated through Rivers and Oceans Expeditions; call 800/360-RAFT. Also during the winter, guided eagle-viewing float trips down the Checkamus River are operated through **CANADIAN OUTBACK ADVENTURES** (604/921-7250).

OTHER OUTDOOR ACTIVITIES

Take your sailboard to Alta Lake (where windsurfing started in Canada), just west of Whistler Village, on the other side of Blueberry Hill. Dip your raft, canoe, or kayak into the River of Golden Dreams, north of Whistler Village; it connects Alta Lake to Green Lake. Pull out your fly rod and try for a few trout at Birkenhead Lake, a 40-minute drive north of Whistler. **WHISTLER OUTDOOR EXPERIENCE COMPANY** (604/932-3389) is a broker for guided hikes, mountain horseback riding, river rafting, kayaking, and fly-in fishing trips. In-line skating is hot, and **BLACKCOMB SKI & SPORT** (604/938-7788) offers bargain instruction packages that include skate rentals.

Shopping

The Whistler villages are brimming with apparel, jewellery, craft, specialty, gift, cosmetic, and sports equipment shops. **HORSTMAN TRADING COMPANY** (4555 Blackcomb Wy, Upper Village; 604/938-7725) carries a great selection of men's and women's Bogner and Tsunami fleecewear as well as swimwear, footwear, and summertime casuals. **MISTER WHISTLER** (Glacier Lodge, Upper Village; 604/938-1743) has some of

GOLFING YOUR WAY UP THE SEA TO SKY HIGHWAY

The completion of several world-class golf courses in the 160-kilometre (100-mile) Sea to Sky corridor has been good news for duffers and scratch players alike. It's not Arizona or California, but once the clouds dissipate, the breathtaking mountain scenery more than makes up for the rainy weather.

Between a rock and a wet place might be the best way to describe **Furry Creek Golf and Country Club** (604/894-2224), located 48 kilometres (30 miles) north of downtown Vancouver on Highway 99. Built on a mountainside that slopes (none too gently in some places) to the briny depths of Howe Sound, the course must be seen to be believed. The course is short—6,001 yards from the gold tees—but requires the legs of a mountain goat to walk it. Carts are mandatory.

No less a golfing legend than Arnold Palmer himself ushered in the modern era of Whistler golf when he took a local nine-hole executive course and redesigned it into the **Whistler Golf Club** (604/932-4544) in 1982. From the back tees, this superb recreational layout is just under 6,400 yards, with a slope rating of 128.

Palmer was followed to Whistler by the great architect Robert Trent Jones Jr., who built the stunning **Chateau Whistler Golf Club** (604/938-2095). Situated away from the village on the Blackcomb benchlands, the course is challenging; from the back tees, it's 6,635 yards, with a slope rating of 142. The clubhouse is an architectural marvel that goes well beyond the typical "19th Hole."

Chateau Whistler fairly screamed "Can you top this?" to course architects, a challenge met by none other than the design team of Jack Nicklaus. Nicklaus has had a hand in planning more than 150 courses worldwide, but **Nicklaus North at Whistler** (604/938-9898) is the only one he's ever lent his name to. Alongside the gurgling waters of Fitzsimmons Creek and adjacent to Green Lake, the course has water hazards on 15 of 18 holes. Nonetheless, it has been built with the recreational golfer in mind, with generous landing areas for well-placed drives.

Thirty-eight kilometres (24 miles) north of Whistler, in Pemberton, designer Bob Cupp took advantage of something not often found in mountainous terrain: a broad, flat, sunny valley hemmed in by vertiginous mountain peaks. Many golfers who play all of the Sea to Sky tracks on a regular basis think that **Big Sky Golf and Country Club** (800/668-7900) is the most scenic of the lot. There are two municipal tracks worth mentioning as well. The **Squamish Golf and Country Club** (604/898-9961) is the oldest golf course in the Sea to Sky region. The view of nearby Mount Garibaldi is striking. So are the views at the **Pemberton Golf and Country Club** (604/894-6197). Both clubs welcome visiting players of all handicaps and are memorable for their scenery and playability.

—Steven Threndyle

the best-designed T-shirts, sweatshirts, souvenirs, ball caps, and fleece-wear bearing Whistler/Blackcomb logos. **AMOS & ANDES** (4321 Village Gate Blvd, Village North; 604/932-7202) has a beautiful collection of hand-knit sweaters for both men and women plus cool cotton summer dresses.

KEIR FINE JEWELLERY (3421 Village Gate Blvd, Whistler Village; 604/932-2944) has a pleasing selection of designer pieces created by Canadian artisans, and carries Italian gold and Swiss watches. **NORTH-WEST CONNECTION** (4232 Sunrise Alley, Whistler Village; 604/932-4646) carries Native-designed jewellery and crafts. **BLACK TUSK GALLERY** (4359 Main St, the Summit, Town Plaza, Village North; 604/905-5540) presents a notable collection of Native artworks, ranging from silk-screen prints to sculptures. Natural cosmetics and body treatments from **LUSH** (Delta Whistler Village Suites, Town Plaza, Village North; 604/932-5445) and **THE BODY SHOP** (Blackcomb Lodge; Whistler Village; 604/932-2639) may have originated back in England but have caught on like wildfire here and in Vancouver.

WHISTLER BACKCOUNTRY ADVENTURES (4314 Main St, Town Plaza, Village North; 604/932-3474) not only arranges guided tours and sells fishing licences; it also carries a great selection of fishing rods, tackle, sports gear, and outdoor clothing. **KATMANDU** (4368 Main St, the Marketplace, Village North; 604/932-6381) supplies outdoor and camping gear, and rents, repairs, and sells mountain bikes, snowboards, skis, and snowshoes.

Check out the selection of local books, national best-sellers, magazines, and newspapers at **ARMCHAIR BOOKS** (4205 Village Square, Whistler Village; 604/932-5557). Try a Cuban cigar from the **VANCOU-VER CIGAR COMPANY** (4314 Main St, Town Plaza, Village North; 604/932-6099), where you'll find everything from Monte Cristos and Macanudos to cigar trimmers and cases. If you haven't seen or heard enough of the bears around Whistler, pick up a memento from **BEAR PAUSE** (Eagle Lodge, Town Plaza, Village North; 604/905-0121), which has bear-related collectibles, books, stationery, and cards.

One of Whistler's coolest (and most overlooked) nooks of commerce is **FUNCTION JUNCTION** (at new traffic lights as you enter Whistler from the south), a rustic shopping area located south of Creekside. It's where locals shop for all their household needs, and it's also where you'll find the **WHISTLER BREWERY** (1209 Alpha Lake Rd; 604/932-6185), one of the resort's most popular microbreweries.

Nightlife

Start your evening at **CITTA BISTRO** (4217 Village Stroll, Whistler Village; 604/932-4177), the local nighttime gathering place. Sip a cocktail or have a quick meal before heading around the corner to the **SAVAGE BEAGLE BAR** (4222 Village Square, Whistler Village; 604/938-3337), a theme-based nightclub that features DJs and occasional live bands, and attracts the young-and-beautiful snowboarding crowd. The Wine Bar at the **BEAR FOOT BISTRO** (4122 Village Green, Whistler Village; 604/932-6613) draws a lively crowd. This dimly lit and very comfortable piano bar offers jazz combined with a very congenial bar staff.

If you're looking for a pub atmosphere, there's no better place than the **DUBH LINN GATE** (see Top 20 Restaurants in this chapter), which offers an authentic Irish-pub interior, a fine menu of brews and single malts, and live Celtic music nightly. **TOMMY AFRICA'S BAR** (Blackcomb Lodge, Whistler Village; 604/932-6090) was recognized as the "best place to witness young nubile babes shaking their groove thing." **MAXX FISH** (Blackcomb Lodge, Whistler Village; 604/932-1904) offers a mix of everything from live blues to DJs.

RECREATION

RECREATION

Outdoor Activities

In the early 1980s, Vancouver's population swelled, even as the economy nose-dived, with a massive recession in the resource sector. Many of the new arrivals were young people from other parts of Canada, coming to Vancouver to enjoy an idealized West Coast lifestyle, a place where they could play tennis in the morning, in-line skate to the beach in the afternoon, and, in the late fall, winter, or spring, take to the North Shore mountains for a night of skiing or snowboarding.

Better economic times arrived, but the outdoor recreation lifestyle is stronger than ever. Hundreds of kilometres of new hiking, cycling, and in-line skating trails have been built. Beaches, once crammed with laid-back hippies, are frequented by volleyball players, Frisbee throwers, and skimboarders surfing the water's edge. Woe betide the Vancouverite who does not look good in Lycra. To find out about events going on and places to go, get a copy of the free publication *Coast,* an outdoor recreation magazine available at retail stores, libraries, and community centres in the city.

BICYCLING

Vancouver's superb recreational cycling trails offer expansive views of the sea and mountains as they wind through stands of fir, cedar, and hemlock, and follow the shoreline of numerous bays and inlets. Not all of the treasures are 100 percent natural: you'll find neighbourhoods to explore and places to stop for cappuccino, pizza by the slice, fish-and-chips, or frozen yogurt. Cyclists with more time can explore the Sunshine Coast and Gulf Islands, with the help of the largest ferry system in the world.

All bicyclists are required by law to wear a helmet—failure to don one may result in a fine. It's against the law to cycle while wearing a headset, so keep it in the day pack. Both a headlight and taillight are legally required for cycling near dawn and dusk—and at night, of course. Also, bring a shackle-style U-lock if you plan to stop and shop or walk around—unfortunately, bike theft is rampant.

The best one-stop source for bicycling information is **CYCLING BRITISH COLUMBIA** (332-1367 W Broadway; 604/737-3034; www.cycling.bc.ca; map:C3). Its small library has maps, bike routes, guidebooks, and a competition calendar. Racers should note that time trials and criterions are held each week throughout the summer at the University of British Columbia. Details on upcoming races can be found on their Web site; for off-road cycling, refer to the mountain biking section in this chapter.

The city of Vancouver produces *Cycling in Vancouver,* a good map of bike routes printed on tear-resistant paper. It's distributed by most bike shops and is free. In recent years, there's been a major push by the city's planning department to reduce accidents between cars and bikes by twinning high-volume streets with bike routes a few blocks away. Off-Broadway, which takes riders along Seventh and Eighth Avenues, and Midtown/Ridgeway, which goes along 37th Avenue, are the best east-west routes; the Ontario, Cypress, and Sunrise routes cover the city from north to south. Although you will encounter some cars on these quiet streets, through traffic is deterred by concrete barriers that force cars back onto the main thoroughfares. Here are some of the best rides in Vancouver:

SEASIDE BICYCLE ROUTE / A terrific 15-kilometre (9.4-mile) route linking the Stanley Park seawall (map:D1) with other waterfront pathways around False Creek (map:D2), Vanier Park (map:D2), Kitsilano Beach (map:C2), and Jericho Beach (map:B2), and ending below UBC at Spanish Banks (map:A2). A less-crowded alternative to Stanley Park's seawall, this route offers more rest-stop options: a cappuccino on Cornwall Avenue, swimming at Kitsilano Pool, strolling at Jericho Beach, or kite flying in Vanier Park. Parts of this route follow city streets; look for the green-and-white bike-route signs. Maps can be picked up at several info kiosks along the way. **RECKLESS THE BIKE STORE** (1810 Fir St; 604/731-2420; www.rektek.com; map:P7) is the nearest rental shop.

STANLEY PARK SEAWALL / No cycle visit to Vancouver is complete without a spin around this 10.5-kilometre (6.5-mile) seawall (map:D1). Watch seaplanes taking off and landing in Burrard Inlet, stop and smell the rose gardens, brace yourself for the Nine O'clock Gun, shout out at Hallelujah Point, and gulp great breaths of cedar-scented air while trying not to disturb nesting Canada geese around Lost Lagoon (map:P1). To escape the crowds, venture off the pavement onto other packed-dirt trails inside the park's core. There are many bike-rental shops near the Georgia/Denman Street entrance to Stanley Park. The best known is **SPOKES BICYCLE RENTAL AND ESPRESSO BAR** (1798 W Georgia St; 604/688-5141; map:P2), which combines cycling and coffee, the favourite passions of many Vancouverites.

RIVER ROAD TO STEVESTON / A fun, flat, 36-kilometre (22.5-mile) loop in the suburb of Richmond. Families often do just a portion of this circuit. Park your car on the west side of the Dinsmore Bridge (near the RV park; map:C6). Cycle along the gravel path on the dike to the fishing village of Steveston (map:C8). Once there, buy an ice cream or sample the best fish-and-chips you'll ever eat. The finely pebbled route is level, but twisty in spots. There is no finer place to watch the sun go down than

Garry Point Park (map:C8), just west of Steveston. **STEVESTON BICYCLE** (3731 Chatham St; 604/271-5544; map:C8) rents bikes in the summer months.

GULF ISLANDS / From March to October, cyclists use the BC Ferries dock in the community of Tsawwassen (pronounced "swah-sehn"), at the south tip of Delta, as a departure point for exploring the southern Gulf Islands; Salt Spring, Galiano, Mayne, North Pender, South Pender, and Saturna Islands are the most popular. Accommodation ranges from provincial park campgrounds to a variety of bed-and-breakfasts. Swimming coves, pubs, and shady arbutus trees give welcome relief from the occasional hill. You can also take BC Ferries from Horseshoe Bay at the western tip of West Vancouver. Bear in mind that schedules change seasonally. If you're taking a motor vehicle, be prepared for lengthy lineups during the summer months, and that you will be charged extra for having an overheight vehicle if you have a vehicle with bikes mounted on a roof rack. Call the **BC FERRIES** recorded information line (888/223-3779) or use its Web site (www.bcferries.bc.ca) for sailing times. Vehicle reservations can be made for major routes between Vancouver and Vancouver Island; call 888/724-5223 in BC—604/444-2890 if you're calling from outside the province—or use the Web address: www.bcferries.bc.ca/res/.

CANOEING/KAYAKING

British Columbia doesn't have a kayak or canoe on its coat of arms, but it could. More than 50,000 residents of the province go kayaking or canoeing, and paddlers can take their pick of thousands of lakes and rivers, as well as offshore islands—many of which are uninhabited.

On any day of the year, marine enthusiasts carry on the Northwest Coast Native tradition by paddling modern versions of the *baidarka*, or sea kayak. The sea kayak is longer and sleeker than its whitewater cousin, and some boats are specially constructed for tandem paddlers. Most of the bays and inlets around Vancouver are perfect for even novice paddlers, but taking an introductory course is a good idea. All of the kayak rental shops close to Vancouver offer this type of lessons. Learn the basic paddle strokes and self-rescue techniques, then rent single- or two-person kayaks at Jericho Beach (map:B2), Granville Island (map:Q6), or Deep Cove (map:H1).

Betty Pratt-Johnson is the grande dame of whitewater trips in the province. A number of her books cover flatwater kayaking and canoeing across British Columbia. *Kayak Routes of the Pacific Northwest Coast,* by Peter McGee, and *Sea Kayaking Canada's West Coast,* by John Ince and Hedi Kottner, are indispensable guides to exploring the province's 27,000 kilometres (16,875 miles) of coastline. Marine charts and tide tables are available from most Vancouver marine stores.

The Canoeing Association, the Whitewater Kayaking Association, and the Sea Kayaking Association of British Columbia are useful sources of information about paddle sports in the province. They can be contacted through the **OUTDOOR RECREATION COUNCIL OF BRITISH COLUMBIA** (1367 W Broadway; 604/737-3058; map:C2).

FALSE CREEK/ENGLISH BAY / The waters of English Bay (map:C2) toward Stanley Park, and by Kitsilano Beach and west toward Spanish Banks, offer a mix of benign and moderately challenging conditions. Watch for unpredictable winds and tides around Spanish Banks (map:A2) on the south side of English Bay, and at Lighthouse Park in West Vancouver on the north side. Sea kayakers are prohibited from using the busy freighter-and-cruise-ship lanes (map:E1) between Lions Gate and Second Narrows Bridges. For absolute beginners, the pondlike surface of False Creek (map:R7) offers reassurance, but little natural ambience. Many other paddle-driven watercraft share these waters.

INDIAN ARM / Indian Arm (map:I1) is a finger-shaped fjord that bends northward from Burrard Inlet for 30 kilometres (18.8 miles), deep into the heart of the Coast Mountains. Travel it and you will see impenetrable forests growing on impossibly steep hillsides, rising from the bowline for hundreds of vertical metres. You can rent boats at the **DEEP COVE CANOE AND KAYAK CENTRE** (2156 Banbury Rd, North Vancouver; 604/929-2268; www.deepcovekayak.com) and paddle across Indian Arm—about 1.5 kilometres (1 mile)—to Jug Island Beach or Belcarra Park (map:I1). A paddle to the south leads to Cates Park (map:H1), where Malcolm Lowry wrote *Under the Volcano*. It takes about four hours to reach the head of this glorious fjord. Inexperienced paddlers should beware of swells from the wakes of passing yachts, speedboats, and sailboats. **BELCARRA PADDLING COMPANY** (604/936-0236) is on the other side of Deep Cove (reached via a circuitous route through Port Moody; map:J2) and offers essentially the same paddling experience as starting from Deep Cove does. Custom tours of Indian Arm are provided by **LOTUS LAND ADVENTURES** (800/528-3531; www.lotuslandtours.com). Geared specifically for tourists staying at Vancouver-area hotels, Lotus Land picks you up at your hotel, looks after all of the guiding and equipment rental, and throws in a great salmon barbecue. No paddling experience necessary.

FLATWATER LAKES AND RIVERS / There are several small bodies of water within a two-hour drive that are suitable for easy canoeing or sea kayaking. East of the city, on the north side of the Fraser River, you'll find Alouette Lake, Pitt Lake, Widgeon Slough, and the Harrison River. Canoe rentals are available at **ALOUETTE LAKE**, and there's camping in adjacent **GOLDEN EARS PROVINCIAL PARK** (604/924-2200).

BOWEN ISLAND / Bowen Island is a short ferry hop from Horseshoe Bay, at the west end of West Vancouver. Located right beside the dock, **BOWEN ISLAND SEA KAYAKING** (604/947-9266) rents sea kayaks for short tours from one of its three bases around the island. Tides, winds, and boat wakes can be tricky, but the views in Howe Sound, a major fjord north of Vancouver, are tremendous.

GULF ISLANDS / There is a type of large black fishing bird on the west coast, called a cormorant, that flies only a few inches off the water. Sea kayaking is the best way of getting a cormorant's-eye view of the Gulf Islands, a long archipelago between Vancouver Island and the mainland. The paddling here is done in safe, scenic waters. Pocket-size, pebble-beach coves shaded by rust-barked arbutus trees beckon the weary paddler. If you have your own boat, just get on the ferry and follow your instincts. Beware: although this area is one of the sunniest and most temperate in the province, the water is frigid, even in summer, and the tide can move water unpredictably as it sweeps through the twists and turns of the little straits between the islands. Less experienced kayakers should stay close to shore, where an easy swim leads to safety in case of a spill. These days, it seems as though each of the islands has at least one kayak rental shop. Suggested ones include **GALIANO ISLAND SEA KAYAKING** (250/539-2930), **GULF ISLAND KAYAKING**, also on Galiano (250/539-2442; www.galianoislandseakayaking.com), **SEA OTTER KAYAKING** (250/537-5678) on Salt Spring Island, **MOUAT POINT KAYAKS** (250/629-6767) on Pender Island, and **MAYNE ISLAND KAYAK AND CANOE RENTALS** (250/539-2667).

SUNSHINE COAST / Less-visited than the southern Gulf Islands or Vancouver Island, the Sunshine Coast, north of Vancouver and Howe Sound, offers tremendous paddling opportunities for everyone, from whitewater-rodeo cowboys to families looking for calm lakes to explore. Sechelt Inlet is a 35- kilometre (22-mile)-long combination freshwater and saltwater indentation in the Coast Mountains. Eight marine park campsites are placed en route. At the head of the inlet is where you'll find Skookumchuck Narrows—a whitewater paradise, especially around full moon, when the tides conspire to turn this usually benign stretch of water into a boiling froth. (The word *skookumchuck* is Chinook jargon—a West Coast Native patois—for "powerful.") Sea kayaks are available for rent in the communities of Sechelt, Egmont, and Powell River.

POWELL LAKES CANOE ROUTE / The Powell River Canoe Circuit, located on the Sunshine Coast north of Vancouver, takes in more than 57 kilometres (35.6 miles) of canoeing and 8 kilometres (5 miles) of portages. There are eight lakes in the loop, but easy access to various parts of the route via logging roads makes day trips popular. The entire circuit takes a week to complete and rewards paddlers with good views of coastal rain forest and glimpses of inaccessible, seldom-visited mountain peaks—and a great deal of peace and quiet. This route is best paddled between April and November, since the higher lakes are frozen during the winter months and roads become inaccessible. Call **SUNSHINE COAST FOREST DISTRICT OFFICE** (604/485-0700) for maps and directions.

CLIMBING/MOUNTAINEERING

The Coast Mountains stretch northward from the 49th parallel, the largest portion of a massive cordillera that extends from the Mexican border to Alaska. Within its huge geographical territory, hundreds of unsurmounted summits and cross-country traverses remain to be tackled. Virtually every kind of mountaineering challenge can be found within a day's drive of downtown Vancouver, from frozen-waterfall climbing in Lillooet, a town northeast of Vancouver, to rock climbing the sun-baked granite of the Smoke Bluffs near Squamish, a town north of Vancouver. Spectacular glacier ascents can be made in Garibaldi Provincial Park and on the peaks surrounding the Joffre Lakes Recreation Area east of Pemberton (which is also north of Vancouver, near Whistler).

Some of the best views of Vancouver can be seen from the summit of several prominent peaks that dwarf the city skyline. Most of these peaks are accessible by well-maintained hiking trails. But a word to the wise: fog, rain, wind, and freezing temperatures can turn even the least-technical climb into an ordeal, so always carry extra food and clothing, even for a day trip, and let people know where you're going and when you expect to return.

There are so many hiking and mountaineering organizations in the Lower Mainland that they have their own umbrella group, the **FEDERATION OF MOUNTAIN CLUBS OF BRITISH COLUMBIA** (47 W Broadway; 604/878-7007; map:U7). Trail building, safety and education, wilderness preservation, and public awareness of mountain recreation issues are all part of their mandate. Courses run by the Federation's Canada West Mountain School offer the best introduction to the wilderness currently available.

MOUNT SEYMOUR PROVINCIAL PARK / This mountainous park (map:E0) is a 30-minute drive north from downtown Vancouver. Hiking to the top of the three rounded summits, each slightly higher than the last, provides a surprisingly authentic wilderness experience if you go there midweek, or in the winter on snowshoes. Your reward is an unparalleled view: north into the heart of the Coast Mountains, south beyond the urban sprawl to the Gulf Islands and San Juan Islands, east to the sleeping volcano of Mount Baker in northern Washington State and western Washington's Cascade Range, and west toward Vancouver Island. The 8-kilometre

(5-mile) return trip takes about four hours. Call the park at 604/986-2261 for more information

CYPRESS PROVINCIAL PARK / Black Mountain in Cypress Provincial Park, north of West Vancouver, can be climbed on foot or reached by chairlift. Nearby Cabin Lake is on the Baden-Powell Trail and is a good spot for a refreshing midsummer dip. The two-hour Black Mountain Loop Trail is perfect for introducing the family to the joys of hiking in the mountains. Call the park at 604/924-2200 for more information.

GARIBALDI PROVINCIAL PARK / North-northwest of Vancouver, Garibaldi Provincial Park is accessible from several points along Highway 99 en route to the resort city of Whistler. Diamond Head, the Black Tusk Meadows, Singing Pass, and Wedgemount Lake provide varying degrees of challenge and are suitable for day trips or overnight expeditions. Perhaps the most outstanding landmark is Black Tusk, a volcanic plug that is 2,315 metres (7,595 feet) tall. The trail to its base starts at Taylor Campground. Because of crumbling rock and high exposure, climbing the Tusk itself is only for experienced mountaineers. Contact **BC PARKS** at 604/898-3678 for trail and weather reports.

TANTALUS RANGE / North of Vancouver and halfway along the Sea-to-Sky Highway, which runs from Squamish to Whistler, a vehicle pullout provides a panoramic view of the most spectacular subrange of mountains in southwestern BC. The Tantalus range is a series of jagged, heavily glaciated summits clustered together on the west side of the Squamish River. There are two access points to the Tantalus: the Lake Lovelywater Trail—a canoe is needed to ferry climbers and gear across the swiftly flowing river—and via Sigurd Creek. For detailed information, call the **BC FOREST SERVICE, SQUAMISH DISTRICT OFFICE**, at 604/898-2100. Climbing in the Tantalus is a rugged wilderness experience, on par with just about anything in the Rockies or Alaska, and your group should be well prepared.

INDOOR CLIMBING / Many local rock climbers learn their craft indoors at the **EDGE CLIMBING CENTRE** (2-1485 Welch St; 604/984-9080; map:D1) in North Vancouver. This is the rock climber's version of an indoor jungle gym. The carved holds and textured surfaces present a stunningly realistic simulation of routes and situational problems found on the real crags. All of the routes are rated, with varying degrees of difficulty. Even if you get vertigo standing too close to a guardrail, it's fun to go and watch human spiders in action. You can take courses, rent shoes and harnesses, and play until 11pm, seven days a week. The **CLIFFHANGER** (106 W 1st Ave, near Science World; 604/874-2400; www.cliffhanger.com; map:V5) and **ROCK HOUSE** (3771 Jacombs Rd; 604/276-0012; map:D5) in Richmond are two other popular climbing gyms.

ROCK CLIMBING / For a taste of the real thing, drive 60 kilometres (37 miles) north on Highway 99 to Squamish. The Stawamus Chief is the second-largest freestanding granite outcropping in the world; the only one bigger is the Rock of Gibraltar. There are more than 280 climbing routes on its various walls, faces, and slabs. A vehicle pullout north of Shannon Falls provides an excellent vantage point for seeing climbers in action. Less dramatic but equally challenging climbs can be found in Murrin Provincial Park and on the Smoke Bluffs—Canada's first rock-climbing park. Novice climbers will like the grippy granite and easy moves on Banana Peel, Diedre, Cat Crack, and Sugarloaf. Lessons and guiding are available through **SQUAMISH ROCK GUIDES** (604/892-2086; www. mountain-inter.net/sqrockguides).

DIVING

The clean, cold, and clear waters between Vancouver Island and the Lower Mainland are home to more than 450 fish species, 600 plant species, 4,000 species of invertebrates—and the ghosts of countless sunken vessels. The best time to dive is in the winter, since plankton growth in the summer months often obscures visibility. Both charter and do-it-yourself diving are popular here.

Betty Pratt-Johnson's *101 Dives from the Mainland of Washington and British Columbia* is essential reading for divers. Wreck divers interested in some nautical history should pick up a copy of Fred Rogers's *Shipwrecks of British Columbia*. Get air, tanks, and the latest news on what's hot from **DIVER'S WORLD** (1813 W 4th Ave; 604/732-1344; map:O7). For local knowledge, pick up a copy of *Diver* magazine at dive shops throughout the Lower Mainland and Sunshine Coast.

The federal **DEPARTMENT OF FISHERIES AND OCEANS, FISHING INFORMATION** phone line (604/666-0583) is a good place to start; the department's listings in the Blue Pages at the back of the Vancouver phone book provides numbers for openings and closures for a number of types of fish and shellfish. As well, local fishing shops all provide lots of information and free copies of government regulations, which sometimes change seasonally. **SHELLFISH RED TIDE UPDATES** (604/666-2828) can provide you with the latest information on this naturally occurring toxic plankton that can affect shellfish during various periods of the year.

WHYTECLIFF MARINE PARK / This fine undersea park in West Vancouver contains a variety of marine life in its protected cove and nearby waters. Copper Cove, Telegraph Cove, and Cates Park in Deep Cove (map:H1), all of which are in the same general area, are also local favourites. Be sure to check local regulations before harvesting edibles like crabs or sea cucumbers.

SUNSHINE COAST / With more than 100 dives mapped by local enthusiasts, **POWELL RIVER**, a town north of Vancouver at the top of the Malaspina Peninsula on the Sunshine Coast, is officially the scuba-diving capital of Canada. Charters, rentals, compressed air, and guides are all available through **BEACH GARDENS RESORT & MARINA** (604/485-6267; bgarden@www.coc.powell-river.bc.ca). Wreck diving is the attraction here. Look for the remains of the *Shamrock* off Vivian Island, and the HMCS *Chaudiere*, a World War II frigate and now an artificial reef that was intentionally sunk off Kunechin Point in Sechelt Inlet a few years ago for divers. Rare red coral thrives in these waters, along with octopus and wolf eels. Many divers seek out the underwater mermaid, a sunken statue that resides near the BC Ferries dock at Saltery Bay.

SALTWATER/FRESHWATER FISHING

BC's scenic coastline and unspoiled wilderness are a magnificent backdrop for fishing and make up for the rare occasion when anglers get skunked. Freshwater anglers can catch trout—including the legendary steelhead—char, and salmon. Saltwater anglers can try for five species of salmon, plus rockfish, lingcod, and halibut.

Two government agencies administer sport fishing. The federal **DEPARTMENT OF FISHERIES AND OCEANS** (604/666-6331) regulates saltwater fishing, and the provincial **MINISTRY OF ENVIRONMENT, LANDS AND PARKS** (604/582-5200) regulates freshwater fishing. Licences are required for either type of fishing. You can purchase these at tackle shops throughout the Lower Mainland, which are also great sources of information about where the fish are biting. These shops, and tourist information centres, also have free copies of the provincial and federal sport fishing regulations. The section on catch-and-release in streams and lakes is particularly important for the freshwater angler. Fly fishermen would do well to pick up a copy of Art Lingren's *Irresistible Waters: Fly Fishing in B.C. Throughout the Year.*

HORSESHOE BAY AND HOLE IN THE WALL / Howe Sound, a 40-kilometre (25-mile) inlet that starts at Horseshoe Bay north of Vancouver, is perfect for saltwater fishing. Whether you're out to hook the fish of your dreams or just want a few relaxing hours on the ocean within sight of land (an area of water the locals call "the saltchuck"), **SEWELL'S MARINA** (604/921-3474; www.sewellsmarina.com) offers a fleet of 60 rental boats, as well as a regularly scheduled group fishing tour. Rock cod and salmon can be caught at the legendary Hole-in-the-Wall, a what-you-might-expect geographical feature, several kilometres north of the marina.

RICE LAKE / This lake is in the Seymour Demonstration Forest (604/432-6410) north of Vancouver. To get there, take the Mount Seymour Parkway exit from Highway 1 and follow Lillooet Road past Capilano College to the road's end. The lake is wheelchair-accessible. The Seymour River provides excellent angling opportunities as well.

FRASER RIVER / The Fraser is one of the largest untamed rivers left in the west; its watershed extends almost to the provincial border with Alberta and includes a great hairpin swath of British Columbia. All five species of West Coast salmon make a pilgrimage up the Fraser each year to their spawning grounds—some of which are hundreds of kilometres upstream—at different times throughout the year. Though the salmon fishery has been degraded by overfishing, unseasonably warm water, and loss of habitat as a result of logging and development, make no mistake—the Fraser is still a thriving, abundant ecosystem and one of the most productive salmon rivers in the world. It's also one of the most regulated, as far as fishing is concerned, so ensure you stay abreast of regulations by picking up a free copy of the sport fishing rules at tackle shops when you get your licence.

Because the Fraser empties into the ocean after traversing a wide, urban delta, its water level is subject to tidal influx. Deas Island Regional Park (604/224-5739) in the Vancouver suburb of Richmond (map:E8), south of the city, and McDonald Beach (604/231-0740) at Sea Island (where Vancouver International Airport is located; map:C5) are the most popular places to wet a line close to where the Fraser reaches its terminus. These are also the places on the Fraser where you're most likely to find the rare white sturgeon, a gigantic bottom feeder that often lives to be a century old.

There are salmon enhancement programs at work on several of the Fraser's tributary creeks, with spawning channels and fish hatcheries constructed to improve productivity. Literally hundreds of mountain creeks feed major Fraser tributaries, like the Pitt, Harrison, Stave, Chilliwack, and Vedder (and those are just the main feeders in the Fraser's delta area). Though some of the more popular spots end up to be standing-room-only on weekends, the fishing here can be truly world-class. On the north side of the Fraser, as you move east of Vancouver, the best bets include Rolley Lake, Kanaka Creek, the Ruskin Recreation Area, and the Harrison River. On the south bank, also going east, Glen Valley, Derby Reach, and Matsqui Trail Regional Park are the action places. The Chilliwack River has a tremendous coho salmon run in the fall.

GOLFING

The popular lotus-land image of going skiing in the morning and golfing in the afternoon in Vancouver is not as far-fetched as you might think. Although golf courses aren't in prime condition in December or January, by the time April rolls around, many of the Lower Mainland links are in midsummer shape. Golf has been the fastest-growing activity in Greater Vancouver for some time now, and new courses are being built as quickly as developers can acquire land. The City of Vancouver operates several municipal golf courses, and some privately owned courses are open to the public as well. Here's a sampling of the best.

FRASERVIEW GOLF COURSE / 7800 Vivian Dr at E 54th Ave; 604/280-1818 On some days it seems that every golfer in Canada has descended onto the fairways of this south Vancouver course, which overlooks the Fraser River. Featuring wide-open fairways for most of its 5.8-kilometre (6,346-yard) length, Fraserview is a pleasant course—and the busiest in the province. *Map:F4.*

MAYFAIR LAKES GOLF COURSE / 5460 No. 7 Rd, Richmond; 604/276-0505 "Water, water, everywhere" might be the unofficial motto of this attractive course in the Vancouver suburb of Richmond. Not as tree-lined as some of the more established tracks, but definitely a must-play in terms of challenge and design. Par 72, 6-kilometre (6,641-yard) course. Watch for salmon jumping in some of the water hazards—it's guaranteed to distract your swing. *Map:F6.*

PEACE PORTAL GOLF COURSE / 16900 4th Ave, Surrey; 604/538-4818 Glance to the right on Highway 99 as you enter Canada from Interstate 5 where it leaves Washington State, and you'll see one of the Lower Mainland's oldest courses, the Peace Portal Golf Course, named after the international boundary monument that straddles the border south of Vancouver. Established in 1928, this mature course is open year-round and is a local favourite. *www.peaceportalgolf.com.*

QUEEN ELIZABETH PITCH AND PUTT / Cambie St near 33rd Ave; 604/874-8336 Serious golfers might scoff at the inclusion of a lowly pitch-and-putt in this type of a listing, but this course offers some of the most breathtaking views of the city from its vantage point atop Little Mountain, a former rock quarry and now a spectacular park in the centre of uptown Vancouver. The P&P is great fun and well used. Non-golfers can stroll the adjacent grounds of Queen Elizabeth Park or visit the Bloedel Conservatory while you play through on the third hole. *Map:E3.*

UNIVERSITY GOLF CLUB / 5185 University Blvd; 604/224-1818 A gorgeous course, well-maintained, and a treat to play no matter what the season. You don't need any connection with the nearby University of British Columbia to play here, and many people attend classes under the tutelage of several certified Canadian Professional Golfers Association pros. *Map:B3.*

HIKING

A telltale sign of the popularity of hiking in Vancouver is that David and Mary Macaree's *103 Hikes in Southwestern British Columbia* is now into its fourth edition. A companion volume, *109 Walks in the Lower Mainland,* is almost as popular. The Macarees know their terrain well, but distances and estimated hiking times are not based on the dawdler. Several of the most popular hikes are listed in the Climbing and Mountaineering section; what follows is a more diverse selection.

GROUSE MOUNTAIN / With its gondola towers and lighted ski runs visible from many parts of the Lower Mainland, Grouse Mountain (1,128 metres or 3,700 feet), north of Vancouver, is one of the city's best-known natural landmarks. On a winter's night, the ski-run lights look like a sparkling necklace. In the warmer seasons, purists can traipse up the Grouse Grind trail, adjacent to the gondola-style Skyride track, to the Grouse Nest Restaurant at the base of the ski runs, and follow a ski run to the top; the less energetic can take the Skyride tram up, and watch the hikers down below work their way up. Trail maps are available at the guest services booth at the **GROUSE MOUNTAIN SKYRIDE** ticket office (Grouse Mountain Resorts; 604/984-0661; www.grousemtn.com).

GARIBALDI PROVINCIAL PARK / North of Vancouver is the jewel of West Coast mountain parks, with more than 60 kilometres (37.5 miles) of developed hiking trails. Beautiful Singing Pass can be reached by taking the Whistler Village Gondola and following a well-defined trail over the intriguingly named Musical Bumps. This is particularly beautiful in August, when the meadows are filled with blooming lupines, Indian paintbrush, and saxifrage. Cheakamus Lake, Diamond Head, and Black Tusk meadows are all worthwhile day trips. If you're going to Black Tusk, a huge granite surge, avoid the crowds and mind-numbing boredom of the infamous Barrier Switchbacks by using the alternative Helm Creek Trail (use the same access as the Cheakamus Lake turnoff). Call 604/898-3678 for information.

GOLDEN EARS PROVINCIAL PARK / Although many hikers like the rugged trails of Garibaldi Park and the North Shore, Golden Ears, east of Vancouver, provides some spectacular views of seldom-visited glaciers and mountains. The best part about climbing Golden Ears is that, although it looks incredibly steep from its precipitous west face, the route up the east side (although it sometimes calls for the use of hands on the way) is little more than an exerting hike. Fit hikers can tackle the 1.7-kilometre (5,597-foot) North Ear, but an early start is necessary as the trailhead is almost at sea level. Once on top, you can marvel at the spectacular view of Pitt Lake and Alouette Lake, two large bodies of freshwater nearby. Alouette is suitable for swimming after you descend. This is not a short day trip, and should be attempted only after the upper meadows are free of snow. For detailed information, call 604/463-3513. Access is off Highway 7.

HOWE SOUND CREST TRAIL / Strong day hikers might want to tackle the Howe Sound Crest Trail. It's a 30-kilometre (18.8-mile) trek—and that's just one way—across several summits north of Vancouver, including Black Mountain, Mount Harvey, Mount Brunswick, and Deeks Peak, ending in picturesque Porteau Cove. Portions of this trail can be reached at various points along Highway 99 north of Horseshoe Bay but, to do the whole trip, you need to have somebody drop you off at Cypress Bowl and meet you at Deeks Creek. There are stiff hills and slippery descents en route, and weather can change quickly. Still, this trail has some awesome views of Howe Sound and the Georgia Strait. Call 604/924-2200 for information.

LIGHTHOUSE PARK / On the bluffs above West Vancouver's Point Atkinson, Lighthouse Park features one of the few remaining stands of old-growth Douglas fir trees. The Douglas fir is the second-tallest tree species found in North America, bested only by the California redwood. This park is fun to walk through, regardless of the weather. There are no crowds during the misty, moody winter months. The smooth igneous rock surrounding the lighthouse provides an ideal spot to rest and enjoy a picnic. Eagle nests, rust-red arbutus trees, and the red-and-white lighthouse, casting its beam across the water, complete this beautiful West Coast postcard. Call 604/925-7200 for information.

MANNING PROVINCIAL PARK / A three-hour drive east on the Trans-Canada Highway (Hwy 1) and a relatively short jaunt along Highway 3—take the Hope-Princeton route at the Hope interchange—Manning Park is spectacular when in bloom. In June, stop at the Rhododendron Flats pullout near the highway; in August, see the brilliant carpet of alpine wildflowers at higher elevations. Trained park naturalists are on duty during periods of peak bloom, and the trail to the alpine meadows is ideal for children as well. If they're restless, have them smell the fragrant *Sitka valerian,* a white wildflower known for its mild calming effect. Call 250/840-8836 for information.

PITT RIVER DYKES / The Pitt is a major tributary of the Fraser, and a walk along its dikes can be enjoyed at any time of the year. You can drive directly to Pitt Lake and take in the breathtaking view of the Coast Mountains to the north, then work your way south along the river's edge, past Chatham Reach, and on toward the Pitt's confluence with the Fraser. If you go on different days and wonder where all of the water has gone, your eyes will not have deceived you. The Pitt is subject to changing river levels as a result of tidal activity. There's great bird-watching here, too. Call 604/530-4983 for information.

HORSEBACK RIDING

Cowboys roam the ranges on the Ponderosa-size ranches of the Cariboo and Chilcotin, but city slickers need only don hats and boots (and pants!) for horseback riding in the Fraser Valley.

CAMPBELL VALLEY REGIONAL PARK / This nature park features equestrian trails, cross-country jumps, picnicking, and nature-study areas. Hop off your horse and pick a handful of blackberries at summer's end. From Highway 1 going east from Vancouver, take the Langley 200th St exit southbound. Travel 14.5 km (9 miles), and turn east on 16th Ave for the North Valley entrance. Horses can be rented at Langley 204 Riding Stables (543 204th St, Langley; 604/533-7978).

GOLDEN EARS PROVINCIAL PARK / A great place for both urban cowboys and the saddle-savvy to trail ride. Commercial stables in Maple Ridge organize summer day rides to Alouette Lake. Hitch your horses, swim in the lake, then head 'em home. J. P.'s Golden Ears Riding Stable is 48 kilometres (30 miles) east of Vancouver on Highway 7 (13175 232nd Ave, Maple Ridge; 604/463-8761).

MANNING PROVINCIAL PARK / This park, which is less than three hours' drive east of Vancouver in the Cascade Range, is a spectacular place to ride horseback. Several hundred kilometres of horse trails crisscross the park. Bring your own horse or rent one through the Manning Park Corral (Manning Park Resort; 250/840-8844; www.manning parkresort.com).

HOT-AIR BALLOONING

FRASER VALLEY / Langley Airport serves as the base for several companies specializing in hot-air balloon tours. **FANTASY BALLOON CHARTERS** (Langley Airport, Unit 209, 5333 216th St, Langley; 604/530-1974) specialize in dawn or dusk champagne flights, taking wing once the air is cooler and less susceptible to turbulent currents. It's the most relaxing way to get an eagle's-eye view of Mount Baker, Golden Ears, and the patchwork quilt of rich farmland bordering the Fraser River.

ICE SKATING

Unlike Canadian cities with below-zero temperatures, Vancouver has a mild winter climate that isn't generally conducive to traditional winter recreational activities such as tobogganing and ice skating. Nevertheless, several recreation facilities are open to skaters, and some outdoor ponds are suitable for a quick pirouette or double axel when an infrequent cold snap hits.

When arctic air comes pouring out of the north, many of the ponds in Vancouver parks freeze over. The Parks Board cordons off part of Lost Lagoon in Stanley Park (map:P1) for free public skating until rising temperatures and precipitation make ice levels unsafe. Other ponds are located in Queen Elizabeth Park in uptown Vancouver near 33rd Ave and

Cambie St (map:D3), along the south shore of False Creek (map:S6) near the downtown core, and on Como Lake in Coquitlam (map:K3). For details, call 604/257-8400.

KAREN MAGNUSSEN RECREATION CENTRE / 2300 Kirkstone Rd, North Vancouver; 604/987-7529 Named after an ex-Olympic medallist who grew up in the neighbourhood, this North Vancouver facility is the premier skating rink on the North Shore. *Map:E1.*

KERRISDALE CYCLONE TAYLOR ARENA / 5670 East Blvd; 604/257-8121 This arena on the west side of Vancouver holds special parties to commemorate events like St. Patrick's Day. Open fall and winter; call ahead for a public skating schedule. *Map:C4.*

KITSILANO COMMUNITY CENTRE / 2690 Larch St; 604/257-6983 Year-round public skating is available at this popular recreation centre on the west side of Vancouver. *Map:C3.*

RILEY PARK COMMUNITY CENTRE / 50 E 30th Ave; 604/257-8545 If the ponds on nearby Queen Elizabeth Park aren't quite frozen over, this nearby recreation centre in the centre of uptown Vancouver can provide an artificial alternative. *Map:E3.*

ROBSON SQUARE / 800 Robson St; 604/482-1800 Join power-lunching businesspeople whirling around the outdoor rink on the lower level of Robson Square, in the centre of the city's core, from November until early March. Rentals are not available, so bring your own skates. *Map:S4.*

IN-LINE SKATING

Vancouver was recently named one of North America's top 10 in-line cities by Condé Nast's *Women's Sports and Fitness* magazine. Still, the city's rather hilly geography means that you should have your braking techniques honed, especially if you're going to be out among pedestrians on city streets.

KERRISDALE CYCLONE TAYLOR ARENA / 5670 East Blvd; 604/257-8121 Like many other Vancouver ice-skating arenas, Kerrisdale becomes a popular in-line skating centre when the ice is taken out in the spring , and it even has an energetic street hockey league for boys and girls. *Map:C4.*

STANLEY PARK SEAWALL / Bladers can travel on parts of the 10.5-kilometre (6.5-mile) seawall that circles Stanley Park near the downtown core, taking in the spectacular viewpoints. This is a busy pedestrian and cycling area, and each group takes their rights seriously. Follow the route's rules of etiquette, or you'll find yourself like the terrain: mostly flat. *Map:D1.*

UNIVERSITY OF BRITISH COLUMBIA / On the far west side of Vancouver, skaters can share an undulating cycle path that loops along 16th

Avenue through **PACIFIC SPIRIT REGIONAL PARK** and back along Chancellor Boulevard into University Village. The paved shoulder of Marine Drive, from West 16th Avenue to West 49th Avenue (map:B3), is also prime skating territory. *Map:B3.*

SEYMOUR DEMONSTRATION FOREST / Only in North Vancouver could you go in-line skating through a wilderness environment that has scenery to rival a national park. The existing 14-kilometre (8.2-mile) paved road to the Seymour Dam is slated to be closed to skaters and cyclists sometime in 2000, to be replaced by a brand-new trail paved specifically for bikers and bladers. Interpretive trails into old-growth forests are planned for the future. Take the Capilano Road exit from Second Narrows Bridge, part of the Trans-Canada Highway (Hwy 1), and follow the signs to Seymour Demonstration Forest. For details, call 604/432-6410. *Map:F0.*

KITE FLYING

When the winds blow whitecaps on the waters of English Bay, it's time to unravel the kite strings and join other fliers at one of the seaside parks.

GARRY POINT PARK / The windswept meadows at the mouth of the Fraser River in Steveston, south of Vancouver, are flat and exposed to south and westerly winds. This park isn't visited often by Vancouverites, but it's well worth the trip. If the wind dies, you can always enjoy a beach bonfire. Drive south out of Vancouver across the Oak Street Bridge, continue along Highway 99 to the Steveston Highway turnoff, just before the Deas Island Tunnel, then go west (to your right) along the Steveston Highway as far as you can go. Then turn south (that'll be to your left) to the park. *Map:B7.*

VANIER PARK / This park on Kitsilano Point is a frequent-flyer spot, where many enthusiasts fly high-performance combat kites that engage in exciting dogfights. *Map:P5.*

MOUNTAIN BIKING

Although many recreation-oriented towns claim to be a mountain-biking mecca, there is a good case for making the Vancouver-Pemberton corridor the fat-tire capital of North America. Every possible accessory and kind of bike is available in the area's specialty stores, and some of the finest frames and components are built in Vancouver. Designers test their prototypes on some of the most technically difficult trails to be found anywhere. For mountain biking in Whistler, see the Whistler chapter.

THE NORTH SHORE / The North Shore mountains of Vancouver have become *the* proving ground for riders from all over the continent. The shore's vertiginous terrain and fecund overgrowth provide only half the challenge—the other half is the work of a crew of dedicated trail builders, who have created a fun house of dizzyingly challenging descents on the flanks of Mount Seymour and Cypress Bowl. These trails are word-of-mouth: a comprehensive trail guide and map to the area does not exist. General areas in which you can pick up the trails include: below Cypress Bowl in West Vancouver, behind Grouse Mountain, and in the Seymour Demonstration Forest. **DEEP COVE BIKE SHOP** (4310 Gallant Ave; 604/929-1918; map:H1) can provide details. **BICYCLE SPORTS PACIFIC** (3026 Mountain Hwy; 604/988-1800; map:G1) is the closest shop to the North Shore trails. This terrain is not suitable for novice riders and should never be cycled alone. Frequent riders are asked to help maintain the trails and obey proper etiquette when encountering other users. The **NORTH SHORE MOUNTAIN BIKING ASSOCIATION** (www.nsmba.bc.ca) works hard to keep these trails maintained and open.

PACIFIC SPIRIT REGIONAL PARK / This large tract of land was one of the earliest places to be discovered by mountain bikers, and it remains popular despite trail closures in some areas. Wardens patrol the park and have the authority to fine those who stray. Trails are especially muddy (and uncrowded) after a few days of rain. A great place to get your first single-track fix. Some of the most challenging riding is in the obscure northeast sector of the park. *Map:B3.*

SQUAMISH AND WHISTLER / Once the snow melts and Vancouverites have retired their skis and snowboards for the season, the toys of summer are pulled out. The Sea-to-Sky Country, the local nickname for the area between the towns of Squamish and Whistler, north of Vancouver, offers as much variety for mountain bikers as it does for skiers—wide-open cross-country ski trails, old logging roads leading to magnificent stands of old-growth red cedar, and some of the gnarliest and most technically difficult riding imaginable. Not all of the trails are easy to find, so pick up the *Squamish-Whistler Mountainbike Trail Guide* (produced by Elaho) or *Mountain Bike Adventures in Southwest British Columbia—50 Rides* (Mountaineers Books). The two can't-miss races are the Test of Metal (Squamish) held each June and the Cheakamus Challenge (Whistler) in September. The Cheakamus's 63-kilometre (32-mile) course features gear-grinding ascents, white-knuckle descents, and a great post-race party.

Novices will enjoy the Lost Lake Loop. Stop for a refreshing dip either at the public beach on the south side of the lake or at a clothing-optional dock on the east side. For greater challenge and a bit more solitude, Brandywine Falls (Whistler) and Cheakamus Lake (Whistler) are ideal trips, often scheduled by one of the local guiding companies, such as **BACKROADS BICYCLE TOURS** (604/932-3111) and **WHISTLER OUTDOOR EXPERIENCE COMPANY** (604/932-3389). Hard-core riders will head straight for legendary trails like the Emerald Forest, A River Runs

Through It, Northwest Passage, and the Rebob Trail. Bike rentals are available throughout the valley.

NATURE OBSERVATION

Although the intrusion of civilization has pushed aside the habitat of indigenous flora and fauna, in Greater Vancouver many areas still exist where one can observe the rhythms and life cycles of the natural world. Birds, fish, whales, and other mammals are constantly foraging for food in the same places where Native people hunted them centuries ago. The Fraser River Delta is a favourite stopping point for migrating flocks of snow geese, brants, and terns.

Many clubs and associations provide detailed information on nature observation in the province. The **VANCOUVER NATURAL HISTORY SOCIETY** (604/737-3074) holds field trips and has a birders' hotline that tells where rare birds have been spotted. The umbrella organization for the province is the **FEDERATION OF BC NATURALISTS** (604/737-3057), which can provide details on area clubs.

BIRD-WATCHING / Naturalists come from all over the world to the **GEORGE C. REIFEL MIGRATORY BIRD SANCTUARY** (604/946-6980) on Westham Island at the mouth of the Fraser River, 10 kilometres (6 miles) west of Ladner. More than 250 species of birds can be sighted; the peak viewing season is between October and April. This wetlands environ-ment is especially attractive to shorebirds like herons, geese, and ducks. Occasionally, migratory birds from Asian countries lose their way and end up here, drawing crowds of ornithologists seeking to cross another exotic bird off their life lists. Kids love to feed seeds to the quacking hordes of ducks that are looking for a free handout. Take a picnic, sneak into a bird blind, or climb up a viewing tower—particularly in November during the Snow Goose Festival.

FARM ANIMALS AND ZOOS / The Zoological Centre (604/856-6825) in Aldergrove, a town east of Vancouver, near Abbotsford, is open all year. Its well-treed, parklike 48 hectares (120 acres) are home to 126 species of animals, including tigers, wolves, zebras, rhinoceroses, bears, elephants, parrots, flamingoes, ostriches, bison, and many others—all roaming freely. You can walk, cycle, or drive through the farm, a favourite with kids. Drive 48 kilometres (30 miles) east of Vancouver, along the Trans-Canada Highway (Hwy 1); take the 264th St exit.

MAPLEWOOD FARM / 405 Seymour River Pl, North Vancouver; 604/929-5610 Teeming with domestic animals, North Vancouver's municipal park farm is a great hit with kids. Its Rabbitat and Goathill areas are particularly popular for petting farm animals. Visitors to the 2-hectare (5-acre) farm can also take part in daily milking-by-hand demonstrations. Watch for special family events like the Sheep Fair in May, the Farm Fair in

September, and Christmas Caroling in December. From Vancouver via the Second Narrows Bridge, exit 23-B (Deep Cove/Mt. Seymour exit), turn left at the second traffic light. *Map:G1.*

RICHMOND NATURE / 11851 Westminster Hwy, Richmond; 604/273-7015 This park offers everything you always wanted to know about bogs (and there's a lot of interesting things to know!). Interpretive trails and a Nature House, complete with salamanders and snakes, make this a hidden gem in the suburban sprawl. *Map:E6.*

SALMON SPAWNING / The **CAPILANO SALMON HATCHERY** (604/666-1790), a federal government fish hatchery set on the Capilano River among majestic red cedars and lush huckleberry bushes, is a family favourite. Meander through the self-guiding facility, where information panels describe the life cycles of Pacific salmon, then watch juvenile fish in the ponds, or see returning salmon from the ocean jumping up a series of chutes (from July to December). This park also boasts some of the tallest trees still standing on the Lower Mainland—the Giant Fir is more than 500 years old and 61 metres (200 feet) tall. Open daily. Drive up Capilano Rd in North Vancouver, take the first left past the suspension bridge onto Capilano Park Rd; proceed about 1.5 km (1 mile) to the hatchery. *Map:E0.*

Every four years (2002, 2006, 2010 . . .) it's worth taking the six-hour drive (one way) to the **ADAMS RIVER** for the fall sockeye run. Fish return every year, of course, but these are the peak years, and that's when seeing them come back is truly spectacular. This is one of the great life-cycle stories in nature, in which salmon that have spent their entire lives on the Pacific Ocean return up the Fraser River and Thompson River to spawn and die. Head west from Salmon Arm on Highway 1 to Squilix, then northeast on the paved highway for 3.8 km (2.4 miles) to the junction just after the Adams River Bridge. Call BC Parks (250/851-3000) for information.

WHALE WATCHING / For grey whales, the best lookout locations are on the west coast of **VANCOUVER ISLAND**, a five-hour drive from Vancouver (including the ferry ride between Horseshoe Bay in West Vancouver and Nanaimo). Migrating grey whales can be seen beginning in late November, but are more often seen in March and April, as they travel between their Arctic breeding grounds and Mexican calving lagoons. Many whale-watching boat charters operate out of the west coast communities of Tofino, Bamfield, and Ucluelet. There are good land viewpoints in the **LONG BEACH** area, all of which have telescopes and are accessible by car. The Wickaninnish Centre at **WICKANINNISH BEACH** is a prime viewing spot. Call Pacific Rim National Park (250/726-4212) for more information.

STRAIT OF JUAN DE FUCA / BC's second-largest city, **VICTORIA**, is one of the best places in the province for spotting killer whales. In fact, you may even see a pod from the deck of the ferry on your way over to Vancouver Island. **SEACOAST EXPEDITIONS** (250/383-2254) in Victoria offers guaranteed sightings of killer whales on its three-hour trips, available by special arrangement June 1 through September 15. Listen to orcas chatting on the hydrophone (a type of water microphone). A naturalist is on board to educate visitors about the flora and fauna encountered en route. Seacoast also makes two-hour excursions to Race Rocks Ecological Reserve and Lighthouse to view California sea lions and Steller's sea lions, along with harbour seals, porpoises, colonies of cormorants (large fishing birds) and bald eagle nests.

RIVER RAFTING

For a sheer adrenaline rush, it's hard to beat a day's rafting on one of the province's many stretches of white water, interspersed with a lazy drift through calm patches. Watch for deer nibbling on shoots and leaves near the water's edge, bald eagles whirling on air currents overhead, or even grizzled prospectors panning for gold (all kinds of wildlife!). River rafting is regulated (for safety reasons) by the provincial government under the Commercial River Rafting Safety Act.

CHILLIWACK RIVER / Located 96 kilometres (60 miles) east of Vancouver, this river is popular just after spring runoff, which occurs from about early May to mid-July, for one-day rafting trips. Chilliwack River is also popular with whitewater kayakers. Contact **HYAK WILDERNESS ADVENTURES** (604/734-8622).

FRASER RIVER / Most one-day Fraser River excursions are offered from May to the end of August. Customers travel in motorized rafts downriver from Boston Bar to Yale (communities along the Fraser Canyon), about four hours' drive east of Vancouver. Raft Scuzzy Rock, China Bar, and Hell's Gate with experienced operators like **KUMSHEEN RAFT ADVENTURES** (800/663-6667).

NAHATLATCH RIVER / The Nahatlatch River, a four-hour drive north of Vancouver, seethes with boiling chutes of white water from May to mid-August. Join the Nahatlatch experts, **REO RAFTING ADVENTURES** (604/684-4438), for a wild ride through ominous-sounding rapids like the Meat Grinder, Lose Your Lunch, and the Big Chill. Free overnight camping is available at REO's private campsite.

THOMPSON RIVER / The emerald-green waters of the Thompson River provide a pleasant mix of casual floating and stomach-churning white water. Rafters follow the Thompson southward from Spences Bridge (about a four-hour drive from Vancouver, east and then north along Highway 1) to the take-out point at Lytton, where the clear Thompson joins the murky, silt-laden Fraser. The trip includes thrilling rapids like the Devil's Kitchen and the Jaws of Death. Contact **HYAK WILDERNESS ADVENTURES** (604/734-8622).

RUNNING/WALKING

Especially during peak periods, such as lunch hour and after work, there are so many runners on the municipal pathways that visitors to Vancouver might be forgiven for asking, "Is there some kind of race happening today?" Once you include in-line skaters, mountain bikers, triathletes, and race walkers, it seems as though the entire city is clad in Lycra tights and carrying water bottles. Exposure to fitness starts early, with jogging moms pushing their infants in specially constructed strollers, and continues into the golden years, with local Masters racers (competitors 40 and over) routinely running faster than men and women half their age. More than 50,000 runners participate annually in the **SUN RUN**, a 10-kilometre (6.2-mile) race for elite athletes and joggers alike, which is held each April in downtown Vancouver. A complete list of running events may be found in the running calendar of *Coast*, the outdoor recreation magazine.

AMBLESIDE PARK / As the name implies, this West Vancouver park is a great place for a beachside amble or jog. Watch cruise ships, freighters, barges, and even the odd battleship passing underneath Lions Gate Bridge into Burrard Inlet. Start at the east end of the park, where the Capilano River enters the ocean, and follow the seawall west. Great views across the First Narrows, Lions Gate Bridge, and Stanley Park. *Map:C0.*

CENTRAL PARK / The wooded trails of Central Park, near the boundary of Vancouver and the suburb of Burnaby, begin at the boundary, just off Kingsway. Track athletes regularly use Swangard Stadium for interval workouts. For runners who wish for more diversity, a fitness circuit featuring a variety of exercise options is available nearby. *Map:F4.*

KITSILANO BEACH/VANIER PARK / A 5-kilometre (3-mile) network of flat asphalt and dirt paths skirts Vanier Park on the Kitsilano side of Burrard Street Bridge. The paths follow the water around Kitsilano Point and past the Vancouver Museum, the Pacific Space Centre, the Maritime Museum, and Kitsilano Beach. In the summer, Kitsilano Beach is the Vancouver home of the bronzed and muscle-bound, and there's always a game of beach volleyball or street basketball happening. *Map:N5.*

LOST LAGOON, STANLEY PARK / The 1.6-kilometre (1-mile) trail that encircles Lost Lagoon is an easy stroll and a great spot for watching nesting Canada geese in the springtime. There are often hundreds of ducks and other waterfowl to view all year, too. At intervals, the fountain in the centre of the lagoon emits a fine spray in a pattern that you have to watch for a few minutes to figure out. *Map:P1.*

PACIFIC SPIRIT REGIONAL PARK / Surrounding the University of British Columbia, this park contains 50 kilometres (31.1 miles) of walking and jogging trails through deciduous and coniferous forests, including Camosun Bog. Trails vary in length; you can enjoy a short stroll or you can take a more vigorous walk all the way from the Fraser River Estuary to Spanish Banks. The Visitor Centre is located on the north side of 16th Avenue, just west of Cleveland Trail. *Map:B3.*

STANLEY PARK SEAWALL / The longest seawall in Canada (10.5 kilometres/6.5 miles) is a great place to jog or walk. Plaques set in the wall at 0.5-kilometre intervals detail the wall's history. Runners and walkers can also detour into the park. The seawall is a brisk, nonstop, two-hour walk. *Map:P1.*

SAILING

Perhaps no sport quite defines the West Coast lifestyle like sailing. From two-person, high-speed catamarans to double-masted schooners, virtually every kind of sailboat can be found in the waters around Vancouver. Some of the best cruising is in Georgia Strait, where the landmass of Vancouver Island shelters many tiny bays and inlets that make perfect anchorages. Sailors wishing to charter boats for self-sufficient expeditions must pass tests administered by the International Sail and Power Association or Canadian Yachting Association; you can receive ISPA and CYA certification through **LAND'S END SAILING SCHOOL** (1195 W 13th Ave, Suite 104; 604/818-8984 or 877/818-7245; www.landsend.bc.ca; map:D3). **COOPER BOATING CENTRE** (1620 Duranleau St; 604/687-4110; www.cooper-boating.com; map:Q6) on Granville Island and **WIND VALLEY SAILING SCHOOL** (at the foot of Beach Ave; 604/685-7757; www.windvalley.com; map:Q5) both offer combination learn-to-sail cruises and classroom lectures to develop navigation and other nautical skills.

ENGLISH BAY / During the summer, Cooper Boating Centre (604/687-4110) will take you on three-hour cruises in English Bay on 6- to 12-metre (20- to 40-foot) yachts. Cruising in English Bay can also consist of a leisurely sail into spectacular Howe Sound, where salmon, killer whales, and dolphins are often seen.

GULF ISLANDS / Several sailing schools offer five-day cruise-and-learn trips around the Gulf Islands, including Land's End Sailing School (604/818-8984 or 877/818-7245) and the Sailing School on Salt Spring Island (422 Sky Valley Rd, Salt Spring Island; 250/537-2741; fcomm@ saltspring.com). Or you can rent a yacht, with or without a skipper, and cruise the islands to discover the solitude of arbutus-lined coves, the charm of neighbourhood pubs and restaurants, and the thrill of watching marine life, such as harbour seals, whales, porpoises, and sea otters.

PRINCESS LOUISA INLET / This is a saltwater bay carved deep into the Coast Mountains wilderness. Located on the Sunshine Coast north of Sechelt, its calm waters and cascading waterfalls make it an ideal sailing destination. Farther north, the Desolation Sound Marine Park is also a favourite summertime objective.

CROSS-COUNTRY SKIING

The moist, mild climate of the south coast means that skiers take their chances on conditions when skiing locally. In Vancouver, cross-country skiing can be either as casual as a trip around a golf course or city park during one of the city's infrequent snowfalls or as extreme as a multiday expedition into the heart of the Coast Mountains. Cross-country skiers generally divide into two groups: aerobic-sports enthusiasts, who prefer striding or skating along specially manicured, machine-grooved tracks, and backcountry skiers, who blaze their own trails into the wilderness. The former can take classes in skate skiing, waxing, and racing strategy, while the latter will be interested in telemarking, backcountry navigation, avalanche awareness, and winter camping. Near Whistler, is where you'll find the Spearhead Traverse, a multiday high-mountain trip, where the skiing is almost entirely on glaciers. Local weather conditions can change rapidly, and extra food and clothing should always be brought in a day pack. Winter backcountry ski courses are taught through the **FEDERATION OF MOUNTAIN CLUBS OF BRITISH COLUMBIA'S CANADA WEST MOUNTAIN SCHOOL** (47 W Broadway; 604/878-7007; map:V8). For cross-country skiing in Whistler, see the Whistler chapter.

CYPRESS BOWL / The groomed trails closest to Vancouver are at Cypress Bowl on the North Shore. You'll find 16 kilometres (10 miles) of groomed, track-set trails radiating from historic **HOLLYBURN LODGE.** Five kilometres (3.1 miles) of trail are lit for night skiing. A backcountry trail to the top of Hollyburn Mountain is also navigable, but it is quite steep in places and not suitable for children or inexperienced skiers. Nevertheless, the view over the city and into the Coast Mountains is unforgettable. Because Cypress is the closest place for Vancouver parents to take their kids for an authentic winter experience, it's not really a place to get away from it all. Rentals and lessons are available, though. **CYPRESS MOUNTAIN SPORTS** (604/878-9229) in West Vancouver's Park Royal Mall is the nearest full-service cross-country shop to the trails. Call 604/419-SNOW for weather and trail information, and the park can be reached at 604/926-5612.

GARIBALDI PROVINCIAL PARK / The alpine meadows of Singing Pass, Black Tusk, and Diamond Head, which yield an awesome profusion of wildflowers in the summer, are blanketed with several metres of snow each winter. These three areas are prime backcountry skiing territory, with conveniently located small huts for protection from the elements. backcountry skiers travelling in any areas within Garibaldi Park should be entirely self-sufficient, and everyone should be trained in avalanche safety. The park can be reached at 604/898-3678.

MANNING PARK RESORT / Three hours east of Vancouver, Manning Park Resort offers skiers everything they could ask for: cross-country trails especially designed for skating and classic techniques, hundreds of square kilometres of rugged Coast Mountains ski touring, and even a challenging little downhill area for perfecting telemark turns. **SIGGE'S SPORT VILLA** (2077 W 4th; 604/731-8818; www.sigges.com; map:C3) in Kitsilano organizes bus trips from Vancouver that can include transportation, rentals, and lessons. Manning is a good place to take kids, and the ticket prices won't break the bank, either. Overnight accommodation is available in wonderful log cabins or at the main lodge. The park can be reached at 250/840-8822 .

MOUNT SEYMOUR PROVINCIAL PARK / Mount Seymour is another local favourite, especially for those with backcountry skiing aspirations. The skiing between First (Pump) Peak and Second Peak can be excellent, especially after a big snowfall. Outside the downhill ski-area boundary, skiers must stay close to the marked trail, especially in foggy weather. It's common for skiers or snowshoers to become lost in this bluff-filled, confusing terrain. In the past three years, the back bowls beyond the ski area have become popular with snowboarders, too. Call 604/718-7771 for weather and conditions; 604/986-2261 for guest services and instruction.

DOWNHILL SKIING/SNOWBOARDING

With the possible exception of Salt Lake City, no city in North America boasts such excellent skiing facilities within a two-hour drive from downtown as does Vancouver. The closest areas are on the North Shore. Cypress Bowl, Grouse Mountain, and Mount Seymour all have respectable vertical drops and are ideal places to learn the sport. The crown jewel, though, lies 90 minutes north of Vancouver, at the resort city of Whistler, North America's largest ski destination (see the Whistler chapter).

CYPRESS BOWL / Cypress is the largest downhill facility on the North Shore and can be a fantastic place to ski after a big snowstorm. For the advanced skier, Cypress Bowl boasts some excellent mogul skiing, especially the Top Gun run underneath the Sky Chair. The half pipe draws lots of local boarders, too. Cars driving the Cypress Bowl road should be equipped with tire chains or good, winter-tread tires. For conditions and weather information, call 604/419-SNOW. For ski school programs, call 604/926-5346. *www.cypressbowl.com.*

GROUSE MOUNTAIN / Closer to Vancouver, the ski runs and lit trails on Grouse are visible from most parts of the Lower Mainland. You can take the bus from downtown right to the base of the mountain, where you're shuttled to the top on the Skyride, an aerial tram that gives a spectacular view of the city, and all the way across Georgia Strait to Vancouver Island. Although Grouse's slopes are a fraction of the length of those found at Whistler, it's still a great place to go for a quick ski fix. The snow report phone number is 604/986-6262; for guest services, call 604/980-9311. *www.grousemtn.com.*

HEMLOCK VALLEY / Tucked in a side-valley tributary of the Fraser River, Hemlock is one of the least-conspicuous ski areas in the province. Its quaint day lodge and older, slower lifts make it a throwback to the days when even downhill skiing was an adventure sport. But that's a good thing, since powder skiing here often lasts longer than it does at more crowded destination resorts. Some slopeside accommodation is available through privately rented cabins. General information and the Hemlock Valley snow phone is 604/797-4411.

MOUNT SEYMOUR / This ski area lies within the provincial park of the same name and is where many Vancouverites are exposed to skiing or snowboarding for the first time. The learn-to-ski programs are inexpensive and are often operated in conjunction with the local schools. There's a great tobogganing area at the south end of the parking lot. Seymour's somewhat irregular terrain also makes it popular with snowboarders looking to ollie off buried stumps and logs. All-season tires or chains are recommended for the road to Seymour. Call 604/718-7771 for weather and conditions; 604/986-2261 for guest services and instruction. *www. mountseymour.com.*

SNOWSHOEING

Snowshoeing is a tried-and-true way of getting off into the backwoods snowy terrain that is often too uneven for cross-country skiers.

MANNING PROVINCIAL PARK / Three hours east of Vancouver, Manning has extensive snowshoeing terrain in its vast backcountry. As with any winter backcountry activity, snowshoeing entails being wary of avalanches and changing weather conditions, as well as having mountain navigation skills. The park can be reached at 250/840-8822.

MOUNT SEYMOUR PROVINCIAL PARK / Over the Second Narrows Bridge, 16 kilometres (10 miles) north of Vancouver, Mount Seymour offers snowshoe rentals and instruction. Snowshoers can skirt some of the winter cross-country trails, including Goldie Lake Loop, Flower Lake Loop, and Hidden Lake Loop. Guided snowshoeing tours and rentals are operated through the Mount Seymour ski school (604/986-2261). Call 604/718-7771 for snow conditions.

SWIMMING

Vancouver's 11 sandy beaches are fine for swimming, even in slightly brisk temperatures. Lifeguards patrol in June, July, and August. Favourite swimming beaches include English Bay (site of the annual **NEW YEAR'S DAY POLAR BEAR SWIM**), Sunset Beach, Kitsilano Beach (especially after a strenuous session of beach volleyball), Jericho Beach, Locarno Beach, and Spanish Banks. Jericho, Locarno, and Spanish Banks are also popular with cycling and windsurfing crowds.

KITSILANO POOL / North foot of Yew St; 604/731-0011 Kitsilano Beach has a gigantic outdoor saltwater pool adjacent to English Bay. It is heated to 26°C (79°F) and has a graduated depth, making it ideal for both children and strong swimmers. *Every day (Victoria Day to Labour Day); map:N6.*

NEWTON WAVE POOL / 13730 72nd Ave, Surrey; 604/501-5540 Because the waters of Vancouver are protected from the ocean swells of the Pacific Coast, surfing is not part of the city's aquatic culture. But in the suburb of Surrey, south of Vancouver, a wave-action leisure pool generates 1-metre (3-foot) waves for bodysurfing. There are also two water slides, a wading pool, steam room, whirlpool, weight room, and even a licensed lounge. *Every day; map:L7.*

SECOND BEACH OUTDOOR POOL / Stanley Park; 604/257-8371 Along the Stanley Park seawall, the newly refurbished Second Beach outdoor pool is popular with locals and visitors alike during the summer months. *Every day (late June to Labour Day); map:O1*

SPLASHDOWN WATERPARK / 4799 Nulelum Way, Tsawwassen; 604/943-2251. The owners of Splashdown Waterpark have taken advantage of Tsawwassen's sunny location—less than half the annual rainfall of downtown Vancouver—to construct a giant 3-hectare (7-acre) park, featuring 11 waterslides. There's a full range of summertime fun to be enjoyed here, including volleyball, basketball, and a minigolf course. It's a great place to pack a picnic and is perhaps the most reliable spot in the Lower Mainland for getting a suntan. *Every day (Victoria Day to Labour Day).*

UNIVERSITY OF BRITISH COLUMBIA AQUATIC CENTRE / 6121 University Blvd; 604/822-4521 UBC has Olympic-size indoor and outdoor pools with a sauna, steam room, whirlpool, exercise gym, and toddler pool. Open late into the evening for public swimming. *Every day; map:A3.*

VANCOUVER AQUATIC CENTRE / 1050 Beach Ave; 604/665-3424 In the West End, overlooking Sunset Beach, the Vancouver Aquatic Centre features an Olympic-size indoor pool, sauna, whirlpool, and toddler pool. *Every day; map:Q5.*

TENNIS

Keen tennis players can perfect their topspin lob or two-fisted backhand year-round on Vancouver's 180 public courts, even though the outdoor season officially runs from March to October. Most public courts are free and operate on a first-come, first-served basis.

STANLEY PARK has 21 courts (the wait can be lengthy during peak periods), 17 by the Beach Avenue entrance (map:O1) and four by Lost Lagoon at the foot of Robson (map:Q1). From April to September, you can book a Beach Avenue court for a small fee. **QUEEN ELIZABETH PARK** courts (33rd Ave at Cambie St; map:D3) are centrally located in the city but can be quite hot when there's no breeze. **KITSILANO BEACH PARK** has 10 courts near the ocean, with a concession stand nearby for a cool drink or french fries. **JERICHO BEACH PARK,** behind the Jericho Sailing Center, offers great rugby viewing on the pitch south of the courts while you wait your turn (map:B2).

WINDSURFING

Although Vancouver is practically surrounded by water and exposed to breezes from every direction, capricious conditions can test the patience of high-speed sailors looking for waves to jump and steady, consistent winds. But the light winds often found on the beaches of the city's West Side are ideal for learning to windsurf.

WINDSURE WINDSURFING SCHOOL (604/224-0615; map:B2) operates out of the Jericho Sailing Centre. Their specialty is an intensive six-hour course that guarantees results. **PACIFIC BOARDER** (604/734-7245; map:B2) in Kitsilano sells boardsailing equipment and wet suits, along with surfboards and body-boards.

For some of the most consistent wind conditions in North America, drive an hour north from Vancouver to the town of **SQUAMISH**—the name comes from a Native word meaning "place where the wind blows." The Squamish Spit is a human-made dike that separates the saltwater bay of Howe Sound from the frigid waters of the Squamish River. Skim out on your board within view of the Stawamus Chief, Shannon Falls, and Howe Sound. Conditions are best from May to August, when afternoon thermals generated by warm air create steady, consistent conditions. The water is cold, so a thick wet suit or dry suit is mandatory, especially if you are still developing your jibing and water-start skills. The **SQUAMISH WINDSURFING SOCIETY** (604/926-9463) administers the park, charging a daily fee to pay for rescue boats, washroom maintenance, and liability insurance. To get to the spit, follow Highway 99 north to Squamish and turn left at the Cleveland Avenue intersection. Turn right on Buckley Avenue as it turns into Government Road. Follow Government Road as it loops back past the Railway Museum and the BC Rail yards (on the left). A sign on the right directs you to the 4-kilometre-long gravel road.

Call 604/926-WIND to get the wind report, which is updated several times each day.

Spectator Sports

Like other North American cities of comparative size, Vancouver is what's known as a "small-market" franchise. Sports owners here don't have the lucrative TV deals or other revenue streams to lay out big bucks for marquee superstars. Complicating matters is the fact that the biggest competition a sports franchise has is a sunny day—Vancouver boasts a significant population that would rather be playing sports than watching them. Add to these woes the fact that fans of the Lions, Canucks, and Grizzlies have suffered through many losing seasons, and you can see why golfing on a sunny Sunday might be preferable to watching yet another disheartening defeat. That said, the best bet is likely to watch the Vancouver Canucks play NHL hockey at GM Place, even if the alternately loved and reviled Pavel Bure is no longer in town.

BC LIONS FOOTBALL / BC Place Stadium, 777 Pacific Blvd; 604/589-7627 The BC Lions play in the Canadian Football League (CFL). A longer, wider field and only three downs to make 10 yards means that a passing game predominates, making it a far more exciting sport than its American counterpart. Action is the name of the game in this league, which is decades older than the National Football League (NFL). Avid fans enjoy home games downtown from June through late October; the season culminates in the Grey Cup championship. Tickets are available through Ticketmaster (604/280-4444) and at the gate. *www.bclions.com; map:T5.*

HASTINGS PARK HORSE RACING / Near the intersection of Hastings St and Renfrew St; 604/254-1631 From April to November, the thoroughbreds race at the Hastings Park racecourse, on the grounds of the Pacific National Exhibition. It's easy to get caught up in the excitement of an afternoon's racing. Racing season runs from mid-April to November, Wednesday through Sunday. Post time is 6:15pm weekdays and 1:15pm weekends and holidays. General admission is $3.50 ($1.50 for seniors, free for children 15 and under), and clubhouse seating on the table terrace is $7.50 for two and $15 for four. *www.hastingspark.com; map:F2.*

VANCOUVER CANUCKS HOCKEY / GM Place, 800 Griffiths Wy; 604/899-4667 Although the National Hockey League has been diluted by the addition of too many teams and a punishing regular season schedule, a well-played hockey game is still the most spine-tingling spectacle in pro sport. You don't need to know anything about the rules to watch; it's all pretty self-explanatory. The hometown Canucks have had a few bright, shining moments during their 25-year history, but their inconsistent ways and failure to live up to potential have led fans to a peculiar breed of cynicism. Still, the faithful stick with the team through good times and bad, and that makes getting tickets a challenge—especially when popular opponent teams are playing, such as the Montreal Canadians and Toronto Maple Leafs. Tickets are available through Ticketmaster (604/280-4444) and at the gate. *www.orcabay.com; map:V5.*

VANCOUVER 86ERS SOCCER / Swangard Stadium, intersection of Boundary Rd and Kingsway; 604/589-7627 Vancouver's diverse ethnicity has created a ready-made audience for soccer, especially among homesick Brits, Portuguese, and Italians. The Vancouver 86ers played their first season during the year of Expo 86, and promptly won four straight Canadian soccer league titles before switching to the A League, a seven-team international circuit. The season starts in early May and winds up in September. Tickets are available through Ticketmaster (604/280-4444) and at the gate. *Map:F4.*

VANCOUVER GRIZZLIES BASKETBALL / GM Place, 800 Griffiths Wy; 604/899-4667 Basketball ain't just shooting hoops any more, not in the showbiz world of the National Basketball Association. Sometimes diehard roundball fans have to look beyond the fireworks, jugglers, mascots, rock music, and acrobats to see what's going down on the floor. But that's just as well, for the hometown Grizzlies have set records for losing and general ineptitude throughout the first three seasons of their existence. The fans shrug it off; there's always next year, or another coach. There's simply not a bad seat in their arena, which is officially known as **GENERAL MOTORS PLACE** and irreverently as "The Garage." It's home to the Grizzlies and the NHL Canucks, and is one of the most luxurious and well-designed sports stadiums in North America. Sellouts are uncommon, though it sometimes gets pretty busy; walk-up seats are usually available. Season runs from October to May. Tickets are available through Ticketmaster (604/280-4444) or at the gate. *www.orcabay.com; map:V5.*

Index

Music in the Morning, 222–23
musical instruments, 205–06. *See* recordings, CDs, tapes
Mystic Beach, 303

N

Naam, 81–82, 262
Nahatlatch River
river rafting, 359
Nairn Falls Provincial Park, 335
Nanaimo-to-Vancouver Bathtub Race, 173
Nancy Lord, 191
Nat's New York Pizzeria, 82
National Geographic Tree, 143
National Post, 33
National Tilden, 23
Native Peoples
art, crafts, 203–04
art, crafts, Victoria, 300
art, galleries, 166
art, Museum of Anthropology, 149, 204, 262
art, Royal British Columbia Museum, 295
House of Himwitsa, 308–09
Inuit Gallery, 168
Marion Scott Gallery, 168. *See also* totem poles
restaurants, 77
Three Vets, 169
Wickaninnish Interpretive Centre, 308
nature observation, 357–59
Gulf Islands, 361–62
Richmond Nature, 358
Vancouver Natural History Society, 357. *See also* birdwatching; whale watching
Nazarre BBQ Chicken, 82
Neptoon Records, 205
Net Loft, 138
New Grand View Restaurant, 82–83
New Westminster, 18
Met Hotel Bar & Grill, The, 245–46
New Year's Polar Bear Swim, 365
newspapers, magazines, 33
where to buy, 193–95
Newton Wave Pool, 365
Nicklaus North at Whistler, 336
nightlife
bars, pubs, and taverns, 241–47
"Celebrity Hangouts," 217
Celluloid Social Club, 229
history, current listings, 234
jazz, 236, 302, 338
"Late Night Eats," 244–45
lounges, 247–52
music and clubs, 234–41
"Vancouver After Hours," 249
Victoria, 302–03

Whistler area, 337–38
Nike, 155
Nikko Japanese Restaurant, 83
Nimmo Bay Resort, 291
900 West Restaurant & Wine Bar, 83–84, 119, 250
Nine O'Clock Gun, 142
Nitobe Memorial Garden, 170
Noor Mahal, 84
Normandy Restaurant, 44–45
North Shore
lodgings, 131, 132
mountain biking, 355–56
restaurants, 38–39
North Shore Mountain Biking Association, 356
North Vancouver, 18
Karen Magnussen Recreation Centre, 354
Maplewood Farm, 357–58
nightlife, 238
restaurants, 73, 80, 107
Sailor Hagars, 246
North Vancouver Air, 6, 306
Northwest Connection, 337
Number 5 Orange, The, 217, 246
Numbers Cabaret, 238
Nyala Restaurant, 84

O

"O Canada" House, 121
O-Tooz the Energie Bar, 86
Oak Bay Beach Hotel, 291–92
ocean fisheries
US Department of Fisheries and Oceans, 347, 348
Ocean Pointe Resort, 292
Ocean View Lodging, 136
Odyssey, The, 238
Old Cemeteries Society, The, 276
Olde World Fudge, 196
Olympia Seafood Market & Grill, 85
Omnitsky Kosher Foods, 85
Only Seafood Cafe, The, 85–86
opera
Vancouver, 223, 230
Victoria, 301
Opera Club, The, 230
Optaderm, 208
Opus Framing and Art Supplies, 212
Or Gallery Society/KSW, 168
Original Tandoori K. King, 86
Orpheum Theatre, 258, 261
Outdoor Recreation Council of British Columbia, 343
Ouzeri, 86–87

P

Pacific Boarder, 366
Pacific Central Station, 6
Pacific Centre
lodgings near, 118, 120
shopping, 182–83
Pacific Cinémathèque, 228
Pacific Coach Lines, 7, 178

Pacific Opera Victoria, 301
Pacific Palisades, 121–22
Pacific Rim National Park, 306–07
Green Point Campground, 307
Infocentre, 307
Pacific Rim Whale Festival, 307
Pacific Space Centre, 165, 175
Pacific Spirit Regional Park, 175
in-line skating, 355
mountain biking, 356
running, walking, 361
Pacific Undersea Gardens, 299
Pagliacci's, 302
Pajo's, 157
Palisades Extended-Stay Suites, 122–23
Palladio, 201
Palladium Club, The, 238
Pan Pacific Hotel, The, 117, 123
Pan Pacific Lodge, 328
Dubh Linn Gate, 319–20
Panther Décor, 189
Paper-ya, 213
Paperhaus, 213
Park and Tilford Gardens, 170
Park Lock Seafood Restaurant, 87
Park Royal Hotel, 132
Park Royal Shopping Centre, 185
Park Theatre, 227
Parker Place, 156, 268–69
parking
downtown Vancouver, 23
downtown Victoria, 276
Granville Island area, 138–39
Vancouver International Airport, 2–3
parks
Ambleside Park, 162, 171, 265–66, 360
Barnet Beach Park, 171
BC Ministry of Environment, Lands and Parks, 348
BC Parks, 346
Beacon Hill Park, Victoria, 298
Belcarra Regional Park, 171
Campbell Valley Regional Park, 353
Capilano River Regional Park, 171–72
Cates Park, 264–65
Central Park, 172
China Beach Provincial Park, 303
Cypress Provincial Park, 172, 346
David Lam Park, 172–73
Deas Island Regional Park, 349
East Sooke Regional Park, 303
French Beach Provincial Park, 303
Garibaldi Provincial Park, 333, 334, 346, 351, 362–63
Garry Point Park, 173, 355

We Stand By Our Reviews

Sasquatch Books is proud of *Vancouver Best Places*. Our editors and contributors go to great lengths and expense to see that all of the restaurant and lodging reviews are as accurate, up-to-date, and honest as possible. If we have disappointed you, please accept our apologies; however, if a recommendation in this 3rd edition of *Vancouver Best Places* has seriously misled you, Sasquatch Books would like to refund your purchase price. To receive your refund:

1. Tell us where and when you purchased your book and return the book and the book-purchase receipt to the address below.
2. Enclose the original restaurant or lodging receipt from the establishment in question, including date of visit.
3. Write a full explanation of your stay or meal and how *Vancouver Best Places* misled you.
4. Include your name, address, and phone number.

Refund is valid only while this 3rd edition of *Vancouver Best Places* is in print. If the ownership, management, or chef has changed since publication, Sasquatch Books cannot be held responsible. Tax and postage on the returned book is your responsibility. Please allow six to eight weeks for processing.

Please address to Satisfaction Guaranteed, *Vancouver Best Places*, and send to:
Sasquatch Books
615 Second Avenue, Suite 260
Seattle, WA 98104

Vancouver Best Places Report Form

Based on my personal experience, I wish to nominate the following restaurant, place of lodging, shop, nightclub, sight, or other as a "Best Place"; or confirm/correct/disagree with the current review.

_____

_____

_____

(Please include address and telephone number of establishment, if convenient.)

REPORT

Please describe food, service, style, comfort, value, date of visit, and other aspects of your experience; continue on another piece of paper if necessary.

_____

_____

_____

_____

_____

_____

I am not concerned, directly or indirectly, with the management or ownership of this establishment.

_____

SIGNED

_____

ADDRESS

_____

_____

PHONE   **DATE**

Please address to Vancouver Best Places and send to:
SASQUATCH BOOKS
615 SECOND AVENUE, SUITE 260
SEATTLE, WA 98104
Feel free to email feedback as well: **BOOKS@SASQUATCHBOOKS.COM**